A HISTORY OF
THE UNITED STATES

THE MACMILLAN COMPANY
NEW YORK · BOSTON · CHICAGO · DALLAS
ATLANTA · SAN FRANCISCO

MACMILLAN & CO., Limited
LONDON · BOMBAY · CALCUTTA
MELBOURNE

THE MACMILLAN COMPANY
OF CANADA, Limited
TORONTO

A HISTORY

OF

THE UNITED STATES

BY

EDWARD CHANNING

VOLUME VI

THE WAR FOR SOUTHERN INDEPENDENCE

New York

THE MACMILLAN COMPANY

1936

19345

CONTENTS

MAPS

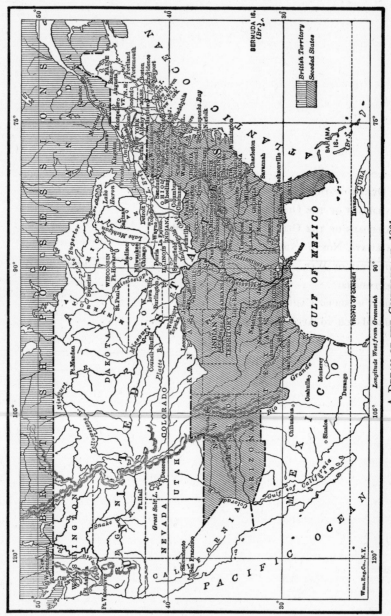

A Dream of the Confederacy, 1861.

(By George McHenry, author of *The Cotton Supply.*)

A HISTORY OF THE UNITED STATES

CHAPTER I

A DIVIDED COUNTRY

"SECESSION by the joint action of the slave-holding States is the only efficient remedy for the aggravated wrongs which they now endure and the enormous evils which threaten them in future, from the usurped and unrestrained power of the Federal Government."[1] So run the words of a resolution introduced by Langdon Cheves of South Carolina on November 14, 1850, into the Nashville convention at one of the sittings of its second session. The moment was inopportune. The adoption of Clay's compromise plan had turned the minds of the Southerners away from their grievances and had led them to look forward with hope to another period of Southern domination of the government of the United States and of the people of the North. None the less, the resolution expressed the conviction of a very large portion of the ruling class in Southern politics and society. The twentieth century historical student finds it difficult to understand how the slaveholders and the slaveholding States could by any possibility have endured aggravated wrongs at the hands of the Federal government, for the Southerners themselves

[1] *Bulletin* of the New York Public Library, vol. xiv, No. 4, p. 240. Earlier, in 1844, Cheves had written a letter to the *Charleston Mercury* which was printed in *Southern State Rights, Anti-Tariff & Anti-Abolition Tract No. 1,* p. 7. He declared that until the South Carolinians could cherish the vital truth that their first and holiest allegiance was to their State, they were unprepared to resist "Abolitionists and Manufacturers."

1

had held that government within their control for at least fifty of the sixty years of its life. Washington, Jefferson, Madison, Monroe, Jackson, Tyler, and Polk were Southerners, and at that moment Zachary Taylor, Virginia born and the owner of many slaves, was occupying the White House. The first five of these Southern Presidents had served for eight years apiece, while not one of the Northern Presidents had been reëlected. Moreover, throughout this whole time, — with scarcely an exception — the Southerners, with the help of their Northern allies, had controlled one or both Houses of the Federal Congress and the major part of the Justices of the Supreme Court of the United States had been Southern in every year of its existence. Not only had the South possessed control of the Federal government, it had constantly and consistently used this power for its own protection. Nevertheless, Barnwell Rhett of South Carolina in the United States Senate in December, 1851, declared that the decadence of the South was due to the operations of the general government and that the North, formerly poor, rioted in prosperity and "not only threatens our liberties, but our existence, itself." Indeed, so he said, the South was "the very best colony to the North any people ever possessed."[1] Another man, Captain Pike, otherwise un-

[1] *Appendix to the Congressional Globe,* 32nd Cong., 1st Sess., p. 46. See also *A Voice from the South comprising Letters from Georgia to Massachusetts and to the Southern States* and Iveson L. Brookes's *Defence of the South against the Reproaches and Incroachments of the North* (Hamburg, S. C., 1850). The former denies that slavery has a demoralizing tendency and the latter undertakes to show that slavery is the only safeguard of a republican government and that the South must not enter into any compromise which will not give it a perpetual equality of political influence in the Union.

On the other side, an anonymous Philadelphian, on June 13, 1850, wrote that the Southern system tended to make every Northerner hostile to slavery and that the time of Congress should be given to a consideration of the case of fugitive white freemen who were being driven from their homes and employments by the short-sighted policy of the Southerners. The extreme Northern view of Southern desire may be seen in a campaign pamphlet of 1864 entitled *Proofs for Workingmen of the Monarchic and Aristocratic Designs of the Southern Conspirators and their Northern Allies.*

known to fame, in the New Orleans Convention of 1855, described the servitude of the South in these words: ". . . From the rattle with which the nurse tickles the ear of the child born in the South to the shroud that covers the cold form of the dead, every thing comes to us from the North. We rise from between sheets made in Northern looms, and pillows of Northern feathers, to wash in basins made in the North, dry our beards on Northern towels, and dress ourselves in garments woven in Northern looms; we eat from Northern plates and dishes; our rooms are swept with Northern brooms, our gardens dug with Northern spades, and our bread kneaded in trays or dishes of Northern wood or tin; and the very wood which feeds our fires is cut with Northern axes, helved with hickory brought from Connecticut and New-York." [1]

By the middle of the century, two distinct social organizations had developed within the United States, the one in the South and the other in the North. [2] Southern society was based on the production of staple agricultural crops by slave labor. Northern society was bottomed on varied employments — agricultural, mechanical, and commercial — all carried on under the wage system. Two such divergent forms of society could not continue indefinitely to live side by side within the walls of one government, even within the walls of so loosely constructed a system as that of the United States under the Constitution. One or the other of these societies must perish, or both must secure complete equality, as Calhoun contended, or the two societies must separate

[1] *Proceedings of the Southern Commercial Convention, held in . . . New Orleans . . . January, 1855* (New Orleans, 1855), p. 10.

[2] Two Southern books published within the present century admirably set forth the view that is expressed in these paragraphs: Thomas C. Johnson's *Life and Letters of Robert Lewis Dabney* (Richmond, 1903) and John C. Reed's *The Brothers' War* (Boston, 1905). The latter author was a Georgia lawyer and a Confederate veteran.

absolutely and live each by itself under its own government. The Southern social system was built on slavery.[1] The conversion of the free labor wage system of the North into a labor system based on slavery was so against the whole tendency of the nineteenth century that this solution of the problem was impossible. It was possible that slavery might have remained a living institution within the limits of the cotton-growing States for many, many decades. Moreover, had the Southern leaders been men of great wisdom and foresight, peaceable secession might have been achieved in 1850. As it was, instead of ameliorating the slave-labor system and confining it to the Cotton States or pushing on separation while it was feasible, the Southerners sought to combat the free-wage-system society of the North by enlarging the area of slave territory and securing the right to carry their slaves with them, without danger of loss, into every part of the country. This attempt to secure the recognition by law of their peculiar institution was against the whole economic, social, and moral sentiment of the times, not merely in the Northern United States, but throughout the greater part of the civilized world. Moreover, for one reason or another, the boundary line of what might be termed the effective slave area was drawing itself farther and farther southward with each decade and almost with each year. Repugnance to the presence of the negro — or free-soilism — was growing in the North and, especially, in the northern portion of Transappalachia. It was perfectly plain, even in 1850, that in every year the North was increasing in man power and in material resources as compared with the South. Inevitably this superiority would sooner or later be translated into

[1] In 1855, Governor James H. Adams, of South Carolina, in a *Message* to the legislature (p. 11), declared "The world owes its civilization to slavery. It exists with us in its most desirable and enduring form. 'It is the corner stone of our republican edifice.'"

elements of political power and the South would lose the
grip on the government of the United States that it had
enjoyed since 1789.

In 1850 there were within the United States twenty-
three million human beings, — white, black, yellow, and
red. Ten years later this number had increased to thirty-
one millions. The "Census" of 1850 designates about two
and one quarter of the twenty-three millions as of foreign
birth. Adding to this number the children born of foreign
parents within the limits of the United States, we get a total
of what has sometimes been called "the foreign population"
of three millions.[1] Usually a line of demarcation has been
drawn between the North and the South at the northern limit
of the States wherein negro slavery was recognized by law.
For purposes of historical discussion, it would be better to
speak of the latter as the Slave States and to divide them into
the Slave States that seceded and those that did not. Over
thirteen millions of the twenty-three million human beings
who formed the total population of the United States in
1850 lived in the Free States and just under ten millions in
the Slave States. But taking the Slave States that seceded
by themselves we get a population of seven and a quarter
millions for Secessia, or the Confederate States. Adding to
the population of the Free States the people of the Slave
States that did not secede, we get a total Northern population
of slightly under sixteen millions in 1850. Going forward
ten years to 1860, the "Census" gives nine millions of people
to the States that seceded and over twenty-two millions to
those that remained within the Union, and of these twenty-
two millions, three and a half millions lived in the non-
seceding Slave States and in the Virginia counties that later

---

[1] *A Century of Population Growth*,
87 note, from the *Compendium of the* *Seventh Census*, 119. See also the
present work, vol. v, 475.

formed the State of West Virginia. It appears, therefore, that
in the ten years from 1850 to 1860, the States that remained
within the Union in 1861 had grown in population out of
all proportion to the States that seceded.[1] It is now easy to
understand how Southerners of the Cotton Belt and of Virginia — Robert Toombs, William Lowndes Yancey, Judah
P. Benjamin, and Edmund Ruffin — should study with care
and view with dismay the statistics of population as they
were printed by the States and by the Federal government.

In almost every Southern book that was printed before
the war, — or has been printed since, — we read of the
Southerners as forming one people — superior to any other
people on the face of the earth. They formed a "most homogeneous population, all of the same blood and lineage";[2]
they were of "gentle" descent, mainly from the cavaliers of
the time of Charles II. This thought left out of mind all
the colored inhabitants — mulattoes and blacks, slave and
free. There were three-quarters as many colored human
beings as white within the Slave States that seceded and one-
half as many colored as white in the Slave States taken as a
whole. And it must be remembered that from ten to fifteen
per cent or perhaps even twenty-five per cent of the colored
people of the States that seceded had white blood in their
veins. By the middle of the century, however, Southerners
had come to look upon the negroes — both mulattoes and
blacks — as property. The claim that the white population
was of English descent and of pre-Revolutionary ancestry
makes one think for a moment of Francis Marion, of the
Petigrus or Pettigrews, the Gaillards, and the Hugers, —
all of ancient French Protestant stock. In New Orleans

[1] *Census* of 1920, vol. i, "Population," pp. 14, 20, 21, etc.
[2] *Speech of the Hon. Langdon Cheves
. . . November 13, 1850,* in U. B.

Phillips's "Literary Movement for
Secession" in *Studies in Southern
History and Politics,* p. 44.

there were representatives of the old French and Spanish
Catholic colonial families. Turning back to the Carolinas,
the names of John C. Calhoun and Andrew Jackson come to
the recollection, — they were of Scotch-Irish descent and
exemplified in their lives many of the best known traits of
their stock. In Charleston, also, was one of the oldest
Jewish groups in the United States and, in the first part of
the nineteenth century, persons of German origin were
prominent in its mercantile life and are now. In the uplands
of the Carolinas, there were descendants of the old Moravian
immigrants and of other non-English settlers who had followed the great valleys from Pennsylvania southward. In
the mountains were descendants of German prisoners taken
with Burgoyne at Saratoga and these are, even to this day,
known as "the Hessians." And, indeed, Jefferson Davis
himself represented a strong and vigorous Welsh stock of
comparatively recent migration from Pennsylvania. It is
no doubt true that the planting aristocracy of the cotton
belts and of the tobacco-growing areas represented for the
most part families that had been on the land before the
Revolution and who had come from England, Scotland, Ireland, and France. But there were many men and women in
the Southern States and even in the States of the cotton
belts who had come to the country since 1800 and even
since 1830.

Looking into the "Census" of 1850, it appears that there
were then 147,532 foreign-born whites in the slaveholding
States that seceded and, in 1860, this number had risen to
233,651. In fact, in 1850, one white inhabitant of the slaveholding States in every twenty was of foreign birth and this
proportion had risen to nearly seven per cent in 1860. In
the latter year, in Louisiana nearly one-quarter of the white
population was foreign-born. And it may be said in passing

that foreigners formed nearly one-eighth of the population of Ohio, one-seventh of that of Pennsylvania, one-quarter of that of New York, and one-third of that of Wisconsin.[1] Also, it appears that of the thirty-six thousand emigrants who sailed from the port of Bremen for the United States in the year 1857, about twenty thousand went to New York and Philadelphia and about sixteen thousand to five Southern ports, one-half of them, more or less, to New Orleans.

The Crescent City on the banks of the Mississippi — one of the most attractive spots in the United States — was to all intents and purposes in 1850 and 1860 a foreign city and even today in many ways it is foreign still.[2] Besides the descendants of the old French and Spanish inhabitants of this city, the new-comers from foreign lands in 1860 numbered 64,621, and of these no less than 24,398 were immigrants from Ireland. The contribution of the Irish race to the South seems to have slipped the minds of most Southern writers, and yet John H. Reagan, the efficient Postmaster General of the Confederacy, was of Irish origin, although born in Tennessee; General "Pat" Cleburne — the bravest of the brave — who gave his life for the Southern cause at Franklin, and General Joseph Finnegan, who defended the Florida boundaries against Union attack, were both Irishmen born. John Mitchell, the Irish patriot, who settled at Richmond before the war, stated that there were forty thousand soldiers of the Irish race in the Confederate army, — one of his own sons was killed at Gettysburg in 1863,

[1] *Census* of 1860, "Population," p. xxix. See also C. E. MacGill in *The South in the Building of the Nation*, v, 595–606.

[2] According to the *Census* of 1860 ("Population," p. xxxi) the foreign-born formed 13.07 per cent of the population of Richmond, 15.55 per cent of Charleston, 38.31 per cent of New Orleans, and 24.13 of Mobile. Of the foreign-born population of the slaveholding South, 4,956 resided at Richmond, 6,311 at Charleston, and 7,061 at Mobile. It appears, therefore, that approximately five-sixths of the foreign population of the South was then living outside of the commercial towns. It is perhaps worth noting that at Mobile there were 3,307 persons of Irish birth.

and another at Fort Sumter in 1864, both of them dying in the cause of the Confederacy. Most of the Irishmen had come to the Southern States to work on the railroads or to do the heavy labor around the wharves of the commercial centers, for the slaves were too valuable to be put to strange occupations or to be exposed to dangerous climatic conditions. Many of these Irishmen had remained in the South, especially at New Orleans and Mobile. Another attractive and interesting element in the population was that of the Jews. They were strong in Charleston, mostly of German and English race, in Richmond, and in New Orleans. Indeed, it is worth noting, perhaps, that the Louisiana Ordinance of Secession was lithographed by Pssow & Simeon at New Orleans and was published by Jos: Korwin (Jaholkowski) who is termed on the title page "Clerk of the Senate of Louisiana" and would appear to have been of Polish race. In Richmond, in Virginia, there were many Jewish families. Samuel Mordecai's "Richmond in By-Gone Days" was published in 1856 in that city and is still an important book of reference, and the first Southern account of the "Battle of Young's Branch," as Bull Run or Manassas was at one time denominated, was lithographed by Hoyer and Ludwig at Richmond. There were so many Germans within the limits of the Confederacy in 1863 that a "Deutsches A-B-C und Erstes Lese-Buch" was published for their benefit at Richmond at a time when paper, ink, and labor were very expensive. From all these facts and from a multitude of others that cannot be brought into a brief statement, it would seem that there were so many white persons of German, French, and Irish extraction and of recent arrival within the States of the South that the white population was by no means "homogeneous" and in many ways was not at all "gentle." It was the wife of Senator Chesnut of South

Carolina who suggested that the eloquence of Southern men was due to the fact that so many of them were of Irish descent.

Apart from the new-comers and from the dwellers in the mountain regions of Virginia, Kentucky, Tennessee, Alabama, Georgia, and especially North Carolina, the whites of the old migration had developed a distinct physique, a distinctive speech, and a characteristic mode of thought. The typical Southern plantation white man was of good height, with a lean body, a thin face, and a characteristic far-off look in his eyes. As he stood, he held his hands a little in front of the median line and his shoulders ordinarily were drawn a little forward. He had a soft sub-tropical intonation and a "plantation patois" that had come to him in part at least from childhood association with the ever-faithful colored "mammy" and his playmates, the "little niggers."[1] His dialect was in a way as marked as that of the New England farmer or of the Northwestern settler in the days before efficient transportation had broken down barriers of speech as well as of occupation. The Southerner was very self-centered and intent on his own affairs, — upon the condition of the crops, the price of cotton, or the run of sugar. For half a century and more the Federal capital had been the rallying point of the more influential political leaders of the South; the State capitals had served the lesser politicians, and the county elections had been the principal meeting ground of local leaders and the voters. Apart from the crops and from litigation over lands and debts, politics was the chief mental excitation of the Southern white, rich or poor. Living in close contact with an alien race, he naturally and necessarily had self-protection always in the very front

[1] See John W. Forney's *Anecdotes of Public Men*, 194: "Every body has noticed how the negro dialect pervades the conversation of the so-called superior race . . . the plantation *patois*."

of his mind. At any moment of the day or of the night, he might be required to strike at once and to strike hard to save his own life and to protect his wife and his children. He possessed a militant nature and brooked no insult from any one — Southerner or Northerner. If he felt aggrieved, he sent the other man a challenge, and if the other man refused to fight, he knocked him down or horse-whipped him at the first opportunity.[1] A diarist described her father-in-law as resolute of will as he ever was, although ninety-three years of age and blind and deaf, — "the last of a race of lordly planters who ruled this Southern world. . . . His manners are unequaled still, but underneath this smooth exterior lies the grip of a tyrant whose will has never been crossed."[2] Of another South Carolinian — the assailant of Charles Sumner — another South Carolina woman wrote, on learning of his death, that personal amiability was the most marked feature in the character of the "kindly, warm-hearted man."[3] These instances are drawn from South Carolina, but they might easily be duplicated as to any of the States of the Southern coastal plain. The Southern planters lived contented and happy lives surrounded by a white peasantry and a black servile laboring class. They believed themselves to be the chosen of the earth and as superior to the fanatics, business men, laborers, to "the mongrels and hirelings" of the North as one set of men could

[1] Thomas Gamble's *Savannah Duels and Duellists* (Savannah, 1923) is an instructive book and has a wider outlook than its title would indicate as Savannahians acted as seconds in the Hamilton-Burr and Clay-Randolph duels.

[2] Mary B. Chesnut's *A Diary from Dixie*, 390.

[3] Mary J. Windle's *Life in Washington*, 52, 53. Southern antagonism to Northerners was well set forth by William H. Russell in a letter that was printed in the London *Times* for May 28, 1861, and was omitted from his book — *My Diary, North and South* — and was reprinted in the *Proceedings* of the Massachusetts Historical Society for February, 1913, p. 310. The result of Russell's observations in Charleston was that there was "nothing in all the dark caves of human passion so cruel and deadly as the hatred the South Carolinians profess for the Yankees," — and he gives several examples.

be superior to another.   To their minds it would be a " dishonor" to be governed by such as these.

Southern writers of recent years and Southerners themselves in the period "befo' de war" have always insisted upon the intellectual training of Southern plantation life, upon the fact that the ruling class was well read and was capable of intellectual advancement, and, indeed, had accomplished much in the way of mental endeavor.   Northern writers, who have largely been of abolition sympathies, have been loath to accept this idea; but there was a great deal of truth in it.   Indeed, some of the most remarkable scientific minds of the United States were produced by this social organization in the generations before 1860.   Of these, the best known and perhaps the greatest, was Matthew Fontaine Maury of Virginia, whose work on the currents of the Atlantic and on the geography of the world has given him everlasting fame.   Another of this group was Basil Gildersleeve, one of the profoundest scholars that America has brought forth,[1] who was born in Charleston, South Carolina. Joseph Le Conte was born on a great plantation in Georgia, the son of the owner of many slaves.   After attending the local educational institutions, Le Conte went to New York to study medicine.   Still later he broke away from that profession and sought the newly founded Lawrence Scientific School at Cambridge in Massachusetts, where he was one of the earliest students of Louis Agassiz, and ended his life as a professor in the University of California.   Surely a society that could produce these men had in it something else than the qualities that Northern writers have usually

[1] "The Creed of the Old South" in the *Atlantic Monthly* for January, 1892, by Basil L. Gildersleeve, and "Why the Men of '61 Fought for the Union," *ibid.*, March, 1892, written by General J. D. Cox, one of the best military men on the Union side in the war, state the divergent views of the two sections admirably.

nations of antiquity, the slaves had been of the master's own color, with few exceptions, and on emerging from slavery, such of them as did emerge, took their place in the mass of the population. But when the black slave of the South bought his freedom and became a free black, his position was one that was full of peril to himself and that was dreaded by the white.

Besides the plantation aristocracy, there were professional men in the South, lawyers, doctors, clergymen, newspaper editors — and each of these owned or hired a slave or a slave family or two, or more. It is astonishing to note how many lawyers and newspaper men there were in the South in proportion to the white population, and it is surprising to observe how closely bound together were the leaders of public opinion in all these walks of life.[1] To be a white man, whether slaveholder or not, was to possess a position in society commensurate with one's ability. Inevitably, in the contest of life, the young man who started with good educational and social advantages rose above the surface more quickly than did the poorer young man who had no such opportunities, but there were innumerable examples of the rapid advancement of men who were distinctly outside the limits of the plantation aristocracy, and there were many Northerners who had gone to the South, married there, and had at once taken place with the local aristocracy. Joseph E. Brown, the war governor of Georgia, is an example of a poor young man who made his way to high station. Governor Quitman of Mississippi was born in New York of immigrant parents, and

[1] Alexander H. Stephens, while incarcerated at Fort Warren in Boston Harbor in 1865, wrote in his diary : "The Southern mind was influenced and misguided by a class of public men, politicians not statesmen, newspaper editors and preachers, who possessed far more ambition and zeal than wisdom and knowledge. . . . They precipitated the Southern people into reassumption of their independence as States, more as an escape from anticipated wrongs than from actual grievance." *Recollections*, 326.

assigned to it. And before closing this paragraph, it may be well to note that Walter Hines Page was born and bred in a small North Carolina town in the years around 1860.

The number of persons who actually held title to negroes as slaves, whether considered in proportion to the white population or as an absolute number, was not large. It has been estimated in 1850 as low as 150,000 and as high as 375,000.[1] Taking 250,000 as a convenient number and supposing that each one of these represented a slaveholding family of five persons on the average, one might estimate the number of white persons directly or indirectly holding slaves as one million and a quarter. All such estimates are entirely devoid of meaning because the white people of the coastal plain and of the neighboring piedmont region believed fully that the prosperity of the South and of themselves depended upon the production of the staple crops by slave labor; and there were few white men in that country, except the hopelessly poor of the pine barrens, who did not expect some time or other to own a slave. Southern society was unified by the presence of the negro and by the constant attacks that were made upon their "peculiar institution" and upon themselves by the abolitionists and other agitators in the North. It was the first time in the history of the world that it was proposed to found a state on the enslavement of human beings of one color by masters of another. Black slaves had been held and were held in Africa by black owners. In the

[1] See De Bow's *The Interest in Slavery of the Southern Non-Slaveholder* (Charleston, S. C., 1860, p. 3). De Bow uses the phrase "actual slave-holders" to include all members of slaveholding families and in that way reaches the conclusion that "the number of actual slaveholders" was about two millions and a quarter. W.

L. Fleming (*The South in the Building of the Nation*, v, 117) states that there were in 1860 "only 384,000 slaveholders, representing probably 325,000 families." See also the *Statistical View of the United States. . . . Compendium of Seventh Census*, 95, and *Census* of 1860, "Agriculture," p. 247.

Senator James H. Hammond of South Carolina was the son of a newcomer from Massachusetts. The Southern whites believed their prosperity to be bound up with the slave system; they looked to their State as to their country. They believed their State to be "sovereign," — whatever the word might mean, — and that their peculiar institution was recognized in the Constitution of the United States and was guaranteed by the provisions of that instrument.

The Southern slave system, as it was in the decade before 1860, appeared very differently to the person who had been born and bred on a Southern plantation, to a visitor from the North or from England, to an abolitionist agitator, and to the negro himself. Andrew Carnegie tells a story that exhibits the essence of the objection to the system. An Ohio judge is represented as interrogating a fugitive slave and upon the colored man telling him that he had plenty of food, good shelter, plenty of clothes, and a good master and that he did not have to work very hard, the white man suddenly asked, why if he had all these things did he run away, and the fugitive replied that the place he had left was open, that the judge could go down and take it, — and resumed his line of march for Canada. Like everything else the goodness or the badness of the system depended upon the point of view. The Northerner was greatly affected by the change in buildings and by the general dilapidated condition of fields and stock as he passed from Pennsylvania southward. It was pointed out, however, that throughout the whole Southern region the white man was master. If he desired things other than as they were, he could provide them at the expense of "the crop." If he preferred to make the largest number of bales of cotton that he could with his labor supply, he had to concentrate all his efforts and those of his slaves on the production of cotton; and when the soil was exhausted to move away to other fields. Under these circumstances, it was not good policy to build large houses and barns. On the greatest plantations, the amount of land was so considerable in comparison with the number of slaves that when one field was exhausted a new field could be prepared within the plantation limits and the master's house would naturally assume a permanent form.[1] By 1850, slaves had become so valuable in dollars and cents that they could not be used profitably except in localities where their labor in gangs could be advantageously employed. So far from there being any necessity for new areas to occupy with slave labor, there were not nearly enough slaves to cultivate the existing cotton area, — more slaves not more land was the need of the South.[2]

Reading some Southern books, one gains the impression that life on a great Mississippi plantation for master and for slave was as near to the ideal state of existence as the world has ever seen. Undoubtedly on the Dabney plantation and on Jefferson Davis's own property of Brierfield and on many other plantations, the conditions were very good.[3]

[1] A discussion of the Southern industrial system is to be found in a book of 304 pages entitled *Notes on Political Economy, as applicable to The United States by a Southern Planter* (New York, 1844). The author was N. A. Ware and the book reflects the ideas of an intelligent Southerner. He gives the cost of slave labor at six cents per day or about one-sixth part of the wages of free laborers and does it by leaving out of account all the cost of maintaining negro children, old people, the sick, and the maimed.

[2] John A. Parker (*National Quarterly Review* for July, 1880, p. 118) noted that the South in seeking for an extension of slave territory contended for a principle which would have been of no benefit to it, because there were then open to slavery "unoccupied lands sufficient to employ all the slaves in the United States and their increase for at least one hundred years to come."

George Melville Weston's *Progress of Slavery in the United States* (Washington, 1857) is an excellent moderate Northern estimate of the system.

[3] Professor Walter L. Fleming described the conditions that prevailed on Davis's plantation in the *Sewanee Review*, xvi, 407–427. Senator Hammond of South Carolina declared that "at no time has the African ever attained so high a status . . . as in the condition of American SLAVERY." Extract from a letter written in 1856 in E. Merritt's "James Henry Hammond" in *Johns Hopkins Studies*, xli, No. 4, p. 112.

On the other hand, there were hard-hearted and cruel masters. Probably the truth in the matter would be somewhere between these two extremes. A manuscript account of life on a Mississippi plantation, that was written a quarter of a century after the war and without a thought of publication, throws much light on the problem. The author says that the life of the slaves on his father's plantation was not one of discontent. The negroes had no conception of the value of liberty and were satisfied with their lot. They would have liked exemption from work, as is the case with most of us, and they had some ill-defined desire for better food and clothing. The profits of their labor went to the master and he endeavored to maintain them as cheaply as possible; "but self interest as well as humanity prompted him to give them quite as full a measure of creature comforts as they were capable of enjoying usefully." Their chief grievance was the inability to go about without a permit, as any colored man found on the highway was liable to be stopped by a white man and turned over to a constable, — although in ordinary times this probably would not happen. The overseers on his father's plantation were chosen for their skill in agriculture more than for their "driving capacities." With one exception, those that this writer knew in his early life were mild-mannered and gentle-hearted men. He states that he saw more "cruelty" in the army from the officers to the white men under them than he ever saw on his father's plantation. He declares that the brutalizing effects of slavery as he knew it had not made the savage inhabitants of equatorial Africa or their descendants more brutal. Nevertheless, the effects of slavery were so terrible on the whites that the benefits conferred by it upon the slaves in no way counterbalanced this; and he, undoubtedly, was thoroughly rejoiced at its ending even through so terrible

a catastrophe as the destruction of the old Southern society.[1]
A visitor, coming afresh from New York, or Chicago or
Boston, or an English man or woman arriving from London
was naturally affected by the slackness of household service
and by the realization that these human beings were the
property of their masters as were the horses and the cattle
on the plantations.   Also, they undoubtedly saw punishment
inflicted, but very few of them ever mention anything but
the most inconsequential whipping, nothing like, indeed,
what the traditional English school boy expected and endured in many of the public schools in those days, and nothing like the severe punishments inflicted on seamen in the
American navy until this very year, 1850.[2]   In any attempt
to appraise the condition of negroes in slavery in the epoch
under review, it must be, in part at least, governed by the
fact that each one of them in the years of his or her greatest
activity and at this period in our history was worth from one
thousand to two thousand dollars.   No planter could have
worked his slaves beyond their capacities or inflicted labor-
destroying punishments upon them without serious loss to
himself.   In point of fact, if the crop were poor, if provisions
were hard to get, it was the white family in the house that
suffered, and not the negroes in the cabins; for whatever else
might happen the bodily capacity of the slaves must be
maintained for the next crop season.   Also it is true that for
a brief period in each year, at cotton-picking time and at the
sugar-making season, labor was severe in the field and in the
sugar house, but it may safely be said that it was never more
severe than it was in the iron-making establishments of the
North or, at times, on the farms of the Free States.   Southern

[1] Professor Francis A. Shoup, a
veteran of the Confederate army, wrote
in the second volume of the *Sewanee
Review* (p. 104) that the result of the
War for Southern Independence was
the emancipation of the Southern white.
[2] See the present work, volume v,
165, 189, notes.

writers and speakers, one after another, tell us that one could see more wretchedness in a day's walk on the streets of New York than one could witness on a tour through the South, — and the slave when old and infirm was cared for on the plantation and not turned adrift to beg or to starve.[1] Indeed, in the story of John Brown's raid on Harper's Ferry, nothing so arrests the attention of the student as the fact that not a slave voluntarily joined the band of "deliverers." And nothing is more noteworthy in the four years of the war than the fact that the white women and children lived through those four years on the plantations in perfect security from the plantation slaves. It is said that after the first months of the war their husbands and brothers in the Confederate army sent their pistols to the people at home; it was not to protect them from the slaves, but that they might have means of defence against "insult and violence" at the "hands of the ruffians who prowled about the country shirking duty."[2]

All treatments of Southern life by Northern writers gave an entirely false assessment of the weaknesses and the strengths of the slave system. They uniformly applied white standards to black life without any comprehension of the actualities of negroid, racial development. This was partly due to the inability of every man and woman to see

---

[1] In 1856, an anonymous pamphlet was printed at Charleston, replying to an address that Dr. Orville Dewey had delivered at Sheffield in Massachusetts. This unknown writer asserts that there are far more fearful sights in the North than the selling of slaves in the South. Indeed, so he asserted, the sale preserved the slave from the misery of the "unemployed hireling," for the sale is merely "the mode by which he is transferred from the master who cannot support him to the master who can." It is the slave's labor only that is sold and bought and not his body and soul: "his body is as much his own as the hired operative's, and his soul as free to engage in its proper occupation." The terrible crimes of the day belonged to the North and not to the South, but when a Southern slaveholder killed a slave in a fit of passion the killing was attributed to the institution and not to the man as it was when a Northern husband killed his wife.

[2] Carlton McCarthy in Southern Historical Society's Papers, ii, 133.

good in unaccustomed ways of living of other persons; but it was more especially due to the fact that in those days knowledge of negroid institutions and conceptions of negroid ideals were very vague and extremely inaccurate. Since 1890, many competent explorers have visited Central Africa and the Congo and have set down in print the results of their observations and of their communings with the natives. Reading these many accounts,[1] weighing them, and trying to draw judgment from them, it appears that it is about as hard for the Ethiop to change his institutional and racial conceptions as it is for him to alter the color of his skin. Both his institutions and his skin are matters of heredity. They have come down from a very remote past and are, even today, being handed on unchanged to future generations.

In his pure condition, undiluted by white or yellow blood, the negro is essentially a communist and a fatalist. He belongs to his tribe. His chief holds powers unknown to any Caucasian governor or king. Slavery is the recognized condition of many men and women in most of the tribes of Africa in their pristine state. Slaves are taken in war, or a man sells himself into slavery to procure protection, or he is enslaved by reason of some criminal act. In any case, the life of an African slave in Africa is in no great degree harder than that of many a free man in his own village and certainly is not as hard as that of the great majority of the women of his tribe. In Africa the woman is looked upon as an asset. The coming of the girl child is welcomed, for at maturity she will bring to her father from five to fifty cows or goats — according to her station in life and the station in life of her husband. Once married, the wife is the maintainer of the

---

[1] Among the innumerable books on central and western Africa reference may be made to A. L. Kitching's *On the Backwaters of the Nile;* John Roscoe's *The Baganda;* Sir Harry Johnston's *George Grenfell and the Congo* (2 vols.) ; and E. Torday's *Camp and Tramp in African Wilds.*

family. She not only cooks the food and keeps the house;
she provides the food, for it is the women who cultivate the
fields. The men devote themselves to the chase and to the
protection of their fields and their families from the enemies
across the border. Once in a while the father helps in house-
building and, in some parts of Africa, occasionally he joins
the women in the field. In most African tribes, if a man
prospers, he obtains more cows or goats and is able to purchase a second wife who is welcomed by the first wife, as her
coming makes lighter the work of the family group. There
is no family in the African conception like that of the Caucasian, and the breaking up of a family bore slight resemblance
to the destruction of family ties according to white man's
ideas. These observations apply only to the uncontami-
nated parts of Africa and to the pure-blooded slaves of
America. The moment there was any considerable infiltra-
tion of alien blood, the negro's physical and mental constitution and moral make-up underwent a change.

J. D. B. De Bow[1] of New Orleans in the "Census" of
1850 undertook to give the first definite picture of the proportionate colors of the Southern population. It appears
that no less than four hundred thousand of the three and a
half million colored persons in the United States in 1850
were mulattoes; and in ten years' time the mulattoes numbered nearly six hundred thousand in a total colored population of nearly four and one-half millions. Indeed, in that

[1] He was a native of Charleston, South Carolina, his father having come there from New Jersey. At the moment he was a professor in the University of Louisiana and the editor and publisher of *The Commercial Review of the South and West*. De Bow's *Compendium* of the seventh census was the first of a useful form of statistical compilation. In 1852 De Bow published three volumes entitled *The Industrial Resources, Etc., of the Southern and Western States*. In 1853 the title of the *Commercial Review* was changed to *De Bow's Review and Industrial Resources, Statistics, Etc.* Volume x, published in 1851, has an index to the first ten volumes which is "fearfully and wonderfully made."

decade, of every one hundred colored births, seventeen were mulattoes.[1] "The white man's burden" in the South, in those days, was to keep the white race white. It is difficult to turn to a Southern book of that time or to a description of Southern life without coming across some allusion to miscegenation. Anyone thinking for a few moments of time must come to some conclusion as to the effect of such conditions on the white families of the South — on the young men and on the young women. Hinton Rowan Helper, himself a North Carolinian, who lived most of his mature life in South America and in California, once wrote of the "Africanized South." On the other hand, one must consider how difficult it was for the census taker, or anyone else, to separate the undiluted black negro from the negro diluted with white blood ; and also how great an effect the story of a mulatto woman killing her daughter to keep her from the life that she herself had been forced to lead must have had. The figures of the census bureau were very arbitrary and imperfect. They do not point to any such black taint of the white blood as so many writers have suggested.[2]

Another topic about which something must be said was the exportation of slaves from the northern Slave States — North Carolina, Virginia, Maryland to the east of the mountains, and Tennessee, Kentucky, and Missouri to the west of them. It is a subject about which it is easy to make statements which are impossible of proof, but which are not therefore necessarily false. Probably thousands of negro slaves were sold southward from the northern Slave States every year from 1850 to 1860. It could hardly have been otherwise, for the demand for labor on the cotton plantations was

[1] *Census* of 1860, "Population," page x ; see also the Bureau of Census's special study by John Cummings entitled *Negro Population, 1790–1915* (Washington, 1918).

[2] Rhodes's *History of the United States*, i, 335–343.

much greater than it was on the tobacco farms. Moreover, it was much cheaper for the planter to import a large part of the food for the slaves from the free labor States adjoining the slave area than it was to produce it himself. It has been suggested that the net income from the tobacco States from their agricultural products was not equal to one per cent on the valuation of the real and personal property and that the balance of the income of the planters and farmers of that region was made up by the sale of slaves to "the South." Or, as another writer stated it, in times of drought or difficulty a child was sold to feed its parents, or the parents were sold to feed the children. It is certain that the premium on the production of negro children in the northern tier of the Slave States was great, for each one born was worth in a very short time about two hundred dollars to its master. It is hardly necessary to go farther. One has only to think for another moment to arouse in his mind many unpleasant surmises as to the results of such a condition of affairs, however we may minimize it, upon both master and slave. Moreover, the traffic, great or small, established an economic bond between the northern region of "tolerated slavery," if one may use such a phrase, and the cotton South and thereby strengthened the political and social forces that bound the two sections of the Slave States together.

In 1850, before the great increase in the money price of slaves, it was probably true that on the best conducted plantations the slave gang was the cheapest and most efficient agricultural labor in the world in terms of the crop produced. It was argued that the food, clothing, and shelter of a slave cost about three-fifths as much as those of a free white laborer. It would seem, therefore, that slave labor would destroy free white competition. And, certainly, for one reason or another, in the agricultural sections of the South

the free white farmer did not prosper in competition with
the negro slave, although the precise reason for this may not
be entirely clear. In those days and since, it has been stated
with more or less dogmatism, that the climate of the Southern coastal plain made it impossible for the white man to
compete with the black man in the field.[1] When the war
came, however, one of the things that compel the student's
attention is the fact that the Southern poor whites and the
men of the Southern piedmont region, enfeebled as they were
supposed to be by malaria and other subtropical diseases,
were able to outmarch the Northern soldiers. They also
proved themselves able to withstand exposure and insufficient nourishment better than their Northern opponents.
It is true that in the years from 1830 to 1860, great epidemics
swept over parts of the South and it is also true that certain
diseases were always present there which were comparatively
harmless in the North. Of the former, the cholera[2] and the
yellow fever appear to have visited white and black impar-
tially. The distinctive Southern disease was "malaria,"
which included in those days a wide range of disorders,
among them what we now denominate ague, dysentery, and
the hookworm. Malaria, properly so called, and fever and
ague are not at all peculiar to the southern South; they were
all present in the Ohio Valley and distressed the settlers of
Ohio, Indiana, and Illinois, as they did the poor whites of
South Carolina or Mississippi. Various forms of dysentery
and the anæmia due to the inhabitancy of the human body
by the hookworm were peculiar Southern diseases; but

[1] Writing to the Secretary of the
English Cotton Supply Association in
July, 1857, Frederick Law Olmsted
maintained that free white labor could
produce more cotton man for man than
the laborers of the African race. He
was referring especially to Texas; but
maintained that this was true save as to
"exceptional malarious and pestilential
regions." *American Historical Review*,
xxiii, 114.

[2] On the cholera in the South and the
West, see the Mississippi Historical
Society's *Publications*, vii, 271.

they were not the effects of a sub-tropical climate.[1] It was the conditions of sanitation, or lack of it, and the habit of going barefooted that made it possible for the hookworm to gain admittance to the human body. Scientific men tell us that the hookworm came from Africa on the slave ship. It was the poorer whites who were more likely to receive the disease and, once started in a community, even in our own time, it is hard to eradicate. The outward effects of the hookworm are visible on the extremities, ulcers appearing on the tibia or shin-bone. It is curious that the disease does not interfere with the use of the legs, the effects of the anæmia being observable in the loosened grasp of the fingers. Nowadays, when the hookworm has been largely banished from the South and malaria, yellow fever, and cholera no longer threaten the community, white labor finds no difficulty in competing with the negro in the cotton field.

In the preceding pages, reference has been mainly to the Cotton States. North of these was a belt of Slave States in which the conditions of production were largely against the utilization of negro labor, for it was only under very peculiar circumstances that black labor was more efficient than white. In the production of grain, in the breeding of cattle and horses, in the preparing of turpentine and rosin, in the mining of coal and iron, and in the working up of iron ore and cotton fibre, this northern belt of Slave States possessed, each of them, large areas in which there were no negroes, or in which the employment of negroes was confined to one or two families for each slave owner. Moreover, as

[1] On the hookworm, see Dr. C. W. Stiles's "Prevalence and Geographic Distribution of Hookworm Disease" forming *Bulletin* No. 10, issued by the Hygienic Laboratory of Washington in 1903. On p. 79 is a study of the prevalence of the disease in the United States and on p. 96 of the economic importance of it. The "Introduction" to the *Bibliography of Hookworm Disease*, published by the Rockefeller Foundation in 1922, is a brief but most interesting account of the matter.

one ascended from the line of five hundred feet of altitude above the sea, the negro population became scantier and scantier, until in the mountain region there were few or no negroes to be found and the white people of the mountains did not belong to the white population of tide-water Virginia and Carolina and the Cotton States. They sprang from other migrations and were closely allied to the people of Pennsylvania. One of the most far seeing of the Southern leaders, Robert Y. Hayne, had devised and pushed forward a project for uniting by railroad the Ohio Valley at Louisville and Covington opposite Cincinnati with the southern Atlantic seaboard at Charleston. The physical and political obstacles to the carrying out of this plan were so formidable that no such road was built and operated in time to divert the commerce of the upland South to the south-east and thus bind the people of this region by ties of interest and affection with the people of the southern coastal plain.[1] As it was, the efforts of the South, in so far as they were directed towards railroad building, centered about a plan to connect the Mississippi Valley at Memphis with the Southern States on the Atlantic. In 1860, a peninsula of population extended from the Virginia panhandle southward to the northern counties of Alabama and Georgia and westward to central Kentucky and Tennessee that had little or no share in Southern life and traditions. It is clear that the Southern leaders, instead of concentrating the cotton interest, should have striven to unite the people of the geographic South by bonds of interest and affection through marriage and commercial intercourse.

Whenever one thinks of the South in the older time, there arises a picture of an agricultural community. And this picture is the true one, taking the slaveholding States as a

[1] See Theodore D. Jervey's *The Railroad, the Conqueror* (Columbia, S. C., 1913) and his *Robert Y. Hayne,* "Book iv"; and *Correspondence of John C. Calhoun* (American Historical Association's *Report,* 1899, vol. ii).

whole, for the profits derived from growing cotton and tobacco by slave labor were so great that it was cheaper to procure manufactured goods from the North and from Europe than it was to produce them. Nevertheless there were manufacturing industries in the South in 1850, and the capital invested and the amount produced were distinctly appreciable and in the decade preceding secession increased in equal proportion with those of the North. Omitting from "the South" Delaware, Maryland, and Missouri, but including the area that later became West Virginia, one finds that the South in 1850 turned out manufactured goods to the amount of one hundred million dollars. The North, including the Slave States north of the Potomac and the State of Missouri, produced nine times that amount.[1] In the next ten years the manufactured products of the South increased to one hundred and ninety-three millions, while those of the North rose to something under seventeen hundred millions.

Cotton spinning and weaving were confined for the most part to the Carolinas. In North Carolina there were many mills, and in Virginia a factory was in operation in the town of Manchester on the opposite side of the James River from Richmond. The most interesting establishment of the kind, however, was the Graniteville Manufacturing Company in South Carolina, nearly opposite Augusta, Georgia. The president of this corporation was William Gregg. In 1854 he presented a report[2] which contained, besides the usual statistical information as to operation and profits, a valuable dissertation on manufacturing in the South and the reasons

[1] *Census* of 1860, "Manufacturing," pp. 729, 730. See also Samuel B. Ruggles's *Tabular Statements from 1840 to 1870*, at foot of pages 10, 16, 22, 28, 34, 37.

[2] *Report of the President and Treasurer of the Graniteville Manufacturing Com-pany, for the Year 1854* (Charleston, 1855). See also William Gregg's *Essays on Domestic Industry; or, An Inquiry into the Expediency of Establishing Cotton Manufactures in South-Carolina* (Charleston, 1845).

why it had not had greater success. The net earnings of the Graniteville Company had been nearly sixty-five thousand dollars for the year, about one-half of which was paid out in dividends to stockholders. He states that the success of his company was not accidental, but was due to the cheap labor supply, the mild climate, the low cost of the raw material, and the home market for the finished goods. He enumerates five causes for the failure of many Southern manufacturing enterprises. The first is the attempt to use cheap machinery and the failure to provide a surplus of water power. Secondly, no mill should attempt to turn out more than one or two kinds of goods: the plant must not be located in a run-down city or town, but should be established where laborers can be attracted to it and, when once assembled, everything should be done to encourage a community spirit among the operatives. Finally, the capital must be sufficiently large not only to provide for the building of the mills and the supplying of the machinery, but also to provide ample working funds. It was the lack of this last that had caused the destruction of many manufacturing enterprises in the South. It is noticeable, that Gregg does not refer to slavery as having anything to do with either the success or the failure of Southern manufacturing enterprises. Undoubtedly, although Gregg does not say so, the real cause of the small development of Southern manufacturing compared with that of the North up to the year 1850 was that every dollar could be more profitably utilized in the production of staple agricultural crops than in operating cotton machinery. At all events, in 1860, of the 5,236,000 spindles in the whole country only 290,000 were in the South.[1]

At New Orleans, at Richmond, and in numerous localities

[1] These figures are taken from Victor S. Clark's *History of Manufactures in the United States*, 558.

in the valleys of the Tennessee and Cumberland rivers there were ironworking establishments and also in northern Alabama and northern Georgia; but Atlanta was then on the very threshold of its career and the deposits of the Birmingham district had not yet been worked to any great extent.[1] Of these Southern ironworking establishments, the Tredegar Iron Works at Richmond stood foremost. This was due to the knowledge and business capacity of Joseph R. Anderson. A general machine and iron business was done there, and steam engines of various kinds and cannon were produced. Counting in the Tredegar, there were in Richmond in 1860, seventy-seven ironworking establishments valued at over three and a half million dollars. Richmond, indeed, was a prosperous and growing manufacturing center, at that time possessing no less than eighty tobacco factories, fifteen flour mills, two cotton factories and one woolen factory, and many boot and shoe makers. All in all, these iron works and other manufacturing establishments in the capital city of Virginia were valued at about twenty-five million dollars.[2] It is remarkable how one comes across evidences of manufacturing impulses and of their fruition in most out-of-the-way places. In 1851, E. Steadman published at Clarksville, in Tennessee, "A Brief Treatise on Manufacturing in the South." He gave many examples of what had already been accomplished in that direction and he advocated strongly the Southerners working up their own productions themselves. Again in 1856, the "American Cotton Planter" for December of that year printed a list of awards given at the Alabama State Agricultural Society's meeting for the best Southern articles of manufacture of

[1] See descriptions with maps in John P. Lesley's *Iron Manufacturer's Guide* (New York, 1859).
[2] *An Illustrated and Descriptive Catalogue of Manufactures of Tredegar Iron Works. Joseph R. Anderson & Co.* (Richmond, 1860), p. 14. For a summary of the manufactures of that time, see J. H. Colton's *Progress of the United States*, 19–21.

cotton, leather, farming implements, and machinery. This publication was issued at Montgomery, the capital of the State, and aspired to be "to the South what the 'Country Gentleman' is to the North — a first class family paper." All this evidence shows that the South, even the Far South, had drawn away from the anti-manufacturing attitude of the 1830's, and the manufacturing activity in the Confederate States during the war reënforces this idea.

In 1850 the social fabric of the Northern States was on the verge of the tremendous change that marked the beginning of the industrial revolution which has extended from 1861 to our own time. But even then, notwithstanding the hampering effects of Southern tariff or anti-tariff legislation, the industrial products of the North were already considerable as compared with those of the South, although trifling as compared with what they were to be in 1870. In 1860, the capital invested in manufacturing enterprises in the South was ninety-six millions of dollars; in the North nearly ten times that amount. And the annual products of manufactures were valued in the South at one hundred and fifty-five millions and in the North at more than ten times that amount.[1] By far the greater manufacturing activity in the North in those days was in the States to the eastward of the Ohio River; the States west and north of that river and Kentucky also were devoted mainly to agricultural pursuits. The farms of New England, central New York, and central Pennsylvania were able even then to feed a very large proportion of the people of the manufacturing cities, towns, and villages. The farms of Transappalachia in 1849 exported wheat, corn, and hogs, through the northeastern gateway to the amount only of some four million bushels of wheat, two million barrels of flour, three and a half million bushels

[1] *Census* of 1860, "Manufactures," p. 729.

of corn, and one hundred and fifty thousand barrels of pork. In that year there was a large and constant exportation of pork and corn from the Ohio Valley States[1] southward by the river to feed the slaves of the great plantations of the cotton and sugar area.

In the North as in the South, the most difficult problem at this period was to procure an adequate supply of labor. The closing of the slave trade had put an absolute ending to any legalized importation of bond servants from Africa, but the immigration of free white laborers from Europe was not restrained by law in any way. Immigrants were coming by the thousands and the hundred thousands and had been coming for some years, and the stream of them was so great by the middle of the decade that serious social and political problems arose. One effect of this flow of immigration had been to replace the native-born factory operatives by foreigners to a very great extent. This in turn had led the active and enterprising young men and women and some of the older of the native-born to seek the richer lands of the western country; and in 1849 and the following years, the gold discoveries of California drew hundreds of thousands of the most enterprising and restless of native Americans to the Pacific coast either to the mines or to commercial enterprises connected therewith or to the farming areas to produce food for the gold seekers and merchants. What with the incoming tide of immigrants and the outgoing flood of westward pilgrims of native stock, the proportion of foreigners and their children to the native-born had become distinctly noticeable. In the State of New York, one-quarter of the total population was composed of recently arrived immigrants and their children; in eastern Massachusetts the

---

[1] These figures and those in ch. xiii are taken from an unpublished study   made by Professor Albert L. Kohlmeier of Indiana University.

case was even more striking, and in Philadelphia and in Baltimore, the non-native American population was proportionately very large; most of these people in the Northeastern States were newly arrived immigrants from Ireland and Germany. In the Northwestern States, there were comparatively few Irish men and women, but there were large numbers of Germans, Scandinavians, and Poles. Some of the Western States were very active in diverting immigration toward themselves. In 1852, Wisconsin, for example, had a "Commissioner" in New York City whose business it was to turn the tide of immigrants toward his State. In 1853, he printed his first report.[1] It appeared that he had established an office in New York City and provided himself with pamphlets in English, Norwegian, German, and Dutch, booming Wisconsin. He found it difficult to circumvent the runners and tavern keepers and possibly rival "commissioners" who tried to keep the immigrants away from his office. He reports that in the second half of the year 1852 5,225 emigrants had actually started for Wisconsin on the Erie Railroad, and 4,561 had gone "partly with destination for our State." He stated that 2,372 other emigrants had started for Wisconsin on the Hudson River Railroad and 456 more had begun their journey to that State by steamboat.

All in all, there were two and one-quarter million persons of alien birth within the limits of the United States in 1850 and over nine-tenths of these were living north of Mason and Dixon line. The proportion of foreign-born to natives was not very large, but the immigrants congregated in the

[1] See *First Annual Report of the Commissioner of Emigration of the State of Wisconsin* (Madison, 1853). See also Livia Appel and Theodore C. Blegen's "Official Encouragement of Immigration to Minnesota during the Territorial Period" in the *Minnesota History Bulletin* for August, 1923, pp. 167–203. Nathan H. Parker's *Minnesota Handbook for 1856–7* gives an interesting picture of that Territory just before the panic of 1857.

commercial cities of the seaboard and in Chicago and Milwaukee and in rather well-defined areas in the agricultural States of the Northwest. Anyone going to Philadelphia, New York, or Baltimore could hardly fail to become conscious of the existence of a non-native element in the population and would be quite likely to jump at an entirely wrong conclusion as to the proportion of the immigrant population in the North as a whole.

The commerce of the country was then carried on almost entirely by Northern people and by Northern capital. In 1850 the ocean-going American mercantile marine was at its very highest point of efficiency and the coastwise commerce was also very extensive. New York was the center of commercial activity, both export and import. To it came the products of the farms of the North outside of central and eastern New England and to it came a very large proportion of the products of the Southern plantations. In fact, apart from Baltimore and New Orleans, the transoceanic trade of the Southern commercial seaports was very small. New York, also, and, to a smaller degree, Philadelphia and Boston, controlled the marketing of manufactured goods, not only to the interior of the North, but to the South as well. In 1860, at the time of the Southern secession, it was estimated that the South actually owed over two hundred million dollars to the merchants of the Northern commercial cities, especially to those of New York. The ship-building and ship-owning industry of the United States was at the very acme of its life in 1850. The clipper ships of Boston, New York, and Baltimore were renowned throughout the world for their speed and safety. They even competed with the steamships on the North Atlantic in the carrying of passengers from the United States to Great Britain. A few years were to see the substitution of the iron steamship for the wind-propelled wooden vessel, but few persons anticipated the doom of the clipper ship.

The growth of the country in population and in wealth after 1840 and especially after 1850 was marvelous, whether considered as a whole or with reference to the States that seceded, or to those States that remained in the Union. It is true, of course, that the science of statistics was in its infancy in those days, at least within the United States, but looking over the figures that are available and bearing in mind their crudeness, one may reach a few conclusions that are probably not very far from a reality. It appears that in 1850 the Southern States which later seceded contained practically one-third of the wealth, real and personal, of the entire United States. In the next ten years, however, the material progress of that portion of the country was not as great as was that of the North.[1] In 1850 and again in 1860, not one of these Southern States contained real and personal property put together to the value of one billion dollars; in 1850, New York State was valued at over one billion. In 1860, Ohio and Pennsylvania had passed the billion dollar mark and New York City itself had approached closely to the two billion dollar mark.[2] In 1861, in a debate in the Senate at Washington, Senator Wigfall of Texas had

---

[1] Thomas P. Kettell, on p. 4 of his *Southern Wealth and Northern Profits*, prints some figures showing that the South had been growing with great rapidity since 1850. In that year he states the assessed value of the North and West at $4,118,781,600, and in 1858 this amount had risen to $5,537,413,663. In 1850 the South had $2,947,781,366, which had increased in eight years to $4,620,617,564. As the figures of 1850 were taken from the Federal census and those for 1858 from State censuses, there probably were some considerable discrepancies, but the growth of the South was remarkable as compared with that of the North, whether the figures are absolutely exact or not. A criticism of Kettell's work was published at Philadelphia in 1861 with the title of *Notes on "Southern Wealth and Northern Profits."*

[2] *Census* of 1870, "Wealth and Industry," p. 10. This subject is analyzed in a volume issued by the Census Office in 1907 under the title, *Special Reports of the Census Office . . . Wealth, Debt, and Taxation*, p. 43.

declared that the North had no money with which to finance
a war, while the South gathered gold from the cotton stalks.
Senator Wilson of Massachusetts replied that the manufacturers of Massachusetts took a bale of Southern cotton
and returned it to the South in the shape of manufactured
goods with its value increased fivefold, and that the working
men and women of his State had deposits in the savings
banks within the State to the amount of forty-five million
dollars, which was larger than the total deposits of the seceded States in all their banks by all classes of their people
put together.[1] When the "Census" of 1860 was published,[2]
it appeared that in the decade before the war, not only had
the States of the Northeast increased in wealth, but California, in the ten or dozen years of its history, as a part of the
United States, had accumulated property to the value of
two hundred and seven million dollars. The wealth of
Illinois had increased from one hundred and fifty-six millions
to eight hundred and seventy-one millions and that of Iowa
from twenty-three millions to two hundred and forty-seven.
Some men in the South, like J. D. B. De Bow, anticipating
this result of the disproportionate development of the two
sections of the country, had striven by a course of commercial
and political propaganda to arouse the people of the South
to take a more active part in the commercial and industrial
development of the country. Something had been accomplished, but there was not the capital or the personal incen-
tive among the Southern people to accomplish so great a
design. Instead, they remained on their plantations, closed
their eyes, and contented themselves with counting the
wealth of prominent Southern persons and families. They

---

[1] The Crittenden Compromise — A
Surrender. Speech of Henry Wilson of
Mass., February 21, 1861.

[2] Census of 1860, "Mortality, Property &c.," p. 295.

pointed to the fact that in 1860 the Gordon plantations in Mississippi[1] were valued at over one and a half million dollars, that the Burnsides and the Chews of New Orleans were worth three millions apiece, that Wade Hampton was a two-million-dollar man, and that the James Bruce estate of Virginia was estimated as amounting to nearly four millions, including over three thousand slaves.[2] It seems never to have occurred to them that these fortunes could have been easily duplicated in New York City alone, for there the Astors were credited with possessing forty-one million dollars worth of property, William B. Astor himself being credited with twenty-five millions, — the richest man in America in those days of small fortunes. Among other New Yorkers, the Roosevelts and the Wendells were credited with three millions each, the Wadsworths and the Wrights with two apiece, and there were besides, the Brevoorts, the Lorillards, the Stuyvesants, and the Vanderbilts, the Van Rensselaers, and others of lesser possessions.[3] Of course, it is men and ideals and not money that make a nation and give the direction in which progress shall move. But when one thinks of taking a radical and far-reaching course of action, it is well to look the cold facts of numbers of men and millions of dollars squarely in the face. The Southern leaders were either unwilling or incapable of doing this very thing.

[1] Mississippi Historical Society's *Publications*, vi, 247.

[2] *The Virginia Magazine of History*, xi, 330.

[3] These figures are taken from *The Wealth and Biography of the Wealthy Citizens of the City of New York* (10th ed., 1846), Reuben Vose's *Rich Men of New York Series No. 4* (1862) and his *Wealth of the World Displayed* (New York, 1859).

NOTES

I. General Bibliography. — McMaster's comprehensive work stops with the election of 1860. The eighth volume, covering the decade from 1850 to 1860, which was published in 1919, is extremely useful. James Ford Rhodes, in the first five volumes of his *History of the United States Since the Compromise of 1850* has treated the subject in a broadminded way and simple language. He has minimized certain lines of thought, as that of the part played by the naval vessels during the war. In 1917, Mr. Rhodes published a volume with the title *History of the Civil War, 1861–1865*, which was a " fresh study of the subject," but he used his own book " as one of many authorities." Nicolay and Hay's *Abraham Lincoln, A History* (10 vols.) is in reality a survey of the period covered in the present volume and can be usefully illustrated by referring to the original papers in the *Complete Works of Abraham Lincoln*. Daniel W. Howe's *Political History of Secession* (New York, 1914) and Walter G. Shotwell's *The Civil War in America* (New York, 1923) are able and discriminating accounts of the period. Emerson D. Fite in his *Presidential Campaign of 1860* and his *Social and Industrial Conditions in the North during the Civil War* has treated one side of the problem with ability and interest. Professor John C. Schwab of Yale University in his *Confederate States of America* (New York, 1901) did for the South what Professor Fite did for the North in the second of his two volumes. Woodrow Wilson in his *Division and Reunion* in the " Epochs of American History " series, William E. Dodd in his *Expansion and Conflict* in the " Riverside History of the United States," vol. iii, Nathaniel W. Stephenson in his *Abraham Lincoln* and in his two small volumes in " The Chronicles of America Series," H. J. Eckenrode in his *Jefferson Davis, President of the South*, and Professor Albert Bushnell Hart in his volume on *Slavery and Abolition*, in the " American Nation " series, have provided brief and stimulating accounts of these years from different points of view. Titles of other works on this topic, down to the year 1906, are provided in the last-named book, pp. 324–343, and, to 1912, in Channing, Hart, and Turner's *Guide to the Study and Reading of American History*, pp. 421–461.

Several volumes of *The South in the Building of the Nation* have material on the years from 1850 to 1865, especially the articles in volume v by Ulrich B. Phillips, Logan W. Page, and Davis R. Dewey.

Of the larger books by contemporaries those by Jefferson Davis,[1] Alexander H. Stephens,[2] Horace Greeley,[3] and Henry Wilson[4] had great vogue in their day, but now are recognized as monuments of reminiscence and compilation and not as authoritative history.

II. **Descriptions of Southern Life.** — Frederick Law Olmsted's books describing his journeys through the South give a lifelike view of things as they appeared to the eyes of a Northerner fresh from the North.[5] The *Autobiography of Joseph Le Conte* (New York, 1903) relates the story of the childhood and youth on a Georgia plantation of a very remarkable man. Read in connection with his " Race Problem in the South " in the volume of the Brooklyn Ethical Association entitled *Man and the State* (pp. 347–402) one gains a very different conception of Southern society from what he obtains from a perusal of Olmsted's stimulating volumes or from J. E. Cairnes's *Slave Power* (London, 1862) that was once a leading authority on the subject from the non-slave-section point of view.[6] A book that has been extensively used is William H. Russell's *My Diary North and South* (2 vols., London, 1863). It consists of letters written to the London *Times*, of which he was special correspondent. Those relating to the South have been gathered into a convenient little volume entitled *Pictures of Southern Life, Social, Political, and Military* that was printed at New York in 1861. Naturally there was some editing of these letters in their transfer from newspaper page to printed book; the student, therefore, will seek the originals in the London *Times*. A familiar book is John B. Jones's *A Rebel War Clerk's Diary at the Confederate States Capital* (2 vols., Philadelphia, 1866). It is interesting, but was considered by his contemporaries as unreliable and "crammed with street rumors." Possibly the most instructive book is Mary B. Ches-

---

[1] *Rise and Fall of the Confederate Government* (2 vols., New York, 1881) and *Short History of the Confederate States of America* (New York, 1890).

[2] *Constitutional View of the Late War between the States* (2 vols., Philadelphia, 1868–1870).

[3] *The American Conflict* (2 vols., Hartford, 1864–1866).

[4] *History of the Rise and Fall of the Slave Power in America* (3 vols., Boston, 1872–1877).

[5] Olmsted's books are *A Journey in the Seaboard Slave States* (New York,

1856); *A Journey through Texas* (New York, 1857); and *A Journey in the Back Country* (New York, 1860). Upon these was based *The Cotton Kingdom* in two volumes (New York, 1861) and an identical work entitled *Journeys and Explorations in the Cotton Kingdom* was published at London in the same year.

[6] Another British subject, Robert Russell, in his *North America, Its Agriculture and Climate* (Edinburgh, 1857), gives a good sober account of the United States as an agricultural country.

nut's *Diary from Dixie* (New York, 1905). Her husband was in Richmond during a part of the war as military aide to President Davis. Mrs. Chesnut's references to plantation life are illuminating. Mrs. Susan D. Smedes's *Memorials of a Southern Planter* (Baltimore, 1887) is very highly regarded by students of Southern institutions. Her father, Thomas L. Dabney, while born in Virginia, lived the greater part of his life in Mississippi and managed a large number of slaves. He cannot be regarded as a typical planter, and it is very doubtful if his plantation or the life thereon, either of blacks or of whites, was typical, — he distrusted Jefferson Davis and did not believe in secession. In 1858 Thomas R. R. Cobb " of Georgia " printed *An Inquiry into the Law of Negro Slavery in the United States of America. To Which is prefixed, An Historical Sketch of Slavery.* The bound volume is marked " Vol. I," but no second volume was ever issued. A few copies of the " Historical Sketch " were bound separately with the first two chapters of the " Inquiry " added as an appendix. A rather detached view of Southern life can be obtained from the perusal of Catherine C. Hopley's *Life in the South; From the Commencement of the War. By a Blockaded British Subject* (2 vols., London, 1863) and the Rev. William W. Malet's *An Errand to the South in the Summer of 1862* (London, 1863). Possibly the best book of the type is Eliza F. Andrews's *The War-Time Journal of a Georgia Girl* (New York, 1908). This, again, relates primarily to war topics, but the side lights of the relations of the whites to the blacks are certainly interesting. A book that gave considerable comfort to the Southerners in the 1850's was Nehemiah Adams's *South-Side View of Slavery.* He was a New England clergyman whose abolitionistical conception of slavery received a rude shock during a three months' stay in Georgia and possibly led to a somewhat one-sided description.[1] Two most interesting glimpses of Southern society as they exist in latter-day Southern recollection are William Cabell Bruce's *Below the James* (New York, 1918) and Harry S. Edwards's *Eneas Africanus* (Macon, Ga., 1920). A readable Southern view of slavery and the struggle over it is Edward A. Pollard's *Black Diamonds* (New York, 1859).

[1] For other titles, see William K. Boyd and Robert T. Brooks's "Selected Bibliography and Syllabus of the History of the South, 1584–1876" (*Bulletin* of the University of Georgia, vol. xviii, No. 6, pp. 89–119).

CHAPTER II

CALIFORNIA, OREGON, AND JAPAN

NINE days before the treaty of peace with Mexico was signed at Queretaro, James W. Marshall on January 24, 1848, picked up the lumps of gold that immortalized his name and gave California a beginning such as no other state or country up to that year — within the range of modern history — had ever had.[1] Marshall had constructed a mill for Colonel Sutter on the South Fork of the American River at Coloma, about thirty-five or forty miles from the site of the later Sacramento. In the course of digging the mill-race and the pond into which it led, Marshall turned the water off and on. One morning he suddenly spied a queer-looking bit of rock on the floor of the sluice-way. It was soft, it was malleable, and it had an appearance of gold. He showed it to his men, but, although excited, they never thought that there might be large quantities of gold there or near at

[1] Early accounts are George G. Foster's *The Gold Regions of California* and J. Ely Sherwood's *California: Her Wealth and Resources*, both published at New York in 1848. David T. Ansted in his *Gold-Seeker's Manual* (New York, 1849) has brought together much interesting material about the gold deposits.

Among the books that found an early place were Henry I. Simpson's *Emigrant's Guide to the Gold Mines* (New York, 1848). The author of *Emigration for the Million . . . California* (London, 1848 or 1849) refers to California as the "Italy of Western America." Another interesting publication of the time is *Notes on California and the Placers. By One who had been there.*

Other books that deserve mention are T. J. Farnum's *Life, Adventures and Travels in California* (New York, 1849), Fayette Robinson's *California and Its Gold Regions* (New York, 1849), and William G. Johnston's *Experience of a Forty-Niner* (Pittsburg, 1892). The title page states that the author was a member of the first wagon train of 1849. Twenty-three engravings reproduced from drawings made "on the spot" are in William R. Ryan's *Personal Adventures in . . . California, in 1848-9* (2 vols., London, 1850).

hand. In due course, Marshall rode to Sutter's Fort and handed over the specimen to his employer. Together they experimented with it, decided that it was gold and endeavored to keep the discovery to themselves. This was impossible. A workman at Coloma paid a carter with a lump of gold and the existence of the precious metal[1] in the Sierras in no long time became public property.

For years the presence of gold in California, especially in the vicinity of Los Angeles and in the neighboring mountains, had been known. In 1841 or 1842 Thomas O. Larkin, later United States consul at Monterey, sent gold dust to New Bedford by the *Braganza*. In 1842, gold was found near Santa Barbara, and in the same year Abel Stearns sent twenty ounces of gold from California to Philadelphia.[2] And, again, in 1846, Larkin in one of his articles in the New York "Sun" stated that "north of the town of the Angels" placer gold could be picked up to the amount of ten dollars a day. It is possible that this common knowledge of the existence of gold and of silver also made men, who were then in California, take at first a very languid interest in the new discovery. On March 18, 1848, the "California Star," which was published at San Francisco,[3] noted that "Gold has been discovered in the Northern Sacramento Districts about forty miles above Sutter's Fort." Two

---

[1] John S. Hittell's *Marshall's Gold Discovery, A Lecture* (San Francisco, 1893) ; what purports to be "Marshall's Narrative" of the discovery is in *The Century*, xix, 537.
[2] Dr. Hugh Quigley's *The Irish Race in California, and on the Pacific Coast* (San Francisco, 1878) p. 146. In the manuscripts collected by the California Historical Survey Commission, there is an interesting letter dated "Rancho Chino . . . 1842" stating that "the grate noys of gold at St. Fernando" had induced the principal men there

to leave "to See what discovers they can make." See also the *Calhoun Correspondence* (American Historical Association's *Report* for 1899, ii, 1068) and A. Robinson's *Life in California* (New York, 1846) p. 190. A footnote to p. 324 of the 1869 edition of R. H. Dana's *Two Years before the Mast* states that his ship —the *Alert*— brought home a small quantity of gold-dust in 1836.
[3] From a manuscript copy in the Bancroft Library at Berkeley, California.

weeks later, on April 1, there was in the paper a paragraph on the "mine of gold," but little interest was expressed. On May 20, at length the "Star" announced that the gold fever or "Yellow Jack" had reached San Francisco. A "fleet of launches" had recently left for the Sacramento "closely stowed with human beings, led by the love of 'filthy lucre.' . . . Was there ever anything so superlatively silly?" At about the same time, on May 26, Larkin wrote a long letter from San José which contains the first mention of Marshall's discovery in the "Larkin Papers." [1] Nothing was heard, so he wrote, but "Gold, Gold, Gold. An onze a day, two a day, or three — everyone has the gold or yellow fever." Already several thousand dollars worth of gold had been taken in payment of goods and carpenters were asking six dollars a day. Nine men in ten whom he met on the street asked him if he had "left home to look for gold." By June 10, the editor of the "Star" himself had succumbed to the fever and printed an editorial displaying belief in the reality of the mines and that they would powerfully affect the future of San Francisco as well as that of the Valley of the Sacramento, — and so they did.

Before the end of September, 1848, notices of the discovery of gold in California appeared in the columns of the Eastern newspapers. Specimens of the precious metal reached Washington in time to find mention in President Polk's last annual message of December, 1848. In the spring of 1849, twenty thousand men were said to be waiting on the banks of the Missouri River for the first oppor-

---

[1] On April 25, 1849, Samuel H. Willey wrote to Larkin from Monterey that "one or two men are now and then seen walking the streets" and that the soldiers are "getting up appetites for the mines." In later life Dr. Willey summarized the history of these years in a little book entitled *The Transition Period of California* (San Francisco, 1901). Walter Colton in his *Three Years in California* (p. 247 and on) has a good deal of first-hand information on the early gold fever.

tunity to cross the plains on their way to the land of gold.
Somewhere between eighty thousand and one hundred and
fifty thousand persons reached California within the year
1849.[1] The accounts are vague and conflicting. Many
gold-seekers were easily discouraged and returned home or
proceeded northward to Oregon; but by the end of the year
there were one hundred thousand new-comers in California.
They had come from New England and from Missouri and
the country between; they had come from Virginia and
South Carolina and from Louisiana and Texas. They had
come from the British Isles and the European continent, and
from China, Australia, and the islands of the Pacific. In
1850 and in 1851, the current of immigration continued.
In the latter year, fifty-five million dollars worth of gold was
taken from the California soil. Clever men and shysters
looked upon the movement as one to be encouraged. They
published "Guides" and sold tickets.[2] They invented instruments to make easy the work of the gold-seeker. Among
these was Don José D'Alvear's "Goldometer" which worked
on the magnetic principle, or was advertised so to do, in the
Columbia, South Carolina, "Telegraph" for January 12,

[1] Thomas Butler King in his *California: The Wonder of the Age* (New
York, 1850, pp. 8, 15, 22) gives the
population of California as 15,000 in
1848 and 120,000 in 1850. In the
"Memorial" of 1850 (J. Ross Browne's
Debates, "Appendix," p. xxiii) the
population is given on January 1, 1849,
at 26,000 and one year later at 107,069.
Owen C. Coy of the California Historical Survey estimates the population of
"Central California" in 1852 at 207,000,
of whom about 36,000 were in San
Francisco. The *Census* of 1850, p. 972,
gives the number in California as 92,597,
which number is repeated in the *California State Almanac for 1856*. The
*Hand-Book Almanac for the Pacific
States: . . . for the Year 1862* that was

published at San Francisco contains, on
p. 92, a list of the counties of California
with the population of each, which is
substantially repeated in the *Hand-
Book* for 1863. The *Census* of 1850
(p. xxxvii) gives the foreign population of California as 22,358. Of these
6,454 were born in Mexico, 877 in South
America, 660 in China, and 319 in the
Sandwich Islands.

[2] *The Boston Daily Bee* of March 13,
1851, contains an advertisement of the
"American Ticket Office" and states
that cheap, comfortable, and speedy
passage would be provided by the
"Great Southern and Western Passage
Company" to all parts of the Southern
and Western States.

1849. This instrument would be sent to any one for the sum of three dollars with the "Gold-Seeker's Guide" so wrapped as to escape "the inspection of postmasters."

The tide of migration to the newest El Dorado was so great that existing facilities were severely taxed and gold seekers sailed around Cape Horn in coasting schooners that were hardly fit to voyage the sounds of New England.[1] In 1848, before the gold discovery had become known in the East, William H. Aspinwall had organized the Pacific Mail Steamship Company. The first vessel from New York by way of Cape Horn reached Panama on the last day of January, 1849, and was immediately crowded with gold-seekers awaiting passage for San Francisco. Soon, many steamers were plying from New York to Aspinwall and from Panama to San Francisco [2] and each month the railroad across the isthmus provided better facilities. But, oftentimes, hundreds of gold-seekers remained helpless in fever-stricken Panama for weeks and months. Those who belonged to the migrant pioneer type or who came directly from the farms of the Old Northwest, the plantations of the South, or the trans-Mississippi settlements followed the land route over the prairies and through the mountains.[3] Some of them even essayed to cross the greater part of the continent with what they could put into a handcart. From the Great

[1] For an account of these voyages, so far as they relate to Massachusetts immigrants, see Octavius T. Howe's *Argonauts of '49* (Cambridge, 1923).

[2] In December, 1852, the Pacific Mail Steamship Company had nine steamers plying between New York and New Orleans and Aspinwall and fifteen steamers on the Pacific. These left Panama on the arrival of the mail from the United States. The fare was from $35 to $65 from New York to Aspinwall; from $10 to $25 across the

Isthmus; and from Panama to San Francisco "on the most Favorable Terms." Freight from New York to Chagres was seventy cents per foot, and from Panama to San Francisco $100 per ton. Circular in the "Larkin Mss." in the Bancroft Library.

[3] Accounts of early overland journeys are *Extracts from the Diary of William C. Lobenstine*, Oliver Goldsmith's *Overland in Forty-Nine* (Detroit, 1896), and the *California Letters of William Gill . . . 1850* (New York, 1922).

Salt Lake one route lay westward over the Sierras. This was the most available way except in the winter months when snow filled the passes, — then the fate of a belated party was apt to be most tragic.[1] Southward from the Utah Valley, another line went through the arid regions to Southern California, the worst part of the way bearing the appropriate name of Death Valley.[2] Considering the inadequacy of the means of transportation, the ignorance of many of the migrants, the physical incapacities of some of them, and the epidemic disorders that infested portions of the route, it is remarkable that so many of them reached California, and even more remarkable that so many of them were able later to make their way back to their old homes.

The summer and autumn of 1848 saw a continuing exodus from the existing settlements in California to the mines. These people had already passed through the pioneer period. They attended strictly to their own affairs, and let other persons and property severely alone. With the coming of the gold-seekers, the "Forty-niners," the scene changed. Most of them were conscientious persons, but there were desperados from Australia, "plug-uglies" from New York, and others to whom the distinctions between mine and thine

[1] The discomforts and dangers of the Utah-Nevada route are vividly set forth in T. Turnbull's "Travels from the United States across the Plains to California" in the *Proceedings* of the State Historical Society of Wisconsin for 1913, pp. 151–220. The historic disaster befell what is known as the "Donner Party" in 1846–1847. No contemporary records of this expedition have come down to us, but accounts have been compiled from letters of the survivors written in later years and by two of the survivors who were children at the time of the expedition. C. F. McGlashan's *History of the Donner Party* (4th ed., San Francisco, 1881) gives heart-rending details; Eliza P. Donner Houghton's *Expedition of the Donner Party* (Chicago, 1911) records family recollections, including her own — but she was only four years old at the time — and Virginia Reed Murphy's "Across the Plains in the Donner Party" (*Century Magazine*, July, 1891, pp. 409–426) was likewise written by a person who was a child at the time of the disaster, but it has realistic illustrations, some of them from photographs of the country traversed.

[2] William L. Manly's *Death Valley in '49* (San José, Cal., 1894).

were not clear. The temptations were great, for the miners necessarily often left the produce of their labors in their tents, hidden away as well as they could. Sometimes they carried their treasure with them. Then, too, with the existing difficulties and cost of transportation, food and clothing possessed famine values. All in all, the temptation to steal and to kill was great and the probability of punishment uncertain and remote. It was under these circumstances that the miners and merchants decided that they must have some kind of definite government. They would have been content with a territorial organization; but Congress was so dominated by the question of free-soil or slave territory that it was impossible for it to enact any law as to the disposal of the lands acquired by the Treaty of 1848. The Federal representative in California was an army officer — Colonel Bennet Riley. He had no constitutional authorization to govern civilians, except orders from the President through the War Department. These directed him to continue the existing government by military law, — which it would seem difficult to defend on any ground except that of necessity. It is supposed that President Taylor sent an emissary or emissaries to California to incite the people there to take the matter into their own hands, draw up a constitution, and apply to Congress for admission to the Union as a State. Whether this supposition is absolutely correct or not, this was precisely what the Californians proceeded to do. Some of them held a meeting and issued a call for a convention. Thereupon the governor fell in with the movement, which he could not very well help doing, and also issued a call for a convention, somewhat varying the details as to apportionment and time of meeting. The convention met at Monterey on September 1, 1849, and held its final session on October 13. To it came representatives from all portions of the population : the miners, the merchants, and the old Californians.[1] Among its members were men who had come from the North, from the Old Northwest, from the South, and from outside the United States, mainly from England. The New York constitution provided the framework for the new instrument, as it did for so many of the newer States. Apart from the ordinary questions of organization, the debates turned upon the exclusion of negro slavery and on the extension of the proposed State to the eastward. There was practically no opposition whatever to the exclusion of slavery. The old Mexican-Californian population had not possessed slaves and did not want them. The new-comers from the South were, for the most part, from the non-slaveholding Southern classes, or from those who held very few slaves. They had no desire to introduce the slave-system into their new homes and spoke and voted solidly in favor of prohibition.[2] The Northern settlers and miners had come to California to work out their own salvation, and they did not at all relish having negro slaves laboring side by side with them in the fields and in the mines.

[1] John Ross Browne's *Report of the Debates in the Convention of California, . . . 1849* (Washington, 1850) and President Taylor's "Message" of January 24, 1850 (*House Executive Document*, No. 17, 31st Cong., 1st Sess.), p. 729 and on, contain practically all the documents. Bayard Taylor attended some of the sessions of the convention, and the pages of his *Eldorado*, giving his impressions of that body, partake of the nature of an original document. Rockwell D. Hunt's "Genesis of California's First Constitution" (*Johns Hopkins Studies*, xiii, No. viii) and his "Legal Status of California, 1846–49" in the *Annals* of the American Academy of Political and Social Science for November, 1898, pp. 387–408, treat the matter from a legal and constitutional standpoint. Cardinal Goodwin in his

"Question of the Eastern Boundary of California" (*Southwestern Historical Quarterly*, xvi, 227–258), and in his *Establishment of State Government in California* (New York, 1914) has summarized the whole matter, as Robert G. Cleland has in much briefer form in his *History of California: The American Period* (New York, 1922), ch. xviii.

[2] Owen C. Coy in *The Grizzly Bear*, xix, p. 1, says that negroes were held as slaves in California as late as 1853 and that Indians were apprenticed until the age of twenty-five, under conditions that closely resembled servitude. Interesting material on this general subject is in *The Journal of Negro History*, iii, 33–54, and in the *Report* of the American Historical Association for 1905, i, 243–248.

Indeed, when a Southern slaveholder appeared within the mining territory and proceeded to set his slaves to work, he was summarily excluded.[1] As a Mexican province, Alta California extended eastwardly to the limits of the old French Louisiana or, at all events, to the line of the Treaty of 1819, or to the parallel of 42° north latitude and to approximately the 106th meridian. If the proposed State extended to the 1819 line, it would have included what are now the States of Nevada and Utah. By 1849, there was a large settlement of the Mormons in the Utah Valley. With the Sierras intervening between them and the Sacramento and San Joaquin, under the existing conditions of transportation, it would be practically impossible for them to be represented in the legislature of the new State. There was a good argument, therefore, for restricting the eastern line to the Sierras. There may have been a few persons in the convention who thought that if the eastern boundary of the proposed State were fixed at the 106th or 114th meridians, in no long time it would be divided by an extension of the Missouri Compromise line (36° 30′). This would provide a State to which slaveholders might carry their slaves with some chance of profit. The real issue in the convention, however, seems to have been as to which line would arouse the least friction in Congress, and it was finally decided by an overwhelming vote in the convention that the new State should be bounded on the east as it is today.

Somewhat connected with the boundary question was the agitation that arose in California in the course of the next

---

[1] Cardinal Goodwin's *Establishment of State Government in California, 1846–1850*, pp. 110–112, gives the instance that is supposed to have led to the prohibition. Opposed is the statement in J. D. Borthwick's *Three Years in California* (London, 1857), p. 164, that there were many slaves in the mines and that in any town or camp of any size there was always a negro boarding-house.

decade for a division of the State by an east and west line.[1]
The supposition that has almost always been put forward
has been that this was a scheme on the part of the slaveocracy
to add to the territory open to slavery by taking California,
south of Monterey, out of the free soil area and leaving the
question of slavery open with the expectation that Southerners with their slaves would go to that country in such numbers that they would turn the territory into a Slave State.
This may be so, but the accessible records do not bear out
any such theory.　Northern and southern California differed
in those days economically: the main occupation of the
northern area was mining and commerce; that of the southern was agriculture and ranching.　Any system of taxation
that bore equitably on the people of one section inflicted a
hardship on the people of the other.　Moreover, the
southern region was still distinctly Spanish and Catholic,
while the northern part of the State was American, and
Protestant.　These were the reasons that actuated the
southern Californians in seeking division, and so far as
the records go, it was not slavery in any sense nor any
bond of sympathy with the slave-owners of the Cotton
States.

Before closing this topic of Californian statehood, it will
be well to say a word or two about gold-mining in its various
aspects.　In the twelve months of the year 1851 eighty-
one million dollars worth of gold was taken from the gravels
of California and put into the world's circulation.　Around
the placer mining of those early years has gathered the

[1] See W. H. Ellison's "Movement
for State Division in California, 1849–
1860" in the *Southwestern Historical
Quarterly*, xvii, 101–139.　In the
"Olvera de Toro Collection" under date
of September 15, 1851, there is a copy of
a call for a meeting to effect the speedy
formation of a territorial government
for Southern California.　It represents
Los Angeles forsaken by commerce, her
surplus products of no value, "her
capital flying to other climes," a sense
of insecurity, "and everything tending
to fasten upon her in the guise of
legislation a state of actual oppression."

glamour of romance.[1] Stories are told of this man taking twenty-four thousand dollars out of the soil in one day, of another man with a knife picking out four thousand dollars worth of golden nuggets in a very short space of time. These and other stories are taken as typical. Fifty thousand dollars in those days to the ordinary man seemed a fortune. Therefore, if one could get to California, one could pick up a fortune within a fortnight or a month at most. El Dorado, the Golden State, further enwrapped the truth in glamour. Really, placer-mining was fully as hard work as laying water or gas pipes in the streets of New York. Moreover, not only was the work laborious, but the living conditions were hard and dangerous. Oftentimes the miner stood in the water hour after hour. When the day's work was done, his shelter was of the rudest kind and his food was unusual and oftentimes scanty.[2] In California, the wet season occupied

[1] Joaquin Miller's *Romantic Life amongst the Red Indians* and his other writings give a lifelike picture of the place, people, and time. See also Bayard Taylor's *Eldorado* (New York, 1850), William Shaw's *Golden Dreams and Waking Realities* (London, 1851); Samuel C. Upham's *Notes of a Voyage to California* (Philadelphia, 1878); *The Log of a Forty-Niner . . . kept by Richard L. Hale*, edited by Carolyn H. Russ (Boston, 1923); J. M. Letts's *California Illustrated: . . . The Panama and Nicaragua Routes* (New York, 1853); *California: Its Past History; Its Present Position; Its Future Prospects* (London, 1850). This book describes California after the discovery of gold, but before the admission of the State to the Union, and has a chapter on the "Mormon State of Deseret." Robert E. Cowan's *Bibliography of the History of California and the Pacific West, 1510–1906* (San Francisco, 1914) gives details as to about one thousand titles.

[2] *The Shirley Letters from California Mines in 1851–52*, reprinted in San Francisco in 1922 from the *Pioneer Magazine*, San Francisco, 1854–55, by Mrs. L. A. K. S. Clappe, pp. 137, 138. The writer says that occasionally there are "lucky strikes," as when one person took out of one "basinful of soil" $256 worth of gold; but "such luck is as rare as the winning of a hundred-thousand-dollar prize" in a lottery. Many there were, whose gains "*never* amounted to much more than wages, that is, from six to eight dollars a day." A claim which yielded "a steady income of ten dollars *per diem* is considered as very valuable." For graphic accounts of the methods of mining, the tide of immigration, and mining failures, see the "Fifteenth," "Twenty-second," and "Twenty-third" letters in this book. See also chs. x and xi in Oliver Goldsmith's *Overland in Forty-Nine* (Detroit, 1896). John J. Werth, who wrote *A Dissertation on the Resources and Policy of California*, that was published at Benicia, California, in 1851, calculated that the average miner cleared net about four hundred dollars a year; but his estimate for food and clothing — only three hundred and fifty dollars — seems very small.

most of the winter and spring months, when practically no
work could be done at the placers. Then idleness and suddenly accumulated gold brought their usual results in drink-
ing, gambling, and other dissipations.[1] Scurvy, pneumonia,
and fever of one kind or another took their toll of the miners
and induced many of the survivors to return to their prosaic
homes in the East. No statistics have ever been compiled
of the number of those who died on their way to California,
or who perished from pneumonia and fevers in the wet
season. Nor has any one compiled the statistics of those
who failed to achieve "a fortune" from mining. The perusal of countless narratives of one sort or another, reading
letters, and conversing with old men have convinced the
present writer that most of those who made money in California in the "golden days" were those who supplied the
miners with food, clothing, tools, and drink, or who worked
at the mechanic arts in San Francisco and other centers of
life and commerce.[2] Oftentimes a miner mined with more
or less success until something untoward happened. We
read everywhere of the thousands of Argonauts going to
California in pursuit of the "golden Dream"; but we read
very little of those crowding the ships on the homeward

[1] See *The Shirley Letters*, "Twelfth"
and "Fourteenth" letters.

[2] *The Shirley Letters* (p. 72) celebrate
the prowess of a woman who earned
"nine hundred dollars in nine weeks,
clear of all expenses, by washing," which
probably accounts for the fact that
much laundry work was sent to the
Sandwich Islands in those days. Howe
in his *Argonauts of '49* (p. 133) writes
that a New England man earned $60
a day ferrying passengers to and from
ships at anchor in San Francisco Bay.
On pp. 72, 103 and fol., 119, and 152 of
this book, there is a great deal as to
hardships endured, small pecuniary
profit gained, and the uncertainty of
mercantile life. Indeed, there was
such a fall of prices that, according to
the *San Francisco Letter Sheet* of
February 27, 1850, Haxall flour was
then selling at $10 a barrel in that city,
which was a distinct loss. In 1849,
according to Henry F. Williams in his
Statement of Recollections, in the Bancroft Library, carpenters in the autumn
of 1849 were receiving from $12 to $16
a day for "rare men" and laborers $1
an hour. It is said that at that time the
regular price of a physician's visit was
an ounce of gold worth $16, and money
in April, 1849, was loaning at from 1 to
2 per cent a month.

way. Yet in 1852 fifteen hundred persons were reported to be on the Isthmus of Panama starving and waiting for transportation to New York and thence to their old homes.

North of California, from the forty-second parallel of latitude to the forty-ninth and from the water parting of the Rockies westwardly to the Pacific Ocean, was a vast region of varied riches in soil and trees, fur-bearing animals and fishes. It went by the name of Oregon and was what remained of the still vaster region claimed by the United States before the Treaty of 1846. It was unrivaled among the favored portions of the earth. In its first historical phase, it had been given over to the seeker for furs and fish. Americans had wrestled with Englishmen for these prizes, but in the end the Hudson Bay Company had prevailed, at least in the Valley of the Columbia River. In the mountains to the southward and to the eastward, fur-trappers from St. Louis and the American Fur Trading Company were supreme. Many of the employees of these companies, after their terms of service were over, had settled and were settling in the country around Puget Sound and in the lands to the southward, even to the Willamette Valley, and in no long time were ministered to by clerics of their own faith.[1] In the early forties, or thereabouts, agriculturalists had begun to come over the mountains from the Mississippi Valley and also missionaries to convert the Indians. These took possession of the best lands in the Willamette Valley, opened up the soil, and built homes. All this, of course, was greatly to the disadvantage of the British fur traders. Indian life in that region seems to have been unusually

[1] See ch. ii of *Gleanings of Fifty Years. The Sisters of the Holy Names of Jesus and Mary In the Northwest, 1859–1909* (Portland, Ore., 1909). This book was approved by Archbishop Christie of Oregon. See also the present work, vol. v, p. 511.

precarious, and Indian superstition, coupled with hardships,
led to murders and war, so that the Oregon country was not
an altogether peaceful abiding place.

In the first years Oregon,[1] besides feeding its own people,
supplied the sudden population of California with food. In
the earlier decade, gold and silver were not associated with
Oregon, but the country was powerfully affected by the discovery of gold in California, for the rapid increase in the population provided a market for the products of the Columbia
Valley and the opportunities for sudden gain drew to California many of the most enterprising and restless of the
settlers of Oregon. Fortunately Oregon [2] was north of what
was then looked upon as a region suited to the negro. It
happened, therefore, that the Senators and Representatives
from the Southern States were willing to give it a territorial
government, it being the general impression that slavery
would not prevail there. By 1853 so many people had come
into this favored region and the settlements were so dispersed, extending from Puget Sound to the head of the
Willamette Valley, that it was very difficult to carry on the
government with efficiency and dispatch. In 1853, therefore, the country south of the Columbia River and of the
forty-sixth parallel and west of the Snake River, to the
California line, was set off as the Territory of Oregon. The
remainder of the old territory was denominated Washington

---

[1] A map giving the names of that
day is prefixed to D. Lee and J. H.
Frost's *Ten Years in Oregon* (New York,
1844). A map giving the names of a
later day is appended to Captain John
Mullan's *Miners and Travelers' Guide
to Oregon . . . via the Missouri and Columbia Rivers* (New York, 1865).

[2] In addition to the volume on
Oregon in H. H. Bancroft's history of
the Pacific States and the books cited in
the present work, vol. v, 505, 511, refer-

ence should be made to Joseph Schafer's
History of the Pacific Northwest, originally published in 1905 and revised in
the light of new material in 1918;
Charles H. Carey's *History of Oregon*
(1922) ; and the articles in *The Quarterly*
of the Oregon Historical Society, especially those by T. C. Elliott. Papers
relating to civil affairs in Oregon are in
Senate Executive Document, No. 52,
31st Cong., 1st Sess.

and ultimately included what is now the State of Washington, the present State of Idaho and the western part of Montana. This region contained somewhere between ten and twenty thousand white inhabitants in 1850 and, in 1860, over sixty-four thousand.[1]

While the "movers" and the professional gold and silver seekers were busily employed in the mountains and on The Coast, the United States government was stretching out its arms toward the West Indies, the Amazon, and the lands and islands on the western shores of the Pacific. The precise reason for the activity of the Pierce and Buchanan administrations in the outer parts of the world is not easily discovered. So far as Cuba and northern Mexico were concerned the exigencies of the political situation as viewed by Southern eyes seem to afford an explanation; — Cuba and northern Mexico, if they could be acquired, would afford two more Slave States, — with two Senators each in Congress. Again, as to the Nicaragua filibustering expeditions of Walker and others, the desire to establish new centers of slavery may have actuated and probably did actuate many or most of those interested in those enterprises. The same things in a dimmer form may be supposed to have played a part in the attempt to open Brazil. On the other hand, the active interest displayed by these administrations in the Pacific and in the Islands of the Pacific and the lands bordering on its western margin cannot be in any way regarded as flowing from a desire to extend the area of slavery, and very likely

[1] J. Christy Bell in his *Opening a Highway to the Pacific* (*Columbia Studies*, No. 217), p. 179, quoting from Charles Saxton, gives the white population of Oregon in 1846 as "8,000 souls." G. Hines in his *Oregon: Its History, Condition and Prospects* (New York, 1859), p. 416, states that the population of Oregon in 1846 was not "far from" twelve thousand, chiefly in the Willamette and Cowlitz valleys, on the Clatsop plains, and in the Hudson Bay Company's posts. The *Census* of 1850 (p. 993) gives the population of Oregon Territory at 13,294, Utah Territory at 11,380, and New Mexico Territory at 61,547.

the slave extension element in the other expeditions has been exaggerated.

William Walker was in many respects a most attractive figure. He was a filibuster by inclination from his youth.[1] In 1855 he set on foot a scheme to nullify all of Great Britain's projects in Central America by invading the republic of Nicaragua. After some trouble, he managed to get away from San Francisco and after more trouble to depose the President of Nicaragua and put himself in his place. It seemed as if he were about to make good his hold on that country when he became involved in a dispute with the Accessory Transit Steamship Company, at the head of which was the redoubtable Commodore Vanderbilt of New York. That company at the moment was conducting a vigorous commerce between New York and San Francisco by way of Nicaragua, part of the journey being performed by land transportation. The withdrawal of the steamer service made it impossible for Walker to secure men and supplies. He was obliged to return to the United States. Essaying again to conquer Nicaragua, Walker was captured by a United States naval officer. Again seeking Nicaragua, Walker was again captured and this time was executed. In all of these endeavors, he certainly had the good will of the South, but whether "manifest destiny" or the extension of slave territory was at the bottom of his action is by no means certain. In another aspect the Nicaragua affair was of interest because upon Nicaragua centered, in some way, the scheme for constructing a canal across Central America. The United States was very anxious to complete such an enterprise and Great Britain was also desirous of lessening in any reasonable way the cost of transportation

[1] W. O. Scroggs's *Filibusters and Financiers; the Story of William Walker and his Associates* (New York, 1916) and his earlier article in the *American Historical Review*, x, 792–811.

between the Atlantic and the Pacific. Both countries entered into sundry treaties with Central Americans.[1] The United States representatives acquired possession of a town and the British proceeded to demonstrate their possession of various bits of territory : the Mosquito Coast, Belize, and Honduras. Desirous of avoiding all possible controversies, the United States and Great Britain entered into negotiations which resulted in the Clayton-Bulwer Treaty, so named for the American Secretary of State and the British minister at Washington. By this arrangement, any canal that should be dug was to be neutral and to be at the disposal of the shipping of the world, for a reasonable compensation. Unfortunately, in delivering the British ratification of this instrument to Secretary Clayton, the British minister handed with it a note to the effect that the stipulations in it did not apply to the existing British possessions in Central America, and more unfortunately still Clayton did not at once lay the British interpretation of the treaty before the United States Senate. In the end this matter was settled by the British withdrawing most of their contentions.

With Cuba, the story of these years is even more strange. The government of Spain was in a condition of uncertainty. There appears to have been only one certain thing about it, and that was that any Spanish monarch or minister who looked as if he were about to give up Cuba to the Americans, or to any one else, would have been deposed from throne or office. In 1853 President Pierce sent out as minister to Spain a Frenchman born, but a naturalized citizen of the United States, named Pierre Soulé. He was a resident of

[1] In addition to the official papers and the secondary works mentioned in Note II at end of this chapter, interesting side-lights are shed by letters printed in the *American Historical Review*, v, 95–102 ; Massachusetts Historical Society's *Proceedings* for March, 1856, pp. 75–77 ; and by a " Memoir" presented to the Liverpool Chamber of Commerce in April, 1857, by the Manchester, England, Free Trade and Foreign Affairs Association.

Louisiana and an inconvenient politician to some of those who were powerful there. Secretary Marcy, who held the State Department in Pierce's administration and who was a strong and cautious man from New York, gave Soulé some rather non-committal instructions. But the minister, when he reached Spanish soil, proceeded with alacrity to do whatever he could. It happened he could do very little, as the Spanish government was in an unusually unsettled condition. Moreover, Soulé, as a recreant Frenchman, was objectionable to the Emperor Napoleon. In the upshot, Soulé fought a duel with the French ambassador at Madrid, and, as he could not advance one foot on the Cuban matter, made such use as he could of the case of the *Black Warrior*.[1] This was an American steamer that had been making regular trips between New York and New Orleans, calling at Havana. On the last of these voyages, the Cuban authorities, scenting spoil, fined the captain of the steamer and, in default of payment, held the vessel. Soulé being directed in somewhat incautious language by Marcy to secure satisfaction, proceeded to call upon the Spanish minister, and getting no redress informed him that if he did not receive it within forty-eight hours, he should demand his passports and leave. The Spaniards took him at his word and he left. As the Spaniards would do nothing about Cuba, Soulé, James Buchanan, who was then minister at London, and John Y. Mason, who was minister at Paris, were directed to meet and compile a report on the Cuban question. They met at Ostend in Belgium in October, 1854, for Soulé was unable to stay in France, and drew up what is known as the Ostend

[1] See an elaborate paper by Henry L. Janes entitled "The Black Warrior Affair" in *American Historical Review*, xii, 280. See also James M. Callahan's "Cuba and Anglo-American Relations" and John H. Latané's "Diplomacy of the United States in Regard to Cuba" in American Historical Association's *Report* for 1897, pp. 195, 219.

Manifesto.[1] In this they advised the offering of a large sum of money to Spain for Cuba and if Spain would not receive this money for the coveted island, to seize it. This brought Soulé back to America, but although Buchanan's name was the first signed to the document it did not interfere with his political prospects, but rather improved them.

Combined with this diplomatic or undiplomatic activity as to Cuba was a succession of filibustering expeditions to that island. These are associated with the name of Lopez, a Cuban, who aroused interest and enthusiasm among the young men and some of the old ones of the South.[2] Lopez fitted out an expedition in 1851, eluded capture by the United States authorities, landed on the island of Cuba, and was able to get away without being shot. When he returned to the United States, he was arrested by the authorities, but the jury refused to convict him. He set out, therefore, on another expedition to Cuba. This time, he and his men actually fought a battle with the island authorities, but were speedily overcome and put to flight and Lopez and several Americans were executed by the Spaniards. The United States was so clearly in the wrong that it was forced to make apologies, and the vexatious matters between the two governments were brought to an end for the time being by the Spaniards paying for the detention and despoiling of the *Black Warrior* and promising better for the future.

The Mexican War and the acquisition of California with its gold mines and Texas with its boundless acres turned the thoughts of the people of the United States beyond their own borders and the lands abutting thereon, not only to

---

[1] *House Executive Document*, No. 93, 33rd Cong., 2nd Sess.; in *American History Leaflets*, No. 2; and with other interesting matter in John B. Moore's *Works of James Buchanan*, ix, 260–274.

[2] See *Publications* of the Southern History Association, x, 345–362, J. F. H. Claiborne's *Life . . . of John A. Quitman*, ii, 195–209, and Rhodes's *United States*, i, 216–220.

islands that might become States of the Union with slavery
but to far-off regions whose only connection with the United
States would be that of commerce.   The trade of the United
States between the western coast and the ports of China had
been active for more than half a century, and this activity
had been greatly increased by the sudden rush to California,
following on the discovery of gold therein.   The people on
the western side of the Pacific, however, did not seem at all
anxious to reciprocate.   They preferred to continue to live
the lives that Confucius and Buddha had laid down for them.
The Emperor of China with the King of Korea and the
Mikado of Japan, however else they might differ, were agreed
in keeping their seaports closed as tightly as they could to
foreigners.   Trade in teas, silks, and "china" went on
through the ports of Canton, Hongkong, and one or two
others.   The Opium War, following on the resistance of
the Chinamen to the demands of the English that they
should smoke more opium, led to the opening of more
Chinese ports to the Christian nations.   The Koreans, however, and the Japanese steadily refused to do anything of
the kind.   In fact, they seemed rather bent on limiting
whatever commerce there was with the white people and
with other yellow people, for that matter.   They wanted
to be left alone.   They had an Asiatic Monroe Doctrine of
their own, and had they been a little more up-to-date in
weapons of defence and offence, they might well have carried
out their desires.

From time to time, Japanese fishermen and seamen were
borne away from the shores of the Island Empire.   They
drifted far out into the Pacific and were picked up by American whalemen and traders and carried back to Japan;
but all attempts to penetrate beyond the beach of one or
two harbors or to remain at anchor in Japanese ports were

fruitless. In a similar way American whalemen wrecked on Japanese rocks were handed over to American war vessels through the good offices of the Dutch of Nagasaki; but there the matter ended. The ruling powers of Japan did not want commerce with the outer barbarians; they were living very happy lives of their own and there was no telling what would happen to them after the missionaries and merchants had come in and filled the minds of the Japanese people with other ideas. It so happened that at that time, — in the middle of the nineteenth century — the mediæval aristocracy of Japan, that had usurped power and had kept its consecrated ruler in durance within his own palace, was going to pieces. The time was ripe for the Mikado or Emperor to resume his ruling function with the loyal help and the good will of the great mass of the Japanese. The inception of American intervention was the joint work of several American seamen, merchants, and politicians, but the final impetus that led to success was given by Matthew Calbraith Perry. Exactly why he should have become interested in Japan and the Japanese is not clear, but he began buying books on Japan and reading them years before there was any thought of a formidable expedition to the islands, much less that he himself would be in command of it. There were several Secretaries of the Navy who had more or less to do with the inception of the enterprise, but no sooner had one of these touched the matter, than he left the Secretary's office to become a candidate for the vice-presidency or to write books of fiction. The time was one when the navy was at its lowest ebb, and if a commanding officer of a fleet or an expedition wished to get a fleet or an expedition together, he had to rely largely on his own effort. This was the case with Perry, for he seems to have written his own instructions and to have absorbed to himself whatever ships there were

that were absorbable and fit for his purpose. When the
time came to leave home, he was obliged to sail with one
ship only, the side-wheel sloop-of-war, *Mississippi*. After
discharging other duties, in due season he anchored in the
Bay of Yedo with the *Mississippi*, one other steamer, and
two sailing vessels that he had picked up on the way. A
local magistrate appeared in all the fuss and feathers of a
feudal Japanese official, two swords, helmet, sandals, and
flowing robe. He could not even get sight of the commodore
or admiral, as Perry found it convenient to designate himself, but had to leave his message with a lieutenant. The
governor of the place appeared the next day, but he got only
so far as the captain of the ship; the great man, himself,
did not talk or even look at a middle-size official, — and
thus Perry restored American prestige that had been sadly
lowered by the actions of an earlier American commodore.[1]
Finally, after a Japanese magnate had put his head into an
eight-inch gun to make sure of its size and had lifted a sixty-
four-pound iron cannon ball, it was arranged that suitable
officers should receive Perry on shore and take from him, or
from his representative in his presence, the letter encased
in a gold box which the President or Emperor of the United
States had sent to the ruler of Japan. This having been
done, Perry sailed away, saying he would be back in a few
months with more ships. On his second coming the Japanese
authorities were more clamorous than ever that he should
go to some other port, where they had already spoken to
foreigners, but Perry refused point blank. They asked him
if he would like wood and water or provisions, but he said he
had all he needed and somehow conveyed to them the idea
that he was quite prepared to stay where he was for eight
months or more. There seemed to be nothing for it, but to

[1] See *Senate Executive Document*, No. 59, 32nd Cong., 1st Sess., p. 66.

make a treaty with him, and it was done on March 31, 1854. In its final form this instrument granted no rights of trade to Americans. It merely provided that they could come to Japan, anchor in specified harbors, and buy whatever they needed to take them away. But it was the entering wedge and the beginning of the new Japan.

As to South America, there was no such charm of romance and of silk and tea that there was as to Japan, and China, and Korea; but the lure of the unknown, of cheap hides, and a market for lumber attracted merchants, politicians, and naval officers. The net result was several treaties with Brazil and other South American countries and the exploration of the Amazon by an American naval officer, Lieutenant Herndon. Naturally, this achievement, lacking the glamour of the East, has not received the picturesque chronicling that has given Perry his place in world history, but Herndon's report of his own doings is thrilling, and it has a parallelism of its own with that of Perry's master stroke.[1]

All in all, what with California gold, Oregon wheat and salmon, the opening of Japan, the growth of far eastern trade, and the looking into the Caribbean and the countries of Central America, and, finally, the opening of the valley of the greatest river in the world, these years and these achievements betokened a coming change in the mental attitude of the American people that seems always to portend revolution. In all this change and coming revolution,

[1] The reports of Lieutenants William L. Herndon and Lardner Gibbon on the *Exploration of the Valley of the Amazon, made under the Direction of the Navy Department* were printed in two volumes at Washington in 1853 and 1854; the first volume contains Herndon's report, and the second, Gibbon's, and there are two accompanying volumes of valuable maps. The circumstances under which the expedition was undertaken were stated by Lieutenant M. F. Maury in his essay on *The Amazon, and the Atlantic Slopes of South America* (Washington, 1853), p. 22, and his language naturally aroused indignation in Brazil. The later aspects of the subject are taken up in Professor P. A. Martin's "Influence of the United States on the Opening of the Amazon to the World's Commerce" in *Hispanic American Historical Review*, i, 146.

the people who gained were the merchants and ship owners of the North. Almost alone in the advancing modern world, the South stood still. As it was in 1830 so it was in 1850 and so it was quite likely to be in 1860. Southern forward-looking men felt a certain nervousness which they could not conceal, but which they tried to hide under a recounting of their invincible position in the world of commerce. They possessed, James A. Seddon declared,[1] a monopoly of the production of cotton fibre and if they refused to plant their cotton fields for one, for two, or for three years, the manufacturing nations of Europe and the Northern States of the Union would see the sources of their own prosperity dry up; the Northern lords of the loom, the merchant princes, the wealthy mechanics, and the thriving laborers would feel the gloom of a common cloud. Northern ships would rot at the wharves, factories crumble stone by stone, cities dwindle to half their size, and all this would happen unless the Northern men in Congress would accede to Southern demands for the extension of slavery and slave territory.

[1] *Speech 'of Hon. James A. Seddon . . . in the House of Representatives, January 7, 1847*, p. 8.

NOTES

I. California. — The leading secondary books and the more important official documents are noted in the fifth volume of the present work, p. 584.   In 1850 President Taylor transmitted to Congress several messages relating to California; among them a report by Colonel R. B. Mason, dated Monterey, August 17, 1848.   It describes the beginning of the gold industry (*House Executive Document*, No. 17, 31st Cong., 1st Sess., pp. 528–536).   A report of a later journey by General Bennet Riley, dated August 30, 1849, is in *ibid.*, pp. 785–792.   These papers are in *Senate Report*, No. 18, 31st Cong., 1st Sess., but with different pagination.   Other papers are in *Senate Executive Document*, No. 52, 31st Cong., 1st Sess.

II. Central American Policy. — The important documents are summarized in Mary W. Williams's *Anglo-American Isthmian Diplomacy, 1815–1915;* the bibliography at the end gives the titles of the more important works down to 1915.   The first 262 pages of the third volume of J. B. Moore's *Digest of International Law* contain a most useful summation of the official documents.   Lindley M. Keasbey's *The Nicaragua Canal and the Monroe Doctrine* (New York, 1896) and James M. Callahan's " The Mexican Policy of Southern Leaders under Buchanan's Administration " (American Historical Association's *Report* for 1910, pp. 135–151) are valuable treatments of separate branches of the general subject.[1]   The first two volumes of the *Compilation of Executive Documents and Diplomatic Correspondence relative to a Trans-Isthmian Canal in Central America* are most useful, but the student will necessarily go to the official documents, themselves. Among the older publications, an article in the *Colonial Magazine* in November, 1849, entitled " Mosquito, Nicaragua, and Costa-Rica," gave the present writer some idea of contemporary British opinion. There is an interesting map showing clearly the various proposed canal routes in Robert B. Pitman's *Succinct View* (London, 1825).   The volume embodying the results of a survey that was made under the direction of United States engineers (*The Isthmus of Tehuantepec,* New York, 1852) has a supplementary volume of maps.

[1] See also Gardiner G. Hubbard's "Canal Routes between the Atlantic and the Pacific" in *Science*, iv, 434, with an interesting map. Two contemporary documents are "The Report" on the subject of a railroad to the Pacific presented on August 1, 1850 (*House Report*, No. 439, 31st Cong., 1st Sess,) and E. G. Squier's "Preliminary Report" on the proposed Honduras inter-oceanic railway (New York, 1854).

III. The Opening of the East. — Perry's report, somewhat dressed up by Francis L. Hawks, D.D., was printed as a congressional document. It was supplied with pictures, made before the days of field photography, and contains reports made to Perry by various members of the expedition.[1] Perry also, while in China, embarked Bayard Taylor on his flagship in the guise of master's-mate. Taylor exercised his talents in describing the Japan portion of the expedition in chs. xxix–xxxvi of his *Visit to India, China, and Japan in the Year 1853*. The story is charmingly told by William Elliot Griffis in chs. xxvii–xxxiii of his *Matthew Calbraith Perry* (Boston, 1887), and with more sobriety in ch. ii of Payson J. Treat's *Japan and the United States, 1853–1921*.[2] A Japanese view of the matter is included in Inazo Nitobe's *The Intercourse between the United States and Japan*, ch. ii. A serious, modern American statement of the facts of the case is in Tyler Dennett's *Americans in Eastern Asia* (New York, 1922), chs. xiii and xiv. An earlier and briefer treatment is James M. Callahan's " American Relations in the Pacific and the Far East, 1784–1900 " in *Johns Hopkins University Studies*, xix, Nos. 1–3.

[1] *Narrative of the Expedition of an American Squadron to the China Seas and Japan . . . 1852, 1853, and 1854, under the command of Commodore M. C. Perry* (2 quarto vols., Washington, 1856). These form *Senate Executive Document*, No. 79, 33rd Cong., 2nd Sess. A letter, describing Perry's first visit, and written by the purser of the *Susquehanna*, Perry's flagship, and dated "Japan, 14 July, 1853" is in the *Proceedings* of the Massachusetts Historical Society for April, 1886, p. 258.

[2] Professor Treat has also dealt with the matter in his *Early Diplomatic Relations between the United States and Japan, 1853–1865*. Samuel Mossman in his *New Japan* (London, 1873) and J. H. Gubbins in his *Progress of Japan* (Oxford, 1911) have given brief and readable accounts of the negotiations.

CHAPTER III

THE COMPROMISE OF 1850

ON March 12, 1850, at Washington, William M. Gwin, John C. Frémont, and two companions signed a "Memorial" to the Senate and House of Representatives. In this they recapitulated the recent history of California and recounted the reasons why it was necessary to form a State government. In conclusion, they presented "the certified copies of their State Constitution and their credentials, and asked the admission of the State" and the right to take their seats in Congress. They assured the members of Congress of the anxious desire for the perpetuity of the Union that animated all classes of their constituents and that their patriotism was as broad as the Republic, as deep as their mighty rivers, as pure as the snows on their mountains, and "as indestructible as the virgin gold extracted from their soil." They asked to be permitted "to reap the common benefits, share the common ills, and promote the common welfare, as one of the United States of America." [1] Gwin and Frémont and their fellow emissaries could hardly have chosen a more inopportune moment to present this memorial to Congress, for the Southerners were then in a peculiarly irritated and unreasonable state of mind. In the next year, in a speech at Opelousas, Louisiana, Senator Pierre Soulé declared that a "handful of adventurers" in California had wrested "from the common domain upwards of one hundred

---

[1] John R. Browne's *Report of the Debates in the Convention of California* (Washington, 1850), "Appendix," p. xxiii.

66

and fifty-three thousand square miles of soil, bordering on nine hundred miles of ocean" and extended over it the very proviso that had so aroused the public spirit of the South and that this spoliation had been committed on the slaveholding States under the behests of a salaried military officer.

It was at this time, in the years 1848 to 1850, that the Southern cotton planters were passing through one of those crises in the price of their staple that have greatly affected the minds and hearts of the Southern people and have caused them to look closely into the relative positions of themselves and their Northern fellow-countrymen. It seems to be the sad fate of the cultivator of the soil to be unable to match the productions of his fields with the demands of manufacturer and consumer. At least this had been so as to cotton. In the third decade of the century, the average price of cotton [1] had been so satisfactory to the planters that the crop of 1840 was more than twice that of 1831 or 1832. In almost every year of the next decade the crop increased in size, but the demand for cotton by the spinners in America and in Europe did not increase to anything like the same extent.[2] In 1845, the price went to below six cents a pound at New York, and it is said that three years earlier an Alabama planter had sold seventeen bales of cotton for three and a quarter cents a pound. As is always the case, the politicians and the newspaper men early sensed what was going on in the voter's mind and proceeded to

---

[1] See James L. Watkins's "Cotton and the Currency" in *Sound Currency*, iii, No. 21 (October, 1896).

[2] Some jealousy of Liverpool cotton brokers was beginning to show itself. In the New Orleans Convention of 1855, it was asserted that forty bales of cotton out of every hundred sold were appropriated by the shipping men and brokers of Liverpool: "the cotton planters were mere hewers of wood — overseers of that great estate which was managed by others. . . . England is not a consumer of cotton; she is only a reproducer." *Proceedings of the Southern Commercial Convention held in the City of New Orleans, . . . January, 1855*, p. 25. For the older "forty bale theory" see the present work, vol. v, 427 *n*.

enlarge upon it in political meetings and newspaper editorials. And it must be said that there was good cause for this uneasiness. Whichever way the Southern man might look, his mind was likely to be filled with apprehension. William Gregg in 1854 pointed out that "money and negro capital" were constantly leaving the State of South Carolina for the North. He thought that enough capital had migrated from that State during the last quarter century to have more than quadrupled its agricultural-producing capacity had it been retained at home. It is true that a large part of the annual surplus produced by Southern agriculture went to the North to pay for goods already bought and partly consumed or to buy new supplies of tools, household wares, clothing, and food. If this capital were kept at home and invested in manufacturing activities, it would inevitably result in a great increase in the number of non-slaveholding whites, — and this last condition would be worse than the first. In point of fact the line of profitable slaveholding was constantly moving farther and farther to the southward, and more and more white men in the northern belt of the slaveholding States were exhibiting less and less interest in "the peculiar institution." In 1844, Robert W. Roper informed the State Agricultural Society of South Carolina that the annual importations into that State amounted to the aggregate yearly value of the products of the State. As long as this continued, the South Carolinians themselves were not "free." In 1847, Henry Ruffner of Virginia published an "Address to the People of West Virginia." He stated that the town of Norfolk had lost one-half of its commerce within twenty-five years and that the production of ship tonnage in little Rhode Island was twice that of Virginia, notwithstanding the fact that much of the timber used in the construction of those vessels had actually been carried to the

Northern shipyards from Southern lumber ports. In 1790,
the two sections — the North and the South — were approximately equal; in 1840, there were more people in the
Free States than there were in the Slave States. He quoted
with approval an address of James Bruce, also a Virginian,
to the effect that the average net product of slave labor in
that State was about twenty-two dollars a year for each
slave. It would be a good plan for Virginians to sell their
slaves to the cotton planters and invest this "dead capital"
in usable funds or in manufacturing. Ruffner noted the
striking contrast between the thriving villages, towns, and
cities of the North with the stagnation and decay that was
to be seen in the older Slave States that was broken "only
by the wordy brawl of politics." And, indeed, as early as
1832, Judge Gaston of North Carolina had declared that
slavery was the worst evil that afflicted the South; that it
stifled industry, repressed enterprise, discouraged skill, and
was fatal to economy and progress.[1]

In December, 1848, the excitement among the Southerners in Congress was intense. On the twenty-third day
of that month, two days before Christmas, that day of good-
will toward men, the Southerners in Congress held a caucus
that led a month later to the adoption of an "Address to the
People of the Southern States." This was drawn by Calhoun, was signed by persons who denominated themselves
delegates, and was issued on January 22, 1849. It fills
twenty-three pages of Calhoun's "Works"[2] and begins with
an allusion to "the conflict" between the two great sections
of the Union. This had grown out of a difference of feeling
and opinion as to "the relation existing between the two

[1] *American Catholic Historical Re-*
searches, viii, 71, and D. R. Goodloe's
The Southern Platform (Boston, 1858),
p. 37.

[2] Volume vi, p. 290, of the edition
of 1857.

races" — the white and the black in the South and "the acts of aggression and encroachment to which it has led." It enumerates the making of the Constitution, the Missouri Compromise, and the Prigg case, and then gives the following sentence from the charge delivered by the presiding judge in the case of Johnson *vs.* Tompkins and others: "Thus you see, that the foundations of the Government are laid, and rest on the right of property in slaves. The whole structure must fall by disturbing the corner-stone." Going on, the "Address" asserted that the attempt to recover a slave in most of the Northern States could not be made without "the hazard of insult, heavy pecuniary loss, imprisonment, and even of life itself." The addressers insisted that they should "not be prohibited from immigrating with our property, into the Territories of the United States, because we are slaveholders." They rested their claims not only on the solid foundation of right, justice, and equality, but on the ground that New Mexico and California, which were in dispute, had been acquired by a common sacrifice to which the South had contributed far more than her share of men, "to say nothing of money!" The territories belonged to the States as distinct sovereign communities and all the States and citizens thereof had rights in them. Then they enumerated aggressions that had recently taken place: a bill to repeal all acts recognizing the existence of slavery in the District of Columbia, another to exclude it from California and New Mexico, and a third to abolish the slave trade within the District. These acts of aggression and encroachment threatened with destruction the most vital of the institutions of the South and would probably be followed by the abolition of slavery. Viewing all these things the signers of the address deplored the "want of union and concert" in reference to this solemn question. The South must unite and the North will be brought to a pause. If the conflict did not cease, nothing would remain but "to stand up immovably in defence of rights, involving your all — your property, prosperity, equality, liberty, and safety."

It is noticeable that the addressers did not mention the holding of a convention of delegates from the Slave States. Whether there was any such provision in the earlier drafts of the address is not clear. But it was hardly signed when Calhoun set himself to work to stir up Southern sentiment by writing to various people. Some of these letters have been printed and probably there were many others. On April 13, 1849, Calhoun wrote to John H. Means,[1] an influential politician who was chosen governor of South Carolina in the next year. Calhoun thought that as things were going, the people of the Union would be divided into great hostile sectional parties before four years had elapsed. The only thing that could possibly save the Union would be for the united South to threaten secession, unless the North ceased violating Southern rights. It would be impossible to present such a united front "except by means of a Convention of the Southern States." On March 6, 1850, the Mississippi legislature, following the action of a Convention that had been held at Jackson in the preceding October, after rehearsing the Southern grievances passed thirteen resolutions summoning a convention of the slaveholding States to be held at Nashville, Tennessee, on the first Monday in June, 1850, to "devise and adopt some mode of resistance to these aggressions" and pledging the State of Mississippi to

[1] American Historical Association's *Reports*, 1899, vol. ii, p. 764. On July 9, 1849, Calhoun wrote to Collin S. Tarpley, a Justice of the Mississippi Supreme Court, advocating a Southern convention. The call should be addressed to "all those who are desirous to save the Union and our institutions, and who, in the alternative, should it be forced on, of submission or dissolving the partnership, would prefer the latter." Southern History Association's *Publications*, vi, p. 415. See also an interesting letter from Henry L. Benning to his friend Howell Cobb in U. B. Phillips's *Life of Robert Toombs*, 53.

"stand by and sustain her sister States of the South" in whatever action the convention might determine on.[1]

In the presidential year of 1848, there were three candidates, Zachary Taylor, Lewis Cass, and Martin Van Buren. General Taylor, the man of Palo Alto and Buena Vista, had been regarded as available presidential timber by the Whigs ever since 1846, and President Polk and the Democratic leaders had been equally filled with misgivings. Zachary Taylor was born in Orange County, Virginia, on November 24, 1784. He belonged to a famous Virginia family closely allied with the Lees and the Madisons and also, strangely enough, he numbered among his ancestors Elder William Brewster, the Pilgrim father.[2] He was the owner of a sugar plantation with its gang of slaves. He steadfastly declined to say what his political ideas were and placed himself unreservedly in the hands of two friends. He was not a party candidate "in that straitened and sectarian sense" that would prevent his being "the President of the whole people." He would not lay violent hands upon public officers who had other opinions than his, and would not force Congress to pass laws to suit him. He declared he would hail with entire satisfaction the nomination of any one else, being persuaded that the welfare of the country required a change both "of men and measures."[3] He thought that nominating him for the presidency without asking pledges of any kind was an evidence of the confidence of the Whigs in his "honesty, truthfulness, integrity [that] has but few parallels

[1] Ames's *State Documents*, No. vi, p. 14, from the *Laws of Mississippi, 1850*, p. 521; and St. George L. Sioussat's "Tennessee, the Compromise of 1850, and the Nashville Convention" in *Mississippi Valley Historical Review*, ii, 313.

[2] *Letters of Zachary Taylor . . . from the Originals in the Collection of Mr.*

William K. Bixby (Rochester, N. Y., 1908, p. viii).

[3] *Ibid.*, p. 163 note. There is no adequate life of President Taylor, but the last three chapters of General Oliver O. Howard's *General Taylor*, in the *Great Commanders* series, deals with this part of his career.

anywhere, at any rate none since the days of the Father of his Country."[1] As Taylor would give no pledges, the Whigs could have no platform and so they went before the country without any statement of their policy. The Democrats, the regular Democrats, instead of nominating Taylor as they might have done if the Whigs had not appropriated him, selected as their standard bearer a Northern man, Lewis Cass of Michigan, who had a great reputation in his day, although the reason for it is somewhat indistinct at the present time. Some discontented Democrats broke loose from their party and nominated Taylor, — and he accepted their nomination also. The opponents of slavery, or those to whom opposition to slavery was everything, could not vote for either of these candidates, one a Southern slaveholder, the other a Northern Democrat with Southern principles. They assembled around Martin Van Buren, who now was a Free-Soiler and an opponent of Southern Democratic ideas. He attracted enough New York Democrats to him to give the electoral vote of that State to Taylor and this gave Taylor a majority in the electoral college. Taylor was a minority President in that he received 1,360,099 votes to 1,511,807 votes for Cass and Van Buren put together.[2] On December 10, 1848, Taylor wrote that he "felt neither exultation or gratification" so far as he was individually concerned and that he looked upon the office "more as a bed of thorns than one of roses." His enemies had sought to destroy him by the "vilest slanders of the most unprincipled demagouges this or any other nation ever was cursed with,

[1] *Letters of Zachary Taylor*, p. 161. The same thought was expressed in a letter to his one time son-in-law, Jefferson Davis, dated July 10, 1848 and printed in Rowland's *Jefferson Davis*, i, 209.

[2] These figures are from Greeley and Cleveland's *Political Text-Book for 1860*, p. 239. Slightly different figures are given in James Williams's *Model Republic*, 220, and in a pamphlet entitled *"The Platforms," Containing the Compromise Democratic Platform, adopted at Baltimore, June 1, 1852,* p. 2. The electoral vote is in the *Journal of the House of Representatives*, 30th Cong., 2nd Sess., 442–444.

who have pursued me like blood-hounds,"[1] but Taylor declared the people, when left to themselves, rarely err.

. General Zachary Taylor was inaugurated President of the United States on March 4, 1849. At once he found himself face to face with difficulties fully as great as those that had confronted any previous President since the days of Washington. The administrative offices were entirely occupied by Democrats, and the Southern States, or their political spokesmen, at all events, were on the edge of violent opposition to the Federal government. At first Taylor, remembering perhaps the words that he had written in 1848, designed the replacement of only the higher officials, those answering to generals and colonels in an army, by persons of the Whiggish faith. He very soon found, however, that he had to descend from those of the uppermost positions to those occupying places analogous to captains and lieutenants. He soon became involved in that crater of political difficulties known as New York politics and in no long time surrendered more or less completely to William H. Seward and Thurlow Weed, somewhat to the dismay of the Vice-President, Millard Fillmore, who represented the other wing of the Whig party of the Empire State. Every month, every week, almost every day, the mutterings of the political storm that was sweeping up from the South became more and more audible until, by the middle of 1849, their import could by no possibility be misjudged.

The Southern position was well summarized in the resolutions of the Virginia House of Delegates which were first adopted on March 8, 1847, and affirmed with some additions on January 20, 1849. The opposition of the Northern States to the Mexican War had assumed, so the resolutions affirmed, the form of opposition to the extension of slave

---

[1] *Letters of Zachary Taylor*, 167.

territory, and this desire or design had been affirmed in the attempt to extend the provisions of the Ordinance of 1787 over any territory that might be acquired from Mexico. In other words the wish of the anti-slavery or Free-Soil people of the North was to sweep into the boundaries of non-slave territory whatever of the region south and west of the line of the Florida Treaty might be wrenched from the hands of the Mexicans, with the exception, of course, of the actual existing State of Texas. The Southerners met this attempt to restrict the enlargement of slave territory by proposing to extend the line of the Missouri Compromise westward to the Pacific Ocean, thus including within the area of slave territory the present States of New Mexico and Arizona and the southern part of California. Failing this, they proclaimed their right to take their slaves with them into any part of the national domain of the United States. The Southern attitude of resistance to Free-Soilism in any form had been greatly strengthened by the action of the Northern States following on the decision in the Prigg case in 1842. Up to that time, the Free States had been quiescent, with few exceptions, in the policy of the general government as to fugitive slaves. But, now, one Northern State legislature after another passed laws compelling State officials to protect fugitives, or, at all events, to give no aid of any kind to the pursuers. The whole contest over the Mexican War had brought forth a recrudescence of anti-slavery feeling in the North which was greatly resented by the people of the South. It was under these circumstances that the Virginia House of Delegates resolved once and again [1] that the government of the United States had no control whatso-

---

[1] *Journal of the House of Delegates of Virginia,* January 20, 1849. The resolutions of March 8, 1847, are printed in Herman V. Ames's *State Documents on Federal Relations,* No. vi, p. 4.

ever over the institution of slavery; that all territory acquired by the United States belongs to the several States as their "joint and common property" and that the Federal government could not in any way "prevent the citizens of any state from emigrating with their property, of whatever description, into such territory" and that to do so would "tend directly to subvert the Union itself." The third resolve was not adopted unanimously, but it was adopted and declared that if "the fearful issue should be forced upon the country," the people of Virginia would have to choose between "abject submission to aggression and outrage" or resistance "at all hazards and to the last extremity."

President Taylor at once drifted away from his Southern moorings and proposed to settle the land questions that had arisen, offhand, and before the politicians could get hold of them. He sent an emissary out to The Coast to incite the Californians to draw up a State constitution and demand admittance to the Union. He somewhat euphemistically informed Congress that the course of the Californians "on their part, though in accordance with, was not adopted exclusively in consequence of, any expression of my wishes, inasmuch as measures tending to this end had been promoted by the officers sent there by my predecessor."[1] Accompanying this statement from the President was a letter from General Riley who had been governing California under the authority of the Secretary of War. This letter was dated October 31, 1849. It accompanied a copy of the new constitution and stated that "it is contemplated to put the new government into operation" in December. Riley declared that he would surrender his civil powers to the executive of the new State, — all of this to be done before he could receive any instructions from his superiors at Washington

[1] *Senate Reports*, 31st Cong., 1st Sess., No. 18. p. 2.

and long before Congress could take any action as to the admission of the new State into the Union.[1]

As to Texas and New Mexico, there was the question as to what was the boundary between them. It was an interesting question because whatever might be the status of slavery in New Mexico under Mexican or United States law, there was no question whatever that Texas was a Slave State and that the farther westward the Texan boundary was, the greater would be the undisputed extent of slave territory. The Texans claimed that Texas included all of the eastern valley of the Rio Grande and was not confined, as the old Spanish maps had it, to a much more restricted frontier, — in fact only to the eastern edge of the watershed of the Rio Grande or Rio Bravo del Norte.[2] It must be remembered that slavery, strictly so called, had no existence on Mexican territory, — a painfully analogous institution was there termed peonage. It fell out, therefore, that California, New Mexico, and Utah, when they came into the United States, were free territory and the question was as to whether they were to remain free territory. Did the Treaty of Guadalupe Hidalgo determine forever the status of the inhabitants of detached Mexican territory or only until Congress, acting under the Constitution of the United States, should prescribe what that condition should be? The Southerners said one thing and the Northerners said another and the claim of Texas to extend to the Rio Grande

[1] This statement and the preceding one will also be found in *House Documents*, 31st Cong., 1st Sess., No. 17, pp. 2, 850.

General Riley, in his "Proclamation" of June 19, 1849, stated that his instructions from the Secretary of War "make it the duty of all the military officers to recognise the existing civil government and to aid it." Therefore, apparently, he helped on the making of the constitution and then recog-

nized the government instituted under it! *Ibid.*, p. 777.

[2] The map on p. 500 of volume v of the present work gives an idea of the Spanish-Mexican nomenclature of this region. The Treaty of Velasco of 1836, by which Santa Anna acknowledged the independence of Texas, is in English in Yoakum's *History of Texas* (New York, 1856), ii, 528. According to this translation, Texas is "not to extend beyond the Rio Bravo del Norte."

was equivalent to extending the area of slave territory into about one-third or one-half of the present State of New Mexico. It was suggested that the status of the laws of New Mexico and Utah should be left to the Supreme Court; but this — the so-called Clayton Compromise — was disapproved by both Northerners and Southerners. Taylor met the crisis with the point-blank statement that if the Texans attempted to carry out their threats, or if any other Southerners did, he would lead the army of the United States in person against them. As many of the Southern leaders had been active in securing Taylor's nomination and election, they were somewhat perturbed at the actions of the slave-holding Southern general in the White House. Some of them waited upon him and tried to turn him from his course; they were absolutely unable to accomplish anything; but in no long time death relieved them of his presence, placed Millard Fillmore, a Northern man with Southern principles, in the White House and gave the handling of these problems to the politicians at the other end of Pennsylvania Avenue, — to John C. Calhoun, Henry Clay, Daniel Webster, and their co-workers.

Calhoun, Clay, and Webster, the Great Triumvirate, were now near the close of their wonderful careers. Clay in recent years had been out of Congress, engaged in an effort to repair his pecuniary state by practising his profession of the law. The political crisis seemed to him so urgent that he sought election to the Senate that he might devote the last years or months of his life to the preservation of the Union. The hand of Death was already heavy upon Calhoun, and Webster was living from day to day under the influence of oxide of arsenic and other preparations prescribed by physicians.[1]

[1] Dr. John Jeffries in his "Account of the Last Illness of the Late Hon. Daniel Webster" in the *American* *Journal of the Medical Sciences*, January, 1853, states that Webster for years had had a deep-seated affection of the liver

Clay's compromise plan as it was outlined in resolutions that he introduced into the Senate on January 29, 1850 was to balance concession to one side by concession to the other. To the Northerners, he proposed to give the admission of a free California and the ending of the slave trade in the District of Columbia; to the Southerners, he offered the Territory of New Mexico without the conditions of the famous proviso, that is, without mention of slavery; and the enactment of a drastic fugitive slave law. As to the Texas-New Mexico problem, he proposed to include the disputed lands in New Mexico, but to compensate Texas by paying her existing public debt. Following the resolutions came what was known as the Omnibus Bill including these propositions within the scope of one enactment. This bill in its entirety could not pass the two Houses, but as five separate measures it found enough support and passed.[1] Such was the settlement of 1850 that was supposed to be a finality, — and proved to be nothing of the kind.

The much-heralded Southern Convention met at Nashville on the third day of June, 1850. By that time, Southern enthusiasm had distinctly dwindled. It happened, therefore, that the attendance was much less than had been expected and the delegates who did come could hardly be regarded as representative, as those only from South Carolina had been elected directly by the voters; all the others had been chosen by legislatures or appointed by governors. The presiding officer of the convention was Judge Sharkey of Mississippi, who was distinctly unfavorable to any radical

and that for three years before his death he had been under the care of physicians, frequently taking stimulating drinks under their direction. It is not at all impossible that some impairment of the powers of the nervous system made it difficult for Webster to rise from a sitting posture and gave him "a sense of falling" and, at times, a slight hesitation of speech.

[1] These laws may be most conveniently found in the *Statutes at Large . . . of the United States*, ix, 446, 452, 453, 462, 467.

pronouncement or action.   The Convention finally produced
resolutions and an "Address."   The resolutions, twenty-
eight in number, simply rehearsed the opinions that had been
expressed by Southern legislatures and informal bodies of
one sort or another.   In the sixth, the Convention declared
that the "tolerance" that Congress had given to the idea that
Federal power might be used incidentally to weaken the
slave system in the States was a cause of "the discord which
menaces the existence of the Union."   The "Address"[1]
is more interesting.   It begins with recounting the growing
estrangement between the South and the North; then it
purports to describe the existing situation.   Southern
Congressmen are "habitually reviled by the most oppro-
brious epithets" and Congress has become a grand instrument in the hands of abolitionists to degrade and ruin the
South.   The non-slaveholding States are combined "not
only to wrest from you your common property, but to place
upon your front, the brand of inferiority."   If you were to
yield everything required of you, would things stop there?
In fifty years the non-slaveholding States would have a two-
thirds majority in Congress and a three-quarters majority
of the States and could then amend the Constitution "to
consummate their policy," — namely to abolish slavery.
The Nashville Convention then adjourned after making
provision for another meeting later in the year.

The second session of the Nashville Convention or the
second Nashville Convention was held in November, 1850.
By that time, opposition sentiment had died down in the
South generally.   In fact, South Carolina was the only
State that remained faithful to secession.   The most marked

[1] *Resolutions, Address, and Journal of
Proceedings of the Southern Convention,
held at Nashville, Tennessee, June 3d
to 12th, Inclusive, in the Year 1850.*
Chapter iv of Melvin J. White's *Secession Movement . . . 1847–1852* contains
a clear and brief account of the Nashville Convention.

overturn was in the sentiments expressed by the three great leaders of Georgia, — Toombs, Cobb, and Stephens. They supported the compromise and in the convention of the people of Georgia in December, 1850, obtained the adoption of certain resolutions that were known at the time as the "Georgia Platform." These stated that the people of Georgia held "the American Union secondary in importance only to the rights and principles it was designed to perpetuate," but that the States "may well yield somewhat, in the conflict of opinion and policy, to preserve that Union." That Georgia, while she does not wholly approve the compromise, will abide by it as a permanent adjustment of this sectional controversy, but that the State ought to resist, even to secession, any action of Congress upon the subject of slavery in places subject to its jurisdiction or any act suppressing the inter-state slave trade, or the refusal to admit a State to the Union because of slavery or the modification of the law for the recovery of fugitive slaves.[1] It was on the basis of this platform that Toombs and his associates organized the Union Rights Party. In Mississippi, although the governor, John A. Quitman, and many leading men were in favor of secession, the movement of the people in support of the compromise was overwhelming. A State convention was held, but instead of declaring for secession or declaring against the compromise, it voted that the right of secession was unsanctioned by the Federal Constitution and resolved that the legislature had no right to call the convention without having first given the people of the State a chance to express their opinion as to whether they would have one or not.[2] In fact the revulsion of feeling was so great in Mississippi that Quitman retired from the contest

---

[1] Herman V. Ames's *State Documents on Federal Relations*, No. vi, pp. 29–32.

[2] *Ibid.*, No. vi, p. 30.

for reëlection to the governorship and Jefferson Davis could not prevail upon the voters to elect himself governor in opposition to Senator Foote, who had stood almost alone in Congress among the Mississippi delegation as favoring the compromise.

As might have been expected, the contest in South Carolina was especially keen, for there the influence of R. Barnwell Rhett was still considerable. He was unreconcilable, as were several other South Carolinians of power and prestige. The secessionists were so strong in South Carolina that the only way the anti-secessionists could make head against them was to conduct the campaign on the unwisdom of seceding without the coöperation of other Southern States. In short, the struggle assumed the form of a contest between "Secessionists" and "Coöperationists," in which the "Coöperationists" won. At the same time the South Carolinians asserted the right of secession. This was done by a vote of a convention that was elected to consider the question and met at Columbia in April, 1852. In the preceding December, Rhett in the Senate of the United States had declared that the right to secede from the Union was not granted in the Constitution.[1] It is a constitutional right because the States have not surrendered their sovereignty. He thought

[1] *Speech of R. Barnwell Rhett . . . Delivered in the Senate of the United States, December 15th & 16th, 1851* (Washington, 1851), p. 29. Edward McCrady, the father of General Edward McCrady, the historian of South Carolina, wrote several letters in 1851 and 1852 that were printed in the Charleston *Mercury*. In one of these, he declared that "sovereign and independent States" may assume any obligations that they see fit and, if these obligations are abrogated, any one of these States may "of its own motion" secede. He admits, however, that the other States have an equal right to prevent this secession, if they can. These extracts were communicated to me by Miss Louisa L. McCrady of Charleston, South Carolina. On the other hand, Benjamin F. Perry in the South Carolina House of Representatives, on December 11, 1850, asserted that the dissolution of the Union would be "the most fatal blow which slavery could receive." It would deprive the slaveholders of the protection of a great and powerful nation and fleeing slaves would go off in gangs and the moment they passed the frontier would be safe. Nothing "could gratify the abolitionists more" than secession. *Speech* of B. F. Perry (Charleston, 1851), p. 17.

that if secession was looked upon as a revolutionary right, the Federal government had a right to coerce a State and that if the government had the right of coercion, the State had no right to secede, all of which he thought was entirely wrong. Rhett asserted that Calhoun had been hurried to his grave by the malignity of Senator Foote of Mississippi, who now wished to exhume his body to expose it to dishonor. Another South Carolinian, Langdon Cheves, left a retirement of thirty years to go to the Nashville Convention to try to incite the Southern people to stand up for what he declared to be their rights. Addressing the Convention in burning words, he prayed God to release the faculties of Southern men from "the awful torpor which so utterly benumbs them," to endue them with "some self-respect, with some sense of honor, some fear of shame and degradation." If they would unite, they would scatter their enemies, protect their slave property, place California in the Slave State column, enjoy full rights in all the territory which was conquered by their blood and treasure. If they would unite, they would form one of the most splendid empires. "But submit, — submit! The very sound curdles the blood in my veins. But, O, great God, unite us, and a tale of submission shall never be told." [1] But not even South Carolina would stand by Rhett and Cheves.[2] By May, 1851, Cheves himself had weakened. He wrote that South Carolina should not secede alone "in the midst of her sister States"; but if "we have souls in our bosoms," Southern principles will be triumphant and the present degradation of the Southern

---

[1] This extract from Cheves's speech was communicated to me by Dr. D. Huger Bacot of South Carolina who copied it from the Charleston *Mercury* of November 22, 1850.

[2] See two articles by Professor Chauncey S. Boucher: "The Secession and Co-Operation Movements in South Carolina, 1848 to 1852" and "South Carolina and the South on the Eve of Secession, 1852 to 1860" in *Washington University Studies, Humanistic Series*, vol. v, No. 2 and vol. vi, No. 2.

people will cease.[1] In November, 1850, James Buchanan, viewing the scene from his estate of "Wheatland, near Lancaster," Pennsylvania, stated that a well-organized party in favor of secession or disunion existed in the South. This party was in a minority in every Southern State except South Carolina, but it was active and energetic and, by means of well-written pamphlets which were everywhere in circulation, was seeking to prove to the Southern people that the Union was an injury to all their material interests.[2] Fortunately, the increase of prices, which was due largely to the discovery of gold in California, and the consequent prosperity that prevailed in the South for some years after 1850 drove thoughts of secession away from the Southern mind and justified the stand taken by Daniel Webster[3] in the United States Senate on the seventh day of March, 1850.

Looking backward, it is astounding to realize the accuracy with which Daniel Webster sensed the situation in the South and recognized that a concession on the part of the North, like that contained in the Fugitive Slave Act of 1850, would cut the ground from under the feet of Barnwell Rhett, Langdon Cheves, Robert Toombs, Alexander H. Stephens,

[1] *Proceedings of . . . Delegates from the Southern Rights Associations of South Carolina, Held at Charleston, May, 1851*, p. 9.

[2] From the "William M. Marcy Papers" in the Library of Congress.

[3] The "Seventh of March Speech" was widely distributed in pamphlet form at the time and is in every edition of Webster's speeches. The evidence as to the true attitude of Webster and the influence of this speech have been brought together, with abundant citations, by Professor Herbert D. Foster in the *American Historical Review*, xxvii, 245–270. See also Clifford B. Clapp's "Speeches of Daniel Webster" in the *Papers* of the Bibliographical Society of America, xiii, Part One Opposite Mr. Clapp's title page is a reproduction of a remarkable daguerreotype of Webster taken when he was about fifty-six years of age.

Ideas on the economic possibilities of New Mexico at that time were based very largely on Lieutenant William H. Emory's *Notes of a Military Reconnoissance*. This report was published in book form in 1848. On p. 129 Emory says that the profits of labor in New Mexico were too inadequate for the existence of negro slavery, although peonage which bound the master to take no thought of the laborer in infancy or old age or in sickness might pay. But negro slaves would not repay the cost of transportation.

and Robert Lowndes Yancey, and put off the inevitable crisis
until the North should outstrip the South in man power and
material resources — so much so, indeed, that possibly
secession and war would never come. As one reads his
"Seventh of March Speech" one realizes that Webster was
trying to say to his countrymen : "Make this concession to
our Southern brethren! They love the Union, they want
to remain in it, but they have been led to believe by their
political chiefs that you Northerners are designing their
ruin and the ruin of their social system. The concessions
made in the Compromise Acts as a whole do not amount to
much, apart from the Fugitive Slave Law, for slavery can
never profitably exist in New Mexico and Utah and the
Fugitive Slave Law is only the carrying out of the plain
provisions of the Constitution of the United States." The
abolition propagandists of the North turned upon him with a
fury that showed they realized that what he had done was
to put an end for the time being to their schemings. There
are no more painful, no more unjustifiable, lines in American
poesy than those in John Greenleaf Whittier's "Ichabod,"
describing Webster as the fallen, the lost, the man for whom
"the Tempter" had laid a snare : —

> Let not the land once proud of him
>   Insult him now,
> Nor brand with deeper shame his dim,
>   Dishonored brow.

NOTE

Southern Secession in 1850. — James Ford Rhodes (*History of the United States from the Compromise of 1850* (New York, 1892, i, 105, 187, 190) gives the impression that he regarded the danger of the separation of the Cotton States as not serious in 1849–1852. Essays and monographs that have been written since 1892 and books and manuscripts that were not accessible at that time, but have since become so give a different impression. See P. M. Hamer's *The Secession Movement in South Carolina, 1847–1852*. This is a book of 143 pages and has a useful bibliography at the end containing titles as late as 1917. Chauncey S. Boucher's " Secession and Co-Operation Movements in South Carolina, 1848 to 1852 " in *Washington University Studies* for April, 1918, covers much the same field in smaller compass. Professor Herman V. Ames has printed many useful documents in his *State Documents on Federal Relations* [1] and has set forth the leading facts in an essay entitled " John C. Calhoun and the Secession Movement of 1850 " in the American Antiquarian Society's *Proceedings* for April, 1918. Arthur C. Cole's *The Whig Party in the South* and his essay entitled " The South and the Right of Secession in the Early Fifties " in the *Mississippi Valley Historical Review*, i, 376; R. P. Brooks's " Howell Cobb and the Crisis of 1850 " in *ibid.*, iv, 279; St. George L. Sioussat's " Tennessee and National Political Parties, 1850–1860 " in the *Annual Report* of the American Historical Association for 1914, i, 243; and U. B. Phillips's " Georgia and State Rights " in *ibid.*, for 1901, vol. ii, contain much useful matter. Cleo Hearon's " Mississippi and the Compromise of 1850," in Mississippi Historical Society's *Publications*, xiv, with Hamer's essay will give a good idea of the history of this time in the South and may be supplemented [2] by D. T. Herndon's " Nashville Convention of 1850 "

---

[1] See especially "Number vi. Slavery and the Union, 1845–1861." The editor's notes to these documents are extremely serviceable.

In 1853, some members of the Presbyterian and Congregational churches, wishing to deal with their Southern brethren in the "confidence of Christian friendship" proposed to aid pecuniarily struggling churches of their faiths in the South. They wished to treat their Southern fellow-citizens with fraternal appreciation and to leave the carrying out of the project to their Southern brethren "who are competent to judge of the manner in which the work shall be prosecuted." See the *Annual Reports* of the Southern Aid Society. The last one was issued on November 25, 1860.

[2] See also F. Newberry's paper on "The Nashville Convention and Southern Sentiment of 1850" in the *South Atlantic Quarterly*, xi, 259.

in Alabama Historical Society's *Transactions*, v, 203–237, and by Melvin J. White's " Louisiana and the Secession Movement of the Early Fifties " in Mississippi Valley Historical Association's *Proceedings*, viii, 278, and his *Secession Movement in the United States, 1847–1852.*

Two essays by the Rev. Iveson L. Brookes that were printed at Hamburg, S. C., in 1850 and 1851, with somewhat similar titles [1] give an excellent idea of the views of educated Southern men on the Northern anti-slavery propaganda of that time. Sidney Andrews's *The South Since the War* and Whitelaw Reid's *After the War* were written by two Northern newspaper correspondents who visited the South in the year of Appomattox. They state a few naked facts as to the life of that region that do something to illustrate the ways of thinking that are described in the essays noted in this and the preceding paragraph.

[1] *A Defence of the South against the Reproaches and Incroachments of the North* and *A Defence of Southern Slavery against the Attacks of Henry Clay and Alex'r. Campbell. . . . By a Southern Clergyman.*

CHAPTER IV

FUGITIVE SLAVES AND "UNCLE TOM'S CABIN"

No part of the settlement of 1850 aroused so much bitterness, not even the admission of California as a free State, as did the passage of the Fugitive Slave Law and the attempts that were subsequently made to enforce it. The rendition of fugitives from justice, from service, or from labor goes back to the clause of the Constitution of the United States that provides that a person charged in any State with treason, felony, or other crime and found in another State shall be delivered up on demand of the executive of the State from whence he fled for the purpose of removal from the State of refuge to the State where the crime was committed. Another clause provided that persons held to service or labor in one State, escaping into another, shall be delivered up "on Claim of the Party to whom such Service or Labour may be due." It will be noticed that in both these clauses no specific directions are given, but the matters are left to be dealt with by Congress and the States. In 1791, Governor Mifflin of Pennsylvania had demanded the surrender of three men who were charged with having kidnapped a negro in Pennsylvania and taken him to Virginia to sell him into slavery. The Virginia governor refused to comply and Mifflin thereupon appealed to President Washington.[1] It is generally thought that it was the friction that arose between Pennsylvania and Virginia in this case that led to the

[1] Marion G. McDougall's *Fugitive Slaves (1619–1865)* forming *Fay House Monographs* No. 3, p. 17 and notes, and H. M. Jenkins's *Pennsylvania*, ii, 130.

passage of the law of 1793 which applied both to fugitives from justice and from service or labor. It will be noticed that the wording of the Constitution is peculiar. The fleeing criminal was to be delivered up on demand of the executive authority of the State from which he fled, but the servant or slave was to be delivered on claim of the party to whom the service or labor might be due. The former led to the process of extradition, the latter resulted in the slave owner or his agent personally undertaking the seizure of the slave. The Act of Congress of 1793 [1] proposed to use State officials for the carrying out of these two provisions of the Constitution.

The line between securing the return of a runaway slave and kidnapping a free negro was always an exceedingly difficult line to draw. Naturally, many runaway slaves proclaimed themselves to be free negroes and naturally many a master or slave dealer in pursuit of salable negro property had an exceedingly acute sense of recognition and saw in many a physically sound free black the runaway slave for whom he was searching or pretending to be searching. Where the evidence is so scanty it is extremely easy to overstate the case one way or the other and it is impossible to estimate, even roughly, the total number of blacks and mulattoes who had fled from their legal owners or how many escaped slaves were living in Northern States. In 1826, the Pennsylvania Assembly passed a law making kidnapping a felony punishable by fine and imprisonment at hard labor for from seven to twenty-one years. [2] The title of the law stated that it was passed to aid in carrying into effect the provisions of the Constitution and Federal laws relating to fugitives from labor. Section nine of this law provided that "No alderman

---

[1] *Statutes at Large* of the United States, i, 302.

[2] Richard Peters's *Report of the Case of Edward Prigg*, pp. 16, 17.

or justice of the peace of this commonwealth shall have jurisdiction or take cognisance of the case of any fugitive from labour from any of the United States or territories under a certain act of Congress" of February 12, 1793, or grant any certificate or warrant of removal of any such fugitive under pain of being deemed guilty of a misdemeanor punishable by a fine of from five hundred to one thousand dollars. The jurisdiction of these cases was confided to certain judges who were also somewhat limited in the performance of their duties. The opinion of the Supreme Court of the United States in the Prigg case was delivered by Mr. Justice Story.[1] After rehearsing the facts as to the bringing of the suit and its course through the courts of Pennsylvania, Story stated that the Act of 1793 was clearly constitutional and that the Pennsylvania law of 1826 was unconstitutional and void. He also stated, as one part of the opinion of the court, that as to the authority conferred by Congress on State magistrates by the Act of 1793 a difference of opinion exists in different States whether State magistrates are bound to act under it; "none is entertained by this Court that state magistrates may, if they choose, exercise that authority, unless prohibited by state legislation." In other words the Supreme Court of the United States — by opinion of the majority of the justices — declared that State magistrates need not obey the provisions of the Act of 1793 and that the States by legislation could forbid them to obey it. Of course, the legislatures of States, where the opinion of the people was strongly opposed to the return of fugitive slaves, by law prohibited the State officials from aiding in the return of fugitives from labor, — and thus in effect nullified that part of the Federal law of 1793 and that particular clause of the Constitution of the United States. It is true that

[1] Peters's *Case of Edward Prigg*, 74. The words quoted below are on p. 88.

Chief Justice Taney dissented from that part of the opinion
of the court which denied the right of the State authorities
to protect the master when he is pursuing a fugitive from
his service and declared that if the States are forbidden to
legislate on this subject on the ground that the power is
exclusively in Congress, the State of Maryland "must soon
become an open pathway for the fugitives escaping from
other states." [1]

The Prigg Case arose out of the incursion of Edward
Prigg, a citizen of Maryland, into Pennsylvania in 1837.
Thence he forcibly carried away a negro woman, Margaret
Morgan, who was claimed as a slave by another Marylander.
Prigg had obtained a warrant from a Pennsylvania justice
of the peace directing him to bring Margaret Morgan before
him.   When Prigg did this, the justice refused to take cog-
nizance of the case and Prigg carried the woman and her
children, all of whom had been born in Pennsylvania, with
him to Maryland.   Being in Pennsylvania again in 1839,
Prigg and three other persons were indicted by the grand
jury of York County.   From this beginning the case went
to the Supreme Court of Pennsylvania and then to the Supreme Court of the United States, where the decision that
is noted in the preceding paragraph was rendered in 1842.
Meantime, in 1839, three colored men, members of the crew
of the schooner *Robert Center,* had assisted in the escape of a
negro slave from the town of Norfolk, Virginia.   The
schooner was found in the waters of New York.   Whereupon,
on August 30, 1839, the lieutenant governor of Virginia
applied for the surrender of the three negroes on the ground
that they "did feloniously steal . . . a certain negro slave
named Isaac" and were fugitives from justice.   The demand
was founded upon the committal of an offence peculiarly and

[1] Taney's opinion is in Peters's *Case of Edward Prigg,* 92–99.

deeply affecting Virginians and recognized as felony by the
laws of that Commonwealth.   William H. Seward was then
governor of New York.   He took his own time to consider
the case and finally refused to surrender the three men who
were charged with having stolen a slave because the act,[1] if
it had been committed in New York, would not contravene
any law of that State which did not recognize slavery and
had no statute admitting that one man can be the property
of another or that "one man can be stolen from another."
The two governors thereupon corresponded for some time
until finally, the governor of Virginia wrote a circular letter
to the governors of the slaveholding States, setting forth
what appeared to him to be a "gross and dangerous" per-
version of the Federal Constitution.   He asked them to
earnestly consider what could be done to meet this danger.
He suggested that it remained to be seen whether the expression of one common feeling and one resolution on behalf of
the slaveholding States would not make the adoption of
retaliatory measures unnecessary.

In 1842, George Latimer, a slave who had escaped from
Norfolk, Virginia, was seized at Boston without a warrant,
and writs of habeas corpus and personal replevin proving of
no avail, public meetings were held.   The owner of Latimer
had followed him to Boston.   He was discovered and met

[1] *Correspondence between the Governor of New-York and the Executive of
Virginia*, 41, 45, 109, 114, etc. A portion is in the *Messages from the Governors*
of the State of New York, iii, pp. 869,
915–928. On April 30, 1841, Seward
transmitted to the Assembly resolutions
of the Maryland legislature "declaring
the right of each state to define felony
or crime within its jurisdiction, which
definition should be binding on every
other state." *Ibid.*, iii, 929.

The difficulties that beset Southern
slaveholders in Northern States comes
out in the case of Jonathan and Juliet
Lemmon and their eight slaves. The
Lemmons were Virginians who were
going to Texas with their slaves by the
way of New York City in 1852. The
slaves were carefully concealed, but they
were seen by a free negro named Louis
Napoleon. Legal proceedings followed
until 1860, when five of the seven judges
of the Court of Appeals decided that no
human being could be held as a slave in
the State of New York, unless he happened to be a fugitive. See *Arguments
and Speeches of William Maxwell
Evarts*, i, 3–90.

with so many obstacles — legal and otherwise — to the
recapture of his slave and his removal, that he finally consented to give up all his rights to Latimer for four hundred
dollars cash which was paid to him. Upon the owner's
return to Norfolk the people of that town held a meeting
"to take into consideration the outrageous proceedings of
the Abolitionists." To the Norfolkers, the question seemed
to be whether they would "submit to habitual violations of
their rights . . . or dissolve the Union." They declared
that the people of Boston had shown a lack of decency and a
wish to substitute the desires of the mob for the laws of the
land.[1] These Virginians and many other Southerners had
been aroused by the decision of the Supreme Court of Massachusetts in 1836 to the effect that a slave brought within the
boundaries of that State by his or her master or mistress was
free, as no one had authority to retain any person in service
against his or her will or to carry such person out of the
State to be held in slavery.[2] In 1822 and in 1835, South
Carolina, in order to prevent the entrance of free negroes
into that State, had passed laws directing the sheriff to take
possession of any free negroes coming into the State on
board of a vessel whether in the crew or otherwise and to
detain such free blacks in the town jail until the vessel was
about to depart when the captives would be returned upon
payment of the ordinary fees.[3] These laws gave rise to some
interesting questions of international law which were settled
amicably enough, but as to negro cooks and seamen on
coasting vessels, especially those from Massachusetts, affairs
did not proceed so smoothly. The South Carolinians denied

---

[1] See *Proceedings of the Citizens of the
Borough of Norfolk on the Boston Outrage, in the Case of the Runaway Slave
George Latimer* (Norfolk, 1843), pp. 1,
5, 9.

[2] See the present work, vol. v, 126,
note 1.

[3] Howell M. Henry's *Police Control
of the Slave in South Carolina*, 124–131.

that Massachusetts citizenship conferred rights of citizenship in South Carolina and asked why Massachusetts did not recognize the status of the slaves, — and the Federal government being in the hands of Southerners no relief could be obtained. In 1844, Samuel Hoar of Concord, Massachusetts, then in middle life — he was sixty-six years of age — was sent by Massachusetts authorities to Charleston to take the preliminary steps toward getting a case in train for decision by the Supreme Court of the United States as to the validity of the South Carolina law; but after staying there a week he was "run out of town" by sundry Charlestonians, having accomplished nothing.[1] Upon the other hand, many Northerners were appalled at the idea of being turned into slave-catchers. This feeling took the shape of hostile legislation and sometimes of hostile acts. So far as one can gather from such figures as are available, the actual loss of the slave owners because of runaways was small. In 1860[2] the Census Bureau estimated that in 1850 only one thousand out of the three million slaves were fugitives — or three one-hundredths of one per cent — and how many of these had passed Mason and Dixon's line into the Free States was absolutely unknown.[3] Moreover, the number

[1] Samuel Hoar's letter describing the proceedings at Charleston is reprinted from the Massachusetts documents for 1845 in the *Old South Leaflets*, No. 140. An interesting colloquy occurred in United States Senate between Senators Davis of Massachusetts and Butler of South Carolina. See "Appendix" to the *Congressional Globe*, 31st Cong., 1st Sess., vol. xxii, pt. ii, pp. 1625, 1674. This matter was reprinted in a pamphlet entitled *Proceedings of the U. S. Senate, on the Fugitive Slave Bill, . . . and the Imprisonment of Free Colored Seamen in the Southern Ports*.

[2] See *Preliminary Report on the Eighth Census* [1860], p. 137.

[3] In a pamphlet, dated Washington City, July 18, 1850, and signed "Randolph of Roanoke," it is asserted that the number of fugitive slaves living in seven Northern States was 46,000. This number included those who had escaped in thirty years. The author computed the pecuniary losses of the South in forty years on account of fugitive slaves to be equal to $22,000-000. John Randolph of Roanoke had died fourteen years before this letter was written, and these estimates are guess work; but these or similar estimates were believed by very large numbers of persons living in the Southern States.

of fugitives from the plantations of the Cotton Belt was even smaller. The "Census" of 1850 notes that only sixteen of the nearly four hundred thousand South Carolina slaves ran away in that year. Nevertheless, a correspondent of Calhoun, the South Carolina Senator, writing to him in 1847 on the subject of the sheltering of fugitive slaves by the people of the Northern States, declared they had committed a most barefaced invasion of the Constitution by removing the jurisdiction of those cases from the Southern courts and insisting upon the "cowardly and contemptible contrivance" of a jury trial for the alleged fugitives. Accordingly, the South was "completely absolved from the slightest obligation to observe any faith" to the Northern people.

In February, 1849, a committee of the Virginia House of Delegates presented a report with accompanying resolutions as to how far existing legislation of Congress fulfills the intent and object of the Constitution of the United States in affording an adequate remedy for the recapture of slaves absconding into the non-slaveholding States of "this confederacy" and to suggest such relief as the urgency of the case requires. The report goes back to 1780 and recites the Southern view of the making of the Constitution. It declares that the South "is wholly without the benefit of that solemn constitutional guaranty which was so sacredly pledged to it at the formation of this Union"; and that the conditions were precisely what they had been under the old confederation. No Southerner could go into a Free State to seize his fugitive slave with a view to taking him before a judicial officer and proving his ownership without imminent danger of being criminally prosecuted as a kidnapper, being sued for false imprisonment, imprisoned himself for want of bail, and, finally, "of being mobbed or being put to death in a street fight by insane fanatics or brutal ruffians." Very

few owners of fugitive slaves have the hardihood to pass the
frontier of a non-slaveholding State and seize the fugitive.
In such a "diseased state of opinion" as prevailed in the
Free States, laws were passed which subjected slave owners
to conditions utterly incompatible with the recovery of
fugitive slaves, and some of these laws did not pretend to
conceal the hatred felt to Southern institutions or the
contempt and defiance of the obligations of the Federal
compact. As an illustration, the committee printed in full
an act passed by the Vermont Assembly in 1843. This act
prohibited State courts, State judges, or other magistrates or
executive officers as sheriffs and jailers or citizens of the
State doing anything required by the law of 1793. The
fifth section provided that any Vermonter, whether judge,
sheriff, jailer, or citizen, acting directly or indirectly under
section three of the Act of 1793 should forfeit a sum not
exceeding one thousand dollars or be imprisoned for not
exceeding five years.[1] The State of Pennsylvania had gone
"a bow shot beyond all the rest" in this new legislative war
against the constitutional rights of the slaveholding States.
In 1847 an act was placed on the statute book of that State
making it "highly penal" to kidnap any free negro or
mulatto, forbidding all its judicial officers to have anything
to do with the law of 1793, and providing that if any person
claiming a fugitive slave should under any pretext whatso-
ever violently seize upon any negro or mulatto either with
or without the intention of taking him before a judge he
should be guilty of a misdemeanor and be fined and imprisoned accordingly. The Virginia investigating committee
declared the intention of the Pennsylvanians was that any
such attempted seizure should produce "an assemblage of

[1] Charles L. Williams's *Compiled Statutes . . . of Vermont* (Burlington,
1851), pp. 536–538.

abolitionists, fugitive slaves and others actuated by hostile feelings," a riot would result, the slave would be rescued, and the owner would be arrested and prosecuted. He might be acquitted, but in the meantime the slave would have escaped. The sixth section of this law forbade the use of the public jails of the State to preserve the property of the master from irresponsible mobs, while opening them to the slave as a refuge. In bringing to a close "this disgusting and revolting exhibition of faithless and unconstitutional legislation" — all of which, by the way, was in conformity with the opinion of the majority of the justices of the Supreme Court as stated in the Prigg case — the committee of the Virginia legislature observed that similar embittered feelings against the rights of the slaveholders marked almost without exception the legislation of every non-slaveholding State. The committee thought that it would be difficult to devise an act of Congress by which the rights of slaveholders could be secured, as the current of popular feeling and prejudice was so strongly against the slaveholder. To repress the evil that now threatens to disturb the relations between "the two great divisions of this confederacy," the committee pointed out "in an honest spirit" those remedies which may control it "within the limits of a patient endurance." The committee, therefore, recommended that an earnest effort be made through the Virginia Senators and Representatives in Congress to procure such amendments to the law of 1793 as shall confer on every Federal commissioner, clerk, and marshal, postmaster, and collector of the customs the authority now granted to the judges of the circuit and district courts to give to the claimant of a fugitive a certificate authorized by that act and, when applied to, to issue a warrant for the seizure and arrest of a fugitive slave. Finally, the committee suggested that the penalty for hindering a claimant should be increased and that all members of obstructing assemblages should be deemed guilty of misdemeanors. The report concluded by recommending that the Virginia Senators and Representatives in Congress should use their "earnest and persevering efforts" to have the Act of 1793 so amended as to secure to the slave owners the rights guaranteed in the Constitution of the United States.[1]   On the other hand, in 1848, the legislators of Vermont had resolved that slavery resting on fraud or physical force ought to be prohibited in the territories and abolished in the District of Columbia.   They averred that it was unbecoming the representatives of freemen to legislate "while their eyes are insulted with the frequent spectacle of men, chained, shackled, and driven to market." They declared that unless slavery could be abolished in sight of the capitol the seat of government ought to be removed to some "Free State."

Senator James Murray Mason of Virginia, obeying the command of his constituents and doubtless his own feelings as well, and following Clay's seventh resolution, that more effectual provision ought to be made by law for the restitution of fugitive slaves, introduced a bill into the United States Senate that finally became law on September 18, 1850, without much opposition and with slight notice.   The title was "An Act to amend, and supplementary to, the Act" of 1793.[2]   The important thing about the new law was that it provided Federal jurisdiction for these cases instead of utilizing the existing State judicial establishments.   This

---

[1] See "Report of the Select Committee appointed under a Resolution of the House to enquire into the existing Legislation of Congress upon the subject of Fugitive Slaves," Doc. No. 50, in *Governor's Message and Annual Reports . . . of Virginia* (Richmond, 1848).   This "Report" is also in the *Journal of the House of Delegates of Virginia. Session of 1848–49*, pp. 238–257.

[2] *Congressional Globe*, 31st Cong., 1st Sess., vol. xxi, p. 233, and *Statutes at Large*, ix, 462.

was done by authorizing United States commissioners to
exercise all the powers and duties conferred by this act and
directing the appointing power to enlarge the number of
commissioners from time to time to afford reasonable facilities to reclaim fugitives from labor. These commissioners
were to grant certificates to claimants of fugitive slaves
"upon satisfactory proof being made" with authority to take
and remove such fugitives to the State from which such
person escaped. United States marshals and deputies and
persons appointed by the commissioners were charged with
the execution of the warrants of the commissioners and those
officials were authorized to summon the by-standers when
necessary to insure a faithful observance of the Constitution
and this law. The fugitives might be claimed by the owner
or by an agent appointed by him who might "use such reasonable force and restraint as may be necessary, under the
circumstances of the case, to take and remove such fugitive
person back to the State" whence he or she might have
escaped. In none of the proceedings under this act should
the testimony of the alleged fugitive be admitted, and the
certificate issued shall be conclusive of the right of the claimant to remove such alleged fugitive. Any person hindering
the arrest or attempting to rescue him shall be fined not exceeding one thousand dollars and imprisoned not exceeding
six months and shall pay to the party injured one thousand
dollars for each fugitive lost. The commissioner was to
receive five dollars fee, if the fugitive were set free, but if
he were returned into slavery he was to receive double the
amount, or ten dollars. This provision which appeared to
abolitionists to be a direct incitement to the commissioner
to adjudge the alleged fugitive to be one in fact, was explained on the ground that the labor of making out the certificate justified the double compensation. Ample provision

was made for other compensation — all payments to be made "out of the treasury of the United States."[1]

The question of the constitutionality of the Fugitive Slave Law of 1850 has been often debated and the debate is not yet closed.[2] In most of these discussions attention is solely given to the clause of the Constitution that requires the delivery of a fugitive servant or slave to the master or owner; and this clause taken by itself certainly justifies the fugitive slave laws of 1793 and 1850. There are, however, other parts of the Constitution and there are also sundry amendments. Having these in mind Chief Justice Hornblower of New Jersey in 1836 maintained that the Act of 1793 was unconstitutional because it did not obey the precepts of the Constitution of the United States as to the appointment of the agents to carry the law into effect.[3] In 1854 a case came before the Wisconsin Supreme Court. After hearing arguments, that court declared the Federal Fugitive Slave Law of 1850 to be unconstitutional and void, because it did not provide for trial by jury and because it authorized the exercise of judicial power by officers who could not be endowed with such functions under the Constitution of the United States.[4] This case was carried to the Supreme Court of the United States, and in 1858 Chief Justice Taney delivered the opinion of the court that the Fugitive Slave Law was constitutional.[5] It is an opinion worth reading, because, among

[1] *United States Statutes at Large*, ix, 462.

[2] Professor Allen Johnson has summarized the arguments in the *Yale Law Journal*, for 1922, pp. 161–182.

[3] See *Opinion of Chief Justice Hornblower on the Fugitive Slave Law.*

[4] See *Unconstitutionality of the Fugitive Slave Act. Decisions of the Supreme Court of Wisconsin in the Cases of Booth and Rycraft* (Milwaukee, 1855), reprinted from the *Wisconsin Reports*, iii; and *Argument of Byron Paine, Esq. and*

Opinion of Hon. A. D. Smith, Associate Justice of the Supreme Court of the State of Wisconsin. Daniel W. Howe, in ch. xi of his *Political History of Secession*, gives the essential facts as to this and other leading cases.

[5] This "Opinion" is in Howard's *United States Reports*, xxi, 506. An abbreviated and understandable statement of the "Opinion" is in Eugene Wambaugh's *Selection of Cases on Constitutional Law* (Cambridge, 1915), p. 135.

other things, it denies the right of a State court to interfere on behalf of any one after it has been judicially informed
that such person is imprisoned under the authority of the
United States. A layman ought not to take issue with the
justices of the Supreme Court of the United States, or an
historian to argue with a lawyer, but a suggestion or two
may be possible. Under the fugitive Slave Act of 1850, a
citizen of a "sovereign State" of the Union might be seized
and taken from the State of his birth and residence from
youth up, to be tried for that which is dearer than life — his
liberty — simply on the oath of an inhabitant of another
State. The defenders of the Fugitive Slave Law constantly
reiterated the statement that the cases of the alleged fugitive
slave and of the fugitive from justice were alike and that no
one objected to the extradition of the alleged criminal as so
many persons did to the return of the fugitive slave. In
reality the cases were very unlike. The squint of the law
was the same as to the murderer or the thief, north or south
of Mason and Dixon's line. It was very different as to holding a human being in bondage for life. It was so different,
indeed, that Senator Underwood of Kentucky declared that
trial of the fact of servitude or freedom in a Free State would
be ruinous! Moreover, many people in the North, with
Representative B. R. Johnson of New York, believed it
dangerous "to permit the South to make a hunting ground
of the North."[1] They thought it wrong to subject a free
white man in a Northern State to fine and imprisonment for
giving a cup of water and a crust of bread to a famished
human being.[2] On March 14, 1860, in a debate in the New

---

[1] *Speech of Hon. B. R. Johnson on the
Personal Liberty Bill. In Assembly
[of New York], March 14, 1860.*
[2] Upon conviction and sentence for
aiding in the rescue of a fugitive slave,

John Hossack declared that he had no
sense of guilt. His wife and his eleven
children were dear to his heart, but he
had counted the cost. "Slavery must
die, and when my country shall have

York Assembly, it was asked whether it was fair for "a quarter of a million of slaveholders" to rule with a rod of iron "not only the four millions of slaves" and the "five millions of southern whites" but also the "twenty millions of free people at the free north"? Surely, any law that made twenty or twenty-five millions of white Americans subject to two hundred and fifty thousand or even a million white slaveholders was not in harmony with the preamble of the Constitution of the United States that declared that the government was formed to "secure the Blessings of Liberty to ourselves and our Posterity."

As has already been said, the portion of the negro slave on the plantations of the States that later formed the Confederacy must have been one of unconstrained happiness, if the books and diaries of visiting Englishmen and Southern women can be relied on. The number of fugitives who found their way to the North on vessels from Mobile or Pensacola or from Savannah or Charleston was very small. Most of the fugitives came from the Border States, where the percentage of white blood in the colored population was very much larger than it was farther south. This meant that family ties were much stronger than they were in the blacker regions. Moreover, there was always the prospect of a break-up of the life in the old Kentucky home and the going to the unknown conditions of the plantations of the Cotton Belt. How large the migration was from the Southern States into the Northern States and Canada in the decade of the second Fugitive Slave Law is very difficult to

---

passed through the terrible conflict which the destruction of slavery must cost, . . . the rescuers of Jim Gray will be considered as having done honor to God, to humanity, and to themselves." *Speech of John Hossack* (*Anti-Slavery Tracts*, New Series No. 11).

The rescue had been made at Ottawa in La Salle County, Illinois.

The argument of E. C. Larned on behalf of Joseph Stout, co-defendant with Hossack, is printed in a volume entitled *In Memory of Edwin C. Larned* (Chicago, 1886), pp. 73–130.

ascertain. From the tables printed in the "Preliminary Report on the Eighth Census" it appears that the number of slaves escaping in the "Census year" ending June 1, 1860, was only eight hundred and three.[1] It has been estimated that from fifteen to twenty thousand colored persons entered Canada in the ten years of the second Fugitive Slave Law. It is certain that in places the passage of the Fugitive Slave Law greatly disturbed the negro population. There undoubtedly was a stream of fugitives across the northern frontier and a few instances stand out as indicative of a great deal that we cannot trace. For example, the colored population of Columbia, Pennsylvania, dropped from 943 to 487 in a very short time after the passing of the act, and more than forty members of a fugitive slave congregation in Boston fled almost at once. It is also said that the "underground railroad" was actively used in the first years after the passage of the law. The real effect of the Fugitive Slave Act of 1850 was not so much the increase or diminution of running away from the Slave States or the increase of the free negro colony in Canada, or the spectacular events that are associated with fugitive slave cases; it was that these things put together converted hundreds of thousands of people of the North from a position of indifference or of hostility to abolition to a position of hostility towards the slave power. It induced hundreds of thousands of voters, who cared very little whether the negro was a slave or a free man, to use all means at their disposal to stop the further extension of slavery and to put an end to it whenever they could, constitutionally.

[1] Jos. C. G. Kennedy's *Preliminary Report on the Eighth Census*, pp. 11, 12, 130, 131. These figures have been criticized by experts on the "Underground Railroad." See Wilbur H. Siebert's *Underground Railroad*, 342 and index under "Number"; and see also the articles on "Negro Migration to Canada" in *Journal of Negro History*, v, 22–36.

Wherever the fugitive from labor struck free soil or by whatever means he or she reached that point, there was certain to be somewhere near-by and accessible a white person who would take charge of the fugitive, feed and succor him, and push him on towards some place of greater safety. It is by no means necessary to regard these persons as abolitionists, or Free-Soilers: they were simply men and women whose natural sympathies were aroused by the sight of wretchedness in another human being and who did whatever came to his or her hand to relieve the sufferer. So complete and so successful did the fugitive slave transit from Mason and Dixon's line to Canada become that it came to be called "The Underground Railroad." In some places there unquestionably was an organized system of relief and evasion; but the perusal of such original matter as has come under the eye of the present writer has convinced him that there was much less system and much more spontaneity than has generally been supposed. A black or colored face on the northern side of the Ohio River or of the Pennsylvania-Maryland boundary line exhibiting hunger or fear or lack of raiment would arouse sympathy and bring succor, even at the cost of effort and danger.

The Fugitive Slave Act was signed by President Fillmore on September 18, 1850. Eight days later, on September 26, a man appeared in New York from Baltimore bringing with him a power of attorney executed by a woman who made her mark and did not write her signature, authorizing him to seize and transport to Baltimore a man represented to be her slave. He also had with him a copy of the Fugitive Slave Law, certified as authentic by Daniel Webster, Secretary of State. He appeared before the clerk of the Circuit Court who had been appointed commissioner under the new law and made an affidavit that James Hamlet, who had

lived in New York for two or three years and had a wife
and children there, was the slave of Mrs. Brown and asked for
a warrant to arrest him.   It was at once granted and placed
in the hands of a deputy United States marshal.   The negro
was promptly arrested, taken before the commissioner, who
decided that he was the slave of the claimant, and delivered
him to be taken to Baltimore, and the expenses of the transaction amounting to between seventy and eighty dollars
were paid by the United States.   Eight hundred dollars
were at once raised by the anti-slavery people of New York
City and on the 5th of October, Hamlet was back in New
York, safe with his wife and two children [1] — this time an
undoubted free man.   On the last day of December in this
fateful year of 1850, three men appeared at the farmhouse
of Joseph Miller in Pennsylvania, not many miles from the
Maryland line, seized a colored woman, Rachel Parker by
name, and made off to Baltimore.   A party of eight at once
organized to go in pursuit.   They rode to the nearest railroad station and took a train for Baltimore, arriving there
before the three kidnappers with their prey.   They went
to the public slave pen and were there when Rachel Parker
appeared.   They protested that she was a free-born Pennsylvanian and was not a slave.   The authorities ordered that
she be held for trial and fourteen months later she was set
free and returned to her home.   One of the rescuing party
was not so fortunate, for leaving the train on the return
journey he was never seen alive again.[2]

In February and April, 1851, two fugitive slave cases were
heard in Boston, Massachusetts, but they ended very differently.   The first was that of Frederick Jenkins, who was

---

[1] See *The Fugitive Slave Bill: Its History and Unconstitutionality; with an account of the Seizure and Enslave-* ment *of James Hamlet* (New York, 1850).

[2] *Journal of Negro History*, v, 480.

found by his master's agent serving as a waiter in a Boston coffee house under the name of Shadrach. A warrant was procured and he was arrested while at work. Legal assistance was given on his behalf and occasioned delay and an adjournment of the case.[1] As the jails were not available in Massachusetts for the confinement of fugitives from labor, Shadrach was detained in the Federal Court House. A body of colored folk took advantage of an opened door to gain access to the prisoner and carry him off before the officers could get aid and he was at once sent out of the city and ultimately reached Canada in safety. Another colored man, Thomas Sims,[2] had not the same good fortune. He was also found in Boston, but was arrested on a bogus charge of theft and was then claimed as a fugitive slave. He also was confined in the court house; but this time the building was guarded by an iron chain four feet from the ground. The hearing was lengthy and two able lawyers defended the man, but he was handed over by the commissioner and was escorted by armed men to a brig lying at Long Wharf which carried him back to Georgia. In these cases there had been no bloodshed; but in the third case that occurred in this year, in September, 1851, in Pennsylvania, affairs did not progress so harmlessly. A Marylander named Edward Gorsuch with his son appeared at Christiana in Lancaster County, Pennsylvania, in pursuit of an alleged fugitive from labor.[3] A number of escaped slaves had gathered in a farmhouse at this place. Thither, the Gorsuches went with

[1] See Charles F. Adams's *Richard Henry Dana*, i, 179 and fol., and *The Fugitive Slave Law, and Its Victims*, 10 (*Anti-Slavery Tracts*, No. 18). See also Rhodes's *United States*, i, 209, 210 and *note*.

[2] See *Trial of Thomas Sims, on An Issue of Personal Liberty* (Boston, 1851), and an abolition summing up of fugitive slave cases in *The Fugitive Slave Law*,

and *Its Victims* (*Anti-Slavery Tracts*, No. 18).

[3] See W. U. Hensel's *The Christiana Riot and the Treason Trials of 1851* (Lancaster, Pa., 1911) and *Report of the Trial of Castner Hanway for Treason* (Philadelphia, 1852), *A History of the Trial of Castner Hanway and Others for Treason . . . By a Member of the Philadelphia Bar* (Philadelphia, 1852).

United States officials and demanded the surrender of the alleged fugitives. Shots were fired and the negroes defended themselves valiantly. In the affray, Edward Gorsuch was killed and his son was wounded. The negroes escaped. The case is memorable because some Quaker bystanders being summoned by the deputy marshal refused to aid him and were tried for treason; but no conviction followed. The two cases that attracted most attention and aroused bitter resentments were those of Anthony Burns at Boston and the Oberlin rescue.

Anthony Burns was a Virginia negro, the slave of a man named Suttle. He was early "hired out" to a William Brent, who lived at Falmouth on the Rappahannock River, and afterwards to a man named Foote. Colonel Suttle had other slaves and in due course Anthony was placed more or less in charge of the hiring out of Suttle's slaves, including himself. Finally, he found an employer for himself in the person of a Richmond druggist named Millspaugh and, upon its turning out that this man did not have enough work for him to do, the two struck a bargain by which Anthony was to find jobs for himself and pay Millspaugh a certain sum every night, which time was soon extended to every fortnight; the remainder of his earnings he could keep for himself. By this time, Anthony Burns had learned to read and write and on occasion exercised some of the functions of a minister. He resolved to flee from Virginia to the land of freedom, and to this end his employment at the time as a laborer on vessels at the wharves and the fact that he was not obliged to appear before any white man oftener than once in two weeks gave him every opportunity, and a sudden

In the same year, there was printed at Annapolis the *Report of the Select Committee* of the Maryland House of Delegates on the murder of Edward Gorsuch. On p. 11 the Committee states that under the act of 1850, no Southern master could reclaim his fugitive slave from a Free State "except at the hazard of his life, for the protection of which that law affords no security."

change in Millspaugh's demands forced Burns to act quickly.
In February, 1854, he put his plans into operation, stowing
away on a vessel that was about to sail for the North and
reached Boston in safety. Naturally, Colonel Suttle, to
whom Anthony Burns brought in one hundred and twenty-
five dollars "hire" money each year, was indignant and
Millspaugh to whom he paid an indefinite amount every
fortnight was likewise solicitous for his return. Unwittingly,
Burns apprised them of his whereabouts by writing a letter
to his brother in Richmond, which he dated at Boston,
although taking care to have it postmarked in Canada. It
was handed to his brother's master and the place of his
residence was communicated to Colonel Suttle. That person repaired to Boston with William Brent and the two of
them searched successfully and caused Burns's arrest on
the charge of the theft of jewelry.

At the first opportunity Burns was taken before the commissioner whose business it was to consider fugitive slave
cases. As Burns had recognized Colonel Suttle and told
him how he had escaped, the case was a clear one so far as
identification was concerned. A well-known Boston lawyer,
Richard Henry Dana, the author of "Two Years before the
Mast," at once took up the defence of Burns, and he with
associate counsel did whatever could be done by bringing
forward all points of law and fact to make impossible the
rendition of the fugitive. But in the existing state of the
law, the case was perfectly plain and the commissioner could
do nothing else but to order his surrender to Colonel Suttle.

Meantime the heart of Boston had been stirred to the
very center. People who had no sympathy with abolitionism were determined that no more fugitives from labor
should be seized in Boston and carried out of the State.
Leading anti-slavery men who favored the use of force were

determined that there should be no other failure like that of
Sims. They formed a regular committee which was known
as the Vigilance Committee and was reënforced by militant
abolitionists from outside. They determined that Burns
should be rescued. On Friday night, May 26, 1854, a meeting was held at Faneuil Hall. It was attended by hundreds
of people, many of whom had never before appeared in anti-
slavery gatherings. The crowd was so dense that it was
impossible for the Vigilance Committee to communicate
with the speakers on the platform. They had gathered a
sturdy band and provided a plank to use as a battering ram
and had purchased sundry axes from a neighboring hardware
shop. At Faneuil Hall the speakers were Theodore Parker
and Wendell Phillips. One sentence of Phillips's remains
in the memory: "See to it . . . that Anthony Burns has
no master but his God!" Soon after a stentorian voice
was heard shouting that a mob in Court Square was attempting to rescue Burns. "I move we now adjourn to that
place!"[1] The crowd poured out, gained the Square, and
the assault on the Court House began. The door was broken
sufficiently for the two foremost men at the battering ram,
the Reverend Thomas Wentworth Higginson and a sturdy
but nameless negro, to enter. They were at once set upon
by the officials with swords and clubs. Suddenly one of the
marshal's men, Batchelder by name, was struck down,
mortally wounded. The crowd drew back. At this moment, most opportunely or inopportunely, the Boston Artillery marched into the Square to perform its customary evo-
lutions. The crowd, mistaking the artillerymen for marines
from the Navy Yard, saluted them with groans and hisses
and dispersed.

[1] *Boston Herald*, May 27, 1854, and other Boston newspapers of May and June,
1854.

Meantime, the more pacific anti-slavery people had entered into negotiations with Colonel Suttle for the purchase of Anthony Burns. Suttle's price was twelve hundred dollars cash down. The money was raised and a bill of sale was made out when the United States District Attorney intervened. He objected to having the sale made until the case was adjudicated and to having any sale made in Massachusetts. And could any man be bought or sold in Massachusetts? The bargain fell through. The anti-slavery people now bent their energies to trying to prevent the actual taking away of Burns, for it was clear that when the case was again before the commissioner on the following Monday, he would decide in favor of Suttle. They printed handbills urging the people to "Watch the Slave Pen!!" They sent out by mail other notices requesting the "Yeomanry of New England" to come and lend the moral weight of their presence. "Come down, then, Sons of the Puritans" to be present at the sacrifice and follow him in sad procession. "Come with courage and resolution in your hearts; but, this time, with only such arms as God gave you." They sought to incite the people against the marshal's deputies by stigmatizing them as "Murderers, Prize-fighters, Thieves, Three Card Monte Men, and Gambling House Keepers" who were supplied with money and rum by the United States and employed to trample upon our laws and "to shoot you down if you dare to assert your just rights." On Friday, June 2, a week from the day of the attempted rescue, Burns was embarked on a vessel for Virginia. Eleven hundred soldiers, besides policemen and deputy marshals, escorted him a quarter of a mile from the Court House to the wharf. As they went down State Street, they passed the spot of the Boston Massacre of 1770, where Crispus Attucks of negro blood had lost his life. They marched under a coffin suspended high above the street and labeled "The Funeral of Liberty." They marched under a large Union flag draped in black and hung union down. Occasional threatenings were met with counter movements by the troops, but no one was killed. A single item in this day's work cost the United States government fourteen thousand dollars, and the total expense of returning this one fugitive to slavery was estimated at from forty to one hundred thousand dollars. Resentment had been so aroused in Massachusetts that no other fugitive from labor was ever arrested on her soil. Burns [1] was ransomed by Boston people in 1855 and seven years later died, the pastor of a negro church in Canada.

In September, 1858, two Kentuckians appeared at Cleveland in the northeastern corner of the State of Ohio in search of fugitive slaves. They ran across a negro named John whom they recognized as the slave of a neighbor of the chief slave-catcher. The negro was decoyed out of the town of Oberlin, where he was living, set upon while on the road, and conveyed to Wellington, a station on the railroad line to Columbus. It happened that two young men had recognized John, the negro, as he was being carried away. They raised the alarm and fifty or sixty men or more took up the pursuit to Wellington. The slave-catchers, being appre-

---

[1] All accounts of the Burns affair are based on Charles E. Stevens's *Anthony Burns, A History* (Boston, 1856). A shorter account, also written at the time, is William I. Bowditch's *Rendition of Anthony Burns* (Boston, 1854). An anonymous pamphlet entitled *Boston Slave Riot, and Trial of Anthony Burns* was published at Boston in 1854. Colonel Higginson's recollections of the affair are in his *Cheerful Yesterdays*, 147–166. Although written forty-five years after the event, it is strikingly accurate. Several contemporary letters relating to the affair are printed in the *Proceedings* of the Massachusetts Historical Society for January, 1911, pp. 323–334. An account made up from Higginson's papers is in Mary T. Higginson's *Thomas Wentworth Higginson*, 142 and fol. The present writer has had the advantage of the use of a large collection of newspaper material made by Higginson at the time and now in the Harvard Library. Richard H. Dana's speech as counsel for Burns is in his *Speeches in Stirring Times* (Boston, 1910), 210–233. The best modern account of the affair is in Charles F. Adams's *Dana*, i, 262–295.

hensive, had retired to an attic chamber with their prey. They were assailed by stairway and by ladder; the negro was taken from them, was concealed in the house of an Oberlin professor of theology and moral philosophy,[1] was then sent on his way to Canada,—and was never afterwards seen. With the fatuous shortsightedness of the anti-free-soil men of that time this seemed to be a good chance to vindicate the majesty of the law and teach the people to keep their hands off things that did not concern them. Thirty or so of the rescuers were arrested, but released on their own recognizances to come up for trial when wanted. Leading politicians of the Western Reserve, interpreting the general feeling correctly, offered their services as counsel. The trials that followed were among the most interesting in our politico-juridical history. A verdict of guilty was returned against the first man tried and also against the second, who happened to be a negro. The proceedings then became somewhat embittered; the rest of the accused were remanded to prison with those who had already been declared guilty. At this point, the local authorities intervened and caused the arrest of the slave-catchers under a State anti-kidnapping law. Before matters had gone very far after this, the two parties came to an agreement by which all proceedings were dropped before the Federal and State judges and the Ohioans in jail and the Kentuckians also were released. Possibly it might have appeared to have been a drawn battle.[2] In reality it was nothing of the kind, for public sentiment had been so aroused by the constancy of the men of Oberlin and

[1] See Professor, afterward President, James H. Fairchild's article on "The Underground Railroad" in *Tract No. 87* of the Western Reserve Historical Society (Cleveland, 1895), p. 113.

[2] The best account of the Oberlin-Wellington rescue is in William C. Cochran's paper in *Collections* of the Western Reserve Historical Society for 1920, pp. 118–157, 197–207. The evidence and speeches of counsel are in J. R. Shipherd's *History of the Oberlin-Wellington Rescue* (Boston, 1859).

Wellington, that no more slave catchings were attempted in that part of Ohio,[1] and there, again, as in Massachusetts four years earlier, a powerful public sentiment against any further yielding to the slave power had been aroused.

From the time of Peter the Hermit to Theodore Roosevelt and Woodrow Wilson, mankind has been ruled by the propagandist. Whether right or wrong, he has only to shout loudly enough or write virulently enough and public opinion sooner or later will turn in his favor. He will crush his opponent. The New England literary and oratorical group has a great responsibility on its shoulders. On meeting Harriet Beecher Stowe for the first time, President Lincoln is reported to have said: "So you're the little woman who wrote the book that made this great war!" Born in Connecticut, the daughter of Lyman Beecher, she married Calvin Stowe, who had done much to bring about the introduction of the Prussian educational system into the Middle West. Stowe was then a teacher in Lane Seminary. Soon afterwards he moved to Bowdoin College in Brunswick, Maine, and later to Andover in Massachusetts. Straitened for money, Mrs. Stowe took her pen in hand and wrote stories; at first about the descendants of the Pilgrims and then about "Life among the Lowly" — among the slaves and along the road to freedom. Her knowledge of slaves and slavery was first hand as to the kind of slavery that prevailed in the neighboring Kentucky, as she or members of her family had personally known and helped fugitives fleeing toward Canada and freedom. "Uncle Tom's Cabin" was not a work of literature; it was written in the plain language of genius that the generality of people could read and comprehend and it had suggestions of tragedies of one kind or another that aroused the imagination, but did not exceed the canons

---

[1] See Cochran as above, pp. 158–196.

of respectability of that period in America, in England, in Europe, and in the world.

The original articles in the newspaper attracted some attention. When republished as a more or less connected narrative in book form in 1852, at Boston, success was immediate and great. Within twelve months, hundreds of thousands of copies were sold in America. Before half a dozen years had gone by, millions of copies had been printed and sold all over the world.[1] As the years went by, the book was translated into forty languages or dialects, or more, and even to this day possesses its power among people who never saw a slave and scarcely ever heard of slavery.[2] In dramatized form, the tale of "Uncle Tom," "Little Eva," and "Topsy" appealed to millions of persons in Great Britain, in France, and in the United States who never had read the book. "Uncle Tom's Cabin" did more than any other one thing to arouse the fears of the Southerners and impel them to fight for independence. On the other hand,

---

[1] James Ford Rhodes has noted the popularity of the work in his *History of the United States*, i, 282–285.

[2] At Savannah, in March, 1861, Alexander H. Stephens, then Vice-President of the Confederacy, declared that African slavery was "the immediate cause of the late rupture and present revolution. . . .

"Our new government is founded; . . . its foundations are laid, its cornerstone rests upon the great truth that the negro is not equal to the white man. That slavery . . . is his natural and moral condition.

". . . This stone which was rejected by the first builders, [those who made the Constitution of the United States] 'is become the chief stone of the corner' in our new edifice." *The Pulpit and Rostrum* (New York, 1862), Nos. 26 & 27, pp. 65–78. Rhodes (iii, 324) prints these and other extracts from Henry Cleveland's *Alexander H. Stephens in Public and Private*, 717, where the speech is printed from the *Savannah Republican*. R. M. Johnston and W. H. Browne give a very different version in their *Life* of Stephens (p. 396). In June, 1865, while incarcerated at Fort Warren in Boston Harbor, Stephens set down in his diary his own remembrance of the matter (*Recollections*, pp. 172–175). From this it appears that he himself corrected the reporter's notes. He reiterates the proposition that the "principle of a proper subordination [of the blacks to the whites], let it be called slavery or what not, . . . was the corner-stone on which it [the new Confederation] was formed."

In February, 1863, according to Frederic Bancroft, 750 "Protestant pastors of France" addressed the pastors of Great Britain, asking them to excite a peaceful demonstration of sympathy for the black race. In June, 3,997 British pastors replied most favorably (*Life of William H. Seward*, ii, 341).

the Northern boys who read it in the fifties were among those who voted for Abraham Lincoln in 1860 and followed the flag of the Union from Bull Run to Appomattox. Its influence on the plain people of France and Great Britain was so tremendous that no man possessed of political instinct in either of those countries,—no matter what were his wishes and those of his class,—no ruler of Great Britain or of France could have recognized a Confederacy whose corner-stone rested on the mutilated body of "Uncle Tom."

NOTES

I. The Underground Railroad. — Wilbur H. Siebert's *Underground Railroad from Slavery to Freedom* (New York, 1898) is the standard work on the subject. It is the result of a vast amount of well-directed effort, but in some places is, perhaps, a little credulous, and it is partly based on the recollections of old men. Professor Siebert deserves the thanks of all students of American history for having gathered and preserved in print so much material on one of the most interesting episodes of the past. " Appendix E " is a " Directory of the Names of Underground Railroad Operators." " Appendix C " contains an excellent bibliography, and an interesting map of the underground railroad system will be found facing p. 113. Of all the fugitives, Frederick Douglass stands preëminent by reason of ability and by the number of his published works. The *Narrative of the Life of Frederick Douglass, an American Slave. Written by Himself* was published at Boston in 1845, " At the Anti-slavery Office," *My Bondage and My Freedom* by Douglass was published at New York in 1855, and the *Life and Times of Frederick Douglass. Written by Himself* was published at Hartford in 1882 and a new and revised edition at Boston in 1893. Booker T. Washington's *Frederick Douglass* in the *American Crisis Biographies* has an interest apart from Douglass himself as practically being a history of the adventures of the colored people by one of themselves. Charles W. Chesnutt's little 134-page sketch entitled *Frederick Douglass* in the *Beacon Biographies* will cover the needs of most readers and has a bibliography of fourteen titles at the end.

The number of reminiscences in book form is large. Possibly R. C. Smedley's *History of the Underground Railroad in Chester and Neighboring Counties of Pennsylvania* (Lancaster, 1883) is the most interesting. Marion G. McDougall's " Fugitive Slaves " (1619–1865), *Fay House Monograph*, No. 3 (Boston, 1891), is a useful compilation with a list of important fugitive slave cases and a bibliography at the end.

II. *Uncle Tom's Cabin*. — The standard *Life of Harriet Beecher Stowe* was written by her son, Charles Edward Stowe, and was published at Boston in 1889. Years afterwards, in 1911, he, in collaboration with Mrs. Stowe's grandson, published a much shorter life, also at Boston. The *Life and Letters of Harriet Beecher Stowe*, edited by

Annie Fields (Boston, 1897), includes a great deal of familiar matter. Florine T. McCray's *Lifework of the Author of Uncle Tom's Cabin* (New York, 1889), made up partly from fresh material, is lifelike and interesting. She notes nineteen translations of *Uncle Tom* and states that it was printed at Paris in three daily papers simultaneously. Possibly the best assessment of Mrs. Stowe and her book was that made by Francis A. Shoup in the *Sewanee Review*, ii, 88–104. A " Bibliographical Account " is prefixed to an edition of *Uncle Tom's Cabin* that was published at Boston in 1884. There is an interesting article on Mrs. Stowe by Richard Burton in *The Century*, xxx, p. 699. *A Key to Uncle Tom's Cabin . . . Verifying the Truth of the Work* was prepared by Mrs. Stowe and printed at Boston and again at London in 1853. It purports to give facts and documents, but it lacks the verisimilitude of the book.

Naturally *Uncle Tom's Cabin* aroused comment and produced imitations. Of these possibly the most interesting is *Uncle Tom in England; or A Proof that Black's White*, published in New York with a preface that was dated at London, in September, 1852, and is said to have been printed from an advance copy of an English edition. Baynard R. Hall, the author of *The New Purchase*, wrote something in the same vein as " Uncle Tom " that was printed in New York in 1852 under the title of *Frank Freeman's Barber Shop*, and from the South there came " *Uncle Tom's Cabin* " contrasted with Buckingham Hall, the Planter's Home (New York, 1852). It was written by Robert Criswell and purported to be a " fair view of both sides of the slavery question." As showing one means of working up anti-Southern sentiment,[1] one can read Daniel S. Whitney's *Warren: A Tragedy in Five Acts* (Boston, 1850). It was designed, so the title-page says, to illustrate the protection which the Federal Union extends to citizens of Massachusetts, referring to the supposed fate of a free black who landed at Charleston and found himself involved in the severe laws of South Carolina against persons of that category.

[1] Hattia M'Keehan's *Liberty or Death; or Heaven's Infraction of the Fugitive Slave Law* (Cincinnati, 1859) reproduces in the form of fiction some of the elements of truth that appeared in the story of a fugitive slave woman who killed her daughter to keep her from a return to slavery and from a life such as she, herself, had led. In this case the slave mother is represented as being the half-sister of her master.

There is no adequate bibliography of *Uncle Tom's Cabin* or of Mrs. Stowe's writings, as a whole. The list prefixed to the 1884 Boston edition of *Uncle Tom's Cabin* will serve the needs of most people. Those who wish to go farther may consult the *Catalogue* of the British Museum and its *Supplements,* for that institution at an early day began the collection of editions of the book.

CHAPTER V

PARTIES, POLITICS, AND POLITICIANS, 1848–1859

THESE eleven years were the most significant in our history, for it was then that the Southerners determined to have their own way within the United States, or else to leave the Union, no matter what their numbers might be in comparison with the Northerners; and the people of the Northern States determined in their own minds that the time for concessions had passed and that there should be no more compromise with slave power. It cannot be said that Northerners before 1861 had come to any fixed determination as to the preservation of the existing Union. Rather the determination was to end the expansion of slave territory within the Union, — if the Southerners wished to leave the Union, very many people in the North would have been quite content to let them go. The election of 1848 placed in the White House a Whig President, Zachary Taylor. This result was due in great measure to his popularity as a military hero; it was due also to the fact that no one knew very much about his political opinions. More than all else the reason for the election of this last Whig President was that in 1848, the Democratic party in the North, or in parts of the North, was honeycombed with free-soilism.[1] For evidence, one may refer to the Massachusetts Democratic State platform[2] of 1849. The fifth resolution contained the statement that

[1] The general confusion in New York comes out in the "Diary and Memoranda of William L. Marcy" in *American Historical Review*, xxiv, 448–452.

[2] See *Three Letters of B. F. Hallett, to Col. C. G. Greene*, 4.

the institution of slavery was "a mere municipal regulation." The sixth resolution affirmed that as slavery did not exist by any municipal law in the new territories and as Congress had no power to institute it there "the local laws of any state authorizing slavery can never be transported there, nor can slavery exist there but by a local law of the territories, sanctioned by Congress, or the legislative act of a state in its sovereign capacity." The seventh resolution announced opposition to the extension of slavery to free territories, and the eighth resolution asserted that the Democratic party of Massachusetts "rejoiced to see the people of the territories taking this question into their own hands." At almost the other end of the then settled parts of the United States, in the Territory of Wisconsin, a body of single-minded Free-Soilers broke loose from the old organizations and actually elected one of their number to Congress.[1] Even in the sturdy Democratic State of New York, the members of that party were divided into sections.[2] There were the "Barnburners," who were so called because it was said that they would burn down the barn to destroy the rat; later they were called the "Softs." Those of the party who did not go so far as to be willing to burn the barn were called "Hunkers," because they were said to hanker or "hunker" for the official flesh-pots. The "Softs" opposed the further extension of slave territory, but the "Hunkers" or "Hards," as they were later called, were willing to keep on with their Southern brethren, slavery or no slavery, free soil or slave soil, — some of them or their friends were called "Doughfaces" and at other times were referred to as Northern men with Southern principles.

[1] See Theodore C. Smith's "Free Soil Party in Wisconsin" in the *Proceedings* of the State Historical Society of Wisconsin for 1894, p. 118.

[2] For the complicated political history of New York, see De Alva S. Alexander's *Political History of the State of New York*, vol. ii, especially ch. xiv and fol.

By this time, parties and party organizations had developed into much the same form that they now present. In the "good old days," candidates for office from the presidency downward were put forward by their friends or they put themselves forward.[1] In the beginning of party organization, the members of legislatures or of Congress of one way of thinking held meetings or caucuses, canvassed the qualities of this person or that, and recommended the election of some one man. As the chosen representatives of their parties, these persons would seem to have well reflected the wishes of those who had elected them, — the members of their own party. It soon came to be felt, however, that they were not representative in that they had no recent mandate — that they were out of touch with the actual feelings of their constituents whose wishes would be better expressed by the members of a body who had been chosen expressly to do that one particular thing. In this fashion, the nominating convention came into being. The first national presidential convention[2] was held at Baltimore in May, 1835, and nominated Martin Van Buren for the presidency. It also adopted a rule requiring a two-thirds vote to make a nomination effective. This rule had been adopted three years earlier by a convention that had nominated Van Buren for the office of Vice-President. In 1840, the Democrats again held a national presidential convention at Baltimore and by again adopting the two-thirds rule made it the policy

[1] Frederick W. Dallinger's "Nominations for Elective Office in the United States" (*Harvard Historical Studies*, vol. iv) contains information that will satisfy the needs of all students except the most exacting. These will find ample opportunities for further study in the works cited in Dallinger's "Bibliography." See especially pp. 36–40.

[2] An Anti-Masonic convention that was held at Baltimore in September, 1831, is sometimes regarded as the first national nominating convention; but it had representatives from only thirteen of the existing twenty-four States. This convention, such as it was, put forth a long "Address to the People" that is regarded as the first "platform," see Dallinger's *Nominating System*, p. 36 and fol. Stanwood gives somewhat different views in his *History of the Presidency*, p. 157 and fol.

of the Democratic party. It also adopted a declaration of party principles which was termed "the platform" as the candidate was supposed to stand on it and to be bound, more or less, to carry out its principles. It very soon came to be the custom for the candidates to acknowledge the nomination either by speech or in a letter and to promise more or less pointedly to carry out the platform.[1] In those days candidates were accustomed to stay at home and receive callers or delegations. They answered speeches made by these delegates and they wrote letters. In 1828 an effort had been made to induce John Quincy Adams to address the Pennsylvania Germans in their own language; but he felt it beneath the dignity of a candidate for the presidency openly to seek the office. In 1852, General Winfield Scott was nominated by the Whigs. Advantage was taken of the fact that he had been detailed by the Secretary of War to go to Kentucky to arrange for the opening of a place of refuge for old soldiers. When crowds had gathered to see the most famous American soldier of that time, Scott addressed them. It cannot be said that he was very happy in his harangues. Indeed, the Democrats collected his speeches and printed them in a pamphlet as a campaign document in behalf of their candidate, Franklin Pierce, who remained quietly at home, receiving such delegations of his fellow citizens as chose to journey to Concord, New Hampshire. When the votes were counted, it was found that Scott was hopelessly defeated, but it will not do to draw from that any conclusion as to the desirability or undesirability of a presidential candidate making personal appeals.

[1] The haphazard — or possibly intriguing — mode of nominating presidential candidates comes out in the letters of Edmund Burke to Franklin Pierce in 1852 (*American Historical Review*, x, 110–122) and of John Slidell to James Buchanan in 1856 (*ibid.*, xxvii, 722 and fol.).

In those days as at present, many people supported one candidate or the other in the hope of making an easy if somewhat limited livelihood from gaining an office, provided their candidate should be successful. As has been suggested in a preceding volume, President Washington began the spoils system by refusing to appoint any enemy of the Constitution to a Federal office.[1] Jefferson had reënforced this system by putting into governmental positions enough of his followers to make the balance fairly even. For years thereafter, there had been no change in parties in the White House and therefore when Jackson became President, as the leader of a revolutionary movement, consistency demanded the appointment of his followers to office. But it does not seem likely that he either dismissed or appointed in anything like the proportionate numbers that some writers have suggested. In 1841, the Jacksonians gave way to the Whigs and President Harrison occupied a large part of his one month in the White House in reapportioning the offices, and his successor President Tyler did what he could to undo this reapportionment. In 1845, President Polk dismissed a good share of whatever Harrisonites remained in place. So now, in 1849, when General Zachary Taylor took command of the government he dismissed Democrats and put good Whigs into their places. After his death and the succession of Millard Fillmore, Whigs of a somewhat different stripe replaced the Taylorites, or many of them. In 1853, Franklin Pierce, the new Democratic President and his principal officials, bent a large part of their energies to displacing the Taylor-Seward-Fillmore Whigs with good Democrats. This they did to the number of eight hundred and twenty-three presidential appointees

---

[1] For Washington's statement and his practice as to the civil service, see the present work, vol. iv, 52–56.

and, undoubtedly, a corresponding number of minor officials.[1]
Four years later, in 1857, when another Northern Democrat,
James Buchanan, came in, there was no rest for the office-
holders, for, when a Pierce Democrat had held a job for four
years, was it not high time for him to give place to a
Buchanan Democrat? Upon this William L. Marcy, the
retiring Secretary of State, remarked that he had been credited with the office seeker's doctrine that "to the victors
belong the spoils," but he certainly should never recommend
pillaging his own camp.[2] As these administrations from
1853 to 1861 were mainly in the hands of Southerners,
although President Pierce and President Buchanan were both
natives and residents of the North, it fell out that in 1861 the
occupants of the administrative offices at Washington were
practically all of them Democrats and were most of them
from the Southern States. Of late years, the building up of
a bureaucracy, under the guise of civil service reform, has
tended to cast reproach upon the earlier Presidents. It is
not at all certain, however, that the civil service under John
Quincy Adams or Andrew Jackson, in the second year of his
administration, or James Buchanan, was any more inefficient
than it has been under the bureaucratic system that has
necessarily developed with civil service reform.

The Whig party was born of opposition to Jacksonism and
died in the effort to "swallow the Fugitive Slave Act." It
had no reason for existence other than its devotion to things
that were past. It attracted to itself the rich and well-born
and many of those who were on the way to wealth. It had
no principles, other than opposition to the Democratic

[1] Carl R. Fish's "Removal of Officials" in American Historical Association's *Report* for 1899, vol. i, p. 80.
[2] See *American Historical Review*,
xxiv, 642 *n*. The documents printed
in this number of the *Review* cast an
interesting light on the inner condition
of the Democratic party in the year
1857.

control of the government. Whenever a new political principle developed, its supporters formed themselves into a new
party, and if they showed strength, the Democrats or the
Whigs would take them into their fold. The sixth decade
of the nineteenth century proved to be a time of political
flux in which the advocates of one thing or another grouped
themselves around some hoped-to-be popular designation
or around some name that might attract voters. The
trouble was that there were too many issues: there was
temperance reform, there was abolitionism, or the milder
free-soilism, and there was hostility to the white new-comer.
On these various topics the Whig party in the several States
and the Democrats also did not feel at all sure as to what position would be wisest to take. The result, the final result, was
the death of the Whig party, the abandonment by all other
anti-Democrats of temperance reforms and hostility to foreigners and the coming together on the platform of opposition
to the extension of negro slavery. Free-soilism and temperance
bit into both of the major parties; opposition to the immigrant alone developed into a party with a single principle.

In a preceding volume of this work,[1] attention has been
called to the opposition to the Roman Catholics that developed in Philadelphia, Boston, and New York, in 1844 and in
the years before and after. This hostility assumed a political phase in Philadelphia, and led to the formation of the
United American or American party to the accompaniment of
rioting and bloodshed, about which a good deal was written
at the time. As the Democrats would have and could have
nothing to do with the opposition to the Roman Catholics
who were mostly Irish, the rise of the new party or faction
affected only the Whigs. It happened, however, that the
attention of the people was diverted from the danger of too

[1] See the present work, vol. v, 213-219, 474-479.

rapid immigration to the danger of the extension of slave territory. This took the form of the contest over the Wilmot Proviso and for the moment consolidated the Whig party. It was only for the moment, however, because the triumph of Taylor and Fillmore and the subsequent death of Taylor resulted in the Compromise of 1850 and the consolidation of the Democratic party as the supporter of negro slavery as it existed in the Southern States. As the Whig party could not or would not face the actual issues of the moment, two new parties came into being: the Free-Soilers or Liberty Men and the Know-Nothing or American party.

Immigrants from Germany, from Scandinavia, and from Ireland did not stop coming to the United States with the taking of the Census of 1850. The movement continued, and ten years later the number of foreign-born had nearly doubled, there being four million of them within the boundaries of the United States in 1860, not including the children born in America of foreign parents. For the most part, the Germans and the Scandinavians spread out over the northern portions of the country, but the Irish settled in or near the three cities of debarkation, — Philadelphia, New York, and Boston. Indeed, in 1860, one-quarter of the Irish people in the United States lived in or near those cities. The Germans came over in considerable numbers after the failure of the revolutionary movements in 1848. Many of them settled in New York and Baltimore and some of them found work at Richmond in Virginia.[1] From the religious point of view, these Germans to a considerable extent were free thinkers. In politics and in social relations they were among the most radical groups of the day. In Richmond, they formed a "Social Democratic Society of Working Men" and speedily put forth a sheaf of demands. They wished

[1] *Census* of 1860, "Mortality," "Introduction," pp. lvii, lviii.

for the abolition of the presidency and the Senate, they demanded universal suffrage and the right of recall, they advocated the abolition of Sunday laws, and the taxation of church property, they wanted landed monopoly done away with, the establishment of the eight-hour day, a free asylum for superannuated mechanics, and they wished that the government should take possession of all the railroads.[1] This seems to have been the most complete statement of the desires of the German immigrants, but their societies in Baltimore and New York put forward substantially identical claims. Whether it was their radical religious ideas or their radical political ideas that aroused more dismay in the ranks of the descendants of the colonial families, it is perhaps difficult to say. The Germans were skilled and hard-working people and their services were in demand; but there was great jealousy felt of them because of their advocating changes that did not then fit in with the political and social ideas of the native-born population. It is curious to notice how the first contact with actual democracy affected the greatest German of that migration. In a letter written in 1852, Carl Schurz asserted[2] that there could be little for the future European republic that must find its support in hot-headed professional revolutionists, and in strong-minded ladies of the educated class. His first sight of the new land filled him with "dumb amazement." "Here you see," he wrote, "voluntarily made laws treated with contempt; . . . the crassest religious fanaticism venting itself in brutal acts; on the one hand you see the great mass of the laboring people in complete freedom striving for emancipa-

---

[1] See *An Address delivered by Thomas R. Whitney, Esq., December 23, 1851 . . . on . . . the Seventh Anniversary of Alpha Chapter, Order of United Americans.*

[2] *Speeches . . . of Carl Schurz*, i, 6. The first three letters in this volume are of great interest to students of political institutions.

tion, and by their side the speculative spirit of capital plunging into unheard-of enterprises."

In 1850, there were nearly one million natives of Ireland in the United States and that number had grown to over sixteen hundred thousand in 1860. Owing to the limited extent of their settlements, they had increased within certain areas out of all proportion to the native population. In Boston, there were, practically speaking, no Irish in 1845 ; in 1855 they formed no less than twenty-eight per cent of the total population of that city and something similar was the case in the vicinity of Boston and in the manufacturing towns of the State.[1] The Irish were very poor when they landed, they came in whole families including the aged and the sick, for family feeling was very strong among them. Many of them could not labor and those who did work were obliged to support the other members of the family. It fell out, therefore, that there was, unavoidedly, a good deal of pauperism among them in the early years of their inhabitancy of the New World. The law of Massachusetts then required that each local unit should support its own poor. This put a great strain upon the towns where the immigrants congregated. In May, 1852, the Massachusetts legislature passed an act providing for the building of three State poorhouses and for the reparation of the existing buildings on Rainsford Island for sick paupers. At the same time a law was passed requiring the master or agent of every ship bringing over a defective immigrant to Massachusetts to give a bond of one thousand dollars to indemnify the Commonwealth for any expense that it might incur for his or her care. And every other alien passenger was likewise to give a bond[2] not to become a public charge within

[1] See *Abstract of the Census of . . . Massachusetts . . . 1855*, Table III.

[2] *Acts and Resolves . . . of Massa-chusetts, for the Years 1852, 1853,* pp. 190, 195.

five years. The State poorhouse system became ex-
cessively unpopular among the immigrants and therefore
seems to have served its purpose, but the one thousand
dollar bond was evaded by disembarking at New York and
thence proceeding overland to Boston. The statistics also
contain conclusive proof that owing to unusual environment
and in great measure to new conditions of law and order, the
new-comers gained an exceedingly unenviable notoriety as
convicts, many of them for minor offences. Also it would
seem from the figures that the hardships of the voyage and
the strange conditions surrounding them in the new lands
drove many immigrants out of their senses and into insane
asylums.[1] It would be going too far, in the absence of definite
information, to say that similar conditions prevailed in the
other centers of Irish immigrant population, but there is no
reason to suppose that conditions of living and of labor in
Massachusetts, to any great extent at any rate, were less
favorable to the Irish men and women than they were in
New York and Pennsylvania, although it may be true, as
has sometimes been said, that the execution of the criminal
law and of the law as to the care of the insane was more
effective in Massachusetts than it was in the other States.

The Irishman was a faithful and consistent Roman Catholic. He also had an aptitude for politics. Naturally, he
espoused the Democratic party, for that seemed to be the
party of the poor man and in some ways the Northern wing
of it might be so regarded; although the spectacle of an
Irish immigrant and a cotton-planting aristocrat sitting
side by side in any kind of an organization presents a singular
aspect. It may be that the distance of the Democratic
aristocrat and the nearness of the Whig aristocrat was one
thing that determined the Irish immigrant's political prefer-

[1] *Abstract of the Census of . . . Massachusetts . . . 1855*, pp. 247–252.

ence. In those days, the inspection of immigrants, the regulation and care of balloting and balloting places, and the naturalization of foreigners were all somewhat inchoate. It fell out, therefore, that the Democratic politician, exercising vigor and a certain amount of cool confidence, was able to round up masses of Irishmen — many of whom were probably recent arrivals who had not the slightest legal right to exercise the franchise — lead them to the polling places, and see to it that they voted the correct ticket. In those days balloting was open and undisguised, the tickets were usually printed on different colored papers, and the exercise of the franchise could be easily traced by the political worker. The coming of so many Roman Catholics and their settlement in such definite areas aroused the jealousy of members of other religious bodies and led them to believe many things that were untrue. It also worked to give an exaggerated aspect to some things that were true. In 1839 a nun of unsound intellect fled from a convent in Baltimore to a neighboring house and asked for protection.[1] It was all that the mayor of the city could do to prevent the mobbing of the convent. Wherever the Roman Catholics secured a measure of political strength, they at once demanded that the reading of the Bible should be stopped in the public schools or that a portion of the money raised by taxation and appropriated to education should be placed in their hands to be devoted to the establishment of Roman Catholic schools. There had been disputes between certain Roman Catholic congregations and the bishops and archbishops, as to the title to the property, — to the church and to the ground on which it stood and to the funds of the society. This matter reached the stage at which the authorities at

[1] See Laurence F. Schmeckebier's "History of the Know Nothing Party in Maryland" in *Johns Hopkins Studies*, xvii, Nos. 4–5, p. 54.

Rome felt obliged to interfere and the Pope sent a personal representative — a Nuncio — to investigate the matter and settle it. This ecclesiastic's name was Bedini. At once, a clamor arose that the head of the Roman Catholic Church at Rome was presuming to exercise control over the property of American citizens in America. These people were called Anti-Bedinists. There were numerous matters of jealousy and disputation between the Roman Catholics and other American citizens. In each case, no doubt, there was some ground for jealousy on the part of the old Protestant population; but the main trouble was in the clannishness of the Irish Roman Catholics.[1] They lived apart by themselves and acted on the advice of their priests, who were the educated men among them. There was rioting in Baltimore, in Philadelphia, and in New York. It is impossible to state with any definiteness who was responsible for this. It sometimes ended in bloodshed, it gave rise to much bitterness, and it led to the formation of the "Native American" party. This had its main scene of activity in Philadelphia, but it soon had branches in Baltimore and New York. In 1845, it held a convention at Harrisburg[2] in Pennsylvania and issued an "Address." In this it asked why any Ameri-

[1] "Editor Lynch" of the *Irish-American*, quoted in the *New York Times* for August 30, 1854, informed his countrymen that they were opposed by a powerful secret society on the grounds that "we are impudent and voracious cormorants of petty places under government; that we are ignorant, turbulent, and brutal; that we are led by the nose and entirely controlled by our clergy; that we are willing subjects of a foreign prince, the Pope; that we are only lip-republicans; that we are not worthy of the franchise; that by the largeness of our vote and the clannishness of our habits and dispositions we rule or aspire to rule in America; that

we are drunkards and criminals; that we fill the workhouses and prisons"; and therefore should be deposed from citizenship and rooted out of the American nation. Scisco's "Political Nativism in New York State" (*Columbia University Studies*, vol. xiii, No. 2), p. 95. The state of mind of the native-born population may be gathered from a perusal of Samuel F. B. Morse's *Foreign Conspiracy against the Liberties of the United States*. This was originally published at New York in 1835; the "Seventh Edition" appeared in 1855.

[2] See *Proceedings of the Native American State Convention, held at Harrisburg, February 22, 1845.*

can should object to our "unity of national character."
True patriotism, it thought, would rejoice at the fusion of
all elements into one mass. Nativism was defined as "love
hallowed by liberty." Foreigners who hereafter should
come to the United States should remain in the country
twenty-one years before receiving the franchise. Americans
should make and administer their own laws. The Bible,
without note or comment, was not sectarian, and Church and
State should be separated. When "Americanisms" triumph, then shall "the glory of our native land spread wide
over the Universe, proclaiming it truly to be the blest Asylum
for the persecuted and the oppressed of all mankind." The
coming of the Mexican War with its attendant excitement
over slavery and the extension of slave territory put a speedy
end to this political manifestation.

After 1850, the immigration from Ireland went on with
great vigor and with the increase of immigrants in definite
areas, the opposition to them likewise grew. There now
developed for the first time and the only time before the
present day, secret political organizations. The history of
these is somewhat uncertain, owing to the destruction of the
records, — but the main facts are fairly well ascertained.
There was the Order of United Americans — the "O. U. A.,"
as it was generally termed. This was in some sort the
descendant of the Native American party of the 1840's; but
it was essentially, in the beginning, a social rather than a
political organization. As the years went by the O. U. A.
absorbed many similar independent organizations, as the
American Brotherhood, the United Daughters of America,
the Sons of America, the Benevolent Order of Bereans, and
the American Protestant Association. By 1850, the O. U. A.
was definitely engaging in political activities, possibly
through unofficial action by its members rather than by any

official action as a body. By 1852, there appeared to be in New York City some concerted political effort that was well directed and that had a considerable number of voters behind it. In the fullness of time, this order absorbed the political direction of the whole secret nativist societies. It seems to have centered in the Order of the Star-Spangled Banner, but nothing is certain about its early history. What was certain then was that there existed a uniform and well-directed political movement to defeat the election of certain persons and to promote or defeat specified legislation; secondly, that this movement did not emanate from either of the old parties; and, thirdly, that when persons who appeared to be active in the prosecution of these political designs were asked concerning their activities or their affiliations, they expressed themselves as knowing nothing whatever on the matter. In the beginning, the Know-Nothing movement centered in New York City and was primarily directed against the perpetuation of the existing political conditions there. In 1853, the nativist movement polled two thousand votes and more. Thereafter, it grew with astonishing rapidity in New York City and then extended itself over the State and then into the neighboring States.

The organization of the Know-Nothing Society or movement was interesting. There were three degrees. Those joining the society belonged to the first degree and promised to vote as the society determined. No one could be admitted to the first degree who was not American born and wholly unconnected by family ties with Roman Catholics. The members of the second degree were eligible for office-holding within the order and the members of the third degree were competent to be nominated for office outside of the order. Apparently, members of the first order had nothing to say as to the conduct of the society, which was entirely

within the power of the first two orders acting singly for a
locality or a lodge, or grouped in council geographically.
Although the first-degree members had no part in these
conclaves, they really determined the policy of the society,
for the councils were careful to do nothing that would not
win the support of the members. There was just enough
mystery and formality to excite curiosity and desire. They
were supposed to have a grip, a certain formula of vocal
recognition, their meetings were summoned in a peculiar
manner, and everywhere was the denial of knowledge which
won for them their name. Whatever the structure of the
society or societies or whatever its ritual or grip may have
been, one thing is certain that when in 1854 almost entirely
unknown persons were elected to office in New York City and
in parts of New York State, the politicians of the older parties
were dismayed as they never had been before. 1854 was
the year of excessive disruption of party allegiance in New
York State. The Whig party was divided into "Woolly-
Heads" and "Silver-Grays," as the followers of William H.
Seward and Millard Fillmore were called, and the Democrats
were likewise divided into the "Hard-Shells" who truckled
to the South, or were said to, and the "Soft-Shells" who
were supposed not to do so. Then there were the Temperance men, the Anti-Nebraska men, and the Anti-Renters
who expressed dissent to the peculiar land system of a part
of New York. Besides, there were the anti-slavery people,
some of whom called themselves Free Democrats; others
belonged to the Liberty party and others were denominated
Republicans. It was into such a heterogeneity of politics
that the Know-Nothings suddenly projected themselves and
rolled up over one hundred and twenty-two thousand votes,
with the aid of their "Silver-Gray" allies, to over one hundred and thirty-three thousand for the "Soft-Shelled"

Democrat and one hundred and fifty-five thousand for the "Woolly-Headed" Whigs and their allies.[1] Evidently, unless something should intervene the managers of the Know-Nothing movement were persons with whom the politicians of the Seward type had got to reckon and that without delay.

Outside of New York, Know-Nothingism was more successful than it was in the State of its birth. In Massachusetts, where political conditions were in an extremely fluid state in 1854, the Know-Nothings swept the polls. They cast sixty-three per cent of the total vote; their candidate for governor had thirty-three thousand majority over all opponents. The Know-Nothings elected every member of the Senate and three hundred and seventy-six Know-Nothings to the House of Representatives, which also included one Whig, one Democrat, and one Free-Soiler — and no one else.[2] The legislature was scarcely three days old when it elected Henry Wilson, a Know-Nothing, to the Senate of the United States. Know-Nothingism offered a refuge for politicians and voters who wished to bilk the real issue of the hour, namely, the expansion of slave territory, as provided for in the Kansas-Nebraska Act. It is in this way only that the adoption of the new movement by Southern politicians and voters can be accounted for. They were not Democrats, or if they were Democrats they wanted to get out of the party at least temporarily; those of them who were Whigs no longer could have that place of refuge, for the Whig party was unmistakably in the last throes of the death agony. On the other hand, the unknown management of the Know-

---

[1] Louis D. Scisco's "Political Nativism in New York State," 125 (*Columbia Studies*, vol. xiii, No. 2).

[2] G. H. Haynes's "The Causes of Know-Nothing Success in Massa-chusetts" (*American Historical Review*, iii), p. 68, and his "A Know Nothing Legislature" in Massachusetts, in American Historical Association's *Report* for 1896, vol. i, pp. 177-187.

Nothings decided to enlarge their sphere of operations and break in upon national politics. They held a national council at Cincinnati in November, 1854, and adopted a new ritual by which the leaders hoped that the order could be extended into the South, while retaining its power in the North. In the third-degree oath that was then adopted a member swore that he would discourage and denounce any attempt coming from any quarter to destroy or subvert the Union of these States, that he would use his influence to procure an amicable and equitable adjustment of all political discontents, and that he would not vote for anyone whom he believed to be in favor of a dissolution of the Union.[1] On June 5, 1855, the National Council of the Know-Nothing party, which was now openly termed the American party, met at Philadelphia. At once the Southerners seized control. They ousted the founder of the society from the presidency and put a Kentuckian in his place. They then adopted a resolution, proposed by a Virginian, that the National Council has deemed it "the best guarantee of common justice and future peace to abide by and maintain the existing laws upon the subject of slavery," that Congress possessed no power to legislate upon the subject of slavery in the States or to refuse to admit any State into the Union because its constitution does or does not recognize slavery as part of her social system.[2] That was the end of Know-

---

[1] L. D. Scisco's "Political Nativism in New York State," 136.

[2] On this aspect of nativism, see The Origin, Principles and Purposes of the American Party; L. D. Scisco's " Political Nativism in New York State," ch. vi; George Robertson's The American Party: Its Principles, Its Objects, and Its Hopes; a moderate Roman Catholic view may be found in two printed Addresses by Charles Gayarré, dated New Orleans, June 5, 1855, and September 21, 1855. He had joined the Louisiana American party at the beginning of the year and these Addresses explain why he had to leave it, The views of another noted Southern writer may be seen in Know Nothingism Unveiled. Letter of Judge A. B. Longstreet, dated University of Mississippi, December 19, 1855. He stated that what he objects to in the American party is their " clanship with all characters, . . . their night-working, their needless swearing, their man-serving, party-scheming, office-hunting, stump-

Nothingism as a political force in the United States, although enough persons retained their nativist sentiments to determine the fate of many a politician even as late as the year 1860. In Maryland, too, the Know-Nothing movement possessed vitality after this time,[1] for there was no other political body around which public opinion could assemble. The straits, indeed, to which Southern men with Northern principles were put in these years are well shown by the shamefacedness with which, in later life, they confessed that at this time of party disruption they had joined or had acted with the Know-Nothings.[2]

The Whig party[3] had had an honorable history and was composed of some of the best elements in American political life and in American life. In the South, at one time or another, it was the party of the more prosperous planters and to it belonged some of the greatest figures in Southern history of the quarter century before 1860, as Toombs and Stephens. It was essentially the party advocating union, if such a thing were possible, and "consistent with honor." Oddly enough, the foremost character in the Whig party of the North was William H. Seward of New York, who formed, with Thurlow Weed and Horace Greeley, a political alliance that had great influence in New York until Greeley, being disappointed in not securing a minor official position on the ticket, put an end to the alliance and nursed his wrath for evermore. The foremost Whigs of them all were Henry Clay of Kentucky

speaking, anger-stirring, brother-wounding, and church-inflaming." See also Note at end of chapter.

[1] See L. F. Schmeckebier's " History of the Know Nothing Party in Maryland" in *Johns Hopkins Studies*, xvii, Nos. 4–5. Anna E. Carroll's *The Great American Battle . . . Between Christianity and Political Romanism* (New York, 1856) gives, in semi-fictional form, the objections to Catholicism of a

Protestant member of the Catholic Carroll family of Maryland.

[2] See Thomas Hunt's *Life of William H. Hunt*, 156.

[3] Arthur C. Cole's *The Whig Party in the South* may almost be described as a history of the Whig party, and Henry R. Mueller's *Whig Party in Pennsylvania* (Columbia Studies, vol. ci, No. 2) has a great deal that is instructive on the history of the Whig party in general.

and Daniel Webster of Massachusetts. In the general com-
mingling of parties and issues that centered around the
election of Taylor in 1848, it would seem that even the astute
politicians of that day would sometimes have been hard put
to it to define the principles of the Whig or the Democratic
party or to give any reason for themselves belonging to one
party or another. The intrusion of the Wilmot Proviso into
the garden of politics brought the politicians to their senses
and made them seek the cover of some stable organization.
Democrats who had been quite favorable to the limitation
of slavery hastened to rejoin their old organization and Whigs
who had been upholding strange doctrines likewise reëntered
the political gates. The passage of the Compromise of
1850 was the signal for the disruption of the Whig party and
the revival of the Democratic party. Viewing the outcome,
it seems not impossible that the tyro in politics, President
Zachary Taylor, really had more political prescience than the
most veteran political war horses of them all. The Democrats, having assented to the Compromise, stood for its
"finality." The Whigs were now to dabble with all kinds of
reformations and movements, with Know-Nothingism, with
Free-Soilism, and with Temperance!

The passage of the Kansas-Nebraska Act in 1854 and the
subsequent round of troubles in Kansas brought the political
cauldron to a boil and resolved its contents into their component parts. The Democrats remained Democrats —
those of them that did not become anti-Nebraska men —
and the Whig party as an organization disappeared, although
there were Whiggish remnants to be discerned in the South
in the presidential election of 1860. The Know-Nothings
had essayed to rise to the heights of a national party, but
had fallen into the hands of Southern petty politicians. The
way was now open for a new organization and one sprang

into being that gained control of the government in 1861 and did not relinquish it for a quarter of a century. Like the origin of most great movements, the beginning of the Republican party is somewhat veiled in obscurity. It would seem, however, that its birth actually took place at Buffalo, in 1848, although it did not reach anything like maturity until 1856. It was at Buffalo on the 9th of August, 1848, that a mass convention composed of delegates and of thousands of intelligent and patriotic men and women assembled from far and near, from as far west as Iowa and as far east as Maine. No hall in Buffalo would hold them, so they pitched "the Oberlin tent, capable of containing 10,000 persons" in the city park. The convention organized on the basis of three delegates for each congressional district and six for each State at large. The people had come there to oppose the rising slavery propaganda. They sank as between themselves all minor causes of dissension and planted themselves upon "the national platform of Freedom, in opposition to the sectional platform of Slavery." New York Barnburners, Whigs, and Liberty men worked together and signified their heterogeneity and harmony by nominating Martin Van Buren for President and Charles Francis Adams of Massachusetts for Vice-President.[1] They were easily defeated by Taylor and Fillmore on a platform of nothing whatever.

The repeal of the Missouri Compromise in 1854 brought every man and woman in the country face to face with the

[1] Northampton *Courier Extra* of August 16, 1848. The Democrats gleefully got together various articles that Adams had previously written derogatory to Van Buren, calling him a "servile dough-face" and printed them in an eight-page pamphlet entitled *The Charles F. Adams Platform, or a Looking Glass for the Worthies of the Buffalo Convention*. The tone of this pamphlet may be discerned from the description of the nomination as "the Union of the Houses of Lindenwald and Braintree — a marriage extraordinary between all that is superlative and rampant in modern Democracy, and all that is cold, selfish, austere, and vinegar-like, in the remains of American aristocracy, dying out and tapering off in the third generation."

real issue that underlay all others in the life of the people of the United States. At innumerable isolated points in the northern part of the country, meetings were held and resolutions were adopted denouncing all attempts to extend the area of slavery and pledging those present to exert every effort to prevent it. The first State convention apparently was the one held at Jackson, Michigan, July 6, 1854, and that meeting may well be regarded as the formal beginning of the Republican political organization.[1]

The elections of 1854 in New York and New England and in Pennsylvania turned out generally in favor of the Know-Nothing or American party. Every month, as it went by, saw some occurrence in Kansas that added fuel to the fire of Northern discontent. In October came the Ostend Manifesto, advocating the seizure of Cuba by force if the Spaniards would not sell it for gold.[2] It seemed as if the desire of the Southerners for territory was incapable of satisfaction. Now, besides Cuba, they cast longing eyes on Mexican possessions and the lands extending southwardly from the Isthmus of Tehuantepec to the Isthmus of Panama. Much of this desire and intrigue for additional slave territory

[1] These two sentences are based on A. J. Turner's article entitled "The Genesis of the Republican Party" in the *Wisconsin State Register*, for March, 1898. A reprint of this article was given to me by his son and my colleague, Professor Frederick J. Turner, of Harvard University, who has laid me under deep obligations in many ways. The earlier accounts are most conveniently found in Rhodes's second volume. Theodore C. Smith wrote an interesting article on "The Free Soil Party in Wisconsin" which was printed in the *Proceedings* of the State Historical Society in 1894. See also Professor Smith's *Liberty and Free Soil Parties in the Northwest* in *Harvard Historical Studies*, vol. vi, and his *Parties and Slavery* in the *American Nation* series.

Detailed accounts of the rise of the Republican party are in Francis Curtis's *Republican Party, A History* (New York, 1904), i, chs. vi–ix, and in Daniel W. Howe's *Political History of Secession* (New York, 1914), ch. xiv.
[2] Writing to J. Glancy Jones from London on May 4, 1855, Buchanan stated that the Ostend report was prepared with deliberation and under the conviction that when the offer to purchase the island was made to Spain that the United States would be powerfully aided in accomplishing the object by the influence of the Spanish bondholders and the commercial classes in England and also by the Spanish clergy on whose property the government was levying for current needs. See Charles H. Jones's *J. Glancy Jones*, ii, 370.

had only been suspected by inference, but the Ostend Manifesto brushed all that aside and stated as to one bit of territory — Cuba — the desires of the South in language that no one could fail to understand.

When the year 1856 opened, the political situation throughout the country was very complicated. The Democratic party was united in the South, but was losing, or had lost, much of its strength in the North ; the Whig party was practically lifeless ; and the Know-Nothing or American party having sold itself to the South, the way was open for the establishment of a strong Northern opposition party which should frankly abandon all thoughts of Southern support and rely upon the sentiment of the North as to the further enlargement of slave territory. The Americans met in national convention at Philadelphia in February, 1856. A platform had already been provided by the National Council of the party or order. This pronunciamento entirely evaded the real issues of the hour by openly declaring that laws constitutionally enacted must be enforced until regularly repealed or adjudged null and void by competent judicial authorities. This dodging of the issue was not at all what many northern Americans wished. Being defeated on a motion to deny the binding authority of this platform, a large proportion of the delegates from New England and from some other Northern States withdrew. The regular Americans who remained nominated Millard Fillmore for the presidency. Four years earlier, Fillmore had been greatly favored by Democrats and this nomination was expected to find some response in the South, for Fillmore had set his name to the compromise bills that had been declared to be a finality. The Democrats met in June at Cincinnati. An effort was made by the constructors of the platform upon which the Democratic candidate was to stand to placate all

elements of the party in the North and in the South. A
"political crusade . . . against Catholics and foreign-born"[1]
was not justified or in unison with the spirit of toleration
which distinguishes the American system of government, so
they declared.   They resolved that the principles contained
in the Kansas-Nebraska Act were "the only sound and safe
solution of the slavery question." And so they went on.
The prominent candidates for the nomination were Pierce,
the actual occupant of the White House, Stephen A. Douglas,
and James Buchanan.   They were all able men, well qualified to fill the presidential chair; but both Pierce and Douglas had been closely identified with the unhappy proceedings
of recent years in Kansas.   Buchanan had been out of the
country as Minister to Great Britain and had, therefore,
taken no part in the unsatisfying events of the Kansas-
Nebraska contest.   Buchanan's record was "without a
blemish," according to the Richmond "Enquirer."   In
other words, he was sound on the slavery question.   In fact,
according to the "Enquirer" he had never "uttered a word
which could pain the most sensitive Southern heart."
Buchanan's campaign had been managed, so far as one can
call it a campaign and speak of it as management, by one
of the ablest men in political life, Senator John Slidell
of Louisiana.   At the crucial moment he appeared and
fought the action so successfully for Buchanan that he was
nominated.   The trivial circumstances and the shrewd
management of the Democratic politicians of that time
may be best seen in the correspondence between Slidell and
Buchanan[2] and that between Franklin Pierce and his hench-
men in the preceding time.[3]   Apparently the best recom-
mendation for the presidency in those days was to have been

[1] *Official Proceedings of the National
Democratic Convention, held in Cincinnati, June 2–6, 1856,* p. 25.

[2] *American Historical Review,* xxvii,
709–730.
[3] *Ibid.,* x, 110–127 and 350–370.

in the public eye and to have done nothing in recent years
about which any kind of enthusiasm could arise.

The Republican party was organized on a national basis
at Pittsburg in February, 1856, by a meeting of persons
from a score or so of States. They had no official mandate;
but they represented the desire of thousands and thousands
of men and women — not all of them living in the North.[1]
The first national nominating convention of the Republican
party was held at Philadelphia in June, 1856.[2] It was a
"mass convention" in that there was no prescription as to
the size of the State delegations, and the States cast as many
votes as they had delegates in the hall when the vote was
taken. It really mattered little, for the members of the convention were so enthusiastic, so filled with hope, that they
were determined to reach a conclusion that would be practically unanimous. Justice McLean of the Supreme Court
of the United States, whose place of residence was in Ohio,
was looked upon by many persons as the most likely candidate; but there were many objections to him. For years
he had coveted the presidential office, and there was another
Ohio candidate, Salmon P. Chase, who possessed in some
ways more availability than McLean because he had more
recently deserted the Democratic party. Neither of these
two men really had much chance in the convention, although
for a time it seemed as if McLean could be nominated. The
foremost Republican of them all was William H. Seward of
New York. For some unknown reason, Seward chose this
time to remain in his house when he should have stepped
forward to sound the keynote of the campaign and the
opposition of the North to continued Southern domination.
The result had in it something of the grotesque, for the con-

[1] George W. Julian in *American Historical Review*, iv, 313–322.

[2] See J. F. Rhodes's *United States*,
ii, 182 *note*.

vention, being composed of well-intentioned but undisciplined persons, passed by these candidates or potential candidates and selected John C. Frémont of California as the standard bearer of the new party in its first presidential campaign. The reasons for this selection are still hidden in the dimness of the past. Frémont was the "Pathfinder," that is to say, he popularized paths that other people had found. Possibly to the enthusiasts at the convention the person who had found the paths to the West might also hit upon a route to the White House. Then Frémont was a Southerner by origin and there was a glamour of romance about him, owing to his high-handed marriage with the forceful Jessie, daughter of Senator Benton of Missouri. Frémont's name seemed to be one to conjure with,[1] but there were some difficulties in regard to his actions in California as to certain lands and as to his doings outside of California, in London and New York, in attempts to dispose of those lands. These financial irregularities should have put an end to Frémont's career as a public man forever, — but they did nothing of the kind.[2] It is noteworthy that in the balloting for Vice-President, which resulted in the choice of Senator Dayton of New Jersey, Abraham Lincoln of Illinois received no less than 110 votes. The campaign

[1] A stirring and informing campaign pamphlet was issued at Providence, R. I., in 1856. It was entitled *Facts and Figures for Frémont and Freedom*. Much has been written about Frémont's financial vagaries and these statements have often centered around the Mariposa Estate in California. All land titles in California were more or less upset by the fact of the conquest; but the doubts that were raised were judicially settled in Frémont's favor. The gold-yielding lands that stood in his name were apparently taken over by his creditors and yielded only loss to them; but this was due to lack of proper method in mining and milling.

[2] The sort of political pabulum served to the voters in those days can be seen in "A Plain Statement addressed to all Honest Democrats by One of the People" (Boston, 1856) or *American Abolitionism* by F. G. de Fontaine (New York, 1861). The "Declaration" of the Radical Political Abolitionists at Syracuse, N. Y., in 1855, and the accompanying "Exposition" and "Address" solidified secession sentiment in the South, according to Professor Phillips, — and well they might have done so.

J. Ross Browne's *Resources of the Pacific Slope*, 23.

that followed was exciting. The Democrats were sure of
the electoral votes of the South, but they needed more than
the South could give.[1] Indiana and Pennsylvania were
the pivotal States, for if their votes went to the Democratic
candidate, he would be elected, and without them Frémont
could not win. Apparently for the first time in our political
history large sums of money were subscribed to put speakers
into the field and to provide the mechanical parts of torchlight processions and public gatherings. The enthusiasm
was greater than it had been at any time since 1840, but
Buchanan carried both States and was elected. Northern
Democrats, according to a speaker at Faneuil Hall, in
Boston, in October, 1856, felt that at last the "black snake
of sectionalism" had been broken. The accounts of the
campaign are so conflicting that it is difficult to state with
any exactitude the reasons for the outcome. Probably
the fact that Frémont's father was a Frenchman lost many
German votes in Pennsylvania. It may be that his business
methods did not commend him to the Quakers of the Keystone State. Besides, persistent rumors that Frémont was
a Roman Catholic undoubtedly turned away from him
many Know-Nothing voters.[2] The defeat of Frémont has

[1] The feeling was so tense in the
South against Frémont that Professor
Benjamin S. Hedrick of the University
of North Carolina was dismissed in
October, 1856, for supporting Frémont
and opposing slavery. The feeling
against him may be gathered by the
perusal of a pamphlet entitled *Are
North Carolinians Freemen?* *Read and
Judge* and Professor J. G. de R. Hamilton's article on "Benjamin Sherwood
Hedrick" in *The James Sprunt Historical Publications*, x, No. 1.

Another professor — D. Willard Fiske
of Cornell — declared in writing to a
friend that he resolved to vote for Frémont when that person spoke words
in his hearing that convinced him
of his utter freedom from the stain of

Know-Nothingism and of his opposition to the extension of "our Southern
crime." Indeed, Frémont seemed to be
"the only person entitled to the support
of any one who had read history, of any
one who loved humanity." This letter
was kindly communicated to me by my
colleague, Professor Horatio S. White.

Another professor, a native of California, an historian of that State, and a
philosopher, Josiah Royce, gave his
assessment of Frémont in the *Atlantic
Monthly* for October, 1890, p. 548.

[2] See, for example, *Frémont's Romanism Established. Acknowledged by Archbishop Hughes ; The Romish Intrigue:
Frémont a Catholic!!*, and *Col. Frémont's
Religious History. The Authentic Account. Papist or Protestant, Which?*

been generally welcomed by historians, for it seems reasonably certain that the South would have seceded in 1856 had a sectional President been elected, and certainly the public opinion of the North in 1856 was not in favor of coercing their fellow countrymen back into the Union fold.

NOTE

The Nativism Movement. — There is no modern scientific work treating the nativist movement of 1840 to 1860 as a whole. L. D. Scisco in his " Political Nativism in New York State " (*Columbia Studies*, vol. xiii, No. 2) goes outside of New York, but only incidentally; for New York itself it is a satisfactory account. John Hancock Lee's *Origin and Progress of the American Party*, published at Philadelphia in 1855, relates only to the Philadelphia riotings of 1844. Another account is in *American Catholic Historical Researches*, xiii, 50–64. G. H. Haynes's " The Causes of Know-Nothing Success in Massachusetts " (*American Historical Review*, iii, 67–82) is an interesting study of the immigration problem and of the reasons for the dislike of the immigrant in Massachusetts. Thomas O'Gorman in his *History of the Roman Catholic Church in the United States* [1] in the *American Church History* series, vol. ix, has some interesting matter on the subjects treated in this chapter; see index under " Hughes," " Know-Nothingism," " Bedini." James P. Hambleton's *History of the Political Campaign in Virginia in 1855* [2] contains much instructive material on this subject, although how authentic some of it is may be questionable.

[1] Humphrey J. Desmond's *The Know-Nothing Party* is a moderate and not very extended account of the movement by a Roman Catholic; with it may be read *Startling Facts for Native Americans . . . to be apprehended from Foreign Influence* (New York, 1855).

[2] A " Biographical Sketch " of Governor Wise was issued separately in the year 1856 and is usually bound, with a title page of its own, in copies of the *History*.

CHAPTER VI

"BLEEDING KANSAS"

On May 24, 1854, Anthony Burns was arrested at Boston. Six days later, Franklin Pierce, President of the United States, affixed his name to the Kansas-Nebraska bill. In the following July, the first party of emigrants left Massachusetts for the new Territory of Kansas. The origin of the Kansas-Nebraska Act and of its most important provision is still veiled in obscurity. With the admission of the State of California and the establishment of the Territories of Oregon, New Mexico, and Utah, governmental institutions had been provided for the people living in the regions that were drained by rivers flowing into the Pacific Ocean. Immediately to the west of the Mississippi there were the States of Missouri and Iowa and the Territory of Minnesota. Between these groups of organized communities, there stretched hundreds of miles of exceedingly fertile and desirable land that was entirely without government of any kind. Thousands of fortune hunters and would-be farmers with their families were crossing this region to California and Oregon, to Utah and Idaho. Others were pursuing the old Santa Fé trail to New Mexico and the southwestern markets. How many thousands went over these roads in each year from 1849 to 1855 has never been stated with accuracy. In 1849, forty-two hundred emigrants died on the plains and in 1852 cholera swept into the next world five thousand persons as they were toiling over the prairies and through the

148

mountains.[1] At the great bend of the Missouri River, at
Independence or Westport, the traveller left steamboat and
civilization and began his westward march. This point has
such a geographical significance that at the present day
Kansas City, Missouri, is one of the great railroad centers
of the world. There were Indian reservations and government agencies in this region and there were mission stations.
One of these had been founded by Presbyterians as far back
as 1824, and there were Methodist, Baptist, Friends, and
Roman Catholic missions that dated from 1837 and earlier.
On the Missouri River above Westport was Fort Leaven-
worth that dated back to 1827. At all these places put
together — not counting the soldiers — there was a reasonably stationary white population in 1854 of about fourteen
hundred persons.[2] Taking into consideration the moving
population of the plains, the inhabitants of the Indian
agencies, of the missions, and some isolated settlers, it was
certainly desirable that there should be some form of government between the Missouri and the Rockies. And there
was nothing of the kind, except the will of a military commander or two, or of an Indian trader or some other government agent. There was also a demand for better communication between the settled portions of the Mississippi
Valley and the mining camps and farms of the Rocky Mountains and the Pacific Coast. Projects had been put forward
for the building of a railroad through the country in the
northern area, in the central area, and in the southern area.[3]
The two first of these, whenever built, would pass through
this unorganized territory. A railroad would bring about
active settlement, and higher prices could be obtained for

[1] Grace R. Hebard and E. A. Brininstool's *The Bozeman Trail* (Cleveland,
1922), i, 54.

[2] Kansas State Historical Society's
Transactions, ix, 160, 161. For slightly

different details, see *ibid.*, iii, 422.

[3] See George E. Albright's " Official
Explorations for Pacific Railroads"
in *University of California Publications
in History*, xi, 1–39.

lands.[1] But it was essential that there should be some governmental organization.

Whenever any project was put forward for the establishment of one or more territorial governments in this country of the prairies, there was friction. The effort to extend the principles of the Ordinance of 1787 to the unorganized territorial possessions of the United States aroused passions that ended in the cataclysm of secession and war. This northern region held out no hope for the profitable employment of slaves. The slaveholders could not cultivate the land they possessed with the amount of labor in their control; but they were determined that they should not be debarred from going to any part of the national domain with their slaves and living there, if they could do so with profit and happiness. On the other hand, there were Northern Congressmen in Senate and House who were equally determined that there should be no extension of slave territory, at least north of the Compromise line of 1820, and many persons in Congress and out were opposed to any increase of slave territory north of that line or south of it. These considerations led to the defeat of every bill for the organization of this region into one or more territories from the year 1848 to the year 1854. As to the precise moving force that led to the passage of the Kansas-Nebraska Act, one's Douglas or anti-Douglas prepossessions largely influence the investigator and the historical narrator.

[1] A map showing Indian reservations and agencies and mission stations as they were in 1850 or thereabouts, together with the routes over the plains and in general the geographic knowledge of that time as to the western country, is the "New Map of that Portion of North America, exhibiting the United States and Territories . . . and Mexico, also Central America" that was published by Jacob Monk at Baltimore in 1852. Hebard and Brininstool's *The Bozeman Trail* contains at the ends of the two volumes two very clear maps drawn by Grace R. Hebard and showing the Oregon and Bozeman Trails and the Overland Stage Route. The Indian reservations are given on S. Eastman's "Map of Nebraska and Kansas Territories" (Philadelphia, 1854). E. B. Whitman and A. D. Searl's "Map of Eastern Kansas" (Boston, 1856), shows the mission stations or some of them, the reservations, and the early settlements.

Stephen Arnold Douglas was a Vermonter.[1] In early manhood, he found his way to Illinois and there, like many other ambitious young men, practiced law and politics. His great ability, his winning personality, and his power of elucidating difficult questions to his own satisfaction and to that of his hearers, drove him rapidly upward on the political path, until, in 1847, he entered the Senate of the United States. Douglas married a North Carolinian, the daughter of a prosperous planter, who, after the manner of that time, became interested in a Mississippi plantation with its equipment of negro slaves. As was the case with all the greater men of the forties and fifties — those in national politics — Douglas desired to become the occupant of the Executive Mansion, as the White House was dubbed in those days. How much any one politician was willing to pay for this depends very largely upon the individual point of view. The enemies of Stephen A. Douglas, and first and last they have been exceedingly numerous, imputed to him as mean and low motives as could be imputed to a presidential aspirant.[2] To others—a very small minority of them —

[1] Nine biographies of Douglas have been printed. Those by James W. Sheahan and Henry M. Flint were the work of personal friends, — the latter exists in four forms published in 1860 and in 1863. The others are Robert B. Warden's *A Voter's Version of the Life and Character of Stephen Arnold Douglas* (Columbus, 1860) ; and the biographies by William Garrott Brown (Boston, 1904), William Gardner (Boston, 1905), Allen Johnson (New York, 1908), Clark E. Carr (Chicago, 1909), Louis Howland (New York, 1920), and by Frank E. Stevens in volume xvi (pp. 247–673) of the *Journal* of the Illinois State Historical Society (1924). Of these Garrott Brown's book is an interesting characterization by a Southerner who had lived long in the North. The life mask prefixed to Gardner's book is a striking representation and

the illustrations in Carr's and Stevens's books reveal the salient characteristics of many of the great men of that time. Benjamin F. Butler's appraisal of Douglas at Lowell on August 10, 1860, is well worth reading.

[2] Douglas once denied that he owned a slave or ever had owned one (Allen Johnson's *Stephen A. Douglas*, 273). He added that he had never appropriated to his own use " one dollar earned by slave-labor" from the slaves inherited by his sons from their mother. See also James W. Sheahan's *Life of Stephen A. Douglas*, 437–442. From the statement made in the *Claim of Rob't M. and Stephen A. Douglas* (Washington, 1872) it appears that in 1857 Senator Douglas, as guardian of his minor sons, entered into a contract with J. A. McHatton to take the Douglas slaves, one hundred and forty-two in

Douglas appears to have been no better and no worse than
other Illinois politicians of his time — and, indeed, of other
politicians east and west of Illinois of that day and of this.
Then, too, in assessing Douglas's moral position, it is not
necessary to endow him with a prescience given to only one
or two men in each century. To the present writer, it seems
that the necessity for the organization of some kind of government in this region was great and pressing, and that the
precise mode of settlement hit upon by Douglas need not
have led to very undesirable doings at almost any other
time in the history of the United States. Of course, it may
be said that, as a statesman of presidential timber, he should
have and must have realized what the measure would bring
forth. But one of the first things that the historical student
learns to distrust is the vitality of the prophetic vision of
himself or of anyone in ages past. Prophesying is the most
dangerous of all historical pursuits and also of political pursuits. The Southerners had uniformly objected to the erection of any more territories from which slavery should be
excluded, that is to say, from which they, the leaders of
Southern public opinion and the actual rulers of the South —
and of the United States — should be excluded with their
laborers. The old-time Southerner, born and bred to the
slave-labor system, could not go to a new country and engage
in free-labor employment because he could not get rid of his
inherited attitude towards his fellow men. The young non-
slaveholding Southern whites and the whites in the Southern

number, and work them on his own
lands. The contribution of the Douglas
estate to the joint enterprise was valued
at $118,000, that of McHatton at
$80,000. After the war Douglas's sons
sued the United States government for
one-quarter of a million dollars for cotton seized on this plantation by the
United States army in 1863. Writing in
her *Reminiscences* (p. 69) long after the
war, Mrs. Roger A. Pryor states that
the second Mrs. Douglas one day asked
as to what she could do with the awful
picture of Judge Douglas, bought for
his first wife: "When old Mrs. Martin
pounces down upon us to see how we are
spending her grandchildren's money she
will miss it, and think I have sold it."

States of varied employments going out to make their way in the world could mingle freely with Northern white workers and compete with them in the mine or on the farm. The exposure of this class of Southern whites to free-labor conditions almost invariably made Free-Soilers out of them. The only way to keep them true to the social system of the South was to carry that system alongside of them to whatever part of the country they might go, and this could only be done by opening new territories to the slave system.

The Missouri Compromise of 1820 had consecrated to freedom all the territory north of the parallel of 36° 30′ and west of the new State of Missouri. The Compromise of 1850 had provided for the admission of California into the Union as a State without slavery, although a large part of it lay south of the Compromise line of 1820. New Mexico had been erected into a Territory without any specific requirement as to slavery. It appeared to Robert Toombs and to many others that by these enactments the Southerners had recovered "the principle unwisely surrendered in 1820."[1] Douglas seems to have held similar ideas and to have believed that Congress was free to make new arrangements as to the unorganized territory, north and south of the old Compromise line. He proposed to salve the feelings of the Northern people by providing that the question of slavery or no slavery in the new territory should be determined by the voters at the polls. This idea of popular sovereignty or squatter sovereignty or local sovereignty was not original with Douglas. It went back at least as far as a letter written by Lewis Cass in 1847 to A. O. P. Nicholson of Tennessee.[2]   Most

---

[1] U. B. Phillips's *Life of Robert Toombs*, 119. See also George T. Curtis's *Life of James Buchanan*, ii, 194, and Dr. H. B. Learned in the *Mississippi Valley Historical Review*, viii, 315.

[2] The difficulties created by the "Nicholson Letter" are set forth in papers printed by Dunbar Rowland in his *Jefferson Davis*, ii, 109–117. The passage referred to in the text is variously printed. In William T. Young's

people at that time seem to have agreed that the voters
of any portion of the United States when they drew up a
State constitution had the right to say whether there should
be freedom or slavery in the proposed State and it was
generally held that Congress had no control over slavery
within a State, although it might determine questions of
freedom or slavery for any part of the national domain.
What "popular sovereignty" proposed to do was to give a
similar right to the first settlers in any one Territory or to
later settlers in that Territory to exercise their own sovereign
will as to slavery and practically all other matters. It was
James W. Grimes of Iowa[1] who inquired why under this
doctrine the legislature of Utah could not declare that only
Mormons could enjoy rights of citizenship, — and, indeed,
why should not the Catholics take possession of New Mexico,
the Methodists of Nebraska, and the Presbyterians of Kansas? Moreover, Grimes could not understand by what
moral right a slaveholder going to a slave territory with
twenty thousand dollars' worth of slaves should have so much
more representation in Congress and in the Electoral College
than the Northern man going to a free Territory with an
equal amount of money invested in cattle. Of course, this
was regulated by the "federal ratio" that was one of the
prices for Southern participation in the government under

Lewis Cass (Philadelphia, 1853, p. 323)
it is given as follows: " It [interference
of Congress] should be limited to the
creation of proper governments for
new countries, acquired or settled, and
to the necessary provision for their
eventual admission into the Union;
leaving, in the meantime, to the people
inhabiting them, to regulate their internal concerns in their own way."

Frederick J. Turner traced the idea
of local self-government back to "the
frontier" in his "Western State-Making
in the Revolutionary Era" in the

American Historical Review, for 1896,
pp. 251–269, especially pp. 266–269.
Allen Johnson repeated this thesis in his
article in *The Iowa Journal of History
and Politics*, iii, 3–19. Milo M. Quaife
traced the later history of the dogma in
*The Doctrine of Non-Intervention with
Slavery in the Territories* (Chicago,
1910).

[1] See James W. Grimes's printed
address entitled "To the People of
Iowa," dated Burlington, April 8, 1854,
p. 5.

the Constitution. But the arrangement was evidently becoming irksome to Grimes and to many other Free-Soilers as it had been to the abolitionists for years.

There has also been considerable disputation among the professors who have written on this subject as to why it was brought forward in 1854.[1] To some of them it appears that Douglas's pressing presidential aspiration prompted the proposal at that time. To others and with some degree of probability it seems to have been the result of a bit of local Missouri politics. For some years, the people of the western part of that State had coveted the rich and cheap lands across the river. They waited anxiously for a territorial government to be established, so that they might stake out claims which they could occupy themselves or sell to newcomers from the East. As Congress would do nothing, Missourians had crossed over into the unorganized region in 1852, had set up the ordinary paraphernalia of an election, and had chosen a "delegate" to go to Washington to work for the early establishment of a territorial government. They did this again in 1853, and then it occurred to the Iowans that they might also hold an election in the unorganized region to the west of Iowa and also send a delegate to Washington.[2] It would appear that it was this demand

[1] On the genesis of the Kansas-Nebraska Act, see John A. Parker in the *National Quarterly Review* for July, 1880. He notes (p. 118) that the "primary object of the repeal [of the Compromise of 1820] was to politically strengthen one man [Atchison] and to weaken another" — namely Benton. See also P. Orman Ray's article in the American Historical Association's *Report* for 1914, vol. i, 261–280. He criticized a paper by Professor F. H. Hodder in the Wisconsin State Historical Society's *Proceedings* for 1912; and Professor Hodder briefly replied to Professor Ray's criticism in the *Missis-*

sippi Valley Historical Review, ix, 10. In 1899, Mrs. Archibald Dixon stated the family view of the part taken by Senator Dixon in *The True History of the Missouri Compromise and Its Repeal.* Professor Ray's volume on *The Repeal of the Missouri Compromise* has a workable bibliography as an Appendix.

[2] On this curious episode, see Morton, Watkins, and Miller's *Illustrated History of Nebraska*, i, 145–149; *Proceedings* of the Nebraska State Historical Society, Second Series, vol. iii, 58, 78–88; and Edward McMahon's "Stephen A. Douglas" in *Washington Historical Quarterly*, ii, 231. "Provisional govern-

for cheap lands that was the actual moving cause for the introduction of the bill at this time; and the desire of Iowans as well as of Missourians probably was the reason for the division of the Territory into two parts. It happened that Thomas Hart Benton and David R. Atchison were striving for election to the United States Senate in the autumn, winter, and spring of 1853–1854. As the story goes, Benton, in desperation at having lost the Senatorship which he had held for thirty years and knowing that hundreds of people in western Missouri were anxious for lands across the river, told them that the country was open to settlement and that he himself would bring forward a bill at the next session of Congress to erect a territorial government therein.[1] The only way that Atchison could counteract this move of Benton's was to get his friend, Senator Douglas, to introduce a bill for the erection of a territorial government in the region to the westward of the Missouri line. At all events, for whatever reason, Douglas introduced a bill to erect this whole block of ungoverned land into the Territory of Nebraska and at once became conscious of the fact that it would be impossible to pass the measure. Thereupon, he hit upon the idea of separating the territory into two, Kansas and Nebraska, the dividing line between them being the fortieth parallel.[2] A further proposition was con-

ments" were established in other unorganized regions before and after the Kansas episode — and slavery or antislavery had no part in their formation.

[1] The story comes out in a speech of Senator Atchison delivered at Fayette, Missouri, November 14, 1853, and printed in part in *Letters of John Minor Botts, of Virginia, on the Nebraska Question* (p. 14), and see P. O. Ray's "Genesis of the Kansas-Nebraska Act" in American Historical Association's *Reports*, 1914, vol. i, 264, and "The Missouri Compromise, Its History" prefixed to *The Nebraska Question*

comprising Speeches . . . by Mr. Douglas and seven other Senators (New York, 1854). Professor Allen Johnson in his notice of Ray's *Repeal of the Missouri Compromise* in *American Historical Review*, xiv, 835, throws some doubt on the soundness of Ray's thesis. See also *Address of Senator Atchison to The People of Missouri*, dated Washington, June 5, 1854.

[2] According to the author of the *Illustrated History of Nebraska* that is generally cited under the name of J. S. Morton (i, 150, 151) the division into two Territories was primarily so that

tained in the revamped bill that whenever either of the said
Territories should be admitted to the Union as a State, it
should be "with or without slavery, as their constitution
may prescribe at the time of their admission." In explanation, a subsequent section of the act stated that it was the
true intent of the law "not to legislate slavery into any
Territory or State, nor to exclude it therefrom, but to leave
the people thereof perfectly free to form and regulate their
domestic institutions in their own way, subject only to the
Constitution of the United States: *Provided*, That nothing
herein contained shall be construed to revive or put in force
any law or regulation which may have existed prior to
the act of sixth of March, eighteen hundred and twenty,
either protecting, establishing, prohibiting, or abolishing
slavery." [1]

It would seem that the words that are cited at the end of
the last paragraph should have satisfied the Southerners;
but they did not. The slaveholders wanted an explicit
statement in a law that the Compromise of 1820 was no
longer binding. It was then that Senator Archibald Dixon
of Kentucky proposed to move an amendment providing
that citizens of the United States shall be at liberty to take
and hold their slaves "within any of the Territories of the
United States, or of the States to be formed therefrom,"
as if the Missouri Compromise of 1820 had never been
passed.[2] In the end Douglas placed in the bill a clause
making it clear that the Missouri Compromise, whatever
its standing may have been before 1850, was no longer bind-

one could be settled through and from
Iowa and the other from and through
Missouri. According to this view,
slavery had no part in the original
decision. See also Hadley D. John-
son's statement in the *Proceedings* of the
Nebraska State Historical Society,
Second Series, vol. iii, p. 85.

[1] *Statutes at Large . . . of the United
States*, x, 277–290.

[2] Mrs. Archibald Dixon's *True History of the Compromise and Its Repeal*,
ch. xvii.

ing on any one.[1] Senator Sumner of Massachusetts at once
proposed to amend the bill in diametrically the opposite
direction by providing that nothing in it should be "construed to abrogate or in any way contravene" the Missouri
Compromise. It was a hopeless fight, for at last the solution of the territorial trouble seemed to have been found,
namely, to sweep away the Compromise of 1820 and to provide that the people of any territory could do as they saw
fit as to slavery. It has been supposed that there was an
understanding somewhere and somehow that the southern-
more territory, namely, Kansas, would fall into the hands
of the slaveholders and the other — Nebraska — would be
free soil. There is no evidence of any such understanding,
but it is certain that many Southerners expected Kansas
would fall naturally and easily into the hands of the Missourians and would therefore become slave soil. A somewhat
similar idea seems to have appealed to the Free-Soil Democrats who called themselves Independent Democrats. On
January 19, 1854, three days after Senator Dixon moved his
amendment, Senators Chase from Ohio and Sumner from
Massachusetts and Representatives Giddings and Wade
from Ohio, Gerritt Smith from New York, and Alex. de Witt
from Massachusetts signed an "Appeal . . . to the People
of the United States."[2] The new Nebraska bill, they said,

[1] H. B. Learned in his " Relation of
Philip Phillips to the Repeal of the
Missouri Compromise in 1854" (*Mississippi Valley Historical Review*, viii,
304–317) ascribes a good deal of influence in the matter to Colonel Phillips,
who was then a Representative from
Alabama. According to this view
there was some kind of a conference
between President Pierce and the
leaders including Phillips. Still another
theory was put forward by Galusha A.
Grow, who attributed a leading influence
to the President. In this version,
Pierce is represented as asserting that
the Missouri Compromise being unconstitutional ought to have been repealed
in 1850 (J. T. Du Bois and G. S.
Mathews's *Galusha A. Grow*, 138).

[2] This was widely circulated and
may be conveniently consulted in
American History Leaflets, No. 17,
pp. 9–18. The most important papers
are given in this number and in William
MacDonald's *Select Documents Illustrative of the History of the United States,
1776–1861*, pp. 395–405, and in Herman
V. Ames's *State Documents on Federal
Relations*, No. vi, p. 40 and fol.

would open all the unorganized territory "to the ingress of slavery." The bill was a gross violation of a sacred pledge, a criminal betrayal of precious rights, a part and parcel of an atrocious plot to exclude immigrants and free laborers from the unoccupied region and convert it into "a dreary region of despotism, inhabited by masters and slaves." The blight of slavery will cover the land, and the Homestead Act, if one were ever passed, would be worthless. The signers of this appeal called upon "the People" to be mindful of the fundamental maxim of democracy, "equal rights and exact justice for all men." They concluded by saying that they would not despair, "for the cause of human freedom is the cause of God." William H. Seward, Senator from New York, did not sign this appeal, but in a speech he declared that "the sun has set for the last time upon the guarantied and certain liberties of all the unsettled and unorganized portions of the American continent. . . . To-morrow's sun will rise in dim eclipse over them." By organizing two Territories, the evil was merely postponed until they asked to be admitted as States "slave or free." [1]

Before closing the survey of the opinions of leading men on the subject of the repeal of the Missouri Compromise [2] and the establishment of the Kansas-Nebraska Territories with freedom of action as to slavery, it would be well to give the opinions of two leading men of the South, Alexander H.

[1] Frederic Bancroft's *Life of William H. Seward*, i, 357.

[2] J. Glancy Jones of Pennsylvania well expressed in the House of Representatives in the next year the Northern Democratic view of the Kansas-Nebraska Act of 1854. The act, he said, is not direct legislation at all, but merely a legislative declaration that the acts of 1850 were inconsistent with the act of 1820 and that consequently the Missouri Compromise Act of 1820 was inoperative and void. The Act of 1854 did not repeal the Missouri restriction; it declared it void, and asserted that by the Compromise measures of 1850 the principle of non-interference with slavery in the Territories by Congress was established and that this principle would apply to all Territories hereafter organized. Charles H. Jones's *J. Glancy Jones*, i, 301.

Stephens, afterwards Vice-President of the Confederacy, and John Bell, in 1860 candidate of the Conservatives for the presidency of the United States. Writing to a friend on June 15, 1854, Stephens declared that since the triumph of the Nebraska Bill he felt as if the mission of his life was performed. He had opposed the Clayton Compromise that would have handed over the settlement of these problems to the Supreme Court of the United States and had been looked upon very coldly by his former Southern friends; but now time had done its work "And when the signal guns upon Capitol Hill proclaimed the final passing of the Nebraska Bill I felt that the cup of my ambition was full."[1] Quite the contrary was the attitude of Senator Bell of Tennessee. He tried to get his Southern colleagues to state why they proposed to vote for the Kansas-Nebraska Bill with the anti-Missouri Compromise amendment tacked on. They apparently thought that this would extend the area of slavery; Bell did not believe this. He did believe that the measure would arouse "the fiendish, infernal spirit of disunion at the North" and that the "cauldron of northern agitation and fanaticism would again be brought to the boiling point" and that no more fugitive slaves would be returned from the North.[2]

On the 26th day of April, 1854, a month before the Kansas-Nebraska bill became law, the charter of the Massachusetts Emigrant Aid Company was signed by the governor of the State.[3] It at once occurred to some of the original members

[1] *American Historical Review*, viii, 92.

[2] *Speech of Hon. John Bell of Tennessee in the Senate, May 24, 25, 1854*, p. 19. See also *Speech of J. W. Richardson . . . in the House of Representatives, February 8, 1858*.

[3] The following account of the Kansas episode is based largely on manuscript notes that were taken by William H. Isely when he was studying at Harvard University under the direction of Professor Hart. Later, Mr. Isely became Dean of Fairmount College, Wichita, Kansas. After his untimely death, his widow sent these notes to Professor Hart, who very kindly turned them over to me.

that the charter as drawn up would make each stockholder liable for all the debts of the company. A new charter, therefore, was obtained, this time from Connecticut, and the title of the corporation was changed to the New England Emigrant Aid Company.[1] The original paper capitalization of the company had been set at five millions. But by March, 1855, only twenty-seven thousand dollars had been paid in and the stock account never amounted to more than one hundred and forty thousand dollars. After the beginning the company was managed very wisely by some of the most successful merchants and professional men of New England. The idea was unobtrusively to assist emigrants to Kansas by securing reduced rates from transportation companies, founding a town in Kansas as a nucleus for settlement, sending there steam engines, saw mills, grist mills, and supplies of food and clothing and, in general, so to ameliorate the lot of the emigrant that he would go to Kansas instead of to Nebraska, or Washington, or Oregon.[2] In 1854, the company collected five parties of emigrants numbering about 750, and in 1855, 635 persons left Boston for Kansas under

[1] In 1862, the New England Emigrant Aid Company published a *History* of that organization. Eight years earlier, the secretary of the company prepared a pamphlet entitled *Information for Kanzas Immigrants*, of which the fourteenth edition appeared in 1857. In 1854, the company issued a pamphlet entitled *Organization, Objects, and Plan of Operations, of the Emigrant Aid Company* and in the same year also printed a pamphlet entitled *Nebraska and Kansas*. These three publications were in the nature of circulars to intending subscribers and emigrants. Among the "Isely Papers" are notes from manuscript records of the executive committee, the "Secretary's Minutes," and the letter books. Of the secondary accounts, William Lawrence's *Life of Amos A. Lawrence, with Extracts from his Diary and Cor-*respondence and Eli Thayer's *New England Emigrant Aid Company* published in 1887 and his *History of the Kansas Crusade* published in 1889 are useful.

[2] On p. 8 of the *History of the New England Emigrant Aid Company,* the statement is made that the transportation companies gave it lower rates than were ordinarily charged to individuals. These tickets were sold to emigrants without any profit to the Company. The emigrants went at their own charge under the escort of one of the Company's agents who traveled "at our expense." It never paid "the passage of any emigrant, nor paid any thing towards his passage: we simply organized the emigration of individuals, and relieved it, as far as we could, of its solitude and other inconveniences."

the auspices of the company. These numbers seem very small, but the spectacle of one party after another coming up the Missouri River and disembarking at Westport startled the people of western Missouri who had expected to seize upon all the best lands in the Territory. Moreover, Eli Thayer, the originator of this enterprise, and other abolition orators talked loudly of what could be accomplished with the five million dollars that were to be paid into the capital stock. Thayer even prophesied that a cordon of Free States, stretching from Minnesota to the Gulf, would be established and that then the company would colonize the Border Slave States with free white men. Southern orators took up the challenge; they declared that the Emigrant Aid Company was shipping out "paupers and hirelings" to Kansas "like so many cattle."[1] The Missourians stopped the further passage up the river and thus compelled the emigrants to take the overland way through Iowa and Nebraska.

In 1856 or 1857 the New England Emigrant Aid Company practically ceased to function[2] and its place was more than filled by innumerable societies and committees. These held meetings, raised money, and spent it to further the interests of the free settlers of Kansas in every possible way.

[1] Quoted in the New York Tribune of December 5, 1855, from the St. Louis Intelligencer of December 1. " Isely Papers."

[2] In 1862, the Emigrant Aid Company or a committee of it had in consideration the colonization of the South. In 1865, it set on foot a plan to transfer the surplus young women of Massachusetts to Oregon and other parts of the West and applied to the legislature of the State for a grant of money for that purpose. This was referred to a joint committee of the two Houses which reported that it was inexpedient to legislate on the subject although Governor Andrew, himself, had recommended it. One sentence of this report is worth noting : " Inexcusable shall we be, — utterly blind to the lessons of the past, — if we do not recognize it as our true policy, to leave industry, emigration, and, more than all, the disproportion of the sexes, to regulate themselves, or to be regulated by the providential course of events and influences." See Massachusetts Documents, 1865, Senate, No. 156.

In 1867, the charter of the Company was amended with a view to making it possible for it to encourage emigration to Florida and to the South; but nothing came of this.

No one can say how much money was raised or paid out or how many settlers were aided, and it is impossible to disentangle the expenditures of these committees from those of individuals. It is enough to say that the stream of free migration to Kansas continued and that money was provided when absolutely necessary for the needs of the settlers.[1] The constant agitation and the news of the passage of these bands of assisted emigrants aroused the interests of thousands and thousands of persons in the States west of the mountains and throughout the Northwestern settled country. Men and women, impelled by the pioneer spirit, left their half-cleared farms and such buildings as they had erected and took up the march for the new land of promise. At one time in 1857, one thousand emigrants were said to be arriving in Kansas every twenty-four hours, and in May of that year the population of the Territory was estimated at from seventy to eighty thousand.[2]

At first the Southerners, living under the assumption that Kansas was already theirs, seem to have taken little interest in emigration to that Territory. As will be seen, they tried to grasp the administration of the territory, and when one company of Northern emigrants after another came up the Missouri, they stopped that avenue of approach to Kansas. Their attitude was well expressed by the "Baltimore Patriot" in the declaration that "God and geography have

[1] These statements are based on the "Jackson Papers" in the Massachusetts Historical Society's Cabinet, containing a mass of accounts, etc.; upon copies of letters written by William Barnes, Secretary of the New York State Kansas Committee, in April and May, 1856, in the "Isely Collection"; on the *Report of the Proceedings of a Convention of Delegates from Kansas Aid Societies* held at Cleveland in June, 1856; and on Frank P. Stearns's *Life*

and *Public Services of George Luther Stearns* (Philadelphia, 1907).

[2] Nathan H. Parker, on p. x of his *Kansas and Nebraska Handbook for 1857-8* (Boston, 1857), gives the population of Kansas and Nebraska in March, 1855, as less than 10,000; "Now, in March, 1857, it will probably exceed 75,000" (p. x). See also his *Iowa as It Is in 1855; a Gazetteer for Citizens, and a Hand-Book for Immigrants* (Chicago, 1855).

given the commercial control of the new territory to the Southern States and all the British Abolitionists in New York and Canada cannot deprive us of it." [1]   Nevertheless, by the end of 1855, the Southerners began to be alarmed. In November, Senator A. G. Brown of Mississippi suggested a plan for the State to purchase three hundred slaves in her own name and send them to Kansas with three hundred of her young men "to defend them with ballots and, if necessary, with bullets." In Alabama, a certain Thomas J. Orme stated that if the people of Alabama would raise one hundred thousand dollars, he would lead five hundred settlers to Kansas and he declared that he had the names of over one hundred volunteers already. In February of the next year, a bill was introduced into the Georgia legislature to appropriate fifty thousand dollars to be raised by a tax on slaves for the purpose of making Kansas a Slave State. The idea was to send young men there, and it was stated that after great effort the Muskogee Emigrant Aid Company had only succeeded in raising $950. Another member asserted that Georgia could not compete with Massachusetts which was emptying her poor houses of native and foreign paupers and sending them to Kansas. Besides, he stated as a "sad fact" that young men sent from Georgia to Kansas, on reaching that place, joined the opposition. Moreover, there was a "rising cloud," and it would be better for Georgia to keep her young men at home to defend her in case of trouble than to send them to the Northwest. A writer in the "Frontier News" appealed to the South to rally. They must not stand by looking on while a "paradisical garden" was being established for decoyed, stolen, and runaway slaves. "Birds of darkness are on the wing — the day will soon dawn — the battle will soon commence. Arouse and fight a good fight!

[1] *New York Tribune*, July 19, 1854, from the *Baltimore Patriot*.

Let the eagle of victory perch upon your banners. Steady, men! Forward!"[1] About this time also, Atchison wrote a letter to a gentleman at the South. Let your men come forth to Missouri and Kansas, well armed and with money to support them for twelve months. Let them come on in squads "as fast as they can be raised, well armed. We want none but true men."[2] How many men reached Kansas in response to these and other stirring appeals is not known. The only party that has a definite history was the one that was led into Kansas by Major Jefferson Buford.[3] He was an Alabamian from Eufaula. He tried to stir men of means to contribute. Some donations came in, but the Georgia legislature declined to appropriate twenty-five thousand dollars for the purpose of aiding emigrants to Kansas. Contributions came in to the amount of nearly fourteen thousand dollars. The total expenses are said to have been over twenty-four thousand and the balance of about ten thousand dollars was paid by Buford himself, who sold some of his slaves to provide the necessary funds. Four hundred white men from Georgia, South Carolina, and Alabama composed the expedition. They were unarmed. At least they did not carry rifles, although presumably they had pistols and knives, or some of them had. They were supplied with Bibles at the cost of the Baptist Church in Montgomery. Their progress was rather leisurely, but they reached Westport at about the end of April. Half a century later, an old man wrote that the people of that town had been glad to see them come and "doubly glad when they went away finally."

[1] Quoted in the *Herald of Freedom*, Lawrence, Kansas, February 17, 1855.

[2] Printed in T. H. Webb's *Information for Kanzas Immigrants* (Boston, 1857), p. 13.

[3] See Professor Walter L. Fleming's article entitled "The Buford Expedition to Kansas" in *American Historical Review*, vi, 38–48. Approximately the same matter is in Professor Fleming's article in the *Transactions* of the Alabama Historical Society, iv, 167–192, which was reprinted by the Society in 1904 as "Reprint No. 7." This article has a bibliography on the last page.

Instead of settling in one place, the Buford men scattered over the Territory. About two weeks later, they were gathered together to aid the United States marshal in arresting some Free State men at Lawrence and were there when the hotel and printing presses were destroyed. Buford is reported to have been against this destruction, but it was he who in a great measure made it possible. After he had been in Kansas a couple of months, Buford left for the South to try to stir up public sentiment, but he had slight success. He returned to Kansas and early the next year left the Territory forever, and most of his men drifted away from it.

The first authentic enumeration of the people of Kansas was taken in 1860.[1] It appears that the total free population was then 107,204 and the enumerators could find only two slaves in the Territory. Of the free people, 37,501 came from the States of the Northwest and only 4208 from New England. New York and Pennsylvania together furnished nearly thirteen thousand or only fifteen hundred less than the immigrants from all the States of the Upper South, excluding Missouri. Ohio and Missouri each gave over eleven thousand inhabitants to Kansas.[2] Ohio exceeded Missouri by 250 and, therefore, was the greatest single contributor to the peopling of the new State before 1860. It is interesting to note, however, that the twelve hundred persons who went to Kansas from Massachusetts outnumbered the one thousand and seven immigrants from all the States of the Lower South put together.[3] Studies of pioneer society publications and biographical dictionaries only reënforce the general

[1] *Census* of 1860, "Population," pp. 616–623.

[2] Professor Allyn A. Young has given these facts in a somewhat different setting in *The South in the Building of the Nation*, v, 620–624.

[3] I have been greatly aided in writing this account of early Kansas by some statistical studies that were made by Professor Cornelius J. Brosnan of the University of Idaho, while studying in the Graduate School of Harvard University.

story that is told by the "Census" of 1860.[1] Taking the
last permanent residence of one hundred colonists of Kansas
somewhat at random, one finds that fifty-five came from the
Northwest, fourteen from New York and Pennsylvania,
fourteen from New England, ten from Missouri, five from
the other Border Slave States, and only one from all the Cotton States. Studying the nativities of these same persons,
it appears that twenty-seven were born in the Northwest,
nineteen in New York and Pennsylvania, and eighteen in
New England. Of the rest, eleven were born in Germany,
four in England, and one in Wales. Furthermore, only seven
of these one hundred persons were influenced in any conscious way by the New-England Emigrant Aid Company
or by any similar society or committee. Seventy-six of the
one hundred were mainly influenced by economic motives
and seventy-seven — practically the same persons — were
"movers" who had moved from one to seven times before
reaching Kansas. The origin of the various elements of the
Kansas population comes out in a study of the State origin
of the political bodies that debated and in a measure determined the fate of the Territory. The first of these was the
legislature that met in 1855 — the "Bogus Legislature,"
as the Free State men called it. It had been elected by the
pro-slavery men and all but one of its members were pro-
slavery, and this one promptly resigned. There were forty-
five of them in all, leaving out the Free Stater; of these,
sixteen were born in Kentucky, twelve in Virginia, five in

[1] Redpath and Hinton, on p. 9 of
their *Hand-Book to Kansas Territory*
(New York, 1859), made a very good
guess as to the population of Kansas.
The " recent elections," so they wrote,
" indicate a population varying between
70,000 and 90,000. The best judges
estimate it at 80,000." They thought
that the census year of 1860 would show
a resident population of 100,000, — and
so it did, and more. These figures have
been analyzed by William O. Lynch in
an article on " Popular Sovereignty and
. . . Kansas" in the Mississippi Valley
Historical Association's *Proceedings*, ix,
pt. iii, p. 380. This is followed by an
article by Mary J. Klem on "Missouri
in the Kansas Struggle."

Missouri, nine in other Slave States, and only three in the Free States, Ohio and Iowa. It will be noticed that this list gives the nativities, not the last permanent residence, and probably most of these came directly from Missouri. The Topeka Convention was the answer of the Free State men to the invasion of the Missourians. Of its members, ten were natives of the Middle States, eight of the Northwest, four of New England, ten of the Upper South, and only two from the Cotton States. Finally in the Wyandotte Convention, that was held in 1859, and made the constitution under which Kansas came into the Union, there were fifty-two members; of these, twenty were born in the Northwest, eleven in New England, eleven in the Middle States, six in the Upper South, and four outside of the United States, and not one of these constitution makers was born in Missouri.

The first years of the history of Kansas as a Territory were filled with commotions of one sort or another. Many of them were of the regular frontier type, — claim jumping and the like; others were designed to take possession of the Kansas government by outvoting the actual settlers. Western Missouri seems to have had ideas of its own, for it was the people of that part of the State who had driven away the Mormons, — and their doings had met with no disapproval by the State government or by that of the United States. Many pro-slavery Kansas societies were formed in Missouri: the Social Band, the Blue Lodges, the Sons of the South, the Self-defensive Associates, and others. The members of the last-named body pledged themselves "when called on by the citizens of Kansas" to go to their assistance to expel from that Territory those "who had been exported" to it by the "Abolition Aid Societies." The Kansas-Nebraska Act had hardly become law when Missourians passed the border, staked out claims to the best lands within easy reach, and returned to Missouri. In November, an election for a Territorial Delegate to go to Washington to represent Kansas in the House of Representatives was held. Seventeen hundred Missourians are said to have crossed the border, voted in the election, and then returned to their homes. They prevented the Free State men from voting, and the Territorial governor, appointed by President Pierce, ratified their action. Later the pro-slavery settlers and their Missouri allies elected a territorial legislature of their own stripe. It was upon this that the Free State men likewise elected a legislature of their own, held a convention, drew up a constitution, and applied to Congress for admission to the Union as a State. This convention was presided over by an extraordinary character named "Jim" Lane.[1] He had been a "volunteer" colonel in Mexico, had been lieutenant governor of Indiana, and, as one of the Congressmen from that State, had voted for the Kansas-Nebraska bill. Precisely why he was in Kansas is uncertain. The wish to obtain an easy divorce from his wife, whom he left behind in Indiana, probably had something to do with it; but the Missouri Border Ruffian territorial legislature would not grant it to him. A few weeks later he became the presiding officer of the Free State convention at Topeka and carried the proposed constitution and memorial to Washington. When the latter was examined carefully, it appeared that the signatures of the members of the convention were all in one handwriting.

The Missourians evidently expected that the Free State men would meekly submit, for they were "tender feet" and

---

[1] Three views of the Kansas troubles may be obtained by reading Thomas Wentworth Higginson's *A Ride through Kanzas* (*Anti-Slavery Tracts*, No. 20), Samuel C. Smith's *Reply to "T. W. H."*, dated March 23, 1903, and Professor Leverett W. Spring's "Career of a Kansas Politician" in *American His-torical Review*, iv, 80–104. There is a *Life* of Lane by John Speer. It was not only written by him, but was printed by him at "Garden City, Kas." in 1896. Some years before, Speer had obtained a Federal office through the efforts of Senator Lane.

belonged to the non-duelling, non-fighting North. But the Kansas Free-Staters, after the first shock of surprise had passed away, applied for arms, and undertook to defend their rights. The Missouri people had received or had taken arms from the Missouri State arsenal. These were old-style Springfield muskets that had been served out to the militia and were well enough when used against men armed with the same sort of weapons or without weapons of any kind. When the appeal for arms with which to defend themselves came from the Free State settlers of Kansas to the officers of the Emigrant Aid Company, they — in their unofficial capacities — responded by sending to Kansas one hundred and then more hundreds of Sharps rifles.[1] These were the newest and best breech-loading guns then in existence. They could be easily and rapidly reloaded and shot accurately for a much greater distance than the old United States muskets. The presence of these modern weapons in Kansas changed the attitude of the Missourians, for any Free State man with a steady arm, good eye-sight, and a Sharps rifle could shoot down an approaching slavery advocate long before the latter had gained effective distance with the ordinary rifle. The Southerners burst into flames of reproach against those who used and those who provided Sharps rifles. Several considerations occur to the historical student at this point. The first question is how many Sharps rifles ever got into the hands of fighting Free State men? Of course, any answer to this conundrum is full of doubt, but it would

[1] W. H. Isely's "The Sharps Rifle Episode in Kansas History" in *American Historical Review*, xii, 546–566. Professor Isely prints a statement by General Deitzler describing his going to Boston and receiving an order from the executive committee of the Emigrant Aid Company for one hundred rifles. This statement was written in 1879 and cannot hold against the public denial of the officers at the time that the Company had ever sent or paid for sending weapons to Kansas. Some of the leading members of the Company did get up a subscription and pay for the rifles and for sending them to Kansas.

appear to have been the case that in all, not more than three hundred and sixteen Sharps rifles ever reached the hands of actual Kansas Free State men and were employed in shooting down Border Ruffians from Missouri or genuine pro-slavery settlers from anywhere. The rifles struck terror to the souls of the Southerners. They apparently had expected it to be necessary only to look truculently at a "hireling" or a "pauper" from the Northeastern States and he would at once depart for Iowa. When, however, the Free-Stater stood his ground with a Sharps rifle in his hand, the chance of the representative of Southern chivalry ever getting within reach was slight. Why the Southerners did not raise ten or twenty thousand dollars and send three hundred or six hundred Sharps rifles out to Missouri, instead of spending their time in declamation, is one of the unravelled mysteries of historical research.

Another problem that confronts the investigator is how much blood was actually shed in Kansas, how much of it was Free State blood, how much of it was Slave State blood, and how much of it was claim-jumper blood. The letters of the Southerners declare that pro-slavery men were persecuted, slaughtered, and driven off their farms; those of the Northerners tell of the murderous propensities of the Missouri Border Ruffians and the meek behavior of the Free State men.[1] Then the delver into the past comes to a series

[1] An example of abolition propaganda is *The Reign of Terror in Kanzas* that was published at Boston in 1856 with startling illustrations. On November 14, 1856, eleven Kansans, who were held prisoners at Lecompton, wrote to Governor Salmon P. Chase of Ohio the following moderate statement as to the origin of the troubles in the Territory: "Since early last spring this Territory has been overrun by numerous bands of non-settlers from Missouri and other Southern States, whose only object, and these avowed ones, has been to rob, plunder, and murder our citizens for the purpose of enriching themselves, and by so doing compel the people of Kansas — those who came here as peaceful settlers, and for honest and quiet purposes only — to acknowledge and obey laws imposed upon us by the same species of fraud. These marauders also held in blockade all the roads leading into the Territory from any point where provisions and other articles necessary to our sustenance

of glorifications of the resistance of the Northerner to the
Southerner and the more or less heart-felt approbation of
the doings of John Brown at Pottawatomie and at Osawatomie. He is somewhat startled to find that in the "Waka-
rusa War" there was no fighting, and that the drunken Governor Shannon was completely hoodwinked by the Free
State men at Lawrence. The best estimate of the number of
lives sacrificed in Kansas during those troublous times was
that it "probably exceeded rather than fell short of two hundred." [1] This estimate includes isolated killings of claim-
jumpers and organized lynchings, like that at Pottawatomie,
where John Brown and some of his followers murdered five
defenceless and extremely objectionable men in somewhat
cold blood. [2] It also includes the losses sustained at the
"Battle" of Osawatomie, at which the pro-slavery men lost
from five wounded, according to their own accounts, to
thirty-two killed and fifty wounded, according to their
opponents' statement, while the Brownites lost two killed,

could be provided, thereby reducing
many of our people to the verge of
starvation. At last we were compelled
to resort [to] the natural rights of man,
protect and support our lives by the
only means left us — force — for there
was no law in Kansas for the protection
of people of our political sentiments."
"Isely Papers" from the "Chase
Collection."

[1] This is the estimate made by the
Commissioners of Claims, under act of
February 7, 1859, in the report from the
Committee of Claims made to the House
of Representatives, March 2, 1861, p. 93
(*House Reports*, 36th Cong., 2nd Sess.,
No. 104).

[2] In 1878 — twenty-two years after
the event — James Townsley stated in
writing that he drove John Brown and
the others to the scene of the massacre.
His statement, although made so long
after the time, has been generally
accepted. See Villard's *John Brown*,

ch. v and bibliography with notes on
pp. 608 and fol.; F. W. Blackmar's
Charles Robinson, ch. x; William
Phillips's *Conquest of Kansas*, 316;
F. B. Sanborn's *John Brown*, ch. ix;
W. E. B. Du Bois's *John Brown*, 153;
Higginson's *Cheerful Yesterdays*, 206;
and hostile views in H. P. Wilson's *John
Brown*, ch. v, and in George W. Brown's
Reminiscences of Old John Brown
(Rockford, Ill.).

Villard's declaration in his *Brown*,
p. 265, that it was "idle to assert that
Kansas would never have been free, had
it not weltered in blood in 1856," and
statements made by Amos A. Lawrence
and by Professor Spring at meetings of
the Massachusetts Historical Society
in May, 1884, and March, 1900, incited
Franklin B. Sanborn to read four papers
at four separate meetings of the same
society in November, 1907, February
and May, 1908, and March, 1911.

two wounded, and three missing, according to their own
declarations; or thirty, according to the pro-slavery-ites.

The best way to understand the psychological effect of
the Kansas tragedies on the minds of men, North and South,
is to bring together a few events in their chronological sequence and to remember that those were the days when
occurrences were trumpeted forth in the editorials of the
ablest newspapers that this country has ever seen; — Barnwell Rhett's Charleston "Mercury," James Gordon
Bennett's New York "Herald," Horace Greeley's "Tribune," and the "Picayune" of New Orleans. It was on May
21, 1856, that Buford's men with the sheriff or the marshal
and sundry Border Ruffians rode into Lawrence, arrested
some of the Free State leaders, destroyed the "hotel" that
had been erected by the Emigrant Aid Company for the
convenience of the colonists, broke the printing-presses of
the two papers that were published in the town, and retired.
This performance, that has come down in history as the
"sack of Lawrence," was followed one day later by a murderous assault on Charles Sumner. As the Border Ruffians
were riding or plundering, Sumner was delivering a speech
in the Senate, criticizing Senator Butler of South Carolina,
in language that was unpleasant in the halls of Congress even
in that decade. On the 22nd, while Sumner was sitting
hemmed in by his desk after the adjournment of the Senate,
a kinsman of Butler's struck him over the head with a heavy
cane and repeated the blows until Sumner sank bleeding to
the floor, — Senators Douglas, Toombs, and Slidell were near
at hand and did not intervene.[1] It was two nights later that

---

[1] Douglas stated that he did not
interfere because he was afraid that his
doing so would be misrepresented, owing
to his hostile relations to Sumner.
Senator Toombs of Georgia, who also
was at hand, approved of Brooks's
action. He wrote to George W. Crawford, May 30, 1856, that the Yankees
were greatly excited about "Sumner's
flogging. They are afraid the practice
may become general and many of
[their] heads already feel sore. Sumner

John Brown directed the killing of the victims of Pottawatomie. It is difficult to say which of these occurrences was
the most brutal, or which had the most effect on the public
mind, North or South. Put together they advertised the
fact that lands were to be had in Kansas, aroused the fighting instinct of hundreds and thousands of men and women,
— no more Kansas colonies needed to be raised; "they
raised themselves." Also they convinced President Pierce
and his advisers and the managers of the Democratic party
that if they were to succeed in the presidential election in
the coming autumn, the excitement as to Kansas must be
allayed. Thereupon, the President appointed a good man,
John W. Geary, governor of the Territory and ordered
a detachment of the United States army to be sent
there.

Governor Geary's letters to President Pierce throw an
interesting light on this period of Kansas history.[1] There
was not a territorial officer "competent or willing to discharge the duties" of the office to which he had been ap-

takes a beating badly. He is said to
be ill tho' I don't believe it." And
Junius Hillyer wrote to Howell Cobb,
two days earlier, from Monroe, Georgia,
that Brooks and Sumner have had some
sport in the Senate. "When you see
Mr. Brooks give my respects to him
and offer him my sympathy and most
sincere regard." On the other hand,
one Southerner, Gazaway B. Lamar,
wrote to Howell Cobb that the assault
was "unjustifiable, unmanly, illtimed,
illadvised, injudicious to the cause of the
South, and totally indefensible as to
time, place and manner." *Proceedings*
of the Massachusetts Historical Society
for June, 1913, p. 486. An excellent
account of the assault is in Walter G.
Shotwell's *Life of Charles Sumner*,
ch. xxiii.

As recently as 1915, this assault was
justified by the "Historian of the
Daughters of the Confederacy" in an
address delivered at San Francisco.

[1] See *American Historical Review*, x,
124, 350–354; John H. Gihon's *Geary
and Kansas* (Philadelphia, 1857). The
abolitionist view may be seen in Higginson's *Ride through Kanzas* and
somewhat changed by the years in
chapter vii of his *Cheerful Yesterdays*.
There is " A Defense" by Samuel D.
Lecompte in Kansas State Historical
Society's *Transactions*, viii, 389.

The doings of Geary and Walker, his
successor, in Kansas led certain members of the Mississippi State Convention to feel doubtful of the soundness of
Pierce and Buchanan as to the introduction of slavery into Kansas. Jefferson Davis defended Pierce, denouncing those who charged Pierce with aiding
the Free-Soilers in Kansas as uttering
" a slanderous falsehood." *American
Historical Review*, x, 357.

pointed, so he wrote. This statement is worth noting when
one considers that at that time, and before and since, territorial offices have been the last resource of the efficient
politician. The dangers and hardships of frontier life have
had no attraction for those who could secure good positions
in the departments at Washington. So it was left for the
pecuniarily ambitious and importunate office-seekers to
secure the appointment to Indian agencies and Territorial
offices, — and the farther away the office and the more delicate the duties, the feebler seems to have been the occupant.
At all events, Geary wrote that one of the three Territorial
judges was still in Pennsylvania and had been there for
twelve months and the United States marshal was so old
and uncourageous that he could not serve a writ without
a military escort. Three months later he wrote to the President that, as his chief was aware, no man in the Union more
heartily despised the "contracted creed of the abolitionists"
than himself; but the persecution of the Free State men in
Kansas had not been exceeded by that of the early Christians.
Geary's ambition and policy were to be absolutely impartial.
Whenever any man in Kansas appeared determined to fight,
whether he was a Border Ruffian or a Free-Stater, Geary
turned the United States cavalrymen upon him. Kansas
became quiet, Buchanan was elected and inaugurated, and
Geary was dismissed from his office.

Presumably as a part of the same movement to secure
quiet and peace in Kansas in the election year, Senator
Toombs of Georgia on the 24th day of June, 1856, introduced
a bill that provided for a census of the inhabitants of Kansas
and the election of delegates to a Territorial constitutional
convention. The bill further provided that the constitution
formulated by this convention should be submitted to the
voters of Kansas for ratification or rejection. This particu-

lar bill was not adopted; and when the election actually
took place, for some reason that is now not perfectly clear,
the Free State men refused to take part. It appears that the
apportionment had been made in a peculiar manner by the
Territorial legislature and there were other irregularities that
displeased the Free State men. The result of this abstention
was that nearly every person elected to the Convention was
in favor of slavery. Governor Geary wrote to the President
that the members of the Convention assembled and before
organizing voted that "no person should be entitled to a
seat in the Convention *unless he was in favor of making Kansas
a Slave State.*"[1] The Convention was held at the town of
Lecompton and the constitution that it drew up was known
as the Lecompton constitution. The Free State voters outnumbered the Slave State voters. They saw no objection
to taking part in the election of members of the proposed
legislature under the constitution and procured for themselves a majority of the members of that body. Under these
circumstances the leaders of the Lecompton Convention
hit upon "a nice little scheme" to secure the adoption of the
constitution by the voters with a clause in it recognizing the
ownership of slaves within the State. This was done by
providing in the body of the instrument that owners of slaves
then in Kansas should continue to enjoy their rights in slave
property and the question to be placed before the voters
was whether they would accept this constitution with slavery
or accept it with no slavery. Whichever way they voted,
they accepted the constitution with its clause for the protection of existing rights to slave property within the Territory or State. The Free State men again refused to vote.
The constitution was adopted by a large majority of a fraction of the voters of the Territory.

[1] *American Historical Review*, x, 354.

When the constitution and its peculiar features became known at Washington, Douglas at once visited the President. He reflected severely upon the action of the Lecompton Convention,[1] and finding the President in favor of it, declared he should oppose the ratification of the constitution. At the end of the interview, President Buchanan exclaimed that he desired Douglas "to remember that no Democrat ever was successful in opposing the policy of an administration of his party." To which Douglas, rising and looking into the face of the President, replied, "Mr. President, permit me most respectfully to remind you that General Jackson is dead." From that time on in speech, in letter, and in conversation, Douglas strenuously opposed what he regarded as the treachery of the President, his appointees, and the pro-slavery men of Kansas and Missouri. He carried with him so large a proportion of the Northern Democrats in and out of Congress that it was impossible to force any resolution through that body admitting Kansas under the Lecompton constitution. Thereupon the proposition was made that the constitution as such should be laid before the voters of the Territory with the understanding that if Kansas were admitted to the Union as a State under its provisions, a fairly liberal grant of land should be made to it. This was done, and in August, 1858, the Kansas people rejected it by a vote [2] of nearly six to one — and again the question comes to one's mind, Why had the Free State men refused to take part in earlier voting contests and why had they changed their minds?

The answer to the question that is propounded at the end of the last paragraph seems to lie in the action of Senator

[1] There is an interesting article on Lecompton and its buildings by Wilbur Cortez Abbott in the *Journal of American History* for 1909, p. 628.

[2] Daniel W. Wilder's *Annals of Kansas* (ed. 1886), p. 240.

Wilson of Massachusetts and a few men who were of his way of thinking. He went to Kansas unofficially and by conference with leading men there induced them to change their attitude and make their numbers tell through the ballot box rather than by Sharps rifles and bowie knives and bludgeons.[1] Senator Wilson had always been opposed to the doctrine of force and he represented that group of Kansas Free State supporters of which Amos A. Lawrence was the leading spirit. For a time John Brown and those who stood with him had had their way. By 1857, however, it had become fairly clear to nearly everybody that Kansas was saved to freedom and that the path of wisdom was to suppress any and all attempts that would lead or might lead to a collision with the United States government. This proved to be difficult, for when men have once proceeded on the blooded path, it is very hard for them to walk in any other. So it was in this instance, and every infraction of the peace by a Missourian led to a bit of border warfare which in turn brought together on the frontier units of the Missouri militia and reprisal after reprisal. This "Jay-hawking" was connected so far as Kansas was concerned with the names of James Montgomery and John Brown.[2] Altogether, this portion of Kansas history is not pleasant reading by the historical student of the twentieth century. In 1859, another constitutional convention met, this time at Wyandotte. It was entirely in the hands of the Free State men. A constitution of the normal western type was drawn up and in 1861 the State was admitted to the Union as one of the last acts of the Buchanan administration.

[1] Henry Wilson's *History of the Rise and Fall of the Slave Power in America*, ii, 537 and fol.

[2] See "Documents Illustrating the Troubles on the Border, 1858," edited by Jonas Viles in the *Missouri Histori-* *cal Review*, i, Nos. 3 and 4, and ii, No. 1. The Free State side of the matter comes out in a letter from Montgomery to G. L. Stearns in Stearns's *Life of George Luther Stearns*, p. 235.

NOTE

Kansas Bibliography. — The bibliography of Kansas is bewildering. The State Historical Society has produced twenty volumes,[1] more or less, of one kind or another; some of the more important articles are noted in the preceding pages. Of the formal histories of Kansas, Daniel W. Wilder's *Annals of Kansas* (Topeka, 1875) contains a mass of information (new edition, revised and enlarged, Topeka, 1886). Of the shorter accounts, that by Leverett W. Spring in the *American Commonwealths* series strongly expresses the anti-Brown side. This point of view is best set forth, perhaps, in Sara T. D. Robinson's *Kansas: Its Interior and Exterior Life* (Boston, 1856); (10th ed., Lawrence, 1899). Of the almost numberless books describing journeys and sojourns in Kansas, the three that have attracted the present writer most are T. H. Gladstone's *The Englishman in Kansas,* which was printed with an introduction by F. L. Olmsted at New York in 1857, C. B. Boynton and T. B. Mason's *Journey Through Kansas . . . made in the Autumn of 1854* (Cincinnati, 1855), and *Six Months in Kansas. By a Lady* (Mrs. Hannah A. Ropes, Boston, 1856). Of the county histories that of Wyandotte County seems to be the most satisfying, especially for the pre-territorial time. *A History of Lawrence, Kansas* by Richard Cordley (Lawrence, 1895) and John H. Gihon's *History of Kansas* preserve the local point of view. At the end of Spring's *Kansas* is a bibliography, but it does not include newspapers or many pamphlets. It does give a list of congressional documents that the author used. Of these the " Report of the Special Committee appointed to Investigate the Troubles in Kansas " (*House Reports,* 34th Cong., 1st Sess., No. 200) containing the evidence taken by the committee has been of service. The report of the committee appointed to examine into the claims of citizens of Kansas for property taken or destroyed from November 1, 1855 to December 1, 1856, is a remarkably useful and satisfying document (*House Reports,* 36th Cong., 2nd Sess., No. 104).

[1] *Transactions* — iii, 226–337, iv, 520–745, v, 156–633 — form together a documentary history of Kansas in the period covered in this chapter.

CHAPTER VII

THE DECIDING YEAR OF 1857

THE Massachusetts anti-slavery radicals held a Disunion Convention at Worcester in January of this year, and in March the Supreme Court of the United States delivered itself of the Dred Scott decision which Southerners expected would silence Northern Free-Soil opinion. In neither case did the event turn out as expected; but public opinion was so changed in the North that thenceforward compromise with the South was an impossibility. Ever since 1841, William Lloyd Garrison and the ultra anti-slavery people — the abolitionists — had argued for separation from the Slave States.[1] In 1842, Garrison declared that the repeal of the Union was the measure of one's patriotism and piety. Opposition on the part of the more moderate anti-slavery people brought to Garrison's mind the message of Isaiah to the people of Jerusalem and before the end of the decade, he had changed the heading of "The Liberator" to "No UNION WITH SLAVEHOLDERS. The United States Constitution is 'a covenant with death, and an agreement with hell.'" In justifying this statement, he printed a quotation from William Ellery Channing, in which that preacher declared that on this subject of slavery the "FATHERS, IN FRAMING THE CONSTITUTION, SWERVED FROM THE RIGHT." Channing added that no blessing of the Union could compensate for the enslaving of human beings; "nor ought this bond to be

[1] Lindsay Swift in his *William Lloyd Garrison* (Philadelphia, 1911), ch. x, admirably summarized the Northern disunion sentiment of 1841–1844.

perpetuated, if experience shall demonstrate that it can only continue through our participation in wrong doing." In 1844, Wendell Phillips moved a resolution which did not at all meet with the views of the moderate anti-slavery people, but is memorable as enunciating the feelings of Garrison and Phillips. It reads: "The only exodus of the slave to freedom, unless it be one of blood, must be over the ruins of the present American Church and the grave of the present Union." However others changed, Garrison and Phillips remained firm in their convictions. Slowly the disunion sentiment spread among the anti-slavery people, until by the time of the Mexican War, it embraced a large proportion of them in New York, New Jersey, and Pennsylvania, as well as in New England. With the passage of the Compromise of 1850, the excitement died down and the ultra-abolitionists were left almost to themselves. The Kansas-Nebraska Act again brought them to the front. On the Fourth of July, in that year (1854), the abolitionists held an open-air celebration at Framingham, in Massachusetts. Over the platform, Massachusetts was represented as chained to Virginia "by links of cotton, and crouching under the slave whip of the latter." It was at this time and place that Garrison held a species of auto-da-fé,[1] in the course of which he burned a copy of the Fugitive Slave Law, the decision remanding Burns to slavery, the statement of the court as to the treasonable nature of resistance, and finally, "holding up the U. S. Constitution, he branded it as the source and parent of all the other atrocities, and consumed it to ashes on the spot, exclaiming, 'So perish all compromises with tyranny! And let all the people say, *Amen!*'" Evidently, whatever else he may have been, William Lloyd Garrison was a consistent disunionist.

[1] *The Liberator* of July 7, 1854.

The formation of the Republican Party and the possible election of a Republican President for a moment turned the thoughts of the anti-slavery people into other channels. The election of James Buchanan seemed to them to involve "four years more of Pro-Slavery Government." Believing the existing Union to be a failure "as being a hopeless attempt to unite under one government two antagonistic systems of society, which diverge more widely with every year," [1] over ninety citizens of Worcester united in an invitation to their "fellow citizens of Massachusetts" to meet in convention to consider the "practicability, probability, and expediency of a Separation between the Free and Slave States." The convention met and was attended by "a highly respectable and most reliable body of earnest men and women" from different parts of Massachusetts. There were speeches, including two from Phillips, one from Garrison, and one from Higginson, pastor of a "Free Church" in Worcester, and in 1862 colonel of the first regiment of freed slaves embodied under the authority of the United States government to fight for the preservation of the Union. [2] Among the letters read to the convention was one from Henry Wilson, one of the Massachusetts Senators. He wrote that he had read the call of the convention with sincere and profound regret because the movement would put a burden upon the anti-slavery cause to which so many years of sacrificing toil had been given. The American people love their country, the movement at Worcester would only serve to array against those who are battling to arrest the further extension of slavery, "that intense, passionate

---

[1] *Proceedings of the State Disunion Convention, held at Worcester, Massachusetts, January 15, 1857* (Boston, 1857). See also the Garrisons' *William Lloyd Garrison*, iii, ch. xvii.

[2] Frank P. Stearns's *Life and Public Services of George Luther Stearns* (Philadelphia, 1907), p. 285, and T. W. Higginson's *Army Life in a Black Regiment.*

and vehement spirit of nationality which glows in the bosoms
of the American people." He could have no sympathy or
connection with any such movement. It was upon the
statements in this letter that Garrison and Phillips hung
their remarks. The former asserted that those whose
reverence for God is greater than all human institutions
"will go for a dissolution of this blood-stained Union."
Senator Wilson desired to aid the anti-slavery movement
and advance his own political interest at the same time.
Theodore Parker did not attend the meeting, but wrote
that he could not consent to disunion because it would
separate the abolitionists from the slave population. Garrison thought, on the other hand, that a dissolution of the
Union would smite slavery to the dust, — "Whoever else
may falter, or counsel delay, or take refuge in hypocrisy,
I go for uncompromising hostility to slavery every where,
and, therefore, for No UNION WITH SLAVEHOLDERS."
Wendell Phillips agreed that Wilson's letter showed him to
be no fit leader in the anti-slavery cause. Also, he asserted
the Union has not produced men. Daniel Webster said
that the virtue of the colonial institutions was that they
produced Washington. Phillips announced that "the sin
of the Union is that it manufactured Webster."[1] The
Reverend Mr. Higginson said, "You call us traitors and
fanatics. That is what we came here to be." You say we
are weak, "Give us five years and let us see." You say that
some of us are "old flints that won't strike fire, and some are
young steel, that won't give out sparks. . . . Open the
doors of your powder magazine and let us try."[2]

Among the letters written in response to the invitation to
attend the convention was one from Professor Calvin E.

[1] *Proceedings of the State Disunion*   [2] *Ibid.*, p. 29.
Convention (Boston, 1857), p. 45.

Stowe,[1] the husband of the writer of "Uncle Tom's Cabin."
If he were in despair as to the Republic, as they seemed to
be, he should take the course that they proposed to take.
But when he reflected that "the really determined, aggressive slaveholders of the country are probably less than
150,000 against more than 20,000,000 of people" and their
cause sustained by falsehood and violence, and what wonderful progress has been made in the anti-slavery cause during
the last twenty-five years, the Andover professor thought
it to be "the part of wisdom to hold on and vote, and help
the 20,000,000 turn the 150,000 with their corruptions out
of the house, (which they had no business ever to occupy,)
and not allow the 150,000 to turn out the 20,000,000, to
whom the whole justly belongs." One or the other must
be done, and that soon, wrote Professor Stowe.[2] The Convention appointed a committee to summon a larger convention to be held some time during the coming summer or
autumn. Circulars were printed and sent out and private
letters were written, asking the people of "ALL THE FREE
STATES" to meet at some convenient point in October next
"to consider the practicability, probability, and expediency
of A SEPARATION BETWEEN THE FREE AND SLAVE STATES,"
thus repeating the identical phrases of the original call for
the Worcester convention.[3] The response was far beyond
what the leaders could have expected, for by September more
than six thousand persons, of whom two-thirds were voters
and the remainder presumably women, had sent in their

[1] *Proceedings of the State Disunion
Convention,* "Appendix," 18.
[2] Two years before, in 1855, Samuel
J. May, Lewis Tappan, Gerrit Smith,
and other persons, styling themselves
"Radical Political Abolitionists," con-
vened at Syracuse, New York. Among
other things they resolved that slavery
was "an unsurpassed crime," that "the

Constitution requires the Federal Government to abolish slavery in all the
States," and they would consent to no
dissolution of the Union which would
"leave the slave in his chains." *Proceedings of the Convention of Radical
Political Abolitionists* (New York, 1855),
pp. 5, 6, 7.
[3] *The Liberator,* July 24, 1857.

signatures to a repetition of the call.[1] Those signing were
residents of Maine and the other New England States, of
New York, New Jersey, and Pennsylvania, and of the States
of northern Transappalachia: Ohio, Michigan, Illinois,
Indiana, Wisconsin, Iowa, and Minnesota. The largest
number from any one State, east or west, was seventeen
hundred from Ohio; and Cleveland, therefore, was chosen
as the appointed place of meeting. But the convention was
never held, because the sudden and terrific pecuniary pressure of the panic that struck the country made it impossible for any large number of persons to leave their business
or to spend what little available money they had in railroad
fares and lodging expenses.

To comprehend the history of the period covered in this
volume, one must try to realize that in the North there was
a considerable body of anti-abolition sentiment. There
were the merchants of New York, Boston, Philadelphia,
and other commercial towns, and the mill owners and cotton
brokers. These business men and manufacturers had intimate business relations with Southerners or with the representatives of Southerners and many of them knew intimately
— and favorably — Southern planters who had been their
customers for years. Besides, of course, their financial
interests bound them more or less closely to the South.
Possibly this was not so true of the cotton brokers and
manufacturers as it was of the merchants trading to the
South, although it must be said that many prominent cotton
men of the North voted against Frémont in 1856 and against
Lincoln in 1860 and in 1864. These men believed that the
Southerners had cause for complaint in the spoken and written words of the Northern abolitionists. Beginning about

[1] *The Liberator*, September 25, 1857, and a broadside entitled " Call for a Northern Convention."

1845 there had been a constantly growing dislike of negro laborers on the part of the white inhabitants of Massachusetts, New York, Pennsylvania, and some other States or parts of States. In the first forty years of the century the free negroes of the North had advanced socially by entering the trades and by doing a large amount of the rough labor of the three great Northern cities. With the coming of the Irish friction began, for the free blacks were performing tasks that were suitable to the newly arrived immigrant. This feeling of antagonism took the form of riots and fights, and ended in petitions to legislative bodies for action. How far this general feeling of hostility to the free black impelled voters to join the Free-Soil movement cannot be stated, but there is good reason to suppose that it impelled more men to vote for the Republican candidate in 1860 than did any sentimental desire for the rights of the colored person. And, finally, it must be kept in mind when one comes to the question of emancipation of the slaves during the war and of the reaction of this opinion on those subjected to the draft.

In his Inaugural Address, President Buchanan stated that the question as to when the people of a Territory could decide whether they should enter the Union as a free State or a slave State, was "a judicial question, which legitimately belongs to the Supreme Court of the United States, before whom it is now pending, and will, it is understood, be speedily and finally settled. To their decision, in common with all good citizens" the new President said he should cheerfully submit.[1] Three days later, on Saturday, March 7, the Supreme Court announced its decision in the case of Dred Scott against Sanford.[2] A vast amount has been written about this case because of its great importance in determin-

[1] John B. Moore's *Works of James Buchanan*, x, 106.
[2] The name is incorrectly spelled Sandford instead of Sanford in Howard's *United States Reports*.

ing the sentiment of the country, both of the North and of the South; the details are, nevertheless, somewhat obscure. Dred Scott was born a slave in Virginia on the Blow estate. He was sold to Dr. Emerson, a surgeon in the United States army. He accompanied his new master as a household servant, at one time living with him in the free State of Illinois, at another time in the Territory of Wisconsin, far to the North of the Missouri Compromise line. While at these Northern posts, the slave married a woman purchased by Dr. Emerson and two children were born to them. Dr. Emerson then went to the army post at St. Louis in the Slave State of Missouri, taking the Scott family with him. Six years later he died leaving all his property, including the Dred Scott family, in trust to his widow and to John F. A. Sanford, her brother. From this time on, Dred Scott and his wife and children were a burden to the Emerson estate. Dred seems to have been a rather inefficient negro, who may have made a good household servant, but was hardly capable of looking out for himself and his family. Having no use for him or them, Mrs. Emerson "hired" him out, but he never seems to have stayed long on one job. As the family was held in trust, Dred, his wife, and children could not be sold or given away. In 1850 Mrs. Emerson married Dr. Calvin C. Chaffee, a Massachusetts Representative in Congress, and the possession of the Scott family became even more objectionable.

As far back as 1846, Dred Scott and Mrs. Dred Scott brought suit against Mrs. Emerson for their freedom in a Missouri State court. There were four suits in all, two brought by Dred and two by Harriet his wife. The first of each pair was in the form of a petition for permission to bring suit. The others were for alleged assault and battery on the part of Irene Emerson and illegal imprisonment for twelve hours. The object of these suits was to get a decision that Dred Scott, a man of color and Harriet Scott, a woman of color, were free persons, for the assault and imprisonment alleged could not have been committed on a slave. The jury in the State Circuit Court brought in a verdict to the effect that Dred Scott was a free man. The case was thereupon appealed to the State Supreme Court. In 1852 that court ruled that although Scott may have been free in a free territory, yet by voluntarily returning to a Slave State he had resumed his status as a slave. In November, 1853, a new action was begun, this time in the United States Court at St. Louis. To bring this case Dred Scott was described as a citizen of Missouri and the suit was brought against John F. A. Sanford, a citizen of New York. Thence the case drifted legally until it appeared on the docket of the Supreme Court of the United States at Washington. There it rested for years until the winter of 1856–57, ten years and more from the date of the original action. The beginnings and persistencies of the Dred Scott suits have never been satisfactorily explained. Probably, they were a part of the radical abolitionist propaganda.[1] On July 4, 1854, Dred Scott affixed his mark to a document that lends color to this view. It was in the form of a letter to his "Fellow-Men," and purported to lay before them the

---

[1] One story is that Arba N. Crane, when a young lawyer, meeting Dred Scott in Roswell M. Field's office, persuaded Scott to sue for his freedom. This cannot relate to the suits brought in 1846, for Crane was then only twelve years of age. Another idea is that Taylor Blow was at the bottom of the whole business. F. Trevor Hill attributes the origin of the actions to the design of some lawyer to get a large fee from the accumulated wages of the Scott couple (*Decisive Battles of the Law*, p. 117). As the suits were for assault and battery and false imprisonment, and not for wages, as Hill supposed because he could not find the papers, the motive of cupidity would not seem to apply. Mr. Edward F. Rowse of St. Louis kindly looked up this matter for me at the Court House in that city. The papers are printed in John D. Lawson's *American State Trials*, xiii, 220 and fol. Helen T. Catterall has an interesting article on "Some Antecedents of the Dred Scott Case" in the *American Historical Review*, xxx, 56–71.

record of a suit which he had brought to gain the freedom
of himself, his wife, and children. He was a negro of pure
African blood, whose ancestors were brought into this
country and sold as negro slaves. The United States Circuit Court judge at St. Louis read from the constitution of
the State of Illinois that slaves could not be introduced
into that State and that "any violation of this provision
should effect the emancipation of the person from his obligation to service." He also read a clause from the Missouri
Compromise Act and said that while Dred Scott was in
Illinois and Wisconsin he was a free man "just as good as my
master." After a while, the judge said that as soon as his
master got him back in Missouri "my right to be free was
gone; and that I and my wife and my children became
no-thing but so many pieces of property." Dred Scott, or
rather the person who drew this appeal, wrote: "I thought
it hard that white men should draw a line of their own on the
face of the earth, on one side of which a black man was to
become no man at all, and never say a word to the black
man about it until they had got him on that side of the
line. So I appealed to the Supreme Court of the United
States." And now he besought his fellow men for help in
his day of trial. "Will nobody speak for me at Washington,
even without hope of other reward than the blessings of
a poor black man and his family?"[1]

The story of the sudden appearance of the case on the
surface of the Supreme Court room is as indistinct as is the
earlier part of it. Apparently it had not interested anyone
in particular until the election of James Buchanan in the
autumn of 1856 convinced many good men of the South that

---

[1] *The Case of Dred Scott. In the
Supreme Court of the United States.
December Term, 1854.* This pamphlet
also contains "The Record" of the
proceedings in the Circuit Court of the
United States for the Missouri District.
The letter is reprinted in Lawson's
American State Trials, xiii, 243, note 4.

the current of sentiment in the North had turned to their side. The Supreme Court as then constituted comprised the Chief Justice, Roger B. Taney, and eight Associate Justices. Five of the nine, including the Chief Justice, were Southerners. For sixty years the Supreme Court had been acquiring prestige in the eyes of the American people. Throughout its history, up to 1857, it had consisted of amiable, learned, and elderly gentlemen — for the most part — all of them expert in the art of rationalizing the Constitution to suit the needs of the passing hour. In the United States, political parties represent public opinion in the making. It is the business of the Supreme Court to register the will of the people of the United States or of the ruling part of it, as it is from time to time determined. Whenever it mistakes the will of the people, a revolution has resulted, as in the case of the triumph of Jacksonism in 1832 and as was to be the case in the years immediately following 1857. It is generally supposed that one of the Southern Associate Justices suddenly made up his mind, of his own motion, and induced the Chief Justice and his other Southern brethren to seize the opportunity offered by the Dred Scott case to vindicate the right of the slave owner to take his slave property into any Territory of the United States and that a negro descendant of negroes could never be a citizen of the United States within the meaning of the Constitution. It seems not unlikely that there was a moving force behind this determination stronger than Mr. Justice Wayne, the Southern Associate Justice, and stronger than James Buchanan, the President-elect of the United States. It is possible that the impulse came from Jefferson Davis and the other Southern political leaders in Congress, — but no proof of this has, as yet, appeared. Public opinion has shrouded the doings of the Supreme Court with an

almost impenetrable gloom; the Justices are supposed to think in silence, and when they meet in conclave to keep the least whisper of their conclusions away from the outer world. In a case of political interest, such as the meaning of citizen or the validity of the Missouri Compromise, there would seem to be no good reason why the Supreme Court should inclose itself in secrecy. At all events, when President Buchanan, in his Inaugural, announced that in a few days the Supreme Court would decide the slavery question; and when, two days afterward, the Supreme Court did so endeavor to do, charges of conspiracy and of undue influence were made which have not yet died down.[1]

Chief Justice Taney's "Opinion," which was that of the Court, covers fifty-five pages of Howard's "Reports." The question he said was simply this: Could a negro, whose ancestors were imported into the country and sold as slaves, become a member of the political community brought into existence under the Constitution of the United States and as such become entitled as a citizen to sue in a court of the United States as specified in the Constitution? He thought not. He was simply expressing the ordinary Southern view that was stated in the Virginia constitutional convention of 1776 that "slaves, not being constituent members of our society," could not pretend to any benefit from the maxim that all men are by nature equally free and independent.[2] Chief Justice Taney stated that the legislation and histories of the revolutionary time and the language of

---

[1] E. S. Corwin, in his notice of Warren's *Supreme Court* in the *American Historical Review*, xxviii, p. 135, states that Justice McLean's "perpetual candidacy for the presidency precipitated at last the calamitous Dred Scott decision." John Bassett Moore (*Works of James Buchanan*, x, 108) after printing letters from Justices Catron and Grier to Buchanan, dated February 19 and 23, 1857, outlining what would be the action of the court, adds — as a contribution of his own: "the action eventually taken in the case seems to have been brought about by the activity of the minority rather than of the majority of the court."

[2] See the present work, vol. iii, 204 n.

the Declaration of Independence show that slaves and their descendants, whether slave or free, were not then acknowledged as a part of the people, "nor intended to be included in the general words used in that memorable instrument." Going on, he maintained that for more than a century before the Revolution, negroes had "been regarded as beings of an inferior order, and altogether unfit to associate with the white race, either in social or political relations; and so far inferior, that they had no rights which the white man was bound to respect;[1] and that the negro might justly and lawfully be reduced to slavery for his benefit." And again, after repeating the words of the Declaration "that all men are created equal," he stated it to be "too clear for dispute, that the enslaved African race were not intended to be included, and formed no part of the people who framed and adopted this declaration." Having proved to his own satisfaction and to that of the Southern people generally that the negro was not a member of the society that adopted the Declaration and framed the Constitution, there was no way that he or his descendants could attain citizenship except by positive legislation passed in conformity with the Constitution of the United States, and no power to do this had

[1] These words were often taken at that time by abolition writers to mean that Taney "decided" that the negro had no rights in 1857; whereas what he was trying to prove was that at the time of the making of the Constitution and for half a century before, the negro had no constitutional rights. See E. H. Bristow in *The Century* for May, 1895, p. 157, and also two letters in *ibid.*, for October, 1883, p. 957. In the fifth edition of Samuel Nott's *Slavery, and the Remedy* that was published in 1857, there was a "Review" of the Dred Scott case (pp. 121–137). Nott sent a copy of this to Chief Justice Taney and received a long letter from him, dated August 19, 1857 (*Proceedings* of the Massachusetts Historical Society, for March, 1873, p. 445). In this letter Taney discussed the relations of the whites and the blacks and stated how difficult it was for anyone who had not lived in the South to comprehend the relations which exist between master and slave, which were generally "kind on both sides." There were "painful exceptions," but so there were when both parties were of the same race and the weaker and dependent one was not "legally a slave." Taney added that more than thirty years before, he had manumitted his slaves except two who were too old to provide for themselves, and these he had supported as long as they had lived.

been given to Congress in the Constitution or in the amendments that had been made thereto. It followed, therefore, that Dred Scott was not and could not be a citizen in the meaning of the Constitution and therefore could not sue,[1] and that the Missouri Compromise was unlawful and could confer no rights. Of course it is impossible in a page or two to summarize a fifty-five-page opinion of so skilled a master of the English language and of a man so learned in American history as Chief Justice Roger B. Taney. All that can be said is to reiterate that he stated the Southern view of the matter admirably. Of course, if Taney were right and the negro had no status in society at the time of the formation of the Constitution, he and his descendants were, so far as citizenship in the United States was concerned, in a position of an immigrant from England, France, or Germany, whose political rights within the United States depended solely upon positive enactments of Congress. The other Southern Justices for the most part agreed with the Chief Justice, although they varied their language somewhat. One of the Northern Justices, Benjamin Robbins Curtis of Massachusetts, expressed the Northern view with equal cogency and learning. He stated that, as a matter of actual fact, negroes were citizens in several Northern States in the epoch of the Constitution and that the phraseology of the Declaration was entirely applicable to them. And that Congress possessed the power to legislate for the common possessions of the United States as to property in slaves in common with any other property, thus expressing and

---

[1] J. S. Black, Buchanan's Attorney General and later his Secretary of State, asserted that the decision meant "that under the Constitution, slavery in the Territories is not only, *not* within the power or control of Congress either to inhibit or establish, but that warrant for it's lawful existence during the territorial form of Government is found in the very letter and spirit of that solemn compact of Sovereign States." "J. S. Black Papers," vol. 27, in the Library of Congress, under date of January 31, 1860.

justifying the Northern attitude. As to which was right, it
is impossible to give an unqualified answer, for undoubtedly
the Declaration and the Constitution were understood differently by the people living north and those living south of
Mason and Dixon's line; moreover, the Southerners were
living in the memories of the past, while Northern society
and politics had gone on with the current of world history,
— and the institution of slavery was utterly opposed to the
moral sense of the civilized world in the year 1857. It may
be added that the South Carolinians in ratifying the Constitution in 1788 had no thought other than Taney now expressed, — they had no idea whatever that they were conferring potential citizenship upon the slave population of the
State. On the other hand, free negroes exercised the franchise in North Carolina under the constitution of 1776 unless
Judge Gaston was misinformed [1] — which is very unlikely —
and the Supreme Court of Massachusetts in 1783 had declared that no one could be a slave in Massachusetts after
the adoption of the State constitution with its memorable
declaration that "all men are born free and equal." [2]

The announcement of the opinion of the Supreme Court
in the Dred Scott case aroused such a storm in the North as
the country had seen only on two or three occasions before.
Technically, the only thing decided was that the Supreme
Court of the United States and the Federal Circuit Court of
the Missouri district had no jurisdiction because Dred Scott
was not and could not be a "citizen" within the meaning of
the Constitution, and therefore the suit must be dismissed.

[1] Judge Gaston's opinion is quoted
from Devereux and Battle's *North
Carolina Reports*, iv, 25, in *The Equality
of all Men before the Law, Claimed and
Defended* (Boston, 1865), p. 11: "It is a
matter of universal notoriety that under
it [the North Carolina constitution of
1776] free persons, without regard to
color, claimed and exercised the
franchise" until it was taken away from
colored persons by the amended
constitution of 1835. See sections vii,
viii, ix, of the constitution, and the
"Amendments" of 1835, Section 3 of
Article 1.

[2] See the present work, vol. iii, 559.

As by-products, the majority of the judges in reaching this decision had incidentally rendered other decisions or quasi-decisions, — one of these was that mere residence in a Free State did not prevent a negro from returning to the condition of slavery on returning to a Slave State. Another, a third, was that Congress could not exclude slavery from the national domain by a law and therefore that the Missouri Compromise and probably the law confirming the Ordinance of 1787 were illegal. As the matter appeared to a committee of the Vermont legislature, if these "doctrines" were enforced as constitutional law, the lives, liberty, and property of Vermont citizens were without protection; they could be reduced to slavery with impunity, their persons imprisoned, and their property destroyed. Indeed, no Free State could exist for any length of time under the doctrines enunciated by a majority of the court, and no free man or community could remain a member or partner of a union "where his dearest and most cherished rights were cloven down and destroyed." [1] The "Springfield Republican," which was then one of the two or three most influential anti-slavery newspapers in the country, declared that the Supreme Court had given no judgment and had simply dismissed the case for want of jurisdiction. "Everything beyond this uttered by the Court is just as binding, as if it were uttered by a Southern debating club and no more." [2] Samuel J. May, an anti-slavery clergyman, writing from Syracuse, New York, on March 16, 1857, asserted that the "egregious wickedness" of concessions to the demands of slaveholders "for the sake of the Union" ought to be exposed, and its worthlessness to all who love liberty and hate oppression ought

[1] *Report of the Select Committee on Slavery, The Dred Scott Decision, and the Action of the Federal Government thereon* (Montpelier, Vt., 1858).

[2] Quoted in Steiner's *Roger Brooke Taney*, 391.

to be shown up. The Ohio legislature expressed its opinion in declaring that the Supreme Court had taken occasion to "promulgate extra judicially" certain doctrines that were contradictory to well-known facts, repugnant to the Constitution and "subversive of the rights of free men and the free States" and that every free person born within the limits of any State is a citizen thereof. Abraham Lincoln in Springfield, Illinois (June 26, 1857), declared that according to his way of thinking, the decision was erroneous. The Supreme Court had often overruled its own decisions and "we shall do what we can to have it overrule this. We offer no resistance to it." The decision, Lincoln stated, was not unanimous, was biased, was based on assumed historical fact, and it is not disrespectful to treat it "as not having yet quite established a settled doctrine for the country." [1] In reality, instead of settling anything in the minds of the people of the North, what the Dred Scott decision did was to unsettle their belief in the impartiality and justice of the Supreme Court of the United States.

In the South the action of the Supreme Court in the Dred Scott case was looked upon as the final word. The highest voice in the United States had spoken and had declared for the interpretation of the Constitution that Southerners had looked upon as the true interpretation for the last ten years, at least. On March 17, 1857, Colonel Josiah Gorgas noted the decision in his "Journal" and said that "Considerable sensation" had been created by it. The principal points decided, according to him, were that a "negro could not be a citizen within the meaning of the constitution of the U. S."; that "mere residence in a free State does not prevent the

---

[1] Nicolay and Hay's *Complete Works of Abraham Lincoln*, ii, 321. For the circumstances attendant upon this speech, see the same authors' *Abraham Lincoln, A History*, ii, ch. v.

slave from resuming his conditions of slavery "; and that
"the principles of the Ordinance of '87 excluding slavery
from the Territories N. W. of the Ohio, were unconstitutional." Colonel Gorgas thought that this decision ought to
be a final disposition of "this vexed question which has heretofore assumed such a threatening aspect." Dred Scott,
having served the purposes of the abolitionist propagandists,
was sold with his wife and two children to Taylor Blow on
May 13, 1857, for the purpose solely of the "*emancipation*
of the family, and if they are not as Speedily emancipated as
possible the papers will be withdrawn & other means used to
effect that object." [1] As a matter of fact Dred Scott
was emancipated and his family with him. He died in a
couple of years and they disappeared from the sight of
history.

In the summer of 1857, there occurred a financial crisis.
The causes of this particular crash are unusually obscure.[2]
There had been the usual over development that consumes
"fixed capital." In America, there had been a most rapid
building of railroads in the region between the Alleghanies
and the Mississippi, and in Great Britain there had been
a large investment in factories, railways, and buildings of
one sort or another. This feverish activity was due in great
measure to the sudden addition of large sums of gold to
the world's stock of the precious metals as the result of the
discoveries in Australia and in California. The precise
amount is not known, but it seems reasonably certain that

[1] I am indebted to Professor Albert
Bushnell Hart for permission to use a
letter from C. C. Chaffee to Montgomery Blair inclosing a copy of the
indenture of sale of the Scott family.

[2] See Hunt's *Merchants' Magazine*,
December, 1857, p. 659; and Rhodes's
History of the United States, iii, 50 and
note to p. 51. D. M. Evans, in his
*History of the Commercial Crisis, 1857–
58*, " Section the Fifth," has a great deal
of interesting and valuable information
that seems to show that conditions were
fully as bad in Great Britain as they
were in the United States.

in the year 1857 and the nine years preceding, eight hundred million dollars' worth of gold and silver had been added to the world's stock [1] and had caused a rise in prices of from twenty to forty per cent with a consequent derangement of business, social ideas, and transactions of all kinds.[2] Furthermore the settlement of the Northwestern States and Territories had gone on with tremendous vigor. Immigrants were coming in increasing numbers year by year and many of them were going to the farthest western settlements. The accounts that one finds in papers and diaries are almost unbelievable. In 1856, lots in Minneapolis could be bought one day and sold the next at an advance of fifty to seventy-five per cent. Prices were going up so rapidly that no one supposed that they would ever decline. It was in these circumstances that "Wild Cat" and "Red Dog" banks and bankers came from parts unknown,[3] issued "shin plasters" and other forms of paper money — sometimes the notes of a dead bank elsewhere — and then silently stole away. Suddenly in August, 1857, the revulsion came in the form of the failure of the Ohio Life Insurance Trust Company of Cincinnati.[4] Notwithstanding its name, it does not appear that the institution ever wrote any life insurance or carried on an ordinary banking business. It served as a species of

[1] Hunt's *Merchant's Magazine* for June, 1858, p. 684; the California *State Register and Year Book* (1859), p. 264. Reuben Vose in his *Wealth of the World Displayed* (New York, 1859), p. 28, gives the total gold production of the United States for the last twenty years, including California, North Carolina, Alabama, etc., at $600,000,000. Slightly different estimates are in Edward H. Hall's *Great West* (New York, 1864), p. 88, and in the successive reports of the Director of the Mint, but these last relate to the gold received at the government offices and not to the amount actually mined.

[2] Horace White's "Money and Its

Substitutes" (*Economic Tracts*, No. vi), p. 11. For the effect of the Columbian discovery, see *ibid.*, p. 9, and the present work, vol. i, 143.

[3] Sydney A. Patchin's "Developing of Banking in Minnesota," in *Minnesota Historical Bulletin* for August, 1917, pp. 111–168, contains much unusual and interesting information on this subject.

[4] On the beginning and course of the panic, see *The Magazine of Western History*, ii, 170; *Studies* of the University of Nebraska, vol. v, 164; Return I. Holcombe's *Minnesota in Three Centuries*, ii, 508–511; and McMaster's *United States*, viii, 283.

"clearing house" for Western banks, corporations, and institutions and it possessed a branch establishment in New York
City. The chief official of this branch was termed the
cashier. Either he used the bank funds for himself or loaned
a considerable portion of them imprudently to a railroad in
which he was interested.[1] At all events the "Ohio Life"
closed its doors on August 24, 1857, and at once banks all
over the West and in New York City itself found themselves
in difficulties. Instead of combining and assisting the Ohio
Life to meet its obligations and reopen its doors and thereby
preserve business and credit all over the country, the New
York banks, with one exception, suspended specie payment,
although they had in their vaults more gold than was
necessary to redeem their paper notes.[2] The Philadelphia
bankers caught the infection, suspended specie payment, and
refused to cash cheques. In October, Borup and Oakes,
the best banking firm in the Northwest, was compelled to
close its doors. And so the panic spread, carrying down
industrial institutions of all kinds and throwing working
people out of employment all over the country. In Philadelphia and in New York City there were many German
immigrants engaged in mechanical employments. These
Germans were well organized and peculiarly susceptible to
the influence of radical agitators. For some weeks they
held meetings and conducted parades, carrying banners
with inflammatory inscriptions and adopting resolutions
demanding work and the despoiling of the rich. In a few
months, the banks reopened and the factory machinery
turned again, but the industries of Pennsylvania especially
and the progress of the settlement of the West had received
a severe check from which recovery was slow.

[1] John E. Russell's *The Panics of*   [2] *Ibid.*, p. 19.
1837 and 1857, p. 17.

The principal interest of the panic of 1857 and the slow recovery that followed was in its effect on Northern political opinion and especially in its effect upon the fortunes of the Democratic party in the North. It is one of the axioms of our political history that the party in power is responsible for any financial reverse that may happen and for the hard times and lack of employment that follow and severely affect the working classes. In 1856 and again in 1860, the pivotal States of the North were Pennsylvania, Indiana, and Illinois. Especially, Pennsylvania with its large electoral vote was essential for the safety of the Democratic party and likewise for the election of a Republican President. Buchanan as a Pennsylvanian and as having a long time been in the public eye of his fellow citizens had received a good sized majority in the election of 1856. Pennsylvania was deeply interested in the production of iron, although her iron industry was not as highly developed even in comparison with her population as it is today. Of course, in these years of feverish railroad building from 1849 to 1857, the Pennsylvania iron workers had had full employment, but when the demand for railroad iron fell off, as it did in 1857 with the sudden cessation of railroad building, the demand for iron workers disappeared. In 1852 pig iron was selling at $19 a ton and at $42.50 two years later. In 1858, "anthracite foundry pig" was selling at Philadelphia for a little over $22 a ton and imported Scotch pig iron, which had been selling for $44 in 1854 at New York, was selling for $22 in 1858.[1] In 1858, these figures were translated into political facts by the rejection, in Pennsylvania, of all but three of the Democratic candidates for the Federal House of Representatives; — as Buchanan wrote to his niece, Harriet Lane, "Well!

[1] These figures are taken from   (New York, 1911), pp. 208, 238, 239. George H. Hull's *Industrial Depressions*

we have met the enemy in Pennsylvania & we are theirs."
He added that in the interior of the State the tariff was
"the damaging question." In Philadelphia, according to
him, the wrongs of Kansas had melted the hearts of the
voters.[1]

[1] Moore's *Works of James Buchanan*, x, 229.

NOTE

The Dred Scott Case. — The decision was reported by Benjamin C. Howard and printed in Howard's *United States Reports*, xix, 393. It was published in advance as a separate pamphlet of 239 pages entitled *Report of the Decision of the Supreme Court of the United States . . . In the Case of Dred Scott versus John F. A. Sandford. December Term, 1856* (Washington, 1857). Curtis's opinion begins on p. 170 and runs to the end of the pamphlet. Synopses of the opinions are given in Thayer's *Cases on Constitutional Law*, i, 480 (on pp. 493–496 is a long note discussing various aspects of the case) and in Eugene Wambaugh's *Selection of Cases on Constitutional Law*, 491–506. George T. Curtis's *Memoir* of his brother, B. R. Curtis, has a long and justificatory chapter (vol. i, ch. viii) on the Dred Scott case, in which he prints at length the letters that passed between his brother and the Chief Justice and makes the statement that Taney added eighteen pages to his original opinion before it was printed. Bernard C. Steiner, in his recently published *Life of Roger Brooke Taney*, ch. xii, necessarily devoted considerable space to this episode in Taney's life, and Charles Warren in his *History of the Supreme Court* has naturally gone into the subject at length (vol. iii, ch. xxvi) as it is a landmark in the annals of that tribunal.[1] E. S. Corwin's " The Dred Scott Decision, in the Light of Contemporary Legal Doctrines," in the *American Historical Review*, xvii, 52–69, presents the most modern and the most satisfactory treatment of the matter. Another modern and much briefer view is given in Otto Gresham's paper read before the Chicago Law Club in January, 1908. Of the older critical essays that by John Lowell and Horace Gray, Jr., in the *Law Reporter* for June, 1857, and also printed separately at Boston in the same year, has especial interest.

---

[1] George Ticknor Curtis's *Argument . . . in the Case of Dred Scott* was printed with that title. Other interesting pamphlets of the time are Thomas Hart Benton's *Historical and Legal Examination of that Part of the Decision . . . which declares the Unconstitution-* ality of the Missouri Compromise Act (New York, 1857); *A Review of the Decision . . . in the Dred Scott Case by a Kentucky Lawyer* (Louisville, 1857); and *The Dred Scott Decision with an Introduction by Dr. J. H. Van Evrie* (New York, 1859).

CHAPTER VIII

"THE IMPENDING CRISIS" AND JOHN BROWN

"THE Impending Crisis of the South: How to Meet It," by Hinton Rowan Helper, was published at New York in the year of the Dred Scott decision.[1] The author was a native of North Carolina who had lived in California [2] and had learned to contrast free labor with slave labor. His father resided in an upland North Carolina town and was a slave-holder [3]; and was not a "poor white" in the ordinary meaning of that phrase. The object of the book was to demonstrate to the Southern people that their part of the country, industrially, economically, and socially, was not keeping pace with the North. At the time, the book was looked upon as a bit of anti-slavery propaganda, but Helper's later writings give color to the idea that he regarded the negro as undesirable on account of his inefficiency, whether slave or free.[4]

[1] In 1860 an "Enlarged Edition" was published with a preface stating the details of publication up to that time. Estimates of the number of copies sold or given away run up to one million.

In 1854, Henry C. Carey printed in the New York *Tribune* and later in pamphlet form a similar, but briefer, study entitled *The North and the South*.

[2] See John S. Bassett's "Anti-Slavery Leaders of North Carolina" (*Johns Hopkins Studies*, xvi, No. 6, pp. 11–26) and Helper's *Nojoque*, 11.

[3] Helper's *Noonday Exigencies in America*, 157.

[4] See Helper's *Nojoque; A Question for a Continent* (New York, 1867) and *The Negroes in Negroland* (New York,

1868). On the title page of the latter book he describes himself as the "Author of 'The Impending Crisis of the South,' 'Nojoque,' and other writings in behalf of a Free and White America." In the first sentence of the "Preface" to *Nojoque* he declares that "God's simple truth would be told" were he to state that "the primary object of this work is to write the negro out of America, and that the secondary object is to write him . . . out of existence."

On p. 16 of Alfred H. Stone's article in the *Publications* of the University of Virginia (*Phelps-Stokes Fellowship Papers*, 1915) are these words: "In truth, it was not slave labor but negro

He was a firm believer in the supremacy of the white race. He favored slow emancipation as a means of freeing the South from the encumbrance of the negro; he had no particular interest, apparently, in freeing the negro from the shackles of slavery.

Helper approached the problem of the effect of the presence of the negro on the South from the statistical standpoint, using the "Census" of 1850 as his authority.[1] It happened that that "Census" had been taken under the supervision of J. D. B. De Bow, the professor and publisher of New Orleans. As the work of a Southerner it was difficult for Southerners to dispute the validity of the figures. It appeared that in 1790 New York State contained 340,000 inhabitants and Virginia more than twice as many; in 1850, New York State had a trifle over three million inhabitants and Virginia less than half as many.[2] In 1791, the exports of New York were valued at two and one-half million dollars and those of Virginia at something over three millions. In 1852, New York exported eighty-seven million dollars' worth of goods and produce and Virginia less than three millions. In 1790, the imports of New York and Virginia were about the same; in 1855, New York imported

labor which was, at bottom, responsible" for the "economic loss entailed upon the South through long generations of dependence upon unskilled, untrained negro labor." A similar sentiment is in Stone's article in the *American Historical Review*, xiii, 779.

[1] Something of the kind had been done earlier by E. Steadman in his *Brief Treatise on Manufacturing in the South* (Clarksville, Tennessee, 1851, p. 20). He contrasts the growth of Massachusetts and Tennessee in the last ten years. In 1840 Massachusetts had a population of 739,699 and in 1850 of 994,271 and Tennessee in 1840 of 829,210 and in 1850 of 1,023,116.

The difference in the ratio of increase in the two States was due, according to Steadman, to the comparatively small amount of capital invested in manufacturing in Tennessee as compared with Massachusetts.

[2] According to the *Census* of 1860 ("Population," p. iv) New York State had in the census year 3,880,735 inhabitants and Virginia 1,596,318. Helper repeats many of the comparisons made in *The Impending Crisis*, using the *Census* of 1860 in his *Noonday Exigencies*, 168–196 (New York, 1871). It is in this book that he uses the terms "Guineaized North Carolina" and "Africanized South."

goods to the value of $165,000,000, while Virginia imported less than one million dollars' worth. As to the real and personal property in 1850, in those two States, the Virginians possessed lands, livestock, dwellings, negro slaves, and everything else that could be valued to a total of nearly four hundred millions; while that of New York State excluding any human beings was over one billion dollars. Indeed, in 1856, according to Helper, the valuation of real and movable property in New York City alone exceeded that of the whole State of Virginia, slaves and all. And so he went on, contrasting Massachusetts and North Carolina, Pennsylvania and South Carolina, and then the Free States and the Slave States. Everywhere the same lesson was to be read as in the case of New York and Virginia.

After this beginning, Helper proceeded to take an inventory of the productions of the Free States and the Slave States. He arranged this study in the form of tables. For example, he stated that in 1850, the Free States produced just under five hundred million bushels of wheat, corn, beans, etc., to the value of three hundred and fifty-one million dollars, and the Slave States, eighteen million bushels less of agricultural products that were valued at forty-five million dollars less than were those of the Free States. He added "So much for the boasted agricultural superiority of the South." He then passed on to agricultural products that were valued in pounds — hay, hemp, hops, tobacco, butter, cheese, cotton, sugar, and rice. Putting them all together, the products of the Free States in 1850 were valued at fifty-nine million dollars more than were those of the Slave States, and the farms and the domestic animals of the Free States were worth more than were those of the Slave States to the amount of one billion dollars. Helper maintained that if the South rid itself of slavery and established freedom of labor, in a few years its products would be worth an additional billion dollars; or, to put it in another way, the slave system was costing the South one billion dollars a year. Incidentally he enunciated the thesis that the slaveholders of the South owed to the free Southern whites the sum that slavery had cost the South for a term of years. He concluded with a chapter on "Southern Literature" and an interesting discussion of illiteracy in the North and in the South.[1]

Helper's "Impending Crisis" at first aroused interest in the South as well as in the North. It came out in 1857 and thirteen thousand copies were put on the market in that year. Arrangements were making to print a cheap edition of one hundred thousand copies when the Panic of 1857 drove that, as it did so many other things, from people's minds. In 1859, the matter came up again. What purported to be a briefer rendering was printed as a "Compendium of Helper's Impending Crisis" and sold for sixteen cents a copy or was given away. This was put forth and endorsed by committees and by sixty-eight Congressmen, among them John Sherman, Justin S. Morrill, and Elihu B. Washburne. Helper's book was by no means the first Southern criticism of slavery, nor was it the first Southern criticism of slavery from the statistical standpoint. The earlier books or pamphlets had fallen harmlessly on unheeding ears. At first the "Impending Crisis" likewise aroused no particular

[1] *The Union: Being a Condemnation of Mr. Helper's Scheme* of uncompensated emancipation was published at New York, probably in 1859. It was written by "One who has considered both Sides of the Question" and advocated remunerated emancipation. His figures in general teach the same lesson as Helper's, although his conclusion is very different. Much earlier, in 1847, Henry Ruffner, D.D., of "Lexington, Va.," had printed at Louisville in Kentucky an *Address to the People of West Virginia*. In this he showed to his own satisfaction that slavery was injurious to the public welfare and might be gradually abolished without detriment to the rights and interests of slaveholders.

resentment. When the book was adopted by the Republicans and distributed in considerable numbers as a bit of propaganda, Southern sentiment turned against it and raged with ferocity. Any person distributing the book in any Southern community or owning a copy of it was dealt with. A statement was made that no person who endorsed the book was fit to be Speaker of the Federal House of Representatives and this led to the defeat of John Sherman after eight weeks of heated debates and thirty ballots. Possibly, the reason for Southern resentment in 1860 for what had attracted slight attention in 1857 was the constantly increasing prosperity of the South. In 1850 the cotton crop was reported as worth seventy-eight million dollars and in 1860 at two hundred and thirty-six millions. The tobacco crops had doubled in value and the principal commodities used by Helper in his argument were worth three hundred and forty-two millions in 1860 as against one hundred and thirty-eight millions in 1850. Yet in 1859, when the South was at the height of this prosperity, the leaders of the Republican party of the North were proposing to print and disseminate as a campaign document a book condemning slavery on account of the figures contained in the "Census" of 1850 ! Also in this time of great prosperity flowing from the exportation of these commodities grown by slave labor, it might well be that the slave owners would feel that any and every attack on the "peculiar institution" of the South was an attack on themselves and on the prosperity of the Southern States. Moreover, one of Helper's most striking arguments, that of the supremacy of the Northern hay crop over the total yield of the staple agricultural crops of the South, no longer held good in 1860,[1] for in that year the Northern hay

[1] The figures for 1850 are taken from Helper's *Impending Crisis* (ed. 1860, p. 50). The 1860 amounts of the staple products are taken from the *Census* of 1860 (" Agriculture" p. 185 and fol.) ; the 1860 prices, except that of hemp, are

crop was valued at three hundred and twenty-five million dollars and the six great Southern staples at three hundred and forty-two millions.

Among the criticisms of Helper's book,[1] two stand out partly because of the States from which they presumably emanated. The first of these was a pamphlet of eighty pages, entitled "Appeal to the Common Sense and Patriotism of the People of the United States." The author's name on the title page was Louis Schade, "of Iowa." The pamphlet was printed at Washington in 1860. The author strove to stir up the sympathies of the people of the North by rehearsing the awful story of San Domingo. Indeed, there is no more extraordinary contradiction in the whole history of this sixth decade of the nineteenth century than the reiterated insistence of the Southerners as to the peacable and affectionate disposition of their slaves and the horrible situation which they depicted would have happened had not John Brown's raid been nipped in the bud, — and it might be said that the security that the women and children of the South enjoyed during the four years of the war on the lonely plantations and in Richmond, itself, attests the truth of one of these statements and the utter falsity of the other. Nevertheless, this author, Schade, appears to think that a book like Helper's would bring carnage and blood to the South. At the end, he attempts to counteract the lessons of "Helperism" by saying that the book is full

---

taken from the *Third Annual Report* (1860–61) of the New York Chamber of Commerce, p. 286 ; the price of hemp is taken from the table at the end of Brent Moore's *Study of . . . the Hemp Industry in Kentucky.*

Interesting comparisons can be made by a perusal of the *Report of the Secretary of the Treasury . . . for the Year ending June 30, 1855* and the "Report from the Register of the Treasury enclosed therein."

[1] The Southern view of Helper's book is expressed in Alexander R. Boteler's *Speech . . . on the Organization of the House,* delivered January 25, 1860. He declared it as "objectionable," a "most infamous publication," and the "abominable Helper book," etc.

of "fallacious deductions," that it was directed against the free white laborers of the North in that it advocated the people of the South producing their own necessaries of life. And yet Helper's book, which advocates the withholding of Southern money from the North, was commended by Senator Seward and sixty-eight Republican members of Congress. Schade points out that, according to the register of the United States Treasury Department, Southern staples were exported in the year ending June 30, 1859, to the amount of one hundred and ninety-six million dollars' worth. Adding to this amount the goods of lesser moment sent out from there would give a total of two hundred and twenty million dollars out of the total of three hundred and thirty-five million dollars' worth of exports from the whole United States, north and south. Or that the exportations of Southern products were nearly double in value that of the Northern products in the year covered by this report. And it was the money that the South thus obtained that went to pay for Northern brooms, shoes, tombstones, and provisions. At the end of the pamphlet are nineteen conclusions, the nineteenth being that the advocates of Helper's book are enemies of the country, and their doctrines, if carried out, would leave the American people at the mercy of the "European despotic Powers." The other book was written by "Saml. M. Wolfe" of Virginia and purported to be "Helper's Impending Crisis Dissected." It was published at Philadelphia in 1860. He points out that in "The Land of Gold," which was published at Baltimore in 1855, two years before the appearance of the first edition of the "Impending Crisis," Helper had argued that slavery was a beneficent institution and that the slaves were a great deal better off than the free negroes. Like the Iowan, Louis Schade, Wolfe argued that Helper was undermining the prosperity of the North.

The slow industrial development of the South up to 1850 was due, in great measure, to the lack of an adequate supply of labor. This defect in the Southern industrial system could have been overcome by dispensing with the negro population, slave or free, or by greatly increasing it. Either solution of the problem was full of difficulty. An effective industrial white population could not and would not live side by side with negro slaves. No one in the South desired a large free negro population and the presence of even small numbers of free negroes had led to schemes of deportation. The results had been insignificant and with the condition of ocean travel as it was in 1850, the deportation of several million blacks — free or slave — was out of the question; and therefore the establishment of a white industrial population was an impossibility. The only practicable way, therefore, to solve the labor problem of the South was to import more slaves from Africa,—and in large numbers. The matter came up in successive commercial conventions.

The origin of the Southern commercial conventions is unknown. Industrial conventions were no new thing; for instance, in 1827, persons interested in iron making had assembled at Harrisburg in Pennsylvania to incite Congress to give added protection to the iron industry of that State. In 1831, the Friends of Domestic Industry met in General Convention at New York. This convention had issued an "Address . . . to the People of the United States" and accompanied it with long reports of committees on the conditions of industry. In 1838, there were conventions at Augusta, Georgia, and at Richmond and Norfolk in Virginia. Finally, in 1847, an "Internal Improvement Convention" had been held at Chicago. The activity of the Northern industrialists did not at once lead to a similar display of energy on the part of the Southerners, but in 1852 a convention was held at New Orleans.[1] This convention may have come together owing to the propaganda published by De Bow in his "Review," and it is possible that he might be regarded as the originator of the succession of Southern commercial conventions that were held in the next few years until secession put an end to them. Whatever the official outcome of the successive conventions may have been and whether they represented a conscious movement or not, there is no doubt whatever that the mere fact of delegates from all or many of the States of the South coming together, year after year, and comparing views, brought Southern independence nearer to the thoughts of many people.

The discussions in the conventions taking them as a whole ranged over all the subjects of human activities of that time. Three things come out prominently, however. The first is the great and ever-present desire of the Southerners for independent commercial intercourse with the outer world. This took the form of the advocacy of one or more Pacific railroads,[2] the eastern termini to be within the limits of slave territory and also independent communication by steamship to be established with Europe. Another topic that constantly crops up is the desirability of the South establishing its independence of Northern manufacturers, and this could be best accomplished by the upbuilding of manufacturing industry in the South. There was a great deal of declamation on these topics, many reports from committees, and many solutions proposed. A study of the debates so far as

[1] William W. Davis has an interesting and important article on the "Ante-Bellum Southern Commercial Conventions" in the *Transactions* of the Alabama Historical Society, v, 153–202. It would be well if the proceedings of these conventions could be reprinted from the local newspapers of the day with the above essay as an explanatory introduction.

[2] John P. Davis's *Union Pacific Railway* has an account of the earlier political history of the trans-Mississippi railway projects.

they can be rescued from the newspapers and from De Bow's "Review" does not exhibit Southern business capacity in a very favorable light. But it was hardly to be expected that persons who had never taken part in the management of large enterprises should have realized the difficulties of the establishment of railroads or have thought of any better way of bringing it about than State ownership. In fact, with some notable exceptions, the operative enterprise of the South was directed toward cotton raising, for that was the most profitable of all enterprises. The rates of profits, however, were constantly declining. It has been calculated [1] that the value of a slave had risen from fifteen hundred pounds of cotton to ten thousand pounds in the first fifty years of the century. It is unquestionably true that it was only the planter who was cultivating the best soil who could clear a profit of any size under these conditions and that the plantations in less favored regions were yielding no profit at all. Granting that negro labor and slavery must be maintained or the Southern social system would go to pieces, a lower price for slaves must be brought about. This could only be done by direct importations from Africa, — by openly and avowedly reinstating the African slave trade as a profitable and lawful commercial undertaking. It was in 1854 that the Grand Jury of Williamsburg District, South Carolina,[2] "presented" the law abolishing the African slave trade as a public grievance. If the trade were reëstablished, it would be a "blessing to the American people," — so declared the Grand Jury. It was also asserted by some people that if the price of slaves were lessened and the ownership of slaves brought within the reach of practically all white

[1] Ulrich B. Phillips's "Black Belt Labor" in the *Publications* of the University of Virginia, *Phelps-Stokes Fellowship Papers*, p. 34.

[2] W. W. Boddie's *History of Williamsburg* (Columbia, S. C., 1923), p. 315.

persons, south of Pennsylvania and the Ohio River, the institution would be popularized in the northern belt of Slave States. From many points of view the reopening of the African slave trade was highly desirable. That the conscience of the civilized world was fixedly set against this does not seem to have occurred to the advocates of the reëstablishment of the trans-oceanic traffic in human flesh. The project was first brought before a Southern Commercial Convention by Mr. Gaulden of Georgia, at Savannah in December, 1856.[1] At that time the proposition did not arouse active discussion. It came up again at Knoxville in 1857, at Montgomery in 1858, and especially at Vicksburg in 1859. L. W. Spratt of Charleston in a "Speech upon the Foreign Slave Trade" which he delivered before the legislature of South Carolina in 1858 stated the Southern view in categorical form.[2] Opening the foreign slave trade would give prosperity, progress, and political power to the South, so he maintained. At the moment slaves were so high in price that only the planters of the black belts could afford to buy them, for they could not be purchased at prices that would enable them to be used on "the lighter lands in the older States" and they could not be employed at mechanic trades in competition with cheaper labor elsewhere. Until they could be so employed, there could be no advancement in population. With the reopening of the trade, the old lands could be cultivated, Southern mechanics could compete with mechanics in other parts of the world, the South could

[1] See the Richmond *Dispatch* for December 11, 1856, De Bow's *Review*, xxii, 221, and W. E. B. Du Bois's "Suppression of the African Slave-Trade" (*Harvard Historical Studies*, No. i, 170). See also the *Congressional Globe* 34th Cong., 3rd Sess., Appendix, p. 364 and 38th Cong., 1st Sess., *Senate Executive Document*, No. 56.

[2] Printed in pamphlet form at Columbia, S. C., in 1858. The prohibition of the African slave trade in the provisional constitution of the Confederate States naturally aroused Mr. Spratt to renewed effort and he caused a long communication to appear in the Charleston *Mercury* for February 13, 1861, which is reprinted as "Appendix M" to the 1863 edition of J. E. Cairns's *Slave Power*, pp. 390–410.

produce its own supplies, railroads and steamboats would begin to pay returns on money invested in them, and the South would stand "resplendent in the prosperity to be poured upon us by the teeming thousands from the plains of Africa." According to Mr. Spratt there were now three and a half million slaves to six million masters, or three million masters without slaves. There is not a white man in the South who would not own a slave if he could, but at the present prices many cannot buy them. Turning to the political aspects of the case, he stated that while the Union is a democracy, the South is not a democracy, but is "perhaps the purest form of aristocracy, the world has ever seen." And, unlike other aristocracies, it is based upon natural and necessary principles.

Mr. Spratt, who made the speech that is partially analyzed in the preceding paragraph, was possibly the most persistent and outspoken advocate of the reopening of the slave trade, not only before the legislature of South Carolina, but in the later commercial conventions. In 1857, Governor James H. Adams of South Carolina laid the matter before the legislature of that State in a message [1] declaring that our system of slavery has "elevated the African to a degree of civilization which the black race have never attained in any other age or country." Had the slave trade never been closed, the equilibrium between the North and the South would not have been destroyed. The South needed more labor. Governor Adams felt that he would be "wanting in duty" if he did not urge the legislature to withdraw its consent to the act declaring the slave trade to be piracy.

[1] This part of the "Governor's Message" is reprinted as an "Appendix" to the *Report of the Special Committee of the House of Representatives, of South Carolina, on . . . Slavery and the Slave Trade* (Columbia, S. C., 1857). Pettigrew's *Report of the Minority* was printed at Columbia in the same year. An interesting statement of Pettigrew's position is in Wm. Henry Trescot's *Memorial of the Life of J. Johnston Pettigrew* (Charleston, 1870), p. 36.

In conclusion, he again stated that more slaves are necessary to a continued "monopoly in plantation products,"
to the full development of the agricultural and mechanical
resources of the South, and to the restoration of the South
to an "equality of power in the General Government."
This message was referred to a special committee of seven.
The majority report signed by six members was made in
1857 and was accompanied by a minority report signed by
J. Johnston Pettigrew. The majority asserted that a more
general ownership of slaves among the white population of
the South was desirable and they concluded by offering
three resolutions directing the Senators in Congress to propose the abrogation of the eighth article of the Treaty of
Washington, to support any proposition to repeal the act
declaring the slave trade piracy, and that a copy of the report and resolutions be sent to the governor of each Southern
State. Johnston Pettigrew traversed most of the opinions
advocated by the majority. He maintained also that the
reopening of the trade would decrease the value of the
slaves already in the South to one-half of the present price
at a general loss of somewhere around a hundred thousand
dollars to the State. He declared that cheap negroes were
not equivalent to cheap labor, because the existing slave
population of the South had been attuned to labor for three
generations of servitude. The true remedy for the troubles
that were besetting the people of South Carolina was to
promote scientific agriculture and make the existing land
and labor more productive.

The arguments put forth by Johnston Pettigrew in his
"Minority Report" of 1857 may be said to have formulated
essentially the public opinion of the northern belt of Slave
States. Then, too, many slaveholders believed with Washington and Jefferson that better management of the soil

would cure the ills of the planter. Whether this was so or
not, many planters in Kentucky and Virginia still adhered
to the ideas of 1832, that slavery was an evil and should
be done away with at the first possible moment. And many
other Virginians and Kentuckians, while willing to die for
the perpetuation of Southern social institutions, would have
opposed most vigorously the reopening of the African slave
trade, had the matter ever come within the range of practical
politics. As the years went by, the tide of opinion in the
commercial conventions in favor of the reopening of the
trade gathered force ; but how far this increase reflected
real public opinion in the South may well be questioned.
It is worth noting, however, that in December, 1856, the
Federal House of Representatives voted that it would shock
"the moral sentiment of the enlightened portion of mankind"
to revive the African slave trade.[1] Already in August,
1856, Congress had voted eight thousand dollars to carry out
the anti-slave-trade laws.[2] But it is worthy of note that in
March, 1858, a bill to import two thousand five hundred
Africans to be indentured for fifteen years or more passed
the lower House of the Louisiana legislature and was defeated in the State Senate by only two votes. It was in
the same year that the collector of Charleston was actually
applied to for a clearance for a vessel to go to the African
coast and return with "emigrants." [3] In 1858, Edward A.
Pollard, the newspaper writer of Richmond, Virginia, suggested the importation of Africans under the permission of
existing laws. These might come as apprentices and when
they had reached the South they themselves might find it
convenient to "live in bondage." [4]

---

[1] *Journal* of the House of Representatives, 34th Cong., 3rd Sess., p. 105.
[2] *Statutes at Large*, xi, 90.
[3] W. E. B. Du Bois's *Suppression of*
the African Slave-Trade (*Harvard Historical Studies*, vol. i), p. 177.
[4] *Black Diamonds* (New York, 1859),
p. 63. See also p. 52.

The attempts that were made by the United States and by European nations, especially by Great Britain, to put an end to the African slave trade by seizing slavers on the African coast seem to have been fairly efficacious in the earlier time, but, beginning with 1840, the number of slaves exported from Africa appears to have constantly increased. In 1850, Mr. Hutt, the chairman of a committee of the British House of Commons, reported that in 1842, thirty thousand slaves were exported from Africa, and that the number had risen to seventy-six thousand in 1846, to eighty-four thousand in 1847, and that the trade, at the time of the report, was "in a state of unusual activity." [1] He added that the British admiral, then in command on the West African station, had declared that the number of slaves exported from the coast depended upon the commercial demand and not upon the strength or efficiency of the British squadron. As the decade preceding secession progressed, the activity of the slave traders increased.[2] There can be no question about the fact although it would be impossible to prove any specific point. No doubt, also, many loose statements have been made on the subject. Dr. W. E. Burghardt Du Bois, in his "Suppression of the African Slave-Trade to the United States of America," has brought together a mass of unpleasant material on this subject. He quotes Stephen A. Douglas as saying in 1860 that more slaves had been imported into the Southern States in the preceding year than had ever been imported before in any one year, even when the traffic was lawful. It has also been stated that eighty-five ships were fitted out at New York in eighteen

[1] *Report of the Agent of the Colonization Society of the State of Indiana* (Indianapolis, 1855), p. 10.

[2] James S. Pike (*First Blows of the Civil War*, p. 492), writing in February, 1860, says that the revival of the African slave trade that had taken place within a very few years was due to "the demoralized condition of the law-officers of the federal government, judges included."

months for the slave trade [1] and there are interesting stories
of vessels being hastily constructed on the Maine coast for
the express purpose of making one slave-trading trip to the
coast of Africa before capture or destruction. In "Appendix
C" Du Bois gives "Typical Cases of Vessels Engaged in the
American Slave-Trade." In the years 1851–1860, he cites
the cases of eighty-five ships. It might be easily argued
that if these were the known ships, the total number engaged
in the trade was very much greater. On the other hand, as
Henry R. Jackson pointed out, most of the vessels that were
brought into the light of trial were engaged primarily in the
transportation of slaves to Brazil, where slavery was still
legal and the slave trade regarded as an entirely worthy
branch of commerce. The consideration just adverted to
tinges all the accounts and discussions of the slave trade of
this time. It is impossible to separate the vessel whose
primary destination was the United States from the vessel
whose primary object was to carry slaves across the Atlantic
to a market anywhere, — and it is not at all certain that
slaves, landed in Brazil or Cuba, would find their way to
the United States; they might or they might not.[2]

[1] *The Wanderer Case; the Speech of
Hon. Henry R. Jackson of Savannah,
Ga.* (Atlanta, 1891), p. 55. An interested student might read with profit the
evidence in the case of "The Schooner
Wanderer, and Cargo" to see upon what
slim foundations important historical
statements are often made. The anti-
slave-trade laws are summarized in
Judge Wayne's charge to the Grand
Jury of the sixth circuit court on
November 14, 1859, in the *Forty-third
Annual Report of the American Colonization Society* (Washington, 1860) pp. 53–
70. In the ten years to May 1, 1862,
twenty-six vessels were "arrested and
bonded" as slavers in the southern district of New York, but in the cases of
four of them the libel was dismissed;

Senate Doc., No. 53, 37th Cong., 2nd
Sess.

[2] *An Exposition of the African Slave
Trade* that was published by the
Society of Friends at Philadelphia in
1851 contains heartrending accounts of
the capture and transportation of
slaves. Brantz Mayer's *Captain Canot;
or Twenty Years of an African Slaver*
(New York, 1854) gives an exceedingly
favorable view of the trade (see especially pp. 102–106). Nathaniel Haw-
thorne's edition of Horatio Bridge's
Journal of an African Cruiser (New
York, 1845) and Commander Andrew
H. Foote's *Africa and the American
Flag* (New York, 1854) relate many
experiences from personal observation;
and see his *African Squadron: . . .*

While so many men from Captain Canot to Governor Adams and Mr. Spratt were engaged in plans to increase the slave population of the United States, John Brown was leading "a forlorn hope" to put an end to the institution, once and for all. Like so many men of one idea in ancient and in modern times, John Brown in earlier life had herded cattle and tended sheep. Long vigils and hours of solitude had led him to that excessive contemplation which seems to be the breeding ground of fanaticism. At any rate, in early manhood it was borne in upon him that his ultimate task in this world was to put a termination to negro slavery in the South. At one time, he seems to have wandered around parts of the Southern country in the guise of a surveyor and to have familiarized himself with favorable spots for the carrying out of his plans. The idea was with him all through his Kansas experience. His raid into Missouri in 1858 was in the nature of a dress rehearsal for the final tragedy. His plan was to establish a strong point in the mountains of the South, attract slaves to it, arm, and colonize them there so they might be able to defend themselves from all comers. Presumably, the further development of this scheme would involve a series of strong points and colonies and become, indeed, a rallying ground for slaves of the whole South, — a place where they would be free and secure without undergoing the hardships of the underground railroad and the flight to Canada. The impossibilities of carrying out this plan have occurred to many commentators, but they never entered the mind of John Brown.

To carry out his great scheme, John Brown secured two thousand dollars in money, a couple of hundred Sharps rifles, and some bundles of pikes. These last were elongated

Reviewed . . . by Commander A. H. Foote, U. S. N. (Philadelphia, 1855). More popular accounts may be found in the Atlantic Monthly (lxxxvi, p. 451); The Century (xxvi, p. 115); and Scribner's (viii, p. 113).

bowie knives stuck on poles and looked wickeder than they were. How many persons outside of John Brown and his little band knew of these preparations and intentions is concealed in the mists of time. At that moment it was the interest of those who were or might be implicated in the affair to keep all knowledge of it to themselves. Since the war, it has been the desire of many persons to connect themselves or their forbears with so important an adventure. Between the two it is impossible to reach any conclusion. It may well be that no one, not even John Brown, had any accurate knowledge of what he was going to do, — beyond the vague scheme of arousing the negro slaves and providing them with arms. At all events, his following was very scanty and the means at his disposal very small.

The plan to revolutionize Southern society, for it was nothing else, would have been put into operation in 1858 had it not been for the treachery of a man whom Brown had employed to train his men in the rudiments of military art, for if everything went well, they would be captains and colonels and generals within a few months. This man, however, thought he saw greater profit in revealing what he knew of the scheme to persons in Washington. The headquarters of Brown's army were in Canada and there at Chatham on May 8, 1858, Brown held a constitutional convention for his proposed republic [1] and a constitution was adopted. It comprised forty-eight articles and provided for the formation of a state within the United States. In short, Brown's scheme was to appropriate a certain portion of the soil of the Southern States, form a government thereon, and then secede from the United States and the States wherein this new republic might be situated. He was about to make

[1] See *Calendar of Virginia State Papers*, xi, 271–349, and Richard J. Hinton's *John Brown and His Men*, 179, 619–637.

war on the existing society of that part of the United States; but it was to be done with the utmost regularity. It is on this constitution-making that those hostile to the memory of John Brown — and many of his partisans also — have based the claim that he was insane. He may have been so, but in any discussion of insanity or of what constitutes a maniac it is perhaps well to remember that the line between the sane and the insane is very tortuous and exceedingly difficult to draw and that success or failure is hardly a secure metewand with which to measure one's sanity or insanity. Besides, in the march of history, Thermopylæ was as desperate as Harper's Ferry, and when one comes to turn over the beginnings of great events, Captain Parker of Lexington on the 19th of April, 1775, or the embattled farmers at Concord Bridge a few hours later on the same day, were likewise tempting fate. In each case success followed; Greece was freed from Asiatic control, — for a time; the colonies became the United States, — with the aid of France; and within five years from the death of John Brown, the Emancipation Proclamation came from the pen of Abraham Lincoln. In dying, John Brown achieved the success that evaded him when living.[1]

In July, 1859, John Brown with a dozen or so white followers, one daughter and one daughter-in-law, and four negroes appeared at a farmhouse in Maryland about five miles from Harper's Ferry — Kennedy Farm — and settled down in three-quarters seclusion. There were great delays in assembling the forces of the new republic at the farmhouse and neighboring cabin, and even greater delays in assembling the revolvers, pikes, and rifles that were essential for the

---

[1] "John Brown's body lies a-mouldering in the grave, But his soul goes marching on" was an inspiration to many a weary and forlorn Union soldier; but its origin is obscure. See Rhodes's *United States*, ii, 416 *note*, and *The Continental Monthly*, i, 735.

success of the undertaking. How it happened that the
neighbors suspected nothing is difficult to understand and is
a tribute to the good management of this part of the enterprise, especially as some of the men nearest Brown lost heart
and deserted, even the one who held the office of Secretary
of State of the Provisional Government. At length on
the sixteenth day of October, 1859, in the early evening,
John Brown led his army of eighteen or twenty men from the
Kennedy Farm and took up the line of march for Harper's
Ferry. No one stopped them. They crossed the Potomac,
seized and held the bridges, and gained possession of the
United States arsenal at that place, occupied the town,
captured the persons of leading men of the neighborhood,
and then stopped. This is the most difficult quarter of a
day in John Brown's life to understand. Why did he remain
at Harper's Ferry, why did he not go into the hills and place
himself and his following in a position where nothing but
starvation could have conquered them? No one ever will
know. Fate or the Unseen Power impelled him to keep in
the center of the stage entirely unconscious, no doubt, that
that was the place for him.

As the telegraph carried through the Southland the news
of the appearance of old John Brown of Pottawatomie at
Harper's Ferry with an armed following and his incitement
to slaves to desert their masters and follow him, the excitement became intense until it grew beyond all bounds of
reasoning. For years, Southerners had insisted that slavery
was a most beneficent institution, that the slaves were
happy, happier than anyone else in the United States.
Now, the presence of a score or two of men at Harper's
Ferry within a hundred miles of Washington aroused them
to frenzy; they saw San Domingo painted on the faces of
their slaves, their property taken from them, their wives

and children slaughtered, and they themselves either dead
or exiled. In reality the most astounding thing about the
Harper's Ferry episode, apart from its effect on the public
mind, South and North, was the absolute lack of desire on
the part of the slaves of the neighborhood to take advantage
of the freedom and the weapons that were held out to them.
Had there been a sane and sensible governor of Virginia at
Richmond at the time and one who had the salvation of
Virginia and of Southern society, and the welfare of the
United States, at heart, he would have minimized in every
possible way the exploit of this little band at Harper's Ferry
and consigned the leader and some of his followers to the
Virginia Western Insane Asylum as hopeless lunatics. It
could not be so, save in the very exceptional circumstance of
there being a man of first-class calibre in the Virginia gubernatorial chair. In the existing apprehensiveness of the
Southern mind,[1] in the ingrained feeling of all Virginians
east of the Shenandoah that Virginia and not the United
States was the nation to which they owed allegiance, only a
man of the strongest and most forward-seeing capacities
could have done other than what Governor John A. Wise of
Virginia did. He issued a proclamation, he called out the
militia, he ordered the cadets of the military school to march
on Harper's Ferry, and he implored the Federal government
for aid. President Buchanan and Secretary of War Floyd

---

[1] This comes out vividly in the
address that was delivered by Samuel
Hall, commissioner from Georgia, to the
North Carolina legislature. Among
other things he pointed out that
"Predatory bands [Brown's armies]
were marched into peaceful communities to excite insurrection — apply
the midnight torch — rob and murder
— to destroy the means of subsistence
— to poison the wells — to alarm our
sleep — . . . and when the desperadoes
were arrested and punished, they were
elevated to the honors of martyrdom;
all the restraints of religion were cast
aside, and the crucifixion of the Savior
of mankind blasphemed by impiously
comparing with it the execution of a cut
throat and a thief." In the next
paragraph he declared that "Among a
people not dead to all sense of virtue and
decency, such a party could not
prevail."

despatched a body of United States Marines to Harper's
Ferry and placed them under command of Major Robert E.
Lee of the regular army.   Even so, in spite of overwhelming
odds, the fighting was prolonged and it was only after a
desperate defence that the party surrendered, except some
who had been killed and others who had managed to flee
to the mountains and make their way to Pennsylvania and
to the North, even to Canada.   Then followed the governor
and the politicians and interviewed the middle-aged leader
of men as he lay wounded.   They were surprised at his sanity and entire truthfulness.   He had no desire to conceal
anything.   Last of all came his trial at Charlestown, the
county seat.[1]   At first the judge suggested that there should
be an inquiry into John Brown's sanity, but this Brown
put aside with scorn.   It had suddenly occurred to him with
the foresight which is given to those in the grasp of death
that every hour's delay, every day's delay, every week's
delay, until the inevitable execution came, would strengthen
the tide of Northern feeling against slavery.

On December 2, 1859, John Brown was hanged in the public square of Charlestown in the presence of fifteen hundred
soldiers.   "So perish all such enemies of Virginia!   All
such enemies of the Union!   All such foes of the human
race!" declared the colonel in command of the Virginia

---

[1] Three contemporaneous accounts
were printed: one of them, *The Life,
Trial and Conviction of Captain John
Brown* (New York, 1859), has some re-
markable and largely imaginary pictures
of the tragedy; another, entitled *The
John Brown Invasion, An Authentic
History of the Harper's Ferry Tragedy*
(Boston, 1860), has as frontispiece an
engraving from a photograph by
Whipple that exhibits a man of stern
purpose; and Osborne P. Anderson's
A Voice from Harper's Ferry (Boston,
1861) gives incidents prior and subse-

quent to its capture by one of the
captors.

Three accounts by eye-witnesses,
written long after the event, are worth
noting: Alexander R. Boteler's "Recollections of the John Brown Raid"
(*The Century*, July, 1883); Capt.
John H. Zittle's *Correct History of the
John Brown Invasion* (Hagerstown,
Md., 1905); and Elijah Avey's *Capture
and Execution of John Brown* with
thirty illustrations, printed at Elgin,
Ill.

troops. Three weeks and a half earlier (November 8, 1859), while lying on his pallet in prison, Brown had written to his "Dear Wife, & Children *every One*." [1] He declared that he was quite cheerful, having "the peace of God which passeth all understanding" and "the testimony (in some degree) of a good conscience, that I have not lived altogether in vain." He wrote that he could die believing that to seal his "testimony (for God, & humanity) with my blood: will do vastly more to advance the cause (I have earnestly endeavoured to promote) than all I have done *in my life*." He asked his wife and children to remember that Jesus of Nazareth had suffered a most excruciating death and that the prophets, apostles, and Christians of former days went through "*greater* tribulations than you & I" and besought them to think of the crushed millions. On the next day he added the following postscript: "I cannot remember a night so dark as to hinder or prevent the coming day: nor a storm so furious, & dreadful: as to prevent the return of warm sunshine; & a cloudless sky: but beloved ones do remember 'that this is not your rest': 'that in this world you have no abiding place or continueing city.' To God & his Infinite grace I always commend you."

---

[1] These sentences are taken from the original letter in the Cabinet of the Massachusetts Historical Society. The letter has been printed with slight variations in Vincent Y. Bowditch's *Life and Correspondence of Henry Ingersoll Bowditch*, ii, 377, and in F. B. Sanborn's *Life and Letters of John Brown*, 585.

NOTE

John Brown. — A list of the biographies of John Brown is in Oswald Garrison Villard's *John Brown, 1800–1859. A Biography Fifty Years After* (Boston, 1910). Of those mentioned, Sanborn's *Brown* and Du Bois's *Brown* are more sympathetic than Villard's own book. An extremely hostile work is Hill Peebles Wilson's *John Brown, Soldier of Fortune, A Critique* (Lawrence, Kansas, 1913). The histories of Kansas pay much attention to Brown, as do the works on Governor Charles Robinson.

Of the books and articles dealing directly with the attack on Harper's Ferry, the following may be mentioned: John E. Cook's *Confession* (Charlestown, 1859); and United States Senate *Report*, 36th Cong., 1st Sess., No. 278. In the *Publications* of the Southern History Association, i, 165–195, is an interesting account of "John Brown's Raid" by Andrew Hunter, who was appointed by Governor Wise of Virginia to conduct the prosecution. This paper was written some time after the event. It may be supplemented by certain letters from and to Hunter printed in the Massachusetts Historical Society's *Proceedings* for June, 1908, pp. 509–518, and December, 1912, pp. 243–249. In vols. i, 196, and iii, 302, of the *Publications* of the Southern History Association is a "Bibliography of John Brown" by Thomas Featherstonhaugh; preceding the second installment is an article on the Harper's Ferry affair. With John Brown was captured a carpet-bag containing papers and letters. These are printed in the *Calendar of Virginia State Papers*,[1] xi, 271–349.

Many of those more or less nearly connected with John Brown's raid, on one side or the other, have left behind them reminiscences and, sometimes, letters of value as original documents. See the lives and works of recollection of Samuel G. Howe, George L. Stearns, F. B. Sanborn, Thomas Wentworth Higginson, and John Murray Forbes. A collection of John Brown manuscript material is in the Boston Public Library.

[1] For a statement of the important points in these papers, see the *Boston Evening Transcript*, December 24, 1901, reprinted from the *Richmond Times*.

CHAPTER IX

ABRAHAM LINCOLN AND THE ELECTION OF 1860

THE career of Abraham Lincoln casts a doubt on all our ideas of heredity and of education. Elaborate genealogical studies of his forbears have been published.[1] An examination of them has failed to disclose any ancestor in England or America who possessed anything approaching the qualities of mind and command of Abraham Lincoln. As to education, he had nothing that a pedagogical professor of the present day would recognize by that word. Whatever there was of home instruction was exceedingly limited in amount and poor in quality and he never attended school for more than a year in all. As a boy, he knew nothing of child labor regulations; whatever work there was to do that he could do, that he did. Tradition and recollection — which are much the same — portray a boyhood and early manhood that were absolutely impossible in view of his later career. He is represented as more or less of a boor, as ill-clothed, ill-mannered, and as painfully embarrassed on social occasions. Yet this man took his wife from one of the best houses in central Illinois, became one of the half dozen leading lawyers

[1] Lea and Hutchinson's *The Ancestry of Abraham Lincoln* (Boston, 1909) and Waldo Lincoln's *History of the Lincoln Family; An Account of the Descendants of Samuel Lincoln of Hingham, Massachusetts, 1637-1920* (Worcester, Mass., 1923). A delightful short essay on *The Parents of Abraham Lincoln* by William E. Barton was printed at Charleston, Illinois, in 1922. It contains the gist of a much longer work of four hundred pages by the same author entitled *The Paternity of Abraham Lincoln* (New York, 1920). Dr. L. P. Clark in his "Psychologic Studies of Notable Historic Characters" has analyzed Lincoln from one point of view; it is to be hoped that other psychologists will attack the problem. For more formal Lincoln books, see Note at end of chapter.

of his State, sent his eldest son to an eastern college, and produced the most perfect piece of English prose that has yet been written in America.[1]

Henry Watterson, a Confederate soldier, in May, 1909, spoke these words of Abraham Lincoln [2]:

"Born, as lowly as the Son of God, in a hovel; reared in penury, squalor, with no gleam of light or fair surrounding; without graces actual or acquired; without name or fame or official training; it was reserved for this strange being, late in life, to be snatched from obscurity, raised to supreme command at a supreme moment and intrusted with the destiny of a nation. . . . That during four years, carrying with him such a weight of responsibility as the world never witnessed before, he filled the vast space allotted to him in the eyes and actions of mankind, is to say that he was inspired of God."

Whatever his ancestry, whatever his early life, in 1832 Abraham Lincoln enlisted in the Illinois troops at the time of the Black Hawk War and was chosen captain of the local company. In 1834, when not quite twenty-six years of age, he was sent to the Illinois legislature and twelve years later in 1846 was chosen one of the Illinois Representatives in the Congress of the United States. In Washington, he achieved slight distinction, although his speeches there and in New

---

[1] For the evolution of Lincoln's literary style, see a paper by Daniel K. Dodge in the University of Illinois *Studies*, vol. i, No. i. On pp. 50–52 is an excellent account of the composition of the Gettysburg address. Samuel A. Green gives several early instances of the use of the idea set forth in the phrase "government of the people, by the people, for the people" in Massachusetts Historical Society's *Proceedings* for May, 1901, p. 92.

[2] John B. Castleman's *Active Service*, 64. In 1868 or thereabouts, Horace Greeley wrote the following which was not printed until after his death: "Looking back through the lifting mists of seven eventful, tragic, trying, glorious years, I clearly discern that the one providential leader, the indispensable hero of the great drama — faithfully reflecting even in his hesitations and seeming vacillations the sentiment of the masses — fitted by his very defects and shortcomings for the burden laid upon him, the good to be wrought out through him, was Abraham Lincoln." The *Century* for July, 1891, p. 382.

England during his term of service must have made him
known to many people. He was not reëlected to Congress,
and, returning to Illinois, betook himself energetically to the
practice of the law. The passage of the Kansas-Nebraska
Act brought him to the front. He had no particular liking
for the negro; in fact, he would have been glad to deport
every negro from the limits of the United States, if he could
have done it. He thought that every man and woman, of
whatever race or color or circumstances of life, had an in-
alienable right to the produce of his or her labor.[1] In 1856,
a convention of Kansas Aid Societies at Buffalo, New York,
appointed Lincoln one of the "National Kansas committee,
of wise and upright men, to whose discretion the whole conduct of our sacred cause shall be intrusted." In 1858 he
contested the Illinois senatorship. Precisely why he did so
is not known, but it may well be that Lincoln entered into
the fray to prevent a coalition between Douglas and the
Republicans, more especially those of the Northeastern
States. He began the contest with a pronouncement[2] that
dismayed his friends by declaring that "'A house divided
against itself cannot stand.' I believe this government
cannot endure permanently half slave and half free. . . . .
It will become all one thing, or all the other." Uncon-
sciously, Lincoln had struck the keynote of the history of

---

[1] The distinction between the Free-
Soiler and the abolitionist was that the
former believed slavery to be politically
and industrially undesirable and economically and humanly wrong. The
abolitionist believed it to be morally
wrong. As to the latter, Henry J.
Van Dyke in his *Character and Influence
of Abolitionism* (Washington, 1860)
declared that abolitionism had no
foundation in the Scriptures, led to utter
infidelity, had been promulgated by
misrepresentation and abuse, and was
the chief cause of the strife that agitates

and the danger that threatens the
country.

[2] There is nothing new in politics or
elsewhere. In 1850 Edward B. Bryan
had printed at Charleston, South Carolina, a tract asserting the necessity of
separation from the North. "Our
people," he wrote, "are opposed in
interests, at variance in opinions —
they are at war, inevitable, unavoidable
war . . . the house is divided against
itself. It must fall." Ulrich B. Phillips's *Literary Movement for Secession*,
p. 40.

the United States for the next seven years. Douglas and his friends sought to reunite the Democratic party and to attract to it whatever Republicans, old Whigs, or Know-Nothings they could find who were dissatisfied with the uncompromising attitude of Lincoln and of those who believed with him that the preservation of the existing Free-Soil area was of more importance than anything else on the political horizon. At first Lincoln and Douglas spoke separately on different platforms and then, at Lincoln's instigation, held a series of joint debates.[1] It was at one of these that Douglas challenged the accuracy of Lincoln's "house divided" assertion and received the reply that it was the pronouncement of a higher authority than either Judge Douglas or himself. In the midst of one of these debates, at Freeport, Lincoln suddenly asked Douglas whether, in view of the Dred Scott decision, the people of a Territory could exclude slavery from their midst, and Douglas answered that, by unfriendly local legislation, the people of any Territory could make it hazardous for a slave-holder to bring his slaves within its limits.[2] Although there were enough hold-over Senators in the Illinois legislature to reëlect Douglas to the United States Senate, nevertheless Lincoln had forced himself into a position of equality with Douglas and had made it impossible for a great many members of the Democratic party to support the latter for the

---

[1] In 1860, a volume was issued at Columbus, Ohio, entitled *Political Debates between Hon. Abraham Lincoln and Hon. Stephen A. Douglas, in the Celebrated Campaign of 1858, in Illinois.* It is the original of all later editions. The most complete of all is the one edited by Edwin E. Sparks and published in the *Collections* of the Illinois State Historical Library, vol. iii ("Lincoln Series," vol. i). The most usable edition is that issued at New York in 1912, with an "Introduction" by George Haven Putnam.

[2] The Mississippi delegation to the Charleston Convention bore with them a copy of Douglas's Freeport speech. Murat Halstead's *Caucuses of 1860*, p. 3. See, however, O. M. Dickerson, "Stephen A. Douglas and the Split in the Democratic Party" in the *Proceedings* of the Mississippi Valley Historical Association, vii, 196.

presidency. In 1860, Lincoln delivered one of the most carefully prepared speeches of his life before an audience at the Cooper Institute in New York City and made a marked impression upon all who heard him. He then journeyed through New England to visit his son who was at school at Exeter, New Hampshire, and spoke at several places on the way.

The condition of parties in the United States in 1860 was most peculiar. The Whig party was dead, but there were still remaining many voters, North and South, who thought of themselves as Whigs and undoubtedly would have voted for Henry Clay, if they had had an opportunity. Then there were the Free-Soilers, who were not abolitionists, but disliked the idea of having colored men and women — whether slave or free — in their neighborhood. They had formed a national party, but by this time had come to realize that no party on the single issue of free-soilism could ever gain important success in national affairs. There were also the remnants of the Know-Nothing organization which had been very successful in New York and Massachusetts and had established a national organization. It went to pieces when it was seized upon by Southerners who hoped to find in it some neutral political niche where they could stand free from the slavery forces of the South and the Free Soil and abolitionist propagandists of the North. Besides there were newcomers from Germany and Scandinavia in the States west of the Appalachians and north of the Ohio. These immigrants did not know much about the colored man or slavery; but they did want cheap land and a market for the products of their farms and of their workshops. They had come to have political influence in the States of their adoption because of their numbers and because of their freedom from old political prejudices. By

1859 or 1860 the Democratic party was so broken by internal discords that it might almost be regarded as moribund, as far as national politics were concerned. By 1860, the Republicans had definitely gone away from the Douglas-ites and stood for distinctly Northern desires,[1] economically and socially, and formed, therefore — quite irrespective of the slavery issue — a sectional political party. In other words, it stood for those things that had been denied to the people of the North by the Southern rulers of the country during the half century or more that they had been in control of the Federal government.

The national convention of the Republican party was held at Chicago in the middle of May, 1860.[2] Undoubtedly there was a feeling in the air that the new organization stood a good chance of securing the control of the government and with it the offices in the departments at Washington and all over the country. It fell out, therefore, that abolitionists, like Joshua R. Giddings, Thaddeus Stevens, George William Curtis, Horace Greeley, and Eli Thayer attended. Then there were politicians, pure and simple, who saw the chance of a lifetime to get in on the political "ground floor." Most of these had no national reputation before 1860, but many of them were to gain immortality of one kind or another in the years to come. Some of them, however, were already well known, as David Wilmot and Andrew H. Reeder both of Pennsylvania, Francis P. Blair, a relic of Jacksonian days, who had deserted Democracy for Republicanism and was

---

[1] William E. Dodd, in his "Fight for the Northwest, 1860" (*American Historical Review*, xvi, 774–788), has a most interesting analysis of the political conditions prevailing in that part of the country before and during the campaign of 1860, with a suggestive map.

[2] See *Proceedings of the National Republican Convention, Held at Chicago,* *May 16th, 17th & 18th, 1860* ("Press & Tribune Documents for 1860," No. 3). The doings at Chicago, Charleston, Baltimore, and Richmond are chronicled in Murat Halstead's *Caucuses of 1860. A History of the National Political Conventions . . . Compiled from the Correspondence of the Cincinnati Commercial.*

at Chicago with his two sons, Francis P. Blair, Jr., and Montgomery Blair. Among the newer men and representing the newer elements in the population were Gustavus Koerner of Illinois and Carl Schurz of Wisconsin. The convention met in a building that had been especially constructed for the occasion to hold ten thousand persons and bore the name of "the Wigwam," and there were wide spaces about it that could accommodate eight or ten thousand more. The scenes the night before were hitherto without parallel in national party conventions, and the earlier sessions of the body itself were remarkable for indecision. For a moment it seemed as if the two-thirds rule of the Democratic party for the nomination of the presidential candidates would be adopted, — for it must be remembered that a very large and influential portion of the new party had come over from Democratic organizations.

The platform, as it was written, broke away from the issues of 1856 and, so far as slavery was concerned, confined itself to fulminating against the enlargement of the slave area. It branded the recent reopening of the African slave trade as a burning shame. The old idealism had mostly evaporated, but after a dramatic struggle, the actual words of the opening part of the second paragraph of the Declaration of Independence were inserted in the platform and the admission of Kansas as a State was demanded. The remainder of the platform had to do with things that intensely interested the rank and file of the Western members of the organization, and the voters of the two most important States in the Union, from the point of view of numbers in the electoral college — New York and Pennsylvania. For the new-comers to the Northwest, a free homestead policy and no change in the requirements of naturalization were demanded. For the Pennsylvanians, the encouragement of the industrial interests of the whole country was set forth as eminently necessary.[1] It was these clauses in "The Platform" as it was read to the delegates that aroused the most enthusiastic and the longest-continued "bursts of applause" — according to the newspaper report of the proceedings.   In addition, river and harbor improvements were advocated and the construction of a railroad to the Pacific was demanded. In short, an attempt was made to meet the wishes of all the discordant elements of the voting population of the North who were not hopelessly tied up to the Democratic party.   "Free speech, free soil, free labor, and free men" were inscribed on the Republican campaign banners.[2] When the time came to place in nomination candidates for the presidency, no less than twelve names were put forward. These were, besides Lincoln and Seward, Frémont, Sumner, Dayton, Chase, Cameron, Wade, McLean, Bates, Reed, and Collamer. To these was added on the second ballot, Cassius M. Clay of Kentucky, who received two votes. Mention of the names of Lincoln and Seward evoked "prolonged," "immense," "tremendous," "warm," and "great" applause. When the confusion began to die down, an Ohio delegate, on behalf of the delegation from that State, put in nomination — apparently for the second or third time — "the man who can split rails and maul Democrats — Abraham Lincoln." Thereupon, after great applause, Mr. Logan of Illinois moved that three cheers be given for all the candidates, but he was declared out of order and then the convention proceeded to vote. As had been

[1] This was a direct bid for the votes of the anti-Buchanan Democrats or "State Rights Democrats" as they called themselves. These had held a convention at Harrisburg on April 13, 1859, and had demanded a revision of the revenue laws to "permanently protect the labor and industry of the country."

[2] "This insulting inscription," according to Col. W. N. Bilbo in an Oration delivered at Nashville on October 12, 1861, justified the statement that the declared purpose of the North was the complete subjugation of the South.

expected, Seward received 173½ votes, Lincoln 102, Cameron of Pennsylvania 50½, and the remainder of the 465 votes were divided among the other nine nominees.

Undoubtedly the great mass of the delegates to the convention and of the lookers-on had gone to Chicago with the expectation that William H. Seward of New York would be nominated, and that without any contest. He had long been in the public eye. He had been governor of New York and had later been elected Senator and had occupied that office for a period of eleven years. By reason of his close association with Thurlow Weed, the editor of the Albany "Evening Journal," Seward was supposed to be one of the ablest political leaders in the United States, although exactly which part of any especial transaction was Seward and which was Weed might not be entirely clear.[1] In a moment of enthusiasm, Seward had trumpeted forth the alarum of the "higher law" and had rung the changes on the "irrepressible conflict." To many persons, he seemed to be the real radical leader of the country. In reality, he or Weed or both of them had made three or possibly four stupendous blunders from a political point of view. The first of these was Seward's posing or seeming to pose as a radical. The second was in 1857; when the Lecompton issue was before the people of the United States, he sat in his tent and refused to leave it to lead the people forward. Earlier in his career as governor of New York, he had espoused the cause of the Roman Catholics and had gained for them a partici-

---

[1] M. McGowen, writing from Albany in May, 1864, declared that Lincoln's honesty and Seward's lack of it led to the former's nomination at Chicago in 1860. Seward, to his mind, was an organ in the hands of the organ-grinder — Thurlow Weed. He played tunes that would pay best: "anti-mason, anti-rent, anti-temperance, anti-school system, were all used in their turns; and then, anti-slavery was to be the anti that should make him president." See also Charles F. Adams in the *Proceedings* of the Massachusetts Historical Society for December, 1872, and Charles K. Tuckerman in the *Magazine of American History*, xix, 499.

pation in the financial grants of the State and localities to public education.[1] It was an act of justice and had been done many years before, but this did not in any way redeem it or the doer in the eyes of the remnants of the Know-Nothing party which held the balance of power in two of the most important States in 1860 — Indiana and Pennsylvania. The fourth blunder was in making hopeless the political aspirations of Horace Greeley, a great newspaper editor and a man of most indefatigable energy when thoroughly aroused. As Greeley was not elected to the convention from New York, he appeared there as a delegate from Oregon. After the first ballots had been counted, Andrew G. Curtin and Henry S. Lane, the one a candidate for the governorship of Pennsylvania, the other for the governorship and senatorship of Indiana, appeared at Chicago and made it clear to many members of many delegations that an enemy of the Know-Nothings could not carry either one of those States.[2] The night between the first and second days of the convention was a busy time, indeed. The very size and exuberance of the hangers-on of the delegations that promoted Seward's interests proved to be a disadvantage. When the second ballot was taken, Seward received 184½ votes and Lincoln 181. Cameron had only two votes and his name was withdrawn by the Pennsylvania delegation. There were 465 votes in all, making 233 necessary for a choice. When the third ballot was announced, it appeared that Lincoln had 231½ votes; thereupon the chairman of the Ohio delegation arose in his place and announced the change of four votes from Salmon P. Chase to Abraham Lincoln. The applause was enthusiastic, thunderous, and deafening! When quiet was at length restored, Mr. McCrillis of Maine declaring

[1] See the present work, vol. v, 217.
[2] Editorial by Greeley: "Last Week at Chicago" in the *New York Daily Tribune*, May 22, 1860.

that "the young giant of the west has become of age," announced a change in the votes of his State from ten for Seward and six for Lincoln to 16 for Lincoln. Then the chairman of the Ohio delegation again addressed the chair and announced a change in the vote of his State to 46 for Lincoln. Finally, Mr. William M. Evarts, chairman of the New York delegation, moved that the nomination of Abraham Lincoln be made unanimous; — and this was done. After many more speeches had been made in which Seward's friends sought to explain what a great man he was and with what feelings of sadness they deserted him, Hannibal Hamlin of Maine was nominated for the vice-presidency and then, after more speeches, more resolutions, and excursions, the convention adjourned without day.

The Democrats met in convention at Charleston, South Carolina, on April 23rd and separated to come together again at Baltimore and at Richmond as separate, different, and antagonistic bodies. As a meeting full of fate for the American republic, for Northern industry, and for Southern social institutions, this Charleston Convention was without parallel in our history. There were few of the great men of the Democratic party among the three hundred and more whose names are given in its "Official Proceedings." Caleb Cushing of Massachusetts was a man of national figure and of changing faiths. He was elected presiding officer. Another Massachusetts man was Benjamin F. Butler [1] of Lowell, who signalized himself by fifty-one times casting the only vote that was given for Jefferson Davis for the office of President of the United States. Of New York's seventy delegates, hardly a name of distinction appears except that of August Belmont. Of the Southern members, the name

---

[1] For a severe arraignment of Douglas, see *Speech of Gen. Benj. F. Butler, in Lowell, August 10, 1860.*

of William L. Yancey is the only one that attracts attention. From Ohio, the names of George E. Pugh of Cincinnati and David P. Rhodes of Cleveland arrest the eye. Going back to Georgia, one comes to the name of W. B. Gaulden of Huntsville, who was said to be the largest slaveholder of his day, and from Alabama there was L. P. Walker who, before a year had passed, became Secretary of War of the Confederacy. In fact it was a meeting of men representing Southern interests and experienced party workers from the South and the North. At once friction appeared when Walker moved that it was the duty of the Federal government to afford "adequate protection and equal advantage to all descriptions of property" as well within the territories as upon the high seas and in every place subject to its legislation. This was moved as a pendant to a resolution that had been brought forward by a Pennsylvanian to the effect that citizens emigrating to "Federal Territory" retained their right to slave and other property, and that the attempted exercise of anti-slavery legislation by a territorial legislature is unconstitutional and dangerous. Other resolutions that were brought forward by other members affirmed the Cincinnati platform of 1856, approved the Dred Scott opinion, and asserted that the Republican party was organized on "strictly *sectional* principles, and its hostility to the institution of slavery, . . . is war upon the principles of the Constitution and upon the rights of the States." There were many others. They were all referred to a committee. The majority presented a report advocating the adoption of the Cincinnati platform with some alterations curbing the power of a Territory to regulate slavery. Moreover, there were resolutions demanding the protection of persons and property on the high seas and in the Territories, the acquisition of Cuba, and the building of speedy communication between the Atlantic and the Pacific coasts. A minority of the committee, including all the New England delegates, — excepting Mr. Butler of Massachusetts, — the delegates from New Jersey and Pennsylvania and all those from the Northwest, and, with conditions, those from New York resolved that the principles of the Cincinnati platform were unchangeable, but added that the questions of rights of property were judicial in their character and should be determined by the Supreme Court of the United States. They also resolved that the government should protect its citizens, provide a railroad to the Pacific coast, acquire Cuba, and that the anti-fugitive slave laws of the States were revolutionary in their effects. B. F. Butler also affirmed the Cincinnati platform with an additional resolution as to the protection of the citizens of the United States, whether native or naturalized. When the contest was at its height, William Lowndes Yancey of Alabama obtained the floor and spoke for an hour and a half.[1] He declared that the Democrats of the North had not come to the high ground that must be taken, namely, that slavery was right and must be aggressively protected. The Southerners had begun to distrust the Northern Democracy. Neither he nor his colleagues from the State of Alabama were in favor of the dissolution of the Union, but if constitutional principles as he had enunciated them did not prevail at the ballot boxes, a dissolution of the Union was inevitable. Senator Pugh of Ohio replied to him, thanking God that an honest

[1] The speech was printed in a twenty-page pamphlet, with the Alabama Protest, at Charleston in 1860. A synopsis is in Halstead's *Caucuses of 1860*, p. 48.

Benjamin F. Perry of South Carolina in an address entitled *To the Democracy of the Fifth Congressional District in South Carolina* stated the reasons why he did not go with his fellow delegates.

Some Southerners, he contended, thought that neither Congress nor the territorial legislatures could exclude slavery or impair it; others insisted that it was the duty of Congress to protect slavery in the Territories by the passage of a slave code; — and the South Carolina democracy split on this question at Charleston.

man from the South had at last spoken. The growing weakness of the Northern Democracy was due to the policy that the South had forced upon the Northern Democrats, and now they were told that they must put their hands in their mouths and their mouths in the dust. "Gentlemen of the South, you mistake us — you mistake us — we will not do it."

Precisely what occurred during the course of the joint debate between Yancey and Pugh is not stated in the official proceedings. When the convention met on the sixth day of its deliberations, the presiding officer took it upon himself to admonish the members as to the necessity of preserving order. Thereupon, the members became involved in a hopeless discussion and recommitted the whole matter to the committee on resolutions. In the evening both the majority and minority members of that committee reported. Then the convention three times refused to adjourn and finally adjourned over Sunday. When they came together on Monday morning, the presiding officer and others of the convention sought to explain away their doings on Saturday, — but without much success. The members of the convention then voted that they would do this and would not do that. Thereupon LeRoy P. Walker, chairman of the Alabama delegation, presented a written communication. In it he stated what the democracy of Alabama in State convention had resolved. As the national convention of the party at Charleston had refused to conform to the desires of the Democrats of Alabama, it became the duty of the Alabama delegation to withdraw from the convention.[1]

[1] The statement of the Alabama delegation announcing their withdrawal is on pp. 55–59 of the *Official Proceedings of the Democratic National Convention, held in 1860, at Charleston and Baltimore.* See also an article by James L. Murphy entitled "Alabama and the Charleston Convention of 1860" in *Transactions* of the Alabama Historical Society, v, 239–266. Sir Robert Lowe, afterwards Lord Sherbrooke and Chancellor of the British

The South Carolinians followed them on similar ground that the national convention had not done what the State convention demanded and so did the delegates from Mississippi, Florida, Texas, and Arkansas. The Texan delegates stated the condition succinctly and truthfully, that if the principles of the Northern Democracy are represented by a majority of the delegates from that section, "we do not hesitate to declare that their principles are not only not ours, but, if adhered to and enforced by them, will destroy this Union." It would appear, therefore, that the question as to whether it was the duty of the Federal government by legislation to protect slave property within the Territories of the United States or to leave the matter to the determination of the Supreme Court was ground for a dissolution of the Union,[1] — that active or passive adherence to the extreme demands of the slave power was the measure of one's democracy.

The Southerners having gone, the remainder of the delegates proceeded to vote for President. Among those remaining were a few from Georgia and Arkansas, and the question arose as to whether the convention could vote without the absent delegates or whether the few remaining delegates from a State could vote after the majority had retired. In the end the presiding officer decided that in order

Exchequer, who had visited the "States," set down for Sir George Cornewall Lewis in 1859 his views as to the existing American union : (1) The States were afraid of each other; (2) "They find in federation some slight counterpoise to democracy"; (3) They had free trade within themselves and protection from the outer world; (5) The South, alone, would be in a danger of a servile war; and (7) "The long rivers of America render separation difficult. The Mississippi runs through ten States." A. Patchett Martin's *Life and Letters of . . . Viscount Sherbrooke*, ii, 147, and *Letters of . . . Sir George Cornewall Lewis*, 365.

[1] Archbishop Hughes of New York in a letter to Bishop Lynch of South Carolina stated that there was a Southern conspiracy to bring about the election of Lincoln as the best means to force secession on the South. See also *Speech of Horace Maynard of Tennessee*, March 20, 1862, and Wm. D. C. Murdock's *Address to the Democratic Party* (Washington, 1864).

to secure the nomination, the candidate must receive votes equivalent in number to two-thirds of the original number of the convention. Stephen A. Douglas of Illinois, James Guthrie of Kentucky, Daniel S. Dickinson of New York, R. M. T. Hunter of Virginia, Andrew Johnson of Tennessee, and General Joseph Lane of Oregon were nominated. The vote was then taken and Douglas received 145½ votes, the remainder being scattered among the other candidates mentioned above and three more. Ballot succeeded ballot. For two days they kept on balloting, Douglas receiving from 147 to 152½ in fifty-seven ballots, needing 202 to secure the nomination under the ruling of the presiding officer, Caleb Cushing, although the remaining delegates were only 252 in number.[1] When the convention came together on the tenth day, Thursday, May 3, 1860, a motion was made that when the convention adjourned, it adjourn to reassemble at Baltimore on the 18th day of June and that the Democratic party in the several States fill the vacancies in their respective delegations; and it was so voted.

The Democratic National Convention reassembled at Baltimore on Monday, June 18, 1860, with Caleb Cushing again in the chair.[2] On opening the meeting, he directed that only the States that were present at the time of the adjournment at Charleston should be called. For the next few days, the discussion was about admitting or not admitting delegates who had been chosen since the breaking up of the convention at Charleston. A committee examined this subject and some others. It reported on June 21 and its report was ushered in by a sudden sinking of the front of the stage and orchestra, throwing the settees and their

---

[1] *Official Proceedings of the Democratic National Convention held in 1860,* pp. 72, 74 and fol., 182.

[2] The doings at Baltimore are chronicled on pp. 93–181 of the *Official Proceedings of the Democratic National Convention of 1860,* and in Halstead's *Caucuses of 1860,* p. 159.

occupants into one wedged mass, from which they extricated themselves and fled to distant parts of the house and it was an hour or two before the convention could resume its deliberations. After the disruption at Charleston, the seceders had assembled in solemn conclave and adjourned to meet at Richmond on Monday, June 11. They came together at that place at the appointed time. Mr. Erwin of Alabama was chosen as presiding officer and declared in his key-note speech that the "serpent of 'Squatter Sovereignty' must be strangled." After a little more speech making, this segmentary convention adjourned to meet again at Richmond on the 25th day of the month. Many, possibly most of the delegates at Richmond, except the South Carolinians, went to Baltimore. At all events, there were three kinds of delegates there — the regulars, who had remained faithful to the organization at Charleston, the seceders, and a third group of those who had been elected to take the places of some of the seceders. It was only after a great deal of confusion that the Charleston secessionists were kept out of the Baltimore meeting. When that had been finally achieved and the newly elected delegates had been admitted, Caleb Cushing retired and with him went another group of members including Benjamin F. Hallett,[1] Alexander Lincoln, George B. Loring, and Benjamin F. Butler. This group of seceders with some of the Charleston withdrawers met together at Baltimore with Mr. Cushing, again, as presiding officer. Besides the Massachusetts men whose names have been given, there were James Barbour, Henry P. Garnett, and R. H. Glass from Virginia, T. Butler King from Georgia,

[1] The objections to "squatter sovereignty" were admirably stated by Hallett at Boston on September 12, 1860: " a petty Legislature, the creature of Congress, . . . may intervene as a sovereign. Citizens of the South may go with their slave property into the Territories, in spite of all the power of Congress to prohibit, but the Territorial Legislature may disfranchise the slaveholder, and take away his property as soon as he gets there."

Bradley T. Johnson from Maryland, George H. Gordon, E. Barksdale, and Joseph R. Davis from Mississippi, and L. P. Walker and W. L. Yancey from Alabama. Harmony now prevailed in the two assemblies of the national Democratic Convention. The regulars nominated Douglas without any further trouble and the seceders placed before the country John C. Breckinridge, as their candidate for the presidency, and Joseph Lane of Oregon for the second office. At the end of the voting, although it was late, there was a general call for Yancey and he stepped forward in some sort as the chief architect of the ruin of the great historical Democratic party. He declared that the "storm clouds of faction have drifted away, and the sunlight of principle, under the Constitution, and of the Union under the Constitution, shines brightly upon the National Democracy." He announced that he was neither for the Union nor against the Union and that he would let Mr. Douglas rest "beneath the grave of squatter sovereignty." At eleven o'clock, the seceding convention adjourned *sine die* and on the 26th day of the month, its nominations were ratified by the South Carolinians and a few others who met at Richmond.

The National Constitutional Union Convention met at Baltimore[1] on May 7, 1860. Its members were old line Whigs and others who could not act with either portion of the Democratic party or with the conglomerate Republican organization. Among its members, one looks almost in vain for familiar names. Erastus Brooks of New York, W. G. Brownlow and H. Maynard of Tennessee, William L. Sharkey of Mississippi, Leverett Saltonstall, George S. Hillard of Massachusetts, and John M. Morehead of North Carolina are the only ones that are recognizable by the present writer. There were 254 delegates in all. Most of them

[1] Murat Halstead's *Caucuses of 1860*, pp. 104–120.

according to Murat Halstead were "eminently respectable" and most of them, also according to Halstead, were "somewhat stale in politics." They nominated John Bell of Tennessee[1] for President with Edward Everett of Massachusetts for Vice-President. The platform was of two paragraphs only and its creed was the Constitution, the Union, and the Enforcement of the Laws. The spirit of the members of the convention was exuberant and one would gather by the speeches they made that they had every reason to expect success,—whereas, in reality, they had no reason to expect anything of the kind. The ticket was known as the "Kangaroo Ticket" because the hinder part was stronger than the head, or longer, at any rate.

The presidential nominations, four in number, having been made, the campaign at once began. Lincoln stayed at home in Springfield, Illinois, receiving letters and delegations, but refusing to make speeches or to write letters except in the most general terms. Lincoln seems to have regarded himself as no abolitionist or to have seen some radical difference between an abolitionist and a Free-Soiler and to have thought that, as he did not believe Congress could constitutionally interfere with slavery in the States, the Southerners had no right to look upon him as a dangerous man. Many of his utterances on the slave question, however, had been so uncompromising that, although he constantly made this exception as to the power of Congress, Southerners were united to a man in the belief that Lincoln, if he were elected, would hem in the Slave States with free soil,— as with a wall of fire,— firm in the expectation that sooner or later, and probably sooner, slavery would perish within them. Lincoln

---

[1] G. W. Miller's speech at Indianapolis on September, 17, 1860, is a lively arraignment of *The Political Record of the Hon. John Bell* and is worth reading.

There is an article by Joshua W. Caldwell on John Bell in the *American Historical Review*, iv, 652-664.

refused to make any further statement of his views on the slavery question. He had already talked on the subject and had written many letters, "If they will not hear Moses and the Prophets, neither will they be persuaded though one rose from the dead." Naturally he did not gain one vote in the South. Whether he would have gained any if he had explained his position as fully as he might have done in reference to the statements he had made in the past may well be questioned. As a matter of fact he did not do so and was regarded by the Southerners as their uncompromising foe,— and they were right. Much as they disliked Lincoln and feared him and those about him and those working for him, the Southerners detested Douglas more. He had said over and over again that he did not care which way slavery went, whether up or down, but they could not forgive him for opposing the admission of Kansas to the Union under the Lecompton constitution. His doctrine of squatter sovereignty was worse, if possible, than Lincoln's theory that the Union must ultimately become either free or slave. He even penetrated far into the South and was heard,— but that was all. The Breckinridge people and the Bell and Everett followers made slight noise in the campaign and the Douglas Democrats did not show much enthusiasm except in a few isolated places. It was left for the Republicans, scenting offices from afar, to expend money and energy. They marched in immense torchlight processions, in uniforms with oilcloth capes to keep off the drip from the smoking, flaring lamps and wide-awake hats which protected their faces and distinguished them from the followers of other presidential aspirants. The Republican cause was fairly certain to win in the North and by reason of the preponderance of Northern electoral votes to secure the election of their candidate. The one hope of the Democrats and of the Bell and Everett men was to carry the election into Congress where it would be settled by vote of the Senators and Representatives who had been elected two or more years before. There was no irreconcilable difference between the Douglas Democrats and the Bell and Everett men. There were no Sumners and Yanceys in their ranks.[1] If they could combine and carry the vote of the State of New York, for instance, the election would be taken into the House. Many persons feared and others hoped that this would happen, but as it turned out, the diversion of three electoral votes of New Jersey from Lincoln to Douglas was the measure of success of this manœuvre.

The Republican campaigning was on two main lines. One of these was of a distinctly anti-slavery character as may be seen in a "Speech" of Carl Schurz, delivered at St. Louis on the first day of August, 1860. He declared that the discussion of what system of labor or what organization of society promotes best the moral and intellectual development of man could not be arrested. Slavery demanded the absolute ascendancy of the planting interest which was utterly incompatible with the principles upon which "the organization of free labor society" rests. The Southerners stressed the anti-slavery utterances of the Republican candidate and possibly sometimes exaggerated them. On September 4, 1860, the Honorable William B. Reed addressed the National Democratic Association at Philadelphia in the interests of Breckinridge. Lincoln's election, he asserted, would be full of evil to the Union and to Pennsylvania. Since his nomination, Lincoln had maintained a prudent silence, but earlier he had spoken out on the slavery question. On one occasion he had declared that those who denied

[1] See *Union and Republican Parties. Address of the Union Electoral Committee to the Union Men of New York.*

freedom to others deserved it not for themselves and "under a just God cannot long retain it." Again, Reed declared that Lincoln had prophesied that his friends would fight for this cause four years hence, "even stronger than you now fight for it, though I may be dead and gone." It followed, therefore, according to Reed, that if the Republicans were successful in 1860 on the somewhat temporizing platform of Chicago, they would be out and out abolitionists in 1864. Concluding, Reed pointed the moral by referring to the opposition to the return of fugitive slaves that was then manifesting itself so strongly in Wisconsin, — "And this, say what you please, is Republicanism." Toward the end of October, Samuel J. Tilden — a leading New York Democrat — in a printed letter, analyzed the aims of the Republican party.[1] He asserted that it was an organized agitation by a majority of one community against the social system of a neighbor. Seward had recently stated that the Republicans did not authorize Lincoln or Congress to vote any laws about slavery in Virginia. What Seward really taught, according to Tilden, was the doctrine of "the irrepressible conflict" which meant that the Northern States could not preserve their social and industrial system without overturning that of the South. They proposed to subvert the relations now existing between the white and black races by a combination of a majority of the people of the Northern States against the unanimous opposition of the whole people of the Southern States. In a later paragraph of the same letter, Tilden stated that the area of slave production is receding and must continue to recede. His argument was that the constantly increasing demand for cotton fibre brought about constantly increasing demand for slave labor which could not be answered but in "the slow course of

---

[1] *The Union! Its Dangers!! And How They Can Be Averted.*

nature." The price of slaves had so increased that wheat
grown by slave labor on the southern bank of the Ohio was
at least twice as costly in 1860 as in 1850, but wheat could be
produced by free labor and improved machinery on the
northern bank of the Ohio River as cheaply as it was grown
ten years before. He concluded by predicting that Lincoln's election would bring about a crisis and the South
must face the question of submission to an intolerable
policy or defeat the Republican candidate. Samuel J.
Tilden was unique as a scholarly Northern Democrat who
could write letters with as effective a sting in them as the
keenest abolition propagandist of New England and New
York. In every Southern speech, in every Southern letter,
the song was always the same, — the danger to the Southern
social system — in so far as it rested on slavery. It is interesting, therefore, to turn to campaign documents in some of
the Northern States as in Pennsylvania, and find there an
entirely different political outlook. In the "Miners' Journal," published at Pottsville in Pennsylvania, one comes
across exhortations to citizens of that town and of the county
of Schuylkill to do their duty in the coming election and
vote for the Republican candidate who stood for freedom
in the Territories, an adequate protective tariff, the "Constitution and the Union," and the supremacy of the law. A
firm, consistent, constitutional resistance to the aggressions
of slave owners would set forever at rest the agitation of
slavery issues in the republic. In another issue of the
same paper, the Republicans are described as standing for
the Union, protection, free men, free lands, while the people
on the other side stood for slavery, disunion, corruption, and
free trade. All the friends of protection and freedom and
opposed to free trade and slavery extension should vote for
the Republican candidates and make the corrupt democracy,

the destroyer of the country's prosperity, "quail before the majesty of the honest voters" of Schuylkill County.[1]

When the returns came in and were tabulated, some very interesting things were noted. Lincoln had received 180 of the 303 electoral votes and his election was, therefore, certain without any doubt or fear of constitutional contest.[2] In the popular vote, however, he had received only 1,866,452 votes as against 2,813,741 votes for his three opponents. He was a "minority" President, therefore, as had been James K. Polk, Zachary Taylor, and James Buchanan before him.[3] Except for some votes cast in the western part of Virginia — that part of the State that is now West Virginia — Lincoln received not a single vote in any of the States that seceded.[4] In the States west of the Appalachians and north of the Ohio River, Lincoln received only twelve or fifteen per cent more votes than his opponents combined. In Illinois itself, he received only 11,946 more votes than Douglas. It would seem that if the Democrats had united on one candidate and had made some slight concession on the economic issues, the election so far as it depended on that part of the country might have gone the other way. It was free land and internal improvements at public expense that turned many of the newer voters into the Republican ranks in 1860.[5] A study of the Breckinridge vote brings

[1] For these notes from the *Miners' Journal* of Pottsville, Pa., I am indebted to Mr. Morris K. Turner of Lykens, Pennsylvania.

[2] The electoral vote is taken from the *Journal of the House of Representatives*, 36th Cong., 2nd Sess., pp. 309–312.

[3] McPherson's *Hand Book of Politics for 1868*, p. 372; Greeley's *Political Text-Book for 1860*, p. 239. In 1856, Buchanan received 1,838,169 votes to 2,215,798 for Frémont and Fillmore combined. Slightly different figures are given on p. 220 of James Williams's *Rise and Fall of 'The Model Republic.'*

[4] Rhodes in his *United States* (ii, 501, note 1) gives the popular vote as compiled in Greeley's *American Conflict*, i, 328; according to this estimate Lincoln received 26,430 votes in the Slave States, which somewhat differs from the present text which gives the figures for the seceded States only.

[5] See W. E. Dodd's article on "The Southern Struggle for the Northwest" in the *American Historical Review*, xvi, 774 and compare them with the map in Logan Esarey's *Indiana*, ii, 663.

some queer surprises. In Connecticut, the aggressive slavery candidate received nearly as many votes as Stephen A.
Douglas; in Pennsylvania, an attempted fusion gave Breckinridge 178,871 votes to 268,030 for Lincoln. From a
study of some of the local returns, it would seem that many
people voted for Breckinridge, because they thought that
it was the surest way to avoid secession. South Carolina
still appointed her presidential electors by a vote of the
legislature. In the rest of the soon-to-be Confederate States
856,524 votes were cast. Of these 436,592 were given to
Breckinridge, 345,919 to Bell, and 72,084 to Douglas. The
856,524 voters elected 80 presidential electors, while
1,524,334 voters in the States of the Northwest chose only
66 electors. And it may be noted that the 1,151,618 voters
in the two States of Pennsylvania and New York in 1860
were represented in the electoral college by only 62 presidential electors, all of whom cast their votes for Abraham Lincoln. The over-representation of the Slave States had an
historic past and was one of the so-called compromises of the
Constitution. It is noteworthy, however, that in that
great instrument, the phrase is "three fifths of all other
Persons," — the word "persons" is noticeable. In 1860,
however, slaves had become property, pure and simple, but
the over-representation of the South went on and it is still
a fact that the outcome of the war and the passage of the
Thirteenth, Fourteenth, and Fifteenth amendments has
not remedied this condition of affairs; in fact it has increased
the over-representation of the white voters of the former
members of the Confederacy.

There was no question whatever as to the validity of
Lincoln's election, it was unquestioned. The only way it
could be met was by secession. At one time, Southerners
had hoped and expected that the diversity of candidates

might throw the election into Congress, in which case one
of the candidates, other than Lincoln, might be chosen.   In
any event the Southerners might have gone on governing
the country for at least two years longer if they had not
seceded.   All the estimates made at the time seem to show
that the South would have had a majority in the Senate and
in the House of the 37th Congress.   Had the Southern
Senators and Representatives remained in their places, not
one of Lincoln's appointments need have been confirmed [1]
and not a bill embodying any part of the Republican program
need have passed either House of Congress.

At once, as soon as the result of the election was known,
South Carolina and other States seceded and a cloud of compromise schemes appeared in the North.   It seemed to many
persons living within the United States at that time, that if
Bell and Everett had been elected, secession and war would
have been averted for another decade, and that if that
had been done, the North would have gained so much in
strength that the Southern States would never have seceded.
History, of course, deals only with those things that have
happened, but this belief has been so persistent that it is
well perhaps to pause a moment to consider it.   Unless all
the analyses of Southern social and economic conditions that
have been set forth in the preceding pages are wrong, it
may well be that the election of Bell and Everett would
have postponed secession and war for years and perhaps
forever.   Undoubtedly, a very large part of the support of
the Republican party came from persons who had no scruple
of conscience, but had great desire to hold public office, and

[1] See   Alexander   H.   Stephens's
"Speech against Secession" delivered
before the legislature of Georgia, November 14, 1860, in Henry Cleveland's
Alexander H. Stephens, 694–713, and
Senator Andrew Johnson in *Congressional Globe*, 36th Cong., 2nd Sess.,
Pt. 1, p. 309.   For another estimate,
see Rhodes's *United States*, ii, 501,
note 2.

presumably the number of out and out abolitionists who voted for Lincoln was small. The rest of the Lincoln voters were those who wished for a change in the economic policy of the Federal government. It would seem that if Bell and Everett had been chosen, and Lincoln, Douglas, and Breckinridge relegated to the background, no Southern State would have seceded and there would have been no war, and in the fullness of time, slavery would have yielded to the new spirit of the nineteenth century, or, at all events, to the spirit of the twentieth century. Besides, as we shall see before another hundred pages are read, the South was drawing nigh to the close of the period of cotton supremacy. In 1861, supposing there had been no Southern secession and no war, the Southern cotton crop would have been nearly unsalable and financial ruin would have overtaken many of the slave barons of Mississippi and the other Cotton States. Economic distress might have brought them possibly to a realizing sense of the archaic character of production by slave labor and might have led to a movement to replace "the institution" by white labor wherever it was feasible to do so under the existing circumstances. As events shaped themselves, two forces made any such outcome impossible,— the one was the aggressive secession desire on the part of the leaders of Southern political opinion; the other was the adamantine determination of Abraham Lincoln to yield not one jot or one tittle to the desires of the South for an extension of slave territory. He was willing to guarantee to them that Congress would not interfere with slavery in the States where it existed. That could be put into the Constitution, but that one foot more of the national territory should be devoted to slavery was impossible. As to the Southern leaders, they were few in number, they represented no great body of slave owners;

in fact there were only 384,884 slave owners in the whole country and many of these were in States that did not secede and many more were in States that had not seceded before the inauguration of the new President on March 4, 1861. But the aggressive leaders of the Southern slavocracy dominated Southern political opinion. They had brought about the existing crisis — at least so it would seem — to serve as a pretext for secession and, having succeeded in that, they were absolutely opposed to any sort of concession to the North. And they were absolutely right, if the Southern social system were to live, it must live under its own government. It was so out of tune with the opinion of mankind that it could not exist under the domination of any other rulers of the white race. It is extraordinary that any set of people should have likened themselves, as many typical Southerners did, to the lords and ladies, to the thanes and squires of the pages of Sir Walter Scott and not have realized that a mediæval state of society could not exist in the modern world. Years later, in 1877, W. L. Trenholm, a South Carolinian, describing the growth of the nineteenth century in industry and in the arts wrote that the "whirl and rush of this progress encompassed the South on every side. . . . Yet alone in all the world she stood unmoved by it; in government, in society, in employments, in labor, the states of the South, in 1860, were substantially what they had been in 1810."

NOTE

Books on Lincoln. — Up to the time of Lincoln's death his life had attracted little attention from literary men and biographers. Since then, some five thousand titles centering about Lincoln and his career have accumulated.[1] There is no satisfactory life of that God-inspired man. Ida M. Tarbell's *In the Footsteps of the Lincolns* and Nathaniel W. Stephenson's *Lincoln . . . as Revealed and Deepened by the Ordeal of War* together, form a study of Lincoln's ancestry, training, and achievement that satisfy many of the canons of modern historical writing. These books have been made possible by the productions of earlier writers, especially of Nicolay and Hay's ten volumed work entitled *Abraham Lincoln, A History*[2] and another set of twelve volumes edited by them with the title of the *Complete Works of Abraham Lincoln,* — to which should be added a volume of *Uncollected Letters,* edited by Gilbert A. Tracy, and a mass of material printed for the first time as an appendix to the second volume of the " New edition " of Miss Tarbell's *Life of Abraham Lincoln.* Few men have been more frequently pictured than the Great Emancipator. *The Photographic History of The Civil War* gives many representations of the great President and Frederick H. Meserve's *Photographs of Abraham Lincoln* (Privately Printed, New York, 1911) is a most interesting volume as showing the enigmatic character of Lincoln and Lincolniana.

[1] In 1903 a *List of Lincolniana in the Library of Congress* was printed at Washington. Three years earlier Daniel Fish published at Minneapolis a list running to 135 pages of *Lincoln Literature.* These lists supplemented by auction catalogues will give an idea of the extent and character of this bit of historical literature.

[2] Nicolay printed a *Short Life of Abraham Lincoln* in 1904 and his daughter, Helen Nicolay, published *Personal Traits of Abraham Lincoln* in 1912. In 1891, Lucius E. Chittenden published his *Recollections of President Lincoln and His Administration,* which was said to have been based on "notes" presumably made at the time. In the same year two small volumes entitled *Lincoln, His Life and Times . . . Together with His State Papers* were published. They were compiled by Henry J. Raymond, one of the leading men of the period, and are still serviceable containing, as they do, text and quoted matter in one consecutive whole.

CHAPTER X

SECESSION

THE motives and reasons that led the men and women of the South into secession are as inscrutable now as they were in 1860 and in 1861. We can understand Robert E. Lee's motive for action. He stated it in writing to his cousin Lieutenant Roger Jones of the United States army: — "I have been unable to make up my mind to raise my hand against my native State, my relatives, my children & my home." [1] These feelings impelled him to resign his commission in the United States army rather than accept the chief command of the forces that were to be used to coerce Virginia back into the Union. Thomas R. R. Cobb's actions are also comprehensible as he related them in a meeting of the General Assembly of the State of Georgia on November 12, 1860. It was then that he told the assembled legislators how on the night of the 6th of November, "I called my wife and little ones together around my family altar, and together we prayed to God to stay the wrath of our oppressors, and preserve the Union of our fathers. . . . And when the telegraph announced to me that the voice of the North proclaimed at the ballot-box that I should be a slave, I heard in the same sound, the voice of my God speaking through His

[1] For similar sentiments, see letters to his sister and to his brother, also dated April 20, in J. William Jones's *Life and Letters of Robert Edward Lee*, 133, 134. See also a letter written on January 23, 1861, in *ibid.*, p. 120. In the letter to Lieutenant Jones, Lee also stated that he sympathized with him — entirely agreed with him in his "notions of allegiance" to the Union.

256

Providence, and saying to His child, 'Be free. Be free.'"[1]
The actions of the Federal judge and the Federal Grand
Jury at Charleston in South Carolina on November 7, 1860,
are intelligible. The foreman of the jury declared that "the
verdict of the ballot-box on yesterday has swept away the
last hope for the permanence of the Federal Government of
these several States," the jury, therefore, declined to proceed with its duties and the judge, putting off his gown,
resigned his office and left the bench.[2] The twentieth
century student finds himself unable to understand how it
was that the great mass of the men and women of the South
went into the ranks of secession, body and soul, and were
accompanied by hundreds and thousands of men and women
from the Border States, from those States that never seceded
and where the pressure of slavery was slight. And this
feeling of unanimity did not die down during the years of
war and calamity, for in May, 1865, a Northern officer
stationed in Georgia, wrote to his mother in Massachusetts
that a "very great number of the officers and soldiers of the
rebel army can in no more way be considered 'led' than the
men of our army are. They have a strong personal conviction of the justice and right of their cause."[3] And as late
as the year 1874 Senator B. H. Hill of Georgia, who had
played his part as a member of the Confederate Congress
throughout a portion of the war, declared that the right to
regulate their own affairs and the conviction that independence was necessary to preserve that right were the reasons
for secession; "slavery was the particular property which,

[1] *Confederate Records of . . . Georgia*,
i, 175.

[2] W. W. Boddie's *History of Williamsburg* (Columbia, S. C., 1923), p. 340.

[3] I am indebted to my friend and
colleague, Professor James Hardy
Ropes, for a sight of the letters written
by Captain and Major John C. Gray
to his mother and sister and to John C.
Ropes, and of the letters written by
Ropes to Gray. Being very close to
what historical students call "unconscious material," these letters from two
remarkable men present a series of interesting pictures.

it was believed, was endangered without independence, and which, therefore, made the assertion of secession necessary"[1]: but, he added, it was not the great fundamental right for which the Southern States seceded.

In 1860, the great majority of the Southern people believed that the people of the North — at any rate those who had voted for the election of a "Black Republican" President — wished to annihilate them. According to the "Richmond Examiner," "every Yankee had hated every Southern citizen from the day of his birth." If the South submitted to Lincoln's election, it must be content to prepare deliberately for the abolition of slavery from Delaware to Texas. Writing at Concord, New Hampshire, Franklin Pierce, on November 23, 1860, stated that the election of Lincoln was beyond all doubt constitutional, but the people of the Southern States looked beyond to see what it implied and were amazed at the sympathy manifested for "Old Brown" which was shown by the election as governor of John A. Andrew "a man who justified the armed invasion of Virginia last year; and they believe that the people of Massachusetts are acting deliberately."[2] Parson Brownlow of Tennessee once stated that "the curse of the Country" had been the abuse of the people and the institutions of the other section by the ministers and he might have added by the newspapers. A few examples of Southern propaganda will be in place. It was in 1858 that Mary J. Windle wrote from Washington to a newspaper of Charleston, South Carolina, of which she was a regular correspondent, that the representatives of the

[1] Southern Historical Society's *Papers*, xiv, 485. See also Walter A. Montgomery in the *Fourteenth Annual Session [of the] State Literary and Historical Association* of North Carolina, p. 35: "There can be no doubt that secession was resorted to by South Carolina and the six Gulf States for the protection of slavery."

[2] *American Historical Review*, x, 365. See also the *Proceedings* of the Massachusetts Historical Society for January, 1921, p. 185, and the *Journal of the State Convention* (Jackson, Mississippi, 1861), p. 86.

North by refusing to accept the Lecompton constitution were "unanimous only in sending up as a sacrifice to heaven a dissevered Union." There were men then in Washington, — she was evidently referring to Douglas — who to gain their ends would practice "the defiance of every law, human and divine, which, in former times, filled the ice-house of Avignon with dead, and defiled the waves of the Seine with corpses."[1] Shortly after the election John M. Daniel, the owner and editor of the "Richmond Examiner," one of the noteworthy papers of that city and of the South, in an editorial stated that it made comparatively little difference whether "we are to be governed by a gentleman or ruled by a baboon. . . . But with Lincoln comes something worse than slang, rowdyism, brutality, and all moral filth; something worse than all the rag and tag of Western grog-shops and Yankee factories. . . . With all those comes the daring and reckless leader of Abolitionists."[2] This idea that the abolitionists were behind Lincoln was widely prevalent. In New Orleans, in 1860, William H. Holcombe printed a pamphlet.[3] His thesis was that separation from the Union was the only way to preserve slavery and with freedom the negro would rule the South. "When Lincoln is in place, Garrison will be in power," for opposition to slavery is the sole cohesive element of the Republicans. Nevertheless the slaveholders

---

[1] Mary J. Windle's *Life in Washington* (Philadelphia, 1859), p. 265. Jefferson Davis thought so well of Mrs. Windle that he recommended her to Ethelbert Barksdale, editor of the *Clarion* of Jackson, Mississippi. One of Mrs. Windle's Charleston employers, R. Barnwell Rhett, wrote to John Bigelow on November 14, 1860, that if a representative of the New York *Evening Post* came to South Carolina to report the proceedings of the Secession Convention, "He would come with his life in his hand, and would probably be hung." Bigelow's *Retrospections*, i, 305. For one Southerner's idea of the New Englander, see James Williams's *Rise and Fall of ' The Model Republic*,' 75–77, reprinted with remarks by General Charles F. Adams in the *Proceedings* of the Massachusetts Historical Society for May, 1906, p. 254.

[2] *The Richmond Examiner During the War* (New York, 1868), p. 6.

[3] *The Alternative: A Separate Nationality, or the Africanization of the South* (New Orleans, 1860), pp. 1, 3, 15.

would carry out the designs of Providence and establish
"a vast, opulent, happy and glorious slave-holding Republic,
throughout tropical America — future generations will arise
and call us blessed!" This picture of a slave empire or
republic extending from Mount Vernon on the Potomac to
the "Palaces of the Montezumas" within sight of the
mighty Popocatepetl comes again and again before one's
eyes in Southern books.[1] As an independent nation, according to Senator Hammond of South Carolina, the South
would have no need for an army or a navy, for " Cotton
is king." In the South, the slaves, in the North, the wage
earners constitute "the very mudsills of society."[2] Two
years later, in February, 1862, Governor Brown of
Georgia[3] asserted that secession was due to the "outrageous
usurpations of power and aggressions upon our rights
committed by the Federal Government, and the absolute
degradation to which the Southern people were exposed if
they submitted to the rule of Mr. Lincoln, who was elevated to power by the abolitionists and protectionists of
the North." Later on, Brown completely lost himself in
a maze of words, declaring that the South "threw off the
yoke of bondage" and refused to be "hewers of wood and
drawers of water" for a haughty and insolent people.[4]

[1] For Buchanan's proposed intervention in Mexico, see article by H. L.
Wilson in *American Historical Review*,
v, 687.

[2] *Congressional Globe*, 35th Cong., 1st
Sess., Pt. i, pp. 961, 962. *Selections
from the Letters and Speeches of the Hon.
James H. Hammond* (New York, 1866).
Hammond's *Speech* delivered at Barnwell Court House, October 29, 1858,
was printed in pamphlet form and
deserves perusal by all students of this
period.

[3] *Official Records*, ser. iv, vol. i, p.
918. This vehemence of language was
not curbed by the chastening influences
of war and disaster. In January, 1864,

Benjamin wrote to his old friend and
compatriot of Plaquemine Parish that
no "crime is too revolting for this vile
race, [the Yankee] which disgraces
civilization and causes one to blush for
our common humanity." Benjamin
had no doubt that hundreds of thousands of people at the North would
take "fiendish delight" in a universal
massacre of the Southern people in one
night. They could then exterminate
the blacks and "become owners of the
property which they covet and for
which they are fighting." Bigelow's
Retrospections, ii, 122.

[4] Robert Toombs's ideas as to the
reason for secession come out in "A Re-

Southern ministers felt the same thrill of fear and indignation. In 1862, the Reverend J. H. Thornwell of
Columbia, South Carolina, asserted [1] that the Southerners
were struggling for constitutional freedom, they were
not revolutionists, they were resisting revolution: "Our
fields, our homes, our firesides and sepulchres, our cities and
temples, our wives and daughters, we must protect at every
hazard." The secession conventions held the same tone.
The preamble of the Alabama Ordinance of Secession declared that [2] the election of Lincoln "by a sectional party
avowedly hostile to the domestic institutions and peace and
security of the people of the State of Alabama" is a political
wrong of "so insulting and menacing a character" as to
justify secession. And the Confederate Congress itself in
an "Address . . . to the People of the Confederate States"
asserted that "Compelled by a long series of oppressive and
tyrannical acts, culminating at last in the selection of a
President and Vice-President by a party confessedly sectional and hostile to the South and her institutions these
States withdrew" from the Union.

At the risk of piling Pelion on Ossa, it might be well,
perhaps, to reënforce the lessons taught in the preceding
paragraphs by some further statements by Southerners at
the time, of the reasons that led them to risk their all in an
attempt to secure their independence. The first of these
is in the shape of resolutions that were adopted by the Mississippi legislature in 1860. According to these, the Constitution of the United States recognized property in slaves and
the election of a President by the voters of one section on the
ground of "an irreconcilable conflict between the two sec-

port" that was presented to the Georgia
Convention on January 29, 1861.
Journal of the Georgia Convention, 104–
113.

[1] *Our Danger and Our Duty*, 5, 6.
[2] *Journal of the Congress of the Confederate States*, i, 8.

tions, in reference to their respective systems of labor" justifies the slaveholding States in separation.[1] The next year the Mississippi State Convention issued "A Declaration of the Immediate Causes which Induce and Justify the Secession of the State of Mississippi from the Federal Union." [2] In this document, they affirmed that their action is "thoroughly identified with the institution of slavery," for a blow at slavery is a blow at civilization and, as it was on the point of reaching its consummation, Mississippians must either submit to the "mandates of abolition" or secede from the Union. They give no less than seventeen "unquestionable facts" to justify their action for "utter subjugation awaits us in the Union" with a "loss of property worth four billions of money." Some of these points are amplified in an address which was made by a Commissioner from Mississippi to the State of Tennessee in January, 1861. In it he asserted[3] that it was the unappeasable hatred which the party behind Lincoln had ever cherished for slavery and slaveholders that justifies secession and, should it cost every drop of blood and every cent of money, Mississippi would never submit. Governor Moore of Alabama, after a little incitement by ardent secessionists issued an address[4] which well displayed the spirit of the time and place. The Black Republicans had controlled nearly every one of the non-slaveholding States for years. They had nullified the Fugitive Slave law, they had robbed the South of slaves worth millions of dollars, and had threatened pursuers of fugitive slaves with the penitentiary. They had invaded the State of Virginia and had sent emissaries into Texas who had "burned many towns,

[1] "Jefferson Davis Mss." in the Library of Congress.
[2] *Journal of the State Convention* (Jackson, Miss., 1861), pp. 86–88.
[3] *Journal of the State Convention* (Jackson, Miss., 1861), p. 152 and fol., and see also Mississippi Historical Society's *Publications*, vi, 91.
[4] William R. Smith's *History . . . of the Convention . . . of Alabama*, 14.

and furnished the slaves with deadly poison for the purpose of destroying their owners." Governor Moore then took the rôle of seer and prophesied that when the Republicans were fully successful they would alter the Constitution. Then the "irrepressible conflict" would end, for the South had been notified that it would never stop until "the foot of the slave shall cease to tread the soil of the United States." John H. Reagan visited Sam Houston,[1] the hero of San Jacinto, who was then governor of Texas and was opposed to secession. He told Reagan that "the people are going to war on the question of slavery, and the firing of the first gun will sound the knell of slavery." Another Texan, a clergyman, said that like Ephraim of old, the Texans had fed on wind, when they had no time to waste. The men who had elected Lincoln were those from whom had gone up a "frantic, furious cry" for an anti-slavery constitution, Supreme Court, Bible, and God. They were the fathers and feeders of the whole anti-slavery war. If you anger them they will, if they can, overwhelm you with destructive lava "hot as the hellish passions of their own black hearts, foul as streams from the sewers of Pandemonium." The Southerners were born to "freedom and equality." Shall Texas hold her property and the lives of her citizens "at the mercy of such caitiffs, or receive them as her superiors? or the man of their choice — the embodiment of all their fanatical malignity, the representative of all their enmity — as our Chief Magistrate? No!" [2]

It is a relief to turn from these Southern contemporaneous diatribes to some remarks made after the war by Charles O'Connor, one of the leading Democrats of New York. He declared that secession was a tactical error. Instead of

[1] *Memoirs, with Special Reference to Secession and the Civil War* (New York, 1906), p. 105.

[2] James C. Wilson's *Address Delivered in Gonzales, Texas, November 17, 1860.*

seceding, the Southerners should have retained possession
of Maryland and of Washington and maintained relations
with European powers; in that case the Northerners would
have been forced to attack and the Southerners would have
won the day. In 1887, Henry R. Jackson of Georgia [1]
asserted that the secessionists had their rights as tenants
in common to the flag, to the army and navy, and to all the
property of the United States and they had relinquished
them all. They had asked for the right to carry their property into the Territories and by secession had abandoned
forever all vestige of right to those Territories and had faced
the appalling danger of defending on the field of battle the
only right they did not surrender — the right to govern
themselves. But it must be said that there was a widespread
belief in the South that secession would be peaceable.[2]

The great mass of the white inhabitants of the Cotton
States sincerely believed that they were in danger of persecution and of disaster and that their "honor" demanded

[1] *Letter from Henry R. Jackson . . .
with Explanatory Papers*, 15. See also
"Address" of Hon. Charles J. Jenkins
printed in the report of a *Public Meeting
of the Citizens of Richmond County
[Georgia], December 24th, 1860*. In 1862,
in a letter vindicating his refusal to follow his State into secession, the Hon.
Joseph Segar pointed out that all the
fifteen Slave States lost 803 slaves in the
year 1860 valued at from four hundred
thousand dollars to eight hundred
thousand; in November, 1861, one
Virginia county alone lost one thousand
slaves worth five hundred thousand
dollars.

[2] In February, 1861, Thomas R. R.
Cobb was in Montgomery as a member
of the committee that was engaged in
preparing a constitution for the Confederacy. On the 8th day of the month,
he wrote to his wife in Georgia: "The
news from So. Car. to-day indicates a
little more chance for war, but it will be
a small matter." Southern History

Association's *Publications*, ix, 275. On
the 15th, he wrote again (*ibid.*, ix, 279):
"The almost universal belief here is
that we shall *not have war*." As is well
known the Confederate Congress, when
it met, provided that the postal officials
of the Confederacy should render their
accounts to the United States until the
close of the financial year in June, 1861.
See *ibid.*, vi, 314; *American Historical
Review*, xii, 66–74; and John H.
Reagan's *Memoirs*, 132.

It is interesting to note also that
when the Confederate agents, Yancey,
Mann, and Rost, reached London in
May and June, 1861, they used the
United States legation at Westminster
in order to get in touch with one an-
other. And another Confederate agent,
early in July, applied to the legation for
Mann's address. See "Diary of Ben-
jamin Moran" in *Proceedings* of the
Massachusetts Historical Society for
May, 1915, p. 441 and note 2.

independence. For three-quarters of a century, they had exercised power out of all proportion to their numbers as the original price of their coöperation in the government. In 1860, the fifteen Slave States put together contained about eight millions of white people and the State of New York about four millions, but the Slave States had thirty Senators to speak for them and the people of New York only two. The people of the three coterminous States of New York, Pennsylvania, and Ohio, with a greater population than the fifteen Slave States put together, had only six Senators combined. Moreover, the working of the "federal ratio" gave the Slave States ninety Representatives and one hundred and twenty electoral votes, while the State of New York had only thirty-three Representatives and thirty-five electoral votes.[1] So rapidly were the Northern States growing, that it was a question of no long time, when they would overbalance the South — "federal ratio" and all — in Congress and in the electoral college.[2] It was Jefferson Davis, in 1864, who informed two Northern emissaries that the Southerners had seceded "to rid themselves of the rule of the majority."[3]

For generations, the Southerners had filled the departments at Washington and had occupied most of the offices in the army and navy and in the diplomatic and scientific services. The triumph of the Republican party of the North meant a distinct economic loss to many a Southern family and a distinct social loss to many a Southern woman. For years, Washington had been a Southern town, — "an

---

[1] *Arguments and Speeches of William Maxwell Evarts*, i, 191.

[2] In 1840, the Free States had 168 electoral votes to 126 for the Slave States, including Maryland and Missouri; in 1860, the Free States had 183 electoral votes, the Slave States 120.

See *Journal of the House of Representatives*, 26th Cong., 2nd Sess., pp. 251–254 and Daniel W. Howe's *Political History of Secession*, 401–404.

[3] Nicolay and Hay's *Abraham Lincoln*, viii, 210.

overgrown tattered village which some late hurricane had
scattered along the river's edge."[1]   Southerners had given
the tone to whatever society there had been at the capital.
Now, they would have to forego the salaries that came from
the departments, abandon their Washington houses, and
retire to their plantations.   Not only this, they would have
to realize that Northerners were sitting at their desks, drawing the salaries that they had drawn, and, so far as the
"mongrel" Yankees were capable of it, leading the society
of the capital, and, worst of all, governing the nation and the
Southerners, too.   Gideon Welles, who had been a Democrat, but was one no longer, wrote in his "Diary"[2] that he
thought that Calhoun's real aim was to secure special privileges for the South, "something that should secure perpetuity
to the social and industrial system of that section."   It was
the lesser men, according to Welles, — "the shallow political
writers and small speechmakers" who advocated disunion,
which they thought would enrich the South and impoverish
the North and would enable them to dictate to the country
and to the world.   Admiral David D. Porter compiled a book
entitled "Incidents and Anecdotes of the Civil War."   The
stories related in it undoubtedly were written long after the
events, but as Porter had known a great deal of the South
and of Southerners, he was capable of understanding what
he saw and heard.   He relates that on the night when the
news of the secession of South Carolina reached Washington,
he escorted a Southern lady to the White House, whither
she was going "to tell the President the good news."   She
told Porter, so he wrote, that the Southern people could not
be berated by the Black Republicans and would take refuge
in a monarchy.[3]   On a later page, he asserted that if the

[1] Columbia Historical Society's *Records*, v, 195.
[2] *Diary of Gideon Welles*, i, 377.

[3] The idea that Southern secessionists
would have welcomed a monarchy was
widespread; but there is little evidence

Southerners had been given "fat" offices they would have stuck to the flag until it blew away; but when it came to giving up offices, they determined to secede and to establish an office for each one of themselves. Porter's language is undoubtedly overdrawn and his statements of fact reflect the recollections of an old man; but his description states with a fair degree of accuracy the actualities of the situation which Jefferson Davis, when he became President of the Confederate States, found to his cost.

The secession sentiment was strongest in the Cotton States and diminished in intensity as one proceeded northward, except among the old tobacco-growing aristocracy of Virginia. In Alabama, it is true, there was a distinct line of cleavage extending lengthwise of the State from the Tennessee River to the Gulf and there were men of mark and influence in the Cotton States who doubted the expediency of secession at that time and some of them questioned the validity of the reason generally assigned by ardent disunionists. Jefferson Davis himself was a conservative by inclination and seems to have been forced into the leading place by the feeling that his own political fortunes depended upon it. In 1858, he spent some time in the North with Mrs. Davis, partly on account of her health, and was impressed by the general fairness to the South of the people with whom he associated.[1]

to be found justifying this belief. On January 10, 1861, Senator Alfred Iverson of Georgia declared that "there is not one man in a million, as far as I know and believe, in the State of Georgia, or elsewhere in the South, who would be in favor of any such principle." *Congressional Globe*, 36th Cong., 2nd Sess., Pt. i, p. 311.

[1] Davis, writing to Franklin Pierce from Washington on January 17, 1859, stated that his northern tour had convinced him "that temperate, true men could effect much by giving to the opposite section the views held by the other. The difference is less than I had supposed," *American Historical Review*, x, 360. Davis's New England speeches and the one which he felt it necessary to deliver before the Mississippi legislature upon his return home were printed at Baltimore in 1859 in a 56-page pamphlet entitled *Speeches of the Hon. Jefferson Davis, . . . during the Summer of 1858*. They may be more easily found in Rowland's *Jefferson Davis*, iii, 271–360.

Alexander H. Stephens, one of the three leading men of Georgia, made a speech to the Secession Convention of that State in January, 1861. He declared that Georgia should not "take the extreme step before some positive aggression upon our rights by the general government." He was opposed to secession as a remedy against "anticipated aggressions" and his judgment was against the policy of immediate secession for "any existing causes." [1] A wave of political hysteria swept over the Far Southern States and carried into the ranks of secession thousands of men who had opposed disunion up to that time and, within a few weeks, Davis and Stephens had accepted the two highest political offices in the new Confederacy.

One of the distinctive lines of thought that separated the North and the South was on the question of the constitutional position of the States within the Union. In the North, the general opinion was that the Union was sovereign and the States part of it. In an earlier time, some of the original Northern members of the Union under the Constitution had regarded themselves as entitled at any time to take back powers that they had delegated to the general government. The resolutions of the Hartford Convention are directly to this point. The economic inter-dependence of the Northeast and the Northwest and the extremely profitable relations that existed between the manufacturing

---

[1] Louis Pendleton's *Alexander H. Stephens*, 180; Johnston and Browne's *Stephens*, 380. The speech was printed at the time in a thin pamphlet. While a prisoner at Fort Warren in Boston Harbor, after the war, Stephens kept a journal or diary. As he was then expecting to die within any twenty-four hours, this manuscript may be supposed to contain his convictions. It was printed in 1910 with other matter in a volume entitled *Recollections of Alexander H. Stephens . . . and Some Letters and Reminiscences* with a biographical study by Myrta L. Avary. After his release from prison, Stephens set to work to justify his doings and those of his comrades in secession by writing *A Constitutional View of the Late War Between The States* (2 vols., 1868, 1870). It aroused so many animadversions that Stephens in 1872 produced another volume entitled *The Reviewers Reviewed: A Supplement to the "War Between The States."*

and commercial parts of the Northeastern States and the
slaveholders of the South had combined to bring about a
change in the constitutional ideas of the people of the North
which had found expression in Daniel Webster's famous
speeches in reply to Hayne and to Calhoun. The idea that
the people of the United States formed one nation had been
powerfully reinforced by the coming of the immigrant from
abroad. These people had no conception of a "State" or
sentimental attachment to a "State." They had come to
America to better their condition or to gain political freedom,
and sometimes from a combined motive to achieve both of
these objects; and some of them had come to the United
States because here they could enunciate opinions on religion
and on government as they could not in the old homes.
Whatever reasons impelled their migration, they came to
The United States and looked upon it as their adopted
country. In the North, even in 1860, there were to be found
many people who still looked upon their State, the State of
their birth and their nurture, as the entity to which they
owed their allegiance, and, indeed, in 1857, as we have already seen, a movement for secession had been started
in Massachusetts, itself. Furthermore, in the eyes of
many men and women, who were not abolitionists, technically speaking at any rate, the idea of an indefinite
continued connection with slaveholders was displeasing,
but, probably, this would not have taken the form of any
concerted measure of withdrawal from the Union. Speaking roughly and at hazard, it may be stated that the
great majority of the people of the North believed that
they owed their duty first to the Union and secondly to their
State.

In the South, the consensus of constitutional opinion was
entirely unlike that which has been described as the prevalent

idea that was held by the people of the North.[1] In the South, or perhaps one might better say, in the South of the coastal plain every white boy and girl grew up to regard himself or herself as born into the service of his or her State and as owing, not merely allegiance, but devotion and life itself to her protection and to the furtherance of her wellbeing. The only feeling of solidarity that comes out in the writings of Southern people, in the generation before 1860, is that of the community of interest of the slaveholding aristocracy and their white neighbors.[2]

The first State to take the fateful step of secession was South Carolina. And this was fitting, for that State for a generation had been on the verge of separation more or less complete. On Monday, December 17, 1860, the South Carolina Convention of the People met in the Baptist Church in the town of Columbia.[3] Mr. D. F. Jamison, a delegate from Barnwell and the author of a life of Bertrand Du

---

[1] William H. Trescot (*Memorial of . . . J. Johnston Pettigrew*, p. 8) thus stated the Southern idea: "The existence of large hereditary estates, the transmission from generation to generation of social and political consideration, the institution of slavery, creating of the whole white race a privileged class, through whom the pride and power of its highest representatives were naturally diffused, all contributed to give a peculiarly personal and family feeling to the ordinary relation of citizen to the Commonwealth." It followed, therefore, when the State seceded "the question of duty was settled for Southern men." On the other hand, Major Robert Anderson's wife wrote on February 7, 1861, that she had "no faith in those people [the South Carolinians], after all their broken pledges, their false dealings, and the lies they have promulated about you and your garrison."

[2] A Southern book that had great vogue in the South just before the war was E. N. Elliott's *Cotton is King, and Pro-Slavery Arguments* (Augusta, Ga., 1860).

The condition of Southern sentiment in 1861 may be obtained by reading the "Letters to Secretary Chase from the South" which Albert Bushnell Hart contributed to the *American Historical Review*, iv, 332–347.

[3] *Journal of the Convention of the People of South Carolina* (Charleston, 1861) pp. 3–5. The next day, December 18, the Convention met at Charleston where it carried on its business and adopted the famous ordinance of secession. In 1862, another edition of this *Journal* was printed at Columbia, together with the journal of the subsequent sessions of the Convention and an appendix of nearly 400 pages containing documents of various kinds and of great interest, from the declaration of the immediate causes which justified the secession of South Carolina to the "Report of the Chief of the Department of the Military."

Guesclin, took the chair and in his speech of acceptance
stated the case for South Carolina — and for the rest of the
seceding States — as well as it ever was stated. He declared that it was the fixed determination of the members
of the Convention to throw off the yoke of the Federal
government and to provide new safeguards for their security.
There were two dangers to fear : overtures from without, and
precipitation from within. The door was forever closed to
all further connection with "our Northern confederates," for
they could offer no new guarantees. And then he went on
with the regular list of the sinful doings of the Northerners :
placing the burden of support of the government on the
industry of the South, showering Congress with abolition
petitions, and exposing the Southern settlers of Kansas to the
emissaries of Emigrant Aid Societies armed with Sharps
rifles and Colt's revolvers "to swell the butchery of Southern
men." He asserted that the Constitution had been trodden
under foot by the Northern States, that there was no common
bond of interest between the North and the South and all
efforts to preserve the Union would be fruitless. As the smallpox was then raging in Columbia, the Convention adjourned
to Charleston, where it speedily adopted the famous Ordinance of Secession that was signed by all the members of the
Convention. This body had been set up by the legislature
without any special election and this was the ordinary mode
of procedure in the Cotton States. There was, in truth, no
need of a special mandate from the voters, for the secessionists were so active and so much better organized than the
Union men, in those States, and had so much more effective
control of "public opinion" that their opponents generally
bowed to the inevitable and gave their votes with the secessionists. Most of the conventions appointed commissioners
to go to the other States, report what their own State had

done and do what they could to convince the legislatures and the politicians of the backward States of the necessity of immediate and radical action. Of the first group of seceding States, Louisiana and Texas submitted the question of secession to the voters. In Georgia, several leading men opposed the movement,[1] but when the tide of public opinion rose high, they turned about and took their places in the front rank of secession. One of these, Howell Cobb, in taking the chair of the Provisional Congress of the Confederacy declared that it was a meeting of "sovereign and independent States, who by their solemn judgment have dissolved the political association which connected them with the Government of the United States."[2]

Seven States having seceded, a meeting of delegates was held at Montgomery, the capital of Alabama, in February, 1861.[3] They formed themselves into a deliberative body and proceeded to adopt a fundamental law for the Confederacy.[4] The need seems to have been urgent or to have appeared urgent to the committee and the Convention, for no attempt

[1] *Journal . . . of the Convention of the People of Georgia* (Milledgeville, Ga., 1861), p. 20.

[2] *Journal of the Congress of the Confederate States of America*, i, 16.

[3] There is some uncertainty as to the summoning of the Montgomery Convention, see *Journal of the Convention of the People of South Carolina* (Columbia, S. C., 1862), p. 169; *Journal of the Congress of the Confederate States of America*, i, 9 and an article by A. J. Gerson in *Report* of American Historical Association for 1910, p. 181. E. A. Pollard's *Echoes from the South* (New York, 1866) contains ordinances of secession, the Constitution of the Confederate States, and sundry addresses and speeches conveniently between two covers. The Constitutions of the United States and of the Confederate States are printed in parallel columns in Jabez L. M. Curry's *Civil History of the Government of the Con-*

federate States (Richmond, 1901). The provisional and permanent constitutions of the Confederate States are printed in the *Statutes at Large of the Provisional Government of the Confederate States of America* that was edited by James M. Matthews and printed at Richmond in 1864. They were also printed separately at Montgomery and at Richmond in 1861. Douglas S. Freeman has enumerated the official publications of the Confederate government on pp. 502–506 of his *Calendar of Confederate Papers* (Richmond, 1908).

Interesting letters from Thomas R. R. Cobb of Georgia to his wife are dated Montgomery, February, 1861 (Southern History Association's *Publications*, xi, 147–185).

[4] A. L. Hull's "The Making of the Confederate Constitution" in Southern History Association's *Publications*, ix, 272–292.

was made to adjust the new fundamental law to the extraordinary conditions of a Confederacy where each State was sovereign when it went into it, remained sovereign after it got in, and established a government that necessarily possessed some of the elements of sovereignty itself. The most notable departure from the organic law of the old United States was that there was no adequate provision in the new constitution for a separate and distinct Supreme Court, which was the most outstanding feature of the organic law drawn up by Hamilton, Madison, Gouverneur Morris, and their co-workers. Furthermore, the power of the executive branch as compared with the legislative branch was augmented by providing that the President of the new Confederacy might veto separate items in appropriation bills. There were also some other provisions that would make it impossible for the President and Congress of this new Confederacy to do those things that the South had so bitterly complained of in the old Union. Possibly the most interesting provision in this constitution was the preservation intact of the "federal ratio." This gave to those States of the Confederacy that possessed many slaves in proportion to the whole population, as Alabama and Mississippi, a distinct preponderance in the councils of the new government, out of proportion to their white population or to the votes cast. Another feature that strikes the eye of the student is the provision prohibiting the reopening of the African slave trade.[1] As we have very slight means of forming an opinion

[1] It is worth noting that the Georgia Convention itself adopted all the existing Federal laws relating to the inter-State slave trade, but substituted imprisonment for from five to twenty years for the death penalty provided in the United States law and that no slave shall be received who had been imported "from beyond sea" since December 20, 1860. *Journal of the . . . Convention . . . of Georgia*, 59, 60. On January 26, 1861, the Mississippi State Convention (*Journal*, p. 78) resolved that it was not "the purpose or policy of the people of the State . . . to reopen the African slave trade." When the Confederate constitution reached South Carolina, L. W. Spratt,

as to the reason for including or excluding anything from this
constitution, we can only surmise that this prohibition was
placed in the new organic law to make easier the recognition
of the Confederacy by England and by France, the two
countries that had been most ardent in the attempts to suppress the African slave trade; and it is possible that it was
put in in the hope that it would attract the slave exporting
States to the northward to join the new Confederacy. This
first constitution was to be provisional and the President
and Congress, appointed under it, were to remain in power
only until the spring of 1862.

It is exceedingly difficult to comprehend what the secession
leaders and the people of the first group of seceding States
thought their relations to the new government and to one
another would be. The South Carolina Convention, that
adopted the secession ordinance, following the example of
some of the revolutionary bodies of 1775, did not adjourn
but remained in existence and generally in session for over a
year.[1] It proceeded to establish a complete government for
South Carolina with an army and officials and everything
that pointed to an active, continuing, constitutional life as a
national entity.[2] When the provisional constitution of the

who had ardently advocated the reopening of the African slave trade (ante, p.
213) said that no one who looked upon
the slave trade as wrong could be a firm
believer in slavery, that the prohibition
was "a great calamity" and that a new
irrepressible conflict was sure to rise.
John Bigelow's *Retrospections*, ii, 41.
On April 5, 1861, the South Carolina
Convention proposed to amend the Confederate constitution to make the slave
trade prohibition "elastic" and to
prohibit the admission of any State to
the Confederacy in which "African
slavery does not, by law, exist." *Journal*, 539.

[1] See the *Journal of the Convention of
the People of South Carolina, Held in*

1860, 1861 and 1862 (Columbia, S. C.,
1862). It is noticeable that on December 24, 1860, a prominent citizen
addressed a letter to the "Convention
of the Independent State of South
Carolina," p. 81; and this form was not
uncommon. An "Address of the People of South Carolina, Assembled in
Convention, to the People of the Slaveholding States of the United States"
was adopted on December 22, 1860.
It is printed on pp. 467–476 of the above
and fifteen thousand copies were printed
and distributed in pamphlet form at the
time.

[2] *The Journal of the . . . Convention
. . . of Georgia* (1861), p. 43, contains
resolutions that recited the reasons that

Confederacy appeared the majority of the South Carolina
Convention did not take altogether kindly to it. They at
once drew up a series of proposed amendments to the new
organic law, which would provide for the reopening of the
African slave trade and would forbid the membership of
any non-slaveholding State within the new organization.
But events marched too rapidly. It soon became evident
that it would be well to postpone any revision of the new
Confederate organic law until the government became better
established and in no long time the opposition to the existing
order of things within the Confederacy was transferred from
the South Carolina Convention at Columbia to the Confederate Congress at Richmond.

Around the election of a President for the new provisional
government, there is likewise a dense cloud of uncertainty.
It would seem that the most logical candidate would have
been one of the leaders of the secession movement : — William
Lowndes Yancey, Barnwell Rhett, Robert Toombs, or
Howell Cobb, or even the veteran statesman of Georgia,
Alexander H. Stephens. Instead of taking any one of these,
the members of the Convention with a considerable degree
of activity selected Jefferson Davis of Mississippi, who, up
to that time, had been looked upon rather as a conservative.
It cannot be said that Davis disapproved of secession,
ultimately, or even at the moment when it occurred; but
he apparently took no leading part in bringing about the
actual separation at the time and in the precise mode that
was adopted. It appears also that he, himself, would have
preferred the leadership of the military forces of the new

---

impelled the State of Georgia to resume
her sovereignty and independence.
Subsequent resolutions, that were not
adopted, declared that Georgia would
not tolerate any interference with her
rights under "the Laws of Nations" and
authorized the governor to issue Letters
of Marque and Reprisal, *ibid.*, pp. 103,
280.

government.[1] Edward A. Pollard, a newspaper man of
Richmond, who wrote several books on the Confederacy, in
a memoir of Jefferson Davis that was published in 1869,
set forth the theory that the whole course of secession, constitution making, and election of President was "managed"
by a small coterie of Southern Congressmen of whom the
leader was Davis himself, first at Washington, then at
Montgomery.[2] It may well have been so, because the
movement was very well organized and prosecuted. But
nothing that can be called evidence has been brought forward so far that would justify any such theory. A study of
all available material would seem to point to the conclusion
that the movement was rather the culmination of a long
series of dissatisfactions and was promoted by persons who
were exceedingly well qualified to stir up dissensions and
organize revolutions. When the Secessionists came to
Montgomery and faced the absolute necessity of at once
establishing a governmental organization, they naturally
based it on the Constitution of the United States to which,
for the most part, they had no objection whatever. In point
of fact the burden of their song had been the violation of
that Constitution by the people of the North. When they
came to look about for a chief magistrate, they undoubtedly
canvassed the merits of several leading men. The ablest of
these was Robert Toombs of Georgia. He had served his
State faithfully and well at Washington, was a master of
finance, and a man of courage and conviction; but he had
infirmities of character and habits that, at this point of time,
seem to have made impossible his appointment as chief

[1] Also it is interesting to note in this
connection that Governor Pickens of
South Carolina on January 23rd wrote
to Davis that as soon as the States could
meet at Mongomery they should elect
Davis Commander-in-Chief of the Confederate forces. The selection of the
civil officers was of not so much consequence. Rowland's *Jefferson Davis*,
v, 45.

[2] *Life of Jefferson Davis, with a Secret
History*, chs. iii and vi.

executive of any government. Howell Cobb and Robert
Toombs and Alexander H. Stephens, all of Georgia, were
considered. The story is that caucuses were held at which
Jefferson Davis's name was brought forward and that the
Georgians, thinking that they had the office securely within
their grasp, were slow in taking definite action, with the result
that Davis was nominated and elected.

Among the leading men of the first group of the Confederate States, there was no one better qualified for the
presidency than Jefferson Davis. For years he had been
a close student of affairs and he possessed a fine mind that
had been well trained and was stored with facts.[1] He had
had administrative experience, at first as an army officer and,
later, as Secretary of War at Washington. In this position,
he had shown himself to be an excellent administrator and a
good judge of fit men to employ for the work he wanted done.
He also was an excellent public speaker. The two factors
that worked against him so far as he himself was concerned
were his chronic ill-health and his knowledge of the art and
practice of war. It may possibly be that the presumed
pacific outlook of the new government was what induced the
members of the Convention to offer a civil place to Davis and
induced him to accept it. The feelings of the Georgia delegation were somewhat salved by the election of Stephens to
the office of Vice-President.

---

[1] Mrs. Jefferson Davis's *Memoir* of
her husband (2 vols., New York, 1890)
and Davis's own books, the *Rise and
Fall of the Confererate Government* and
A Short History of the Confederate States,
give the modern student little satisfying
information. Frank H. Alfriend's and
Edward A. Pollard's books on Davis
view his career from two very different
angles. Of the smaller books, those by
William E. Dodd, Armistead Gordon,
and H. J. Eckenrode give interesting
and varied views of the Confederate
President; and Nathaniel W. Stephenson's *The Day of the Confederacy* is, in a
measure, a review of the great period
of Davis's career. Stephenson's "A
Theory of Jefferson Davis" in *American
Historical Review*, xxi, 73–90 and Walter
L. Fleming's "Early Life of Jefferson
Davis" in the Mississippi Valley
Historical Association's *Proceedings* for
1915–1916, pp. 151–176, give one a
somewhat different point of view.

Davis had scarcely read his Inaugural Address, than difficulties opened before him. It would seem that every leading man in the South expected to have one of the principal offices in the new government. One of the first to state his desire was Barnwell Rhett, who appears to have had the Secretaryship of State in mind, but who would have been content with one of the two important ambassadorships to European powers. No offer of any kind was made to him and within a few months, the editorials of the "Charleston Mercury" were as vehement and as picturesque in denunciation of the Davis government as they had ever been of any of the Washington administrations.[1] Yancey was sent to Europe as head of a mission to secure recognition of the Confederacy. Within a year, he was at home again having utterly failed in this endeavor. He speedily lost confidence in Davis and died in 1863 — a disillusioned man.[2] Toombs was appointed Secretary of State, but within three months, he had quarrelled hopelessly with his chief and had received a commission as brigadier general in the army. There he endeavored to enlighten his superiors as to the method of making war and resigned to seek the seclusion of his Georgia home. In point of fact there were too many able men within the Confederacy, too many ambitious men. Before 1860, these had belonged to distinct parties and political groups; they had come together to consummate what seemed to them to be a great and urgent work. That accomplished, they resolved themselves into their old political and local group-

[1] Rhett's part in the struggle for Southern independence has never been adequately set forth, possibly because his papers are beyond the reach of students. A twenty-eight page pamphlet by "A Contemporary" was published in 1859, but it is simply a reprint from a local South Carolina paper. Printed with it is a remarkable speech by Barnwell Rhett himself delivered at Grahamville, S. C., on July 4, 1859, which might well be read by all persons interested in the subject of the present volume.

[2] An account of this mission is in John W. Du Bose's Life and Times of William Lowndes Yancey, ch. 25; the official papers are printed in Official Records . . . Navies, ser. ii, vol. iii, pp. 191–370.

ings and in Congress at Richmond, in the legislatures of their
States, and in retirement on their plantations, made the
administration of Jefferson Davis at Richmond an exceedingly difficult affair.

It is hazardous, of course, for a Northern student of history, even with the wealth of documentary evidence that has
come to light, to appraise the motives that actuated the
leaders of the Confederate administration in those early
months of its life. Possibly the keynote was the expectation
that separation would be peaceable. Acting on this assumption the work in hand was to organize the new provisional
government on the most efficient administrative basis and
with the least possible expenditure of the time of valuable
men and of the money of the people of the Confederate
States. Commissioners were at once appointed to go to
Washington and arrange with the Buchanan administration
as to the disposition of the public property within the limits
of the seceded States. All this seems a little strange in view
of what happened within a month or two, but turning over
in one's mind Southern ideas of State sovereignty, it is possible to place oneself within the point of view of the authorities at Montgomery. Moreover, public opinion in the
North, judging by the action or inaction of the Buchanan
administration and by the utterances of politicians and the
writings of newspaper men, gave good ground for this idea of
peaceful separation. Certainly it must have been some
such expectation that led President Davis to organize what
might be termed a business administration. For Secretary
of the Treasury, he picked out a prosperous Charleston
lawyer, Christopher G. Memminger;[1] for Secretary of

---

[1] See Henry D. Capers's *Life and
Times of C. G. Memminger* (Richmond,
1893). An interesting "Speech" of
Memminger in the South Carolina
House of Representatives has come
down in pamphlet form. Another,
delivered in 1857, is a sound exposition
of the relations of funded debts, coin

War, he chose L. P. Walker of Alabama, a successful planter and politician. For Secretary of the Navy, he pitched upon Stephen P. Mallory of Key West, Florida, who had become conversant with naval matters, not only of America, but of Europe, as chairman of the Senate Naval Committee. The Postmaster General, John H. Reagan of Texas, proved to be an excellent administrator and Judah P. Benjamin, the Attorney General, was one of the best known lawyers of New Orleans and had served his State in the Federal Senate with distinction.[1] Altogether, it was an exceedingly able group of men of affairs; but within its membership, were only two political leaders of the South, Toombs and Walker, and these almost at once retired. Of the rest, Memminger was a native of Wurtemberg in Germany, Mallory was born on the British island of Trinidad, the son of a Connecticut father, and Benjamin was of Jewish extraction, born on the island of St. Croix in the West Indies within the dominions of the British crown. With the exception of the first two, Toombs and Walker, not one of them could be described as belonging to the old Southern plantation aristocracy. If Davis had been a man of broader political insight he would have gathered about him the representatives of the various leading political elements within the Confederacy. Possibly, if he had done so, the history of the next few years might have been other than what it was. As things were, in February, 1861, it would seem as if the bacilli of peaceable demise were already germinating within the body of the Confederate States.

reserves, and paper money, to one another and to the country and its people.

[1] There is no adequate life of Judah P. Benjamin. Possibly the best account of him is the sketch by Max J. Kohler in the *Publications* of the American Jewish Historical Society, No. 12, pp. 63–85. An earlier account is Pierce Butler's *Judah P. Benjamin* (1906) in *American Crisis Biographies*.

On August 31, 1858, Buchanan offered the Spanish mission to Benjamin. See letter under date in the "Pickett Papers" in the Library of Congress.

The winter of 1860–1861 at Washington was filled with gloom for all lovers of the Union and with joy for those who sympathized with Southern independence. The President, James Buchanan of Pennsylvania, was an experienced and tried Democratic politician of the old school, but he was infirm in body and mind. His one thought was to keep everything as it was, if the Southerners and Northerners would let him, until he could hand over his responsibilities to his successor. He did not believe that secession was constitutional; but he knew no lawful way to deal with it. Buchanan's Secretary of State was Lewis Cass of Michigan. The President's irresolution drove Cass from office and his place was taken by Jeremiah S. Black, like the President, from Pennsylvania and thinking with him on many subjects. The Secretary of the Navy was Isaac Toucey of Connecticut. Many people looked upon him as a Southern sympathizer and believed that he purposely distributed the small number of efficient naval vessels, so that only one of them was within reach when Lincoln came into office. The other members of Buchanan's official household were all Southern men. Howell Cobb, Secretary of the Treasury, resigned to preside over the Montgomery Convention, but Jacob Thompson, Secretary of the Interior, and John B. Floyd, Secretary of War, retained their places until they were forced out of them by Black and Edwin M. Stanton, who had been appointed Attorney General when Black was elevated to the Secretary-ship of State. When commissioners appeared from South Carolina to arrange with the Federal authorities as to the public property within the State limits,[1] President Buchanan received them as private gentlemen and told them that

---

[1] *Official Records*, ser. i, vol. i, pp. 111, 120–125; *Journal of the Convention . . . of South Carolina* (Columbia, S. C., 1862), pp. 484–502; and S. W. Crawford's *Genesis of the Civil War*, 146, 147.

their business was with Congress and not with the Executive. The critical period in Buchanan's administration was reached when it became necessary to decide what should be done with the forts and arsenals within the limits of the seceded States. Governor Moore of Alabama seized the forts at the entrance of Mobile Bay some days before the State Convention passed the secession ordinance, — and in this way settled Buchanan's troubles in that quarter.[1] At Pensacola, the Federal authorities abandoned the navy yard, but retained possession of Fort Pickens at the entrance of the harbor. The governor of Georgia easily possessed himself of the fort at the entrance of the Savannah River.

In Charleston Harbor, in South Carolina, there were three forts : the old Castle Pinckney on an island near the city was held by a caretaker and his family, Fort Moultrie, on Sullivan's Island near the site of the famous revolutionary fortification, and, in the harbor on a shoal spot, an unfinished casemated work of the type of the first half of the nineteenth century. It was already named Fort Sumter and one hundred workingmen were laboring upon it. In Charleston itself there was a Federal arsenal containing a small stock of rather obsolete arms. In the arsenal and at Fort Moultrie there were half a dozen officers of the regular army and fifty or sixty men. The three forts were in plain view from the city. When the South Carolinians ejected the collector of customs and took possession of the custom house and also of the post-office, they plainly expected that the forts and the arsenal would be handed over speedily and peaceably to "the sovereign State of South Carolina." It was not so to be, for the authorities at Washington would do nothing except agree to maintain the existing state of affairs. Floyd and those who advised with him evidently thought that secession

[1] Fleming's *Civil War in Alabama*, 61.

would be peaceable — if no aggressive action were taken
by the secessionists. It happened, therefore, that when
the Federal commandant at Charleston transferred some
stands of arms from the arsenal to the forts, he was replaced
by another officer, Major Robert Anderson. By birth
Anderson was a Kentuckian; his wife was the daughter of
a Southerner, General Clinch of Georgia. Anderson had
every desire to do his duty, — but what was his duty?[1]
Floyd, the Secretary of War, directed him to hold the forts,
but he also authorized him to surrender rather than sacrifice
the men of his command. As Moultrie was practically
dominated by the neighboring sand hills, Anderson felt
nervous for the safety of his men. On the day after Christmas, 1860, he secretly removed them to Fort Sumter where
they would be secure from sudden assault.[2] To say that the
Charlestonians were excited by this transfer of a company of
heavy artillery from one fortification to another, would be
stating the case very mildly. They at once seized Fort
Moultrie, hoisted thereon the "palmetto flag" of South
Carolina, began the construction of batteries on the southern side of the harbor, and sent remonstrances against
Anderson's actions to President Buchanan. The latter
replied truthfully enough that he could not order Anderson
back to Fort Moultrie, because it had been occupied by
some Carolinians and the State flag hoisted over it.[3] This

[1] Writing on December 24, 1860, to
Edward W. Hincks, Anderson stated
that sand hills, 160 yards from the wall
of Fort Moultrie, which was only 14
feet high would make it impossible for
"the 60 effective men" of the garrison
to hold out long enough for their friends
to come to their succor. See also E. D.
Townsend's *Anecdotes of the Civil War*,
p. 10. The story down to the end of
February, 1861, is told in the "Report"
of a select committee appointed to consider the President's "Message" of

January 18, 1861 (*House Report*, No. 91,
36th Cong., 2nd Sess.). Buell's memorandum and Floyd's endorsement are
printed on p. 19.

[2] *Official Records*, i, p. 2; see also
S. W. Crawford's *Genesis of the Civil
War. The Story of Sumter, 1860–1861*,
Abner Doubleday's *Reminiscences of
Forts Sumter and Moultrie in 1860–'61*
(New York, 1876), pp. 58–71.

[3] William H. Trescot was Acting
Secretary of State during a large part of
this period and afterwards performed

satisfied them for the time being. For a couple of months, there was friendly intercourse between Anderson and the Charlestonians, parties from the fort going to the city every few days to purchase fresh provisions for the use of the garrison and the workmen.

The actions of Secretary Floyd in these months are veiled in a mass of documentary evidence that is replete, in certain directions, but from which it is difficult to trace a connected story. Floyd could have ordered work to cease on the Charleston forts at any time, but he did nothing of the sort, so far as we know. The Confederate government at once took control of the military affairs of the Confederacy, sending General Braxton Bragg to take charge at Pensacola, and General P. G. T. Beauregard to take control at Charleston. In both places, State troops were put under their command. Beauregard was a Louisianian by birth and a West Pointer by education. His appointment to Charleston was the first step on the part of the Davis government to unify the military control of the Confederacy, although it had few if any soldiers of the rank and file at its disposal. Under Beauregard's direction, the fortifications that had already been begun for the subjugation of Sumter were pushed forward and in a short time batteries commanded it from both sides of the harbor. In January, 1861, an attempt was made to reënforce Anderson and supply him with provisions by means of the steamer *Star of the West*, which was

the duties of unofficial adviser to commissoners from Montgomery. In February, 1861, after his return to South Carolina, he wrote down his recollections of these events and some ten years later rewrote them. This later narrative he loaned to General Crawford who used a part of it in his *Genesis of the Civil War*. The original narrative is printed in the *American Historical Review*, xiii, 531. It is of extreme value

as, unfortunately, all of Trescot's books and manuscripts were burned a few years ago. See also the statement of James L. Orr in Southern Historical Society's *Papers*, xii, 60. The "Correspondence" between the South Carolina commissioners and President Buchanan in December, 1860 and January, 1861, is in the *Journal of the Convention . . . of South Carolina* (Columbia, 1862), pp. 484–502.

supposed to have sailed from New York without the knowledge of the outer world. As she stood into Charleston
Harbor with the United States flag flying, she was fired on
by one of the newly established batteries and, being unarmed,
at once turned about and sailed back to New York.[1] Anderson made no attempt to protect her, possibly because he did
not know that she was bringing men and supplies to him.

Another charge that has been made against Secretary
Floyd was that he used his official position to supply the
intending secessionists with arms and ammunition with
which they could defend themselves against attack by the
United States or even to assail it. This matter was made the
subject of several inquiries, soon after hostilities commenced;
but the facts brought out at that time have not yet found
their way into acceptance by historical writers and, indeed,
are somewhat difficult of interpretation. It does seem that
orders were given to send certain pieces of heavy ordnance
from the Pittsburg arsenal, ostensibly to unfinished fortifications at the mouth of the Mississippi River, and that this
had been prevented by the action of the Pittsburgers in
refusing to permit the guns to be removed until a counter-
manding order was received from Washington.[2] As to
small arms, the actualities of the case are hard to understand.
It would seem that the greater part of the muskets within

[1] Slight attention was paid to this
affair in the North or in the South. It
appears, however, that the New York
Assembly on January 11, 1861, resolved
that the insurgent State of South
Carolina had "virtually declared war"
and it tendered to the President of the
United States men and money "to
enable him to enforce the laws, and
uphold the authority of the Federal
Government." *Journal of the . . .
Convention . . . of Georgia* (Milledgeville, Ga., 1861), p. 25.

[2] See John N. Boucher's *A Century*
and A Half of Pittsburg and her People,
ii, 150–153. The official statements
are in *House Report*, No. 85, 36th Cong.,
2nd Sess., p. 10 and fol. and *House Report*, No. 16, 37th Cong., 2nd Sess.
This is often known as the "Potter
Report" on the loyalty of clerks and
others persons employed by the government. Lt. Col. Maynadier's *Reply
. . . to the Charges* contained in this
report also has interesting matter.
Buchanan stated his side in a letter
written October 21, 1861 (J. B. Moore's
Works of James Buchanan) xi, 225.

the possession of the United States government in 1858 and 1859 were in Northern arsenals. These consisted of three varieties of guns, old Springfield flintlock muskets, old muskets that had been altered to percussion muskets, and newly manufactured Springfield percussion muskets. The Ordnance Bureau at Washington was anxious to get rid of the old flintlock muskets which took up a great deal of storage room and could never be made into thoroughly serviceable weapons. The Bureau tried to sell the old stock and at one time seemed on the point of doing so to persons who intended to export the muskets out of the country and work them off on the less developed peoples of the world. This plan fell through and some thousands of these guns were sold to the Southern State governments. It also appears that the Bureau, either with or without instigation from Secretary Floyd, sent South some thousands of the altered flintlock muskets [1] and it is not unlikely that the government factories at Harper's Ferry and at Fayetteville used their machinery to change guns owned by some of the Southern States from the flintlock to the percussion pattern. All in all, it seems to the present writer that the United States arsenals in the Southern States contained rather less than their due share of the small arms and small arms ammunition of the United States government. Finally, Floyd left office not on account of any dissatisfaction with his political acts by the Buchanan government, but because he had authorized certain transfers of bonds — in connection with the financing of Western military operations — that were against official propriety, to say the least. It does not appear that Floyd himself received any pecuniary gain from these transactions; but they laid

[1] *House Report*, No. 85, 36th Cong., 2nd Sess., see especially pp. 2, 22, 32; Maynadier's *Reply;* and *John P. Branch Historical Papers*, vol. iv, 84–86, which differs somewhat from the official *Report;* and General Josiah Gorgas's statement in Southern Historical Society's *Papers*, xii, 93. The whole matter is amply treated in Rhodes's *United States*, iii, 238–240.

him open to criminal prosecution.[1] Naturally, like a practiced politician, he based his resignation on his inability to concur with the feeble measures of resistance to Southern demands that the Buchanan government authorized.

In 1860 and in 1861 at the outbreak of hostilities, there were arms and ammunition in the Southern States that had not come from the Federal arsenals, especially in Virginia and in South Carolina.[2] The latter had been collecting them for some years and had imported heavy guns and ammunition from abroad. Virginia had also bestirred herself after the John Brown raid and had accumulated a stock of small arms and the Richmond mob had prevented the transportation out of the State of certain guns that had been cast for the United States government at the Belona Foundry in or near Richmond.[3] The stock of heavy ordnance and small arms and ammunition that enabled the Confederate authorities to set on foot an army in the early days of the war before extensive importations of arms and machinery had been

[1] See *Report* of the Select Committee appointed to investigate the facts as to the Indian bonds (*House Report*, No. 78, 36th Cong., 2nd Sess.).

[2] As far back as 1851, South Carolina had been procuring heavy guns from the Tredegar Works at Richmond. The John Brown raid gave new vigor to preparations for defense; see the *Minutes of the [South Carolina] Military Commission . . . August 4th, 1859.* The *Journal of the [Mississippi] State Convention* of 1861 contains the "Annual Report" of the adjutant general of the State (p. 221). The old arms in the arsenal had been overhauled, but there seem to have been very few of them. In June, 1860, a contract was made with the Ames Manufacturing Company of Massachusetts for 1700 "sets of accoutrements," of these 500 had been received. In December, 1860, the State purchased 5000 "U. S. altered percussion muskets" which were stored at Baton Rouge. The adjutant general

thought that there were about 150 stand of percussion rifles in the State that had not been included in this return. Altogether it would seem that up to the hour of secession, the Mississippi authorities had made very slight preparations for war.

[3] The Richmond *Examiner*, April 2, 1861. Even before the John Brown raid, Virginia had revamped her militia law, and it was made over again in March, 1860. In 1857, Governor Wise had stated that there were then flintlock muskets in the State for 100,000 men. In January, 1860, a statement was made in the Virginia Senate that the State then owned 80,000 flint muskets of which 40,000 could be percussioned and 20,000 converted into carbines. It was also said that the State arms factory was expected to turn out 10,000 muskets in that year. Altogether, Virginia's military preparations, even in 1861, do not seem to have been very efficient.

made from abroad and before much war material was turned
out in the South itself came from the arsenals and forts
within the seceded States, and especially from Harper's
Ferry and the navy yard at Norfolk.[1] Before leaving the
subject of State armaments, it may be well to notice that
some of the Southern States were purchasing arms and
ammunition at New York months after the passage of the
secession ordinances and that the seizure of one of these
consignments by Federal officials on the wharves at New
York brought forth indignant remonstrances from the
Southern State purchasers and apologies from Fernando
Wood, who was then mayor of the City of New York.[2] It
may also be noted that in 1860–61, some Northern States,
notably Massachusetts, were accumulating arms and ammunition at their own expense from abroad.

The winter of 1860–61 at Washington appeared very
different to the people of that time from what it appears to
the historical student of today.[3] In fact the people of the

[1] Wm. H. Peters made an elaborate
*Report of . . . Property taken . . . at
the Navy Yard, Gosport, . . . near Portsmouth, Virginia.* The schedule (Appendix B.) includes more than 500 guns,
ranging from field howitzers to an 11-
inch "Columbiad." There were also
old style guns and cartridges, percussion
caps, powder, and over 17,000 shells.
The possession of this ordnance and the
machinery taken at Harper's Ferry
which was valued at over $200,000 gave
the Confederacy a fairly even start in
those two respects with the Union; see
ibid., pp. 101–117, which gives an
"Inventory of Musket Machinery taken
at Harper's Ferry."

[2] *"No Compromise with Treason."
Remarks of Mr. Schenck of Ohio.* This
speech was delivered in the House of
Representatives on April 11, 1864.
On p. 6, he says that on the receipt of
two telegrams from Robert Toombs,
dated Milledgeville, January 24, 1861,
asking if arms consigned to the State of

Georgia had been seized in New York,
Wood replied that he regretted to say
that the arms had been seized by the
State police, but that "the city of
New York should in no way be made
responsible for the outrage."

[3] One's ideas as to the policies pursued by Northern and Southern political leaders in Washington, from November, 1860, to March, 1861, are so strongly
tinged by his sympathies and his
knowledge of facts that were unknown
to people living then, that the account
written out by Henry Adams at the
time is of extreme interest (Massachusetts Historical Society's *Proceedings,*
June, 1910, pp. 658–687); his later
thoughts on the subject are in *The
Education of Henry Adams,* 98–105.
George Luther Stearns was in Washington in December, 1860, and wrote to
William S. Robinson "the result of my
observation." This is partly printed in
Frank P. Stearns's *George Luther
Stearns,* 238–240. It is noticeable that

North were divided into four groups, (1) the Buchananites,
who represented the old Northern dough-faces or Northern
men with Southern principles; (2) the abolitionists, who
were glad to see the Southerners go and the sooner they went
— and the farther — the better; (3) the Northerners who
had elected Lincoln, but were willing to compromise with
the South to bring the seceded States back into the Union;
and (4) a few determined men with Lincoln at their head who
were resolved that there should be no more compromise that
would lead to any possible extension of slave soil. It is easy
to understand the attitude of Buchanan and those who
worked with him.[1] For years they had been intimate
associates of the leading Southern politicians who were,
many of them, men of ideas and of social distinction as well as
of intrepidity in action. It is difficult to shake off one's life
associations within a few weeks or within a few months.
Besides, Buchanan, as he stated in his defence of his own
administration,[2] had no power to use coercive measures,
either constitutional or material, and Congress, which was in
the hands of his opponents after the departure of Southern
Senators and Representatives, would not give him any
power. So long as the Southerners committed no overt act,
he held that he could not take any measures under the old
laws that had come down from the beginning of the govern-

Stearns's advice was to "keep quiet"
and wait for the Southerners to show "a
wish for a reconciliation!"

[1] The "Report of a Meeting" at
Williamsport in Pennsylvania on
December 12, 1860, asserted that it was
the duty of all good citizens to save the
Union without inquiring "whether
fanaticism North or South was most to
blame" and that any concession is better than "a pertinacious adherence to
opinion at the expense of civil war and
National ruin." Sentiments of approval of Buchanan's inaction were
voted by the Common Council of the

City of New York in January, 1861
(*House Mis. Doc.*, No. 15, 36th Cong.,
2nd Sess.). The fluidity of opinion is
well shown in the eight reports presented by the select committee of thirty-
three on the "Disturbed Condition of
the Country" (*House Report*, No. 31,
36th Cong., 2nd Sess.).

[2] *Mr. Buchanan's Administration on
the Eve of the Rebellion* (New York,
1866), pp. 125–127. See also George T.
Curtis's *Life of James Buchanan*, ii, ch.
xvii; Buchanan's "Message" of Dec.
3, 1860, precedes this discussion.

ment. If he had wished to coerce the South or any individual within its boundaries it is difficult to see how he could have done so. The military force at his disposal, apart from the militia of the several States which could be called out only under peculiar circumstances, comprised a little army of only sixteen thousand [1] men and of these only one thousand or so were in garrisons east of the Mississippi. Of course it may be that far-seeing Southern secession leaders, acting through Secretary Floyd, had so disposed of the soldiers of the regular army that they could not be of service to the Washington government; [2] but it must be conceded that there were none too many soldiers west of the Mississippi in the winter of 1860–1861.

In October and December, 1860, and March, 1861, General Winfield Scott, the commanding officer of the United States army, wrote several letters. [3] In the earliest of them, he stated that he thought that the right of secession might be conceded and be balanced by the right of the Federal government to reëstablish by force its former territorial limits. Scott wrote that it was quite likely that the Southern forts might be seized even before secession and recommended that they should be so garrisoned that none of them could be taken by surprise. It is said that Floyd at a reception in Richmond that was tendered to him after his resignation, asserted that

[1] In Provost Marshal General Fry's *Final Report*, dated March 17, 1866, (pt. i, p. 6) the total number of officers and men of the regular army on January 1, 1861, is given as 16,402 present and absent. Of these 14,657 are returned as present. Slightly different figures are given on pp. 101, 102. In a memorandum made by Adjutant General E. D. Townsend in 1875, the stations of the troops in the years 1858–60 are given; see *Battles and Leaders of the Civil War*, i, p. 7 note. A map accompanying this article shows the distribution of the forces in 1860. See also the

statement in *Mr. Buchanan's Administration*, 102–106.

[2] It has often been said that the secessionists intended to seize Washington and Georgetown as soon as the movement began and that several thousand men in the city and in the country round about were prepared to act. See William D. C. Murdock's *Address to the Democratic Party* (Washington, 1864) p. 10.

[3] "Appendix A" to Adjutant General Edward D. Townsend's *Anecdotes of the Civil War*.

Scott had desired to transfer the army of the United States to
those forts as speedily and quietly as possible, and added,
that if he had been able to do this "the Southern Confederacy would not now exist."[1] In a letter to Seward dated
March 3, 1861, General Scott suggested four alternatives
that might be adopted in the existing condition of affairs.
The first of these was to adopt Senator Crittenden's conciliatory propositions; the second was to collect the duties on
foreign goods outside the ports of the seceded States; the
third was to conquer the seceded States by invading armies.
This might be accomplished in two or three years with three
hundred thousand disciplined men, led by a general of the
capacity of Wolfe. If this had been written after the secession of Virginia, North Carolina, and Tennessee, Scott
presumably would have raised the size of the field force
required to half a million men or so. As it was, he thought
that the destruction of Southern life and property would be
frightful and that there would be an enormous waste of
Northern life and treasure. It was after writing these lines
that Scott thought of a fourth alternative which was "Say
to the seceded States, 'Wayward Sisters, depart in peace.'"

Opinion in the North was distinctly divided on the question of compelling reunion or of accepting separation into
two or more parts as a necessary and perhaps desirable conclusion. Scott himself outlined four possible divisions of the
United States and others have speculated more or less
definitely on the subject. One of the obstacles to a division
on the line of slavery and freedom or of the Missouri Compromise was the nearness of the northern end of the Virginia
Panhandle to Lake Erie and the nearness of the Kentucky

---

[1] Townsend's *Anecdotes*, p. 8. In
a foot-note to this passage it is
stated that "The army had been
unnecessarily scattered under Secretary
Floyd's administration" and that his
assent was necessary to enable Scott to
move troops from remote posts to the
East.

boundary at Covington, opposite Cincinnati to Lakes Erie
and Michigan.[1] A Northern State extending from Maine to
Oregon, three thousand miles in length and one hundred miles
in width at its narrowest part was plainly out of the question. Nevertheless, many good people in the North, entirely
reputable merchants and honorable men in every way,
thought that some kind of compromise recognizing separation, presumably not on any such impossible geographic lines,
would be the best way out of the conflict and would be in
itself advantageous. Indeed, there might be three or four
divisions formed within the existing United States as Winfield Scott suggested, and with Canada added to these and all
held together by some federative bond or league, it is possible
that the war might have been avoided, and, some people
think, the United States would be better off today were each
part of it within the government of its own inhabitants.

Scott's statement as to the departure of the "Wayward
Sisters" was entirely in keeping with the wishes of the
abolitionists. Horace Greeley, in the New York "Tribune"
wrote that if the Southern States want to leave the Union,
they have an absolute moral right so to do. Wendell
Phillips asserted that President Lincoln had "no right to a
soldier in Fort Sumter." Senator Henry Wilson of Massachusetts was not a disunionist, but a speech that he delivered
in Congress on February 21, 1861, would seem to show that
he was not adverse to cutting loose in some way from the
slaveholding States. Finally, Fernando Wood, mayor of
New York City, publicly suggested the secession of Man-

---

[1] In 1862, George McHenry printed
at London a fifteen page pamphlet
answering the question of the title
page, — *Why Pennsylvania should Become One of the Confederate States of
America*. It is accompanied by an
interesting map reproduced in part as
the frontispiece of this volume. The
secession of Pennsylvania was advocated
by Francis Hughes, a candidate for the
Senatorship from that State in February, 1861. See two tracts entitled
"To the People of Pennsylvania" and
"A Plea for Compromise . . . dated
Bloomsdale, Feb. 4, 1861."

hattan Island and Long Island and the formation of them into a free port which would, in great part, control the commerce of the New World. Shortly afterwards he addressed a great open air meeting and most earnestly advocated the coercion of the seceded States![1]

Attempts to compromise the questions at issue and thereby to bring back the seceded States or even to prevent secession had two origins, one in Congress that culminated finally about the compromise plan of Senator Crittenden of Kentucky,[2] and another that came from Virginia and led to what was known as the Peace Conference at Washington. Soon after Congress met in December, 1860, in its last session under Buchanan, a committee of thirty-three members of the House of Representatives was appointed to see if some way could not be found out of the difficulties that beset the Union. It soon became evident that nothing could be done through that committee, and attention was turned to Crittenden's compromise plan. This scheme really granted nearly all that the South could ask including an amendment to the Constitution that Congress could take no action as to slavery within the States, yielded somewhat on the question of slavery in the Territories, and proposed to leave everything else to the Supreme Court. This was the most likely of all these schemes. The plan that was evolved by the Peace Conference likewise proposed an amendment to the Constitution which had seven sections.[3] By these the Mis-

[1] Rhodes's *United States*, iii, 369, 372.

[2] It is possibly worth noting that one of Crittenden's sons was in the Confederate army throughout the war and another in the Union army, being promoted to the rank of Major General of Volunteers for his services at Shiloh. See Alexander K. McClure's *Recollections*, 374.

[3] Lucius E. Chittenden's *Report . . . of the Conference Convention* (New York, 1864), p. 472, 590. It was held at Washington in February, 1861. Chittenden also reviewed the matter in his *Recollections of President Lincoln* (New York, 1891), p. 23 and fol. George S. Boutwell attended it as a delegate from Massachusetts. In ch. xxiv of his *Reminiscences of Sixty Years* (New York, 1902) is one of the best accounts of the affair. See also the *Report* from the Virginia Commissioners

souri Compromise line was to be partly restored, this time in the Constitution itself where it would be safe from the opinions of the justices of the Supreme Court. When any new State was to be admitted to the Union, either north or south of this line it might come in with or without involuntary servitude, as its constitution might provide. By the second section, no new territory should be acquired unless by treaty, with some exceptions, and such treaty must be ratified by four-fifths of all the members of the Senate. Sections three and four restrained the Supreme Court from interpreting the Constitution to give Congress power over slavery or to prevent the States from enforcing the provision of that instrument as to fugitive slaves. Congress should provide compensation for the escaped slaves. Furthermore, the foreign slave trade should be forever prohibited by constitutional provision. On the other hand, no section of the Constitution, including this proposed amendment protecting slavery and slaveholders, should be amended or abolished without the consent of all the States. The first section, that relating to the territorial question, was adopted by the votes of nine States to eight, Virginia being one of the eight. Indiana did not vote on the question and New York and Kansas were divided. The distribution of sentiment shown in these votes clearly portended the failure of the conference and of any proposition emanating from it.

None of the compromise plans that have been mentioned nor any other had any chance of adoption. The Southern seceders were flushed with success and hope for the future; they saw their machinations of ten or twenty years about to bear fruit and were not at all disposed to give way except on their own terms. Northern men of affairs of that time and

to the Peace Conference in Washington in 1861. The Georgia delegates, assembled at Milledgeville, considered a compromise plan; see *Journal of the Public and Secret Proceedings*, p. 15.

many historical students since have reprobated, more or less severely, the inaction of President Buchanan and his advisers and have likewise condemned the attempts made by Seward and Charles Francis Adams and other Northern men to keep alive the debate on compromise and conciliation throughout those long winter months, until the time came for the inauguration of the new President and the reorganization of the government at Washington. Until that should be accomplished it would seem that prudence and policy pointed to the continuance of pacific relations with Virginia, Kentucky, North Carolina, and Tennessee, — the States that stood at the moment between the country of secession and the doubtful area of the North, which included within its limits the capital city of the United States. It may be true, and probably is, that Seward absolutely misjudged the actualities and possibilities and that he was walking as in a dream. But political leaders do not always say what they think and sometimes permit their hearers and others around them to believe that which they themselves do not believe. Moreover, Seward and Thurlow Weed were two of the most farseeing, successful politicians then on the stage. And they were guided by one whose political prescience and wisdom were greater than theirs, who was unsurpassed in modern history, — Abraham Lincoln.

Lincoln is generally represented as a person of rather aimless volubility, but probably the aimlessness of his flow of talk belonged to the limbo of other traditions that have gathered around him. Certainly the months of his life between the election in November, 1860, and the inauguration on March 4, 1861, witnessed a sphinxlike silence. Southerners who wrote to him for a statement of his views were informed that he had stated them hundreds of times already and that if they would not read what was then in

print they would not read anything new that he might say.
Stephens's speech declaring that the election of the Republican candidate did not justify secession induced Lincoln to
write to him in a conciliatory manner, but nothing came
of this effort. However, when Weed inquired of Lincoln
what should be done about accepting the Crittenden Compromise, or when Lincoln heard from others as to what
Seward and Weed proposed to do, he at once intervened and
put his foot down in a way that no one could fail to understand.[1] With his Southern connections and the accurate
information that Lincoln must have possessed as to the
motives and temper of the Southern people, it must have
appeared to him, as it did to Winfield Scott, that if there
were no more compromise, either the South must be permitted to remain outside of the Union or be brought back
at the cost of hundreds of thousands of lives and of billions
of property and treasure.

[1] See Lincoln to William Kellogg, December 11, 1860; to E. B. Washburne, December 13, 1860; to Thurlow Weed, December 17, 1860; to T. J. Hale, January 11, 1861; and to W. H. Seward, February 1, 1861: *Complete Works of Abraham Lincoln*, vi, 77, 78, 82, 93, 102.

NOTE

Confederate Official Documents. — The Confederate States government began its career with the publication of documents: — "Acts and Resolutions of the . . . Provisional Congress," the "Constitution for the Provisional Government," "Estimates of Appropriations," etc., etc [1] Then there came a mass of military papers; — "Adjutant General's Orders," "Orders" governing conscription and official "Reports" of committees of Congress appointed to examine into the reasons of lack of success in various directions which include "Official Reports of Battles," etc. Large bundles of printed departmental orders and military papers are in the State Library at Richmond. Specific references to some of them are given in the footnotes of this volume. The *Journal of the Congress of the Confederate States of America, 1861–1865* was printed in seven volumes at Washington, 1904–5. It forms *Senate Document*, No. 234, 58th Congress, 2nd Session. The Southern Historical Society began in June, 1923, the publication of the "Proceedings of First Confederate Congress" (Serial No. XLIV). This is compiled from the abstracts of the debates printed in the newspapers of the time, mainly from the Richmond *Examiner*. James D. Richardson printed two volumes of *A Compilation of the Messages and Papers of the Confederacy, Including the Diplomatic Correspondence* (Nashville, 1905). Volume i contains Davis's "Messages" and accompanying papers: volume ii contains the "Diplomatic Correspondence." The second and third volumes of the second series of the *Official Records of the Union and Confederate Navies* contain the correspondence of the Confederate Navy Department with its agents in Europe and their correspondence with those who worked for them, forming together one of the most remarkable exhibits of Confederate skill to be found anywhere; and also the correspondence of other Confederate agents in Europe.

[1] *Provisional and Permanent Constitutions, together with the Acts and Resolutions of the First Session of the Provisional Congress, of the Confederate States* (Montgomery, Ala., 1861). *Acts and Resolutions of the Second Session of the Provisional Congress of the Confederate States* (Montgomery, Ala., 1861). *Acts and Resolutions of the Third Session of the Provisional Congress of the Confederate States, held at Richmond, Va.*, (Richmond, 1861).

There is a bibliography of official publications of the Confederate States in Douglas S. Freeman's *Calendar of Confederate Papers*, 502–521. Charles N. Baxter and James M. Dearborn's *Confederate Literature . . . now in the Boston Athenæum* (1917) will open the way into storehouses of official and unofficial material.

CHAPTER XI

FROM SUMTER TO BULL RUN

THE fourth day of March, 1861, came and with it the peaceful inauguration of Abraham Lincoln as President of the United States. In his address he declared his intention to repossess Federal government property in the South that had been seized by the Secessionists. Acting on Seward's suggestion, he closed with an appeal to the mystic chords of memory that bound together the hearthstones and sepulchres of the American people throughout the land.[1] The issue as to whether there should be peace or war lay with the Southern Secessionists and not with him. They had no oath registered in Heaven to destroy the government of the United States, while he was about to take an oath to "preserve, protect, and defend" the Constitution of the United States. Some weeks earlier, Jefferson Davis, as President of the Confederate States, had taken a similar oath. From

[1] Professor D. K. Dodge has an interesting account of the writing of the closing lines of the First Inaugural, in the University of Illinois *Studies*, vol. i, No. i, p. 47. There are graphic descriptions of the inauguration by C. F. Adams, 2nd, in the *Proceedings* of the Massachusetts Historical Society for February, 1909, pp. 145–154 and in L. E. Chittenden's *Recollections of President Lincoln*, ch. xiv. A dozen years earlier, Jefferson Davis, then Senator from Mississippi, in the Oregon debate had said that if "nothing would satisfy the North short of the destruction of this institution [slavery], then was the time for dissolution come; but let us separate peacefully, and with good feelings towards each other. Let not the battlefields of our country be stained with the blood of brother fighting against brother;" Rowland's *Jefferson Davis*, i, 213. Quite the opposite were the sentiments of General Grant's Aunt Rachel. She lived in Virginia and owned many slaves. In a letter to one of the Grant sisters, Aunt Rachel informed her that if she was "with the accursed Lincolnites, the ties of consanguinity shall be forever severed;" Jesse G. Cramer's *Letters of Ulysses S. Grant* (New York, 1912) p. 27, and see also p. 159.

that day to the end, more than four years later, neither
Lincoln nor Davis could give way, and the Confederacy
demised by the action of military men and the capture and
incarceration of the Southern Chief Magistrate.

It is extraordinary how little we know of the inner pro-
cesses of the great men of the world and how different are
the assessments of them by their contemporaries and by
historians, half a century later. To men of his time, Lincoln
appeared to be weak and vacillating and to be actuated more
by the desires of the moment than by any firm settled policy.
Nowadays, we realize that Lincoln was a man of marvellous
power in the management of men and that he had political
foresight almost without parallel among the men of mediæval and modern times who have risen sufficiently above
the mass of mankind to cause their doings to be recorded in
documents and assessed by students. He had had a long
and excellent schooling in political leadership and management and his successes as a jury lawyer had been based on the
same talent for putting two and two together in such a way
that the resulting combination would be exactly what he
wished and which was, as a rule, incomprehensible in advance
to those about him.[1] In organizing his administration, he
found himself face to face with the grave problems that beset
him throughout the next four years. If he were to pick the
heads of departments from the anti-slavery wing of the Republican party, he would certainly alienate the support of
the protectionists and free land elements among his sup-

[1] A. G. Riddle in his *Life of Benjamin
F. Wade* (new ed., Cleveland, 1888), p.
316, states the case for Lincoln in these
words : "Due allowance has never been
made for Mr. Lincoln's position. Seeing all the most advanced saw, he also
saw what they would not — the slow,
the tardy, the reluctant. For these he
must wait. It required all. To rush
forward with the van, like an old
prophet, to risk all mayhap was to lose
all. In this and in his grand docility
to be taught by each day of its needs, at
the feet of the war itself, consists the real
greatness of the man. Constantly he
grew with the people, till he filled their
entire vision."

porters that had made his election possible and he would set
against him all persons who cared little or nothing for slavery,
but cared a great deal for the perpetuation of the Union.
He therefore drew his principal advisers from differing shades
of Republicanism and from the Northern Democratic element that was very strong in the States bordering on the
Ohio River upon whose action success or failure in the coming
contest must depend.   The office of Secretary of State he
offered to his leading competitor in the Chicago Convention,
Senator William H. Seward of New York, who for years
had been one of the anti-slavery leaders.   For Secretary of
the Treasury, he picked out another of the candidates at
Chicago, Salmon P. Chase[1] of Ohio.   Like Seward, Chase
had been governor of his State and a leader among the Free-
Soilers, but his antecedents were Democratic and not Whig.
For Secretary of War, circumstances, over which Lincoln had
had no control, compelled him to offer the place to Simon
Cameron of Pennsylvania.   He was one of the leading politicians of the Keystone State and was generally regarded
then and has been since as a man devoid of scruple when the
advancement of his party or himself was concerned and it
must be said that in these endeavors he had been singularly
successful.   Lincoln had directed his representatives at
Chicago to make no bargains ; but they had done so to secure
the votes of the Pennsylvania delegates and he felt in honor
bound to carry out their agreement.   Besides, Cameron
represented the protectionist desire of the Pennsylvanians.
Another rival at Chicago, Edward Bates of Missouri was

[1] Robert B. Warden's *An Account of
the Private Life and Public Services of
Salmon Portland Chase* in 838 octavo
pages (Cincinnati, 1874) contains long
extracts from Chase's diaries and from
his letters.   In the same year Maunsell
B. Field printed a small volume entitled
*Memories of Many Men and of Some
Women* in the last pages of which Chase
figures prominently.   Professor Eugene
Wambaugh has an appreciative and interesting 40 page sketch in the *Great
American Lawyers* series, v, 329–391;
and Professor Hart wrote a brief biography of Chase for the *American
Statesmen* series.

appointed Attorney General.   He was the nearest approach to a Southerner that Lincoln could induce to come into the administration.   Two members of the Cabinet were Democrats or of strong Democratic connection.   One of these was Montgomery Blair of Maryland who became Postmaster General and the other was Gideon Welles [1] of Connecticut who took upon himself the very arduous duties of Secretary of the Navy.   Montgomery Blair was the son of Francis P. Blair, the newspaper editor of Jackson's time.   Through his own and his wife's family connections, the new Postmaster General exercised power in fields far removed from the carrying of the mails and was able to intervene, sometimes most usefully, in other departments than his own.   Welles had been a newspaper editor and a political leader in his own State and in the neighboring State of New York.   His manners and his mode of expressing his opinions aroused resentment sometimes; but with Blair and Cameron, he knew about all of the politician's art that was not already at the fingertips of the new President himself.

When Buchanan laid down the office of President of the United States, the departments at Washington were filled with Southerners and with Southern sympathizers.   By this

---

[1] The *Diary of Gideon Welles* in three volumes was published at Boston in 1911.   Unfortunately the word "diary" is a misnomer.   The most interesting part of it, namely Chapter I, entitled "The Beginning of the War," as is stated in a footnote, was written several years after the event.   In the manuscript of this chapter in Washington is an entry of Stanton's death in 1869 which is not in the printed text.   It would appear, therefore, that "several years" after the events described means 1869 or later.   As to the other parts of the "diary," there are several sets or copies of the manuscript; and the manuscript that served as the basis of the text that went to the printer is corrected and rewritten in pencil and sometimes in ink without any indication as to when these changes were made.   It is difficult, therefore, to look upon any statement in the three volumes as belonging to the year of the event.   This is very disappointing, especially the fact that the entries relating to the first year of the war cannot be regarded as in any way contemporary.   In making this analysis, I have been greatly aided by a study of the manuscript made by Howard K. Beale of Chicago.   There is also a mass of letters in the Welles Manuscripts in Washington, but they contain little useful information.

time the Spoils System had come to be the recognized basis of political success. Had the triumph of the Republicans been nothing more than an ordinary political overturn, there would have been a great reconstruction of the clerical forces in Washington and in many other parts of the country. It was absolutely necessary for the life of the republic to cleanse the Departments of all those who were not in hearty sympathy with the cause of the Union and to appoint to their places persons who were faithful.[1] The first weeks of the life of the new administration were a most strenuous time of reconstruction and reorganization of the clerical forces in the departments at Washington and of the civil service throughout those portions of the country that remained loyal to the Union. Moreover, taking into consideration Lincoln's lack of administrative experience and the altogether over-tutored experience of his official advisers in political removals and appointments and also their diverse political antecedents, the task confronting the new President was stupendous. How many officials were removed or how many offices were filled or refilled partakes largely of guess work. Professor Fish in his writings on the civil service[2] has estimated that in the four years and one month of Lincoln's presidency he removed 1457 out of a possible 1639 officials. These figures cover the whole period; some offices were vacated two or three times in those four years. It is

[1] *House Report*, No. 16, 37th Cong., 2nd Sess.

[2] Professor Fish has treated this subject at length in the *American Historical Review*, viii, 53–69. He also necessarily touches on it in his *Civil Service and the Patronage*, 169 and fol. and in his "Removal of Officials" in the *Report* of the American Historical Association for 1899, vol. i, pp. 67–86.

Benjamin Moran in his "Diary" under date of September 17, 1861, says that Charles Francis Adams, his chief at London, told him that President Lincoln had a book in which all foreign posts were noted and that when he was hard pressed, he would call for it and if there were a vacancy, from mission to consulate, he would offer it to the applicant. Moran's own colleague applied for the Chicago postmastership and got the secretaryship of the legation at London.

impossible, therefore, to state anything as to the number of removals in the first month or two. Moreover, these figures, which are based on a study of the "Executive Journals," tell us nothing about the displacement of the mass of the clerical forces in the Departments at Washington and in the Federal offices in those States that remained within the Union. All we can do, therefore, is to say that the "Departments" at Washington and the civil service generally throughout the North were thoroughly reorganized. Had they been more thoroughly reorganized, it would have been better for the Union cause, for there were Southern spies in the Federal service throughout the war.

While it was wholly justifiable to reconstruct the civil services, it is regrettable that more attention was not paid to retaining the officers of the army and the navy in those services. Each and every one of these men had taken an oath each time he received a commission to be faithful to the United States. General Emory Upton points out[1] that in the army and the navy, the obligation to observe this oath was regarded with sanctity, but that it could be voided by resigning, provided that the resignation was accepted. In the mental and moral chaos that prevailed in the first weeks after Lincoln's inauguration, when Major General Winfield Scott's "Wayward Sisters depart in peace" was the psychological rule at Washington and in the country, it was only necessary for an officer of the army or the navy to offer his resignation to have it accepted and with its acceptance went release from the oath of allegiance, and the officer was free to go South and lead an army against the govern-

---

[1] *The Military Policy of the United States*, p. 240. This section is entitled "Furnishing Military Leaders for the Rebellion." This book was published by the government in 1904 and deserves much wider recognition than it has received by students. See also the *Official Army Register* (1860, p. 41 and September, 1861, p. 61) and Southern Historical Society's *Papers*, xxx, 34.

ment of the United States with a clear conscience. Had their resignations been refused, many of them would have remained true to the oath, and those who did not could have been sent to Fort Lafayette or some other place of incarceration. Had some course like this been pursued, the Confederacy would have been deprived of nine-tenths of the men who commanded its armies and its ships. It is an interesting speculation as to what would have happened had the Confederate States not had the services of General Cooper, General Gorgas, Robert E. Lee, the two Johnstons, and Longstreet, on the land, and Raphael Semmes and Franklin Buchanan on the water.[1]

Before dismissing from mind the matter of one's allegiance or one's duty to the old Union or to the new Confederacy and thinking of how difficult it was for men like those whose names have just been given to decide which was the path of duty, it will be well, perhaps, to bring together some of the leading instances of divided relationships that have struck the eye as one has proceeded through the books. The most dramatic of these is the tale of the two men, one a Confederate, the other a Union officer, who lay mortally wounded beside a captured Confederate battery after one of the last charges at Petersburg in 1865. They recognized each other's voices. They were brothers.[2] Proceeding from the humble to the exhalted, one comes to Mrs. Abraham Lincoln's half-brothers and sisters.[3] Mary Todd Lincoln was one of eight

[1] On April 30, 1861, a General Order was issued from the Adjutant General's office stating that the President of the United States directs that all officers of the army, except those that have entered since April 1st, shall take and subscribe anew the oath of allegiance to the United States.

[2] Joseph W. Keifer's *Slavery and Four Years of War*, ii, 196. Another interesting incident is that of the Terrell brothers of Bath County, Virginia. They both became brigadier generals, one in the Union army was killed at Perryville, in Kentucky, in October, 1862; the other in the Confederate service was killed in the Wilderness in 1864. Oren F. Morton's *Annals of Bath County, Virginia*, 143.

[3] T. M. Green's *Historic Families of Kentucky*, 210, 215, 216, etc.

children, daughter of Robert S. Todd's first wife. On her
death, the father married again; this time a woman from
Staunton, Virginia. She, too, had eight children. The
three sons all served in the Confederate army, one was killed
at Shiloh, the second at Vicksburg, the third at Baton Rouge.
And of the daughters, two were the wives of officers in the
Confederate army. General George B. McClellan [1] had a
cousin in the Confederate service, who acted successively
as chief of staff to Generals J. E. B. Stuart and Wade Hampton. General Meade's [2] wife, Margaretta Sergeant of Philadelphia, had two sisters, one of them was the wife of Governor
and General Henry A. Wise of Virginia; the other was the
wife of Lieutenant Thomas B. Huger of the Confederate
navy. Admiral Farragut and General Thomas were Southerners who remained true to the flag; Admiral Porter had
two nephews in the Confederate naval service, and Samuel
P. Lee,[3] the commander of the Union fleet in the James
River at the time of the siege of Petersburg, was the cousin
of Robert E. Lee.

Apart from the reconstruction of the civil service, the most
serious and pressing problem that beset the new administration was as to what should be done with the two coastwise
forts in the South that were still garrisoned by Federal
troops. These were Fort Sumter in Charleston Harbor and
Fort Pickens at the entrance of Pensacola Bay. The Lincoln
administration inherited the agreements or quasi-agreements
that had been entered into by officials of the Buchanan government with the Southerners. Exactly what these were
does not seem to be susceptible of definite statement, but it
does appear that no change in the status of these posts could

[1] P. S. Michie's McClellan, 4–7.
[2] G. Meade's Life and Letters of
George Gordon Meade, i, 17.
[3] F. W. Alexander's Stratford Hall
and the Lees, p. 179. Admiral Lee's
wife was the sister of Postmaster
General Montgomery Blair.

be made by the Federal administration without notification in advance to the local authorities at Charleston and Pensacola.   In case of war on an extended scale between the North and the South, these fortifications had no importance. Economic and strategic considerations would lead to the prosecution of the war on other fields than South Carolina and Florida, and Sumter and Pickens might well have been presented to the Southerners.   But in war sentiment and psychology often overrule the dictates of military strategy. It was impossible for the Federal administration to give up either one or both of these posts to the Confederates — in 1861 — and it was impossible to provision and reënforce either Pickens or Sumter as they should be if they were to be held in the face of attack by the Southerners.   The only thing that the Washington government could do was to prolong the existing state of affairs, — in other words to keep on doing what Buchanan and his advisers had been doing in the last months of his administration.   The burden of making the first move must be placed upon the South, for in that way only could the sentiment of the North be brought to the support of any attempt at coercion.   Of course, this was as patent to the Confederate government at Montgomery as it was to the Union government at Washington.   It led to the appointment of commissioners by the Davis government to negotiate "the settlement of all questions of disagreement between the two governments,"[1] — in other words to secure the recognition of the Confederate States of America as an independent power.

In due course, the commissioners from the Confederate government at Montgomery appeared at Washington and sought to approach the Lincoln administration in as calm and deliberate a fashion as diplomats from France might be

[1] *Statutes at Large of . . . the Confederate States* (Richmond, 1864), p. 92.

supposed to go to London in the present month (March, 1925) and open negotiations with the British ministry as to the airplane service of the two countries.   They really seem to have had no thought whatever but that the new President and his Secretary of State would receive them in a friendly manner and come to some amicable understanding without any unnecessary delay.   And they had good grounds for their belief.   The Southerners had always insisted that the abolitionists, speaking through their oratorical and editorial organs had stated the opinion of the North, — and it was this misconception that was responsible in great measure for the secession of Southern slaveholding States.   As a matter of fact, the apathy in the North was profound.   An English observer, William H. Russell,[1] the famous war correspondent who was in the United States on a tour of investigation for the London "Times," reported that nobody in New York seemed to take much interest in the insults that were daily being offered to the Federal government by the people of the Southern States and, indeed, that arms and ammunition were being sent forward by every steamer from the wharves of New York to those of Southern ports.   Under these circumstances, the Confederate commissioners when they sought to open communication with the President of the United States through Secretary Seward were astounded

---

[1] Russell's letters were printed in the London *Times* and should be read in their original setting. Portions of them with additional matter were printed in different forms: *Pictures of Southern Life* (143 pages, New York, 1861). Certain passages in this book gave great offence to Southerners ; and Northerners were perhaps equally offended by passages in Russell's later books also made up from his letters to the *Times:* *My Diary North and South* (two editions, 1863), *Civil War in America* (Boston, 1861), *Canada; Its Defences . . . being* a . . . *concluding volume of My " Diary, North and South."* The letter on the campaign of July, 1861, was printed by itself at New York in that year under the title of *The Battle of Bull Run.* An interesting comment on Russell's books is Andrew D. White's *Letter to Wm. Howard Russell, LL.D. on Passages in his "Diary, North and South"* (Syracuse, 1863).   Letters from Russell in John Bigelow's *Retrospections* (as in, vol. i, 358, 369) give a somewhat different idea of Russell from that which one obtains from his books.

when Seward, acting under orders from President Lincoln,
refused to receive them or any official letter from them.
Then came forward two Justices of the Supreme Court who
undertook to act as go-betweens and had somewhat ill
fortune. How far Lincoln knew of these negotiations is a
mystery. The evidence seems to show that Seward, who
was still permeated with the thought that with time and
kindness Southerners would return to the fold, acted on his
own authority. The Southerners were thoroughly deceived
and no doubt they died in the belief that Lincoln and
Seward were consummate deceivers or worse.[1]

It is quite impossible for the present-day writer to portray
Lincoln and Seward as they appeared to one another in the
month of March, 1861. Seward had been governor of New
York and for a dozen years or so had been one of the half-
dozen leading figures in the Senate of the United States.
Lincoln coming from a small town in what was then "the
West" had seemed to him to be a petty politician whom circumstances had placed over himself at Washington. We,
now, can conceive that Lincoln with his mind filled with the
future, foreseeing with his wonderful prescience the oncoming
war and the necessity of holding the Ohio Valley to the Union,
and burdened with the task of keeping the heterogeneous
elements of the Republican party in working harmony and
combining with them every Democrat, whether Breckinridge
or Douglas, and every Bell-Everett Whig who would work
with him, undervalued the political power of Seward and his
mentor Thurlow Weed and was impatient at the ill-timed
insistence of his Secretary of State as to the necessity of
doing this or doing that and doing it now. As we see him,

---

[1] See J. A. Campbell to Nathan
Clifford, April 18 and 29, 1861, in P. G.
Clifford's *Nathan Clifford*, 277, 279;
Campbell's *Reminiscences and Docu-*
ments *Relating to the Civil War*, and
Henry G. Connor's *John Archibald
Campbell*, ch. v.

Lincoln was a "Master of men," incomparably above anyone who has ever walked the American stage. His business at the moment was to make Seward, Chase, Cameron, Blair, and Welles work together and to make sure that it was the Montgomery government that fired the shot that would begin the war and unite Northern hearts. Under these circumstances, he concealed his thoughts by telling stories and by various awkwardnesses of body and of habit that were a part of his mode of gaining his ends. To Seward, the situation finally became impossible.[1] In a strange moment of hallucination he wrote out on paper "Some Thoughts for the President's Consideration, April 1, 1861" which he actually presented to his Chief. In these, he advocated, in no uncertain language, doing something radical and doing it at once, making the administration work in harmony, provoking war with some outside power and thus bringing together again the dissevered Union in defence of Americanism. Lincoln read the paper thoughtfully and remarked quietly that if this thing "must be done, I must do it" and then put the paper away and never showed it to anyone as long as he lived. Three years and three months later he spoke with the same authority although more openly to his official advisers in Cabinet meeting assembled, when he told them that he himself must be "the judge how long to retain in and when to remove any of you from his position. . . . My wish is that on this subject no remark be made nor question asked by any of you, here or elsewhere, now or hereafter."[2]

[1] Frederic Bancroft's *Life of William H. Seward* in two volumes (New York, 1900) has the merits of modern scholarship. The greatest monument to Seward is the printed text of his diplomatic despatches in the *Papers relating to Foreign Affairs, 1861–1864*, and in the *Official Records*. The footnotes to Bancroft's *Seward* are a useful guide to these publications. The "Thoughts" are printed on pages 132–133 of the second volume of Bancroft's *Seward*.

[2] Nicolay and Hay's *Abraham Lincoln*, ix, 339.

President Lincoln had been in office a very short time when it became evident that the garrison[1] at Fort Sumter must be reprovisioned and reënforced, if Anderson were not to withdraw; and if he withdrew peaceably, the rightfulness of secession would thereby be acknowledged by the government of the United States.   Three men now come to the front who were destined to play important parts in the next four years; these were Gustavus Vasa Fox, Montgomery C. Meigs, a lieutenant in the United States army, and David D. Porter, a lieutenant in the navy.   Fox was connected by marriage with the Blair family.   He had resigned from the navy to seek his fortune in private life, but was now anxious to serve his country as best he might.   He thought that Sumter could be supplied by means of a fleet of transports accompanied by several tugs which could tow in strings of small boats in the night time, laden with provisions and soldiers, and these could be protected in a measure by one of the larger warships.[2]   Anderson's supplies were running so low

[1] Two of the officers of Fort Sumter compiled accounts of the episode: S. W. Crawford's *Genesis of the Civil War, the Story of Sumter* was published in 1887 and reprinted in 1896 with a somewhat different title. In 1876, General Abner Doubleday, who was a captain in the garrison in 1861, printed a volume of *Reminiscences of Forts Sumter and Moultrie in 1860-'61*. Under October, 1864 and January, 1865, in the "Ropes-Gray Letters" (Mss.) are notes of conversations with General Foster who had also been a captain in the garrison at Fort Sumter. Foster stated that Major Anderson thought he was the divinely appointed instrument for the prevention of bloodshed and was "like a stricken man" when he received Beauregard's announcement that he should open fire. Foster also stated that if the wind had been from another quarter, the fire would have compelled surrender at once, but that when the capitulation was arranged, the smoke and heat "had in great measure passed away and was no cause of the surrender of the fort." A detailed account of "The Bombardment of Fort Sumter, 1861" by Captain O. L. Spaulding of the United States army is in the *Report* of the American Historical Association for 1913, i, 177-203. See, also M. Scrugham's "The Peaceable Americans of 1860-1861" in *Columbia Studies in History*, xcvi, No. 3, pp. 78-104; and N. W. Stephenson's *Lincoln*, 443-447. Other citations are given in the Note at the end of this chapter.

[2] Montgomery Blair contributed to *The United Service* magazine for March, 1881 (pp. 358-384) "Confederate Documents Relating to Fort Sumter." These are exceedingly interesting, but the preliminary matter partakes of the insecurity of recollections. The documents show that it was the exigencies of secession and confederation that postponed the attack until the new government at Washington was some-

that something must be done at once or he would be obliged
to hand over the fort to the Confederates.   Meigs and Porter
had the problem of holding Fort Pickens on their minds.
Soldiers had been transported to the anchorage off Pickens,
but an agreement existed with the Confederate authorities
there to preserve the existing condition of affairs.[1]   Lincoln
and Seward, Fox, Meigs, and Porter consulted together
about these projects and communicated neither with Welles,
the Secretary of the Navy, nor with Cameron, the Secretary
of War.   This failure to work through the usual channels
has been attributed to Seward's self-sufficiency and to Lincoln's ineptitude; but it may well be that the underlying
reason was the presence in those departments of many Southern sympathizers.   At all events, acting under an order from
the President that was countersigned by Seward, the Sumter
expedition was secretly prepared at New York.   Then,
suddenly, Porter appeared at the Brooklyn Navy Yard and
presented a written order of the President giving him command of the *Powhatan* for special service.   This was the
vessel which had been refitted to protect, as far as possible,
the expedition going to the relief of Fort Sumter.   As Porter
was sailing down the bay, he was overtaken by a telegram
from Seward calling his ship back to her original duty : but
as this was signed by Seward and not by the President,
Porter sailed on and accomplished his task of reënforcing Fort

what organized.   Fox's own statements
are contained in letters and memoranda
that are printed in the *Publications* of
the Naval History Society, ix, 3–44.
A letter from George W. Blunt — of the
"Pilot Book" — dated New York,
September 27, 1866, gives some personal
recollections of the attempts to relieve
Fort Sumter in January and April, 1861
(*Home Journal*, September 7, 1892).

[1] An interesting side-light on the
condition of affairs is in a letter of
Stephen R. Mallory dated March 22,
1861.   In it he writes that as the
entrance of United States naval vessels
into Pensacola harbor would compel the
Southerners to fire "the first gun" he
induced Buchanan and Toucey to
countermand orders that had been
given and that he and Captain Barron
then proceeded to Pensacola and
"warned off" every man-of-war as it
appeared.   *American Historical Review*,
xii, 105.

Pickens which was held by Federal soldiers throughout the war.

Notwithstanding this mishap, the Sumter expedition proceeded. Misfortune still attended it, bad weather dispersed its component parts and the transports found themselves off Charleston bar in heavy weather without their protecting warship and without the coöperating tugs. Meantime, Lincoln and Seward had performed their part of the agreement, if one can call it so, with the Southerners that no change would be made in the conditions of things in Sumter without due notice being given. Upon receipt of the information from Seward that Fort Sumter was to be reënforced and supplied with food, the Confederate Cabinet at Montgomery at once took action. It is exceedingly difficult at this point of time to understand their mode of reasoning.[1] A few men more or less at Sumter and food for another month or so would make little difference in the ultimate course of events. But aggressive action on the part of the Confederates would at once bring on the crisis that true policy forbade. On the other hand, it is not unlikely that an attitude of acquiescence in the re-victualing of the fort might bring about the withdrawal of South Carolina from the Confederacy and also the firing on Fort Sumter would compel the Border States to take one side or the other and thus to a very great extent transfer the scene of war, of destruction, and of desolation from the Cotton States to those to the northward of them. It is said that Robert Toombs was the only man at the Confederate Cabinet table who argued against action, asserting that the first shot fired from the Confederate batteries would convert their friends in the

[1] Pleasant A. Stovall's *Robert Toombs*, 226. According to the *Mobile Mercury*, as stated in a speech delivered by Horace Maynard at Nashville, on March 20, 1862, the people of the seceded States were sinking into a fatal apathy and patriotism was oozing out. If something decisive were not done

North to enemies and would bring a swarm of hornets around their ears. Nevertheless, a telegram was sent to Beauregard at Charleston directing him to open fire on Sumter, if affairs demanded it. The despatch was no sooner sent than the high officials at Montgomery appear to have regretted their action. Beauregard, himself, also seems to have been undecided. He sent some of his staff officers to Sumter to demand the surrender of the fort. Of these, Roger A. Pryor of Virginia and Louis T. Wigfall of Texas, were eminent politicians, and a third was one of South Carolina's Senators in the United States Congress, or had been, James Chesnut, Jr. All three were ardent Secessionists and at once upon Anderson's refusing to surrender, gave the order to fire. They did this notwithstanding the fact that Anderson told them that he would be obliged to surrender within two days, if he were not supplied with food. The first gun[1] boomed forth at daybreak on April 12, 1861. On the after-

---

soon they would become disgusted with Southern independence. In this speech the statement of Roger A. Pryor made at Charleston on April 11, 1861, is given as follows: "Strike a blow! The very moment that blood is shed, Old Virginia will make common cause with her sisters of the South."

[1] The story of opening fire on Fort Sumter and inaugurating war is so extraordinary that one can hardly believe it, although it was so well remembered by many of the participants at a later time. See Mary B. Chesnut's *Diary from Dixie*, 31–41; W. E. Dodd's *Statesmen of the Old South*, 221. This last is the substance of a conversation that Professor Dodd had with Roger A. Pryor on December 30, 1909. It is the latest recorded "recollection of an old man" on Sumter. There was great competition at the time for the honor or dishonor of having fired the first shot and it is not yet definitely settled; see *South Carolina Historical and Genealogical Magazine*, xii, 141: *William and Mary Quarterly*, xx, 69; and Southern Historical Society *Papers*, index volume under "Fort Sumter." There is an interesting article on Edmund Ruffin in the *John P. Branch Historical Papers*, iii, No. 2, especially pp. 116–123. In 1860, Edmund Ruffin printed an extraordinary book entitled *Anticipations of the Future*. It purported to be extracts from letters written by an Englishman in the United States to the London *Times* in the years 1864 to 1870 and had an appendix of 73 pages entitled "The Causes and Consequences of the Independence of the South" which had first been printed in a Richmond newspaper in 1856.

Edmund Ruffin was an indomitable Secessionist. When South Carolina seceded and Virginia did not, he abandoned his home and became "a citizen of the Confederate States." When the last hope of Southern independence faded, he wrapped the Confederate flag about his body and committed suicide at his home in Amelia County, Virginia.

noon of the next day, Anderson surrendered.[1] Eighteen
days later, Lincoln, writing to Fox, observed that both of
them had anticipated that "the cause of the country would
be advanced by making the attempt to provision Fort Sump-
ter, even if it should fail; and it is no small consolation now
to feel that our anticipation is justified by the result." Earlier, on April 8, Major Anderson had written to the Adjutant
General of the army that "my heart is not in the war, which
I see is to be thus commenced."

On the reception of the news from Charleston, a thrill of
indignation swept over the North. Every month since the
secession of South Carolina, as letters to Major Anderson
clearly show, the resentment felt by many, many Northerners toward the people of the South had grown more and
more embittered. Now, the Secessionists had fired on the
emblem of national authority flying over the walls of a

---

[1] *Publications* of the Naval History
Society, ix, 44; also in the *Proceedings*
of the Massachusetts Historical Society
for December, 1877, p. 394. On this
phase of the subject, see J. T. Scharf's
History of the Confederate States Navy,
18 and fol. Anderson's letter is in the
"Stanton Papers" vol. i, in the Library
of Congress.

Two Massachusetts men visited Fort
Sumter within a day or two after the
departure of Anderson. The first was
William Appleton, a Boston merchant
and cotton manufacturer, who had gone
South for his health and arrived off
Charleston Harbor in time to see the
bombardment of the fort. It seemed
to him to be "a most awful wreck;
one cannot realize that no one should
have been killed." Mr. Appleton was
well received at Charleston by his
friends and after staying a week or so
with one of the great rice planters,
departed for home (*Selections from the
Diaries of William Appleton*, 238). The
other New Englander was Caleb Huse,
who visited Sumter on his way to England to buy munitions for the Confeder-

ates. After viewing the fort, he remarked to one of his comrades, "What
in the world made Anderson surrender?" and he goes on to say that the fort
was no more damaged for defence than
if a boy had snapped marbles at it and
was impregnable against the Confederate artillery. The wooden quarters had
taken fire and the fort had been very
uncomfortable, but at the time of the
surrender all that danger had passed.
"Eventually his command might have
been starved out," but when Anderson
left he took several barrels of pork with
him and, Huse adds, there were no boats
or scaling ladders with which to make an
assault, as Anderson must have known.
Caleb Huse's *Supplies for the Confederate Army*, pp. 11,12.

Gideon Welles wrote to his wife on
April 14, 1861, that it was remarkable
"that opposite parties should be firing
at each other for two days without any
one meeting with harm." An interesting article on "The Chances of being
Hit in Battle" by William F. Fox, the
author of *Regimental Losses* is in the
Century for May, 1888, pp. 93–106.

national fortress. Patriotism, the necessity of defending "the sacred symbol of free government," even at the cost of one's own life, overwhelmed all other considerations. This wave of emotion was never better expressed than in Whittier's words [1] : —

> "'Shoot, if you must, this old gray head,
>   But spare your country's flag,' she said."

Wendell Phillips, on April 21, declared he would not recant or retract anything he had said, but now, for the first time in his "anti-slavery life," he spoke "Under the stars and stripes. . . . Today the slave asks God for a sight of this banner." Stephen A. Douglas at once came out into the open: "There are only TWO SIDES to the question. Every man must be for the United States government or against it. There can be no neutrals in this war ; only patriots or traitors." Benjamin Franklin Butler, the Massachusetts Democrat who had voted fifty times and more for Jefferson Davis at the Charleston Convention, proclaimed "We will hold as a brother, him who stands by the Union; we will hold him as an enemy, who would strike from its constellation a single star. . . . Our faces are set South, and there shall be no footstep backwards. . . . THE DAY OF COMPROMISE IS PAST." The Roman Catholic Archbishop Hughes of New York wrote to Bishop Lynch of South Carolina that "since violence, battle, and blood-shed" have occurred, he dared not hope for peace. The psychology of men's actions is often beyond the ken of the historian ; but in this case sentiment overruled every other consideration in the North, — and in the South.

[1] For the historical setting of these lines, see the Confederate Colonel H. K. Douglas in the *Century* for June, 1886, p. 287 ; and articles in the Boston *Evening Transcript* for May 9, 1900; and the *Atlantic Monthly* for November, 1902, p. 717.

On April 15, Lincoln issued a proclamation calling for
seventy-five thousand militiamen for three months to put
down disturbances in the Southern States that were too serious for the law officers of the government to suppress. In
taking this action he followed the precepts of the old laws ;
but it may well be that he felt that the obligations of his
oath to observe, protect, and defend the Constitution over-
rode any and every consideration of possible departure from
the absolute letter of those acts of Congress.[1] Whatever
the legality or illegality of his action, the answer was startling. In a few hours militia regiments were recruited to
their full strength and on their way to Washington. The
first soldiers to reach the capital came from Pennsylvania,
but they came practically without arms and equipment.[2]
They were followed by the Sixth Massachusetts Regiment
in uniform and armed. In those days the railroad connection between the North and the South was broken at New
York by the Hudson River, at Philadelphia by the Delaware,
and at Baltimore the cars were hauled by horses from the
terminus of the railroad from Philadelphia to the terminus
of the railroad to Washington. A very large portion of the
Baltimoreans, probably a large majority, sympathized most
heartily with the Southern cause. That city also had been
for generations the abode of a large and active disorderly
element which oftentimes preferred to gain its object by
rioting and physical disturbance rather than by the force of
argument or by the ballot-box. The first portion of the train
bearing the United States soldiers was hauled safely from

[1] Upton's *Military Policy of the
United States*, ch. xvii.

[2] Samuel P. Bates's *Martial Deeds of
Pennsylvania*, 121 ; and his *History of
Pennsylvania Volunteers*, i, 6, 7 ; *Official
Records*, ser. i, vol. ii, p. 7 and fol.,
especially p. 16. These days are
graphically described in C. P. Stone's
"Washington in March and April,
1861" in *Magazine of American History*,
xiv, 1–24 ; in W. R. Thayer's *John Hay*,
i, ch. v ; and in W. B. Bryan's *History of
the National Capital*, ii, 460–481.

one station to the other.[1] Then crowds gathered along the route, anchors and sand were dumped on the track, and other obstructions were placed there. It became necessary for the soldiers to leave the cars and proceed on foot. They formed between the lines of the Baltimoreans who jeered and threw stones at them. Then a musket went off accidentally, it is said. This brought on the trouble which was plainly near at hand. The soldiers deployed and fired and the Baltimoreans returned to the attack with all kinds of missiles and firearms. Then the police appeared and escorted the soldiers to the other station where they entrained and proceeded on their way to Washington. This event occurred on the 19th of April, the anniversary of Lexington and Concord, and the blood shed at Baltimore was the first of the war. The Sixth Massachusetts was followed by the famous Seventh New York Regiment, by two other Massachusetts regiments commanded by General B. F. Butler, and then came an in-pouring of troops from the North. After the rioting of April 19, the Baltimoreans destroyed the railroad bridges leading into the city. The soldiers from the North then made their way by steamer to Annapolis. There they expected to entrain for Washington, but it was found that the railroad tracks had been torn up and the rolling stock damaged. At once military rule was established. Soon communication was opened with the capital and Baltimore was occupied by Union troops.[2] Washington City was safe from attack.

[1] On the Baltimore riot, see G. W. Brown's "Baltimore and the Nineteenth of April, 1861," in *Johns Hopkins Studies*, Extra Volume iii. The author was mayor of Baltimore in 1861, but the account was written in later years, — after 1880. There is also something in G. L. P. Radcliffe's "Governor Thomas H. Hicks of Maryland and The Civil War" in *ibid.*, series xix, Nos. 11–12. The official version is given in a *Memorial of the Mayor and City Council of Baltimore* (Baltimore, 1861). A very lifelike and inaccurate picture is in The "*Southern Rights*" and "*Union*" *Parties in Maryland Contrasted* (Baltimore, 1863). Other citations are enumerated in Rhodes's *United States*, iii, 362 and fol.

[2] Colonel Scott, a nephew of General Scott, who was with Butler in April, 1861, "afterwards joined the rebels." G. S. Boutwell's *Reminiscences*, i, 286.

The picture of Anderson's little band of sixty officers and men in their unfinished, poorly supplied Fort Sumter, attacked by thousands with heavy guns throwing a concentric fire is one of the most curious spectacles of modern history. On the Southern side, the competition for the honor of firing the first shot and the great rejoicing in the "victory" strikes one with amazement as one reads it in cold blood, half a century later. On the other hand, the capitulation of Major Anderson before one of his soldiers had been killed and his being regarded as a hero by the people of the North fills one with even greater concern. From the fall of Sumter to the battle of Bull Run on July 21 following, for exactly one hundred days, the people of the North and of the South passed through a period of enthusiasm and exaggeration that likewise has few parallels, fortunately. The people of the South, confident in the belief that one Southerner could whip five Northerners, proceeded to the conflict with the elation that people now go to a football game. The people of the North had even less respect for the Southern slave owners who "had never done a day's labor in their lives." On either side victory was certain within ninety days.

The attack on Fort Sumter and the proclamation of President Lincoln calling for troops brought on a definite alignment. Already, the seceded States, or several of them, had sent commissioners to exhort the people of the tobacco States to urge them to join the Southern Confederacy. It was the natural and logical course for them to take. It happened, however, that in most of the northern part of the slaveholding area, there were very many persons who had no interest in the institution of slavery and who were closely allied, economically and socially, with the North.[1] In Virginia,

[1] Nevertheless Walter A. Montgomery states that the members of the conventions of North Carolina, Virginia, Tennessee, and Arkansas feared for the safety of slavery and were "greatly influenced" by that fear in their

the people of the western part of the State, as a whole, had no affiliation with the slave system and resembled their cousins and relatives on the opposite side of the Ohio River much more than they did their fellow citizens in the Shenandoah Valley and in the old Virginia to the eastward of the Blue Ridge. In North Carolina, there were many small farmers who owned no slaves and, in some parts of the State, slavery as an institution had no existence and never had. The eastern portion of Tennessee closely resembled the upper regions of North Carolina, while the central portion contained many small manufacturing concerns; but in the western part slavery was well established. In Arkansas, there were areas of cotton planting, where slaves were numerous, but in other parts of the State there were few or no slaves. Virginia seceded on April 17, Arkansas followed on May 6, Tennessee on May 7, and North Carolina on May 20.

The secession of Virginia [1] demands a paragraph or two.

determination to resist the coercion of the Southern States: North Carolina State Literary and Historical Association's *Publications*, Bulletin No. 15, p. 35. Other material is in *The North Carolina Booklet*, xi, 1–16 and xv, 177–202, and in *James Sprunt Historical Monographs*, No. 1. W. K. Boyd's "North Carolina on the Eve of Secession" in the American Historical Association's *Report*, for 1910, pp. 167–177,

explains a good many matters for the Northern student. Governor Vance, in a lecture delivered in Boston in 1886, said that Lincoln's call for men knocked every prop from under the Union men, Clement Dowd's *Life of Zebulon B. Vance*, 441. In a letter written in 1862, Vance stated that after sixteen months of war, the advocates of secession no longer held the ear of the people. *Ibid.*, 74.

[1] The traditional view is stated in Beverley B. Munford's *Virginia's Attitude toward Slavery and Secession*.

P. G. Van Winkle, in the United States Senate on April 21, 1864, stated that the omission of the words "by them" in the Virginia Secession Ordinance entirely changed the meaning of the phrase contained in the Ordinance of 1788.

Herewith are the corresponding passages from Virginia's Ordinance ratifying the Constitution of the United States and from the Secession Ordinance of 1861: —

"that the powers granted under the constitution, being derived from the people of the United States may be resumed by them whensoever the same shall be perverted" etc.

David Roberston's *Debates . . . of the Convention of Virginia* (Richmond, 1805), p. 469.

"that the powers granted under the said constitution were derived from the people of the United States, and might be resumed whensoever the same should be perverted" etc.

[Virginia] Ordinance of Secession.

For sixty years and more, the doctrine of State sovereignty had been firmly held by the ruling class of Virginia. This dogma was now to be used to force the State out of the Union and to carry with it some of its leading citizens to whom State allegiance was paramount. In reality the cause of Virginia's secession was a long-drawn-out conspiracy of the slave-owning class within the State to preserve their domination therein and to remain united with the other States that were organized with the institution of slavery as the basis; but the social bond was far stronger and much more decisive than the economic relation. The Virginia "sovereign" State Convention met at Richmond on February 13, 1861. The majority in this body was distinctly unionist and the governor, "honest" John Letcher, had been elected as a Union man. Unfortunately, Richmond in the heart of the slave-owning region, was still the capital of Virginia and State officials living there were powerfully influenced by local opinion. The sessions of the Convention continued for months and many of the western members left for their distant homes. When Lincoln issued his call for men, the slave-owning Secessionists summoned a volunteer meeting of their own which exerted so heavy a pressure upon the members of the regular Convention that a Secession Ordinance was passed by that body[1] on condition that it should be submitted to the voters for ratification.[2] Without awaiting the result of this vote, the "sovereign" convention, the

[1] Nevertheless Governor Letcher, in September, 1863, said that "Virginia went into this contest after the most serious and calm consideration." *Journal of the Senate of . . . Virginia . . . Extra Session* (Richmond, 1863), p. 9.

[2] The Secession Ordinance declared the union existing between the State of Virginia and the other States under the Constitution of the United States, dissolved as of April 17, 1861, " when the same shall be ratified by the qualified voters of the Commonwealth." Nevertheless, the Convention a few days later and four or five weeks before the voters gave their suffrages for or against ratification, passed an ordinance absolving Virginians from all obligations of obedience to the United States, and even made an alliance with the Confederate States.

State government, and the people of eastern Virginia made active preparations for levying war on the Federal government.[1] Ultimately, the majority of those who voted gave their suffrages for the ratification of the Secession Ordinance.

As has been stated above, the people of the eastern and western parts of Virginia were by no means united on the subject of secession or on any other subject for that matter. There was slight sympathy and few points of contact between the inhabitants of the old settled tidewater region and the lands at the foot of the mountains, or the piedmont as it was usually termed in Virginia, and the people living in the mountain valleys stretching westwardly and northwestwardly to the Ohio River.[2] These people owned very few slaves and were employed in varied farming on a small scale, in mining, and in transportation. Access to the outer world for their products was either down the rivers to the Ohio or eastwardly by the Baltimore and Ohio railroad to Maryland. They had no direct transportation connecting them with the older settled parts of Virginia and the rulers of that State had not, up to 1861, shown much interest in supplying the desires of the people of western Virginia for railroad connection with the seaboard at Richmond or Petersburg. The inhabitants of western Virginia belonged largely to the migration that had come through Pennsylvania and had penetrated southward into the valley of East Tennessee. In other words, they were not offshoots of the old Virginia

---

[1] Governor Letcher stated that these ordinances were "authorized by that vote of the people which ratified the ordinance of secession, for they were the consequences of that ordinance and of the war which was impending when it was ratified!"

[2] On the earlier history of the friction between the two parts of Virginia, see Charles H. Ambler's *Sectionalism in Virginia from 1776 to 1861*, Alrutheus A. Taylor's "Making West Virginia a Free State" in the *Journal of Negro History*, vi, 131–173, and two unpublished essays in the Harvard College Library: Edward Conrad Smith's *The Trans-Alleghany Borderland, 1861*, and Carter G. Woodson's *The Disruption of Virginia*.

families. Whenever it had become necessary to break up one or two plantation households, one of the sons, in some instances the father and mother, with some or all of the slaves had sought new lands in those regions where slave labor would be profitable,— they had gone to Kentucky or Tennessee or farther south to Alabama and Mississippi, but not to western Virginia. It fell out in this way that the people of western Virginia had few ties of interest or of blood with those of the eastern part of the State.[1] By 1860, western Virginians had formed, numerically speaking, a large proportion of the white population of the State; but they were not represented in the State legislative body to anything like their numerical strength. This was due to the representative system of the Old Dominion which had grown up when the Virginia white people were a fairly homogeneous body. It was based partly on the ownership of property and, included in that designation, were the slaves. More-

[1] Many books have been written on the formation of West Virginia. There is still room for a work that shall satisfy the needs of the student. A brief and understandable work is J. C. McGregor's *Disruption of Virginia* (New York, 1922), but the number of pages on the actual secession of western Virginia from its "parent State" is not large enough to express what the author had in mind. Three chapters (vi–viii) in James M. Callahan's *Semi-*

Centennial History of West Virginia, a hundred pages (319–423) in Virgil A. Lewis's *History of West Virginia* (Philadelphia, 1889), and a whole volume, and a very one-sided one, by Granville D. Hall entitled *The Rending of Virginia* leaves the reader still in the dark.

The population of the several parts of Virginia is given as below in the *Report* of the State auditor for November, 21, 1861:

	Total Number of White Males Over 21	Total Whites	Free Negroes	Slaves	Total Population
Tidewater	44,060	215,534	32,841	179,502	427,877
Piedmont	50,650	231,778	16,044	248,849	496,671
Valley	35,539	176,153	5,841	37,204	219,198
Trans. Alleg. So-west	31,526	168,881	1,486	19,025	189,392
Trans. Alleg. No-west	48,893	255,201	1,027	6,448	262,676
Total	210,668	1,047,547	57,239	491,028	1,595,814

over, in arranging State taxation, a slave was valued at only three hundred dollars at the outside, whereas in 1860, a "prime slave" was worth from $1500 to $2000. It was quite within the bounds of human nature that the people of the older settled portion of Virginia should oppose in every way any change in the State constitution that would deprive them of political power and of financial privilege. In successive State constitutional conventions, the western Virginians had sought amelioration of these political and financial disabilities, but without much success. They had been equally unsuccessful in securing the appropriation of money from the State legislature to give them adequate facilities of communication with the Potomac valleys. Now, when the Virginia Convention voted the State out of the Union,[1] the people of western Virginia decided to set up for themselves as an independent State and ask for admission to the Union as such.[2] In order to accomplish this result in conformity with the Constitution of the United States, the inhabitants of western Virginia found it necessary to deny the legality of the action of the Virginia Convention. They, therefore, instituted a Virginia State government which they claimed to be the rightful State government and which was recognized as such by the administration at Washington. The western Virginians then drew up a constitution for a

[1] An Ordinance of the Wheeling Convention of June 13, 1861, declared "without authority and void" all acts of the Virginia Convention and of the Executive acting under it, tending to levy war against the United States or to separate "this Commonwealth" from the United States.

[2] The spirit of the people of the Northern Virginia Panhandle was shown in the reply of Andrew Sweeney — mayor of Wheeling — to Governor Letcher's order, issued on April 20, 1861, directing him to take possession of all federal buildings in Wheeling in the name of Virginia, adding that "Virginia has seceded." The next day, Sweeney reported that he had taken possession of the custom-house and other public buildings, and also of the public documents "in the name of Abraham Lincoln, President of the United States, whose property they are." Much interesting matter is to be found in the *Congressional Globe* of May 21, 1864, and also in a separate pamphlet entitled *Speeches of the Hon. Joseph Segar and Hon. L. H. Chandler.*

separate State and applied to Congress for admission, the newly formed government of the State of Virginia giving its permission as required by the Federal Constitution. When the matter came up at Washington, there was opposition, for the constitution of the proposed new State recognized the condition of slavery. Neither Congress nor the administration was in any mood to admit a new Slave State to the Union. It appeared, however, that there were not many slaves, comparatively speaking, within the limits of West Virginia and it seemed undesirable to place disabilities on the few slaveholding families. They compromised the matter by adopting gradual emancipation, and in 1863, the State of West Virginia was admitted to the Union.

In the eastern part of Virginia, in the estuary of the James River was Fortress Monroe and opposite on the other side, the town of Norfolk with a United States naval arsenal. Fortress Monroe was one of the largest and possibly the strongest fortification on the coast and its continued occupation was vital to the retention of Washington as the Federal capital, for it practically dominated the entrance to Chesapeake Bay. Some time before the secession of Virginia, the authorities at Richmond had shown jealousy over the activities of the United States officers at Fortress Monroe who had mounted guns commanding the approaches to the fort on the land side; but beyond a legislative inquiry nothing was done. On the other side of the channel leading into the James River on a shoal was another fortification known as the Rip Raps. Together the two closed the James to commerce. On the southern side of the river was the port of Norfolk and on the opposite side of the harbor from the town was a United States navy yard which, in those days, was one of the most important centers of construction and ship repairing on the coast and also possessed one of the best dry docks in the country. At the time of the secession of Virginia several of the few important United States warships were at this navy yard for repairs. In the yard itself was a large stock of naval guns and ammunition. Norfolk should have been held by the Federal forces if it were in any way possible, and if not held should have been destroyed absolutely, — ships, dry dock, machinery, and war implements of all sorts. Unfortunately, the commanding officer was old and refused to take any responsibility. The ships were damaged in a half-hearted way, the dry dock was only partly destroyed, and vast quantities of warlike material fell into the hands of the Confederates. The town of Norfolk was distinctively Southern in sympathy. When the news of the secession of Virginia came, the Union flag was hauled down and a "splendid Sic Semper Tyrannis" Virginia State flag was raised in its stead to the accompaniment of the applause of the population.

The composition of the Northern and Southern armies in 1861 was much alike and in many ways was extraordinary. No uniforms could be supplied by either government. Most of the soldiers were clad in their civilian garments. Some of the more permanent militia companies had uniforms, but frequently each company in the regiment had its own uniform and whichever was the case, the clothing was entirely unsuited to campaign purposes. The arms were of various types from the new Springfield rifle to shotguns. The soldiers were generally overburdened with impedimenta of one sort or another and some of the privates of the Confederate service went to the front with a trunk or two filled with clothing and food and attended by a body servant. Company and regimental drills were about all that could be had and there were no units above the brigade or division in either army. For the most part, the officers on either side were hardly better fitted for marching and fighting than were the privates.   On either side, men who had been in the service and had resigned, left their pursuits of peace and reëntered the army.   On the Northern side were Ulysses S. Grant, a clerk in a store on April 15, 1861 ; William T. Sherman, at the head of a horse railroad; and George B. McClellan, the president of a steam railroad.   On the Confederate side, were "Stonewall" Jackson, at the moment a professor in the Virginia Military Institute; Gustavus W. Smith, street commissioner in New York; and Leonidas Polk, a bishop of the Episcopal Church.   The Southern soldiers enjoyed the great advantage of having at the outset half a dozen remarkable men at their head: Robert E. Lee, J. E. Johnston, Albert Sidney Johnston, P. G. T. Beauregard, Braxton Bragg, and James Longstreet.   Albert Sidney Johnston was killed at Shiloh, otherwise these men were in high command at the time of Appomatox and their presence with the Southern armies was worth many regiments, divisions, or army corps.   On the Union side, there were no such outstanding military figures in the early months.   Winfield Scott had had a great career, but he was infirm and past work.   The high officers on the staff, the adjutant general, the quartermaster general, the commissary general, had all "gone South," leaving the department full of the second grade permanent officers, most of them old and all of them inert.   In July, 1861, the army in front of Washington was commanded by Irvin McDowell, a West Pointer, who had remained in the service after graduation. The forces near Harper's Ferry were commanded by Robert Patterson, a native of Ireland.   He had won distinction as a general of volunteers in the Mexican War, had been picked out by Governor Curtin of Pennsylvania to command the State volunteers, and had been taken over by the Federal

government.   McClellan commanded the Ohio State troops
and possibly some other soldiers who had crossed the Ohio
River into western Virginia and with him, as second in command, was General William S. Rosecrans.

As the weeks and the months dragged on, nothing was
done except to march to and fro about Harper's Ferry and
build fortifications on the southern bank of the Potomac.
Indeed, the victory of McClellan, or rather of Rosecrans,
in the mountains of western Virginia on July 11, was the
only event of any moment and seemed at the time to be so
important that Congress gave a vote of thanks to McClellan.
Meantime volunteers were coming into the army and the
terms of the militiamen would be up within a few weeks.
The people, the Congress, the administration, and the soldiers themselves were all anxious to go forward.   Indeed,
the obvious thing was for the army to brush aside the Confederates who stood on the road to Richmond, to occupy that
town, and to end the war, there and then.   Scott withstood
the pressure as long as he could and then gave way.   He
ordered McDowell with the troops in front of Washington
to drive the Confederates from Bull Run or Manassas
Junction and to follow them as far as he could.   Scott also
directed Patterson to cross the Potomac, drive the Confederate General Joseph E. Johnston up the Valley or at all events
to occupy his attention so thoroughly that he could not go
to the aid of Beauregard at Manassas or send any considerable portion of his force to him.   As McDowell's army
moved forward, it was accompanied and followed by members of Congress, newspaper correspondents, and many other
spectators.   In some way, Johnston found it possible to
shake himself loose from Patterson and join Beauregard.
This he did with the greater part of his men on July 20 and
most of the rest of them reached the battlefield on the after-

noon of July 21, 1861. It is impossible to say what might have happened had Patterson done otherwise than he did, but it is certain that his orders were so confused that he did not know what was expected of him and did exactly the wrong thing. After two days and a half of marching, McDowell with his men found themselves in face of a considerable Confederate force stationed behind Bull Run. McDowell's attacks with artillery and infantry were well designed and many of them were well carried out; but they were not pushed home. Accidents and the unexpected presence of all of Johnston's men changed the successful Union attacks of the morning to unsuccessful attacks in the afternoon. Some of the Union militiamen turned and fled and their examples spread along the lines.[1] Soon practically the whole army, newspaper correspondents, and spectators were mingled in one tumultuous flight back to Washington. The soldiers threw away clothing and arms and some regiments that were marching toward the field of battle, turned and fled "at the sound of cannon" from afar. Among the fleetest horsed correspondents was Henry Villard who was trying to outstrip all his comrades to get possession of the telegraph line from Washington to New York for his paper; but he was passed by an officer on a fine black charger, without a hat and without a sword, whom he recognized as Colonel Ambrose E. Burnside who then commanded a brigade and who shouted to him as he passed "I am hurrying ahead to get rations for my command!"[2] That the Confederates did not pursue the Federals further and go into Washington with them was due to the fact that the Southern army had been severely handled and that the extent

[1] Graphic incidents of the flight are related in a paper printed in the *Proceedings* of the Massachusetts Historical Society for March, 1909, p. 186. A contemporary account is George Wilkes's *The Great Battle* (New York, 1861).

[2] Villard's *Memoirs*, i, 197.

of the panic was not known at the time and in fact a repetition of the attack was expected.[1] In looking back at this first large armed conflict of the war, several things come to one's mind. In the first place, had the Union attack been delayed an hour the Confederates would have attacked with all the disadvantages that the offensive implies across a river and up steep banks. In the second place, as things were, a little greater efficiency on the part of the Northern officers would have given the decision to the North. As it was, the historical student after reading report after report, memoir after memoir, and letter after letter, can only assert that the catastrophe at Bull Run was one of those accidents that so frequently occur in war and that can never be absolutely avoided. For a few days, the North was dazed, stocks went down, money went up, and people sat around with their hands folded in despair. Then, almost as by magic, the scene shifted and stern resolve took the place of the hysteria of the Hundred Days since Sumter. Lincoln called for volunteers. The best blood of the North in all ranks of society, in the East, in the Ohio Valley, and on the shores of the Great Lakes responded. The new men went into the conflict with a determination and a spirit that has seldom been seen and never excelled. To the Southerners the war seemed to be over and the time to have arrived for them to

[1] On page 120 of volume v of Dunbar Rowland's *Jefferson Davis* is a letter from Davis to Beauregard. It is dated August 4, 1861 — two weeks after the battle — and was written before any friction had arisen and while the events were fresh in the memory. "Under the circumstances of our army and in the absence of the knowledge since acquired, if indeed the statements be true, it would have been extremely hazardous to have done more than was performed." Davis added, "You will not fail to remember that so far from knowing that the enemy was routed, a large part of our forces was moved by you in the night of the 21st to repel a supposed attack upon our right, and that the next day's operations did not fully reveal what has since been reported of the enemy's panic." On February 18, 1865, Davis stated in writing that (*ibid.*, vi, 493) disaster was averted at Manassas in July, 1861, by the arrival of General E. K. Smith — "acting without orders." Moreover, it was "only after repeated and urgent instructions" that Johnston moved from the Valley to Beauregard's assistance.

go home and attend to their own private affairs.   Volunteering stopped and, even in South Carolina itself, it proved to be
impossible to raise sufficient troops to garrison the seacoast
defences against attacks that were likely to be made by the
Federal naval forces.

NOTE

Bull Run and Its Aftermath. — Besides the reports and despatches that are given in the *Official Records*, a most interesting local contemporary account of the battle was published at Richmond in 1862 with two very life-like maps. It was written by T. B. Warder and Jas. M. Catlett and was printed under the title of *Battle of Young's Branch or Manassas Plain*. Almost from the very day of the battle, disputations arose between President Davis and the Confederate commanding generals and between the Union General Patterson and the authorities at Washington. Beauregard's side is set forth by his son-in-law, Alfred Roman, in the first volume of *The Military Operations of General Beauregard* (New York, 1884) and Beauregard, himself, printed an 187-page *Commentary on the Campaign and Battle of Manassas of July, 1861* (New York, 1891). Johnston's view of these matters is set forth in his own *Narrative of Military Operations during the Late War between the States* (New York, 1874). Gustavus W. Smith, who came into the controversy after the battle of Manassas, but drew up the paper that was signed by the three generals charging Davis with having prevented an autumnal invasion of the North, printed his side of the case at New York, in 1884, in a biographical work entitled *Confederate War Papers*. Davis resented the statements made by his generals in 1861 and in practically every year thereafter, and these animadversions form a large part of the matter printed in the last six volumes of Rowland's *Jefferson Davis, Constitutionalist*.[1]

General Robert Patterson's participation, or rather the lack of it, in the campaign is very well set forth by Colonel Thomas L. Livermore in a paper entitled "Patterson's Shenandoah Campaign" in *Papers* of the Military Historical Society of Massachusetts, i, 3–58. Patterson stated his own side of the case in *A Narrative of the Campaign in the Valley of the Shenandoah in 1861*. This was printed at Philadelphia in 1865 and was reprinted in the same year and, in 1873, a 190-page "Appendix" of letters, most of them of a complimentary nature, was bound with the *Narrative* itself for private distribution.

[1] In this connection it is interesting to read in a letter from Davis to his wife, dated June 23, 1862: "I wish he [J. E. Johnston] were able to take the field. Despite the critics who know military affairs by instinct he is a good soldier, never brags of what he did do, and could at this time, render most valuable service." Rowland's *Davis*, v, 284. A convenient summary of the affair by Leslie J. Perry is in the *Papers* of the Southern Historical Society, xx, 95–108.

CHAPTER XII

"COTTON IS KING"

AT first glance, running over the statistics of population and production of the States that seceded and of those that did not secede, viewing their differing economic interests, and bearing in memory the outcome, one is amazed at the hardihood of the Southern leaders in pressing their people into inevitable and hopeless conflict. In reality, their cause was not at all hopeless, nor was defeat inevitable; and it did not seem to be nearly as hopeless as it was to the Southern leaders whose horizons were bounded by their own little locality and who possessed neither the training nor the desire to study the social, economical, and international relations of the countries of the world. Three fixed beliefs strongly affected them: the one was that cotton was "King" and that the cessation of exportation for a few months, or years at most, would bring the nations of Europe to their knees in supplication to the Southerners to plant cotton,[1] and would even bring about the recognition of the Southern Confederacy by Great Britain and France.

[1] See Senator Hammond's speech of March 6, 1858, in the *Congressional Globe* under that date. The speech is given with somewhat different phraseology in a tract entitled *To the People of the South* . . . *By Troup* (Charleston, 1860) and in *Selections From the Letters and Speeches of the Hon. James H. Hammond* (New York, 1866, pp. 316, 317). See also speech of Zebulon B. Vance of North Carolina in the *Congressional Globe*, 36th Cong., 1st Sess., ii, 1160.

According to F. W. Sargent in a partisan pamphlet printed at London in 1863 with the title *England, the United States, and the Southern Confederacy* (p. 30), the "Southern policy, *Cotton is King, and Slavery is his Prime Minister*, constitute the key to every act which has disgraced the foreign relations of the United States with other powers."

The second idea was that the North would not fight, that
secession would be peaceable. The third idea was that if
the Federal government did attempt to coerce the South,
the people of the Ohio Valley would not rally behind
Lincoln and his Black Republicans. In all these three
expectations the Southern leaders were wrong.

Several Englishmen travelled through portions of the
Southern land and later printed their impressions in newspapers or books. They were overwhelmed by the amount
of cotton that they saw and by the place that it occupied in
the thoughts and the speech of the people whom they met.
Of these Englishmen the most eminent was William H.
Russell, the correspondent of the London "Times." He
reported that the governor of South Carolina said that if
his State stood alone, it must win, and Russell wrote that
the doctrine of "cotton is king" was to the Charlestonians
a lively all-powerful faith without distracting heresies or
schisms. It was only necessary, so the people told him, at a
dinner party in that city, to shut off the supply of cotton
for a few weeks and there would be a revolution in Great
Britain where four millions of people depended upon the
Southern Cotton States for their bread. Russell thought
that some of his Southern friends were persuaded that the
Lord Chancellor of England presided over the deliberations
of the Peers, seated on a cotton bale, and not on a wool
sack.[1] Southerners were unanimous in believing that
England would be compelled by her necessity to recognize
the Southern Confederation as an independent power before

[1] Some extracts from the original
edition of Russell's *My Diary, North and
South* are reprinted in the *Proceedings*
of the Massachusetts Historical Society
for October, 1905, pp. 327–331.

On December 15, 1860, Barnwell
Rhett visited the British consul at
Charleston to find out, if he could, what
would be the policy of Great Britain
after secession. Apparently the interview did not terminate hopefully, as the
two were wide apart on the question of
the African slave trade (*American
Historical Review*, xviii, 784).

the end of October, 1861. Superficially, there was a good deal to be said in favor of this theory.

From 1830, and especially since 1840, Great Britain had been practically dependent upon the Southern United States for the cotton fibre on which its most important manufacture depended, and, indeed, on which manufacturing and one might say British industrial and commercial life depended, for if the purchasing power of the cotton manufacturing counties was impaired, there would be a great falling off in the demand for goods of all sorts and varieties. Originally, that is to say, in the infancy of cotton spinning and weaving by power, England had secured her supply of the fibre from Brazil, the West Indies, and India.[1] By 1830, the cotton of the Southern United States had become a formidable competitor with these other sources of supply, and by 1841 the American supply had become so large comparatively that on a graphic chart the Indian, Egyptian, Brazilian, and West Indian lines have to be carefully looked for.[2] The reason for this replacement of all other cotton fibres by that of the upland South was that this was best suited to the needs of British spinners and was the cheapest. This was due to the peculiarly favorable conditions of the climate and soil of the Southern black belts to which must be added cheap and easy transportation and intelligent management on the part of the white planters, not only in the preparation of the soil, the care of the plant, but also in the cleaning and packing of the fibre for the market. The cotton plant grows under many conditions of soil and climate, but, to reach its best development for the manufacturer's purposes, it

---

[1] J. F. Royle's *Culture and Commerce of Cotton in India* (London, 1851) and P. B. Smollett's *Cotton Supplies from India* (read before The Cotton Supply Association, Manchester, January 11, 1860).

[2] The *Atlas of American Agriculture* issued by the United States Department of Agriculture, pt. v, section A, has maps and text relating to cotton production, prices, and acreage.

must have special conditions, for it is peculiarly susceptible to adverse influences during the growing season. The soil of the black belts was singularly suited chemically to the needs of the short staple, green-seed, upland cotton plant, and so were the rainfall and the temperature. To thrive and produce advantageously, cotton requires abundant rain for a short time at the beginning of the crop season, less moisture thereafter, and clear weather at the time of picking. If there is insufficient moisture, the seed will not germinate and the young plant will not grow. If there is too much moisture thereafter, the weeds will outstrip the cotton plant, and choke it to death. And if the storms come and the rains fall in the picking season, the fibre becomes filled with dirt and loses its resiliency. In other words, it becomes much more difficult to use, even if it is not entirely unfit for spinning. The laborers in the cotton fields need not have any great degree of skill, but there must be an adequate supply of such labor at the planting and the picking season. Experience since the war has shown that white labor possesses greater efficiency in the cultivation of cotton than free negro labor, but, unquestionably, controlled negro labor in the years under review was more effective than any other labor that was then applied to the cultivation of the cotton plant. It was vastly more efficient than the ryot labor of India or the extremely inefficient labor of Brazil and the West Indies in those days. It happened that the rainfall and the temperature and the soil of the Southern United States were more exactly suited to the needs of the cotton plant than the rainfall and temperature of any other cotton region on the world's surface. Furthermore, the peculiar distribution of rivers in the cotton areas provided easy and economical transportation from the plantations of the Cotton Belt to the ports of oceanic transshipment.

Also, the short staple Southern upland cotton was exactly fitted to the existing machinery of British and New England cotton mills. This fibre, while shorter than that of the Sea Islands or of Egypt, is free from imperfections, or joints, or bents. Indian cotton was often dirty, and the transportation was expensive before the opening of the Suez Canal, — and the rivers of India were of slight assistance in carrying the cotton from the place of growth to the seaboard. The Egyptian cotton was of fine quality and was low in price, but the amount that could possibly be produced under the conditions of labor and irrigation then prevailing in Egypt was so small that it did not and could not compete with the coarser and shorter fibre of the upland United States.

About 1850, there was a tremendous development of cotton production within the United States, and a correspondingly great increase of the machinery of cotton spinning and weaving in Great Britain,[1] and the United States, and on the European continent.[2] In the years 1849–1851 something over one million bales of American cotton were annually imported into Great Britain. In the years 1858–1860, nearly two million bales were imported in each year out of a total importation of nearly two million four hundred thousand bales from all sources of supply.[3] In other words,

[1] On the English cotton industry and the supply of the fibre, see G. R. Porter's *Progress of the Nation* (ed. 1912, London), ch. xvi (B).

[2] J. E. Horn's *La Crise Cotonnière et les Textiles Indigènes* (Paris, 1863).

[3] The figures in the text are based upon two researches made by John B. Read Jr., of Cambridge, and Edward C. Storrow Jr. of Needham, Massachusetts. These in turn are based on tables in the London *Economist;* the *Statistical Abstract for the United Kingdom;* G. R. Porter's *Progress of the Nation;* James A. Mann's *Cotton Trade of Great Britain* (London, 1860) ; George

McHenry's *Cotton Trade* (London, 1863); his *Paper . . . Relating to the Approaching Cotton Crisis* that was printed by the House of Representatives of the Confederate Congress at Richmond, December 31, 1864 ; his *Cotton Supply of the United States* (London, 1865) ; and upon James L. Watkins's *King Cotton: A Historical and Statistical Review, 1790 to 1908* (New York, 1908). There is an interesting article in *The Friend* for the 4th month, 7th day, 1863, p. 243.

G. F. Jentsch of Reichenbach, Silesia, has suggested that the changes in clothing customs due to the breaking

except in a very few years in the two decades ending with 1860, England had been absolutely dependent upon the South for the raw material of its principal industry. Under these circumstances and taking a merely superficial view, the Southern idea that American cotton ruled Britain's economic existence seemed to be well founded; but, in this as in all other economic discussions, it is well to look carefully beneath the surface.

In 1860 the Southerners believed that the supply of upland-grown cotton was so necessary to British well-being that the moment it was cut off by Confederate embargo or Federal blockade the spinners of Lancashire and of Scotland would put pressure upon the British government to bring about the recognition of the Confederacy as a separate nation, and to intervene with naval and military forces to secure the much-needed raw material. The South seceded, the North imposed a blockade, Confederate emissaries were taken from a British vessel and no recognition of Southern independence was made, the blockade was not raised by the British navy, and the manufacturers of Manchester and Glasgow seemed to rejoice rather than to repine at the absence of new fibre. They did not put pressure upon the British ministers and even seemed to deprecate the forcible seizure of cotton. A study of the statistics of production which was published in the "London Economist" of those years gives the answer to the question as to why these manufacturers acted in this wholly unexpected manner — and these figures were accessible to Southern leaders in 1860 as they are to us today. It appears from this study that the production of cotton and of manufactured cotton goods had greatly outstripped the demand. In ordinary times, it is usual to have about two

down of the old class system of central Europe powerfully affected the demand for a cheap clothing material, — which was satisfied by the introduction of cotton cloth.

years' supply of fibre and goods in the warehouses of the
manufacturing towns and of the leading distributing centers
throughout the world. In the decade preceding secession,
not only had the production of fibre increased, but the in-
stallation of machinery for spinning and weaving cotton
had grown in almost like proportion and had been running
on full time. Instead of there being the usual two years'
supply of cotton and goods on hand in the storehouses and
in all the primary markets of the world in 1861, there was
then a three years' stock [1] both of fibre and of goods in
Britain and in the warehouses of Europe, Africa, and Asia.
In other words, there was a fifty per cent over-production of
cotton and of cotton goods. Moreover, the greater part of
the 1860 cotton crop had already been exported from the
South before the firing on Fort Sumter and the enforcement
of the blockade. It happened, therefore, that British manufacturers and distributors of cotton goods shut down their
factories, — or placed them on half-time, — closed their
warehouse doors, and waited complacently for the coming
of the time when they could sell their manufactured goods
for two, three, or four times the present prices. [2] It was the
closing of the factories owing to the over-supply of manufactured goods on hand that threw the operatives on their
own resources. It was not until the winter of 1862–1863
that there was a cotton famine in England. In 1861 and
1862 the British cotton interests and the French cotton inter-

[1] McHenry's *Cotton Trade*, 49–51.

[2] On July 11, 1862, Richard Cobden
wrote to Charles Sumner that in the
winter of 1861–62 there was "a large
stock of cotton in the hands of *rich*
spinners and merchants and they were
interested in keeping out cotton."
There were also those who had over-
speculated in cotton goods and were
glad of "a rise in the raw material

which enabled them to get out of their
stocks." *American Historical Review*,
ii, 307. See also John Bright to
Sumner, January 11, 1862, in Massachusetts Historical Society's *Proceedings*,
November, 1911, p. 157; John Watts's
The Facts of the Cotton Famine (London,
1866), p. 356; and R. A. Arnold's
History of the Cotton Famine (London,
1864), p. 44.

ests, also, exercised a restraining power on the governments of those two countries.[1] On the ninth day of January, 1862, the British steamship *Bohemian* arrived at Boston, Massachusetts, from Liverpool with seven hundred bales of cotton on board for the New England mills and a "large quantity of cotton and wool for New York." In the first nine days of 1862 fifteen thousand bales of cotton had been shipped to New York from Liverpool and "upwards of five thousand" bales to Boston, and in the whole of that year seventy thousand bales of cotton, valued at a little more than six million dollars, were imported from Liverpool to New York. In 1863, one hundred and three thousand bales of cotton, valued at over thirteen million dollars, were sent from England to America, and probably more.[2] By the spring and summer of 1863, however, the demand for cotton fibre had become insistent in Great Britain. But by that time other factors had come into play to compel those in power to decline to take any steps to aid the Confederacy; — Lincoln had issued the Emancipation Proclamation, Vicksburg and Gettysburg had been fought and won or lost, and the old anti-slavery element in Great Britain had had time to reorganize and to put pressure upon the politicians at Westminster, and in the years 1861 and 1862 Britain's need of American wheat had been acute. As some lines in the "Continental Monthly" expressed it in August, 1862,

---

[1] As J. M. Mason of Virginia, the unrecognized Confederate commissioner at London, wrote: "The cotton manufacturers, who might have brought great influence to bear in favor of the Confederacy were not, until 1863, in favor of recognition, because they had large stocks of cotton goods on hand"; Virginia Mason's *Public Life . . . of James M. Mason*, p. 265.

[2] *Boston Daily Advertiser*, Jan. 9, 1862, London *Economist*, Jan. 11,

1862, and *Hunt's Merchants' Magazine*, Feb. 1864, p. 136.

In "Moran's Diary" under date of Sept. 8, 1864, is a note to the effect that by that time the great supply of cotton from India had caused a demand for bullion in England. This coupled with the fear of a sudden peace in America — with cheap cotton from the United States — had produced "an incipient panic." See also Morley's *Gladstone*, ii, 79.

Wave the stars and stripes high o'er us,
Let every freeman sing,

. . . . .

Old King Cotton's dead and buried: brave young Corn is King.

As to the relative importance of American cotton 'and American wheat to Great Britain in these years and in some of the years before them considerable dispute has arisen.[1] Whatever the relative importance of the two may have been is not entirely easy of ascertainment, but there can be no question whatever as to the necessity that Britain was under of getting wheat from outside the United Kingdom during the years 1861 and 1862, and the only place from which this food grain could be procured in those particular years was from the United States and from that part of the United States that was then waging war to put an end to the Southern Confederacy. The importation of wheat and flour in large quantities into Great Britain goes back to 1840. But for nearly twenty years thereafter, the American supply was only an adjunct to the total importation. In 1860 and for the next few years, there was a succession of short crops in the United Kingdom and on the European continent. It fell out, therefore, that the importations of necessary food could not be made into Great Britain from the Baltic and the Black Sea countries. It was under these circumstances that the British necessarily turned to the United States. In 1859 ninety-nine thousand "quarters" of "wheat and flour" were imported into Great Britain from the United States; in 1860 there were imported over two million quarters, in 1861 over three and a half million quarters, in 1862 over five million, and in 1863 something

---

[1] This matter is admirably summed up by Professor E. D. Fite in the *Quarterly Journal of Economics* for February, 1906, pp. 259–278. See also Professor L. B. Schmidt's article on "The Influence of Wheat and Cotton on Anglo-American Relations during the Civil War" in the *Iowa Journal of History and Politics* for July, 1918.

under three million. It thus fell out, that at the precise
time the British cotton industry did not want cotton fibre
from the seceded States, the British people desired wheat
from the farms of the Old Northwest, Michigan, Wisconsin,
and the other Northern States. For the time being wheat
had usurped the position of royalty in the economic fabric
of the United Kingdom that cotton had occupied.

Before dismissing definitely from mind the subject of
cotton and its influence on the fortunes of the Confederacy
it will be well to glance at the condition of cotton within the
Confederacy and in the minds of Confederate leaders in the
years of the war. Whatever his excellences and his limitations may have been, Jefferson Davis certainly succeeded in
arousing the distrust and the hatred of many Southerners
quite as fully as he did those of Northerners. Prominent
among these was Joseph E. Johnston, a Confederate general
whose superior abilities never seem to have been recognized
by Davis. It is certain that Davis doubted the military
capacity of Johnston, and that hundreds of thousands of
people in the Confederacy regarded that general as the one
military figure beside that of Lee who could secure safety
and independence for them. After the war Johnston wrote
his memoirs [1] and naturally expressed great bitterness against

---

[1] J. E. Johnston's *Narrative*, 422, and
Roman's *Beauregard*, ii, 419 and 674.
The other side of the case is set forth
in Capers's *Memminger*, 355, and in
letters from Memminger and Trenholm,
his successor in the Treasury Department, in Rowland's *Davis*, viii, 41–51,
— also in part in the "Appendix" to the
*Life and Reminiscences of Jefferson
Davis*, 441–443.

In February, 1862, former Governor
Moore of Alabama wrote to Davis
deprecating "the leaky blockade system." He advised the prohibition of
all exportation of cotton to demonstrate
the fact that "our cotton crops are a

necessity to the commerce of the world.
If it is not, the sooner we know it the
better . . . if it is, European nations
should know it, and should also know
that our consent to their obtaining it is
an essential part of the transaction."
Official Records, ser. iv, vol. i, p. 905.

Texas tried a system of public exportation of cotton, but Confederate officials interfered. See a printed letter
signed by W. J. Hutchins, Chief, Texas
Cotton Office, dated November 20,
1864; and Governor Murrah's *Message*
to the Extra Session of the Tenth Texas
Legislature.

Davis and his government. Among other things he stated, what was not at all an uncommon idea in the South, that the Confederate government should have bought up every available pound of cotton that was in the South at the outbreak of the contest, shipped it to Europe, stored it in warehouses, and used it from time to time as a basis of credit wherewith to purchase ships, arms, and munitions for the South. This idea has met with favor with many writers, but there are some reasons for the belief that the Davis side was the correct one. It was pointed out by members of the Davis government that practically the whole of the cotton crop of 1860 had passed out of the limits of the Confederacy before Jefferson Davis and his associates could have realized that secession was not to be peaceable and that the Northern people would fight for the Union. Furthermore whatever cotton was remaining within the limits of the Confederacy in May, 1861, was needed there to be worked up in the mills and by the families of the South. It has also been asserted that had there been an abundance of cotton at that time there was no money with which to buy it or to hire the ships to carry it across the ocean, and that there were no ships which could have conveniently entered Southern harbors, that could have been bought or hired at that particular time for this purpose. There would seem some ground for these assertions although it is impossible to state the matter with any degree of certainty.

Whatever may have been the merits of cotton and wheat and the wisdom or unwisdom of the Davis government as the leading causes of the defeat of the Confederacy, it is certain that it was practically impossible for the British government to recognize the Confederacy until it had fairly and openly demonstrated its independence as one of the nations of the world. The ruling upper class of Great Britain could scarcely have felt otherwise than hostile to the rapid and continuing growth of the United States and to have welcomed, with some degree of sympathy, a disruption of that power into two parts. In the first place, the United States was the one great example of a successful democracy, and in Britain the still unrepresented "middle class" was becoming more and more restive and more and more clamorous for admission to the voting class. Anything that would destroy the preëminence of triumphant democracy in the United States would postpone and perhaps make unnecessary a favorable answer to this growing clamor for political power. To the Englishman, the seat of democracy appeared to be in the North and the seat of aristocracy in the South.   Indeed, it was not unnatural that the British rulers should accept the Southerners' valuation of themselves, especially when it was the people of the North who came into rivalry with them in commerce and industry.   The Southerners supplied Britain with cotton fibre for her looms and obtained from England, directly or indirectly, a very large part of the manufactured goods that they needed for themselves and their slaves.   They would have bought a larger quantity of British commodities had it not been for the tariff which was imposed on the Southerners by the people of the Northern States.   It was in the latter section, therefore, that British manufacturers and British shipowners found their rivals. In 1860, the United States Congress had passed a new tariff bill which had been approved by President Buchanan as one of the last acts of his presidential career. This was the Morrill Tariff which marked a turning point in the financial policy of the United States.   All in all, there would seem to be good reason for the sympathy that was felt towards the Secessionists and the aversion toward the North that undoubtedly actuated the doings of many of those in authority

in the British government. As justifying the view expressed
in the preceding lines, it may be added that in 1867 Parliament was obliged to yield to the "middle classes" and admit large portions of them to a share in the government.

The British had freed the slaves throughout the limits
of the Empire and had felt so strongly the iniquity of holding human beings in bondage that they had paid money
taken from the British tax levy to the dispossessed slave
owners of the West Indies. At first sight it seems not a
little incongruous that they should have entered into any
kind of an alliance with the slaveholders of the Southern
states. That they did so is partly to be accounted for by
the fact that the British anti-slavery leaders, having accomplished their task within the limits of the Empire, had turned
their attention to other fields of activity. The apathy was
due also in part to Lincoln's declaration in his Inaugural
Address that he had no objection to an amendment to the
Constitution to forbid the Federal government to interfere
with "the domestic institutions" of the several States, and
that he was willing that this amendment should be made
"express and irrevocable." The first Confederate commissioners to Great Britain used this passage from the first
Inaugural on every possible occasion to convince all Englishmen with whom they came into contact that the North was
fighting the South for dominion and power and not to accomplish any philanthropic purpose. Moreover, Lincoln for
a year and a half persistently held the same language and
curbed the efforts of Union politicians and generals to release
slaves from their obligations. It is easy for us, looking backward and realizing that very large and important portions of
the country were firm defenders of the Union and had no sympathy with abolition, to recognize the absolute soundness of
Lincoln's position. It is not at all to be wondered at that

British ministers and British society should have taken the Washington government at its word and viewed the conflict solely as an attempt to rebuild the power of the United States,—to revivify what had been the greatest successful democracy in the world.[1] Nevertheless, it is worth noting that on May 21, 1861, the Confederate commissioners wrote to Robert Toombs — the Southern Secretary of State — that they were satisfied that the public mind of England was entirely opposed to the government of the Confederate States of America on the question of slavery; and it was the sincerity and universality of this feeling that embarrassed the British government in dealing with the question of the recognition of the Confederate States.[2]

On April 15, 1861, President Lincoln issued his proclamation calling for seventy-five thousand men [3] to suppress insurrection. Two days later President Davis by proclamation invited applications for "letters of marque and reprisal" authorizing the holders to attack and capture vessels flying the flag of the United States and bring them into ports of the Confederacy for adjudication. Another two days elapsed and President Lincoln replied with a proclamation declaring a blockade of the ports of the seceded States in pursuance of the laws of the United States in such case provided.[4] On June 2nd, 1861, a schooner, the *Savannah*, sailed from Charleston flying the Confederate flag and soon after captured a Union merchant brig and was herself captured by the United States man-of-war *Perry*. In due course, the officers and seamen of the *Savannah* found themselves

---

[1] For this side of British opinion see two articles in *Blackwood's Magazine* for October, 1861, and January, 1862. They are entitled "Democracy Teaching by Example" and "The Convulsions of America." Immediately following the former is an article entitled "Meditations on Dyspepsia!"

[2] *Official Records . . . Navies*, ser. ii, vol. iii, p. 216. The phraseology of this printed text is slightly different from that of the letter in the "Pickett Papers" in the Library of Congress.

[3] *Statutes at Large*, xii, p. 1258.

[4] *Ibid.*, xii, p. 1259.

at the bar of a United States court charged with piracy.
On hearing of this the Richmond authorities sequestered
an equal number of Union officers then in their hands and
announced that the same fate would be meted out to them
that was inflicted on the crew of the *Savannah*.[1] Fortunately
the jury that had their case in hand disagreed on October 31,
1861. The crew of the *Savannah* disappeared beyond the
historian's horizon [2] and the sequestered Union officers were
restored to the ordinary status of prisoners of war. From
that time the Union authorities were obliged to regard the
Confederates as possessing belligerent rights and this chain
of proclamations and trials brought the question of the status
of the Confederacy before the nations of the world.[3]

The government of Great Britain was then and during the
whole course of the war in the hands of a coalition ministry.
The Prime Minister was Lord Palmerston. He was an old
man and died in October, 1865, within two days of his eighty-
first birthday. In 1861, he was still possessed of much of
the sprightliness and vigor of his youthful days and also of
much of the arbitrary disposition that he had shown when
formerly in power and place. The Foreign Secretary was
Lord John Russell who succeeded to the family earldom in
May, 1861. Earl Russell was a man of marked ability and
marked influence, but as a later English statesman declared,
"You couldn't tell what he was doing round the corner."

---

[1] See *A Memorial of Paul Joseph
Revere and Edward H. R. Revere*, 68–106.
P. J. Revere was one of the Union
officers selected as hostages for the
crew of the *Savannah*.

[2] See *Trial of the Officers and Crew
of the Privateer Savannah, on the Charge
of Piracy* (New York, 1862). Davis's
"Message" of July 20, 1861, is on page
120 of vol. i of *Messages and Papers of the
Confederacy* and in Rowland's *Davis*, v,
115. See also *Official Records* . . .

Navies, ser. i, vol. i, 28; vol. v, 691;
and *Official Records*, ser. ii, vol. iii,
5, 29, 41, 680. William M. Evarts's
address to the jury for the prosecution
is in his *Arguments and Speeches*, i,
91–213.

[3] The somewhat misty ideas of the
Lincoln administration as to the status
of the Secessionists are discussed by
C. F. Adams in the *Proceedings* of the
Massachusetts Historical Society for
October, 1912, p. 23.

He has usually been regarded by American writers as favoring the Confederacy, but Southerners of that time and since have held a very different tone, — and, indeed, his path was so difficult and tortuous that one might well misinterpret his actions. The Chancellor of the Exchequer was William Ewart Gladstone, who was then on the threshold of his great career. Two other strong men, George Cornewall Lewis and the Duke of Argyll were also in the government, and there were others, possibly as eminent in British political annals, but who did not come within the ken of American history in those years. These men did not work well together, for their political antecedents were somewhat diverse. Moreover, their hold on office was precarious, for they were not strong in the House of Commons. Palmerston was a remarkable political manager of great experience, and he saw as clearly as did Charles Francis Adams, our minister at London, that the non-voting democracy of Great Britain would never consent to a war on behalf of slavery against the one government in the world that represented successful democracy.[1] Considering the political careers of the first three members of this ministry, it is somewhat amusing to read that Lincoln and Seward and Chase at Washington were intent only on the number of votes that this measure or the other might bring and were not at all like the above-mentioned British trio who ruled England by their superior wisdom, talents, and authority. The Duke of Argyll [2] and

[1] On January 3, 1862, John Bright wrote to John Bigelow (*Retrospections*, i, 441) that "the town populations — the non-conformist congregations, the quiet religious people, and generally I believe the working men — these have done much to put down the war cry." Among the prominent Englishmen to take the side of the North was William E. Forster, who was elected for the first time to the House of Commons in February, 1861. See his *Life* by T.

Wemyss Reid, i, ch. ix. Forster was a man of courage and sagacity.

[2] "Letters of the Duke and Duchess of Argyll to Charles Sumner" are in the *Proceedings* of the Massachusetts Historical Society for December, 1913. An equally interesting series of "Bright-Sumner Letters, 1861–1872" is in *ibid.*, for October, 1912. "Letters of Richard Cobden to Charles Sumner, 1862–1865" are in *American Historical Review*, ii, 306–319.

the Duchess were strong friends of Charles Sumner and were in constant correspondence with him, and so, too, was John Bright, one of the strongest men of his day.

When the news of the beginning of actual hostilities reached England, it was followed by proclamations and by accounts of the cutting off of the capital city of Washington from communication with the North. Finally, when Lincoln called for more soldiers to put down the Southerners, the British ministers felt that they could not look upon five million people as "pirates" or as engaged in "an unlawful combination." Moreover, if the Federal government recognized the belligerency of the Confederacy by declaring it to be in a state of blockade, it could hardly be expected that Great Britain would hesitate for any long time to recognize the Confederates as belligerents and even as forming an independent nation. The Queen issued a proclamation recognizing the Confederate States as belligerents.[1] The proclamation also, as a matter of fact, recognized the right of the Federal government to establish a blockade and also it warned all British subjects to obey the behests of the Foreign Enlistment Act of 1818.

At the outset, the hope of the Confederates for recognition as an independent nation by the leading countries of Europe was very strong. It might well have been so, for on April 16, 1861, Governor Pickens of South Carolina wrote to President Davis that the British consul at Charleston had said he was authorized to inform him that if the United States government blockaded the Southern ports or declared them to be no longer ports of entry Great Britain would immediately recognize the independence of the seceded States.[2] Three months later, on July 19, the

[1] This proclamation can be conveniently consulted in Mountague Bernard's *Historical Account of the*   *Neutrality of Great Britain*, 135.
[2] Rowland's *Jefferson Davis*, v, 63.

British and French consuls at Charleston opened negotiations with the Confederate government through an intermediary. They wanted to secure the adhesion of the Confederate government to the Declaration of Paris of 1856 without recognizing it as such by having direct negotiations with it; but the authorities at Richmond declined to accede to the first clause in the Declaration abolishing privateering or to have anything to do in the matter, except in direct negotiation with representatives of the two foreign governments, and so the matter ended.[1]

One of the first acts of the Confederate government was to despatch a diplomatic commission to Europe to try to influence public opinion in its favor and to secure,[2] if possible, the recognition of the Confederate States as an independent nation. At the head of this commission was William Lowndes Yancey, who certainly was one of the ablest Southern men then in political life. He and the others had no difficulty in reaching London and they aroused a good deal of sympathy for the Southern cause, but there their progress stopped. The news of the battle of Bull Run greatly heartened them and they reported that it had produced a profound impression, both at London and at Paris; but in the same letter they informed the Confederate Secretary of State that since their arrival in England[3] they had not received "the least notice or attention, official or social from any member of the government." In December, 1861, they received a reply[4] to two letters that they had sent to the British Foreign Secretary in which he wrote that "in the present state of affairs, he must decline to enter into any

---

[1] See *American Historical Review,* xxiii, p. 826.

[2] "Journal" of the Confederate Congress, i, 89 (*Senate Document,* No. 234, 58th Cong., 2nd Sess.).

[3] *Official Records . . . Navies,* ser. ii, vol. iii, p. 237.

[4] *Ibid.,* ser. ii, vol. iii, p. 310.

official communication with them." Yancey returned to
his Alabama home chastened in spirit and convinced that
the South did not have the place in the world's esteem that
he had supposed it held. The Richmond government had
already taken measures to replace its first group of commissioners by other men and had selected John Slidell of Louisiana and James M. Mason of Virginia. Slidell was a New
Yorker who had settled at New Orleans, had been one of
the master spirits of the Democratic party, a senator from
Louisiana, and was the uncle of August Belmont, the representative of the great European banking house of Rothschild.
Slidell had remarkable powers of intrigue which he had
shown on many occasions. Mason well represented the
plantation aristocracy of his day, but he was not at all fitted
for the part he had to play in London. It was Benjamin
Moran, one of the secretaries of the American legation, and
therefore a prejudiced person, who described Mason as
listening to a debate in the House of Commons and covering the carpet about him with tobacco juice. Moreover,
Mason was the author of the Fugitive Slave Law. He had
a very difficult part to play in England, and was not at all
assisted in his work by other Confederate agents as Captain
Bulloch and Caleb Huse, both of whom seem to have had
authorizations from the Confederate government to act
independently of him.

The United States minister at Westminster was Charles
Francis Adams of Massachusetts, the son of John Quincy
Adams and the grandson of John Adams, both of whom
had represented the United States in England. Charles
Francis Adams had been with his father in England as a
boy, had attended an English public school, and had spent
some of the most impressionable years of his life in contact
with English boys and their families. He had thereby gained

an insight into English characteristics that was of great
benefit to his country at this crisis. Moreover, as was the
case with his father and grandfather, Adams had some
qualities peculiar to the English race; and when it came
to a contest of polite aloofness, he could outfreeze even the
coldest-mannered British man. In November, 1861, the
law officers of the Crown had in consideration the question
of the status of a neutral vessel bearing belligerent despatches, and had given an opinion, that was partly modified
later, that the carrying of such despatches subjected such a
vessel to seizure and condemnation.[1] It was at about the
same time that Palmerston conferred directly with Adams
as to the doings or probable doings of the captain of an
American warship, the *James Adger*, that was then or had
been at anchor at Southampton. Either the captain of the
James Adger had stated, or someone had stated for him, that
he was there to intercept emissaries coming from the Confederate States or to possess himself of despatches of the
Confederate government to their agents in Europe. Palmerston told Adams that the seizure of a Cunarder bringing
despatches across the Atlantic would raise serious questions [2]
and he hoped that something might be done to avoid the
difficulty. As it happened, Adams was able to assure
Palmerston that the *James Adger* had sailed, or was about
to sail, and no such incident, therefore, would occur off the
mouth of a British harbor. In truth, the dictates of international law, as they had been laid down by Lord Stowell
in the epoch of the Napoleonic Wars, would be intolerable
in the days of steamships and on the very edge of the period

[1] See Palmerston's letter of November 11, 1861, in Arthur J. Dasent's
John Thaddeus Delane, ii, 36.

[2] J. Bigelow's *Retrospections*, i, 404;
the *Letters of Queen Victoria* (London,
1907), iii, 593–597; C. F. Adams's
Charles Francis Adams (*American
Statesmen* series), 221–225; his *Studies,
Military and Diplomatic*, 394–396;
and *Official Records . . . Navies*, ser. i,
vol. i, 128, 224–227.

of communication across the Atlantic by electric telegraph or cable. Moreover, the incident certainly shows Palmerston in a distinctly favorable light as striving to fend off an explosion of British public opinion which he and his ministry could not withstand and which might be disastrous to continued friendly relations between his own country and the United States.

At almost the same moment of time, Captain Wilkes of the United States warship *San Jacinto*, while at anchor in a West Indian port, read in a newspaper that Mason and Slidell were about to pass through the Bahama Channel on the British mail steamer *Trent* from Havana to St. Thomas, where they expected to embark on another steamer for England. Wilkes was bound homeward from a prolonged cruise on the African coast and had received no instructions whatever from Washington, except to make the best of his way to the United States. Looking into such books on international law as he had in his cabin, he made up his mind that these emissaries were removable from a neutral steamer, as embodied despatches from a belligerent power or as rebellious citizens of the United States. Either from ignorance or from motives of compassion, he did not seem to realize that they were removable because the ship was performing an unneutral act and that she with her belongings should be taken into port for adjudication of the case by a court possessing admiralty jurisdiction. On November 8, 1861, he intercepted the *Trent*[1] and sent his first lieutenant,

[1] The son of the minister to England, General C. F. Adams, presented an elaborate paper on the "Trent Affair" to the Massachusetts Historical Society in November, 1911. It is printed in the *Proceedings* of that date, pp. 35–148. It was also reprinted in pamphlet form, without the letters, in the following year. Leslie J. Perry treated the affair most interestingly and with his unusual skill in the *New York Sun* for April 19, 1896. Professor Thomas L. Harris has compiled a whole volume on *The Trent Affair*, including a review of English and American relations in 1861, which is a convenient hand-book and contains references that would take the student far into the subject.

a Virginian, Fairfax by name, on board. Mason and Slidell and the steamer's officers made some objections to these proceedings. But in the end, after a show of force, Mason and Slidell and their immediate attendants were rowed to the *San Jacinto*. Captain Wilkes then permitted the *Trent* to proceed on her voyage, although, unknown to him, she had in her mail-room despatches from the Confederate government to its agents in Europe, which she was carrying contrary to the terms of the Queen's Proclamation and which would have rendered her liable to condemnation according to the opinion of the British law officers. But, on the other hand, as a British statesman wrote, by not bringing the *Trent* into port for adjudication, Wilkes had placed himself in the position of a belligerent and had then refused to act the part.

When Wilkes reached the United States with his prey, he was given an hysterical welcome. Congress voted him a gold medal and a former Attorney General of the United States and one of the ablest men then living, Caleb Cushing, wrote that Mason and Slidell were contraband of war and were liable to seizure wherever found, and that Wilkes's act was absolutely legal.[1] In London and throughout England, the excitement was intense; a British ship had been stopped by a United States war vessel; her decks violated by a boarding party who had even presumed to take

---

[1] Cushing's letter was dated December 6, 1861. Previously, on November 18, William Beach Lawrence — one of the foremost authorities on International Law of that day — wrote to a friend that the United States had a perfect right to obstruct Mason and Slidell's passage and that no difficulty with England need be apprehended from the "course pursued by Commodore Wilkes."

R. H. Dana, 3rd, in the *Proceedings* of the Massachusetts Historical Society for March, 1912, p. 508, pointed out that Mason and Slidell were still "citizens" of the United States and that the independence of the Southern Confederacy had not been recognized by a single nation. He reprints Lord Stowell's dictum authorizing one belligerent to stop the ambassador of his enemy. General C. F. Adams's comment on this article is in *ibid.*, p. 522.

from her certain of her passengers. Half a century before
British naval captains had stopped American ships time
and again and taken from them persons whom they claimed
to be British subjects. Of course, as is so often the case,
there was a distinction which it was difficult for most persons to see, for Mason and Slidell belonged to the civil service of another belligerent, for by this time, although most
unwillingly, the Washington government had been obliged
to admit that the Confederates possessed the rights of belligerents. The British government acted with a precipitancy
which was due, in part at least, to their own weak condition
in the House of Commons. In fact the newspapers lashed
the nation into fury and mob rule reigned in London and
elsewhere. Talking over the case with one of the law officers
of the Crown, a representative of the American legation
drew from him the statement that what the British government objected to was the failure to take the *Trent* into port
for adjudication. "It would not do," he said, "for naval
officers to constitute themselves captors and judges at the
same time." Upon the American suggesting that if Wilkes
had taken the *Trent* into port the British people would
have been even more violent, the English official assented.
Indeed, at this very moment, or within a few weeks, the
British authorities themselves were sheltering Confederate
warships whose captains had seized and burnt United States
vessels at sea without having even dreamed of asking for a
legal decision as to the ownership of the property destroyed.
The British minister at Washington was directed to demand
the immediate return of Mason and Slidell, and if this demand
was not at once acceded to, to close his office and return
home. The earlier draft of this letter had been even more
peremptory and had been modified on the advice of the
Prince Consort who was then on his death bed. Soldiers

were also ordered to Canada. It chanced that some of the
officers' baggage was put on the steamer *Bohemian* bound
for Portland, Maine. Learning of this, the collector at that
port asked Seward as to what should be done.[1] He at once
replied,[2] January 8, 1862, that facilities "for landing and
transporting to Canada or elsewhere troops, stores and munitions of war of every kind without exception or reservation
should be accorded to the British officers or agents."

While the excitement was at its height in London, a story
found its way into print that General Scott, who was then
in France, had stated that the seizure of Mason and Slidell
had been ordered by the Washington government. Fortunately, an Englishman, who had been acquainted with
Scott for years, happened to meet him in Paris and at once
wrote to Lord Russell that Scott denied that he had ever
said anything of the kind and that when he reached England
he did not know that Wilkes had left the African coast.
What he did know was that orders had been given to the
captain of the *James Adger* and to two or three other naval
commanders to seize the commissioners dead or alive, if
they were found on any Confederate vessel. The matter
was so important that Scott signed a public letter to that
effect which was printed widely in the newspapers and
undoubtedly did something to calm British public opinion.[3]
Early in December, also, the London Meeting of Quakers
or Friends presented a memorial to Palmerston and Russell.
In this they declared that there were no two nations so
closely united by ties of blood, language, religion, constitu-

---

[1] *Documents . . . of the State of
Maine, 1862*, Part second, Senate No. 6.
[2] *Official Records*, ser. ii, vol. ii, p.
186. Curiously enough, in the preceding November, Palmerston had
directed that no American soldiers
should again enter British territory, —
but there is no reason to suppose that
Seward knew of this. See also L. C.
Hatch's *Centennial History of Maine*, ii,
444; and Frederic Bancroft's *Life of
William H. Seward*, ii, 245.
[3] Bigelow's *Retrospections*, i, 387.

tional freedom, and commercial interest as Great Britain and the United States. War between them would be a scandal to Christianity and an injury to the progress of the human race. The people of Great Britain had made vast sacrifices for the abolition of the slave trade and of slavery in their own possessions. It would be deeply humiliating to find their country "in active coöperation with the South and slavery, against the North and freedom." [1]

Meantime at Washington, President Lincoln appears to have had grave doubts as to the soundness of Captain Wilkes's action. Secretary Welles, if we may believe his "Diary," likewise had exceedingly grave doubts as to the legality of Wilkes's performance; but the condition of affairs was so critical at that moment from political and military points of view that Lincoln acted with even more than his accustomed deliberation. Had Seward been a profound student of international law and a skilled diplomatist, he would have seized the first opportunity to restore the prisoners on the ground that as the *Trent* had not been brought into port for adjudication, the whole proceeding was unlawful. But it is doubtful if the niceties of international law appealed to him or if he was fully conscious of them, and he was exceedingly responsive to public opinion. Moreover, he had just concluded a somewhat acrimonious series of letters practically inviting the British government to declare war against the United States, but fortunately Charles Francis Adams had taken it upon himself to give his own interpretation to them or not to take any action whatever. When it became evident that the commissioners must be surrendered, Seward sat himself down to write a despatch justifying the action of Wilkes on the general

---

[1] F. G. Cartland's *Southern Heroes or The Friends in War Time* (Cambridge, 1895), p. 7.

grounds of international law and justifying the surrender of
Mason and Slidell as made necessary by an ancient and long-
continued policy of the United States government. Mason
and Slidell were restored to the deck of a British vessel and
in due time reached an English port, and their further doings
justified the assertion of the Duke of Argyll that two Southerners, more or less, in Great Britain and France, would
make no difference in the conduct of affairs by the rulers of
those countries.

Another question to arise between the United States and
Great Britain was as to supplying arms and ammunition to
the Confederates and providing them with vessels with which
to prey upon the commerce of the United States. Upon
the oncoming of hostilities, agents of the United States
government, of the Confederate government, and of several
States, north and south, appeared in England and very soon
despatched great quantities of warlike material to their
principals in America. At first the authorities at Washington with their ideas that the Southerners were rebels and
traitors looked askance upon the business of supplying them
with the weapons with which to make good their independence. After belligerent rights were accorded to them, this
contention could no longer prevail and it became as legal to
send arms to the Confederates as it was to the Federal
government or to the States of the Union. Whether it was
legal to do so or not is one of those nice questions of international law that seem to be susceptible of different answers,
according to one's point of view. On the one hand, there
would seem to be no doubt that England might sell a musket
or two or a hundred or so to a belligerent and be clearly
within her rights; but when the traffic grew into great pro-
portions and neutrals provided the means by which a belligerent could continue fighting, the case possibly assumed

another aspect, — but the traffic went on throughout the war.

As to providing ships of war, sheltering them, and permitting them to secure coal and provisions and to repair their engines and hulls, the case might be very different. Some years before, in 1849, the "Central Power of Germany" had procured a steam frigate in the United States and had invited American naval officers to cross the Atlantic and take part in the organization of a German naval force. The United States Secretary of the Navy seems to have seen no objection to the project. Ultimately, John M. Clayton, Secretary of State, intervened and prevented the sailing of the steam frigate and the officers.[1] At the outset of the contest, the British authorities acted with great circumspection and prevented the refitting of the Confederate steamer *Nashville* for war purposes.[2] In point of fact the position of England was somewhat delicate. And, indeed, in April, 1861, Richard Cobden had written that if France, with whom there was still some amount of friction and jealousy, could keep a few swift steam corvettes at sea in case of war between the two countries, the insurance on British vessels would be raised so high that their owners would have to seek foreign registry or see their ships rot at their docks.[3] In other words the Declaration of Paris of 1856 abolishing privateering would be no bar to the use of a government vessel as a commerce destroyer. One of the first Confederate emissaries to reach England was Captain James D. Bulloch[4] of the Confederate navy. The Southerners having been recognized as bellig-

---

[1] See *Petition and Papers of Conrad W. Faber & Leopold Bierwirth in Relation to the War Steamer United States.* This case and several others have been treated at length in F. W. Gibbs's *Foreign Enlistment Act* (London, 1863), p. 47.

[2] *Report of Committee on Confederate Navy Department,* 228.
[3] John Morley's *Life of Richard Cobden,* 565.
[4] See his *Secret Service of the Confederate States in Europe* (2 vols.).

erents, it might be possible for him to procure suitable vessels for destroying commerce which could be commanded by Confederate naval officers. Soon after his arrival, Bulloch secured legal advice and proceeded to build the vessel, later known as the *Alabama*. In the earlier months of the war, some members of the British government seem to have felt that there was no distinction between selling a belligerent a warship or ten thousand muskets. As the *Alabama* approached completion, Adams made serious representations. The ministry laid the matter before its legal adviser, but unfortunately at the precise moment that the vessel was about to sail he took to his bed and ultimately became insane. Before other legal luminaries could be consulted and could draw up an opinion recommending the seizure of the ship, she had sailed. Her armament and her munitions were transported in another vessel from England and placed aboard her outside of British jurisdiction; but she was built to receive an armament and the mere fact that it was not on board when she left England did not seem to release her and all who had to do with her construction from the pains and penalties of the Foreign Enlistment Act. The *Alabama* was only the first of several vessels to be constructed or purchased by the Confederates within Great Britain. Later, several cases were brought into the courts to get a judicial interpretation of the Foreign Enlistment Act. The Confederate agents had done their work so skilfully that it was impossible to secure evidence that would justify the condemnation of these vessels, and the British government was obliged to purchase them or to adopt other measures to prevent them from getting to sea. In September, 1863, it was actually proposed to send a very strongly drawn remonstrance to the Confederate commissioner in London, but at the last moment other means were adopted to make clear the determination of the British government to enforce its neutral obligations so far as it could, under the defective Foreign Enlistment Act[1] and the over-careful judges in admiralty.

In 1862, two documents were circulated in England that deserve mention as showing the working of the English middle-class mind.[2] One of them was a leaflet labelled "Cotton," addressed to the "Working Men of Lancashire & Cheshire." It was signed "A Lancashire Artisan" and stated that the Southern leaders, before secession, had determined on a policy with which they expected to gain the sanction of England to the perpetuation of the slave system and of unpaid labor. These Southern leaders, among whom were Pryor of Virginia, Mann of Georgia, and Vice-President Stephens of the Confederacy had declared that the South had a monopoly of the production of cotton and the world could not wrest it from her. If the supply of Southern slave-grown cotton was stopped, English factories would close and her commerce would cease. In one year's time a revolution would be rampant in England. But the working men of Lancashire and Cheshire disappointed the "Enemies of Freedom." "Fellow Working Men, — Are you not satisfied that the Cotton in the Rebel States is held there in defiance of your wants, to force you to riot, to violence, and . . . to spread apprehension and ruin throughout the manufacturing districts, to compromise all industrial classes, and imperil the very peace of Europe." The other docu-

---

[1] On May 2, 1863, Cobden wrote to Sumner that Russell " was *bona fide* in his aim to prevent the Alabama from leaving, but he was tricked and was angry at the escape of that vessel." *American Historical Review,* ii, 310. There can be little doubt at the present time that Russell was uncertain as to what the British law really was; but that it was his intention to make British neutrality an actuality.

[2] English public opinion in varying aspects is seen in Leslie Stephen's *The " Times" on the American War: A Historical Study* (London, 1865). An interesting and brief anti-Confederate pamphlet by C. S. Miall was published at London in 1863 with the title, *The Proposed Slave Empire: Its Antecedents, Constitution, and Policy.*

ment was a broadside marked "Proof" and was apparently a
petition to be signed and presented to the House of Commons, but whether it ever was presented is not known.   The
signers, so the petition stated, are suffering from the want of
a supply of American cotton.   This was due to the fact that
the British government had recognized certain insurgents as
belligerents and thereby justified the blockade, and, secondly,
that when the port of New Orleans had been opened to trade,
the insurgent President had commanded the Southern people
to burn their cotton in the belief that "our sufferings"
would goad us into aiding his policy.   The petitioners
implored the House to address Her Majesty not to recognize
the American insurgents "who keep three million human
persons in the condition of cattle."   They mention the
Alabama and declare that in case of war with the United
States, such pirates would be launched against English commerce, and remarked the exultation of the Irish who hoped
that in case of an insurrection on that island, Ireland would
be recognized as a belligerent by the United States.[1]   When
the supply of cotton fibre in England became seriously low,
and a demand was made by some Southern sympathizers
that the blockade should be broken, the Duke of Argyll
pointed out that it would be cheaper to support all the idle
factory operatives out of the public treasury than it would
be to go to war with the United States.

As the long period of indecision and the entire absence of
the Army of the Potomac from the field of war, or at any
rate from active campaigning continued, governmental
opinion in Great Britain and in France grew more and more
favorable to the adoption of some scheme that would bring

[1] On March 31, 1863, President
Thomas Bayley Potter and other
officers of the "Union and Emancipation Society" of Manchester, England,
issued an address to the Chambers of
Commerce of Great Britain and Ireland,
protesting against building and fitting
out vessels of war for the Southern
Confederacy in defiance of British law
and in derogation of British national
honor.

about a truce between the contending parties in America for some months at least, in the course of which it might be possible to bring the two contestants together and also to obtain a supply of cotton and tobacco.[1] The details of this matter, of course, are very vague and it is very easy to over-estimate the importance of this, of that, or of the other shred of evidence that comes into one's hand. It would seem that the mind at the bottom of the business was John Slidell, but the moving force, so far as there was one, was the Emperor Napoleon III. It is difficult to penetrate into the inner recesses of Slidell's mind and to lay one's hand on anything that he did, and it is even more difficult to do either one of these things with the third Napoleon.[2] He seemed to be friendly toward the United States, and he must have been aware of the strong anti-slavery feeling among the mass of the middle-class population of France. It is possible, of course, that he merely wished to deliver a stroke that would increase his prestige at home and in Europe and it may well be that he already had in mind the Mexican scheme upon which he later embarked.[3] The plan, as it finally took shape,[4] was that the British and French ministers at Wash-

[1] C. F. Adams, 2nd, has written several articles on different phases of the general theme of our relations to Great Britain during the years 1861–1865. The first contribution was in his life of his father in the *American Statesmen* series, chs. ix–xix. This book was published in 1900. In 1911, he again approached the topic in the last two chapters of his *Studies, Military and Diplomatic, 1775–1865*. In addition he contributed articles to the *Proceedings* of the Massachusetts Historical Society in the years 1903, 1906, 1911, 1912, and 1914. In the last years of his life, he made several trips to England for the purpose of collecting material with a view to preparing a new and much larger biography of his father, but death came before anything was published.

[2] L. M. Sears (*American Historical Review*, xxvi, 255–281) gives some interesting glimpses of Slidell. Others may be gathered from the documents printed in *Official Records . . . Navies*, ser. ii, vol. iii. W. R. West has given an informing analysis of "Contemporary French Opinion on the American Civil War" in *Johns Hopkins University Studies*, xlii, No. 1.

[3] H. H. Bancroft's *History of the Pacific States . . . Mexico*, vi, 1–332.

[4] See a letter from Earl Granville, dated April 10, 1887, in Massachusetts Historical Society's *Proceedings* for November, 1915, p. 62. This whole subject is treated in James M. Callahan's *Diplomatic History of the Confederacy*, chs. iv–xi.

ington should jointly address themselves to the United States government and make the proposals which had emanated from Napoleon or from Slidell. It is one thing, however, to propose and it is quite a different thing to convert one's intentions into actual fact. The British government constantly held back and refused to make any effective gesture and no third participant in the proposed action could be found, for Russia, from whom Napoleon had possibly hoped something, was occupied with the affairs of Poland and did not trust, to put it mildly, the good faith of her recent opponents. It fell out in this way that the proposed mediation could not be accompanied by any show of force or by any threats. Nevertheless, the possibility of intervention remained and in October, 1862, seemed about to result in England's taking the decisive step of recognizing the independence of the Confederate States. The project had gone so far that a Cabinet meeting had been summoned to authorize Earl Russell to take action. Thinking that everything would go as projected, Mr. Gladstone in a speech at Newcastle, announced that Jefferson Davis had already made a nation and forecasted a speedy recognition thereof by Great Britain.[1] This pronouncement gave the signal for renewed efforts on the part of those Englishmen who were hostile to Southern independence and all that it implied. Antietam had somewhat restored the hope that Northern coercion would be successful and the announcement of the forthcoming Emancipation Proclamation gave the British anti-slavery people something to work with.

[1] See C. F. Adams's *Studies Military and Diplomatic, 1775–1865* (New York, 1911), p. 402 and fol., and his later "A Crisis in Downing Street" in *Proceedings* of the Massachusetts Historical Society for May, 1914.

According to an entry in Moran's "Diary" under the date of October 24, 1862, Lord Russell told Mr. Adams that Mr. Gladstone had been rebuked for "his indiscreet Newcastle Speech." He told him that "no change of policy . . . was contemplated and that if any should be decided upon he would give Mr. Adams early notice of the fact."

At this time — in the summer and autumn of 1862 — the Confederate propaganda in England was active and successful. With the announcement of an emancipation policy, the English enemies of slavery and all those Englishmen who were opposed to putting pressure on the Federal government to bring about any cessation of hostilities in America, — all these people now redoubled their efforts of speech and pen. In all probability about one hundred separate publications attest the activity of the Confederate agents in England and of their sympathizers there, and more than double that number attest the industry of English anti-slavery men and women. It also seemed clear that another shortage of the British wheat crop would necessitate the importation of large quantities of grain from the United States. And, finally, the prospect of war with America or strained relations with that country greatly disturbed business men and manufacturers in England[1] and they made known their anxieties to the people in power. Gladstone's announcement also aroused the resentments of other members of the ministry. One of them, George Cornewall Lewis, took it upon himself to publish a reply and there is no doubt whatever that Palmerston saw that the time was not ripe for recognizing the Confederacy. No proclamation was issued and Adams did not find it necessary to close the American legation and ask for his passport, as he had been instructed to do in case Great Britain recognized the independence of the Southern Confederacy. The publication of Lincoln's Emancipation Proclamation of January 1st, 1863, aroused the anti-slavery people and the working men in England. Great emancipation meetings were held in different parts of the country. Delegations waited on the American minister.

---

[1] Benjamin Moran's Ms. "Diary" in the Library of Congress, under date of November 11 and 12, 1862.

The working men of Manchester voted an address to President Lincoln and the Emperor Napoleon expressed the hope [1] to the American minister at Paris that "the United States would be better off next year than now."

In the spring of 1863, renewed efforts were made by the friends of the Southern Confederacy to bring about recognition. This time they proposed to put parliamentary pressure on the government through action of the House of Commons. The story is an obscure and also a complicated one. Presumably, like the preceding effort, it had its origin in the brain of John Slidell working through the Emperor of the French and the persons chosen to bring about the hoped-for result were no longer the responsible ministers at Downing Street, but unofficial members of the House of Commons. The person whose name was connected with the motion was John A. Roebuck. At about this time he delivered a speech at Sheffield which exhibited the condition of his mind and also that of the minds of many of the Confederate sympathizers in Great Britain. In this speech, he asserted that the Northerners were so cruel that "they forgot charity, they forgot Christianity, they made themselves a spectacle to the world of cruelty, corruption, and horror." He declared that the Southerners would fight to the death for independence and had already conquered the North. At about the same time, a tract was printed at London advocating the recognition of the Southern Confederacy. In it, the Northern people are represented as "struggling to retain their fellow countrymen of the Gulf States in worse than Egyptian bondage." It must also be said that some members of the ministry found the Emancipation Proclamation difficult to understand, for it set free the slaves only in the States and parts of States then in rebellion, — it was simply

[1] See Moran's Ms. "Diary" under date of January 2, 14, and 16, 1863.

a war measure and was not the announcement of an emancipation policy. To the anti-slavery English men and women and to the non-voting democracy of Great Britain, it appeared in an entirely different light, for it was the first time that the government of the United States had actually expressed a determination to put an end to human slavery in any part of the States where it then existed. Again they brought active pressure to bear upon the members of the ministry with whom they had influence and through them upon the rest. It was under these circumstances that information was conveyed to Mr. Roebuck that the government would oppose the adoption of the motion that had been introduced by him and that he would better withdraw it. He did so; and three weeks thereafter Vicksburg and Gettysburg so changed the military situation in America that it was evident to all but the most ardent Confederate sympathizers in Great Britain and France that the possibility of intervention had forever passed away.

In September, 1863, a Russian fleet entered the harbor of New York and in October following another Russian fleet anchored in San Francisco Bay.[1] Their coming to American shores was the direct result of the lessons furnished by the success of the *Alabama* and other Confederate cruisers in destroying American merchant vessels. In the preceding winter of 1862–1863, the Russian government had been more than ordinarily occupied with repressing disturbances in Russian Poland and had aroused more than the ordinary amount of resentment among the people of England and of some other European countries. Intervention and possibly a European war seemed to be probable in the near future.

---

[1] Professor F. A. Golder has reconstructed this episode from the Russian archives in *American Historical Review.* xx, 801–812. He also has printed some interesting extracts from the letters of Edouard de Stoeckl, Russian Minister to the United States from 1857 to 1868, in *ibid.*, xxvi, 454–463.

According to the Declaration of Paris of 1856, privateering could no longer be practiced, but the *Alabama* had shown that a commissioned vessel of a belligerent navy might prey with success on the seagoing merchant ships of another belligerent. It occurred to someone in the Russian admiralty or naval service that in this way Russia could deal a blow at England which might put a speedy termination to England's interference on behalf of the Poles. The general plan seems to have been for the Russian squadron to rendezvous at New York, to sally forth on the commercial oceanic lanes the moment that war should be declared between Great Britain and Russia, and to capture and sink every British vessel that it met. In a similar way, the Pacific fleet would rendezvous at some convenient point and take up the work of destruction in that quarter. When the Atlantic portion of the expedition reached New York, its appearance was welcomed with great rejoicings, for it seemed to the Americans that its coming was a mark of sympathy shown by the Russian government for the cause of the Union, and that at all events its presence on the American coast would act as a deterrent to any possible declaration of war on the United States by Great Britain. The San Franciscans likewise received the Russians with enthusiasm and Admiral Popov declared his intention of defending the city and port from the Confederate cruisers *Sumter* and *Alabama* in case they passed the Golden Gate and attacked it. What effect the presence on the Atlantic and Pacific coasts of a dozen presumptive *Alabamas* had on the mind of the British ministry nowhere appears in printed documents or letters. It is impossible to conceive that the British admiralty should not have realized the true character of these expeditions and should not have made known their apprehensions to the other members of the government. Indeed, it was at about this time that military and naval men were sent from England to the United States to report upon the ability of that country to conduct hostilities against Great Britain. Their reports were alarming. By pursuing defensive tactics against the Confederates the Washington government, in a few weeks, could place a hundred thousand trained soldiers on the Canadian frontier and, by abandoning the blockade for a time, could turn loose on the Atlantic lanes of commerce, hundreds of swift armed cruisers that could sweep British merchant shipping from the ocean. Already, the battle of the *Merrimac* with the wooden ships of the United States navy had destroyed the wooden navies of the world, and the large improved monitors like the *Weehawken* could have sent to the bottom any vessel in the British or French navies. Moreover, some British statesmen of that time appear to have agreed with Seward that war with a foreign power would have brought the two parts of the United States together, for a time, at least.

The Confederates had built within their own country some formidable armored vessels, but these were not fitted for service on the high seas. To obtain such ships it was necessary to go to England and France. Accordingly, contracts were made with the Lairds in England and the Armans in France for the construction of several iron-clad sea-going vessels, provided not only with heavy guns but with rams. There was a great deal of mystery about these proceedings, and in the underworld of governmental machinations and contemplations many things are obscure and will always remain so.[1] It is certain that at about the same time, Pal-

[1] See John Bigelow's *France and the Confederate Navy*. This contains, interpersed in the text, long extracts from diplomatic papers including those from Slidell, the Confederate emissary.

These are also printed in Bigelow's *Retrospections*, vols. i and ii. The second volume of J. D. Richardson's *Messages and Papers of the Confederacy* contains the official correspondence of

merston and Russell and their colleagues in England and the
Emperor Napoleon in France began to have serious misgivings. Whether a vessel fitted to receive guns on board, but
had not as yet received them, was an instrument of naval
warfare or not, might be doubtful; but when an iron-clad
ship armed with a beak for sinking another ship by ramming
appeared to be approaching completion, grave apprehensions arose as to whether these should be allowed to go
to sea.[1] All of a sudden, orders were given by the British
government to seize the rams, to pay for them if necessary,
but certainly to prevent their leaving British harbors. A
day or two later, appeared Adams's letter containing the
famous minatory sentence that it would be superfluous for
him to say that "this is war." Possibly it was fortunate that
the letter did not reach Earl Russell before the orders had
been given for the seizure of the rams. As to the Armans
rams, the reasons actuating the Emperor of the French are
even more indistinct. The only thing that can be stated

Slidell with successive Confederate
Secretaries of State; and there is an
excellent article by L. M. Sears, entitled
"A Confederate Diplomat at the Court
of Napoleon III" in the *American
Historical Review*, xxvi, 255–281.

Captain Bulloch thought that the
Armans ram, *Stonewall*, would have
been able to break the blockade by the
use of her ram alone. Caleb Huse, the
abnormally astute Confederate agent —
born in Newburyport, Massachusetts,
— tried to get the command of the
Stonewall. He maintained, in 1888,
that if he had she would have reached
the American coast in February, 1865,
driven off the blockading fleets, destroyed New York, and given new
courage to the Southern people. See
Bigelow's *Retrospections*, ii, 452.

[1] On October 8, 1863, Cobden wrote
to Sumner that "the fact that they were
armoured, turreted, and *beaked*, constituted them armed vessels even under

the most lax interpretation of our
Enlistment Act"; *American Historical
Review*, ii, 314.   J. M. Forbes and W. H.
Aspinwall went to England with five
million dollars in bonds to purchase
these vessels, but they had already
been taken over by the British govern-
ment. See, however, Sarah F. Hughes's
*Letters and Recollections of John Murray
Forbes*, ii, 28–66. The *Correspondence
between Her Majesty's Government and
Messrs. Laird Brothers; . . . respecting
the Iron-clad Vessels building at Birken-
head, 1863–4* throws much light on this
transaction and should be compared
with Bulloch's account in his *Secret
Service* and with the documents in the
Official Records . . . Navies. C. F.
Adams has an interesting paper on
"The Laird Rams" in the *Proceedings*
of the Massachusetts Historical Society
for October, 1899. See also the Duke of
Argyll to Sumner, February 16, 1864, in
ibid., for December, 1913.

with any certainty is that a complete change of front on the part of the French government took place. As it was, one of the French rams went to sea, and, after sundry adventures, crossed the Atlantic to Havana, where she was on the day of Appomattox and was promptly handed over to the United States government by the Spanish authorities.

In the spring of 1865, the Confederates made one last effort to secure recognition from the governments of Great Britain and of France. On March 14, 1865, Mason obtained an interview, an unofficial one of course, with the Prime Minister. He tried to interest Palmerston in a barter of the abolition of slavery within the Confederacy for recognition of his government. The aged Prime Minister appeared to take no particular interest in Mason's proposal. By that time, British public opinion had changed so radically that anything of the kind was absolutely out of the question. Some people there were in Great Britain, who still remained faithful to the Confederacy and one of these wrote an article for Blackwood's "Magazine" proving conclusively to his own satisfaction that the Confederacy had won its independence. The article appeared in the January number of the magazine and a few days thereafter came the news that Sherman's sixty thousand men had marched through Georgia from Atlanta to the sea, without meeting opposition of any moment and were then encamped within sight of the southern boundary of the State of South Carolina. From that time on, few persons in England or in Scotland, other than those who held Confederate bonds, had much interest in the South or in the Confederacy. To the mass of the people of Great Britain its fate seemed to be sealed and its collapse a matter of only a short time — a few weeks or months.

NOTE

Northern and Southern Propaganda. — Soon after Sumter, John Bigelow was requested to look after the interest of the United States in the foreign press, and was appointed consul at Paris to give some reason for a prolonged residence at that capital. He proved to be an exceedingly able propagandist.[1] Henry Adams, who was then acting as his father's private secretary, undertook to write the truth to English newspapers, anonymously, of course, or to get it written, and it must be said that he did not do the job very well.[2] Robert J. Walker,[3] Thurlow Weed, William M. Evarts, Henry Ward Beecher, and other Northern men of less eminence appeared in London singly or in groups somewhat to Mr. Charles Francis Adams's dismay. They wrote pamphlets and letters to the newspapers, they exerted all the wiles that they knew of in society and in business and they addressed public meetings. Whether their activities were helpful or otherwise was a matter of opinion.[4]

An ill-natured Southern critic of the Richmond government declared that " All the Jews of Plaquemines Parish " of New Orleans were sitting around the hotels of London and Paris and spending the money of the Southern Confederacy propagating the truth from the Confederate point of view. It cannot be said that they accomplished much. They published a paper in London, *The Index*, complete files of which are exceedingly rare. It was a useful vehicle for the transmission of Southern information from the Confederate authorities to the English

[1] See the first volumes of his *Retrospections of a Busy Life.*

[2] See a *Cycle of Adams Letters* and there is something about these activities in *The Education of Henry Adams.* See also Massachusetts Historical Society's *Proceedings,* 2nd Series, i, 203.

[3] Walker, Northern born, who had been a planter in Mississippi and a Senator from that State, and Polk's Secretary of the Treasury, wrote a series of articles on financial or semi-financial subjects. Among these were three separate letters stamping Jefferson Davis as a repudiationist. These were written with the hope of frightening British financiers from lending money to the Confederacy. They attracted so much attention that De Leon, who was then propagandering on the Confederate side, printed *A Familiar Epistle to Robert J. Walker, from An Old Acquaintance.*

[4] Their experiences are detailed at greater or lesser length in the *Autobiography* of Thurlow Weed, in Abbott and Halliday's *Henry Ward Beecher* (Hartford, 1887) ch. viii, or in Lyman Abbott's *Henry Ward Beecher* (Boston, 1903) ch. x. Beecher's speeches were printed in a volume of 175 pages at Manchester, England, in 1864, for the Union and Emancipation Society of that place. A stout pamphlet of 124 pages, written by Fitzwilliam W. Sargent and printed at London in 1863 with the title of *England, the United States, and the Southern Confederacy* must have appealed to thoughtful English men and women.

press, to the *Times* and others that were devoted to the Southern cause. Among the books and pamphlets issued by the Confederates in London in these years, or issued for them, or in their interests, were A. J. B. Beresford Hope's four pamphlets that appeared in the years 1861 to 1863 and John L. O'Sullivan's *Peace, the Sole Chance now Left for Reunion* (London, 1863). Possibly the best example of a Southern attempt to fire the British heart is Mrs. Greenhow's *My Imprisonment and the First Year of Abolition Rule at Washington* that was printed at London in 1863. The book of this class that has lived to the present day is James Spence's *The American Union . . . and the Causes of the Disruption.* It was published in England in 1862 and was intended to be distinctly favorable to the Southerners, but it contained so much matter derogatory to slavery that the Confederate government overlooked Spence's offer of services as an official propagandist. Edwin De Leon's *Three Letters from A South Carolinian relating to Secession, Slavery, and the Trent Case* was printed for private circulation at London in 1862 and had considerable influence at the time.

The parallelism between *The Times* [1] and *Punch* is very close. Their general feeling is expressed in the words that were printed in the former on July 18, 1862. If Englishmen " ought not to stop this effusion of blood by mediation, we ought to give our moral weight to our English kith and kin, who have gallantly striven so long for their liberties against a mongrel race of plunderers and oppressors " led by " a cold-blooded despot." Ten days after the tidings of Lincoln's assassination reached England, *The Times* announced that he had been " as little a tyrant as any man who ever lived." *Punch* " recanted " in the well-known words, —

> Between the mourners at his head and feet,
>   Say, scurril-jester, is there room for you?
>
> Yes, he had lived to shame me for my sneer,
>   To lame my pencil, and confute my pen —
> To make me own this hind of princes peer,
>   This rail-splitter a true-born king of men.

[1] See Leslie Stephen's *The "Times" on the American War* (London, 1865). This is extremely rare. It is reprinted from a manuscript copy as "Extra No. 37" of *The Magazine of History*.   The animus of three or four of the most influential British papers and periodicals is set forth in Frederick S. Dickson's "Blackwood's" *History of the United States* (Philadelphia, 1896).

In striving to form an opinion as to the underlying reasons for British action, one must read the biographies of men of the day.[1] Especially he must peruse Maitland's *Leslie Stephen*, Trevelyan's *John Bright*, Morley's *Richard Cobden*, the autobiography of the Duke of Argyll, and Bryce's *Modern Democracies* (ii, 413).

[1] Among the most interesting of the anti-Southern publications is the Ladies' London Emancipation Society's series of *Tracts*. These were published under the direction of Emily Faithfull. In No. 8 J. M. Ludlow stated that tenderness toward Southerners or admiration for the gallantry of Southern soldiers "no more palliates Southern slavery, than did the heroic defence of Jerusalem by the Jews of old, palliate the crucifixion of Our Lord." And in No. 12 the massacre of Fort Pillow was described in unchastened phrase that must have caused many an English man and woman to doubt the oft-proclaimed similarity between themselves and the Southern aristocrats.

CHAPTER XIII

THE DECISION OF THE OHIO VALLEY

THE outcome of the struggle for Southern independence was powerfully affected by the course pursued by Great Britain and by France. Had either one, or both of them, intervened, it is barely possible that the United States might have weathered the storm. As matters were, the outcome of secession depended ultimately upon the attitude that the people of the Ohio Valley assumed.[1] If they took the part of their kinsfolk and commercial friends of the South, secession was reasonably certain to be permanent. If they took upon themselves an attitude of neutrality, the case was very doubtful. If they stood squarely behind the Union government, the decision might be prolonged, but success would eventually be with the Union cause. Abraham Lincoln, himself a native of the Ohio Valley, saw with certainty into the future and based his whole policy upon the contingency of rallying the people of that section to the side of the Union. Another Ohio Valley man, Salmon Portland Chase, a native of New Hampshire, who had been governor of the State of Ohio and was now Secretary of the Treasury, confided to his "Locked Diary," on September 12, 1862, that the President "with the most honest intentions in the world,

[1] Senator J. J. Crittenden admirably expressed the truth in a letter to Robert Anderson, dated February 12, 1861: — "I am a Union Man — I condemn secession — all its sophistries do not move me — but I must still regard seceders as Country-men — am at-tached to them as such, & many of them I love as friends — and I look forward, with confidence, to the not very distant day when they will be re-united to us under the glorious Flag of our venerated Union."

and a naturally clear judgment and a true, unselfish patriotism" had yielded so much to "Border State and negro-
phobic counsels" that he now found it difficult not to make
the most fatal concessions. He had already separated himself from the "great body of the party" and distrusted most
those who most represented its spirit.

We of the present day are so given to thinking of the States
of Ohio, Indiana, and Illinois as Northern States that it
would be well to stop a moment and look under the surface
and try to understand the actual conditions of affairs in 1850
and in the ten years following. It is perfectly true that there
were, practically speaking, no negro slaves in the States
north of the Ohio and of Mason and Dixon's line and east
of the Mississippi. The census takers [1] of 1850 found 236
slaves in New Jersey. Their presence there demonstrated
the slowness of the working of any system of gradual emancipation. By 1860 all but eighteen of them had disappeared,
but the census enumerators in that year found two slaves
in Kansas and forty-four more in the territories of Nebraska
and Utah, so that there were then sixty-four persons denominated slaves in what one generally regards as free territory.
In the three Free States of Ohio, Indiana, and Illinois, there
was a system of indenture by which a slave outside of the
limits of one of those States contracted to give his services
within one of them to his master for a term of years. This
was euphemistically termed "voluntary servitude." It is
true that the constitution of Indiana of 1816 declared that
no indenture of negro or mulatto thereafter made outside
of the State should be regarded as valid within it,[2] but there

---

[1] The figures as to slaves in the
Northern States are taken from J. D. B.
De Bow's *Statistical View of the United
States . . . being a Compendium of the
Seventh Census* (Washington, 1854),
p. 82; and from the *Preliminary Report*
on *The Eighth Census, 1860*, by Jos. C.
G. Kennedy (Washington, 1862), pp.
130, 131.

[2] *Revised Laws of Indiana* (1824),
p. 50.

was no prohibition of indenturing within the State. Slavery was prohibited in Illinois by the constitution of 1818, but slaves then in Illinois should be slaves, existing indentures should remain valid and black boys and girls might be indentured for a number of years, and any negro could indenture himself or herself for one year.[1] The most striking example of the working of this system is to be seen in the case of Mrs. Ulysses S. Grant.[2] She had inherited four or five slaves and had at least one of them at Galena, Illinois, who served as lady's maid under indenture. It was this indentured person or slave, that Mrs. Grant took with her to Covington, Kentucky, on a visit to her husband, then in command of the Union army, and she came near being captured with her indentured maid or slave by the Confederate General Van Dorn. The Illinois legislature had adopted, for the most part, the black laws of Kentucky and Virginia, under which emancipation was practically prohibited. Free negroes had been forbidden by law from entering the State and those already there had been strictly regulated.[3] Indeed, Illinois very nearly relapsed in 1822 into the condition of a Slave State.[4] Although the people of these three Free States north of the Ohio did not want slavery in their midst, they were opposed to the coming in of free blacks from any-

[1] *Public and General Statute Laws of . . . Illinois* (1839) p. 32.

[2] *Richmond Times-Dispatch*, February 26, 1905.

[3] *Public and General Statute Laws of . . . Illinois* (1839) p. 501. Other and more restrictive laws were passed in 1829, 1831, and 1833, *ibid.*, 506–508.

[4] See Elihu B. Washburne's *Sketch of Edward Coles, . . . and of the Slavery Struggle of 1823–1824*. The letters relating to slavery are reprinted in *The Journal of Negro History*, iii, 158–195. A brief account is Judge John P. Hands' "Address delivered before the Henry County Old Settlers Association in Cambridge, Illinois" and printed in

The Henry County Advocate for August 20, 1908. The principal facts as to slavery in Illinois were succinctly stated by Judge Woodward in 1807 and printed in Michigan Pioneer and Historical Society's *Collections*, xii, 511–525. See also Massachusetts Historical Society's *Proceedings* for 1867–1869, p. 400, and "Pioneer Letters of Gershom Flagg" in *Transactions* of the Illinois State Historical Society for 1910, pp. 139–183. See also N. D. Harris's *History of Negro Servitude in Illinois, 1719–1864*. There is a good bibliography at the end of the volume, which sometimes has "Slavery" in place of "Servitude" on the title page.

where. In January, 1860, ten free black refugees, turned out of Arkansas, tried to find some place of refuge. They went up the Ohio River, but everywhere the people were opposed to their landing. In a quaintly-worded printed "Appeal to Christians throughout the World" these "Ten Free Colored People" united their testimony against the "unequalled iniquity" that made "merchandize of the deathless soul." "We were weak; our oppressors were strong. We were feeble, scattered, peeled; they, being powerful, placed before us slavery or banishment." They asked all people "to plead the cause of the poor and needy and set him at rest from him that puffeth at him."

The southern part of these three States, that lying south of Zanesville, Columbus, Indianapolis, and Springfield, was settled for the most part from the South and was bound to the South [1] by close economic ties. In Ohio, Cleveland and the towns of the Connecticut Reserve were very Northern in sentiment and in tradition. In Illinois, the great shipping and distributing center at Chicago had very slight affiliation in any way to the Southern country. In Indiana, there was no such strongly defined area of Northern life and prejudice, and the Southern element was unusually strong and aggressive. In 1861, these three States came out squarely for the flag and the Union, and they were aided and joined by Kentucky and by Missouri, which for many purposes may be regarded as one of the Ohio Valley group. Why was this change? It has been attributed to the coming of immigrants

---

[1] According to the *Census* of 1850, over 200,000 Ohioans were from Pennsylvania and about the same number from outside the limits of the United States. The total contribution of the South is given at 146,350. These figures give an entirely wrong impression, as the great mass of the 1,219,432 persons who are described in the *Census* as native-born Ohioans, must have been children of parents who came from the Southern States and had the prejudices and habits of their forebears. See on this general subject D. C. Shilling's "Relation of Southern Ohio to the South" in the *Quarterly* of the Historical and Philosophical Society of Ohio, viii, No. 1.

from Europe, mainly from Germany, but strangely enough many of these were persistent opponents of the coercion of the South throughout these four years. It has also been attributed to a change in the current of the mercantile stream, and in this there would seem to be good reason for the statement that the outlook of the great mass of the people of the Ohio Valley was distinctly different in 1861 from what it had been in 1849. In the latter year, of the one and a quarter million barrels of pork that went from the North-west, nearly one million barrels went down the Ohio and the Mississippi, and in the same year two and a half million bushels of corn went southward with the pork. In the same year, one hundred and thirty thousand barrels of whiskey went from Cincinnati and other river ports for the consumption of the planters and their families. A comparison of these figures with those for 1860 gives some startling results. In this year, only about half a million barrels of pork went southward and eight hundred and sixty thousand barrels of pork went eastward; something over four million bushels of corn went southward and nineteen million bushels went eastward by the Lakes, the canals, and the railroads to the Atlantic slope. In 1849, only sixty-three thousand barrels of whiskey have been traced as going from Kentucky and the Ohio Valley to the Eastern States north of the Potomac. In 1860, over three hundred thousand barrels found their way over the railroads and canals to the markets of those States, while only two hundred thousand barrels went south-ward in that year. Another even more startling change shown by the statistics of commerce is in regard to the ship-ments of wheat and flour from the Northwest to the South and to the Northeast in 1849 and in 1860. In the first of these years, five million bushels of wheat and a little over two million barrels of flour went from the Northwest to the

Northeast, and four hundred thousand bushels of wheat and one million barrels of flour to the southward. In 1860, no less than thirty million bushels of wheat and nearly three and a half million barrels of flour went from the Northwest to the Northeast, and only one hundred thousand bushels of wheat and just under a million barrels of flour to the southward. The figures as to corn, pork, and whiskey denote a radical change in the routes of commerce. The figures as to wheat and flour demonstrate a tremendous change in the weight of the population and of political balance from the South to the North in the States north of the Ohio and west of the Appalachians.

The changes in routes of commerce from the Ohio Valley and the Northwest in the ten or dozen years as described in the preceding paragraph was due, of course, in a great measure to the changing demands of the markets of the East, of the South, and of the world. It was due also to the ability of the States of the Northwest to meet the demands that were made upon them by foreign buyers, and this grew out of the immigration of those years to the wheat-growing States, which made it possible for the farms of the Northern part of this area to supply the wheat required for export. As to the change in the course of the commerce of the Ohio Valley, that was due in part to an increased demand from the Northeastern markets for the products of that region, but this could not have been supplied and the course of commerce could not have changed in those years as it certainly did, had not the building of the railroads in that section been carried forward with a speed that, up to that time, had no parallel in the history of the world.[1] In 1847,

---

[1] Professor Frederic L. Paxson printed a most interesting article on "The Railroads of the 'Old Northwest' before the Civil War" in the *Transac-* *tions* of the Wisconsin Academy of Sciences, etc., xvii, Pt. i. This is compiled from time-tables and railroad reports and the usual books, as Poor's

there were 660 miles of railroad in operation in the States of
the Old Northwest, in Ohio, Indiana, and Illinois.   In 1861
there were 7,653 miles of railroad in those three States.   In
January, 1848, there was not a railroad line connecting
the Ohio River with the Lake.   By the end of that year,
the line connecting Cincinnati and Sandusky had been com-

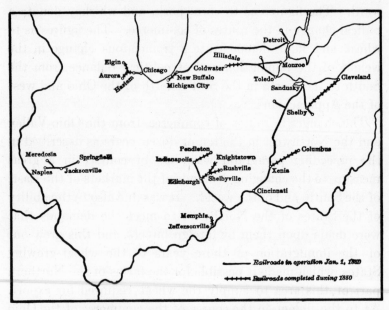

RAILROADS OF THE OLD NORTHWEST IN 1850.

(Reproduced by permission from Professor Frederic L. Paxson's "The Railroads
of the 'Old Northwest' before the Civil War" in the *Transactions* of the Wisconsin
Academy of Sciences, Arts, and Letters, vol. xvii, pt. i, p. 253).

Manual. Included in the study is a
series of maps showing the actual condition of railroads in that section of the
country from 1848 to 1860 inclusive.
Two of these maps are given on opposite
pages of this book through the kindness
of Professor Paxson. Professor C. R.
Fish approached the subject from a
different point of view in the *Report*
of the American Historical Association
for 1910, p. 155, and in the *American
Historical Review*, xxii, 778. Two
other articles, by E. M. Coulter and R.
S. Cotterill, are in the *Mississippi
Valley Historical Review*, vol. iii, 275
and 427. On p. 430 is a map and on pp.
439 and fol. is a statement of the condition of the South in 1850 which may be
compared with one in an earlier article
on the effect of secession on the Mississippi Valley. Curran Dinsmore's
American Railway Guide (New York,
1850) and Ensign, Bridgman and
Fanning's *Lake and River Guide* (New

pleted and was in operation; in 1850 there was not a single
east to west line in those States connecting the Mississippi
River system with the railroads of New York, Pennsylvania,
and Maryland; in 1860 this had been accomplished.[1]
In other words, in 1850, the Ohio Valley had no easy connec-

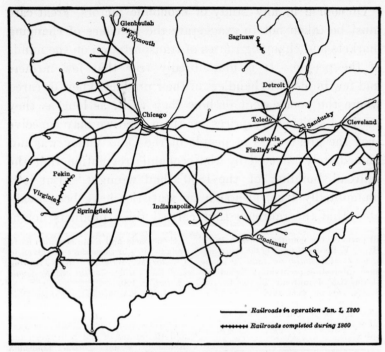

RAILROADS OF THE OLD NORTHWEST IN 1860.

(Reproduced by permission from Professor Frederic L. Paxson's "The Railroads
of the 'Old Northwest' before the Civil War" in the *Transactions* of the Wisconsin
Academy of Sciences, Arts, and Letters, vol. xvii, pt. i, p. 266).

York, 1856) have a great deal of information as to the settlements west of the
Appalachians. The rapid growth of
parts of the country is easily gathered
from Thompson's "Wheat Growing in
Wisconsin" in the *Bulletin* of the
University of Wisconsin, No. 292,
pp. 41–47.

[1] Statistics of railroads in this epoch
are to be found in the *Report of the*
Superintendent of the Census for Decem-
ber 1, 1852 (Washington, 1853); the
volume entitled "Mortality and Miscel-
laneous Statistics" of the *Census* of
1860, pp. 323–334, contains an article
on the "Progress of Railroads" from
1850 to 1860; and the "Transportation" volume of the *Census* of 1880,
pp. 308 and fol., has extensive tables
showing the construction of railroads in

tion with eastern markets, except by steamboat up the Ohio to Wheeling and Pittsburg and thence to the Atlantic seaboard, or by steamboat down the Ohio and Mississippi to New Orleans and thence by sail and steam through the Gulf and up the eastern coast.

Of course in any study of economic factors, great care must be taken not to exaggerate the influence of changing markets and changing routes of transportation on the minds of the people. It is undoubtedly true that few farmers and few immediate handlers of their products knew or cared where the goods went or how they went, as long as they received satisfactory prices for them. So we may conceive that the great mass of people of the Ohio Valley was not immediately affected by the economic revolution that the railroad building of the 1850's had wrought.[1] But it is undoubtedly true, although no statistics have been available, that the railroads that carried these products north-

---

all parts of the country down to 1880. Henry V. Poor's *Manual of the Railroads of the United States, for 1869–70* has a most interesting preliminary "Sketch" of the rise of railroads in the United States. On pp. xxvi, xxvii, is a statistical study from which the following table has been compiled showing the miles of railroads in operation at these dates:

STATES	1840	1850	1860
New England	527	2,508	3,660
Middle	1,566	3,202	6,706
Western	89	1,276	11,064
Southern	636	2,035	9,182
Pacific			23
Total	2,818	9,021	30,635

Some facts and some citations as to freight rates in those days are given in Chester W. Wright's "Wool-Growing and the Tariff" in *Harvard Economic Studies*, v. 150.

[1] In the South the idea that the Ohio Valley was dependent upon the southern market for its very existence was widespread. Cut off that market and the States of the Northwest and Kentucky would perish. Louisiana and Mississippi offered the free navigation of the Mississippi River to the people of "friendly States." *Journal of the Congress of the Confederate States,* i, 9 and *Journal of the [Mississippi] State Convention,* p. 24. On the contrary the fact of the closing of the Mississippi seems to have convinced many people in the Northwest that only a strong central government could secure to them their right to the navigation of the river. See on this general subject W. C. Cochran's "The Dream of a Northwestern Confederacy" in the *Proceedings* of the Wisconsin Historical Society, 1916, p. 213.

ward to the Lakes and eastward to New York, Philadelphia,
and Baltimore, must have brought into the West large
quantities of eastern and European manufactured goods in
exchange and these must have been of a different quality
from those produced on the farm and of a very different
grade and price from similar goods that had been imported
by the way of New Orleans, or had been produced in the
factories of Cincinnati and Indianapolis. So we may suppose that something akin to a changing mental outlook and
mode of living occurred, especially in the last years of the
decade, in countless homes in southern Ohio, Indiana, and
Illinois and in Kentucky, Tennessee, and western Virginia.
But how far any such considerations may have altered political or social conceptions must always remain matter for
debate. It is evident, however, that the influx of capital
to build these railway lines and the coming in of railroad
men from the engineer of the line to the Irish laborer on the
roadbed, and the facility with which news and communication with the East followed hard on the opening of each mile
of railroad could not have done otherwise than upset the
social and mental outlook of practically every man, woman,
and child in that region.

A quarter of a century ago or a third of a century ago, it
was customary to lay great stress on the influence of economic factors; now it is more often the case to emphasize
the sociological or psychical change that is wrought by
changed modes of living and by the general operation of economic factors. Possibly the best way to analyze problems
of progress or of change in human outlook would be to combine all these various factors into one, for surely one's mode
of living exercises a very important influence on one's mode
of thinking. Whatever the path of progress was, whether
economic or mental, it is certain that the outlook of the

people of the Ohio Valley changed most materially in the decade ending in 1860. The only portions of that country that were not affected by these changing conditions were those counties and districts in which it was possible to grow the great Southern staples, cotton and tobacco, by slave labor. Practically the greater part of the western and central Tennessee was occupied by a slaveholding community which became more prosperous as one approached the Mississippi River, and this region of slave production extended northwardly into southwestern Kentucky, and there were also districts in the central part of the State where southern staple crops were grown by slave labor. Eastern Tennessee and eastern central Tennessee and the eastern half of Kentucky were essentially regions of small farms and of small industrial plants. One of these days, perhaps, some student will draw an industrial map of these States and on it exhibit the preferences of the people for union or disunion in 1860. So far as this has been done, the coincidence is remarkable. It may be said, roughly speaking, that about one-third of the people and possibly one-quarter of the productive capacity of Tennessee were allied with Northern markets and possessed free labor prepossessions; but many of the families living in these portions of the State were allied socially and by marriage with slaveholders. As one would draw on such a map the line of area hostile to secession it would become more marked as one ascended into the mountainous region of the eastern part of the State, and the same thing would be true of Kentucky, except there the line would be drawn further westwardly.

The firing on Sumter and Lincoln's call for men produced a tremendous and far-reaching effect in these two States. Tennessee, following the lead of Senator Bell and other powerful men, seceded; but this was done in the face of the opposition of the great mass of the people of the eastern part of the State and especially of the great valley of East Tennessee;[1] but there, as in southwestern Virginia, the Unionists were not as well organized and as powerful politically as were the Secessionists. The governor of Kentucky, Beriah Magoffin, had a difficult part to play. It is probable that his personal sympathies were somewhat torn between the two sections of the State. In answer to Lincoln's call he declared that the whole proceeding was unconstitutional and that Kentucky would not send a man. He tried to set on foot a policy of neutrality.[2] Had this been successful, it would of course have been of the greatest assistance to the Confederates, as it would have prevented military movements through the State, and Louisiana, Mississippi, and Alabama would have been accessible to the Northern forces only by way of the Mississippi and the Gulf of Mexico. The Washington government met this by sending Anderson, the "hero of Fort Sumter" and a native of Kentucky, into the State to organize armed resistance to the Secessionists. It also sent emissaries into eastern Kentucky and eastern Tennessee and provided them with arms and ammunition. They established a camp in the Cumberland Mountains which served as a rallying point to the loyalists, not only of Kentucky but also of Tennessee.[3] When the legislature of

[1] O. P. Temple's East Tennessee and The Civil War (Cincinnati, 1899); History of Tennessee (Nashville, 1887), pp. 477–617; F. G. Cartland's Southern Heroes or The Friends in War Time, 302 and fol.; J. R. Neal's Disunion and Restoration in Tennessee; and J. Fertig's Secession and Reconstruction of Tennessee.

[2] Conditions in Kentucky in 1861 were graphically set forth by Senator Jacob M. Howard of Michigan in a speech on "Military Interference with Elections" on March 24, 1864. See

also "An Address" and "A Letter" from Joseph Holt to the "People of Kentucky" dated May 31 and July 13, 1861; Nathaniel S. Shaler's article on "The Border State Men of the Civil War" in the Atlantic Monthly, lxix, 245, and pp. 226–281 of his Kentucky in the American Commonwealths series; and Thomas Speed's Union Cause in Kentucky (New York, 1907).

[3] See letter from Lieutenant Nelson to Fox dated Maysville, September 25, 1861, in Correspondence of Gustavus Vasa Fox, i, 379.

Kentucky came together it found that the Union men were in the majority. They voted down the motion for calling a convention, and the Confederate sympathizers soon realized that they were in a minority. For some months Kentucky maintained its neutrality, and when it was broken it was broken by the advance of a Confederate force that seized the town of Columbus on the Mississippi River and this gave opportunity to General Grant, who was then in command at Cairo, to occupy the town of Paducah at the mouth of the Cumberland River. From that time Kentucky became the theater of military operations and from the beginning to the end of the war was also the scene of a more or less illicit trade with the Confederates.

Of the three States between the Ohio River and the Lakes, the State of Ohio was most nearly akin to the States of the northeastern part of the country. When Lincoln called for men William Dennison, a Republican and a Union man, was in the governor's chair. He acted promptly and energetically and the majority of the people of the State came squarely into line behind him. This State was one of the first to respond, and it was the Ohio State troops under McClellan who crossed the river and made it possible for the people of western Virginia to oppose successfully the efforts of the people in the eastern part of the State to coerce them back into the Old Dominion. Throughout the war, Ohio remained faithful to the Union cause, although there were times when she seemed to be distinctly wavering. The situation in Indiana was much more critical. That State had no important shipping port on the Lakes and, indeed, its northern portion was still somewhat sparsely settled. In the election of 1860, the position that Indiana would take had been exceedingly doubtful. The Republicans had resorted to a dubious piece of political trickery.[1] Their

---

[1] Logan Esarey's *Indiana*, ii, 659; W. D. Foulke's *Oliver P. Morton*, i, 66.

real candidate for governor was Oliver P. Morton, but he was so pronounced a Free-Soiler that it was thought best to nominate Henry S. Lane for that office and to place Morton in the second position on the ticket. The understanding was that if the Republicans were successful in electing Lane and Morton and a majority of the members of the legislature, that body would elect Lane Senator from Indiana and Morton would succeed to the gubernatorial chair. The Republicans were successful and Morton became governor of Indiana. He retained his office during the war, although the legislature that was elected in 1862 was exceedingly hostile to him. Sumter was fired on, Lincoln called for men, and Indiana enthusiastically stepped into line[1] and furnished more men than had been asked for.

The condition of affairs in Illinois was more serious than in either Ohio or Indiana.[2] Southern Illinois had been settled by people to whom slavery had no terrors. The extreme southern portion was so fertile that it had received the name of Egypt and was entirely suited to the slave gang system. As one advanced northward the character of the soil and of cultivation and the desires of the people changed; but in 1860, the population of the southern half of the State was still distinctly Southern. When the time came and Senator Douglas pronounced squarely for the Union, sentiment changed even in the southernmost counties. The quotas were filled up and when Representative John A. Logan called for men to follow him into the field on the Union side, there was a hearty response, even in the southernmost part of the State. The keynote of Lincoln's policy is now clearly discernible. Without the active, hearty

---

[1] See Professor James A. Woodburn's "Party Politics in Indiana during the Civil War" in the *Report* of the American Historical Association for 1902, vol. i, p. 225.

[2] The *Memoirs of Gustave Koerner* (ii, 96–152) contain interesting matter on these months in Illinois.

coöperation of the people of the Ohio Valley or of a very large part of them, the seceded States could not be brought back into the Union, — and that support could not be had on the basis of a fight for the negro. The loyal people of Kentucky and of East Tennessee were not slave owners to any great extent. There were few slaves in West Virginia and there were no slaves in Ohio, Indiana, and Illinois. Pecuniary interest in slavery did not affect the loyal people of the Ohio Valley to any great extent. But they had no marked sympathy with emancipation and were certainly not willing to risk their lives and their fortunes to compel their slaveholding kinsfolk and neighbors to free their slaves.

The Union of their fathers, the Union for which Henry Clay had devoted his life, was very dear to them, and when its existence was threatened, they rose in its defence. It was for these reasons that Abraham Lincoln set his face sternly against the introduction of slave emancipation into the contest, — although this position seemed to many of his supporters to be wholly unjustifiable. And, besides this lukewarmness for the cause of emancipation, the new President wished to employ every Democrat who would fight for the Union, — and this seemed to many radical Republicans but a little way removed from sin. As we look backward and see the abolitionists and the radicals hounding Lincoln to pursue a policy that would be fatal to freedom, we can only marvel at the strength of will and power of patience of this greatest of Americans. But having made up his mind, and conscious of his own uprightness, Abraham Lincoln stood firm.

With Missouri and the politicians and people thereof, [1]

---

[1] T. L. Snead's *The Fight for Missouri from the Election of Lincoln to the Death of Lyon* (New York, 1886) is the best account of the contest. It is written

President Lincoln had even more troubles and more perplexities than he had with the dwellers in the Ohio Valley
itself. Missouri was a Slave State, but there were few slaves
and fewer slaveholders living in it and they had none of the
political cohesion and social power that their fellow slaveholders in the Cotton States enjoyed. The slaveholders
and their sympathizers were confined chiefly to St. Louis
and the older settlements along the Mississippi and to the
western part of the State; the intervening portion was
inhabited mainly by a population of small farmers who could
not profitably use slave labor in production, but who for
the most part had no great sympathy with anti-slavery
propaganda. Thomas Hart Benton had represented the
State in the United States Senate for nearly a generation,
but he had been defeated for reëlection in 1852 mainly on
account of his lack of sympathy with slavery and had found
refuge in the House of Representatives. Many of the best
known Missouri political leaders of 1850 had been slave
owners or had sympathized with slavery. The commander
of the United States army in the West with headquarters
at St. Louis was General William S. Harney.[1] He was a
Southerner and was now somewhat past middle life, but was
still strong in body and in mind. Realizing the actual condition of affairs, he sought to temporize and to see that no
conflict arose between the two portions of the people of
Missouri. The legislature of the State was in the hands

from the Southern standpoint and
should be supplemented by the perusal
of R. J. Rombauer's *The Union Cause in
St. Louis in 1861* (St. Louis, 1909).
In the *Continental Monthly* for April,
1862, there is an unsigned article
entitled "The War between Freedom
and Slavery in Missouri." Possibly
the best accounts are chs. xiii–xv of
Lucien Carr's *Missouri* in the *American
Commonwealths* series and Professor S.

B. Harding's article on the subject in
the *Report* of the American Historical
Association for 1900, i, pp. 85–103.
    [1] See L. U. Reavis's *Life and Military
Services of Gen. William Selby Harney*
(St. Louis, 1878), ch. xvi. General
Sherman was in St. Louis at the beginning of the trouble and in his *Home Letters* (p. 197) disapproves of the policy of
the Blairs.

of the slaveholding element, and the governor, Claiborne F. Jackson, sympathized ardently with the cause of Southern independence. He suggested to the legislature that a convention should be elected to consider the question as to what Missouri should do in the crisis. The legislature so voted, the election was held, and the convention met on the last day of February, 1861, at Jefferson City, the capital of the State, and promptly adjourned to St. Louis. When a resolution declaring that there was no adequate cause for secession came to the vote, there was only one negative,[1] but the convention also passed a resolution advising the withdrawal of Federal troops from the seceding States. In fact, the great mass of the members seem to have wished that Missouri should remain unpledged, for the moment at least. One member declared himself to be a slave owner and also declared that he was not willing to sacrifice other interests to the slave interest. Another member, an immigrant from Austria, stated that he had known war and revolution, but he declared that the German immigrants to Missouri would stand by the government and the Union, as they knew from experience that there was "no peace and no liberty without union." The Secessionists were dismayed and enraged by the action of this "sovereign" convention. They determined to persist in their projects, and Governor Jackson replied to Lincoln's call for men that it was unconstitutional and revolutionary, "inhuman and diabolical," and that the State of Missouri would not furnish one man "to carry on any such unholy crusade." Alarmed by the attitude of the governor and his secession adherents, Francis P. Blair, who was then living at St. Louis, secured the appointment of Captain Nathaniel Lyon[2] to the

[1] *Journal and Proceedings of the Missouri State Convention . . . March, 1861,* "Proceedings," p. 216.

[2] James Peckham's *General Nathaniel Lyon and Missouri in 1861* (New York, 1866) and chs. x–xiii of Ashbel Wood-

command of the Federal arsenal at St. Louis. In May,
General Harney entered into an agreement with Sterling
Price, who had been president of the convention but was at
the moment heading a movement for the preservation of the
existing state of affairs in Missouri, to the effect that nothing
should be done to disturb the peace. This action of Harney's aroused the distrust of Blair and he procured his
removal. Under the leadership of Blair and Lyon, the
arsenal was secured and then an attack was made on a body
of State troops that was encamped just outside of St. Louis
and was under the influence of Governor Jackson. The
attack was by St. Louis people, principally Germans who
had been for some time engaged in military training for
their own protection. They captured the troops without
any trouble, but, while returning with their prisoners to the
city, firing occurred and some persons were injured. Civil
war then followed in Missouri. It went on with varying
fortunes and ended in the triumph of the Union cause, but
only at considerable cost of men and money, both of which
could have been well employed elsewhere.[1] Nowadays,
historical students are coming more and more to the belief
that a temporizing policy such as General Harney was pursuing, when relieved from command, would have been better
for Missouri and for the cause of the Union.

The part played by the railroad building of the decade
before 1860 in the States north of the Ohio and west of the
Appalachians has already been described. Possibly the
influences of this great development of transportation have

ward's *Life of General Nathaniel Lyon*
(Hartford, 1862) give the Blair-Lyon
side of the controversy. An interesting
account of this bit of St. Louis history
is in Galusha Anderson's *Story of a
Border City during the Civil War.*

[1] An idea of the conditions of life in
Missouri and Arkansas during the war
can be obtained by a perusal of Wil-
liam Monks's *History of Southern Mis-
souri and Northern Arkansas* and
William Watson's *Life in the Confederate
Army*, chs. xvi-xxiii. Professor E. M.
Violette has given an excellent account
of this period in his *History of Missouri*
(New York, 1918).

been exaggerated although it does not seem so to the present writer. To judge fairly the effect produced by this connection of the Northwest with the Northeast one must take into consideration the entire lack of connection between the Northwest and the old South. Way back in the thirties there had been a project of building a railroad from Charleston to the Ohio River at Cincinnati, or at some other available point. This project had fallen through owing to various causes which need not be mentioned here. The Georgians had built a line of railroad connecting Savannah with Chattanooga, but between Chattanooga and the Ohio River there was no direct railroad communication in 1860. The Southerners, instead of making every effort to connect the Northwest with the Cotton Belt by land communication had diverted their energies in railroad building to connecting the Mississippi Valley with the Atlantic seaboard. This enterprise had taken the shape of the Memphis and Charleston Railroad, which was something of a misnomer because the connection at Chattanooga was with Savannah and not with Charleston.[1] Undoubtedly this line of transportation bound the cotton-growing States closer together; but it was not a closer bond between them that was needed so much as any kind of a bond between them and their cousins and food-providers of the Ohio Valley. The condition of transportation North and South of the Ohio River can be seen at a glance from the map on the opposite page. By 1860 the Louisville and Nashville Railroad had penetrated southwardly to the line of the Memphis and Charleston Railroad, and in the season of navigation the Tennessee

---

[1] The map on the opposite page is reproduced from Theodore D. Jervey's *The Railroad the Conqueror* (Columbia, S. C., 1913). There are a few important omissions. These may be supplied by referring to the maps in Appleton's *Steam Guide* (December, 1861) and Dinsmore's *Railroad and Steam Navigation* (July, 1860).

River served as a highway from the Ohio River to the
Memphis and Charleston Railroad.   But these lines of transportation, although they loom large in the history of the
trade between the lines in the next four years, really were
nothing when compared with the oversupply of railroad
facilities to the people of the Northwest.   And, finally, this

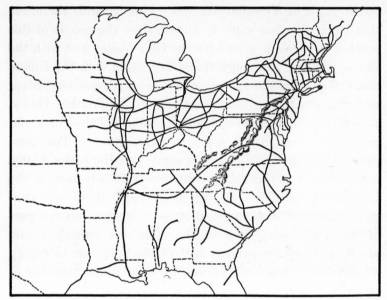

RAILWAYS, NORTH AND SOUTH, 1860.
(Reproduced by permission from Theo. D. Jervey's " The Railroad the Conqueror,"
p. 42).

shortsightedness of the Southern statesmen in not pushing
forward this connecting link between themselves and their
kinsfolk of the Ohio Valley brought it about that when war
came, there was limited transportation service between
Kentucky and Tennessee and the Atlantic seaboard.

It is hard for us living in the days of railroads, aeroplanes,
and the radio to realize the importance of the transportation
problems of sixty and seventy years ago.   The northwestern

portion of Virginia, the region that is now known as the
State of West Virginia, stood directly athwart any direct
route from Kentucky and Ohio to the valleys of the Potomac
and the James.   Next to nothing had been done to provide
this region with transportation facilities.   It lay within the
Ohio Valley although forming a part of the Atlantic seaboard state of Virginia.   It was quite natural, therefore,
that when the time came to choose sides the people of this
portion of Virginia went with the Ohio Valley and with the
Union.   When Kentucky threw her lot in with the Union,
the Valley with the exception of the mid-Tennessee River
region was with the North and against the South.   Had it
been otherwise, the whole strategic problem of the war would
have been other than it was.   In the four years,' Tennessee
gave 31,000 men to the Union army and Kentucky 75,000
more[1] and, together, they contributed 75,000 men to the
Confederate armies.   As the case stood, there was constant danger that some inopportune movement on the part
of the abolitionists and of the Northern radicals would
arouse so much resentment in the Ohio Valley as to nullify
all President Lincoln's efforts, to keep it on the side of
the Union.   And the actions of these very well-meaning
people of the North in 1862 and again in 1864 came near
undoing all that Lincoln had accomplished in holding this
region for the side of the Union in 1861.

[1] This matter is admirably treated
by C. C. Anderson in his *Fighting by
Southern Federals* (New York, 1912).   See also J. O. Murray's *Jefferson Davis*,
42, 43.

NOTE

General Bibliography of the War. — The United States government[1] has printed the records of the armies and navies of both sides in three remarkable publications: *The War of the Rebellion: A Compilation of the Official Records of the Union and Confederate Armies*, in 130 volumes (Washington, 1880–1902). The last volume is a general index to the separate volume indexes. The work is divided into series and volumes, and beginning with series i, vol. xxiv, pt. i, there is a serial number to each volume also. It has a valuable accompanying atlas. This work is variously cited by makers of books as *Official Records*, or simply *O.R.*, as *War Records*, as *W.R.*, and in various other forms.[2] This set is practically the basis of all recent, scholarly extended works on the war.[3] The companion publication on the navy, in thirty volumes, is entitled *Official Records of the Union and Confederate Navies in the War of the Rebellion*. Series ii, volume i, of this work contains important statistical data. This publication is conveniently referred to as *Official Records . . . Navies*. A third set of volumes published by the government is *The Medical and Surgical History of the War of the Rebellion* (8 vols., quarto); pt. i, vol. ii, pp. xxxiii–clv, is a serviceable " Chronological Summary of Engagements and Battles " including those of the navy. Frank Moore's *Rebellion Record* (11 vols.) was published during the war. It contains interesting information with documents, all of which, however, must be verified if used in argumentation. Harper's *Pictorial History of the Great Rebellion* (2 vols.)[4] gives contemporary ideas with

[1] The *Final Report . . . by the Provost Marshal General*, in two parts, contains a mass of useful information, as Document No. 35, "Laws Relative to the Raising of Troops," and No. 36, "Proclamations and Orders of the President." It is usually cited as Fry's *Report* and forms vol. iv, Parts i and ii of *House Executive Documents*, No. 1, 39th Cong., 1st Sess. Table of contents of the "Appendix" is on p. 100 of Part i.

[2] Rowland's *Davis*, x, 168–281, has a "List of Letters and Indorsements" of Davis printed in the *Official Records*.

[3] Before the publication of the *Official Records*, students were obliged to rely on the ex parte evidence extracted from military officers by the partisan Committee on the Conduct of the War and published in 8 volumes as its *Report* (1863–1866).

[4] Besides the contemporary publications mentioned in the text, reference should be made to articles written by eminent participants in the war or by distinguished students of the conflict. Of these is the series entitled *Campaigns of the Civil War* published by the Scribners, the four large volumes published by the Century Company, entitled *Battles and Leaders of the Civil War*, the articles in the *Century*, especially in the years 1884, 1887, and 1888, and the *Confederate Military History* (12 vols., Atlanta, Ga., 1899).

many interesting pictures, and *The Photographic History of The Civil War* (10 vols.) gives one a vivid impression of the scenes of those stirring days. The *Papers* of the Military Historical Society of Massachusetts are mainly confined to the campaigns of the Army of the Potomac, but a few *Papers* relate to events in other fields.

Nicolay and Hay's *Abraham Lincoln: A History* in ten volumes is in reality a detailed narrative of the war from the Union standpoint and the *Complete Works of Abraham Lincoln* in twelve volumes, also edited by Nicolay and Hay, read with the biography will satisfy the needs of all but the most exacting student as to the Lincoln side of the political history of the time and also of much of the military history. There is no work on the Southern side comparable to Nicolay and Hay's *Lincoln* and there is no adequate life of Jefferson Davis. Dunbar Rowland has edited his letters, papers, and speeches in ten volumes under the title of *Jefferson Davis, Constitutionalist* (Jackson, Mississippi, 1923). Unfortunately, Dr. Rowland did not preface the printed documents with an authoritative memoir.[1] The *Personal Memoirs of U. S. Grant* (2 vols., New York, 1886) is one of the most remarkable works of its kind. It must have been founded in large part on documentary evidence and if not, the writer's memory was phenomenal. Of the innumerable lives of this greatest of American military men, that by C. A. Dana and J. H. Wilson (1868) and that by Hamlin Garland (1898), while very different in outlook, are the best. The man himself appears in his true character in the *Letters of Ulysses S. Grant to his Father and his Youngest Sister, 1857–78* (New York, 1912). General Lee never wrote any memoirs or autobiography, but *Lee's Dispatches*,[2] that were printed from the collection of Wimberley Jones de Renne of Wormsloe, Georgia, in 1915, and the *Recollections and Letters of General Robert E. Lee by his Son, Captain Robert E. Lee*, which is composed to a great extent of letters to his family, together give one an interesting insight into his character and thoughts. Of the formal biographies, that by Armistead L. Long (New York,

---

[1] A comparison of some of the material in Rowland's book with the corresponding matter in the *Official Records* shows that one contains Davis material that the other does not and that where the same document is printed in both places, it is evident that the printing in Rowland's book is from one copy and that in the *Official Records* from another of the same letter, and probably such differences as appear as to punctuation, spelling, capitalization, etc., are due to different standards of editing.

[2] This is sometimes cited as *Lee's Confidential Dispatches to Davis*, from the binder's title.

1886) is perhaps the best, but Jefferson Davis in a letter written in 1887 at the time of its appearance reflected most severely on two of the statements in it, and it would seem with some justification. Of the more readable biographies of Lee those by John Esten Cooke and Thomas Nelson Page are to be mentioned; but there is no satisfying life of the great Confederate general.

CHAPTER XIV

THE CONDUCT OF THE WAR

IN the organization of the army, the Confederacy gained a six months start on the North. It had at its head five or six of the most efficient men of the old army: Adjutant General Cooper, Quartermaster General Joseph E. Johnston, Commissary General Northrup, and Colonel Josiah Gorgas, who proved to have a genius for building up the Confederate ordnance service.[1] In the field there were two efficient organizers and disciplinarians, P. G. T. Beauregard and Braxton Bragg. There was no departmental system to hamper these officers and they could build the new army from the ground up. So well did they do their work that there was astonishingly little change in the personnel of the upper places of the Confederate army: the men who were there in 1861, were there in 1862 and, for the most part, in January, 1865. On the other hand the Union administration was obliged to make use of the old departmental machinery at Washington which was suited to a small army scattered throughout the country, but was not fitted to set on foot an army of hundreds of thousands of men and supply it with the best materials for war that the period could produce.

Both North and South, the Presidents were troubled by

[1] There is a sketch of the life of General Josiah Gorgas in vol. xiii of the *Papers* of the Southern Historical Society. The present author has had the advantage of reading in manuscript, the journal kept by General Gorgas from some time before the war to the close of the conflict. For this he is indebted to General Gorgas's son's widow, Mrs. William C. Gorgas, and to Mr. Charles Moore, Chief of the Manuscripts Division of the Library of Congress.

the performance, or lack of performance, of this general or
that, and both Presidents were sorely tried by the doings of
the politicians, many of whom thought that the appointment
and control of generals and colonels was on all fours with that
of postmasters and customs collectors. As long as the people
stood behind them, military failure could be borne with, but
when the political leaders interfered, there was trouble. At
first the South Carolinians and, later, the Virginians seem
to have expected to govern themselves as independent
sovereign entities. But they bowed to the inevitable when
war came and consented for its duration to place power in
the hands of the Confederate government at Richmond.
In the beginning, there were no parties in the Confederacy,[1] but scarcely had Congress begun its sessions in
Virginia than the old political alignments reappeared and
from that time on greatly increased the perplexities of
Jefferson Davis. In the North, the "war powers" of the
President came at once into operation,[2] greatly to the dismay
of many men in Congress and elsewhere. Before long, when
little or nothing had been accomplished by the military,
earnest and exceedingly able members of Congress determined to take upon themselves, so far as they could, the
management of the war.[3] They secured the establishment of

[1] See on Southern party divisions,
Boucher's "*In Re* That Aggressive
Slavocracy" in *Mississippi Valley
Historical Review*, viii, 13–79. Jefferson
Davis, in the brief "Autobiography"
that was first printed in 1890, the year
after his death, wrote that in the
selection of a Cabinet he was relieved
from the usual difficulties that beset a
President of the United States; "for
there were no 'sections' and no 'party'
distinctions. All aspirations, ambitions, and interests had been merged in
a great desire for Confederate independence." Rowland's *Jefferson Davis*,
i, p. xxviii.

[2] In May, 1862, President Lincoln
addressed a letter to the House of
Representatives and to the Senate
taking full responsibility for himself and
the "Cabinet" as a whole for certain
acts attributed by the House to
Cameron and censured by it. Raymond's *Lincoln*, i, 248; *Complete
Works*, vii, 189.

[3] These were Zachariah Chandler
and Benjamin F. Wade. For Chandler,
see the biography issued by the Detroit
"Post and Tribune" and W. C. Harris's
*Public Life of Zachariah Chandler,
1851–1875* (Lansing, 1917).

a Committee on the Conduct of the War that interfered most sadly with the carrying on of military enterprises and no doubt caused the loss of thousands of lives and the expenditure of millions of dollars that might otherwise have been avoided.[1] The Union government — and its generals — were also greatly affected by the doings of the newspaper correspondents. The war correspondent was just coming into being, for the Crimean War had seen him for the first time in his modern form. In the next few years, hundreds of enterprising men followed the armies or went with them, visited the departments at Washington, and sought to interview statesmen and generals wherever they might be found. Many of these men had already achieved reputations[2] in the newspaper world and others were soon to gain them. Among them were Whitelaw Reid, Henry Villard, and Charles A. Dana, who with Horace Greeley and Henry J. Raymond, formed a group of able, well-intentioned, patriotic men,— however unfortunate some of their doings may have been. Southern newspaper men were so thoroughly limited in the scope of their news-getting that it amounted almost to a censorship; but items crept into the Southern papers from "soldiers' letters" home that afforded some information to Northern generals, but not nearly as much as Lee and his lieutenants got from the New York papers.

While the New Jersey-born Adjutant General Samuel Cooper[3] was organizing the Confederate army, Davis sent

[1] Eight volumes of ex parte testimony and unofficial reports and letters were issued under the general title of "Report of the Committee on the Conduct of the War." They have been largely superseded by the *Official Records.* An article by W. W. Pierson in the *American Historical Review* (xxiii, 550–576) takes a much more favorable view of the committee and its works than is taken by the present writer.

[2] See a very interesting article on "The Newspaper Problem . . . during the Civil War" by J. G. Randall in *American Historical Review,* xxiii, 303–323.

[3] Davis's acquaintance with Cooper dated back to the period before the Mexican War and the two had worked together when Davis was Secretary of War and Cooper Adjutant General. In 1877, Davis wrote to Fitzhugh Lee

the Maryland-born Raphael Semmes to the North to purchase military material. He had no difficulty in entering
into contracts for munitions and for the delivery of military
materials at a later time. Every one was willing to deal with
him, for there was as little expectation of war among the
people of the Northern States at that time as there was
among the mass of the Southern population. His work done,
he embarked on a steamer for Savannah, which entered that
port with the United States flag at the peak and the Confederate flag at the fore, and reached Montgomery eight days
before the guns opened on Fort Sumter.[1] At almost that
time, the Confederate government despatched Caleb Huse,[2]
a native of Newburyport, in Massachusetts, to England to
purchase supplies for the Confederacy. He reached Charleston, immediately after the surrender of Sumter, passed
through Baltimore a few days after the attack on the Sixth
Massachusetts regiment, and, by way of New York and
Montreal, found himself on a steamer at Portland, Maine,
bound for Liverpool. In England and in Europe, he had
great success in buying arms and munitions and the machin-

that those who were in "a position to
know what he [Cooper] did, what he
prevented, what he directed, will not
fail to place him among those who contributed most to whatever was
achieved." Rowland's *Davis*, vii, 533.
There is a sketch of General Cooper's
career by General Fitz. Lee in Southern
Historical Society's *Papers*, iii, 269.
Cooper married a grand-daughter of
George Mason of Gunston Hall, and was
thus the brother-in-law of Senator
James M. Mason, the Confederate
Commissioner to Great Britain.

[1] Semmes's *Service Afloat*, 83–88.
The instructions from Davis, himself,
are in Rowland's *Jefferson Davis*, v, 54;
and see P. Kean's *Report of Evidence*
on the Confederate Navy Department,
p. 354.

[2] See Caleb Huse's *The Supplies for
the Confederate Army. How They were
obtained in Europe and How paid for*,
(Boston, 1904). These are the "recollections of an old man," but apart from
details must have some degree of
authenticity. A sketch of Huse's career
is in Massey's *Reminiscences*, 131–136.

The Southerners also captured arms
from their Northern opponents or
picked them up on the field of battle.
Many of these had been purchased by
Federal agents in Europe. A report
in the Archives at Richmond states
that when some of these guns were
fired the "cones" blew off endangering
the lives of the men using them. In
some others the vent was not bored
through at all. At one time the
ammunition wagons of one brigade of
Stonewall Jackson's force carried three
kinds of cartridges for the brigade
muskets. Southern Historical Society's
Papers, xiv, 140.

ery wherewith to make them.[1]   Until these began to arrive,
the Confederate authorities were obliged to refuse the services of thousands of volunteers.   The first flow of Southern
soldiers was largely composed of the aristocrats of the Cotton
Belt and a better body of men for the business in hand was
probably never seen.   Their ideas of war were distinctly
peculiar.   It was not easy to bring into order regiments
composed of officers and men, all of whom had money in
abundance and were more accustomed to give orders than
to obey them.   From the beginning to the end, President
Davis directed the efforts of successive secretaries of war:
L. P. R. Walker, Judah P. Benjamin, General Randolph,
James Seddon, and General Breckinridge.   Benjamin later
was an admirable Secretary of State, but he did not show his
qualities in the war office, possibly because of the great shortage of munitions and equipment.   Otherwise, these men
seem to have been hardly more than chief clerks to whom
Davis played the part of master.[2]   Throughout the upper
grades of the Confederate service, there were graduates of
West Point and the complaint against the West Pointers
was as acute in the South as it was in the North.

President Lincoln's difficulties were very different from
those that faced Jefferson Davis, and, as far as the organization of the army went, they were much greater.   Lincoln

---

[1] In 1862, one hundred thousand
"Musket Shells" were contracted for
by Beverly Kennon for the use of the
Confederate naval force at New Orleans.
They were of "no use to the naval
service. . . . In ramming down the
rammer, the shell frequently exploded"
— and thus explosive bullets were not
used in actual fighting by the Confederates.   *Report of Evidence taken before a
Joint Special Committee of Both Houses
of the Confederate Congress to Investigate
the Affairs of the Navy Department*, 396.
[2] In October, 1861, Davis wrote to

General Beauregard that his letters of
October 20 and 21 "have just been
referred to me, and I hasten to reply
without consulting the Secretary of
War."   This habit grew on Davis.   In
November, 1862, he wrote to Randolph,
then Secretary of War, that his moving
troops and appointing persons were not
at all approved of and the next day
Randolph resigned his office.   Rowland's *Davis*, v, 151, 371, 374.   An
interesting defence of his course is in
ibid., v, 216.

had no military training — except some weeks of service in the Black Hawk War — and his lack of training in that and in other ways was not at all compensated by his first Secretary of War, Simon Cameron, and, possibly, was over-supplied by his second Secretary of War, Edwin M. Stanton.[1] At first Lincoln relied on General Scott and the lesser officers in the War Department. These acted slowly and conservatively. The first Federal armies were more State organizations than were those of the Confederacy. West Pointers, who had left the service and gone into private life, returned to the career of arms; but it took time to select the efficient men among them and place them in positions where they would do the most good. One remarkable Southern officer of the old army remained in the Union service, General George H. Thomas. The authorities at Washington found it difficult to give him employment at all suited to his capacities because he was a native of Virginia, although he had married a woman from Troy — New York. This departmental disorganization and the conservatism of those who remained in the service greatly delayed the building up of an efficient Federal army. When that was finally brought about, the conservatism of the Department resulted in its refusal to adopt a scheme of large military units or to accept the new arms and machinery of war that modern invention had supplied,— as the breech-loading rifle and the rapid firing gun.[2] In the autumn of 1861, McClellan succeeded Scott as chief of the Federal forces. He exhibited remark-

[1] The part played by Stanton in the war is not yet comprehensible. From one point of view, he appears to have been a constant and consistent marplot; his outstanding virtue was his golden patriotism which redeemed many faults and mistakes without number. Three biographies of Stanton have been written by G. C. Gorham (2 vols., Boston, 1899); by F. A. Flower (Akron, Ohio, 1905); and by J. E. Doyle (Steubenville, Ohio, 1911).

[2] See W. C. Dodge's *Breech-Loaders versus Muzzle-Loaders* (Washington, 1864). General J. H. Wilson in his *Under the Old Flag* repeatedly adverts to the opposition of the older officers of the regular army to adopting the new weapon.

able organizing ability and brought discipline and military cohesion within a few months into the Army of the Potomac that remained with it through years of campaigning, disaster, and success.

In the beginning and throughout the war, the Confederate government obtained munitions, clothing, and equipment from Europe. These were inadequate for its needs and had to be supplemented by the products of the South. In that section there were iron mills, woolen mills, and cotton mills; but the output of all of these was far less than the demand that was suddenly placed upon them. The Southerners had persistently deplored governmental interference with private industry. They approached the solution of the new problem with hesitation and showed little of the ability that was displayed in the production of munitions of war. The government appointed officials to purchase equipment and these entered into relations with the existing establishments.[1] They contracted with the mill owners to purchase a portion of their output on a cost-plus basis. The profit in the early years was not to exceed seventy-five per cent! Even so, the mill men were unwilling to sell to the government. The conscription acts placed a club in the hands of the Confederate representatives and by the middle of 1862, the supply of white labor to the factories was almost entirely in the hands of the military officials.[2]

[1] There is an interesting article on "The Control of Manufacturing by the Confederate Government" by C. W. Ramsdell in the *Mississippi Valley Historical Review*, viii, 231–249. See also "An English Merchant" in *Two Months in the Confederate States*, 266–278.

[2] On April 7, 1864, the agent of the "Manchester [Virginia] Cotton and Wool Manufacturing Company" wrote to Colonel Munford, the Secretary of Virginia, that nearly all of their laborers being detailed men, they were to all intents and purposes under the control of the Confederate government which required their whole product (Department of Archives, Virginia State Library). This note was communicated to me by Miss Kathleen Bruce of Richmond, who has for some years been studying the history of the Tredegar Iron Works. The facts stated above are abundantly confirmed by other entries in manuscript and in print, as the *Journal of the Convention . . . of South Carolina* (Columbia, 1862) p. 355.

It happened, therefore, that if a mill owner would not sell to the Confederate government, he was likely to find that the soldiers who had been detailed to work for him had been called to the colors. Moreover, the raw materials could be obtained oftentimes only from a distance. Before long the Confederate Quartermaster's Department exercised practically a priority control over shipments.

The Confederate government exercised a less effective control over the railroads than it did over the factories. The railroads were few in number and did not run in the directions that military traffic necessarily took owing to the strategic problems that had to be faced.[1] Moreover, the lines were short and were broken up by the refusal of important cities to permit them to pass through, and frequently connecting lines had different widths of track. Between the Savannah River and the James, there were half a dozen changes. Where two railroads came together and were of one gauge, the cars of one were not allowed to go on the rails of the other for fear they would never come back. The most serious break was at Petersburg, where the road from Wilmington stopped at the southern edge and that to Richmond began at the western limit. The route from Richmond by the way of Petersburg and Wilmington was the only continuous north and south line on the Atlantic slope within the limits of the Confederacy. In a similar way the Memphis and Charleston road was the only continuous east and west line in the Southern country between the Mississippi and the Appalachians. Many of the gaps were filled during the war, but by the time this was accomplished, either the strategic problems had changed or the roads had so deteriorated

---

[1] See C. W. Ramsdell's article on "The Confederate Government and the Railroads" in *American Historical Review*, xxii, 794–810. An article on "Trade and Transportation along the South Atlantic Seaboard before the Civil War" by H. D. Dozier is in the *South Atlantic Quarterly*, xviii, 231.

that it made little difference whether they connected or not. The constant depreciation of Confederate money had seriously affected the railroads as they had not been able to increase their fares in proportion to the rising cost of operation. Under these circumstances, railroad service lessened rapidly, rolling stock gave out, and rails disappeared. Eventually the Confederate government assumed a modified control over the roads, but the transportation problem remained most serious to the end. In 1864 the Quartermaster General stated that a train could not run more than one hundred miles a day on the main line from Georgia to Richmond and that a car could not go five hundred miles without breaking down. When the blockade became strict, Southern railroad managers had to go on with the materials in hand and use the rails from unimportant lines to repair the main routes of traffic. Had the Confederate government realized the part that transportation was to play in the war, it might have taken possession of the railroads or have given them priority as to materials and the employment of "details." If it had done so, it would have greatly strengthened the powers of resistance of the Southern people and might have prolonged the war for another year or so.

The Southerners had believed that without cotton and without the Southern market for their goods, the mills of the Northeastern States would close their doors and their operatives would walk the streets or starve in their homes. It turned out that the demand for the products of Northern factories and farms was so great that within a short space of time every Northern man, woman, and child who was not engaged directly or indirectly in military operations was needed in industry or in agriculture. No army before had been so lavishly supplied with food, clothing, and equipment as were the Union soldiers after 1861. They were weighted down with impedimenta which they threw away at the first moments of fatigue, to the delight of the Confederates. One of the most telling anecdotes of the war was the loudly expressed disgust of Southern soldiers as to the quality of some of the clothing served out to the Northerners. Of course, there was undue desire for profit on the part of manufacturers and connivance with them by Federal officials, but the use of poor materials was due in great measure to the scarcity of the basal products for the machines in the mills and shops. Wool became scarce and high in price. Enterprising manufacturers chopped up old woolen garments, pressed the fibre into a species of felting called "shoddy," and made it into overcoats for the soldiers that disappeared with the first heavy rain. The phrase "shoddy aristocracy" was used to describe the profiteers of that time ; but probably there was a great deal of exaggeration as to the amount and extent of cheating by Northern contractors and manufacturers.[1] In reality, inventive genius made up in great measure for the lack of labor on the farm and in the factory and released men and women for other pursuits. On the farm, horse-drawn machines supplanted human power, and in the factory and in the shoe shop the widespread introduction of machine sewing reduced almost incredibly the number of hands required. Most of these inventions had been made before 1861, but it was the high price of labor in the war time that brought them into common use. The war stimulated the production of iron and gave the United States its opportunity to become a great iron manufacturing country. The discovery and exploitation of mineral oil or petroleum provided cheap light and lubricating material and took the place of the whale oil of the earlier part of the century. The ever-rising price of gold in terms of paper brought

[1] See *House Report*, No. 2, 37th Cong., 2nd Sess., vols. i and ii.

about an increase of the movement of gold-seekers and silver-miners to Colorado, Nevada, Idaho, and California. All in all, the Northern workers, so far from becoming necessitous and craving employment, actually found themselves in a position to dictate to their employers.

The responsibility for the lavish outlay of the Union government has never been ascertained and probably never will be. The task was a new one, money was abundant, and it was better to over-supply the soldiers than it was to under-supply them. Nevertheless, one turns back to the accounts of the doings of the shoddy aristocrats and camp followers and of those between them and the men in the fighting line with some degree of detestation. The sutlers made money out of the cravings of the soldiers and in many a military post in a city or on a sand hill there was extravagance and useless expenditure. In 1864, at Hilton Head, South Carolina, a town had grown up nearly as large as some of the smaller cities of the North, where there was a theatre to seat one thousand persons and where "all the luxuries and all the vices of civilized New York are to be procured." Many officers had their wives and families with them and lived in "great luxury, with good tables and elegant furniture" all supplied from the government's stores and there was a whole street of sutlers' shops, which was known locally as "Robbers Row." At New Orleans and in the cantonments on the Mississippi, the case was even worse, if possible. Everywhere hangers-on of the army were tempted by the great profits' to be realized from dealings in the products of the Southern States which commanded three, four, or five prices in the markets of the North and of Europe. That there was a shoddy aristocracy is not to be wondered at; the wonder is that there were so many honest people left.

One bit of organization that stands out was the administration of transportation by the Northern government. It was recognized that the solution of many things depended upon the efficient transportation of goods and supplies to the army depots behind the lines. Soon it came to be realized that the rapid and effective transportation of army units from one field of operation to another would materially affect the course and the duration of the war. In 1861, the North was over-supplied with railroads; many of them were on the point of bankruptcy. The railroad authorities at once placed their facilities at the disposal of the government, and the military men took possession of the railway lines in the field just as soon as they fell into Federal control.[1] They rebuilt them with speed and efficiency and by 1864, had acquired so much skill that it was an almost hopeless operation for the Confederates to break a railroad line. The names of McCallum and Haupt [2] should ever be borne in grateful remembrance, for with the exception of a few men at the heads of the armies and of the fleets and in foremost positions in Washington, none contributed more to the successful outcome of the conflict than these two. It is easy to exaggerate the importance of this thing or that; but it seems that the transportation of Schofield's Army of the Ohio, thirty thousand strong, from Nashville in central Tennessee to the North Carolina coast in three weeks' time [3] and in the winter season was one of the things that most powerfully contributed to bring the conflict to a conclusion at the time and place of its ending.

[1] *Fairbanks' Pocket Atlas of the United States, and Miniature Railway Guide* (New York, 1859) has a series of State maps showing the railroads, and a map of the United States in 1860 in T. D. Jervey's *The Railroad, the Conqueror* (Columbia, S. C., 1913) facing p. 42, shows the existing railroads, north and south. A remarkably useful map is appended to the "Report" of General McCallum in *House Executive Document*, No. 1, 39th Cong., 1st Sess.

[2] See McCallum's "Report" as above and Herman Haupt's *Reminiscences* (Milwaukee, 1901).

[3] See L. B. Parsons's *Rail and River Army Transportation in the Civil War* (St. Louis, 1899).

The conduct of war is always expensive and is usually
a drain on the resources of the people.[1] Modern methods
of finance were then in their infancy and where the sentiment
was so divided as it was in the North and in the South, the
problem was unusually critical. Outside of England and
some other European countries, borrowing money on a large
scale was comparatively unknown. In war, every government has to face the question as to whether the terrific
expenditures that are certain to arise should be met by taxation or by borrowing or by some combination of the two.
The Southerners had always opposed taxation, partly because any system of the kind was likely to lend itself to the
stimulation of manufacturing in the North at the expense —
so the Southerners believed — of the people of the South.
Governmental expenditures there had been met by taxation
of land and, when some unusual expenditure was contemplated, a State bank was established or bonds were issued
and sold in the North or in Europe. The Confederate constitution limited the taxation of imports and, in point of
fact, the Confederacy had very few imports to tax.[2]   There

---

[1] In R. G. Dun & Co's Statistical
Table for 1862, the number of failures
in the North in 1861 is given as 5,935
in comparison with about 3,000 in each
of the preceding four years, — including
1857. The liabilities in 1861 are given
at $178,000,000 as against $61,000,000
in 1860 and $265,000,000 in 1857. On
the other hand in the seceded States
the failures in 1861 were noted as very
much smaller than in any of the five
preceding years. In a pamphlet addressed *To our Subscribers*, also printed
in 1862, Dun and Company state that
the increased number of failures and
the decreased amount of indebtedness
in 1861 over 1857 was due to the fact
that in 1861 the jobbers were forced
to suspend, while in 1857, it was the
larger banking, importing, and commission houses that were caught. At

the time the South owed to Northern
merchants about $211,000,000, of which
$159,000,000, was due to New York
alone.

[2] The finances of the South have
been admirably described by the late
Professor J. C. Schwab in *The Confederate States of America* (New York,
1901) and by E. A. Smith in his "History of the Confederate Treasury" in
the *Publications* of the Southern History
Association, vol. v, 1, 99, 188. A
fanciful, but interesting scheme is
outlined in a pamphlet signed "J."
and entitled *War Finance* setting forth
a plan to meet the expenditure of the
war by issuing Treasury Notes based
on the cotton which should remain
on the plantations. It was printed at
Charleston in 1861.

was little gold in the South in 1861, as Southern financial operations had been very largely carried on through Northern banks. With the stoppage of the sale of tobacco, cotton, and naval stores, the great resources of the South for taxation purposes disappeared. The war was necessarily financed mainly by loans supplemented by State aid. Paper money was issued and bonds were issued, the latter to be redeemed within a specified time after the recognition of Southern independence. The Secretary of the Treasury, C. G. Memminger, was a successful business man of Charleston and he had good advisers; but the problem that he and the Confederate Congress had to face was practically insoluble. Paper money and bonds were issued and at once depreciated. Prices rose, more paper money and more bonds were put out, and prices continued to rise. Various expedients were resorted to, but it was the everlasting story of inflation. As prices rose, speculators appeared. Even the most unbusinesslike Southerners invested in commodities that were likely to rise in price. When food and hides and material for clothing could not be purchased, a law was passed authorizing the government to impress a certain proportion of the products of the farms. But this, too, proved to be ineffective, for the farmers became adepts in concealment and the impressment officers, or some of them, were corrupt. Southern books are filled with stories of speculators, of high prices, and of the tyrannical "impressment." Northern writers of an economic turn of mind have oftentimes attributed the collapse of the Confederacy to its paper money, over-issues of bonds, and the impressment. On the other side, it must be said, that governments, like railroads, have often operated most effectually when bankrupt and, viewing the management of the finances of the South and of the North, there was not much superiority on the part of the

North over the South. And, indeed, when one makes a
parallel column of the prices in Richmond and in New York
in dollars of paper or of gold, one does not find so marked a
difference as one would expect from the perusal of books.

In the North, the problem was somewhat similar and, in
many respects, it was entirely different. Throughout the
war, Northern exportations to Europe continued and even
increased, and gold and silver came from the farthest West.[1]
Under the circumstances protection was inevitable, and one
increase of duties followed hard upon another. To equalize
the burden an extensive system of internal revenue taxation
was devised.[2] The expenses of the Federal government
grew so vast that no system of taxation sufficed to provide
the necessary funds. Paper money and bonds became the
only refuge. The government made the paper money
legal tender and issued bonds with a lavish hand. In 1862,
it occurred to some one to establish a new form of national
bank system. By this national banks were to be established
in different parts of the country, each one of them to have
right to issue paper money based on the bonds of the national
government. The State paper money issues were to be
taxed out of existence. The plan worked admirably. Currency
was created that had behind it the credit of the United

---

[1] The articles written by Charles F.
Dunbar on the economic and financial
questions that arose during the war, in
the *Boston Daily Advertiser*, form in
themselves most interesting reading.
When he became Professor of Political
Economy at Harvard, a few years later,
he embodied some of the results of his
later researches in articles written for
the *Quarterly Journal of Economics*,
especially an article on "The Direct
Tax of 1861" (vol. iii, 436) and another
on "The Safety of the Legal Tender
Paper" (vol. xi, 223).

[2] Besides the *Reports* of the Secretary
of the Treasury of the United States for
the years 1861–1865 and the financial
articles in the newspapers of the time,
and in *Hunt's Merchants' Magazine*, a
student will read biographies of Chase
and Fessenden, Horace White's *Money
and Banking*, Oberholtzer's *Jay Cooke*,
D. R. Dewey, *Financial History of the
United States*, a stimulating article by
J. Laurence Laughlin in the *Atlantic
Monthly*, lxxxii, p. 47, on "War and
Money: Some Lessons of 1862" and
F. W. Taussig's *Tariff History*, 155–170.
See also Rhodes's *United States*, vol. vii,
using the index under "Gold Conspiracy,"
"Money," and "Paper
money."

States and possessed a certain degree of flexibility. Of course, this system was inflation, but it carried the country through the war. Some of the last loans were floated by means that remind one of the methods employed to raise money in the Great War. In 1864, the conflict was costing the North one million dollars a day and it was a strain that hitherto no people had endured for any length of time.

Ever since the close of the French and Indian Wars of the eighteenth century, the American people had been devoted to peace and, when compelled to war, had relied on "volunteering." In the Revolution the Continental Congress had called upon the States to furnish quotas of men. These demands had been answered in the ways that have been described in preceding volumes: volunteering, payment of money bounties, or of wild lands, and finally some form of draft. In the War of 1812 reliance was placed on the small "regular" army and on the State militia. By the time of the Mexican War, the regular army had grown to be a formidable force, but it was still necessary to rely very largely on volunteers. The first armies of 1861 — North and South — went to pieces after Bull Run and new forces were raised by volunteering. Both in the North and in the South,[1] locally prominent men placed themselves at the head of a movement to raise a company or a regiment. In the South these units were embodied in the State military organizations and then taken into the Confederate army. In the North, they were raised by State authorities with the expectation that they would be absorbed into the Federal

[1] The details of the raising of regiments come out in reminiscences, in contemporary letters of persons connected with the volunteer organizations, in the histories of those regiments and of the States. A few articles have been printed dealing with the subject, as J. D. Hicks's "Organization of the Volunteer Army in 1861 with Special Reference to Minnesota" (*Minnesota Historical Bulletin*, February, 1918, pp. 324–368). J. L. Jones's *An Artilleryman's Diary* (Wisconsin History Commission's *Original Papers*, No. 8) gives one an idea of the monotony and hardship of life in an artillery regiment.

forces. On both sides, the one idea of the new soldier was to get to the front. When a Southern regiment was ordered to a fort on the coast or a Northern regiment was marched to a post in the Indian country, there was considerable desertion. One reads of Southern men going from one company or regiment or even from one State to another to get into an organization that had marching orders. Both North and South, there was chaos. Neither government could provide arms and equipment for the men who came forward. New recruits, drilling with broomsticks for muskets and in the clothes they wore at home, speedily lost a great part of their pristine enthusiasm, especially when they found no camps prepared for them and were fed by contract with some local provision dealer or restaurant keeper. In the confusion, these things were unavoidable, but they made the service less attractive.

In the early spring of 1862, it had become evident that the Federal government had organized formidable fighting machines in the West and in the East. The Confederate authorities tried to induce men then in the army to re-enlist by paying bounties to them.[1] This system not bringing in the men that were needed, recourse was necessarily had to compulsion. The Confederate Congress, therefore, passed, April 16, 1862, a conscription act declaring every white male between the ages of eighteen and thirty-five within the limits of the Confederate States to be in the military service unless unable to perform the duties of a soldier.[2] Following

[1] On March 5, 1862, for example, J. M. F. Harrison of Newbern, North Carolina, distributed posters offering any man who would enlist in his company, $100 bounty money, one-half to be paid by the State, one-half by the Confederacy.

[2] President Davis's message calling for the passage of a conscription act is dated March 28, 1862 (Richardson's *Messages . . . of the Confederacy*, i,

205). The Conscription Act is in *Public Laws of the Confederate States . . . First Session of the First Congress; 1862*, p. 29. Governor Letcher of Virginia, on May 5, 1862, informed the legislature that it was his "deliberate conviction" that the conscription act was unconstitutional; but in the existing condition of affairs, he would not debate the question.

on this law was an Exemption Act. It declared that all State officials, persons engaged in necessary occupations, teachers of schools, and keepers of apothecary shops should be exempt.[1] In December, 1861, and in April, 1862, the Confederate Congress and the Confederate War Department provided that everyone who volunteered for two or three years, would receive at once two months' furlough and a bounty of fifty dollars in money. The response to these forceful appeals was immediate and large and gave the Confederacy the army that fought its battles until the end of 1864. In June, 1862, nearly three hundred and fifty thousand men were in the Confederate army.[2] As to the rest of the white men in the Confederacy between the ages of eighteen and thirty-five, who were not exempt from military service, attempts were made to round them up and get them into the ranks, — and it proved to be no easy task. At first the authorities accepted the statement of any physician within the limits of the Confederacy that a man was physically disabled for service.[3] The State political departments absorbed others for some governors filled up every office within their jurisdiction.[4] Then "necessary occupation"

[1] *Public Laws of the Confederate States . . . 1862*, p. 51. The publication of Professor Albert B. Moore's *Conscription and Conflict in the Confederacy* (New York, 1924) makes it unnecessary to cite all the laws and orders relating to conscription and exemption. In preparing these paragraphs, I have been greatly aided by the researches of Professor A. Sellew Roberts of the University of Illinois.

[2] More exactly the figures are "Present and absent, aggregate" 343,-322; "Present, aggregate" 243,506; "Present for duty" 178,334. Somewhat different figures are given in the New York *Semi-Weekly Tribune* for June 28, 1867, ("Aggregate, present and absent," 412,000).

[3] On May 5, 1862, Governor Letcher

stated that the exemption laws had been grossly abused. Many of those who had applied for exemption had selected their own physicians who received fees for furnishing certificates of disability and these were usually taken by the boards as justifying exemption.

[4] In December, 1863, Governor Letcher informed the Virginia legislature that men who had no right to exemption had "domiciled themselves and their families in soft places, and have thus escaped the dangers of the field," — some of them were "comfortably ensconced in the commissary's or quartermaster's departments." Moreover, he thought the harboring of deserters by the people was a most serious evil and the lack of punishment

had to be defined. Governor Vance of North Carolina decided that making salt from sea-water was essential to the well being of the people, — and soon the salt works harbored the sons of several prominent men. In some places, the profession of school teaching became an active one and apothecary shops or drug stores sprang up over night. In fact, to some persons, almost anything seemed preferable to becoming food for cannon. One reason for the passage of the Conscription Act was the desirability of securing the services of foreigners who were then within the limits of the Confederacy. Many of them had enlisted in 1861 or had volunteered in 1862, but there were others, especially in Texas and South Carolina, who refused to volunteer. When these were conscribed, they took the matter into the courts. The judges generally ruled that a foreigner could not be compelled to serve; but the conscription officers paid little heed to these edicts. In the upper regions of North Carolina, in East Tennessee, northern Alabama, Arkansas, and Texas, there were many persons who had no sympathy with secession.[1] General Gideon J. Pillow, after his flight from Fort Donelson, was appointed conscription officer in Tennessee and northern Alabama. He rounded up hundreds and perhaps thousands of conscripts; but his methods were so drastic that it was felt desirable to make a change. Before long, however, the need for men became so great that he was again brought into the service. There were districts in North Carolina, in Tennessee, and in Alabama where no

of it prejudicial to the army. Judah P. Benjamin, when he was Secretary of War, wrote to Governor Letcher that there were desperate characters in the army who took advantage of the absence of civil authority to commit murder and highway robbery. These were not military offences and under the law, as it was, they could not be tried in a civil court away from the presence of the armies and they could not be tried in a military court.

[1] See George A. Fisher's *The Yankee Conscript* (Philadelphia, 1864) for a lively account of the treatment of Union men in one part of the Confederacy. Another book of the same type is J. H. Aughey's *The Iron Furnace: or Slavery and Secession* (Philadelphia, 1863).

conscription officer ever showed his face. Toward the end of the war, refugees from conscription and deserters from the Confederate army joined together in such numbers that a force was embodied to guard the people of the countryside from their depredations.

The people of East Tennessee, like their neighbors of western North Carolina, were torn in their sympathies between the Union and the Confederacy. Approximately two-thirds of them were for the Union. These voted against secession, elected a representative to the Federal Congress, and refused to volunteer for the Confederate service. When a military force was sent against them, they passed the mountains into Kentucky, were captured, or disappeared into caves and inaccessible ravines until the advance of the Union armies permitted them to return to what was left of their homes. Possibly the most picturesque of all the Southern evaders of conscription were the conscientious objectors.[1] The Exemption Act of 1862 provided that anyone whose conscience forbade him to engage in war might secure exemption by providing a substitute or paying five hundred dollars in Confederate money.[2] Many persons in this way escaped service. To sternly conscientious Quakers, the payment of money to secure freedom from conscription was as objectionable as marching to war. Some of them were arrested and taken to camp and proved to be as recalcitrant there as they had been in their homes. They refused to drill, they refused to shoulder a musket, they refused to march. Sometimes a musket was tied to the conscientious objector, he was put in the ranks, and the man behind ordered to push him for-

---

[1] See **F. G.** Cartland's *Southern Heroes or the Friends in War Time*, 139 and fol. For the case of T. R. Vestal, see J. G. de Roulhac Hamilton's *Papers of Thomas Ruffin*, iii, 364 (*Publications* of the North Carolina Historical Commission.

[2] *Public Laws of the Confederate States of America, Passed at the Second Session of the First Congress; 1862* (Richmond, 1862), p. 78.

ward with the bayonet. Some Confederate officers tried
to make them work on the fortifications or perform other
services behind the lines. It was all one to the conscientious
objector. He was as willing to die a slow death as a speedy
one; he was not willing to violate what he deemed to be his
duty toward God. Many Confederate officers were dismayed when one of these persons appeared, for it was fully
as much against their feelings of humanity to compel one of
these to do what his duty to God forbade, as it was for the
conscientious objector to brave punishment, starvation, or
death for duty's sake.

In September, 1862, the need for men to fill the ranks of
the Confederate armies became so great that a second conscription act was passed.[1] This extended the age limits from
thirty-five to forty-five and in February, 1864, a third act
extended them to between seventeen and fifty.[2] It was this
last law that brought forth the ejaculation, "They are
robbing the cradle and the grave." In reality these conscription acts were not so bad as they looked, because the
boys and the middle-aged men were to be embodied as "home
guards." These could take the place of regular soldiers in
protecting storehouses and guarding prisoners and serve in
the fighting line only in case of great emergency. The
exemption act that followed the second conscription law[3]
did away with some privileges. Even then the plantation
and office-holding classes enjoyed peculiar exemptions and
justified the poor whites' declaration that the struggle was
"The rich man's war and the poor man's fight." This
excused evasion and desertion in the minds of many Southerners. It is stated that one hundred and fifty thousand men

---

[1] *Public Laws of the Confederate States of America passed at the Second Session of the First Congress* (Richmond, 1862), p. 61.

[2] *Public Laws . . . passed at the Fourth Session of the First Congress* (Richmond, 1864), p. 211.

[3] *Public Laws* (Richmond, 1862), p. 77.

were added to the Confederate forces by the conscription acts.[1] Probably the most important effect of these laws was to induce "volunteering." The recital of humorous incidents as a Southern planter becoming a school teacher or an apothecary to save his skin from the dangers of the battle line and the torments suffered by a few conscientious objectors make a mark on the imagination that is out of all proportion to the number of slackers or pacifists. It is certain that many Confederates were strongly contemptuous of the politicians who brought on secession and then refused to fight. Another thing that impresses the imagination, unduly perhaps, is the very lax discipline that ordinarily prevailed in the Confederate army, — soldiers going away and returning apparently almost at will. In time of battle, however, they were always on hand and the least backwardness then brought swift reprisal. The conscription acts aroused stern opposition[2] from those to whom States'-rights were dear and brought the Confederate government into critical relations with two of the strongest States of the Confederacy, Georgia and North Carolina.

The difficulties of securing men for the Northern armies have never been sufficiently realized. Except at brief moments, people of the North were not united for war. The emancipation of the negroes and the dealings with lukewarm Unionists aroused very divergent opinions. Possibly public

[1] *Official Records*, ser. iv, vol. iii, p. 1101.

[2] Howell Cobb on August 5, 1862, wrote to General Randolph, then Secretary of War, that the conscription law was very unpopular and advised its repeal. It had compelled large numbers of volunteers to reënlist and had done its work: *Official Records*, ser. iv, vol. ii, p. 34. On December 17, 1863, the acting head of the conscription bureau declared that the "evil of desertion from the army, with a deter-mination to avoid and even resist future service" is on the increase, the deserters banding among themselves and with the evaders of conscription, to resist the soldiers sent out to apprehend them. Nevertheless a year or more later, President Davis in an "Address" to the Confederate army referred to "the spontaneous and unanimous offer of your lives" with the halting and reluctant service of the mercenaries who are purchased by the enemy (*ibid.*, ser. iv, vol. iii, p. 105).

sentiment might have been so stimulated by a persistent propaganda that men of military age would have felt ashamed to remain in civil life. Possibly a conscription policy might have been put into effect in 1861 and pursued ruthlessly throughout the war. As it was, the Washington government thought that the only way to fill the ranks in 1861 and in 1862 was to stimulate and utilize the ambition and desire for power and place of the local political leaders. It offered them commissions from captain to general, if they would bring to the army the services of a hundred, or of three or four thousand men. This plan had the further advantage of arousing the interest of Democratic as well as Republican politicians. It also utilized the community spirit and, when the company or the brigade went into the service, it lived, marched, and fought under the leadership of men to whom the rank and file had looked for guidance all their lives. The details of recruiting were left to the States and there was a good deal of diversity of method employed. In Galena, Illinois, a meeting was held in the town square. The chairman was a former army officer, Captain Ulysses S. Grant, who was then a clerk in a store in that town. Prominent men addressed the meeting. When recruits were asked for, a hearty response was made and Captain Grant with a ramrod for a sword proceeded to drill them. He declined the captaincy of the company, but offered his services by letter to the War Department at Washington, stating that he felt competent to command a regiment. No reply to this letter was ever made. He had attracted the attention of an Illinois Congressman and, possibly at his prompting, Governor Yates asked Grant to go to Springfield and assist in the enrollment of the new soldiers. From that point, his genius for war pushed him forward and upward. Two Illinois Congressmen, John A. Logan and John A. McClernand, both

Democrats, came out for the Union and entered the service. This method of recruiting also gave the element of local competition within the State a chance to exert its full strength. Oftentimes, a regiment represented a county or a city. The soldiers elected the company officers and the governor appointed the regimental officers. At first sight, this would seem to be a very clumsy way to recruit an army.[1] Many of the officers knew very little about military matters and had little authority. Regimental histories relate ludicrous incidents that happened when one of these political colonels tried to turn his regiment around in order to march in some given direction. The lamentable thing was that the officers knew nothing of the care of the soldier which means so much in war. No doubt military duties were learned rapidly on the march and in battle, but the expense in human life and suffering was terrible. The disasters that befell the Northern armies in the early part of the war were, in a great measure, the result of this want of military training. They must also be attributed to the fact that in the Confederate armies, from the beginning, there were a few officers of military genius, and it takes but one of these to turn many a defeat into victory.

Almost from the outset in the North, bounties were paid to those who stepped forward and volunteered. Many of the soldiers had persons dependent upon them, and the bounty enabled these to leave something behind for the support of mother, wife, or child until they could send home some part of their pay.[2] As the volunteering spirit declined and the need for men grew, the bounties increased until, in 1863, over a thousand dollars were offered for a

---

[1] A good description of the working of this system is in W. S. Moore's "The Rush to Arms in 1861" in *Annals of Iowa*, Third Series, i, 657.

[2] An interesting article by Professor Fish on "Social Relief in the Northwest during the Civil War" is in the *American Historical Review*, xxii, 309–324.

recruit [1] in Massachusetts. The working of the system was described in a "Memorial" of certain well known citizens of Philadelphia in December, 1864. In the beginning, they said, the bounty system had been justifiable and the moderate sums then paid had worked little evil. The payments had been gradually increased and had converted the duty of service to the country into a matter of traffic and a question of gain. To enlist and to desert had become so profitable that "bounty-jumping" was a recognized profession. One Philadelphian had been arrested six times for desertion and each time had escaped. Agents traversed the country buying men and a disgraceful barter system with "runners and bounty brokers" had come into being that was "worthy of Ashantee." In the preceding summer, men enlisting for twelve months had received as high as fifteen hundred dollars apiece. Four of the names attached to this "Memorial" were those of J. Edgar Thomson, Horace Binney, Morton McMichael, and Henry C. Lea. Running forward a bit, it may be noted that the dissatisfaction of those who had enlisted in the early years and had received small bounties took the form of a demand for an equalization of bounty. In many parts of the country, States and municipalities contributed to the support of the families and dependents of the soldiers,[2] and made direct payment of money. This

---

[1] In 1863 in Massachusetts, the State advanced on enlistment fifty dollars and the Federal government sixty-two. Furthermore the State paid twenty dollars a month, or seven hundred and twenty dollars in three years, and the United States three hundred and forty dollars more. As the conflict proceeded advertising was resorted to, either in the form of large posters or paragraphs in the newspaper. One of the most interesting of the latter appeared in the *New York Evening Post* for November 9, 1864.

[2] For instance, in Wayne County, Michigan, a public board was appointed in October, 1862, to report upon the administration of relief in the county to the end of that year. The tables at the end of the report show that nearly two hundred thousand dollars of public money had been paid or pledged for the relief of families of soldiers and in the city of Detroit over fifty thousand dollars had been expended for the relief of some five hundred families.

was not large in any individual case, but put together amounted to a considerable sum. The contributions of public money to soldiers' families diminished as the years went by, partly because the women and the larger children found means of making a living for themselves and partly because countless societies had been formed to look after the soldiers and to care for their dependents at home.

It was not until March, 1863, that the need for men became so acute in the North that it could only be met by some form of compulsion. This led to the passage of the Draft Act.[1] According to this law, when it became necessary to raise a given number of men the government divided the number to be raised among the States according to the total population of each State and not according to the number of males or of males of military age and, at first, gave the States no credit for enlistments in the naval service. The States themselves were divided into districts, each of which was required to furnish a certain number of men. If the State or the district did not furnish the number assigned to it, the deficit was made up by a draft. United States officials visited the houses, listed the male inhabitants of military age and, when this was accomplished, determined by a public drawing the names of those who must go into the service to complete the quota. Any forehanded man could secure

[1] *Statutes at Large*, xii, 731. General Crowder — who had charge of raising soldiers in the Great War — in his *Second Report of the Provost Marshal General* (Washington, 1919), p. 7, calls attention to the report of General James Oakes made in 1865. Oakes was in charge of the draft in Illinois. This report was dated August 9, 1865 (*Official Records*, ser. iii, vol. v, pp. 803–842). At the close he called attention to the faults of the drafting system of 1863–1865 and made recommendations for the raising of soldiers in the future. General Crowder summarized these as follows:

1. Registration by personal report; 2. Regional liability for man-power to be made by the place of residence of the citizen; 3. Responsibility of furnishing quotas to be allotted to the States; 4. Substitutes to be forbidden; 5. Bounties for volunteering to be forbidden; 6. Short periods of service to be abandoned and the duration of the war to be the uniform period. General Crowder adds "It is a notable fact that every one of the lessons thus pointed out in 1865 was followed in the year 1917."

exemption by paying to the government a comparatively small sum of money with which the government could procure a substitute. This law led to extraordinary attempts to fill the quotas by buying soldiers and securing negroes to count as part of the State quota. In New York and in Boston, great objection was felt to this particular form of compulsion. It bore heavily on the Irish immigrants who were strong in those cities and were particularly affected by the competition of the negro laborers. Indeed, in New York, negro strike breakers were at that moment, or had been recently, taking the places of Irish immigrants on the wharves or on some of them. In Boston, the officer in command of soldiers who had been summoned from a harbor fort to protect city property, fired a couple of cannon shot point blank into the mob and that was the end of it.[1] In New York, the governor of the State, Horatio Seymour, had very slight sympathy with the Unionist cause and even less with emancipation. He paid no attention to the repeated requests of the Federal officials and, at the time of the drawing, New York City was practically left to itself. The result was a riot that lasted several days and led to the killing of several persons and the sacking of the houses of abolitionists.[2] Troops were then brought from Pennsylvania, where they were sadly needed at the moment, and the rioters were put down. When another draft was held in the next year, the Federal government took the precaution to have a body of its own soldiers near at hand in case of trouble,— and there was no trouble.

---

[1] *Report of the "Draft Riot" in Boston, July 14th, 1863.*

[2] *Official Records*, ser. i, vol. xxvii, pt. ii, pp. 875-940. Original matter is in E. S. Martin's *Joseph H. Choate*, i, 255; Martha D. Perry's *Letters from a Surgeon of the Civil War*, 57-73;

Moore's *Rebellion Record*, vii, using index under "Draft Riot"; J. R. Gilmore's *Personal Recollections of Abraham Lincoln*, ch. xiv; and see also G. A. Thayer's *The Draft Riots of 1863* and J. T. Headley's *Great Riots of New York*, 136-288.

In New York, in Boston, and possibly elsewhere, the male immigrant upon landing was approached by agents and frequently induced to volunteer by promises of large money payments. In Boston, and probably elsewhere, the business was carried farther. An agent was employed in Belgium. He advertised for emigrants to go to Massachusetts and, on landing, do whatever M. D. Ross, who apparently was an alderman, should tell them to do. In all, four ship loads were landed, one at Portland and three at Boston.[1] The immigrants at once enlisted and the bounties were divided between them and the partners in the scheme. Benjamin Moran in his diary, under date of January 10, 1863, states that a German calling himself "Colonel Nix" was recruiting men in London, paying their passage to America, and dividing the bounty with them when they enlisted there. The British government had complained to Mr. Adams about this matter. All these schemes for importing foreigners were private ventures and Secretaries Seward, Stanton, and Welles and Governor Andrew all four were justified in denying categorically in writing that either the Federal or the State governments had anything whatever to do with enlisting soldiers in foreign countries.[2] As the population of

[1] See *Answers of the Governor of Massachusetts to Inquiries respecting certain Immigrants who have arrived in this Country from Europe, and who are alleged to be illegally enlisted in the Army of the United States, and Other Papers on the Same Subject* (Washington, Government Printing Office, 1864). My attention was called to this pamphlet by Samuel Abrams of Boston. On January 14, 1865, J. C. Gray wrote from Hilton Head that he was delighted to see in the papers that a "cargo of recruits imported by Gov. Andrew from Germany has been rejected by the War Department." Information on this subject is also to be found in M. D. Perry's *Letters from a Surgeon of the Civil War*,

161, and in the *Official Report of the Trial of Anton Probst* and from the evidence given in the *Report of Commissioners on "Paper Credits"* that was printed at Augusta, Maine, in 1871.

[2] The letters are printed in *Senate Executive Document*, No. 54, 38th Cong., 1st Sess., and in *Official Records*, ser. iii, vol. iv, p. 455. Garibaldi was invited by a United States official representative in Europe to come to America and command an army or two, but the matter did not get much beyond that point. See H. N. Gay in the *Century* for November, 1907, p. 63 ; C. F. Adams in the *Proceedings* of the Massachusetts Historical Society for February, 1908, p. 319, and the *Magazine of History* for

Pennsylvania, of New York, and of the northwestern States contained great numbers of German and Polish immigrants and their children, it fell out that there were large numbers of persons with foreign names in the Union armies.[1] In one case, at least, there was a whole German regiment and there was an Irish brigade. All these things, however, were the natural results of the working of the volunteer-bounty system. There were many foreigners and many persons of Irish[2] and German birth in the Confederate military service.

One comes across Irish companies, as the "Emerald Guards." There was a German artillery company at Charleston at the outset of hostilities[3] and William H. Russell[4] said that he saw German companies and regiments in western Tennessee or Mississippi and was told that they formed the best soldiers. The Southerners had agents in Europe, if we can believe the old-age testimony of John Bigelow,[5] who stated that the police of Paris interfered with the departure of a party of Poles because they were under contract to enlist in the Confederate army. The Southerners thought that the Northern success in raising soldiers in Ireland was so dangerous that they actually sent an agent to that island to counteract the Northern officials and set on foot a Southern

March, 1908, p. 159. There are also some entries as to Garibaldi in Moran's manuscript diary. For the last citations I am indebted to H. Donald Jordan of Cambridge.

[1] From New York the figures were, native Americans 203,622, foreign-born 134,178; Wisconsin 47,972 and 31,528. According to the figures in B. A. Gould's *Investigations . . . of American Soldiers*, p. 27, of the 2,018,200 "different white soldiers" enlisted in the United States volunteers 1,523,267 were native Americans and 494,933 were foreign-born. Of the latter, 144,221 were Irishmen and 176,817 were Germans.

[2] See a letter of John Mitchell addressed to the *Dublin Times* and found in the possession of Major Reid Sanders when he was captured. It was printed in *The [London] Times* for February 7, 1863, and is noted by G. F. R. Henderson in his *Stonewall Jackson* (1919), ii, 340, note. See also Dillon's *Life of John Mitchell*, ii, 173.

[3] *Charleston Courier*, February 10, 1862.

[4] *My Diary North and South*, i, 174; ii, 12, 34.

[5] *Retrospections*, ii, 341.

propaganda. He was to explain, among other things, that convents had been burned in Massachusetts, but none had been destroyed in Virginia.[1] Finally, General Duncan, the Confederate commander at Fort Jackson below New Orleans, in his official report to the War Department, stated that until the very end of the action the spirit of his troops was excellent. "They were mostly foreign enlistments, without any great interests at stake in the ultimate success of the revolution. A reaction set in among them." They mutinied and he was obliged to surrender.[2]

A bit of what might be termed historical recrimination has been for Northern writers to recount the services rendered to the Southern people by the negroes in the construction of fortifications,[3] driving teams, and performing many of the countless tasks that are done in modern armies behind the lines; and the Southerners have replied by calling attention to the contrabands and the colored regiments that appeared in the Northern fighting line in 1863. There is no question whatever that Northern commanders utilized the services of negroes whenever they could. Indeed, there is a letter from General Grant,[4] dated August 19, 1862, stating that he was using negroes who "come into camp" as "teamsters, hospital attendants, company cooks and so forth, thus saving soldiers to carry the musket." How far this employ-

[1] Southern Historical Society's Papers, xxiv, 202. On September 30, 1864, J. A. Seddon, the Confederate Secretary of War, sanctioned the enlistment of Irish and other foreign prisoners, and it is supposed that a thousand Irish-Catholic prisoners were enlisted under this authorization (Official Records, ser. iv, vol. iii, p. 694). Eliza F. Andrews, on p. 75 of her Wartime Journal, states that in 1864 the Confederates enlisted a battalion or more from the Union prisoners at Andersonville and elsewhere and

called them "galvanized Yankees."
[2] Official Reports of Battles. Published by Order of Congress (Richmond, 1862), p. 359.
[3] In William P. Johnston's Life of General A. S. Johnston (pp. 416, 417) are several statements showing the reluctance of owners to send their slaves to work on fortifications, even before the close of 1861.
[4] J. Cramer's Letters of Ulysses S. Grant to his Father and his Youngest Sister (New York, 1912), p. 88.

ment of negroes by Union commanders had gone before the issuing of the Emancipation Proclamation in January, 1863, cannot be stated because no accurate records were kept.   As soon as the Proclamation was issued, all question as to the propriety of using negroes in the military service of the United States disappeared; but these are included in the official numbers of enlisted men in the Northern armies.[1]

The story of the employment of negroes by the Confederates is more involved.   It is undoubtedly true that the employment of large numbers of negroes in agriculture and industry relieved white men for service in the field and thus added materially to the military population of the Confederacy, although of course not in anything like their proportion to the whole population.   Free negroes were embodied as soldiers in some of the Southern States, either by virtue of some express law, or because of independent local action.[2] In the beginning, the planters brought or sent their slaves to work on the fortifications and to do other service for "the cause."   Before long, many slaves became incapacitated by reason of strange conditions of life and lack of care, and some of them died.   Also their services were needed on the plantations.   It was felt that the owners should be compensated for the services of their slaves and be paid for those who died while working for the government; but in the condition of affairs in the South it was very difficult to bring this about.[3]

[1] John Eaton's *Grant, Lincoln, and the Freedmen* (New York, 1907) contains a mass of interesting information on the subject of this paragraph.

[2] See Wesley's "Employment of Negroes as Soldiers in the Confederate Army" in *Journal of Negro History*, iv, 239.

[3] On December 29, 1863, a committee of the Confederate House of Representatives reported on the claim of a Virginia slaveholder, for compensation for the death of one of her slaves, while employed on the fortifications around Richmond, that the remedy should be sought from the State authorities, leaving the matter to be adjusted between the local and the general governments (*Report of Committee on Claims in the Case of Mary Clark*). January 22, 1864, Lieutenant Colonel A. L. Rives, writing to Seddon, the Confederate Secretary of War, estimated that if the claims of Virginia for slave property lost in the service of the Confederacy were sustained, the mini-

As the strain of the conflict became severer and the demand for food more urgent, it proved to be impossible for the government or the military commanders to secure an adequate supply of negro labor. The slaves did not like the service. It took them away from their homes and placed them in dangerous situations. They constantly made off for their master's plantation and it was impossible to retrieve them, as they were concealed by the other negroes and also by the whites. In the winter of 1863–1864 the situation became so serious that the Confederate Congress passed an act authorizing the Secretary of War to call upon the States to furnish male negro slaves to the government not exceeding twenty thousand at any one time; but this arrangement proved to be futile.[1] A question of negro labor that attracted more attention in the South was the possibility of utilizing the free colored population for military purposes. The free negroes, with a few foreigners, were the only Southern men who were not compelled in one way or another to serve the Confederate government. Why should the free

---

mum amount required to pay the claims of all the States of the Confederacy would be over $3,000,000 (*Official Records*, ser. iv, vol. iii, p. 40). In the *Journal* of the Virginia Senate from December 7, 1863, through March 10, 1864, Governor Letcher stated (p. 23) that slave owners manifested a disposition to disregard the requisitions for slaves to work on the fortifications and complained that the Confederate government had not paid for slaves who had died or run away and that they had no reason to suppose that it would pay for those that died or ran away in the future. Letcher stated that the Confederate Congress had voted no money for this purpose and was waiting until a still unorganized court of claims should report.

[1] General J. E. Johnston's letter calling attention to the need of more negro labor is printed in Mrs. D. Giraud Wright's *A Southern Girl in '61*, p. 168. An act passed on March 26, 1863, was already on the statute book (*Public Laws of the Confederate States of America Passed at the Third Session of the First Congress*, p. 102). This law had not produced the desired result. The act of February 17, 1864, is in *ibid.*, Fourth Session, p. 235, § 2. Judging by letters written in November and December, 1864, the impressment of slaves under this law does not seem to have had much more efficacy, — and the whole matter clearly shows the great dislike of the slaveholders to the employment of slaves by the military authorities. The Act of February 17, 1864, is printed in the *Official Records*, ser. iv, vol. iii, p. 208; the same volume, p. 933, has a "Circular" of the Bureau of Conscription dated December 12, 1864, for the impressment of 14,500 slaves.

negro be left to serve himself when the efficiency of the army was greatly diminished by the employment of able-bodied white soldiers as teamsters and company cooks and in many other ways.[1] It was, therefore, provided by the same law that all male free persons of color between the ages of eighteen and fifty shall be held liable to perform such duties as the Secretary of War may prescribe in connection with the military defenses of the country, in the production of war material, or in military hospitals. When so employed, each one should receive eleven dollars per month, rations,[2] and clothing. It is impossible to state how many colored persons, free and slave, were employed by the Confederate authorities, but there must have been thousands of them, and, in so far, their employment increased the effective military force of the Confederacy.[3] On March 30, 1865, ten days or so before Appomattox, the Confederate Congress by law authorized the enlistment of negroes as soldiers, but this change of policy came so late that it had no effect upon the contest.[4]

In fighting their "battles o'er again," veterans of the war — both Union and Confederate — and other persons, too, have essayed to give some tangible idea of the relative strengths of the contending armies. Some of them have computed the "military strength" of the North and of the

[1] There is a letter from Provost Marshal F. S. Parker of Georgetown District, S. C., dated November 23, 1863, stating that the free colored population enjoyed singular privileges and immunities, while the white man was risking health and life, and his slaves are busily engaged in agriculture or engaged on the fortifications. *Official Records*, ser. iv, vol. ii, p. 978.

[2] See the act of February 17, 1864, in the *Public Laws of the Confederate States . . . Fourth Session . . . First Congress*, p. 235.

[3] See a letter written by Judah P. Benjamin on August 18, 1863, in Bigelow's *Retrospections*, ii, 38.

[4] For divergent views as to the employment of negroes in war, see T. W. Higginson's *Army Life in a Black Regiment*, ch. iv; Charles H. Wesley in *The Journal of Negro History*, iv, 239; N. W. Stephenson in *American Historical Review*, xviii, 295; W. W. Davis in *Columbia University Studies*, liii, ch. ix; and a letter from General Robert E. Lee in the *Century* for August, 1888, p. 600.

South by seeking the "Census" of 1860 and have based their calculations on that. Others have explored the "Official Records," have seized upon such enumerations of the Southern armies as they have found therein, and have deduced totals from them. State Historical Societies have not been idle, and have put forth statements of the contributions of the individual States to the Southern armies. All these attempts are absolutly futile. For one thing, the military systems of the two contestants were so different that no useful conclusions can be deduced from them. The enrollments of the Northern forces were kept with the business-like care that was usual in that part of the country. The rolls are complete — they are too complete. A computation based on the total number of enrollments of the Northern soldiers tells us too much, for some Northern young men — thousands of them — were in the militia regiments that marched to Washington in April, 1861, volunteered when their three months tour of duty was ended, and volunteered when their next term of service was finished. Each one of these would count as three on the enrollment. Then there was an entirely different sort of person in the "bounty jumper." Some of them enlisted, deserted, and reënlisted — usually under other names — from three to six times. Most assiduous attempts have been made to convert these enrollments into three-year terms of service; but the results do not inspire confidence.[1]

[1] See Colonel Thomas L. Livermore's *Numbers and Losses in the Civil War* (Boston, 1900). A second edition with some changes was issued in the next year. In November, 1904, Livermore read an interesting paper before the Massachusetts Historical Society which is printed in its *Proceedings* for that month, pp. 432–444. According to the United States *Census* of 1890 (" Population," pt. ii, p. 804) there were then living 432,020 Confederate soldiers and sailors and 1,034,073 men (white and black) who had served in the Union army and navy. Livermore, on page 441 of the article just mentioned, includes in the Confederate numbers both whites and blacks, but omits the blacks from the numbers of the Union survivors in 1890. Interesting and somewhat contrary statements are in Livermore's book (p. 50), in the *Final*

Confederate military records were kept — so far as they were kept at all — in a very different manner from those of the North. Muster-rolls were made out, but they were so imperfect that Southern State authorities in awarding State pensions to Confederate veterans or to their widows in some cases, at least, fell back on the testimony of the claimant! In the manuscripts of the late Henry Villard is a paper without title or date. It gives the "Present & absent Aggregate" and the "Present" of all the Confederate armies from March, 1861, to March, 1865. The first category appears to include every person whose name had been placed on the "roll" and who was not known to have deserted or died at the date of the return. The "Present" includes "For duty" and "Aggregate." The former contains only the soldiers who were actually with arms in the fighting line or ready to take their places in it. Comparing these returns with those printed in the "Official Records," one is impressed with their general agreement. Using them, or some similar tabulation, "Our Special Correspondent" [1] in the "New York Tribune" for June 26, 1867, reached the conclusion that "in all 600,000 different men were in the Confederate ranks during the war." These figures do not include the "home guards" and State troops of one sort or another, who performed many services that in the North were done by regularly enrolled sol-

Report of Provost Marshal General Fry forming *House Executive Document*, 39th Cong., 1st Sess., vol. iv, pt. i, No. i, pp. 1, 25; and in Blaine's *Report* of February 16, 1866, on the "War Debts of the Loyal States," *House Report*, No. 16, 39th Cong., 1st Sess., p. 6.

[1] Jubal A. Early (Southern Historical Society's *Papers*, ii, 16) suggests that William Swinton was "Our Special Correspondent," but Swinton was connected with the *Times* and not with the *Tribune*. C. B. Hite — another Con-

federate — in *Current History* for May, 1923, p. 251, states that it is known that Whitelaw Reid wrote the article in question. Henry Villard was in Europe at the time, but the author, whoever he was, certainly used the returns that are preserved among his papers. The *Tribune* compilation is reprinted in C. Gardner's *Acts of the Republican Party as seen by History* (Winchester, Va., 1906), and he has added some computations of his own drawn from the *Official Records* and other publications.

diers. Possibly the most interesting Confederate record
is the "Report" of Colonel E. D. Blake, "Superintendent of
Special Registration of the Confederate States Army." It
is dated January, 1864, and gives the total of volunteers and
conscripts in the six States of Virginia, North Carolina, South
Carolina, Georgia, Alabama, and Mississippi as 566,456.[1]
To this number must be added the soldiers contributed by
Florida, Tennessee, Louisiana, Texas, and Arkansas, and
those who came from outside the seceded States, — and also
the home guards and the State troops.

In an attempt to get at the strength of the Confederate
army recourse has been had to the recorded white population
of the Confederate States.[2] Deductions have been made
from this as to the "man power" of the South by using the
ordinary calculation that one person in five of the total white
population was of military age and therefore a soldier by the
conscription laws, unless exempted. In making this computation allowance has been made for young men who reached
the military age during the four years of conflict. Adding
and subtracting and making all kinds of combinations, it
would seem that there should have been 1,200,000 in the
Confederate army, instead of the 600,000 that the "Confederate Hand-book"[3] states were "enrolled."[4] In other

[1] *Official Records*, ser. iv, vol. iii, pp. 102, 103.

[2] General C. F. Adams has discussed this subject at length in his *Studies: Military and Diplomatic*, 282–287.

[3] *Confederate Hand-book. A Compilation of Important Data and Other Interesting and Valuable Matter relating to the War between the States, 1861–1865*, p. 29. A copy is in the Confederate Museum at Richmond.

[4] Probably the word "enroll" as used in this phrase meant those only who were actually on the muster roll, — and this number, presumably, was somewhere between two-thirds and three-quarters of the total number of soldiers at one time or another present with the colors. Charles A. Dana stated that the Confederates undertook to keep on foot a field army of 200,000 men, and that it was a great strain on the population of the Confederacy. The numbers with the colors in the field, presumably, were about one-third of the total number of soldiers in service at the time, including "details" and men on furlough.

The *Century* for March, 1892 (pp. 792, 956, 957), contained an article by A. B. Casselman on "The Numerical Strength of the Confederate Army." He returned to the matter thirty years later in *Current History* for January, 1923

words, only one man in eleven of military age ever served in
the Confederate army, instead of one man in five, or one
man in four, as is supposed to have been the case with the
South African Boers in their attempt to secure their independence from the British Empire. But this calculation
omits many important considerations. For one thing, the
white population of the *seceded* States was not a unit for
independence. Three hundred thousand of them, or more,
are supposed to have served in the Union armies. Another
hundred thousand, or more, never served in any army, but
retired to the fastnesses of the Southern Appalachians and
bade defiance to the Southern conscript officers. Portions
of the seceded States were occupied by Union forces almost
at once, as northern Virginia and the Eastern Shore. In the
spring of 1862, the northeastern corner of North Carolina
and the southeastern corner of South Carolina passed into
Union hands. In the spring and summer of 1862, New Orleans and the greater part of the Mississippi Valley below
Cairo came into more or less effective Union control. And
so it went on. The region open to the efficient operation of
the Confederate conscription service constantly narrowed,
and with it the military population of the Confederacy.
Probably nine hundred thousand would represent the average effective military population of the Confederacy, and
presumably eight hundred thousand at one time or another
served in the armed forces of the seceded States.[1]

(p. 653). Sundry replies and rejoinders
are in the same numbers of the *Century*
and *Current History* and in the latter for
April, 1924 (p. 113). See also J. S.
Ward in Southern Historical Society's
Papers, xx, 238; G. P. Thruston's
"Numbers and Rosters of the Two
Armies" in *The Olympian Magazine*
of Nashville, Tenn., for November,
1903; R. H. McKim's *The Numerical
Strength of the Confederate Army* (New

York, 1912); and Moore's *Conscription
and Conflict in the Confederacy*, 357 and
note on p. 358. Of the older books see
Gould's *Investigations . . . of American Soldiers* (New York, 1869) and
Phisterer's *Statistical Record of the
Armies* of the United States (New York,
1883).

[1] J. W. Headley in his *Confederate
Operations in Canada and New York*
(New York, 1906), p. 471, gives a table

Whatever the absolute numbers of the two armies may have been, there never were enough soldiers on the Federal rolls for the task in hand. Instead of two or three Northern soldiers for every Southern one, there should have been five or six at least. Owing to the character of the conflict, which was at first a war of coercion, next a war of conquest, and, finally, a war for the destruction of the Southern social system, the defeat of armies in the field did not have that influence that had been the case in the great wars to which men looked back for guidance. Had the Union army defeated the Southern force at Bull Run, in July, 1861, Secession might have collapsed then and there. Six months later, no such outcome would have followed any Federal victory. From Donelson onward the overcoming of a Confederate force should have been followed by an actual occupation of territory, and this was not possible with the forces at the disposal of the Federal commanders in the West or in the East. If Grant had had double the men that he had in February, 1862, he might have occupied all central Tennessee and also pursued the retreating enemy. Had McClellan had double the men at his disposal, it is possible that he might have held Washington, and made good the possession of the Peninsula as he advanced up the Chickahominy. As it was, the western army after a victory was distributed in a "pepper-pot campaign." It settled down in small groups at different points in the occupied territory and when the Confederate army, reorganized and refreshed, reappeared in the field, it was necessary to draw these forces together, abandon

of "the whole number of men enrolled (present and absent) in the active armies of the Confederacy." He gives the aggregate of the "present and absent" on January 1, 1864, as 472,781 and says that if we add thereto at least 250,000 deaths occurring prior to that date, it gives over 700,000 as the total enrollment, and this, according to Headley, includes "very few, if any, of the local land forces." In this study of numbers I have been greatly assisted by Professor Freeman H. Hart of Washington College, Chestertown, Maryland.

the occupied territory, and meet the enemy in battle. After two or three experiences of the kind, the people of conquered Southern territory became afraid to show their sympathy for the North, or perhaps better, their lack of active and enthusiastic sympathy for the cause of the South. In its final stage, the war developed into a campaign for the destruction of the economic foundation of Southern life which entailed sufferings upon the Southern people and aroused a spirit in the South and in the North that it took decades to live down.

The two most lamentable failures of the War were the lack of care of the sick and the wounded and of the prisoners. As to the first of these, medical knowledge and knowledge of the laws of hygiene in 1860 were not where they had been in 1800, but, with a few exceptions, they were not very far removed from it. The great revolution in the care and cure of the body has come almost entirely since Appomattox. The statistics of the war are vague and unreliable, but it seems certain that many more soldiers died from disease behind the lines than were killed in battle or died from wounds received in combat.[1] Bacteria and bacilli were then unknown. Typhoid was typhoid, an act of God, and so was pneumonia. The best care was taken that could be taken under the circumstances and the rest was left to Providence. Fortunately, anesthesia in some form had been discovered and introduced into surgical practice, but in the field service it could not always be employed in the Federal armies, and the supply of anesthetics was frequently absent entirely from the Confederate hospitals in the field and in the town. Moreover, antiseptic surgery had not been thought of, and the supply of surgeons was entirely inadequate to the work that was suddenly thrown upon them. The "trained nurse"

[1] See Note II at end of chapter.

too, was an unknown factor in the care of the wounded, for Florence Nightingale's influence had, as yet, scarcely crossed the Atlantic. Thousands of self-sacrificing, noble spirited women in the North and in the South left their homes and did what they could for those who were fighting for their cause. They soothed the last hours of many a dying youth, but their knowledge of the proper treatment was sadly lacking. In the life of Clara Barton [1] and in the lifelike letters of Katharine P. Wormeley [2] we have several graphic pictures and many more may be found in individual letters and diaries.[3] The care, the good will, the desire, were all there but the training of how to do it and the knowledge of what should be done were not there and could not be there in the years 1861–1865. In a similar way the knowledge of the origin and the life history of the typhoid bacillus was entirely lacking and the knowledge of how to avoid contact with it was very slight.[4] Many other diseases, that we are now familiar with, were then rife in the South and attacked Confederate and Union soldier alike, whenever they came within reach. Of these the hookworm was in some ways the most ghastly and was then absolutely beyond diagnosis.

In the North and in the South those who were compelled by age, sex, or disability to stay at home, did what they could to aid the cause by making bandages, picking lint, and providing comforts for the wounded and for the well. In the

---

[1] W. E. Barton's *Clara Barton*, i, chs. xi-xviii.

[2] Wormeley's *The Other Side of War*. As confirming many of Miss Wormeley's statements, see a small volume entitled *Hospital Transports . . . Compiled and Published at the request of the Sanitary Commission* (Boston, 1863). For conditions in another part of the field, see "An Army Surgeon's Letters to his Wife" in Mississippi Valley Historical Association's *Proceedings*, vii, 306–320.

[3] See Walt Whitman's "Army Hospitals and Cases" in *The Century*, xiv, 825, "Walt Whitman in War-Time" in *ibid.*, xxiv, 840, and his volume entitled *The Wound Dresser, A Series of Letters Written from the Hospitals in Washington*.

[4] Dr. John S. Logan discovered an improved treatment for "hospital gangrene," — then a most dreaded complication. See *Medical and Surgical History*, Pt. iii, 835.

North, they grouped under an organization known as the "Sanitary Commission"[1] which did very good work. In the South there was no such central body, but there were innumerable local societies, as the "Central Association for the Relief of South Carolina Soldiers" or the "Hospital Aid Association" of Virginia. But, when all has been said, it must be admitted that, compared with the strenuousness of the Great War, these citizen efforts were distinctly calm.

According to the best statistics that are procurable some twenty-six thousand Southern soldiers died in Northern prisons and some twenty-four thousand Union soldiers died in Southern prisons,[2] which, compared with the total number

[1] On December 9, 1861, Fred. Law Olmsted, the General Secretary of the Sanitary Commission, presented a *Report* to the Secretary of War which forms the groundwork of all later descriptions of the early history of the Sanitary Commission. It is in *Documents of the U. S. Sanitary Commission*, i, No. 40. Other reports by F. N. Knapp, Special Relief Agent, and by J. S. Newberry, Associate Secretary, are in the same volume and other material is in a second volume; and in a third volume entitled *Military, Medical, and Surgical Essays* prepared for the Commission. Beginning with November, 1863, the *Sanitary Commission Bulletin* was published twice a month until the close of the war. C. J. Stillé's *History of the United States Sanitary Commission* is a painstaking contemporary account. There are no suitable biographies of Olmsted or his principal workers, but there are some letters in ch. iii of the *Letters of Horace Howard Furness*. Other aspects of the medical side of the war may be found in the *Report of Dr. John Swinburne, giving an Account of his Services on the Peninsula* and George H. Gay's *Report* to the Surgeon General of Massachusetts.

There is an almost endless number of books and articles on the local phases of the relief work; among them may be mentioned J. S. Newberry's *Final Report on the Commission in the Valley*

of the Mississippi. It forms No. 96 of the *Reports* of the Sanitary Commission and was also issued separately. Chapter xxii in Whitelaw Reid's *Ohio in the War* is a valuable account of the relief work of the Ohio branches.

[2] On July 18, 1866, the Commissary-General of Prisoners reported to Secretary Stanton that from the records of his office, it appeared that 26,436 Southern prisoners had died in Northern prisons and that 22,576 Union soldiers had died in Southern prisons. In the North there were about 220,000 Southern prisoners and in the South there were about 126,952 prisoners. See *Official Records*, ser. ii, vol. viii, p. 946. These figures have been generally repeated by writers on the War and are given in the *Confederate Hand-book*, p. 37. Various other figures have been given. The most authoritative seem to be those furnished to Mr. Rhodes in 1903 by General Ainsworth who was in charge of the Record and Pension Office. These are printed by Rhodes in his *History of the United States*, v, 507. From this it appears that 211,411 Union soldiers were captured; of these 16,668 were paroled on the field and 30,218 died in captivity. And that 462,634 Confederate soldiers were captured; of whom 247,769 were paroled and 25,976 died in captivity. Rhodes adds that the mortality was "a little over 12 per cent. at the North

of prisoners, gives a proportion of deaths not far from that of the soldiers of the Union army from disease. If these figures are anywhere near being accurate, it would seem that each government cared for its enemy prisoners about as well as it cared for its own soldiers. In reading accounts of former prisoners, one is impressed with the general complaint of lack of food and of brutality and even cruelty on the part of guardians.[1] As to the lack of food in 1860 and the next few years, it must be remembered that the food habits of Northerners and Southerners were then — and are today — different. The Northerner lived on wheat bread

and 15.5 at the South." Somewhat different figures are given in the *Publications* of the Southern Historical Society, iii, 327 n. In these the mortality at the North is given as 13.25 per cent; that at the South 15.37 per cent. In 1923, the Adjutant General's Office estimated that the total number of deaths of Confederate prisoners in Federal prisons was 30,716, of which 5,569 were on account of wounds and 23,591 on account of disease. Data are not available for all the deaths due to disease, but for the nine principal prison depots the deaths due to certain specified diseases were as follows:

Continued fevers	1,109
Malarial fevers	1,026
Eruptive fevers	3,453
Diarrhea and dysentery	5,965
Anæmia and debility	156
Consumption	331
Rheumatism	95
Scurvy	351
Bronchitis	133
Pneumonia and pleurisy	5,042

[1] From Martha D. Perry's *Letters from a Surgeon of the Civil War*, p. 14 and fol., one realizes the hardships suffered by Northern prisoners and the entirely insufficient attention paid to their obligations by the Confederates. General Jacob D. Cox in vol. ii, pp. 536–539, of his *Military Reminiscences* has some forceful observations as to the

treatment of prisoners at Andersonville and Salisbury and as to the condition of the released captives. A dreadful recital is the *Narrative of Privations and Sufferings of United States Officers and Soldiers while Prisoners of War*. This is a report of a commission of inquiry appointed by the United States Sanitary Commission.

On the Southern side, two articles by John W. Jones in the Southern Historical Society's *Papers*, i, 113–221 and 225–327 and by A. W. Mangum in the *Publications* of the Southern History Association, iii, 307–336, are decidedly worth reading. The Southerners have also reflected severely on the treatment of Southern prisoners in Northern prisons. Indeed, it is difficult in any way to justify the mode of handling the problem by the Northern authorities except that necessity compelled them to utilize the services of officers who could not be trusted at the front, — which was also the case in the South. At any rate, that is the best way to explain the troubles at Elmira which are fully related in Clay W. Holmes's *The Elmira Prison Camp*. Another interesting book is W. H. Knauss' *Story of Camp Chase* (Nashville, 1906). There was an interesting controversy as to treatment of the prisoners at Camp Morton in the *Century* (vols. xix–xxi). See also Cox's *Reminiscences*, ii, 63 and ch. ix of E. Y. McMorries' *History of the First Regiment Alabama Volunteer Infantry*.

and fresh meat — beef, mutton; the Southerner for his staple diet had corn bread and salted pig, — "hog and hominy." To him corn pone and fried bacon were digestible and nourishing, but to the Northerner, who suddenly found them his principal diet, the case was disastrous, especially when poorly prepared and badly cooked, as they often were. In a similar way the digestive organs of the Southerner trained to meals of pork and corn bread found fresh beef and wheaten bread far from satisfying. In each case the prisoners were, for the most part, provided with the army ration of their enemy and in each case they found it unsuited to their needs, and not only was it unsuited, but in the conditions surrounding them of inactivity, great climatic change, and of mental discouragement either produced disease or laid their bodies open to the inroads of serious physical disorders. In each case the guarding of the prisoners was left to the home guards, to those who did not get to the front, and in the case of some Southern prisons to those who were ineligible for service even under the rigidly inclusive conscription acts. The soldier who had fought in the battle line recognized the sterling qualities of his enemy and respected him, and as long as the prisoner was guarded by soldiers of the fighting armies he had not much to complain of, although there was a good deal of robbing the captured enemy of his clothing by Southern soldiers, at times even it seems by those in the fighting line and not by the skulkers and the partisans. There also was cruelty visited upon the prisoners in both Northern and Southern prisons; but how far this was anything more than administering the customary discipline of the regular army seems somewhat doubtful. In 1863, a committee of the Confederate House of Representatives inquired into charges that had been preferred against the officer in command of Castle Thunder.

The evidence is extremely interesting reading and sometimes painful. That prison was the place of incarceration of military offenders of the Confederate army and for a small number of Federal prisoners who had been transferred from Libby Prison. The complaints had been made by Confederate soldiers and their friends. It appears that the treatment measured out to them by this particular prison commandant was the "regular army" mode of enforcing discipline of that day. An almost identical story is told as to the Union commanding officers at Fort Jefferson off Key West. The most dreadful story of all and one that is a household word throughout the North is that of Andersonville. This was a prison pen located in southwestern Georgia, where the climate was fairly genial and food supplies were near at hand, — a location, indeed, that seemed to be far preferable to that of Belle Isle near Richmond or Salisbury in North Carolina. It happened that Federal prisoners were rushed southward in numbers before any suitable accommodation had been provided for them in the Andersonville Prison Pen. They were guarded by Georgia Home Guards who seem to have been to a great extent boys of from fifteen to sixteen years of age, and the officers in charge had no qualifications whatever for the extremely delicate and important duties suddenly imposed upon them. The prisoners as they came were obliged to provide themselves with such lodging as they could, to make what sanitary provisions they could, and to cook their own food. They were given the ration of the Confederate troops outside, but they knew not how to prepare it and it was entirely unsuited to them, especially in the conditions under which they had to live. Malaria and bowel troubles set in and before long fifty per cent of the captives were dead or dying. The scandal was so great that a Confederate officer, Colonel Chandler, was sent to investigate. He made a report stating the dreadful condition of affairs and placing the blame where it belonged on the utter breakdown of the Confederate administrative bureaus. This report was sent to Richmond, but President Davis never saw it until after Appomattox. Moreover, Andersonville[1] was within an area seriously affected with hookworm, then and now, or at all events until recent years. It would have been a marvel if the disease which affected the bodies of the natives who brought supplies and of the soldiers who guarded the stockade, had not penetrated within and resulted in an explosive epidemic that has few counterparts.

[1] Dr. Charles W. Stiles visited Andersonville some years ago, noted the health of the inhabitants, cross examined everyone who could by any possibility give him information as to the condition of the prisoners, and reached the conclusion that is stated in the text, and has placed in the author's hands a memorandum for which he wishes to express his profound gratitude.

NOTES

I. Andersonville. — The literature relating to Andersonville is large and scattered. In 1869, a committee of the House of Representatives presented a *Report on the Treatment of Prisoners of War, by the Rebel Authorities*.[1] This relates to other prisons as well as Andersonville, but naturally a large part of it is taken up with the horrors of that particular prison pen. The volume runs to 1157 pages and contains much evidence of no particular value. On p. 126 is Colonel D. T. Chandler's " Report " of his inspection of Andersonville. It is wrongly dated January 5, instead of August 5, 1864. It relates a horrible condition of affairs and advises the replacement of Brigadier General J. H. Winder by someone who united energy and good judgment with " some feeling of humanity." In 1888, Jefferson Davis wrote an article entitled " Andersonville and Other War-Prisons " which was printed in Belford's *Magazine* in 1890 and also separately. Two books on the Confederate side should be mentioned: R. R. Stevenson's *The Southern Side; or Andersonville Prison* (Baltimore, 1876) and James M. Page's *The True Story of Andersonville Prison, A Defense of Major Henry Wirz* (New York, 1908).[2] It certainly is distressing to read of the gaiety and frivolity that marked the sojourn of Eliza F. Andrews in southwestern Georgia not so many miles from Andersonville.

II. Bibliography of Casualties. — *The Medical and Surgical History of the War of the Rebellion* (6 vols., Washington) was prepared under the direction of J. K. Barnes, then Surgeon General of the United States army. The amount of information is surprising and is as easy to get at as that contained in the *Official Records*. With this may be mentioned *Statistics, Medical and Anthropological . . . of over a Million Recruits* (2 vols., Washington, 1875) and " Document

---

[1] This forms *House Report* No. 45, 40th Cong., 3rd Sess., ser. ii of the *Official Records;* it is devoted to prisoners of war, including the martyrs of Andersonville. The subject deeply appealed to Jefferson Davis in his later years as may be seen by following the citations in the index of Rowland's *Jefferson Davis* under " Andersonville" and " Winder." And see also two letters written by him in 1875, in Southern Historical Society's *Papers*, xxxvi, p. 10.

[2] James Ford Rhodes has treated the matter judiciously and at length in ch. xxix of vol. v of his *History of the United States*. His footnotes contain abundant citations and on pp. 508 and 509 he has given over seven hundred citations to the *Official Records*, ser. ii, *House Report*, No. 45, and to the official account of the trial of Major Wirz in *House Executive Document*, No. 1, 39th Cong., 1st Sess., p. 1060.

No. 8 " in the *Final Report*. . . .   *By the Provost Marshal General*
(*House Ex. Document*, 39th Cong., 1st Sess., vol. iv, pt. i) is a " Report of Medical Branch " by J. H. Baxter, the chief medical officer.[1]
This was superseded by the *Statistics*, but can be used when that is not
available. A stimulating book is Benjamin A. Gould's *Investigations
in the Military and Anthropological Statistics of American Soldiers*
(New York, 1869). W. F. Fox's *Regimental Losses in the American Civil
War* (Albany, 1889) and T. L. Livermore's *Numbers and Losses in
the Civil War in America* (2nd ed., Boston, 1901) give rise to serious
reflections of various kinds.

[1] The following figures were compiled
in the Adjutant General's Office at the
War Department in Washington. In
the years 1861 to 1865, 93,443 Union
soldiers were killed in action or died of
wounds or injuries received in action;
and 210,400 died of disease or from
unknown causes. Analyzing the figures
somewhat, it appears that 29,336
deaths were occasioned by typhoid
fever and 15,570 from other disorders
that were classed as fevers, or 44,906 in
all. An almost equal number — 44,558
— died from diarrhea and dysentery.
"Consumption" and "inflammation of
lungs" together carried off 26,468.
Somewhat larger figures are given by
Professor Samuel Dumas of the University of Lausanne in his study of the
Losses of Life Caused by War (p. 45) in
the volume edited by Harald Westergaard and published by the Carnegie
Endowment for International Peace;
but he did not use the *Medical and
Surgical History*. Dr. Joseph Jones in
his *Memoirs*, i, 661, stated that typhoid
fever and pneumonia caused more than
one-half of the deaths from all causes —
gun shot wounds included — in the
Confederate army. Fortunately, no
such epidemic attacked the soldiers of
1861–1865 as the influenza-pneumonia
that destroyed so many lives at the end
of the Great War. Otherwise, deaths
from disease behind the lines in the
American army in the latter conflict
were surprisingly small (Leonard P.
Ayres' *The War with Germany, A
Statistical Summary*, Washington, 1919,
p. 124). In the study embodied in
these pages, I have been greatly aided
by Mr. H. M. Thomas of Ontario,
Canada.

CHAPTER XV

FROM BULL RUN TO GETTYSBURG

THE War for Southern Independence, or the War for the Union, or the Civil War, was very unlike any other conflict, in that political and sentimental reasons often overbore the dictates of military science.[1] The theater of war was peculiar. We can dismiss at once the country beyond the Mississippi, for the campaigns in that region, after the very beginning, had slight significance. The country over which the campaigns were fought was a rectangular space of ground stretching from the Mississippi River to the Atlantic Ocean, and from the Susquehanna and the Ohio to the Gulf of Mexico. The Alleghany Mountains divided it into a western and an eastern battlefield. The western area, from a military point of view, was largely dominated by the course and direction of the Mississippi, Ohio, Cumberland, and Tennessee rivers. The Cumberland and the Tennessee have their sources not far apart on opposite sides of the Cumberland Mountains in Eastern Tennessee, thence they pursue southern, western, and northern courses and empty into the Ohio, a dozen or twenty miles apart. At their extreme southern points, the Tennessee, in northern Alabama, is far away from the Cumberland, whose southernmost point is conveniently marked by Nashville. South of the Tennessee to the Gulf the rivers flow generally from north

[1] General Sherman wrote an interesting article on "The Grand Strategy of the War of the Rebellion" that was printed in the *Century* for February, 1888, pp. 582–598.

to south. When one adds that much of this country was up and down hill, was sparsely settled, poorly supplied with bad country roads, and hardly supplied at all with railroads, one can get an idea of the extreme difficulty of campaigning on a large scale. The only east and west railroad was the Memphis and Charleston, which ran from the first named place on the Mississippi River to Chattanooga where it connected with railroads to Savannah and Charleston by way of Atlanta, and to Richmond by way of Knoxville and Lynchburg. This was the only railroad connection between the western and eastern theaters of war within the limits of the Confederacy, for the road from Vicksburg to Montgomery and thence to the seaboard was not completed between Meridian and the vicinity of Selma until the close of the year 1864. The possession of the lines from Chattanooga eastward gave the Confederates considerable facility for the movement of troops from one theater of war to the other. When, however, in 1862, the Memphis and Charleston road passed into the hands of the Federal forces or, perhaps it would be better to say, was broken up for a long distance by the contending armies, communication between the Mississippi Valley and Virginia was very difficult. At an early period of the war the Union forces became supreme on the Cumberland and Tennessee and were able to utilize these rivers more or less interruptedly throughout the war. A railroad from the Ohio to Nashville and Chattanooga made possible the campaigns of Rosecrans, Thomas, Grant, and Sherman in East Tennessee and to the southward, for, at that time, Knoxville had no rail connection with Nashville except by Chattanooga. Military operations by way of the Mississippi River were greatly influenced by the peculiar character of that mighty stream. Instead of flowing like most rivers between stable banks, the Mississippi

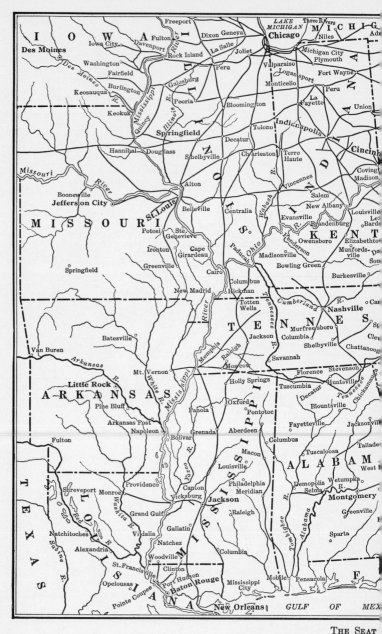

THE SEAT

(Redrawn from Dinsmore

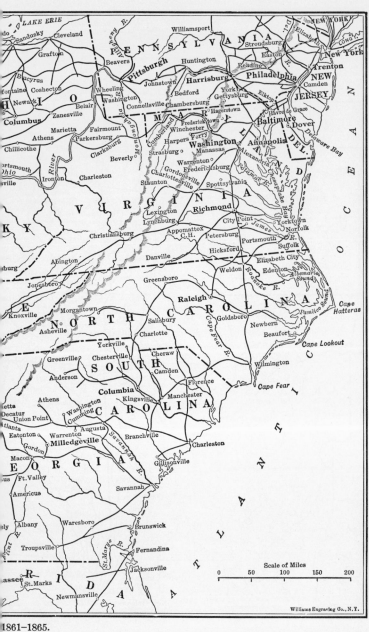

1861–1865.

Guide, New York, 1860.)

occupies the bed of a wide alluvial plain, twisting and turning
in a remarkable degree so that on its course from St. Louis
to the Gulf it sometimes flows in a northerly direction. In
its progress through this alluvial plain it now and then
approaches high lands or bluffs. These places are marked
by towns which serve as centers of distribution and of egress
and ingress from and to the interior. Columbus in
Kentucky, Memphis in Tennessee, and Vicksburg and Natchez also in Mississippi were the most important points of
connection between the river and the land on the eastern
shore above Baton Rouge and New Orleans. These general characteristics of the Mississippi Valley made the task
of the Federal naval and military commanders much easier
than it otherwise might have been; but the comparatively
few points that required defence against combined military
and naval attack greatly favored the Confederates. When
one adds that the summer climate of these southern river
bottoms was peculiarly detrimental to the health of Northern troops, one can get some idea of the difficulties that
faced the Union commanders; — tremendous distances,
sparse settlement, poverty of rail and road communication,
the difficulty of transfer from river to land, and the hostile
character of the climate to Northern bred persons must
constantly be borne in mind when estimating the abilities
of armies and commanders.

The eastern theater of war in Virginia and the Carolinas
was marked by rivers flowing southeastwardly from the
mountains to the Atlantic Ocean: the Potomac, the James,
the Savannah, and countless smaller streams in between.
At the southern end of the mountains, dividing the two
areas was Atlanta where east and west and north and
south railroads crossed. At the northern end of the theater
of war were Richmond and Petersburg where railroads came

together from Charleston, Savannah, Wilmington, and from
Lynchburg, Knoxville, and Chattanooga. Notwithstanding
the many years that this country had been settled, the roads
were very poor and, for long seasons of the year, impassable
and the rivers were not susceptible of use as arteries of transportation as were the rivers of the western area.[1] Along
the eastern shore of North Carolina and extending for long
distances east and west and north and south were Pamlico
and Albemarle sounds accessible from the sea by several
inlets and from the interior by rivers that were navigable
by light draft boats for some distance inland. Northwestwardly from Richmond the Valley of the Shenandoah River,
an affluent of the Potomac, was separated from the rest of
Virginia by the Blue Ridge through which several gaps gave
access to the Valley itself. The Shenandoah flowed into the
Potomac at Harper's Ferry. The Valley, therefore, was an
easy line of approach to Maryland and central Pennsylvania.
Owing to the great fertility of the Valley, it was an important
source of supply of food and forage, and, owing to its topo-
graphical features, it was very difficult to block its use as
a road to Maryland. Virginia, between the Potomac and
the James and the Blue Ridge and the Chesapeake Bay,
was an exceedingly difficult region for campaigning purposes.
Many rivers, large and small, combined with swampy areas,
lay between the Potomac and the James and large tracts
of land had relapsed into the wilderness stage and others
had never been cleared. The roads were very heavy for
military transportation in wet weather. In short, the stra-

[1] John C. Ropes, writing from
Boston in December, 1862, declared
that the "marshy, muddy roads and
rickety bridges" of Virginia with the
constant changes from railroad to
steamboat were inferior to the "ten
beautiful roads for hundreds of miles"
leading out from Ulm even in the
time of Napoleon I. In other words
railroads in connection with difficult bits
of transportation or supplemented by
wagons or steamboats had not as yet
changed the problems of transportation
in the South.

tegic problem presented by the rivers, the Valley of the
Shenandoah, and the wooded areas was most difficult of
solution.

When it became certain that the South must be brought
back to the Union by force of arms — if at all — General
Winfield Scott, sage in counsel but unwieldy in body, set
forth a plan of a complete blockade of the Atlantic and
Gulf ports with the opening of the Mississippi River by
naval and military action.   Probably the matter was somewhat vague in his mind, but the general idea seems to have
been to hold fast the Confederates in the East, while rolling
them up by the occupation of territory following the defeats
of their armies in the West.   With this might well be combined the occupation of all Confederate ports on the Atlantic
seaboard and on the Gulf of Mexico.   Under a single head
an army of half a million men might well have been employed
utilizing the superior railroad and steamboat facilities of the
North to place an overwhelming force first in one and then
in the other strategic area.   Unfortunately, military considerations alone could not govern the problem, and there
was no unity of command before 1864 and it was only with
extreme slowness that men of military genius made their
way into the upper commands.   It was essential to hold
on to the national capital and, from the Southern point of
view, it was no less necessary to defend Richmond which was
not only the capital city of the newly-born Confederacy,
but its loss together with the overrunning of Virginia would
have gravely compromised all hope of foreign recognition,
would have taken out of the Confederacy one of the two
strongest of the seceded States, and would have sacrificed
the possession of the Tredegar Iron Works with the only
heavy metal working machinery in the Confederacy.   It
was for these reasons that the war in the East became local-

ized in Virginia and the seeming importance of Washington and Richmond was so great that soldiers were used in this region who might well have been employed elsewhere. Other Union troops also were stationed to guard the entrance to the Valley of the Shenandoah, to seize and to occupy places on the seaboard, and thus more than one-half of the strength of the Union armies was diverted from the western theater of war. In the West also sentimental and political considerations played very important parts. The protection of the Unionists in Missouri and Kentucky and the secure holding of the latter State were of very great importance. Then there were the Unionists of East Tennessee who were steadfast in the cause, were cruelly treated by the Confederates, and lived on the line of the most available railroad from the Virginia theater of war to the western military area. These considerations led to a dispersal of the forces in the West. One army had for its object the exclusion of the Confederates from central Tennessee and the occupation of East Tennessee. Another army essayed the opening of the Mississippi, the Cumberland, and the Tennessee from the North; and the third was used to occupy the lower Mississippi and to try to join hands with the upper force. These last two armies were necessarily accompanied or preceded by large naval units. In other words, there were six permanent military units operating more or less independently until the autumn and winter of 1863–1864, when Grant was given sole command west of the mountains. Of course, the presence of these Union armies necessitated the employment of opposing Confederate forces, but these, having the advantage of defence and of interior lines, and also the good will of the inhabitants for the most part, were usually much smaller than their Unionist opponents. To the Northern non-military mind in 1861, it seemed that all

that was necessary was to place a force in the field somewhat superior to its Confederate opponent and having
destroyed or beaten him to join the nearest Federal army
and proceed onward with the good work. Indeed, we find
General George B. McClellan writing to Scott in 1861 that an
army from the Northwest might cross the Ohio River and
march up the valley of the "Great Kanawha" and move
on Richmond. This would relieve Washington and bring
about the destruction of the Southern army, "if aided by
a decided advance on the eastern line." Another plan was
to march by the way of Nashville and Montgomery and in
combination with an army coming from Charleston and
Augusta to proceed to Pensacola, Mobile, and New Orleans.
The fancifulness of these plans and possibly of Scott's also
well evince the amateurishness with which the first two
commanders-in-chief approached the problem, and are used
here merely to suggest how little the ablest political leaders,
even Lincoln himself, the War Governors, and the first two
Secretaries of War realized the real problem with which they
were face to face. Considering the force that the Confederates
could put into the field, one million men would have been
none too many to have solved the actual problem. McClellan was always calling for men and was always exaggerating
the numbers of his opponents and minimizing the strength
of his own forces; but it must be said that no general could
have done an effective piece of work with the forces
at McClellan's disposal.

After the disaster at Bull Run, President Lincoln summoned McClellan [1] to Washington, placed him in control

[1] On McClellan's campaigns in the
Peninsula and in Maryland, see the
documents in the *Official Records*.
McClellan's Own Story, that was printed
after his death, is one of the most
lamentable publications that family
piety ever produced and has made it
exceedingly difficult to treat McClellan with fairness. General P. S.
Michie's *McClellan* in the *Great Commanders* series is an admirable study
of his career. Rhodes's chapters in

of the newly raised volunteers and, in November, 1861, appointed him to the chief command of the military forces of the United States. McClellan was a great organizer; and had the capacity to inspire his men with respect for discipline and for himself. When the Army of the Potomac emerged from its camps in the spring of 1862, it was a real fighting force that preserved its spirit and discipline under very adverse circumstances to the end. For one reason or another, McClellan refused time and again to take the field notwithstanding Lincoln's most urgent prompting. This slowness has been attributed to various motives. Some persons have averred that McClellan looked upon himself as a Heaven-sent peacemaker and desired to win the South back without slaughter.[1] Others assert that he greatly over-estimated the numbers of his immediate opponents and under-estimated his own resources in men and material. It is also supposed that he was timid and lacked faith in his own powers of command. Possibly all these put together, combined with other considerations, may have influenced him, and these may have been aggravated by illness. At all events, he did not move, and the Federal government at Washington was mortified by the practical control of the lower Potomac by the Confederates and also by a small

---

volumes iii and iv of his *History* were written with every intention of being fair to McClellan and contain a mass of citations. Colonel T. L. Livermore's and Captain T. G. Frothingham's accounts of McClellan's campaigns in the *Proceedings* of the Massachusetts Historical Society for May, 1917, December, 1922, and November, 1923, are endeavors to do justice. J. C. Ropes and the contributors to the *Papers* of the Military Historical Society of Massachusetts are distinctly unfavorable to McClellan, but the essays in volume i of that series are well worth perusal. The Prince de Joinville's narrative, which was translated from the French by W. H. Hurlbert and printed in New York in 1862, gives an exceedingly lifelike series of impressions, and General Barnard's professional critique of *The Peninsula Campaign and its Antecedents* produces a sense of dismal disillusionment and will serve to prevent any too favorable opinion being acquired by any one.

[1] General Fitz John Porter's description of McClellan as "a man who wisely seeks to heal, as well as to conquer" casts a flood of light on both Porter and McClellan. Katharine P. Wormeley's *The Other Side of War*, p. 53.

but tragic disaster which needlessly had befallen a body of
Federal soldiers on the southern side of the Potomac, above
Washington at Ball's Bluff. When McClellan finally did
move, it is supposed that he was urged thereto by successes
gained by western armies at Mill Springs, Fort Donelson,
and Island No. 10, in January, February, and March, 1862.

In the West, Major General Henry Wager Halleck was
in command after the downfall of General Frémont in the
autumn of 1861. The Confederates were still active in
Missouri and Arkansas, and Halleck, whose headquarters
were at St. Louis, confined his attention largely to Missouri.
At Cairo, just above the confluence of the Ohio and the
Mississippi, General Ulysses Simpson Grant had fourteen
to sixteen thousand men and more. At Bowling Green in
Kentucky, General Don Carlos Buell had other thousands
whose ultimate objective was to be the relief of the Unionists
of East Tennessee. By this time the Confederates had
invaded Kentucky and had occupied Columbus on the Mississippi, and had erected Forts Henry and Donelson on the
Tennessee and Cumberland rivers, just within the Tennessee
line where the two rivers approach each other to within a
dozen miles or so. The main body of the Confederates was
in the vicinity of Nashville under the command of General
Albert Sidney Johnston. Buell seems to have been as unable
to move as was McClellan, — the lack of supplies and need
of wagons were his most appealing cry. Finally, he was
insistently directed to hire private wagons if he could not
get public ones and put an end to the marchings of the Confederates in eastern Kentucky. This task was confided to
General George H. Thomas. At Logan's Cross Roads, some
eight or a dozen miles away from Mill Springs or Mill Spring,
Thomas attacked and overwhelmed a Confederate force
of about the same size as his own, January 19, 1862.

At this time, Halleck, probably with promptings from
Washington, directed Grant to make a reconnoissance in
force to discover the strength and position of the Confederates in the lower valleys of the Cumberland and the
Tennessee. Grant, always prompt in obedience to orders,
sent out a reconnoitering force and reported that the Confederate Fort Henry could be taken by combined naval and
military forces. Halleck therefore ordered Grant, with
gunboats which were then under military direction and the
troops that he had at Cairo and others that might be sent
to him, to capture Fort Henry. The gunboats acted with
despatch and Fort Henry, being peculiarly accessible to
gunfire from the river, soon fell. When announcing this
success Grant wrote that he should at once move overland
to Fort Donelson. This operation proved to be more difficult, for portions of the fortification being high above the
river were inaccessible to naval guns and the defending force
was large. It was commanded by General Floyd, one-
time Secretary of War, General Pillow, once law partner of
President Polk and a general in the Mexican War, and General Simon Bolivar Buckner. The gunboats fired, but without much effect, and the troops battled also without much
result. Grant sought Commodore Foote on his flagship
some distance below the fort to arrange for future operations,
for Foote had been wounded and was unable to leave his
ship. While Grant was away, the Confederates broke from
their entrenchments, attacked the Union soldiers with great
spirit, and drove them back at one end of the line. Returning to the field with all the speed that horse could make,
Grant, finding the haversacks of some dead or captured
Confederates filled with food, said "The enemy is trying to
escape" and ordered an attack to be made at once all along
the line, and by nightfall some of the Union troops had

approached to within assaulting distance of the Confederate works. That night was a terrible one for the Union soldiers lying out in the open in icy sleet, without protection of any kind and many of them without food. It was an even more trying one within the fort, for Buckner reported that at the first attack his line would give way. Thereupon, Floyd, to save himself from capture and possible prosecution for his former misdeeds while head of the War Department, declared he would get on a steamer that was uninjured in the river and hand over the command to Major General Pillow, who at once said "I pass it" and handed it over to Buckner. Floyd and Pillow succeeded in getting away and wrote three reports apiece in an endeavor to explain their actions to President Davis. Ultimately, Floyd was placed in command of Virginia State troops and Pillow became a pursuer of Confederate conscripts.[1] Left to himself, Buckner took the first opportunity to open communications with Grant and ask what terms would be given. To which Grant replied "Unconditional and immediate surrender," adding "I propose to move immediately upon your works." At once Buckner surrendered, February 16, 1862, in accordance with what he asserted were "ungenerous and unchivalrous terms." The phrase "unconditional surrender" caught the public fancy and "Unconditional Surrender Grant" became the newspaper hero of the hour. Unfortunately, the telegraphic operator at Grant's headquarters "went South" taking with him telegrams which Grant had given him to send to head-

[1] The "Reports" and letters are printed in the *Official Records*. Those on the Confederate side were originally printed at Richmond in 1862 with the *Report of the Special Committee on the Recent Military Disasters at Forts Henry and Donelson and the Evacuation of Nashville*. One of the most interesting papers in this last publication (pp. 69–75) is the "Report" of Major W. N. Brown of the 20th Mississippi Volunteers who guarded the landing while Floyd and Pillow fled to the steamer that took them away and left him and his soldiers behind. He also stated the facts in a somewhat more graphic form to Jefferson Davis in August, 1880; see Rowland's *Davis*, viii, 485. An anti-Grant view is given in the *Magazine of American History*, xv, 20.

quarters. Halleck, hearing nothing, became suspicious and communicated his suspicions to the War Department. Only a belated explanation saved Grant from dismissal and arrest. Even then Halleck determined to take the field himself or to give power to another, General A. J. Smith.

In the next month, March, 1862, an army operating down the Mississippi River under the command of General John Pope, with an effective naval force under Commodore Foote, captured Island No. 10[1] and New Madrid on the western bank of the river and opened the way to Memphis, one hundred miles or so below, as the crow flies, and very much farther by water. After the surrender of Donelson, Union gunboats ascended the Tennessee River for a considerable distance and returned safely. By direction of Halleck, the main body of Grant's troops and reënforcements were encamped at Pittsburg Landing near the great bend of the Tennessee River. Meantime Buell's army had advanced overland to Nashville, from which place the Confederates had disappeared.[2] The idea was that Buell should unite with the force at Pittsburg Landing and march to Corinth where the railroads crossed, and thence to Memphis. Meanwhile the naval force would go down the Mississippi to Memphis and, possibly beyond, even as far as New Orleans.

The opening of the lower Mississippi by way of the Gulf had been before the government for some time, but the actual incitement to it seems to have come from concrete

[1] Two interesting accounts of this episode are ch. x in H. Walke's *Naval Scenes and Reminiscences* and E. Y. McMorries's *History of the First Regiment, Alabama Volunteer Infantry, C. S. A.*, ch. ii. Walke was the commander of the *Carondelet* which ran the batteries of Island No. 10.

[2] On March 12, 1862, Jefferson Davis wrote to General A. S. Johnston, who was in chief command in Tennessee and was a friend of many years, that a great many hard things were being said of him and of his precipitate retreat after the capture of Fort Donelson by Grant and asked him to present his report. Rowland's *Davis*, v, 215.

plans proposed by Lieutenant David D. Porter. His suggestion was that Fort Jackson and Fort St. Philip, guarding
the approach to New Orleans, could be reduced or greatly
injured by a bombardment from a mortar flotilla anchored
along the banks of the river below the forts and when this
was accomplished and obstructions in the river removed,
a fleet of sea-going steam men-of-war should run by the forts,
seize New Orleans, and proceed up the river to join hands
with the naval and military force decending that stream.
To coöperate with the naval force in the lower river, twenty-
five thousand soldiers would be required. The government
approved the plan and on Porter's suggestion selected Captain David G. Farragut to lead the naval expedition.
Porter, himself, was given command of the mortar division,
but throughout the operation acted closely in conjunction
with his old friend, Flag Officer Farragut. The military
force was placed under the command of General Benjamin
F. Butler. There were delays inevitable to the prosecution
of so large an enterprise, for the mortar vessels had to be
prepared and navigated from New York and the Chesapeake
to their destination, the necessary naval force had to be
gathered, and a small army transported thousands of miles
by water. Arrived at the mouth of the Mississippi, it was
found difficult to get the heavy naval vessels over the bar
and into the deep water of the river itself. Stores had to
be unloaded and guns removed and then all reshipped again.
In time the mortar vessels were placed in position and, after
the exact ranges had been discovered by careful trian-
gulation, the bombardment was begun and carried on almost
continuously, being directed on Fort Jackson, the nearer of
the two forts.

The Confederates had been in weekly and daily expectation of the descent of an expedition from up river and to make

head against this, troops and artillery had been sent in that direction. They knew of the intended coming of Farragut and his fleet and the attendant army, but relied on the forts and the obstructions placed below them.[1] The Confederates had also been busily engaged in the construction of two formidable iron-clad vessels, the *Louisiana* and the *Mississippi*. The former of these was so far advanced toward completion that her guns had been placed on board, and she had been towed to a position in the river where it was expected she would be of material assistance to the forts. The Confederate commander at Fort Jackson was very anxious to have the *Louisiana* nearer at hand, but with workmen aboard of her completing her motive power, her commander refused to move. The *Mississippi* was launched at about the time that Farragut was ready for his attempt to run past the forts. At length on the night of April 23, 1862, the obstructions were broken sufficiently to permit the passage of the fleet. Very early the next morning, the vessels started on their hazardous journey, the mortar schooners opening fire with redoubled energy. As the vessels went up stream, fire was opened upon them from Fort Jackson and then from Fort St. Philip, but as the heavier vessels came abreast the forts their broadsides drove the gunners

---

[1] Exact citations to the *Official Records* are given in the footnotes of Rhodes's *History of the Civil War* and ordinarily will not be repeated here. Farragut's operations on the lower Mississippi are detailed at length in *Senate Ex. Document*, No. 56, 37th Cong., 2nd Sess., and are well worth reading in the original. Captain Alfred T. Mahan and Professor J. R. Soley have given excellent accounts of the New Orleans expedition in their biographies of Farragut and Porter in the *Great Commanders* series. On the Confederate side, see *Report of Evidence taken before a Joint Special Committee* of Both Houses of the Confederate Congress, to investigate the Affairs of the Navy Department (Richmond, Va.). This committee sat, with adjournments, from September 4, 1862, to March 24, 1863. On April 4, 1863, a military Court of Inquiry assembled at Richmond to examine into the facts attending the loss of New Orleans and its *Proceedings* were printed at Richmond in 1864. Very few publications, if any, give so vivid a glimpse of the difficulties of the Confederates as the 600 odd pages of the evidence printed in these two documents.

from their posts. The *Louisiana* also fired at the Federal ships doing some execution. A ram, the *Manassas*, added its efforts, and fire-rafts and Confederate gun-boats assisted in the general confusion. For a time the *Hartford*, Farragut's flagship, lay aground off Fort St. Philip and caught fire from a fire-raft that was pushed against her. The fire was put out, the ship was backed off and slowly ascended with her consorts. Only one Union vessel was destroyed, but some of the others were considerably injured and a few were unable to get through the barrier. Altogether it was one of the most thrilling and successful episodes of the war. A few days later, April 28, the garrison at Fort Jackson mutinied and its commander was forced to surrender to Captain Porter.[1] The same fate befell Fort St. Philip and some minor fortifications and the *Louisiana* was set on fire by her commander and blown up, fortunately without doing any great damage to the naval vessels within reach. Also when Farragut approached New Orleans, he found the *Mississippi* in flames.

Arrived at New Orleans, Farragut sent a small force on shore to hoist the flag and to receive the technical surrender of the city from the mayor; but the soldiers, who had been stationed there, made good their retreat. General Butler now arrived with his troops,[2] took possession of the forts

[1] General Duncan in command at Fort Jackson reported that great damage had been done to the fort, — "The mortar fire was accurate and terrible, many of the shells falling everywhere within the fort and disabling some of our best guns." Three days later, April 21, he reported that the fort was "in need of extensive repairs almost everywhere" *Official Reports of Battles* (Richmond, 1862), p. 353. On p. 384 of the same volume is a graphic account of the running of the forts by Captain M. T. Squires, who commanded at Fort St. Philip. In the *Continental*

[2] For the Butler side, see his *Private and Official Correspondence*, vols. i, ii, and iii. It does not do, of course, to base too much on these volumes which were put forth by the family. It would seem that much that was charged against him was overdrawn and it would also appear that there was a good deal of speculation and corruption, not only in Butler's time, but later, and in other parts of the Mississippi Valley. A somewhat different story is told in the

Monthly, iii, 560, is a statement of the condition of the forts after the passage of the fleet.

and then of the city, and established himself there as military commander. His position was one of great difficulty, for the people of New Orleans were exceedingly hostile to the Union cause.[1] There were also many foreigners there who claimed protection from the military governor and at the same time proposed to use their immunity to carry on commerce against the interests of the United States. The women, too, the "she-adders" as Butler called them, insulted his officers and men in every way they could think of, until at last one of them, who had repeatedly insulted the Union soldiers, was seen "laughing and mocking" as the funeral procession of a Union officer passed by. Butler sent her to Ship Island with one woman attendant, to have no communication with any one but her jailer. As to the others, he could not arrest them and if they continued to shower insults on the soldiers there was likely to be serious trouble and bloodshed. He therefore issued an order that in the future any woman publicly insulting his soldiers should be treated as a common "woman of the town plying her avocation."[2] For this he was outlawed by Jefferson Davis, was the subject of a debate in the British Parliament, and received many remonstrances from his friends. To these last he replied that he saw no reason to revoke the order: for himself, when he met a woman of the town plying her trade, he passed her by and expected his soldiers to do the same.

"Letters of General Thomas Williams" in the *American Historical Review*, xiv, 304. Edwards Pierrepont's *Review . . . of Gen. Butler's Defense . . . in Relation to the New Orleans Gold* (New York, 1865) gives another interesting side-light.

[1] The execution of Mumford for hauling down the United States flag after the surrender of the city was one of the most questioned acts of Butler's rule. In 1863 he told Colonel McClure it was very painful for him to order the execution and that he would do anything he could for the widow and the family. Ultimately he obtained a place for her in one of the departments at Washington. A. K. McClure's *Recollections*, p. 385.

[2] *Private and Official Correspondence of . . . Butler*, ii, 35. The order itself is in *ibid.*, i, 490. Jefferson Davis's Proclamation declaring Butler to be a felon is in *ibid.*, ii, 557 and in Richardson's *Messages and Papers of the Confederacy*, i, 269.

It is certain that the order put an end to insults to the Union soldiers on the streets of New Orleans.

In April, 1862, a Union army under the command of Grant was at Pittsburg Landing awaiting the arrival of Buell's army from the direction of Nashville on the other side of the river. Among the division commanders of the former force was General William T. Sherman. The soldiers were encamped back from the river for a mile or so in the direction of Corinth. Meantime the Confederates had retreated from central Tennessee and had gathered at Corinth and its neighborhood. They were commanded by Albert Sidney Johnston and Beauregard, who had been sent from the East for some reason or other, and among the subordinate commanders was Braxton Bragg. Owing to accident or to something not perfectly clear, Johnston and Beauregard determined to assail the force at Pittsburg Landing before Buell could join it.[1] They were also incited to make a movement by a sudden attack that was made on one of their outposts which was greatly exaggerated by one of the officers on the spot and seemed to suggest that the Union army was divided. The movement was made with the quickness that marked the Confederates, and at about dawn on the morning of April 6, 1862, their advance came into contact with a reconnoitering force from Sherman's division The Union army was not taken by surprise, but the celerity and weight of the attack were unexpected. The advance force was quickly driven back and the Confederates advanced with great determination on the Union camps and reached them before the Union soldiers had more than time to form.[2] Many of these were fresh from civil life and had

[1] See A. P. James's "Strategy of Concentration" in *Mississippi Valley Historical Review*, Extra Number, November, 1921, pp. 363–372. There is a scathing criticism of General A. S. Johnston in vol. xiii, pp. 354–356, of the Massachusetts Military Historical Society's *Papers*.

[2] The question whether the Union army was surprised at Shiloh aroused

never seen a gun fired in anger. Naturally some of these companies and regiments broke and fled and sought the safety of the river bank. General Lew Wallace with his division was some distance away. He mistook his orders, or took the wrong road, and was thus delayed in reaching the battlefield. Toward night, Johnston was mortally wounded and the command fell to Beauregard who, thinking that enough had been accomplished for the day, stopped the movement. By that time Federal gunboats had begun to open fire on the Confederate positions and the leading division of Buell's army had reached the other side of the river. Grant had never thought of retreat and, when Buell came up, conferred with him as to sending his divisions across the river. Buell inquired of Grant as to whether the shipping at hand would be sufficient to transport the army to the eastern bank in case of defeat. To which Grant replied that the steamers at hand would be quite sufficient for that purpose. That night, Lew Wallace appeared, many of the frightened soldiers returned to their places, and a portion of Buell's army added its strength. The next day, Grant ordered an attack. The Confederates retreated and were pursued some miles beyond the recovered Union camps. Such was the battle of Shiloh or Pittsburg Landing, April 6 and 7, 1862, the bloodiest encounter, considering the numbers engaged, of the war.

Again, as after Donelson, Halleck had misgivings as to

great interest at the time. The Honorable Thomas Ewing, General Sherman's father-in-law, came to his defence in a *Letter . . . to His Excellency Benj. Stanton* (Columbus, Ohio, 1862). He shows that Sherman had his pickets out and that his troops came into contact with the enemy two miles away from his camp. In Beauregard's report, dated Corinth, April 11, 1862, it is stated that "At 5 A.M. on the 6th inst.

a reconnoitering party of the enemy having become engaged with our advanced pickets the commander of the forces gave order to begin the movement"; Beauregard's "Official Letter Book," p. 21. The report is also in *Official Reports of Battles* (Richmond, Va., 1862), p. 181. Three interesting articles on Shiloh — with graphic illustrations — are in the *Century* for February, 1885, pp. 593, 614, and 629,

the quality and skill of his subordinate. He came to Pittsburg Landing, took the field command himself and appointed Grant second in command, giving him no duties to perform. Under these circumstances, Grant applied for a leave of absence. Sherman sought him out, asked if he had any business away from the army, and being informed that he had none, told Grant that he would make a serious mistake in leaving the field; anything might happen there, and if anything did happen, being on the spot, he could take advantage of it; but if he were in St. Louis the lot would fall to some one else. Halleck now gathered a tremendous army and advanced by exceeding slow stages toward Corinth, where Beauregard had entrenched himself with a much smaller force. At length when the Union advance reached the outposts, it found the Confederates gone. The army was then dispersed to occupy the country, a considerable body of troops returning to central Tennessee.

The interest in the West now turns on Tennessee and Kentucky. General Braxton Bragg, in command of the Confederates, marched through Tennessee and invaded Kentucky, presumably seeking recruits and also supplies. The Union army had to be outfitted all over again and there were many newly-arrived regiments which needed hardening to war. It was October before General Buell advanced, and when he did, a well-contested battle took place (October 8, 1862) at Perryville, in central Kentucky. Buell did not take advantage of his opportunities. He was removed and General Rosecrans was placed in command. Thereupon there were other delays, incidental to the reorganization of the army, and it was the last day of December, 1862, before another conflict occurred. This time it was at Murfreesboro', or Stone's River, thirty or forty miles from Nashville. Here, again, the fighting was most strenuous, the losses were very heavy on both sides, and the gain to either combatant slight. The military strength and sagacity of two men on the Union side, George H. Thomas and Philip H. Sheridan, came out prominently in these combats. Otherwise, they were barren of result and left the problem of the care of the Unionists of East Tennessee exactly where it was in the summer of 1861.

In the autumn and winter of 1861–1862 there was astonishingly little movement in the eastern theater of war. Lincoln, alarmed at the growing apathy of the Northern people toward the war and appalled at the tremendous expense incurred in the maintenance of great armies and navies, tried by every means in his power to induce activity on the part of generals and commodores. McClellan brought forward one plan after another, but showed no sign of putting any of them into execution. Flag Officer Du Pont captured the excellent harbor of Beaufort on the coast of South Carolina between Charleston and Savannah, but after that, although soldiers and steamers were sent him, nothing was accomplished, except to care for the fugitive slaves and to divert from McClellan troops that would have been very useful in Virginia. Of the coastwise operations, the capture of Roanoke Island and the occupation of Pamlico and Albemarle sounds inflicted a blow upon the Confederate force that probably justified the diversion of the men and ships from the main objective to that point. The easy capture of Roanoke Island, which was due to the inability of the Confederate government to supply an adequate number of defenders and ammunition,[1] was in one respect unfortunate in that it gave an entirely undue and undeserved prominence to the Union commander, Gen. Burnside, and led to his later being entrusted with operations that were entirely

[1] Southern Historical Society's *Papers*, xxv, 299.

beyond his capacity. In the spring, he was transferred to the Shenandoah Valley. The Union cause in West Virginia was now confided to another political or semi-political general, John C. Frémont. Very possibly, it was McClellan's persistent inactivity that finally induced Lincoln to consent to these outside expeditions; but public opinion in the North demanded the capture and punishment of Charleston, South Carolina, the protection of the Unionist people of West Virginia, and the "doing something for Frémont."

Precisely what McClellan's plans were is extremely doubtful, for we find him writing most vaguely of operations for the main army that were in some respects distinctly fantastical. There was a chance to advance up the Valley of the Shenandoah and driving the Confederates to the eastward and southward to gain Richmond from that quarter. There was a possibility of outflanking Joseph E. Johnston at Manassas by a sudden and direct march from Washington. Again one might cross from the Potomac to the Rappahannock at Fredericksburg and outflank the Manassas position from the other side. Then an army might be landed lower down the Potomac, march across country to West Point on the York River and gain the James below Richmond. And, finally, the army might be transported by water to Fortress Monroe and advance up the Peninsula between the York and the James rivers. Of course, any of these distant operations necessitated the division of the army, so that one part could defend Washington against any sudden attacks, while the other part defeated the Confederate army in the field. But this necessitated another diversion of force from the main attack. Moreover, the views as to the adequacy of the force to be left behind held by the military commander of the main army and by the heads of the government at Washington might well have been very different. McClellan at length, as the spring of 1862 drew on, pitched upon the last of these five plans as the most eligible. Had he chosen the route by the Valley or by Manassas, he might have had at his disposal two hundred thousand men more or less; but when he elected the plan that would take him and his army farthest away from the Valley and from Washington City, it was perfectly certain that his political superiors would insist upon the retention of a very large portion of his total force from the main campaign in the field. This they did and placed in command of the defence of the capital a volunteer general from New York — "to conciliate the agricultural interests" of that State.[1] McClellan seems to have made up his mind that the navy would render him efficient aid and secure him an uninterrupted march with his right flank on the York River or with his left flank on the James. It does not appear that the Navy Department ever gave him such direct assurance and, before he was absolutely committed to the plan, the *Merrimac* appeared and made any thought of utilizing the James out of the question. Finally, it may be said that the geographic knowledge even of the oldest settled parts of the United States was extremely inadequate to the uses of military men.[2] In this case, a river — the Warwick River — was supposed to be very short and to confine itself to the southern side of the Peninsula. In reality, its source was within

---

[1] Ropes's *Story of the Civil War*, i, 251, citing McClellan's *Own Story*, 226. Ropes met McClellan in the winter of 1862–63 and describes him in a letter to Gray dated Feb. 7, 1863, as "standing well, . . . not a weak line in his face. . . . But he lacks that eye which most really able men have. . . . And his countenance is decidedly heavy."

[2] The topography of the Peninsula was well known to the map makers of the years succeeding the surrender of Cornwallis. The maps printed in Stedman's *History . . . of the American War*, in Tarleton's *Campaigns*, Ramsay's *Revolution of South Carolina*, and in Marshall's *Washington* show the Warwick River rising in the vicinity of Yorktown. A sketch of the Stedman map is in the present work, iii, 337. Knowledge of the topography of the Peninsula disappeared from American maps. The Rochambeau Collection, containing maps drawn by the French engineers in 1781, which are now owned by the United States government, was

a mile of Yorktown on the northern shore — instead of being parallel to McClellan's line of march, its course was across it and, being dammed by the Confederates, it proved to be a formidable obstacle. McClellan had postponed movement month after month on account of impassability of Virginia roads in the rainy autumnal, winter, and spring months. When, finally, his men started up the Peninsula from Fortress Monroe in June, 1862, the rains descended and converted the dirt roads into routes of mud. Indeed, the soil of that whole region is so muddy and soft that such roads as there are, even today, apart from one or two modern stone highways, are corduroyed. For half a year, the Federal superiority on the water had given the Union commander great advantage over his opponents who were confined to the land; but now the route chosen placed the two combatants in this respect on a footing of equality.

The Confederate General Magruder at Yorktown had some sixteen thousand men well disposed in fortified positions.[1] McClellan had quadruple, quintuple, sextuple this number as his men came up. Writers on the campaign, some of whom were in the army and others who were not, have asserted over and over again that McClellan should at once have attacked and that inevitably in so long a line a weak spot would have been found. He did nothing of the sort, but called upon Washington for more troops and requested the navy to batter down the Yorktown forts on the river so

not in America in 1862. It would seem that staff officers of intelligence would have studied the historical topography of the Peninsula, but it must be said that a large "Map of the State of Virginia" that was published at Richmond in 1862 has no indication of the Warwick or any other river flowing across the Peninsula.

[1] Magruder's *Report of his Operations*

on the Peninsula was printed at Richmond in 1862 and again at Mobile in the same year. It was first published "By permission of the War Department, in advance of the report of General Lee, through whom, however, it was submitted," — and it shows clearly enough why Magruder never afterwards was given an important command.

that his transports might carry troops to West Point behind
the lines. The navy had no vessels to spare from opposition
to the *Merrimac*, and it is quite improbable that any naval
vessels of that day would have effected much damage to the
shore guns at Yorktown which were perched on a bluff forty
to sixty feet high. McClellan also called for siege guns, and
although somewhat alarmed at his proceedings, the government at Washington sent the guns and an army corps under
General Franklin. Meantime, before McClellan had made
up his mind what to do, Johnston had abandoned his position at Manassas and had concentrated his force in front
of Richmond. He was now directed to take his army to the
Peninsula and aid in the defence of Yorktown. McClellan,
therefore, was soon face to face with thirty or forty thousand
men instead of sixteen thousand.[1] At length, when the
siege guns were ready to open fire, it was found that the
opposing trenches were vacant. The enemy had taken time
by the forelock and made off in the direction of Williamsburg
and Richmond. McClellan followed and in due course
gained the line of the Chickahominy within ten miles or less
of Richmond. So far, all may be said to have gone well
with the campaign, — and slowly.

In November, 1861, McClellan had been placed in
command of all the armies of the United States and had
issued orders to Buell and Frémont, as well as to the generals
in Virginia and Maryland. When he finally determined to
advance by way of the Peninsula, Lincoln appointed him to

[1] McClellan's report with accompanying documents forms vol. xi, pts.
i, ii, iii, of series i of the *Official Records*.
On p. 106 and fol. of pt. i are the original reports of General J. G. Barnard,
chief engineer of the Army of the
Potomac. These should be carefully
compared with letters that Barnard
wrote to McClellan during the campaign that are printed in *McClellan's*
Own Story, and also with Barnard's
book entitled *The Peninsular Campaign
and Its Antecedents, as developed by the
Report of Maj. Gen. Geo. B. McClellan*
(New York, 1864). The body of this
pamphlet was later printed at Washington in 1864 by the "Union Congressional Committee" as a Lincoln
campaign document.

the command of the Army of the Potomac and the President and the Secretary of the War themselves determined upon the movements of the other armies. Naturally, they felt nervous about the military safety of Washington City, because its capture would be equivalent to a great disaster, for European nations were awaiting an opportunity to recognize the Confederacy as an independent nation and Northern opinion was by no means so solidified for the war for the Union as to justify the great loss of prestige that the capture of the capital would have inflicted. Moreover, there appeared in the Valley at this moment one of the few military geniuses that the war produced, Thomas J. Jackson. In the winter of 1861, Jackson was a Union man [1] and voted for the Union candidate to the Virginia convention. When Virginia seceded, he went with it. Jackson was a West Pointer, had served in Mexico, but had resigned from the army and, at the moment, was a teacher in the Virginia Military Institute. Besides his practical training in war, Jackson had employed his spare hours in reading all the available works on military science and the memoirs of the greatest commanders. Indeed, he was accustomed to carry with him Napoleon's "Maxims" and a copy was found in his haversack after his death. Jackson was the embodiment of war, calm in danger, strenuous in conflict, and sparing neither himself nor his men when necessity called.[2] It was such a man who found himself opposed to Banks and

---

[1] See his letter of January 23, 1861. Jackson wrote to a friend that he hoped that Virginia would have no occasion to use certain guns against the Federal government, but he desired to be ready. Furthermore he thought that the Union candidates for the State Convention would be elected.

[2] G. F. R. Henderson's *Stonewall Jackson and the American Civil War* (2 vols., London, 1898) did much to give Jackson the place that he holds in history, but Colonel Henderson's ideas on America and Americans are often based on exceedingly slender foundations. Read in connection with Colonel William Allan's *Stonewall Jackson's Campaign in the Shenandoah Valley* (London, 1912), one gains a vivid impression as to the reasons of the great reputation that Jackson has; but it must be remembered that his reputation

Frémont in the Valley of the Shenandoah. With a little army, in numbers inferior to that of either of his opponents, he attacked first one and then the other and compelled the government at Washington to send one of the divisions, that McClellan had expected to have with him, to the Valley and to retain in front of Washington McDowell's corps which McClellan had regarded as an integral part of the Army of the Potomac. Arrived at the Chickahominy, McClellan insistently demanded that McDowell should march to his aid, and finally he was permitted to do so. Affairs were in this train when, on the last day of May, 1862, General Joseph E. Johnston suddenly attacked at Fair Oaks that portion of the Federal army that had crossed the Chickahominy.[1] In consequence of recent rains this river had risen. The Confederates had destroyed the bridges. McClellan's men had thrown other bridges across the stream, but these were not adequate for the movement of soldiers and guns in great numbers. Notwithstanding the situation of the Federal army and the difficulty of reënforcing it, the results of the first day's combats were distinctly against the Confederates. Advantage was not taken of this at the time, nor was the attack pushed the next day as it might have been. While visiting the front Johnston was severely wounded and Robert E. Lee was placed in command of the Confederate forces in Virginia.

was acquired in campaigns against Frémont, Banks, and Hooker. What would have happened if he had confronted Grant, Sherman, or Sheridan will never be known.

[1] The genesis of this attack was stated by President Davis in a letter to his wife that was dated Richmond, May 28, 1862, and is printed in Rowland's *Davis*, v, 252. In the *Memoirs* (p. 139) of John H. Reagan, a somewhat different statement is made; but this would seem to be an old man's recollection.

In the Southern Historical Society's *Papers*, xx, 106, L. J. Perry makes the suggestion that if McClellan and J. E. Johnston had been continued in their respective commands, the war would have lasted indefinitely, for neither of them believed in fighting, both were skilled in retreating, and "it is doubtful if either had complete confidence in his cause."

General Lee's first military command had been in western Virginia, in the mountains; and, owing to various causes — the inefficiency of his subordinates and a continuous rainfall — he had accomplished nothing. He next went to South Carolina and Georgia to take charge of the defence of the seacoast. He was summoned from this duty in March, 1862, to serve as military adviser to President Davis. Before the change of command, the Confederate government had begun the concentration of additional forces before Richmond, although it is not certain Johnston had been aware of this when he attacked the Union soldiers at Fair Oaks. For about four weeks, from May 31 to June 26, the two armies faced one another, Lee constantly growing stronger and McClellan constantly becoming weaker, owing to the illness of his soldiers, although he received some small reënforcements. Meantime, the activity of Jackson in the Valley and his successes there had so alarmed the authorities at Washington that they had stopped McDowell's march toward McClellan, recalled him, and placed him and other troops in front of Washington under the command of General John Pope who had been brought from the West to defend the capital. When all was ready, Lee sent his cavalry under J. E. B. Stuart to attack the extreme right of the Union army near the York River, and destroy whatever stores he could, and he summoned Jackson from the Valley as secretly and as rapidly as possible.[1] On Jackson's arrival on June 26, Lee struck the Union army and for seven days attacked again and again. Lee now had ninety-five thousand men in

---

[1] Colonel William Allan's *Army of Northern Virginia in 1862*, chs. vii-xix, is an authoritative account of Lee's first great compaign from the Southern standpoint and may well be read in connection with J. C. Ropes's account of the same operation in his *Story of the Civil War*, ii, ch. ii. Captain T. G.

Frothingham's account of the Peninsular Campaign of 1862 (Massachusetts Historical Society's *Proceedings* for November, 1923, pp. 88–122) is an appreciative sketch of the part played by McClellan. See also J. D. Cox's *Military Reminiscences*, i, chs. xii-xviii.

the field to about the same number of Federals.[1] The disposition of the Union army made reënforcement and concentration matters of great difficulty and each unit practically had to fight where it stood. McClellan already had determined to withdraw the army from the York and the Chickahominy to the James. The *Merrimac* had been destroyed by the Confederates and the James River was open to the Federal vessels to within a few miles of Richmond. Of course such a movement in the presence of an army equal or superior in numbers, led by Lee and Jackson, was a matter of exceeding difficulty, especially as part of the way led through a swamp. It was accomplished in the face of the greatest hazard. On July 1, the Federal army found itself most advantageously posted on the crest of Malvern Hill with both flanks adequately protected and with abundant artillery in position. Lee attacked again and again, to be repulsed with terrible loss. Had the Union line gone forward on that afternoon, the war might have ended then and there. As it was, McClellan withdrew his gallant army to Harrison's Landing, where the gunboats on the James River could coöperate with it.

It was at this time that Halleck, newly arrived at Washington to take up his somewhat anomalous post of general-in-chief, chief of staff, and military adviser to the President, visited McClellan's headquarters. That general declared that with thirty thousand new men he could resume the attack on Richmond. As this reënforcement seemed to be out of the question, Halleck decided to withdraw the Army of the Potomac by water from the James and place it once again in front of Washington,—the greatest single disaster of the war.[2]

[1] Livermore in *Numbers and Losses* (ed. 1900), pp. 86,140 gives the numbers in the "Seven Days' Battles" as Union 91,169, Confederate 95,481.

[2] Major J. F. Huntington regarded the order withdrawing McDowell as productive of "greater injury to the Union cause" than any other order

Before the withdrawal could be accomplished, Lee fore-
stalled him, for he realized that the surest method to
relieve the pressure on Richmond was himself to exert
pressure on Washington. By his orders, Jackson made one
of his phenomenal marches and suddenly interposed himself
between Pope's old command and the leading corps of the
Army of the Potomac. Two days later, Lee joined Jackson
with the bulk of his army and inflicted upon Pope a second
Bull Run defeat (August 30) that was far more bloody than
the first, but did not lead to the disorganization of the Army
of the Potomac. After this, two courses were open to the
Confederates, one was to send a portion of Lee's army by rail
to Tennessee, where Bragg was confronting Buell ; the other
was to cross the Potomac and invade Maryland, to threaten
Baltimore and possibly Philadelphia and relieve the Secessionists of Maryland from the weight of Federal power. The
latter plan was chosen and the crossing of the Potomac was
effected without trouble.

At this moment, when everything seemed to be progressing
favorably for the Confederates, a copy of Lee's orders to
one of his principal commanders fell into McClellan's
hands ; [1] for he had again been placed in command of the
army in front of Washington. He took advantage of the
information, sought out the advancing Southerners, and
attacked them at South Mountain. Lee at once drew back,
but — September 17, 1862 — McClellan fell upon him at the
Antietam near Sharpsburg in Maryland and not far from the
Potomac. The battle that followed was one of the most
desperate of the war and ended in the retirement of the Con-

issued during the war "with the possible
exception of that appointing Halleck
General-in-Chief," *Papers* of the Military Historical Society of Massachusetts, vi, 14.

[1] General D. H. Hill's own account
of the "Lost Dispatch" is in the
Southern Historical Society's *Papers,*
xiii, 420.

federates to Virginia. Although repeatedly urged and even
entreated by Lincoln to follow up this advantage and end
the career of the defeated army, McClellan pursued slowly,
and when it was clear that Lee had saved his men, Lincoln
removed McClellan and gave the command of the Army
of the Potomac to Ambrose E. Burnside.

Military critics, both those who served in the war and
those who did not, have almost to a man criticized McClellan
most harshly as a commander, but always laud him as an
organizer. The letters to his wife and those to President
Lincoln, in "McClellan's Own Story," are a severe condemnation of him. Nevertheless from the workshop of
the unmilitary historical student, the outlook is somewhat
different. General Lee's campaign against Grant in 1864,
from the Wilderness to Petersburg, has always been praised
as having inflicted terrible losses on Grant's army. In those
weeks the Union commander lost forty-five thousand "killed
and wounded" out of a total of one hundred and five thousand or so. From the beginning of the Seven Days' battles
to the close of the conflict at Antietam, McClellan inflicted
a loss of forty-one thousand "killed and wounded" upon
Lee's army of ninety-five thousand men![1] We are told
that McClellan, instead of being at the front in the Seven
Days' battles, employed himself in looking after his communications and left the fighting to his subordinates; and,

[1] L. J. Perry in Southern Historical
Society's *Papers*, xxiv, 138–145 ; T. L.
Livermore's *Numbers and Losses*, 86 and
fol., 110 and fol.

Somewhat out-of-the-way and un-
known descriptions of the Peninsular
Campaign which give a much more
favorable view of McClellan are Hiram
Ketchum's *General McClellan's Penin-
sular Campaign* (1864) ; *The Defence of
Richmond against the Federal Army under
General McClellan. By a Prussian*
Officer in the Confederate Service (New
York, 1863) ; and *The Seven Days'
Battles in Front of Richmond . . .
Compiled from . . . the Newspaper Press*
(Richmond, 1862). Dr. Edward War-
ren of North Carolina in *A Doctor's
Experiences in Three Continents*, 302–
305, states that McClellan could have
marched into Richmond the night after
Malvern Hill with as much ease as he
marched to Harrison's Landing.

again, that at Antietam he commanded in person at the
front when he might well have been in the rear. If losses
tell anything in war, McClellan must have shown some
military aptitude in these conflicts, whether he was in the
rear or near the battle line. As to his ability as an organizer, it seems to the present writer that there was something
wrong with the Army of the Potomac. The bravery of the
individual soldiers and the skill of very many of the commanders of corps and divisions was beyond praise. But
there was a slowness of marching before 1864 that was in
painful contrast to the celerity of movement of its opponent.
When battle was joined, there was a constant failure to use
one's full strength that was not remedied until 1865, and
there was a constant failure to follow up advantages that
lost many an opportunity. Moreover, orders were not given
and obeyed as they should have been in war. How far all
this was due to improper organization and how far it was
due to inexperience may be a matter for debate; but in
some of the other armies there was never hesitation to
use the power that one had to the utmost. How far
McClellan was responsible for the over-supplying the Army
of the Potomac with clothing, food, and equipment may also
be uncertain. It is certain, however, that the very luxury
of campaigning material interfered sadly with the movements of the army; and it was not until the Union soldiers
were stripped for the fight that they became the equals
of their opponents. In any assessment that is made of
McClellan's military capacity and in any comparison that
is made between his qualities as a soldier and those of four
acknowledged successful Union commanders, Grant, Sherman, Sheridan, and Thomas, it must be borne in mind that
McClellan exercised his first command in the field at Yorktown, that he was the first person to command an army

of one hundred thousand men on the American continent and that Antietam, his last battle, was a bloody defeat for his opponent. Finally, Lincoln and Stanton in 1862 had not learned the necessity of confiding in the military commanders as they had by 1864.

Instead of occupying the old field of Manassas, Lee took his army to the Rappahannock at Fredericksburg and stationed it in a very strong position on Marye's Heights below that town. Burnside, realizing that action was expected of him and, possibly, also realizing that his former equals, now his subordinates, in command of the units of the Army of the Potomac had slight confidence in him, determined to attack the Confederates where they were, although they were protected by a river, by the slope of steep hills, and by fortifications. On December 13, the Army of the Potomac, or a large part of it, advanced to the attack which was well planned and, had it been pushed in all parts, might possibly have succeeded. As it was, owing to lack of correlation and of enthusiasm, coupled with the strength of the Confederate position and the valor and skill of the Confederates, the attack failed with terrible loss to the attackers and the "horror of Fredericksburg" became one of the most tragic events of the war. Nevertheless, the Army of the Potomac was not disorganized or disheartened and Burnside set to work to maneuver the Confederates out of their position. But everything was against the Union soldiers, the Virginia rains descended and the Virginia roads liquefied. After an ineffectual "mud march" the army returned to its quarters, and Burnside, realizing the lack of confidence that was felt in him by his army and possibly his lack of confidence in himself, tendered his resignation to the President. His successor was "Fighting Joe Hooker," one of the corps commanders of the Army of the Potomac.

In announcing the appointment to him, Lincoln wrote a
remarkable letter in which he adverted to Hooker's failure
to support his chief and suggested to him that while action
was desirable, temerity in the use of a great army was undesirable.   It was an extraordinary letter to write to one to
whom a great place had just been given, and seems to carry
in itself conclusive reasons why the appointment should
not have been made.   It must be admitted that the
Washington government was hard pressed for a successor
to McClellan and Burnside, and Hooker with his soldierly
bearing and successes as a corps commander undoubtedly
seemed to be the most eligible appointee and, indeed, almost
the only one.   Hooker at once set to work with vigor to
reincarnate discipline and enthusiasm in the army and succeeded.   When the roads became dry in the spring of 1863,
the Army of the Potomac once again advanced to the
performance of its task.   This time, Hooker decided to
maneuver Lee out of his entrenchments and crossed the
Rappahannock at some distance from Fredericksburg.
Once on the same side of the river as Lee, Hooker stopped,
his army being enveloped in woods in the Wilderness country, his headquarters being near Chancellorsville.   Why
he should have stopped there instead of moving on into the
open country is difficult to fathom, but stop he did.   Jackson
at once saw the opportunity and suggested to Lee that he
with his "foot cavalry" should march across the front of
the Union army and attack the exposed flank farthest away
from Fredericksburg, while Lee with the main army should
establish the battle in front and a third section should ward
off attacks by General Sedgwick, who with another corps
had crossed the Rappahannock near Fredericksburg.   Jackson's march across the front of the Union army was observed by at least one division officer who reported it to his

chief who in turn transmitted the information to Hooker. It did not seem to interest either of these officers of high rank, who presumably thought the column of dust was raised by the enemy in trying to retreat. Late in the afternoon of May 2, 1863, Jackson attacked and rolled up the right of the Union line, while Lee with the main army attacked in front. Had not the Army of the Potomac been extraordinarily cohesive and disciplined, there would have been grave disaster. As it was, at the moment when the Confederate attack failed Hooker did not order his army forward and, a few days later, he retired behind the Rappahannock, — less than one-half of his men having been in battle. In the evening of May 2, while reconnoitering to find the best approach for another attack, Stonewall Jackson was severely wounded by mistake of his own men and a week later died, and the Confederacy lost its greatest soldier. Why the spirit of inaction so suddenly descended upon "Fighting Joe Hooker" has ever since been a matter of debate. At the time, his enemies — who were many — declared that he was drunk and incapable of performing his duties. Another account states that he was physically incapacitated by the shock of a cannon shot that struck the part of the house near which he was standing or sitting.[1] The drunkenness story has been refuted by abundant evidence. Undoubtedly, he was momentarily stunned, but no such disabling blow could have lasted over forty-eight hours, when he issued the order for retirement. In this way, Lee and Jackson defeated and caused the retirement of a Union force of about double the size of their own.

[1] On May 29, 1863, John C. Ropes wrote to John C. Gray that he had talked with two men who were in the headquarters house when the shell exploded, or within a few minutes thereafter. One of them said that Hooker looked as a man would look "after a pretty severe blow on the head." Another, a staff officer, wrote that "the injury was a severe one, rendering Hooker almost *non compos* for the rest of the day."

Now, a grave question arose as to what should be done with the victorious Army of Northern Virginia. Sound strategy, perhaps, dictated its taking a defensive position in Virginia and sending one-half or one-third its strength to the aid of Bragg and Johnston in the western fighting area. For some reason that is not yet clear, [1] Davis and Lee, or Lee and Davis, determined upon another invasion of the North, where opposition to the war was rapidly developing. Such a movement would procure supplies of food, clothing, and animals which were urgently needed in Virginia. It may be that the desire to free the sacred soil of the Old Dominion from the invader's foot and to carry the war into his own country was the determining factor. Whatever the reason, Lee turned his face to the North and with one of his remarkable movements placed his army across the Potomac and advanced into the heart of southern central Pennsylvania. Lincoln and the Washington government were distressed at this renewed invasion. They directed and implored Hooker to attack, but when this was found to be impossible they removed him and placed General George G. Meade in command on the 25th day of June.[2] It was perilous to change commanders in the presence of the enemy, but Hooker's incapacity to face responsibility was so apparent that nothing else was possible.

By a strange misadventure, Lee found himself deprived of his cavalry. The commander of that force in the Army of

[1] Writing to President Davis on June 10, 1863, General Lee stated that "the decrease of the aggregate of this army," as disclosed by the returns, shows that its ranks are growing weaker and "that its losses are not supplemented by recruits." *Official Records*, ser. i, vol. xxvii, Pt. iii, p. 881.

[2] There are two biographies of Meade, the first by Richard Meade Bache in one volume (Philadelphia, 1897) ; the second, a two volume work (New York, 1913) written by his son, George Meade, and "edited" by his grandson, George G. Meade. The fact that General Meade and Governor and General Wise of Virginia married sisters may have aroused feelings of distrust in the minds of some members of Congress, but there is not the slightest reason to suppose that Meade was ever influenced in the least degree by his wife's Southern connections.

Northern Virginia, General J. E. B. Stuart was one of the
outstanding military figures of the war.   For some reason
he supposed himself to be ordered to ride around the Army

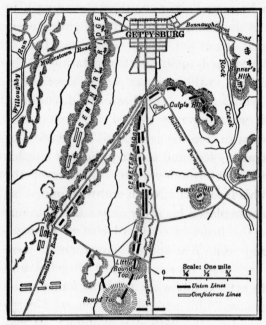

GETTYSBURG, 1863.

of the Potomac
and penetrate
into southern
central Penn-
sylvania.   At all
events, he did so
and for a week
or ten days in
the crisis of the
Confederacy,
Lee was de-
prived of the
eyes of his army.[1]
Hastening for-
ward with ut-
most speed, the
Army of the
Potomac ap-
proached Lee's

line of advance.   Just beyond the little village of Gettysburg,
the Union cavalry came across a body of Confederate soldiers marching toward that town.[2]   The Union cavalry was

[1] There are several interesting articles
on Stuart in the Gettysburg campaign
in the *Papers* of the Southern Historical
Society, especially one by R. H. McKim
in vol. xxxvii, 210–231, and others may
be found through the index volume.

[2] Reports and correspondence relating to the Gettysburg campaign form
parts i, ii, and iii of the *Official Records*,
ser. i, vol. xxvii.   Volume xi of the
Century (1886–1887) contains half a
dozen articles on Gettysburg, including
three by General Hunt, the commander
of the Union artillery in that campaign.
Naturally the Southern Historical Society has devoted much space to this
subject, especially in vols. iv, v, vi, vii,
viii, x, and New Series, v, pp. 55–58.
The best concise account of this
campaign is chapter x of Livermore's
"Continuation" of Ropes's *Story of
the Civil War*, pt. iii, book ii.   Eight
remarkable articles by officers of both
armies are in the *Papers* of the Military
Historical Society of Massachusetts,
vols. iii and iv.

pushed back and an army corps coming up under General
Reynolds, that, too, was driven back in considerable confusion after the death of its commander. It found itself
on a hill overlooking the village and there it was reënforced
by another corps with its commander Major General Winfield Scott Hancock, one of the most brilliant soldiers in the
army. Hancock at once saw the great advantages of the
position for defensive battle. It has often been likened
to the shape of a gigantic fish hook, the curve being
at Cemetery Hill which overlooks the town of Gettysburg,
thence the line, curving around to the right, ended at Culp's
Hill. From Cemetery Hill the line runs along the ridge for
some three to four miles to Little Round Top and to Round
Top beyond. Across from Culp's Hill on the north to the
straight line of the fish hook on the south was about a mile.
By morning of July 2d a large part of the Union army had
come up and been stationed. For some unknown reason,
General Sickles, commanding on the extreme left of the
Union army, instead of stationing his men on the two Round
Tops, took them forward to the level ground in
front.[1] When Lee came on the field he at once saw the
exposed position and determined to attack at that point
and also at the extreme right of Culp's Hill. It took an
unwonted space of time to bring up the Confederate forces
and it was not until the afternoon that the attack was

---

[1] General Meade's recollections as to
General Sickles and one or two other
contested points were set down by him
on paper, March 16, 1870, in a letter
to Colonel G. G. Benedict of Vermont.
This was published in the Philadelphia
Weekly Press of August 11, 1886, and
also in pamphlet form in the same year
with the title of *General Meade's Letter
on Gettysburg*. On November 12, 1863,
Major John C. Gray stated that General
Warren had said that "Sickles would
have been courtmartialed, if he had not
lost his leg." In April, 1864, John C.
Ropes had a long talk with Meade in
which the latter told him that he had
ordered Sickles to prolong the line of the
Second Corps to Little Round Top and
that when he found Sickles's troops
three-quarters of a mile in advance of
that position, he asked him what he was
doing out there; to which Sickles replied
"That he thought they would better
protect Round Top" there.

made.[1] At both ends of the line the Union soldiers were pushed back with considerable losses. At this moment General G. K. Warren ascending Little Round Top in his capacity as an engineer saw at once the importance of that position. He signaled to some Union soldiers that were near the base of the hill to come up; they arrived just in time to prevent its falling into the hands of Confederate troops who had worked their way around the extreme end of the Federal line. It was one of those occurrences in war that makes or loses battles. When night came, the Union army, although it had been defeated at the extreme left, was in stronger position than before; while on the right it had been driven from the post of vantage. Nevertheless it was determined to continue the fight at this point.

The next morning, July 3rd, 1863, the Union soldiers regained possession of Culp's Hill and the ground in front of it, and a strong body of cavalry posted to the southward of the Round Tops was prepared to dispute any further attempt to outflank the Union army in that direction. To Lee the question as to what should be done was of grave import. Should he retire to the Potomac and recross that river into Virginia, incurring all the dangers of pursuit? Or should he make one more effort? He decided to make it. Seek-

---

[1] For years a bitter disputation went on between the biographers of Lee, on the one hand, and General Longstreet and, later, his widow, on the other hand, as to the reasons for the delay on the second day at Gettysburg. The matter is well summed up in a paper by Longstreet, himself, in the *Century*, xi, 628, and by Colonel Allan in *ibid.*, xii, 150. One can read for many, many hours in the biographies of Lee and Longstreet and in the other books on the war and come to no conclusion. Possibly the truth was never stated better than by Jefferson Davis in an article that he wrote on "Robert E. Lee" for the *North American Review* and which is printed in the Appendix to the *Life and Reminiscences of Jefferson Davis by Distinguished Men of his Time* (Baltimore, 1890), p. 411. Whether the failure to occupy Round Top early on the second day of the battle "was due to the order not being sufficiently positive or not" he would leave to others, he wrote. "Lee's natural temper was combative, and to this may be ascribed his attack on the third day . . . when the opportunity had not been seized which his genius saw was the gate to victory."

ing to attack the Union lines at the center, where it was lowest and most accessible, he determined to do this with Pickett's division of Virginia troops which had reached the field of battle that day and was fresh. To aid them, the North Carolina division led by General Pettigrew was to advance on the left, while other troops were to support him on the right and still others to follow on.[1] To prepare for this great assault the Confederate artillery was massed opposite the point of attack. When the time came, one hundred guns opened on the Union position. To this cannonade no adequate reply could be made, because there was not room on Cemetery Ridge for so many guns. What could be done was done. The Confederate cannonade was destructive of horses and material and many soldiers were killed, but nothing in comparison with the amount of noise and ammunition expended. After a time, the Union fire was stopped while some batteries were drawn off and their places taken by others. This was done to prepare the guns for effective work against the infantry attack that was sure to come. It came. Up to that time there had probably been no more splendid military spectacle than those fifteen thousand men marching in open view to the attack. As it was, which presumably Lee did not know, the Union line at the point of assault was somewhat recessed. This gave the guns of batteries on Cemetery Hill the chance to enfilade the advancing ranks. Farther toward Little Round Top

---

[1] Considerable controversy has arisen as to the respective parts played by the North Carolina and Virginia troops at Gettysburg on July 3rd. Of recent years North Carolinians have advanced the idea that their men were first over the Union lines and that the charge should really be called Pettigrew's charge and not Pickett's charge. Naturally this theory has been con-troverted. See especially W. R. Bond's *Pickett or Pettigrew?* (Scotland Neck, N. C., 1888, 2nd ed., 1900) ; W. L. Royall's *Some Reminiscences*, 16–24; J. H. B. Latrobe's *Three Great Battles* (Baltimore, 1863), p. 29 ; the *Papers* of the Southern Historical Society, xxiii, 229 ; and W. H. Trescot's *Memorial of the Life of J. Johnston Pettigrew* (Charleston, 1870), p. 58.

a wooded slope was occupied by a regiment or two which held off the supporting troops in that direction. The artillery in the center opened and was followed by musketry fire, but on went Pickett's men; the foremost of them crossed over the Union lines and advanced even to the cannon. There they were surrounded and those who were not killed, or could not get back, surrendered to the number of four thousand.[1] How many returned unharmed has never been said, but among them was General Pickett. That ended the battle of Gettysburg. The next day both armies remained in position, and on the 5th day of July the Confederates began their movement back to the river.[2] It was swollen by sudden rains and for days could not be crossed, but no attack in large force was made upon it. Such was the battle of Gettysburg which cost the combined armies of one hundred and sixty thousand men nearly fifty thousand in killed, wounded, and missing.[3] On July 4th, while the two armies were resting at Gettysburg, General Pemberton surrendered the garrison of Vicksburg on the Mississippi River to General Ulysses S. Grant.

[1] Captain Young, General Pettigrew's aide-de-camp, stated that the configuration of the ground over which the charge was made was such that "when the left of our line approached his [the Union] works, it must come within the arc of a circle from which a direct, oblique and enfilade fire could be and was concentrated upon it." Trescot's *Pettigrew*, 58. There seems to have been a complete lapse of the necessary orders for the advance of the troops that were to have supported or acted with Pickett or Pettigrew or both of them. Longstreet would not or did not give them and Lee disappears from historical sight for about an hour until the remnants of the charging divisions came streaming back. The Pickett family version is in Mrs. Pickett's *The Heart of a Soldier*, pp. 97–103, and "Editorial Note" on pp. 211–215.

In the study of the campaign of Gettysburg, the author has been greatly aided by the researches of M. L. Wardell of Ingersoll, Oklahoma.

[2] Writing to Davis on July 29, 1863, General Lee stated that on sending back the train with the wounded on July 4, "it was reported that about 5,000 well men started back at night to overtake it." Southern Historical Society's *Papers*, xii, 267.

[3] The losses at Gettysburg in three days were for the Union army 200 for each 1,000 men engaged, and 301 for each 1,000 on the Confederate side. In the Meuse-Argonne campaign of forty-seven days there were 1,200,000 American troops, and the casualties were 120,000. See Livermore's *Numbers and Losses* (pp. 75, 76), and *The War with Germany* (pp. 110, 113), by Colonel Leonard P. Ayres, Chief of the Statistics Branch of the General Staff.

NOTE

Secondary Works. — " Recollections of old men as a source of history," especially of history that pretends to scientific quality, have long been under the ban of " the researcher." With them may be classed historical works laboriously compiled by persons living at the time of the event or even taking part in battles and campaigns. The fact that one's life is contemporaneous with an event or that one took a part, whether leading or humble, in a campaign or battle, does not, except in a very limited way, take the place of training in methods of historical investigation. In fact the prejudices are oftentimes so keen that contemporaneity and participation detract from the value of a book or article. And much the same thing may be said of official reports, which are necessarily written after the event, and in the case of the higher officers are written some time after the event, and based mainly on the reports of subordinates. One gets " local color " and sometimes inspiration from writings of these three classes, and some of them are enumerated in the accompanying note.[1]

[1] Colonel T. L. Livermore's *Days and Events, 1860–1866*, is one of the best books on the war ever printed, and Colonel Theodore Lyman's letters to his wife, written in 1863, 1864, and 1865, and printed under the title of *Meade's Headquarters*, with Livermore's book may pass into the realm of original material. The two volumes entitled *A Cycle of Adams Letters, 1861–1865*, contain many letters from C. F. Adams, Jr. C. A. Dana and J. H. Wilson's *Life of Ulysses S. Grant*, and Wilson's *Under the Old Flag* (2 vols.), and his *Life of John A. Rawlins* have somewhat the same sort of information. An attractive book of this kind is *The Colonel's Diary*, which was kept by O. L. Jackson, of the 63rd Ohio Infantry. General J. L. Chamberlain's *The Passing of the Armies* relates only to the Appomattox campaign. It was written half a century later, but was based on notes "made nearly at the time of the events." A readable book based largely on this is General Morris Schaff's *The Sunset of the Confederacy*.

Possibly, the most vivid of all Confederate personal accounts is General J. B. Gordon's *Reminiscences of the Civil War*. It was written late in life,

apparently without notes, and must be regarded simply as the recollections of an old man. A much more authentic book is General Johnson Hagood's *Memoirs of the War of Secession.* Hagood was in direct command of the Charleston and South Carolina troops at Fort Wagner and at Fort Fisher and Wilmington. The *Memoir and Memorials of General Elisha F. Paxton*, April, 1861–April, 1863, and the history of the Surry Light Artillery by B. W. Jones, a private soldier, entitled *Under the Stars and Bars*, give an entirely different point of view of the workings of the Confederate military system. Contemporary letters written by C. F. Morse, entitled *Letters Written during the Civil War*, give similar information from the Northern standpoint.

Retrospections that make no pretence to any basis of contemporaneous notes are A. R. H. Ranson's "Reminiscences . . . by a Confederate Staff Officer " in the *Sewanee Review*, vols. xxi, xxii, and xxiii; the *Reminiscences* of General Basil W. Duke, C. S. A., and his *Morgan's Cavalry;* and General J. D. Cox's *Military Reminiscences of the Civil War* (2 vols., New York, 1900).

CHAPTER XVI

THE WAR ON THE WATER AND TRADE WITH THE ENEMY

IN 1860 the United States navy was in many ways at its weakest point for two generations. There were a hundred vessels, or so, on the list.[1] Some of these had never been launched, others were wooden sailing ships that had come down from "the Last War with England," — including the immortal *Constitution*. Others were of more modern construction and were greatly liked by the commanding officers of that day because their cabins and berth decks were comfortable and conducive to health. There were thirty-four steam vessels, but some of these were very small, and were tenders to the sailing frigates. Many of the better ships, like the *Merrimac*, were at a navy yard awaiting repairs. The last Congress of Buchanan's time had declined to appropriate money to repair the naval vessels, or to provide them with crews. Also it was more economical to employ the sailing ship than it was to re-engine the steam sloops. Of their kind, the *Congress* and the *Cumberland* were unsurpassed; but they were absolutely unsuited to the needs of warfare in the middle of the nineteenth century, — and many of the steam vessels were not much better. The steam sloops, like the *Hartford*, were the most effective vessels in the navy. They carried a few large guns and possessed a fair amount

[1] "Statistical Data of Ships" in the United States and Confederate navies are given in the first 272 pages of *Official Records . . . Navies*, ser. ii, vol. i, with 21 interesting illustrations. Dr. C. O. Paullin has an altogether too brief article entitled "President Lincoln and the Navy" in the *American Historical Review*, xiv, 284.

of speed for those days. Most of the steam vessels, although small, were well fitted for patrol duty on the African coast and elsewhere. When the war began, it was at once alleged that the cruising ships had been dispersed widely over the Seven Seas with a view to having them afar off, and that the others had been neglected at the navy yards at home. On July 31, 1861, Isaac Toucey [1] wrote to his late chief, James Buchanan, justifying his own actions especially as to the relative numbers of the home and foreign squadrons, and out-of-commission vessels. On the face of it, it would seem that the ships were distributed in an ordinary manner, and that Buchanan had had no money to modernize the navy, even if he had wished to do so. Nevertheless Gideon Welles [2] reflected very sharply on his predecessor and has been followed and exceeded by the writers on the naval history of the war. In truth, in 1861 the United States Navy was obsolescent, and many of its best officers were Southerners by birth, by adoption, or by sympathy.

The new Secretary of the Navy, Gideon Welles, had served as chief of the Bureau of Provisions and Clothing in the Navy Department during the greater part of the Mexican War. With the old bureau chiefs inefficient or sympathetic with the Secessionists and with the tremendous job on hand of building up a new navy and blockading thousands of miles of sea-coast, it was evident that an assistant was needed who combined knowledge of naval matters with administrative capacity. The man was found in Gustavus

---

[1] See Toucey's letter in J. B. Moore's *Works of James Buchanan*, xi, 214. Practically the same disposition of vessels is given in a report made to the House of Representatives in February, 1861, and printed as *House Reports*, No. 87, 36th Cong., 2nd Sess. The committee that made this report stated that the disposition of the naval force was "extraordinary," and reflects the excitement of the hour. A "List and Stations" of vessels in commission, March 4, 1861, is in the first volume of the *Official Records . . . Navies*, p. xv.

[2] This report is printed with the "Message" of the President in *Senate Executive Document*, No. 1, 37th Cong., 1st Sess., p. 85.

Vasa Fox, a native of Saugus, Massachusetts. He had resigned from the naval service and entered the merchant marine, and was now anxious to do what he could for his country. Fox and Montgomery Blair had married sisters, the daughters of Levi Woodbury of New Hampshire,— this gave the Navy Department two votes in the Cabinet instead of one. It made easier the passage of many a measure through Congress, and opened new naval careers to many officers whose Southern or Democratic connections would otherwise have made it difficult for them to gain the confidence of a Northern Secretary of the Navy. The old navy was officered by a disproportionately large number of Southerners. The students at Annapolis had represented the country geographically. After graduation, Northerners had resigned in much greater proportion than Southerners. When the war came, it is astonishing how many of the men from the South remained in the naval service and how able were those who left it for careers in the Confederacy. Of these last, it is only necessary to mention Matthew Fontaine Maury and John M. Brooke.[1]

When the blockade was proclaimed and privateers began to appear upon the ocean, the Navy Department, with or without authority, purchased vessels that could be used on the shallow waters of the Southern States, and when the supply of desirable vessels became scanty, bought almost

---

[1] Of the captains and commanders on the active and reserve lists of the navy, 220 in all, only 49 resigned and "went South." Of the lower ranks, 718 in all, only 199 resigned. Of the engineers, the officers of the Marine Corps, and the warrant officers, 424 in all, only 54 resigned. Taking all grades of the service, including chaplains and doctors, approximately 22 per cent resigned on account of Southern sympathies. These figures are based on a copy of the Register . . . of the Navy of the United States . . . for the year 1861, annotated by Commander, later Admiral, Charles Henry Davis, up to October, 1861. This has been compared with a list prepared by Dr. Gardner W. Allen, with the Register . . . of the Navy . . . to January 1, 1863, p. 108, and with Edward W. Callahan's List of Officers of the Navy of the United States . . . from 1775 to 1900 that was published at New York by L. R. Hamersly & Co. in 1901.

anything that could stay on top of the water and mount a gun or two. It also set about the construction of some up-to-date fighting ships. One hundred and thirty-six vessels were purchased, including fifty-seven sailing vessels, and thirty-six side-wheelers. The sailing vessels could be anchored in the channels leading into Southern harbors, and the side-wheelers were very useful in the rivers and sounds. Usually there was a fighting ship attached to a blockading squadron, but when this was the case she was often at anchor without steam in her boilers, or without much steam in them. It fell out, therefore, that when a Confederate steam vessel essayed to run into a blockaded port or out of it, there was usually no difficulty in getting by the blockading squadron. At the same time, the attempt was dangerous because the tortuous channel might make it necessary to proceed slowly, or one of the blockading steamers might happen to be in motion with a full head of steam. By the autumn of 1861, the difficulties of blockading had become so evident that the experiment was made of closing the port of Charleston by sinking a fleet of vessels laden with stone in the channels leading into it. Sixty vessels were purchased for this "Rat-Hole Fleet," as it was termed in Northern newspapers, at a total cost of one hundred and sixty thousand dollars. The Southerners tried to make capital in Europe out of this experiment by using it to show the helplessness of the blockading fleets, and also to demonstrate by the immorality of the proceeding of permanently closing a port to commerce that the government of the United States was over-stepping all the rules and laws of humanity and also of international law; but they met with slight success. Finally, it should be said that on the rare occasions when a Confederate fighting ship appeared in the midst of a blockading squadron, the vessels that were actually within cannon shot could do little to defend themselves or to prevent the progress of a ship like the *Alabama* or the *Florida*. These episodes afford telling anecdotes for personal memoirs and for more sober narratives; but they really had little or no influence on the course of hostilities. International practice — or law — requires that the entrance to a blockaded port must be hazardous to make the blockade legal, and it certainly was hazardous to attempt to enter any Confederate port after the summer of 1861.

The circumstances of the prisoners taken with the schooner *Savannah* [1] and their indictment as pirates, together with the acknowledgment by the Washington government of the vitality of the Confederate States, induced the Queen of Great Britain and Ireland to issue a proclamation [2] recognizing the Confederates as belligerents, and conferring upon them the rights of belligerents. The Proclamation was dated May 13, 1861, and begins with the usual "whereases." The second of these recited that hostilities have unhappily commenced between "the Government of the United States of America and certain States styling themselves the Confederate States of America." The third whereas declared that being at peace with "the Government of the United States" we determine to maintain a "strict and impartial neutrality" between the contending parties. All British subjects are therefore commanded to observe strict neutrality, and to abstain from violation of the British Foreign Enlistment Act. The Proclamation recites the leading paragraphs of that Act, and then summarizes the things that

---

[1] See *ante*, p. 345.

[2] For the Act of 1819, see *Statutes of the United Kingdom*, vii, p. 901. It is cited as 59 Geo. III, c. 69. The Proclamation is conveniently found in Mountague Bernard's *Historical Account of the Neutrality of Great Britain during the American Civil War*, p. 135. The text of the act is given in F. W. Gibbs's *Recognition: A Chapter from the History of the North American & South American States* (London, 1863), p. 67.

British subjects must not do.   Among these is a prohibition to enter the army or navy of either belligerent, to serve on board any privateer, to fit out, arm, or equip at home or abroad any vessel to be employed as a ship of war, privateer, or transport, to endeavor to break any blockade lawfully established, or to carry "officers, soldiers, despatches, arms, military stores, or material" or any articles deemed contraband by the modern usage of nations.   Nevertheless, the steamer *Trent* carried emissaries of the Confederate States and also despatches, and the *Alabama*, a steamer plainly designed to receive heavy guns, was permitted by Great Britain to take the seas.   The captain, the watch officers, and the engine-room staff of the *Alabama* were Confederates, that is to say they were born within the limits of the United States and were commissioned by the Confederate government.   The sailors almost to a man were British subjects. Yet this vessel, with a crew of violators of the Queen's Proclamation, was allowed to enter a British port and to take on board supplies, and also permitted by the French government to use a French port for purposes of refitting.

The *Alabama* was a fast auxiliary screw steamer and was possibly the best example of her type of vessel then on the ocean.[1]   Her captain, Raphael Semmes, had been one of the most enterprising officers in the United States navy.   After

[1] *The Cruise of the Alabama and the Sumter from the Private Journals and Other Papers of Commander R. Semmes, C. S. N.* was published at London and at New York and, in French, at Paris in 1864.   After the war, Raphael Semmes printed his own account in a book entitled *Service Afloat . . . during the War between the States* (Baltimore, 1887). These books and Arthur Sinclair's *Two Years on the Alabama* (Boston, 1895) give one the story in great detail which is told in briefer compass by Colyer Meriwether in his *Raphael Semmes* (Philadelphia, 1913).   Many important documents are printed in the third volume of the *Correspondence concerning Claims against Great Britain* that was presented before the Tribunal of Arbitration at Geneva and in vols. i, ii, and iii of series i, of the *Official Records . . . Navies.*   Somewhat readable and condensed accounts that are sufficiently accurate for most purposes may be found in C. B. Boynton's *History of the Navy during the Rebellion* and in J. T. Scharf's *History of the Confederate States Navy.*

bringing ship and armament together and destroying a few American vessels, Semmes endeavored to take the *Alabama* into a Confederate port, possibly with some idea of nationalizing her.   Off the entrance to Galveston, he encountered the United States armed vessel *Hatteras*.   She was a converted walking-beam, paddle-wheel steamer with an iron hull, and was in every way greatly inferior to the *Alabama* as an engine of war.   A shot from the Confederate ripped off a section of her iron plates at the water-line and in thirteen or fifteen minutes after the first gun was fired she was sinking. Semmes then put out to sea, and again took up the business of destroying the merchant marine of the United States. The *Alabama's* cruising grounds were constantly shifted [1] to avoid the ships that were on the seas in pursuit of her. Some persons have marveled that the United States Navy Department did not organize a system of convoy, and it has been thought that possibly a few men-of-war stationed at the centers of the routes of ocean travel might have greatly diminished the injuries done to American commerce by the Confederate cruisers.   Apparently, apart from convoying transports on the Mississippi and other rivers, the only attempt made to give this kind of protection to American merchant vessels was in connection with the transportation of gold from California to New York by the way of the Isthmus of Panama.[2]   At one time three vessels were detached from the West Indian squadron to escort these treasure ships through the zone of danger.   It cannot be said that these attempts were entirely welcome to the captains of the

[1] Lew A. Chase has an interesting article on "The Search for the 'Alabama'" in the *Sewanee Review* for July, 1910, pp. 344–358. Information showing the state of the mercantile mind in New York is in "Samuel Hallett & Company's American Circular" dated June 24, 1863.

[2] See Gardner W. Allen's "Naval Convoys" in the *Proceedings* of the Massachusetts Historical Society for May, 1924, and the citations in his footnotes, especially on p. 410.

treasure ships, for they sometimes dropped their escorts behind and made off for New York, trusting to their speed to outrun any Confederate cruiser.

On the 19th day of June, 1864, the *Alabama* met a United States ship of her own class, the *Kearsarge*, off the French port of Cherbourg. Unquestionably the *Kearsarge* was a more formidable ship than the *Alabama*; her hull was clean, her engines in good condition, and her chain cables had been spiked to her sides opposite the engine room. In about an hour the *Alabama* went to the bottom and the *Kearsarge* was uninjured.[1] The result of the combat seems to have been due to the better guns and powder of the Federal vessel and the better gun practice of her crew. Other Confederate cruisers held the ocean for longer or shorter periods and destroyed the property of citizens of the United States. One of these, the *Shenandoah*, at the very close of the war, sailed into Bering Sea and destroyed the greater part of the American whaling fleet there. The money value of the ships and the cargoes destroyed by Confederate cruisers is quite impossible to estimate with any degree of accuracy. A more intelligible way to ascertain the effect of this kind of warfare is to note that in 1862, one hundred and sixty American vessels were sold to foreigners to avoid loss of property by the action of Confederate cruisers, and that in twelve months the proportion of American exports carried in foreign vessels almost doubled.[2] It has often been said that the decline of American supremacy among the commerce carriers of

[1] Besides the papers in the *Official Records . . . Navies*, ser. i, vol. iii, and accounts by Semmes and other officers of the *Alabama* mentioned in note on p. 491, it is interesting to read F. M. Edge's *An Englishman's View of the Battle between the Alabama and the Kearsarge* (New York, 1864) reprinted in William Abbatt's *Magazine of History*, "Extra Number 2," which also contains "The Career of the Alabama" first printed at London in 1864. A description of the combat by the captain of the French warship that escorted the *Alabama* out of Cherbourg Harbor is in *American Historical Review*, xxiii, 119.

[2] F. M. Edge's *Destruction of the American Carrying Trade* (London, 1864), pp. 13–17.

the world was due to the action of the *Alabama* and other
Confederate cruisers and that the war was prolonged by the
damage inflicted by these vessels. In 1860, the United
States was first among the commerce carriers of the world.
Her clipper ships were the marvels of the day for speed and
beauty and their performances in all kinds of weather were
justly celebrated in song and story; but their days were
numbered. The iron hull was slowly replacing the wooden
ship as a commerce carrier and steam was supplanting sail
as motive power. The United States could not, or at any
rate did not, then compete with Great Britain as a maker
of iron. It had fallen out, therefore, that the American
merchant fleet was year by year giving place to that of
Great Britain. The *Alabama* and her consorts hastened
the process which was effectually quickened by the hostile
and unjustifiable actions of British marine insurance under-
writers in giving unduly favorable terms to iron hulls.[1]
Also, the tremendous industrial and agricultural expansion
that was going on in the United States in the dozen or twenty
years after 1861 diverted American capital from the sea to
the land. As to the prolongation of the conflict, it is difficult to see how that was brought about by the *Alabama* and
her consorts. Some American capital was destroyed by
the sinking of American ships and their cargoes and some
commodities that would have been useful in the United
States were sent to the bottom of the sea. It is improbable
that either of these affected, to any important extent, the
campaigns of McClellan and Johnston, Grant and Lee, or
Sherman and his opponents. On the other hand, the
attempt of the Confederates to use British resources for their
own purposes aroused an irritation that partly explains the

[1] These facts are set forth with
abundant figures in W. W. Bates's
American Navigation, The Political
History of its Rise and Ruin (Boston,
1902), especially chs. xix and xx.

failure of the Confederacy to secure recognition as a separate sovereign power by Her Majesty, Queen Victoria. It is impossible to probe into the minds of Palmerston and Russell and other powerful men in Great Britain, but it must have occurred to some of them that the example set by the *Alabama* was of direful omen for Great Britain in wars that were certain to come. And the actions of the Russians in sending a fleet [1] of potential commerce destroyers to New York to await war must have produced some misgivings.

By far the most interesting feature of naval warfare of these years was the introduction of iron-clad vessels, of self-acting anchored torpedoes, and of vessels more or less completely submerged and equipped to explode a torpedo against the side of an enemy ship. The origin and history of iron-clad fighting ships and their introduction into the Union and Confederate navies, like so many historical problems, is veiled in obscurity. [2] The iron-clad ship was no novelty in 1861. During the Crimean War, the French naval authorities had constructed iron-clad floating batteries that proceeded under their own power from Toulon to the Black Sea. They bombarded the Russian batteries at Kimburn in the Crimea and received their fire in return without much damage,— so far as accessible records show. These floating batteries were certainly anterior in point of time to the *Monitor* and the *Virginia*, but how much of a precedent they were is not by any means clear. The attention of British and French naval men in the years between 1856 and 1861 was directed toward providing an iron-clad broadside cruising ship. The difficulty in the way of accomplish-

---

[1] See, for its influence on the Russians in 1863, *ante*, p. 366.

[2] There is an interesting article on "Mail-Clad Steamers" by E. H. Derby in the *Atlantic Monthly* for August, 1861, p. 227, another on "Iron-Clad Ships" by Alex. L. Holley in *ibid.*, for January, 1863, p. 85, and a third by Jacob W. Miller, U. S. N., in *The Record* of the United States Naval Institute for 1879, pp. 513–536.

ing such a design was the great weight of any armor that would effectively protect the above-water portions of a cruising steamship, — either the armor must be very thin or only a portion of the vessel could be protected. In the French ship, *La Gloire*, armor was used of such thinness that nowhere was there effective protection, except against guns of small calibre. On the English ship *Warrior*, heavier plating was used, but the ends of the ship were unprotected. In the 1840's Robert L. Stevens of Hoboken in New Jersey and the Federal naval constructors, or all of them acting more or less together, had prepared the plans of an iron-clad ship that would have fairly good protection for the battery and the machinery. The ends were to be made safe by being provided with a water-tight deck below the surface so that the unprotected above-water portion might be shot away without anything happening to the vital parts of the vessel. By slanting the sides and ends of the armored portion, extra protection would be obtained from the guns of a ship or a fort at the same level. This battery was also to be provided with a beak, after the manner of the ancient war galleys, that could penetrate the side of a hostile ship and put an end to her in that way. The relation of the plans of the 1840's to the first iron-clad ship that actually took part in naval combat is not at all clear. The Stevens battery was never completed and accepted. It would seem that the inventors of that decade tried to do what was entirely impossible in the prevailing condition of engineering science. Nevertheless, the influence of these ideas on those who produced some of the iron-clad vessels of 1861–1865 was considerable, perhaps decisive.

The origin of the naval programs of the Union and Confederate authorities in 1861 is still debatable. Gideon Welles has always been represented as a fossilized Connecti-

cut politician and newspaper man, — possibly because of
his Apostolic appearance and Biblical name. Of course,
it is not to be supposed that Welles was the originator of
the new policy of the Navy Department, but it is not at all
certain that the building of iron-clad fighting ships was a
new policy in the Navy Department in 1861. The government had assisted Stevens and had watched with interest
what was going on in England and in France in the production of armored ships. Many officers of the navy, also, had
become thoroughly interested in the subject. When Congress came together, Welles reported to the President as to
the desirability of investigating the problem of armored
ships and, somewhat later, Congress made an appropriation
of twelve millions of dollars to pay for building some ships.
Three of these were undertaken and in due course of time
were launched and took their place in the fighting line.
These ships were the *Monitor,* the *Galena,* and the *New
Ironsides.* The last named was of the English *Warrior*
type, a partly protected sea-going-cruising ship with unprotected ends. Her plating was not thick. Good fortune
always attended her; but she was the only vessel of her class
that was ever built for the United States navy. The
Galena was so lightly armored that after one action, she
was permanently withdrawn from the fighting line. The
third type of armored ship and the vessel that was first
completed was the *Monitor.* She was built from plans provided by John Ericsson, an immigrant from Sweden. As
to the genesis of his ideas and of the turreted low-freeboard
ship, there is considerable confusion. The Ericssonites
have always looked upon the Scandinavian as the sole inventor of that particular type of war vessel; but an Englishman, Captain Cowper Coles, has also many advocates.
It is said that Ericsson presented plans of an armored

floating battery, with a turret or a cupola, to Napoleon III in 1855 or earlier, but the evidence is dubious. The one thing certain is that Ericsson, largely by reason of his intense belief in himself and because of his skill as an engineer and scientific man, designed an armored fighting ship that did voyage on the troubled waters of the Atlantic seaboard, did fight a floating battery that embodied the Stevens idea, and remained afloat to serve as the prototype of a fleet of improved monitors that rendered effective service to the Union cause and were themselves an important step in the evolution of the modern battleship.

If the story of the building of the *Monitor* is somewhat vague and uncertain, it is no more vague and no more uncertain than the story of the production of her Confederate opponent, the made-over *Merrimac* that was re-christened *Virginia*. The Confederate Secretary of the Navy, Stephen R. Mallory, for years had been the chairman of the Senate committee on the navy. With his business ability and his knowledge of ships and commerce, he was a most useful member of that committee and, being the man that he was, he absorbed a great deal of information. He was the only Secretary of the Confederate naval department and was a most efficient one; but for some unexplained reason he acquired almost at once a large measure of unpopularity with the people of the Confederacy that went with him to the end and seems to have been absolutely undeserved. Almost at once he made up his mind that it would be idle for the Confederacy to try to compete with the people of the North in the production of wooden sea-going steamships. Whatever vessels of that type they required would have to be captured from the enemy or procured in England, or France, or elsewhere. He advocated strongly the production of iron-clad, harbor-defence, blockade-breaking vessels.

He appointed a committee or commission to advise him on the matter, and their report coinciding with his own views, he authorized the building of the vessel that was afterwards christened *Virginia*. Mallory had received sundry plans, how many they were in number and exactly from whom they came, is doubtful; and it is also not exactly clear what the precise connection between them and the United States naval plans of 1846 or 1848 may have been. In the uncertainty it is best to hazard no conjecture as to the actual author or inventor of the *Merrimac;*[1] but it is perfectly certain that the inception of the policy of the Confederacy really belonged to Mallory, no matter who furnished the actual plans for the first ship or for the first two or three Confederate armored vessels. It was extremely desirable to break the blockade of the James River as soon as possible and, if it could be done, to capture or neutralize Fortress Monroe and seal up the mouth of the Potomac River to the uses of the Federal government. It was designed, therefore, to build a vessel for the navigation of the James and the Chesapeake and it was not at all necessary that a vessel designed for this purpose should be able to navigate the open sea and proceed on cruises of months' duration. The general idea of the *Virginia* or *Merrimac* was to take an existing hull, cut off the top of it and build, on the razeed lower

[1] As to the conversion of the *Merrimac* into the *Virginia*, see Mallory's "Report" of May 8, 1861, in *Report of Evidence taken before a Joint Special Committee [Appointed, August 27, 1862] of both Houses of the Confederate Congress,* p. 356. Commander John M. Brooke's statement is on p. 409. The Porter side of the case is given at great length in Naval Constructor John L. Porter's son, John W. H. Porter's *Record of Events in Norfolk County, Virginia, from April 19th, 1861, to May 10th, 1862* (Portsmouth, Va., 1892), ch. xlvii. In the *Papers* of the Southern Historical Society there are many contributions on the subject which can be found through the index volume, and see also William Tindall's "True Story of the Virginia and the Monitor" in the *Virginia Magazine of History,* xxxi, 1–38, 89–145. The Wise family had an idea that Governor and General Wise had directly or indirectly something to do with the production of the *Virginia;* see B. H. Wise's *Life of Henry A. Wise,* 317; J. S. Wise's *End of an Era,* 191, 193; and H. A. Wise's *Seven Decades of the Union,* 279–282.

hull, an iron roof-like structure with a flat top and with sloping sides projecting two or three feet into the water and protecting the point of junction of the wooden hull and the iron superstructure. The ends of the hull were to be unarmored, provided with a water-tight deck, and submerged a foot or two under the surface, and the bow was to be provided with a beak. Haste in building and getting the armored battery into commission was of the utmost importance. It was necessary, therefore, to use whatever means could be found at hand. What happened, therefore, was that the Confederates floated the United States steam sloop *Merrimac* that had been partly consumed by fire and sunk off the Norfolk Navy Yard. Work progressed as rapidly as possible, but delays were inevitable and errors of construction were also inevitable. It happened, therefore, that when the reconstructed *Merrimac*, now the Confederate iron-clad *Virginia*, raised her anchor and proceeded to begin her work of destruction she possessed several grave faults that seriously affected her later career. In the first place, in such an experimental vessel, difficulty was found in attaching the plates to the wooden backing and these easily became loosened. Again, an error had been made in the calculation as to the weights, so that the unarmored ends instead of being submerged were two feet or so above water, thus exposing the rudder chains that ran over the top of the after-deck. Then her beak was so insecurely fastened to her bow that it came off the first time that it was used. Finally, the engines of the *Merrimac* had been condemned and when repaired and made serviceable for temporary use, were able to propel the ship only at the rate of about six or seven miles an hour, and floating light as she was, she still drew so much water that she had to confine her operations to the deeper channels of the lower James and Hampton

Roads. It must be said, again, that the *Virginia* was not built to sail the high seas.

On March 8, 1862, the *Virginia* left her moorings with a gang of workmen aboard and with an absolutely green crew and proceeded on her mission of destruction under the command of Franklin Buchanan. The first vessels she encountered were the two sailing ships, the *Congress* and the *Cumberland.* These were beautiful and effective vessels of the type of a quarter or half a century earlier. Charging the *Cumberland* and utterly regardless of the balls that poured from her broadside guns, the *Virginia* made a great hole in her side and drew away leaving her to sink to the bottom. She then turned on the *Congress*, whose paymaster was Buchanan's own brother. That vessel being aground and her own beak having disappeared the *Virginia* essayed to destroy her by gunfire and succeeded with practically no damage to herself. The *Virginia* then returned to Norfolk, her captain and crew well satisfied with their day's work and looking hopefully forward to the destruction of two or three more of the large wooden vessels of the United States Navy. It happened that while the reverberations of her guns were still sounding as far as Cape Charles, the Ericsson-turreted steamer *Monitor* passed the Capes of the Chesapeake and headed for Hampton Roads.[1]

The *Monitor* was an iron vessel with a raft-like deck composed of wood and heavily plated and extending six feet beyond the hull on the sides and at a greater distance at the bow and stern, thus protecting the anchor-well and the propeller and rudder.[2] Her turret was round with a flat top composed of iron grating and revolving on a central spindle.

[1] The conversion of the *Merrimac* into the *Virginia* had been anxiously followed by the naval officers at Washington, as is seen by the reports made to them and printed in *Official Records, . . . Navies*, vi.

[2] See Note at end of chapter.

When in battle, the smoke from her furnaces came through a hole on the deck under forced draft. Her wheel-house was built of heavy iron logs, well forward. She had two guns of eleven-inch calibre. Nobody had much faith in the *Monitor*, except her designer and half a dozen officers in the navy. She was built at top speed at Hoboken in some one hundred days, was armed with guns that had been provided for another vessel, and sent to sea with officers and crew who had never worked together. Knowledge of imminent attack by the *Virginia* caused the government to send her southward at the very earliest possible moment in tow of a sea-going tug. Heavy weather, which nearly sent the *Monitor* to the bottom, prevented her reaching Hampton Roads before the first appearance of the *Virginia*.[1] On Sunday morning, March 9, the *Virginia* again steamed toward Hampton Roads. She directed her course for the steam wooden frigate *Minnesota*, one of the most beautiful vessels in the "Old Navy," that had gone to the assistance of the *Cumberland* and the *Congress* and had run aground on the side of the channel, where she still remained. As the *Virginia* approached, there emerged from under the side of the *Minnesota* a queer-looking object that was conjectured to be a water tank or a floating magazine. To the astonishment of the officers of the *Virginia*, this object steamed out to meet her. The tank slowly revolved, the mouths of two guns appeared, and two eleven-inch solid shot came crashing against the *Virginia's* iron-clad house, without producing much effect.[2] The Federal ordnance bureau had had little

---

[1] John Ericsson's own account of "The Monitors" is in the *Century* for December, 1885, pp. 80–299.

[2] For the actual engagement, see *Official Records . . . Navies*, ser. i, vol. vii, index under "Monitor," "John L. Worden" and "S. D. Greene." An interesting letter from Lieutenant Greene to his mother, dated March 14, 1862, five days after the fight, is in the *Proceedings* of the United States Naval Institute from November, 1923. An excellent and brief account of this epoch-making encounter is in vol. v, ch. xiii of Nicolay and Hay's *Abraham Lincoln, A History*.

experience with the eleven-inch smooth-bore gun and the life of the *Monitor* was so precious that no chances could be taken. Her commander, therefore, had been strictly ordered to use no more than fifteen pounds of powder at a single charge, — about one-half or one-third of what was used in later battles. Then followed a most curious combat. The *Monitor* was faster than the *Virginia* and drew so little water that she could sail almost anywhere in Hampton Roads without much danger of grounding. As soon as the *Monitor's* officers realized that the guns of the *Virginia* were producing no effect, they closed on her and, had they realized her weak points and had they used heavier charges, they might have inflicted serious damage. The *Virginia*, beakless as she was, tried to sink her antagonist by ramming. She managed to hit her broadside, but the blow produced no effect beyond a dent in her overhanging armor. After the fight had been going on for some time, a shot from the *Virginia* struck the side of the iron log hut that served as a wheel-house on the *Monitor* and blinded Worden, who was looking out through one of the spaces between the iron logs. For some minutes the *Monitor* was absolutely without control of any kind and steered about in all directions. As soon as Lieutenant Greene, second in command, realized that something was wrong in the wheel-house, he turned over the turret to another, made his way forward, and took command. Ultimately the *Virginia* retired to Norfolk with her plating somewhat shaken, and the *Monitor* at the end of the

Southern Historical Society's *Papers*, xiii, 90, contains a reprint of the interesting portion of the documents printed in the *House Report*, No. 1725, 48th Cong., 1st Sess. Among these is Buchanan's "Report" of March 27, 1862, describing the first day's fight and enclosing Catesby Jones's statement as to the combat with the *Monitor*. Some fifteen years later, Jones wrote an account of the combat from memory, adding many details, especially as to the injuries of the *Merrimac*. This is printed in Southern Historical Society's *Papers*, xi, 65 and in *United Service*, viii, 660; and was severely commented on by J. W. H. Porter in his *Record of Events*.

fight — except for the injury to the wheel-house — was absolutely unharmed.[1] This combat and that of the day before spelled the doom of the existing navies of the world.

Meantime, on the Mississippi, new types of vessels had appeared. On the Union side, the ideas seem to have come from James B. Eads, Charles Ellet, and, possibly, General Frémont. Eads's plan was to take ordinary river steamboats and protect with armor their machinery, pilot house, and guns, — so far as it could be done. The first vessels were made over for the army; but the officers were principally from the navy, and, by the middle of 1862, the fleet itself and its appurtenances were transferred to the Navy Department. Gunboats built and armored entirely for war purposes followed these first transformed merchant vessels. The later ones were large, flat-bottomed scows with good engines, heavily armored, heavily armed, and capable of a good rate of speed, and they rendered effective service. Ellet's idea was to convert ordinary river boats into rams by strengthening them fore and aft and giving them some protection against gun-fire.[2] They were also provided with a small armament for defence rather than for offence. The Confederates had anticipated the Union authorities. They had made over existing steamers into rams, but these were not so efficiently protected as were the Ellet rams. When the two types came together off Memphis on June 6, 1862, the Ellet rams triumphed, although at the loss of their inventor and commander.

The Confederates in the Mississippi Valley also undertook

---

[1] In December, 1862, the *Monitor* went to the bottom in a gale off Hatteras and the *Virginia* was set on fire, May 11, 1862, by her crew to prevent her falling into the hands of the Federals. The destruction of the *Virginia* greatly accelerated Mallory's decline in popularity, but the correspondence printed in vol. vii of the *Official Records . . . Navies* shows that he was doing everything in his power to induce Commodore Tattnall to go out and fight.

[2] *History of the Ram Fleet and the Mississippi Marine Brigade . . . The Story of the Ellets and their Men* (St. Louis, 1907).

the construction of several vessels of exceedingly novel
types. One class was composed of small vessels, existing
tug-boats, or something of the kind with an iron turtle-back
top. They carried one gun and were designed for ramming.
Owing to the difficulties experienced in providing efficient
engines and machinery, the *Manassas*, a ram of this class,
never accomplished much. The *Louisiana* and the *Arkansas*
were vessels of the *Merrimac-Virginia* type built for the
purpose from the keel up. The same difficulties delayed
their construction and their speed and power as befell all the
Confederate vessels. The only heavy machinery in the
Confederacy for welding and hammering was at Richmond
and these vessels were built in the Mississippi basin. The
Arkansas made a spectacular dash through the Union fleet,
but she did little damage and was set on fire by her own officers at the apparition of a bogus monitor. The *Louisiana*
might have been a formidable vessel, but when she went
down the river to aid the forts in opposing Farragut's fleet,
she had gangs of working men still on board and her pro-
pelling machinery was so feeble that her commander was
quite unwilling to take many chances and she therefore
proved to be quite harmless. The most interesting of the
Confederate vessels to be built on the banks of the great
river was the armored floating battery *Mississippi*. Her
designers were certain Tift brothers, natives of Mystic,
Connecticut, then residing in Key West. They were
friends and business workers with Mallory. The idea was
to design a hull that could be constructed by ordinary house
carpenters out of common-shaped balks of timber. Upon
this heavy wooden-scow-hull was to be built an iron house
or an iron-plated house into which could be introduced one,
two, or three engines and a few large guns. Of course a
vessel of this type could not proceed far away from a har-

bor, but on the multitudinous rivers, bays, and sounds of
the Confederate States there would be ample opportunity
for her to interfere with blockades and to make difficult or
impossible the occupation by Union forces of amphibious
regions like the sounds of North Carolina and the Mississippi
basin. The building of the *Mississippi* in the outskirts of
New Orleans was a heart-breaking affair for its designers
and contractors. No sooner was the work well under way
than the carpenters struck. The machinery for its propul-
sion proved to be most difficult to procure. It had to be
made at various places, all the way from New Orleans to the
Tredegar Works at Richmond, where two steamboat shafts
were welded into one to provide the main shaft for the
Mississippi, — and the workmen at Richmond also saw their
opportunity and struck for higher wages. In the end, when
Farragut ran by the forts in April, 1862, the only thing to
be done was to tow the partly built ship out into the stream
and set her on fire, her guns at the moment being distributed
at different points on the railroads leading to New Orleans.
Probably there is no better way to understand the handicap
under which the Southerners fought for their independence
than to read the evidence in the inquiry that was held as to
the delays in the construction of the *Mississippi*.[1] Near
Plymouth, in North Carolina, the Confederates built a

[1] The *Mississippi* was designed to
have three engines and three propellers,
two of them to aid in steering the scow-
like craft. The only engines procurable
were those in actual operation on river
steamboats and these had to be altered
over from walking-beam engines to
direct-acting engines. The iron manufacturers at New Orleans either could
not or would not do the work required in
providing new parts and this had to be
let out to contractors in Tennessee,
Georgia, and Virginia. The *Report of
Evidence taken before a Joint Special
Committee of Both Houses of the Confed-*
*erate Congress to Investigate the Affairs
of the Navy Department* (Richmond, Va.)
contains a mass of interesting information as to the attempt to defend New
Orleans, — two plans or diagrams on
pp. 159 and 165 give some idea of the
Mississippi; see especially pp. 192,
235, 373, 394, and 406. See also
"Letter of the Secretary of the Navy"
(U. S. *Senate Executive Document*, No.
56, 37th Cong., 2nd Sess). Accompanying this and in the *Official Records . . .
Navies,* ser. ii, vol. i, are illustrations
showing various vessels of the Confederate navy.

vessel resembling in general the *Mississippi*. Her career
was a short one, but in a few weeks she drove away the
Union forces and fought two actions with naval vessels.
Her career was ended by Lieutenant Cushing exploding a
spar torpedo against her, as she was tied up to the river's
bank for repairs. The last and best of the Confederate
iron-clads was the *Tennessee*, a vessel of the *Virginia* type
with a few improvements. She was built at Selma in the
heart of Alabama and floated down the river to Mobile, where
her guns and fuel were placed on board. She resisted the
attacks of Farragut's fleet, including three river monitors,
for hours before she surrendered,[1] on August 5, 1864.

The first monitor was built at great speed and under
tremendous pressure. As the first vessel of her type in the
world, it was inevitable that she should be defective in many
respects and it was also quite certain that with time and
experience and all the resources of Northern shipyards and
iron works at their command, Ericsson and the naval constructors would within a year or two produce the finest
vessel of that type, and so it proved. The size of the
vessel was increased and the heavily plated deck was fastened more securely to the hull. The wheel-house was
placed on top of the turret and some of the larger monitors
were provided with two turrets carrying four guns. It was
one of these improved monitors, the *Weehawken*, that put
an end to the Confederate ship, *Atlanta*, a vessel of the
Virginia type, in about fifteen minutes and would doubtless
have done the same thing to the *Tennessee*. In 1866, Gustavus Vasa Fox crossed the Atlantic in the *Miantonomoh*, a
large double-turretted monitor and, years later, the *Monad-
nock*, a vessel of the same class, made the voyage across the
Pacific from California to the Philippines.

[1] *Report of the [Confederate] Secretary of the Navy,* November 5, 1864, p. 3.

Among the later vessels in the Confederate navy, the *Oreto*, rechristened the *Florida* after her acquisition by the Southerners, had an interesting story. Her early career as a commerce destroyer was not particularly distinguished, but in May, 1862, she fell into the hands of Captain John N. Maffitt. He at once signalized his command by taking her into Mobile through the blockading squadron in broad daylight. And then, after she had been thoroughly cleaned and repaired and put into as good condition as possible, he took her out of Mobile through the blockading squadron and sailed away. This feat gave great comfort to the dwellers within the Confederacy at the time and to writers on the prowess of the Confederate navy since, but in reality it could hardly have been different, for it was impossible to keep the blockading fleet under weigh with full pressure in the boilers night and day. At all events, the *Florida*, now commanded by Captain Morris, after capturing some merchant ships and destroying them, found her way into the harbor of Bahia, Brazil, and was there discovered by Commander Napoleon Collins of the United States vessel *Wachusett*.[1] Relying on the security of anchorage in a neutral port, the captain and part of the crew of the *Florida* were on shore when the *Wachusett* suddenly collided with the ship. The Federals took possession of her after some resistance, pulled up her anchor, and towed her out to sea. In course of time, the two vessels turned up within Chesapeake Bay and there was great noise of reclamation and, indeed, the United States had very little that could be said in defence of Commander Collins. There was nothing to be done, but to hand the *Florida* over to the Brazilian authorities, salute the Brazilian flag, and express regrets. All these were done or were about to be done, when the *Florida* sank at her moorings and

---

[1] *Official Records . . . Navies*, ser. i, vol. iii, p. 254 and fol.

nothing remained but the apologies and the salute to the Brazilian flag.

Torpedoes and submersible boats [1] had been known since the American Revolution and the beginning of the nineteenth century and are associated with the names of Bushnell and Fulton.[2] A few torpedoes were used in the Crimean War. In 1842, Colonel Colt, the maker of a very well-known type of pistol, blew up a schooner by a torpedo that was exploded by means of an electric circuit, but the first extended use of underwater offensive and defensive weapons was made by the Confederates. The idea of using these weapons extensively seems to have been due to Mallory and to have been defended by the same arguments as he advanced for the building of iron-clad ships. Considering the poverty of the South in metal and metal workers, the showing that was made by the Southerners in the next few years was remarkable. They constructed and used anchored torpedoes that were exploded by contact with a floating object. They also used torpedoes that were anchored and were exploded by electricity operated from a station on shore. The most interesting development of all was the construction and use of a semi-submersible boat and of a boat that was wholly

[1] The best book on the undersea warfare of this time is J. S. Barnes's *Submarine Warfare, Offensive and Defensive* (New York, 1869) which is abundantly supplied with illustrations. There is an interesting article by Admiral Porter on "Torpedo Warfare" in the *North American Review* for September, 1878. In 1882, Commander R. B. Bradford of the United States navy published at the Torpedo Station at Newport, a *History of Torpedo Warfare*, the last half of which is devoted to the years 1861–1865. Of course the subject is taken up in Scharf's *Confederate States Navy*. After the war, Hunter Davidson felt impelled to criticize the claims put forward for Lieutenant Maury's part in connection with the development of the Confederate torpedo service, see Rowland's *Jefferson Davis*, index under "Davidson" and "Torpedo." Davidson also wrote "Torpedoes in Our War" in the *Proceedings* of the United States Naval Institute, No. 86. Many official papers may be found through the indexes of the several volumes of the *Official Records . . . Navies* under "Torpedo," "Davidson," "Maury," and under the names of the ships that were destroyed.

[2] For Fulton's experiments, see the present work, vol. iv, 437 and *note;* and see also the *Baltimore Gazette* for December 12, 1805, for an experiment by a "Mr. Francis" off Dover.

submerged beneath the surface of the water. The first type was known to the Southerners as the "David," presumably in reference to David and Goliath. This type of craft was actuated by a steam engine and therefore had a boiler, a furnace, and a smoke-pipe. When approaching an enemy, she was submerged so that only the wheel-house, the smoke-pipe, and the apparatus for discharging the torpedo were above water. The torpedo was carried at the end of the spar projecting from the bow and was exploded by means of a cord that was pulled by the man in the wheel-house. A boat of this type was practically invisible and in the night time, proceeding slowly so as not to disturb the surface of the water, was actually invisible. One of these "Davids" succeeded in placing a torpedo against the *New Ironsides* and gave her a severe shock, but did not sink her. The most interesting craft, however, was the submersible that was built at Mobile and known as the *H. L. Hunley* from the name of her builder.[1] She seems to have been a practical replica of Fulton's submersible boat in that she was propelled by a screw actuated by man power. Besides a rudder, she had side fins that were expected to direct her course up and down in the water. She was intended to tow a contact torpedo behind her, to dive under a vessel when the towing torpedo would explode and tear a hole in the enemy's hull. From Mobile she was taken to Charleston and after drowning five different crews in experimental trips was finally used as a semi-submersible craft or "David," with a spar torpedo. She succeeded in exploding one of these against the side of the *Housatonic*, a fine new steam sloop of war and sending her to the bottom. When the war was over and the submerged hulks removed from the bar off Charleston, she was

[1] "The Confederate Submarine Torpedo Boat Hunley" by W. A. Alexander of Mobile in *The Gulf States Historical Magazine*, i, 81–91, gives an interesting description of the boat and narrates its career.

found on the bottom one hundred yards distant from her victim. Besides these ways of using torpedoes or explosive bombs, the Confederates constructed bombs of iron in the shape of lumps of coal which were smeared with coal dust and tar to conceal their identity. It is supposed that one of these, placed in the coal bunker of the *Greyhound*, General Butler's headquarters boat, destroyed her at the moment when both Butler and Admiral Porter were on board. Another "infernal machine" was a harmless-looking packing box which was filled with powder and contained a clock that at a given moment would explode a percussion cap. Undoubtedly, one of these machines caused an explosion, fire, and destruction near General Grant's headquarters at City Point on the James River. In a memorial presented to Jefferson Davis in 1864, it was stated that a secret organization of friends of the Confederacy had caused the destruction of ten transports, but how far this was true and to what extent this destruction had been caused by infernal machines is not stated, but it is reasonably certain that several transports were so destroyed. All in all, the destructive effects of the use of torpedoes, more or less submersible boats, and infernal machines of one sort or another, was considerable. More serious, possibly, was the caution that the employment of such means of destruction implanted in the minds of Union naval officers and led them to remain at anchor many a time when they might have accomplished something by risking all, as Farragut did at Mobile Bay, immediately after the *Tecumseh* had gone down before his eyes — destroyed by a torpedo.

The blockade of the Confederate seaports grew stricter and stricter almost every month after the beginning of the year 1862. The seizure of the lower Mississippi by a Union fleet under Farragut closed one of the most difficult inlets

to blockade in the whole Confederate coast line. The great
fleet that lay permanently off Charleston, with the stone
ships sunk in the channel, practically sealed that port; the
occupation of Roanoke Island in February, 1862, gave the
Unionists the control of Pamlico and Albemarle Sounds and
of the rivers emptying into them; and the maintenance of
the blockade of the James River with the occupation of
these sounds practically closed Virginia and North Carolina
to sea-borne trade, except that of the Cape Fear River to
Wilmington. Farther south, the coasts of Florida lay open
to the blockade runner to a great extent, but the conditions of
transportation from Florida northward were then so crude
that heavy goods could not be sent into the Confederacy
through that State.[1] By 1863, therefore, Wilmington,
Mobile, and the Rio Grande were the only available entrances
into the Confederacy from the sea. The effectiveness of
the blockade varied from time to time, owing to changes in
commanders and to the necessity of using serviceable ships
in other directions. It became so efficient, however, by 1862,
that entirely new methods of breaking it had to be adopted.
It was practically impossible for an ordinary sea-going
steamer to carry her cargo from Great Britain into a blockaded port. The entrances to Southern harbors were
generally shoal and tortuous and dangerous for a large
steamer running at full speed. Moreover, her cargo was
liable to capture and the vessel, too, almost anywhere on
the ocean. The practice grew up, therefore, of transporting
goods from European shipping ports in ordinary sea-going

[1] On January 13, 1862, Judah P.
Benjamin, who was then Secretary of
War, wrote to General Lee, then in
South Carolina, that arrangements had
been made to run a cargo of arms and
ammunition from Nassau to New
Smyrna on the Florida coast and asked
him to afford what protection he could
to the vessel in case she was pursued by
a "Yankee gunboat" (Mss. in the
Confederate Museum at Richmond);
but such use of the eastern Florida coast
seems to have been infrequent.

vessels to Bermuda or Nassau on the island of New Providence,[1] one of the Bahamas, whence the goods were taken to Wilmington or Charleston in small, swift, light-draft side-wheel steamers.[2] These vessels would so time the passage that they would reach the coast at about nightfall and then run up or down the shore as near the breakers as possible until they reached the actual inlet. No naval force that had been stationed off Cape Fear could put a stop to blockade running at that point as there were two entrances to the river leading to Wilmington and these were widely separated by the shoal off the Cape. The only practicable way to seal the Cape Fear River to blockade runners was to capture Fort Fisher that guarded its mouth. For some reason the Union military and naval authorities did not bring themselves to the point of attempting this until the winter of 1864–1865,— at a time when it made little difference whether it was captured or not, except that the actual stoppage of the blockade was one more needle plunged into the hearts of the Southerners.[3] The stories of blockade running

[1] From a despatch from Governor Rawson of the Bahamas, dated January 20, 1866, in the British Parliamentary documents for that year, vol. xlix, p. 43, it appears that the imports of goods into the Bahamas in 1860 amounted to £234,029 and to £5,346,112 in 1864; and the exports rose from £157,350 in 1860, to £4,672,398 in 1864. Of the imports in the latter year £3,584,587 represented cotton from Confederate ports. In 1861 two steamers arrived at Nassau from the Southern States and three departed for that destination; in 1864, 105 steamers arrived and 165 departed for the Southern States. Of the 400 sailing and steam vessels which arrived at Nassau from Southern ports in the years of the war, 156 came from Charleston and 164 from Wilmington, The whole report is interesting. It was called to my attention by Everett E. Edwards now of Northwestern University. It is interesting to note that

Governor Rawson said that three-quarters of the clearances were for St. John's, New Brunswick, and added "Their exact destination was not made known."

[2] James Sprunt, at one time purser of the *Lillian* and later a wealthy and respected merchant at Wilmington, printed accounts of blockade running in Walter Clark's *Histories of the Several Regiments . . . from North Carolina*, vol. v, p. 353, in his own *Derelicts* (Wilmington, 1920), and his *Chronicles of the Cape Fear River*. The most interesting Confederate accounts are the *Life and Services of John Newland Maffitt* and Ernest C. Reid's statement of his activities in Massachusetts Historical Society's *Proceedings* for January, 1911.

[3] The rigidity of the blockade varied from season to season. It is impossible, therefore, to make any definite statement that would apply to more than one

are among the most thrilling of the war and perhaps none of them was more thrilling than that of the *Ella and Annie*. In the gloom of a hazy November morning in 1863, the United State cruiser *Niphon* — herself a captured blockade runner — was standing along the coast close to the shore to signal the patrol vessel on the next section. Suddenly the *Ella and Annie*, Captain Bonneau, stood directly for her out of the haze, under a full head of steam, evidently with the intention of putting her out of the way by ramming and then escaping the other patrol vessel. It happened that Commander Breck of the *Niphon* responded quickly to the need. Her helm was instantly put over and the blow was a glancing one. As the two vessels touched, the boarders from the *Niphon* jumped to the *Ella and Annie's* deck, drove the crew below, and captured the ship with her cargo of saltpetre, beef, and pork, rifles, paper, brandy, and hardware. Fortunately a dispute arose as to whether the next patrolling ships had a right to share in the prize money and the evidence that was given in court was preserved in print and has come down to us. The *Ella and Annie* [1] was taken into the navy and, under the name of *Malvern*, served

---

month. On November 29, 1861, the Confederate commissioners in England announced that "more than four hundred vessels have arrived and departed unmolested" from Southern ports; "Pickett Papers" at Washington, under date, *Official Records . . . Navies*, ser. ii, vol. iii, p. 298, — there are frequently slight differences between the manuscripts and the printed text. T. D. Jervey has given some interesting facts on blockade running in a paper on "Charleston during the Civil War" in American Historical Association's *Report* for 1913, vol. i, p. 169–176. A letter from Benjamin to Slidell, dated September 2, 1863, in *Official Records . . . Navies*, ser. ii, vol. iii, p. 882; a "Report" of the Confederate Secretary of the Treasury, dated May 2, 1864, and the "Message" of Davis, dated December 17, 1864, both in the Confederate Museum at Richmond, have other interesting details on the blockade and on the importation of goods from abroad into the Confederacy. An earlier "Message" of the President of the Confederacy, dated December 7, 1863, also has some interesting assertions as to the blockade. In the Library of Congress is a manuscript volume containing entries as to the blockade, made by United States officials at Bermuda and at Nassau; but the entries are too incomplete to add much to our knowledge of the subject.

[1] *Steamer Ella and Annie and Cargo in Prize*, (Boston, 1864).

as Admiral Porter's flagship during the last six months of the war.

As the blockade became stricter and more United States warships appeared upon the ocean, the method was adopted of carrying the cargo from England to Bermuda, Nassau, or to the Mexican town of Matamoros on the Rio Grande River and thence transhipping it into the Confederacy. The surest way to meet this mode of evading the blockade was to capture the vessel bearing the goods from England to the port of transhipment, before she had reached the latter. The first vessel that was taken into port under this plan of operations was the *Springbok*. The Supreme Court of the United States, sitting in Admiralty, declared her cargo to be good prize.[1] Another ship, the *Peterhoff*, was captured while on her way from London to Matamoros and her cargo was likewise condemned. These cases determined the law and practice as to blockade until 1914.

From time immemorial, the general rule of war and of practice between nations has been that when war breaks out between two countries, trade between the people of those countries comes to an abrupt and absolute termination. In practice, however, it has seldom, if ever, been the case and in the years 1861 to 1865, this was especially true. For one or two or three generations, there had been an active commerce between the dwellers in the Ohio Valley and those to the southward of them, and between those living on the northern side of the Ohio River and those inhabiting the country on the southern side of that stream. Intimate commercial relations had thus grown up and these could not be thrown over in a day. Moreover, in the first year of the war, the position of Kentucky was extremely doubtful and

[1] J. B. Moore's *Digest of International Law*, vii, 715, 719. The question of continuous voyages is interestingly handled by Professor E. D. Fite in *The Chronicle* (Poughkeepsie, N.Y.) for May and June, 1919.

it was, therefore, doubly difficult for the Federal authorities to enforce any rules of war that would urge the Kentuckians to take the Southern side. They needed Northern goods and if they continued to get them, it would be an added bond of union with the North. In the several acts of Congress, that were passed during the war, to regulate the commerce of the land frontier, large discretionary powers were given to the President and these were used by him and by the Secretary of the Treasury freely and energetically.[1] Policy demanded the feeding and clothing of the loyal inhabitants of Kentucky and Tennessee, but it was very difficult to prevent goods and food that passed into the possession of the Unionists there from getting into the hands of the enemy either by collusion or capture. As portions of Tennessee, Mississippi, and Louisiana passed into Federal control, it was important to get possession of the cotton, sugar, and naval stores that were on the plantations and to utilize the lands and the available negro labor to produce more. Northern men were encouraged to go South, take possession of abandoned or seized lands, cultivate them with the labor that was on them, and export the produce either to Northern or to foreign markets. In the actual carrying out of any such scheme on the

---

[1] J. G. Randall has printed two articles on certain phases of this general subject in the *American Historical Review*, xviii, 79–96 and xix, 65–79. The *Reports* of the Secretary of the Treasury during the years of the war contain a great deal of information on this matter. Anyone who wishes to get an idea of the intricacies of the regulations can read the three following publications of the government: *Commercial Intercourse with and in States declared in Insurrection, and the Collection of Abandoned and Captured Property* (September 11, 1863); *Additional Regulations concerning Commerical Inter-* course (January 26, 1864); and *Rules and Regulations concerning Commercial Intercourse* (Washington, July 29, 1864). R. S. Cotterill's article on "The Louisville and Nashville Railroad, 1861–1865" in the *American Historical Review*, xxix, 700–715 necessarily throws many sidelights on this matter. The subject is treated at length, with references, in Rhodes's *United States*, v, 274, and fol.

The reaction of the Confederates to this policy may be seen in two orders given by Lee and dated March 29 and April 4, 1864, in D. S. Freeman's *Calendar of Confederate Papers*, 324.

ground, it proved to be difficult to distinguish between the cotton that one grew on the abandoned plantation that had come to be his for a few months or for a year or two and the cotton that had been concealed in a neighboring swamp and might be purchased for a fraction of its real value. Then, too, there was an ever ready market just the other side of the line for small but valuable commodities, as quinine, calomel, and opium. The debatable land between the belligerents was divided into districts and treasury officials went with the armies or followed soon after them and necessarily retired with them. The result of the confusion and of the pressure for the opening of trade or the regulation of that which already existed led to the promulgation of a mass of rules and things of the kind that were practically beyond the comprehension of anyone. The .opportunities for accumulating money easily were so great and so safe that many treasury agents and many military and naval officers succumbed to these temptations.[1] Grant and Sherman were distressed by the traders who followed and flanked the army as they were by the newspapers correspondents. At one time, Grant was so irritated that he issued an order excluding all Jews from the military lines and, apparently at the moment, he considered all the inhabitants of Cincinnati and all the commercial traders of the part of the Mississippi Valley in which he was then operating to be of the Jewish faith. Possibly there is no more characteristic letter to be found in Lincoln's correspondence than the one in which he informed Grant that of course it was all right for

[1] Some illustrative information may be gathered from the *Home Letters of General Sherman*, 229 and fol., from T. W. Knox's *Camp-Fire and Cotton-Field* (New York, 1865), chs. xviii–xlii; and from the *Annals of the Army of the Cumberland . . . also its Police Record of Spies, Smugglers, and Promi-*

nent Rebel Emissaries. . . . By An Officer (Philadelphia, 1863), p. 453 and fol.

In studying this exceedingly intricate subject, the author has been materially aided by the researches of Paul H. Buck of Columbus, Ohio, and A. S. Roberts of Urbana, Illinois.

him to exclude traders from his lines if they were obnoxious, but that he couldn't exclude all the people of a religious faith, and therefore his order was overruled. It is doubtful, however, if the interference of the President was of any permanent benefit to the traders. East of the Alleghanies, in the earlier part of the war, there was a considerable trade through the lines, which also was said to be in the hands of the Jews; but this dwindled as the months and years went by and its place was taken by the blockade runner. In the ways that have been described in this and preceding paragraphs, it appears that two kinds of commerce had grown up to alleviate the condition of the surrounded and generally isolated people of the Confederacy. In 1862 and in 1863, and in the first part of 1864, blockade runners did carry goods from Havana to Mobile, but the number was small and the amount of goods introduced into the Confederacy, or cotton taken out of it, by those vessels was not large. Apart from this, the only intercourse that the beleaguered Southerners, west of the mountains, had with the outer world was by means of the trade through the lines with the North.[1] And, apart from the early commerce over the Potomac, the only commercial communication that the people of the Confederacy, east of the mountains, had with the outer world was through the blockade. Finally, the facilities of transportation between these two sections of the Confederacy were so poor and what railroads there were, were so thoroughly overworked for the supplying of military needs that the people of the two sections seem to have lived quite apart and to have been little influenced in their comfort or discomfort by the trade with the enemy through the other portions of the Confederacy.

[1] See W. L. Fleming's "Blockade Running and Trade through the Lines into Alabama" in *South Atlantic Quarterly*, iv. 256.

In the first years after the war, the history of the struggle was written almost entirely from the military point of view and with the thesis that to the prowess of the Union armies was due the fall of the Confederacy. With the ever-growing sense of the influence of economic factors on the course of human life, it became more and more the habit to attribute the defeat of the Confederates to the working of the blockade, more especially to the working of the sea-blockade. With the greater experience that we of the present day unhappily have of the working of psychological forces in war, it would seem that we must revise our ideas as to the part played by military and naval men and by economic forces, and look more closely into the actualities of existence. It appears that the accounts of Southern life during the war were written mainly by women or by foreigners who happened to be within the Confederate lines. The ladies, naturally, have stressed the difficulties of providing suitable attire and the appearance of belles and beaux in clothes of four, five, or six years before. These accounts are no doubt true and no doubt it was painful for a young person to appear in President Davis's drawing room in antiquated dress, and, undoubtedly, the continued inability to satisfy one's desire for adornment and for the unessential articles of diet, when prolonged, did much to wear down the nerve of "Southern society" and justified the procurement of Leghorn bonnets and Java coffee through the medium of the blockade runners and the interline smuggler to the exclusion of necessities, as bacon and woolen blankets. The blockade and the trade through the lines contributed in another way to break down the morale of the Confederates which led to the final collapse by encouraging speculation and arousing the feelings of envy and hostility that always accompany the sudden rise of the "newly rich." It has been found impossible to place the historical finger on many tangible instances of successful speculation on the part of the Southern people or dwellers in the South, apart from the "Jews of Richmond" and a few others of the kind. The idea, however, was undoubtedly prevalent that someone else was making money while oneself was fighting on the battle line or making over one's old clothes at home. And these feelings undoubtedly had a great deal to do with bringing about the final catastrophe. Moreover, the efficiency of the blockade, like the efficiency of the regulation of the trade through the lines, may well be doubted. It is true that a privately owned blockade-runner was often loaded beyond her capacity and her speed, thereby, seriously interfered with. Indeed, so profitable was the traffic, so great was the demand within the Confederacy for the goods brought in by the unofficial blockade runners, that if a vessel made three voyages in safety, her owners were compensated for their investment.[1] They were thus tempted to overload their vessels and to take risks that led oftentimes to early capture. The story of the government-owned blockade runners is very different. The Glasgow-Belfast iron packet boat, *Giraffe*, was purchased by the Confederate government, rechristened the *Robert E. Lee*, and operated between Wilmington and Nassau on government account. She made thirty trips with the regularity of a ferry-boat. When the Wilmington blockade was strictly enforced in the second half of 1864, one vessel after another fell into the hands of the blockading squadron or was forced on shore, much to the disgust and dismay of General Gorgas who insisted that these misadventures were unnecessary.[2]

[1] According to a report in the *Journal of the Senate of Virginia* in February, 1864, it appears that it oftentimes cost three bales of cotton to send one to market.

[2] From a broadside printed on board the flagship *Malvern* on September 30, 1864, it appears that, in the last sixty days, fifty blockade runners had been captured or destroyed off Cape Fear and among them were three of the best known ships of the blockade running

No statement has ever been made of the amount of cotton taken out or commodities brought in by the Confederate
blockade runners,[1] but Governor Vance made a succinct
statement as to the amounts secured through the blockade
by the North Carolina government. In this we read of
articles advertised for sale on one date by the North Carolina quartermaster. They were valued in all at something
over five million dollars and included 40,000 yards of
army cloth, 10,000 envelopes, and 6,000 great coats. In
1863, the North Carolina-owned-blockade runners brought
in for the account of the State somewhat under two hundred
thousand dollars worth of drugs, medicines, and surgical
instruments. Among these were opium, morphine, chloro-
form, and quinine.[2] It would seem at least open to debate
how far the collapse of the Confederacy can be attributed
to the lack of essential supplies.

fleet, — the *Advance*, belonging to the
State of North Carolina, the *Lillian*
and the *R. E. Lee*, belonging to the Confederate government.

General Gorgas in his "Journal"
states that the arms, steel, tin, and zinc
coming through the blockade on
steamers belonging to his bureau formed
the chief source of supply in 1863.
Later, he notes the loss of six vessels
bringing government stores and severely
commented upon the fact that "our
commanders . . . allow their vessels to
fall unhurt into the hands of the
enemy."

[1] In the "Trenholm Papers," in the
Library of Congress, is a statement
that, up to Nov. 11, 1864, £214,702 had
actually been realized from the sales of
government cotton in England.

[2] These details are taken from a
manuscript of Professor Daniel H.
Hill's chapter on "The State's Blockade
Business" in his forthcoming *History of
North Carolina in the Civil War*, which
he very kindly permitted the present
author to read. A brief statement by
Governor Vance, himself, is on p. 70 of
Clement Dowd's *Life of Zebulon B.
Vance*.

NOTE

General Naval Bibliography. — The volumes of the *Official Records
. . . Navies* are a wonderful storehouse of facts as to the operations
on the water during the war. Many of the documents included in
those volumes were originally printed in connection with the successive
" Reports " of the Secretary of the Navy. There were also inquiries
and courts martial that brought out interesting and valuable information that has been printed separately in some of the official reports
of the committees of Congress and in separate volumes as the *Report
of the Secretary of the Navy in Relation to Armored Vessels* (Washington,
1864) that was made in response to a resolution of the Senate of December 17, 1863. It begins with the building of the iron-clad vessels
and includes the extremely interesting testimony as to the reasons for
the loss of the monitor *Weehawken* (pp. 310–342). Volume iii of the
Report of the Joint Committee on the Conduct of the War for 1865 contains 120 printed pages of testimony as to monitors in general and
light-draft monitors in particular. The *Confidential Correspondence
of Gustavus Vasa Fox*, edited by R. M. Thompson and R. Wainwright
and printed in two volumes in 1918 at New York by the Naval History
Society, is very important. Of the compendious histories of the war
on the water, that prepared by Admiral D. D. Porter and printed in
New York [1] in 1886 is perhaps as authoritative as any, although, of
course, Porter was not a trained historical investigator and possessed
a somewhat constructive memory, which is seen, possibly to the best
advantage, in his *Incidents and Anecdotes of the Civil War* that was
printed at New York in the preceding year. An earlier work was *The
History of the Navy during the Rebellion* by C. B. Boynton, D.D., in
two volumes (New York, 1868). It can hardly be regarded as an
inspired work, but is useful and has some remarkable pictures in color.
F. M. Bennett's *The Monitor and the Navy under Steam* (Boston,
1900) is possibly the best and most up-to-date account, but it is very
brief. Earlier, A. T. Mahan and J. R. Soley wrote two small books,
The Gulf and Inland Waters and *The Blockade and the Cruisers*, that
are still useful. The exploits of the Confederate navy have been set
forth in great detail by J. T. Scharf in his *History of the Confederate
States Navy* which is abundantly supplied with illustrations of men,

---

[1] *The Naval History of the Civil War* printed in a book of 832 double-column
pages, each page being 10½ inches high.

vessels, and naval apparatus (New York, 1887). Dr. Gardner Weld Allen, the author of two interesting books on our navy in two wars, has brought together an admirable library of American naval history and one thousand excerpts from magazines which, most carefully indexed and bound, are in the Harvard College Library. The story of the first iron-clad ships is told by Professor William Hovgaard on pp. 1–27 of his *Modern History of Warships* (London, 1920). In working up this subject, material aid has been obtained from James Phinney Baxter, third of the name, of Portland, Maine.

CHAPTER XVII

THE EMANCIPATION PROCLAMATION

At the outset, Lincoln found himself in a most embarrassing position as to slavery. Rightly or wrongly, the Southern people believed that his aim would be the destruction of the institution upon which their peculiar form of society depended. Lincoln realized that the forceful destruction of slavery would alienate the sympathies of great masses of people in the Ohio Valley and elsewhere,—without whose aid the Union could not be restored. Blinded to all these considerations, the abolitionists attempted to force emancipation at once. Lincoln tried to hold them back, and took every occasion to deny his sympathy with abolition. He also sought to curb all injudicious persons who essayed to ride ahead of him in bringing about the freedom of the black and mulatto slaves. When it became clear that he must bow to the inevitable, he did what he could to secure pecuniary compensation [1] for the slaveholders. The most notable mark in the evolution of the new policy was the attempt to deport the whole colored population of the

[1] Clara Barton stated the matter with great clearness on March 1, 1862: "Our Government has for its object the restoration of the Union *as it was*, and will do so, unless the resistance of the South proves so obstinate and prolonged that the abolition or overthrow of slavery follow as a *consequence* — never an object." She added that "subjugation" would follow as an "incident upon a course of protracted warfare." W. E. Barton's *Clara Barton*, i, 147. On January 5, 1863, John C. Gray wrote that at the beginning of the war some men thought that here was a chance to abolish slavery and they tried to do it independently of the endeavor of the government to unite the country. In some men the attempt to abolish slavery has " developed to the exclusion of all patriotism, . . . In some men this attempt was induced by philanthropy, in others by hatred of the South naturally enough produced by the consciousness of being bullied by them for so many years."

United States, and this led to one of the most remarkable
failures of Lincoln's whole career.

As the war proceeded, the question as to what should be
done with the negroes became every day more urgent of
solution. They penetrated the picket lines of the Union
armies, bringing in food for sale, or seeking food for themselves. It made little difference what opinion as to secession a Virginia or a South Carolina planter held; he either
had a right to his negroes as property, or he had not. If
Virginia had legally seceded and set up as an independent
sovereign power, slave property of an enemy was subject
to capture and condemnation. The idea of the day, however, was that a State could not secede, that the Union was
indestructible, that Virginia was still within the Union, and
that Virginians were still citizens of the United States.
When the negroes appeared, some commanders turned them
back, although they did not like to do it; others provided
them with work and fed them out of the commissary stores
under some semblance of regularity — but it was difficult
to do this without endangering one's standing with the
War Department. At Hilton Head for some months the
negroes of the vicinity were permitted to come freely into
the camp, but the problem of supporting them became so
difficult that the sentries were ordered to allow no negroes
to enter unless they came to sell chickens or sweet potatoes,
or other food products. A brigade surgeon on the Du Pont
expedition related to his family that the negroes seemed to
have no affection for their masters and mistresses, but a
genuine association with the plantation, which to them was
home and country.[1]   In May, 1861, General B. F. Butler

[1] Massachusetts Historical Society's
Proceedings for June, 1923. There is a
great deal of interesting matter on the
general subject of the condition of the
negro in slavery in the "Journal of Miss
Susan Walker, March 3d to June 6th,
1862" in the *Quarterly Publication of the
Historical and Philosophical Society of
Ohio*, vii, No. 1.

was in command at Fortress Monroe, when a Virginia colonel appeared at the picket line and asked for the return of some slaves. He gained audience with Butler and was informed that if the master of the negroes would take the oath of allegiance to the United States, the fugitives would be delivered to him, — and that was the end of it. In commenting on this episode, Montgomery Blair, in a note dated May 29, 1861, told Butler that he was right when he "declared secession niggers contraband of war."[1] From that time the word "contraband" came into common use.

In August, 1861, Congress provided for the confiscation of the property of those who were engaged in treasonable opposition to the government of the United States. While the bill was being considered, on the day after the battle of Bull Run at which negroes were said to have fought by the sides of their masters, an amendment as to the status of negroes was introduced. It provided that if any person held to service or labor in any State shall be used in any way "to destroy this government by the consent of his master, his master shall forfeit all right to him." The amendment received the consent of nearly every Senator from the Free States. Those from the Border States opposed it; but the bill was passed by both Houses and approved by the President.

Lincoln's attitude toward negroes and toward slavery was widely misunderstood at that time, both in the South and in the North. He favored freedom for all men and for all women, everywhere throughout the world; he would have been glad to see the slaves in the United States emanci-

[1] *Private and Official Correspondence of Gen. Benjamin F. Butler*, i, 105, 116. In a letter written in March, 1891, (*ibid.*, i, 102) Major Cary, the Virginian who conferred with Butler as to the reclamation of these colored fugitives, stated that it was in their conversation that he for the first time heard the word "contraband"; but this was the recollection of an old man, and the first appearance of the word in any document of the time is in Blair's letter as above.

pated; but he could not join in the condemnation of the slaveholders as thieves and robbers. Moreover, he realized the
great undesirability of a large free negro population. His
work was to fulfill the conditions of his oath to preserve,
protect, and defend the Constitution of the United States.
As a very practical politician, and as a native of the Ohio
Valley, he knew that the people of that region did not wish
to have free negroes anywhere near their homes and, for
the most part, did not look upon slavery as morally wrong.
To advocate emancipation would be to lose the support of
the Ohio Valley for the Union cause. To oppose emancipation would drive the abolitionists, who were increasing
in strength every week, from the support of the administration. Under these circumstances, he fell in with the deportation idea and suggested to Congress that something should
be done to assist the colonization of free negroes at some
point easier of access than Liberia and more healthful.
Congress replied by voting a hundred thousand dollars to
aid in the resettlement of free colored people residing in the
District of Columbia, and the Confiscation Act itself gave
the President general authority to transport all those made
free by the provisions of the act and who were willing to
go.[1] Propositions came offering lands in the West Indies,
British Guiana, British Honduras, Surinam, Ecuador, and
elsewhere. The most promising proposition had to do with

[1] The history of the emancipation
and colonization schemes comes out in
the "Report of the Select Committee on
Emancipation" that was made on
July 16, 1862 (*House Report*, No. 148,
37th Cong., 2nd Sess.). On p. 19, the
report states the commercial advantages
of colonization in the American tropics
and Appendix No. 4 enumerates the
different places that had been suggested
for colonization, with some description
of the advantages of each. Further
information is contained in the *Report
on Colonization and Emigration made to
the Secretary of the Interior by [James
Mitchell] the Agent of Emigration*
(Washington, 1862). A concise account of the scheme and its failure is
contained in chapter xvii of volume vi
of Nicolay and Hay's *Abraham Lincoln*.
James Mitchell had already printed
several communications on the relation
of the white and African races, in which
he had ardently advocated colonization.

Chiriqui which was situated in the northwestern corner of
what is now the state of Panama.   This territory possessed
a store of coal that could be easily and cheaply extracted from
the soil, — at least so the promoters said.   The plan was
attractive at first sight.   On more careful view, it appeared
that the land was a part of the debatable tract lying between
Panama and Costa Rica.   Also the scientific men reported
that the coal possessed too much sulphur to be of use in
vessels of the navy and that it was doubtful if there was
much coal in Chiriqui.   In August, 1862, President Lincoln
assembled a delegation of colored men at the White House
and addressed them on the subject of the colonization of the
colored race outside the limits of the United States.   It was
in explaining to them as to why they should leave the United
States that he used these words :[1] "You and we are different races.   We have between us a broader difference than
exists between almost any other two races. . . . Your
race suffer very greatly, many of them, by living among us,
while ours suffer from your presence. . . . The aspiration
of men is to enjoy equality with the best when free, but on
this broad continent not a single man of your race is made the
equal of a single man of ours."   Colonized in some favorable
locality, Lincoln thought that the colored men might become
the equals of the best in that region and that would be for
the advantage of both races, not only for the present generation, "but as

> From age to age descends the lay
>   To millions yet to be,
> Till far its echoes roll away
>   Into Eternity."

Notwithstanding Lincoln's appeal, the project did not meet
with any hearty response on the part of the colored people.

[1] *Complete Works*, viii, pp. 2, 9.

In the winter of 1862–1863 a promoter, Bernard Kock by
name, appeared with a statement that he had secured a
hundred square miles of land on Ile A' Vache. It was a part
of the Republic of Hayti where black rules white.[1] He said
that a few thousand negroes arriving on the island in the
spring, by the following autumn would or could gather cotton
to the value of one million dollars. Lincoln and Seward
fell under the blandishments of Herr Kock and so did New
York moneyed men who thought they saw a profit of six
hundred per cent in the scheme. Four hundred or four
hundred and fifty colored persons embarked for Ile A' Vache
in April, 1863; then one misfortune after another befell.
The smallpox went on board the ship with the immigrants;
no preparations had been made for them on the island; fifty
of the colored people died or disappeared within three
months, and in March, 1864, the survivors were brought
back to the United States. Lincoln still held to his idea of
colonization and consulted General Butler on the subject.
He received small satisfaction, for Butler told him that
there were "not enough steamers in the United States to
carry away the colored population."

The next paragraph in the story relates to the attempts of
two Union generals to take the matter out of Lincoln's
hands and settle it for themselves. These were John Charles
Frémont and David Hunter. The former was born in Georgia and the latter in the District of Columbia of Virginian
parents. Why the former should have been sent to Missouri
has never been explained; possibly, it was supposed that

---

[1] Already, in 1861, the government
of Hayti had established an agency at
Boston to promote emigration from the
United States and Canada to Hayti.
James Redpath was the "General
Agent of Emigration to Hayti for the
U. S." His official correspondence
shows great promise of emigration but
little definite information as to fulfill-
ment. Redpath's "Letter Book" is in
the Library of Congress, and see also a
letter to Israel Washburne, under date
of January 12, 1861, in the Washburne
Mss.

he would be a mild emancipationist — as the son-in-law of
Senator Benton — and would not act rashly in that direction at any rate. Frémont went to St. Louis and visited
various parts of Missouri. He was greatly annoyed by the
actions of the Missourians, as one could hardly help being,
no matter what opinion he might have as to slavery or anything else, for in some part of Missouri there was certain to
be a party or a quasi-party, directly opposed to his belief
and prepared to combat it. By August, 1861, one month
after his accession to office, Frémont decided that it was
necessary for him to assume all power within the State of
Missouri. He issued a proclamation, dated at St. Louis on
August 30, 1861, establishing martial law throughout the
State and declaring that all the property of all Missourians
who had or should take arms against the United States was
or should be confiscated and their slaves declared freemen.[1]
On September 2, President Lincoln wrote to Frémont that
the confiscation of property and liberation of slaves would
alarm the Southern Union men and, perhaps, ruin the
Union prospects in Kentucky. He asked Frémont to modify
his proclamation "as of your own motion." As Frémont
refused to do this, Lincoln modified the proclamation himself
on September 11, and some time thereafter removed Frémont to another sphere of activity, which impelled Senator

[1] The documents are printed in the
Official Records, ser. i, vol. iii, p. 466 and
fol., and in the *Report of the Joint Committee on the Conduct of the War* for
1863, pt. iii. Nicolay and Hay have
treated this matter in their *Abraham
Lincoln, A History*, iv, chs. xxiii and
xxiv, and Rhodes has devoted many
pages to it in ch. xvi of his third volume.
General John M. Schofield in his
Forty-Six Years in the Army has put in
print the ideas of one of Frémont's
successors in Missouri. Possibly the
most interesting arraignment of Frémont is to be found in the speech of
Frank P. Blair, Jr., which was delivered
in the House of Representatives on
March 7, 1862 and printed in pamphlet
form under the title of "*Frémont's
Hundred Days in Missouri.*" Frémont's
side of the case had been stated three
days earlier by J. P. C. Shanks, Representative from Indiana, and published
separately as *Vindication of Major
General John C. Frémont against the
Attacks of the Slave Powers and its
Allies.* A much more elaborate statement of the Frémont side is in the
Memoirs of Gustave Koerner, ii, ch.
xxxv ; Koerner was on Frémont's staff.

Benjamin F. Wade to write that "No public man, since
Admiral Byng was sacrificed . . . has suffered so unjustly
as General Frémont."[1]

As the year 1862 unrolled, the administration's attitude
toward the negro and toward slavery took on a new phase.
On February 21, 1862, for the first time in the history of the
United States, an American citizen, Captain Nathaniel P.
Gordon, commander of an American slave ship, was hanged
as a pirate, and this was done in the Tombs Prison in New
York City.[2] Following on this, on April 7, a treaty was
signed between the United States and Great Britain[3] for the
efficient suppression of the African slave trade. In June,
Hayti and Liberia[4] were recognized as independent and
sovereign states by act of Congress, and on July 11, a bill
for the suppression of the slave trade was signed by President
Lincoln. All these things, especially the way in which he
withstood all the efforts that were made to secure a mitiga-
tion of Gordon's sentence, should have convinced every
one, who was at all cognizant of the fact, that Lincoln's
attitude toward emancipation was changing; but it was
only his revocation of Hunter's proclamation on May 19

[1] "Papers" of Charles A. Dana in the
Library of Congress, under date of
February 3, 1862. Another statement
of the case for Frémont is W. Brother-
head's *General Frémont and the In-
justice Done Him by Politicians and
Envious Military Men* (Philadelphia,
1862). Those who had once been
Frémont men found it very difficult to
change their allegiance. And some of
them, of distinct power in other respects,
a generation later declared their belief
in him.

[2] Edward Dicey's *Six Months in the
Federal States* (London, 1863) i, 82–91.
See also Nicolay and Hay's *Abraham
Lincoln*, vi, 99. There are several
interesting paragraphs on the African
slave trade in the "Report" of the
Secretary of the Interior, dated No-

vember 30, 1821; *Senate Executive
Document*, No. 1, 37th Cong., 2nd
Sess., p. 453.

[3] *Treaties and Conventions* (Washington, 1873) p. 388.

[4] For the progress or lack of progress
of Liberia, see Thomas Fuller's *Journal
of a Voyage to Liberia* (Baltimore, 1851).
He was appointed by the Cambridge
(Maryland) African Colonization Society to proceed to Liberia to obtain
information for intending emigrants.
Gardner W. Allen in his *Trustees of
Donations for Education in Liberia*
(Boston, 1923) has necessarily gone
beyond the strict boundaries of the
title of his book. A somewhat gloomy
view of the country and the people is
given in Mary Gaunt's *Alone in West
Africa* (London, 1912).

that attracted attention. General David Hunter's motives
are even more deeply buried in conjecture than are those of
General Frémont. He seems to have been somewhat of a
personal friend of the new President and was one of the men
whom Lincoln tried to push forward to get the deserts that
had heretofore been unattained. Hunter was given the
command of the land forces on the coast of Georgia and
South Carolina. Almost at once the Federal soldiers possessed themselves of islands and plantations, and these were
inhabited by hundreds and thousands of negroes, who remained behind when their masters fled or deserted their
masters and regained their accustomed plantations and
cabins. Some even took possession of the "House" on the
old plantation, and "the day of Ju-bi-lo" seemed to have
arrived. Hundreds of white men and women soon appeared
upon the scene.[1] They came from New England, from New
York, and from Ohio, and other Northern States to look out
for the blacks and to do for them whatever could be done.
With the consent, or under the direction of the government
at Washington, they undertook to employ the colored people
in the production of the long staple, sea island cotton, for
which there was an eager market, and also of enough food
for their own support and some to spare. It was difficult
for men and women who had never seen a negro slave or a
cotton plant to realize the gentle treatment and firm grasp
required to control and encourage the blacks. There were
discontents, and these were added to by reports that the

---

[1] It is interesting to note that
Captain Du Pont was somewhat
dismayed by the influx. He wrote to
Fox that the contraband question was a
very intricate one. He added that the
various "so called agents who come
down here, more or less accredited, the
collectors of cotton, collectors of negro
statistics, the people of God, the best of
the party who want to establish schools,
do not all agree." One thing was
certain, he wrote, that while the most
rabid abolitionist had not exaggerated
the condition of the negro slave "the
transition state has not improved it."
*Confidential Correspondence of Gustavus
Vasa Fox*, i, 106.

Northern government was preparing to export the colored people to Cuba, where they would be sold as slaves. Possibly, it was in part to combat this propaganda that General Hunter of his own motion, on May 9, 1862, issued a general order asserting that the States of South Carolina, Georgia, and Florida, having declared themselves out of the Union and begun war against the United States, "it became a military necessity to declare martial law"; slavery and martial law being incompatible, "the persons in these three States . . . heretofore held as slaves, are therefore declared forever free." [1] It was a week or more before the news of this declaration reached Washington. When it came, Lincoln lost no time in stating that the government had had no part in it and that neither General Hunter nor any one else had received any authorization to issue such a proclamation, that it was void, and that he reserved to himself the exercise of any supposed power to declare slaves free.

General Hunter also undertook to form regiments of blacks for the military service of the United States. Early in May, 1862, he issued an order assembling all able-bodied negroes at Hilton Head. This order took away from the plantations the men working under the orders of an agent of the Treasury Department, at the precise moment when their labors were most needed in the fields to rescue the cotton and other plants from the rapidly growing weeds. [2] Hunter was told that the government would lose half a million dollars, but he paid no attention to this. The negroes were drilled, provided with some sort of uniform, and

[1] See Nicolay and Hay's *Abraham Lincoln, A History*, vi, ch. v; Hunter's proclamation is given on p. 341 of ser. i, vol. xiv, of the *Official Records* and see *ibid.*, ser. iii, vol. ii, p. 52 and fol.; Lincoln's proclamation of May 19, 1862, is in *ibid.*, ser. iii, vol. ii, p. 42.

[2] See "Journal of Miss Susan Walker" in the *Quarterly Publication of the Historical and Philosophical Society of Ohio*, vii, 36–40; and *Letters from Port Royal . . . Edited by Elizabeth Ware Pearson* (Boston, 1906).

partly armed. Then the matter came up in Congress and Hunter was asked by what authority he had organized a regiment of "fugitive slaves." Replying on June 23, 1862,[1] Hunter denied that he had done anything of the kind. His instructions authorized him to employ loyal persons for the defence of the Union and "for the suppression of this rebellion" without any restriction as to color. What he had done was to organize a regiment of persons "whose late masters are fugitive rebels." It is difficult to disinter the later history of this matter from the "Official Records," but it would seem that some of these soldiers were kept together and formed the nucleus around which General Saxton organized the First South Carolina Volunteers.[2] At New Orleans, General Butler found a somewhat different state of affairs, for it appears that the secession governor of Louisiana had embodied a regiment of free blacks to the number of one thousand, more or less. These did not leave with the white militia men on the coming of Farragut, and Butler proceeded to "resuscitate" this colored Louisiana militia regiment. By the end of the year 1862,[3] he had three negro regiments and possibly more in the service.

By the end of 1861, the pressure for negro freedom was becoming intense. In his message to Congress in December, 1861, Lincoln called attention to the Confiscation Act of the preceding August and after suggesting colonization for

[1] Hunter's letter was printed with a prefatory paragraph by the "Emancipation League," as document No. 7. It is interesting to note that Hunter's colleague in command of the naval force, Flag Officer Du Pont, did not agree with him at all. On February 10, 1862, he wrote to Fox, from Port Royal Harbor: "Our independence and nationality are in danger — for God's sake, drop the negro question, it is dying of inanition, without any necessity to place ourselves legally and constitutionally wrong,

thereby offending our weaker brethren." *Confidential Correspondence of . . . Fox*, i, 106.

[2] Higginson's *Army Life in a Black Regiment* (Boston, 1870) gives a lifelike view of South Carolina colored men as soldiers.

[3] *Official Records*, ser. iii, vol. ii, p. 436 and subsequent volumes of this series, using index under "Negroes." See also Professor Charles H. Wesley in the *Journal of Negro History*, iv, 243.

the slaves freed by its provisions, added "The Union must
be preserved; and hence all indispensable means must
be employed." But he added there should be no haste in
determining the extreme measures that are indispensable.
It is clear that in these sentences, Lincoln was thinking aloud
and was purposely permitting his thoughts to be read by
others. He had already formulated suggestions by which
the United States would aid financially the people of any
State that should itself emancipate the slaves within its
limits. Nothing came of this suggestion at the time. This
rebuff did not turn Lincoln from his purpose of holding out
the threat of emancipation to the Southern slaveholders and
soothing the feelings of abolitionists and at the same time
making the way easy for the people of the Border States to
remain in the Union by assisting them out of the national
treasury. In March, 1862, he sent a special message to
Congress. In this he advocated the passage of a joint resolution, pledging the Federal government to coöperate
pecuniarily with any State that might adopt "gradual
abolishment of slavery." He thought that gradual emancipation was preferable to sudden emancipation for both the
whites and the blacks. He called attention to the matter in
his message of December, 1862, as to the preservation of
the Union, which was undoubtedly intended as a threat.
Lincoln hoped that some Border State would respond to
the offer of financial help in emancipation, but none did so
at that time. In April, 1862, Lincoln gave his consent to an
act for the immediate emancipation of all slaves in the District of Columbia with compensation to the owners. It is
interesting to note in this connection that in the autumn of
1861, Garrison had printed in "The Liberator" a memorial
to Congress, asking for the unconditional liberation of the
slaves of rebels, but suggesting "as a conciliatory measure"

that "a fair pecuniary award" should be paid for the slaves of loyal persons, — this to be done to facilitate an amicable adjustment of difficulties, to bring the war to a beneficent termination, and to unite all sections of the country on a basis of universal freedom.[1]

Few things impress more forcibly the student of this epoch than the apathy of the Republican party toward the Fugitive Slave Law of 1850. In November, 1861, and again in June, 1862, persons were prosecuted for offences under this law. One of these was the Reverend George Gordon, president of Iberia College in Ohio. He was convicted of resisting a deputy marshal in his attempt to arrest a fugitive slave and was sentenced to six months' imprisonment and to pay three hundred dollars with the cost of prosecution. In April, 1862, President Lincoln pardoned Gordon on the ground that, although he had encouraged and supported a riotous breach of the law, he had already atoned sufficiently for his offence.[2] The other case was that of John Dean. He was a Washington lawyer who had protected his client from arrest and had himself been arrested.[3] It was not until 1864, and then without any apparent enthusiasm, that Congress repealed the Fugitive Slave Law.

Until the spring and even into the summer of 1862, Lincoln had opposed any plan for an extended emancipation of the slaves with or without compensation. He now took a different view of the matter, but why it is impossible to state. It is generally supposed that the ill-fortune of the Virginia campaigns of 1862 was the determining factor. And it may be that a consciousness of his own responsibility for

[1] Reprinted in the Garrisons' *William Lloyd Garrison*, iv, 35.
[2] *In the Matter of George Gordon's Petition for Pardon* (Cincinnati, 1862).
[3] Noah Brooks's *Washington in Lincoln's Time* (New York, 1895), p. 197. These two cases are summarized in W. H. Siebert's *Underground Railroad*, 377.

those misfortunes, which flowed largely from the appointment of Halleck, may have influenced Lincoln to adopt a
radical departure from all his earlier declarations of policy.
At all events, in the middle of July, 1862, President Lincoln informed two of his Cabinet, Seward and Welles, that
he had it in mind to emancipate the slaves by proclamation,
in case the rebels did not cease their war on the United
States. On July 21, he laid the matter before the Cabinet.
All but one or two of the members agreed with him. It
was suggested, however, that it would be well not to issue
the proclamation at that moment when everything seemed
to be going to pieces, lest it should seem to be "the last
shriek on the retreat." Lincoln realized that the suggestion
was a wise one. He contented himself, for the time being,
by issuing a proclamation calling attention to the Confiscation Act, and warned all persons to cease opposing the government or take the consequences.

What happened in the next two weeks to change Lincoln's mind and to induce him to issue the preliminary
Emancipation Proclamation? Probably several things combined to induce him to change his attitude; but he concealed his intentions as completely as he had ever concealed
his line of action from the opposing counsel and the jury
in any case that he had ever tried in court. Lincoln is
generally regarded as a supreme judge of the trend of political opinion. Within two months after the issuing of the
Emancipation Proclamation, the election throughout the
North went against the government. It is true that in
the first half of 1862 there was a considerable increase of
expressed desire for emancipation on the part of certain
sections of the Northern clergy and of the regular organs of
abolition expression. But, having in mind Lincoln's astute-
ness and calmness in crises, it is difficult to believe that he

could have mistaken these manifestations for a rising tide of Northern desire for negro emancipation.

On August 19, 1862, Horace Greeley wrote what he termed "The Prayer of Twenty Millions" that the laws of the land, which operated to free large classes of negro slaves, should be executed. He declared that on the face of this wide earth there is not one intelligent champion of the Union who does not feel that every attempt to put down the rebellion and to uphold slavery at the same time is preposterous and futile. The President answered Greeley most unexpectedly by telegraph with the desire — so Greeley thought — of seizing that opportunity to place before the public statements that he had already drawn up. This is Lincoln's well-known letter of August 22, 1862.[1] As to the policy which he, the President, seemed to be pursuing — using Greeley's own words — Lincoln replied that he did not mean to leave any one in doubt. He would save the Union and save it the shortest way that it could be done under the Constitution. If there were those who would not save the Union, unless they could at the same time destroy slavery, he did not agree with them. On the contrary, Lincoln wrote: "If I could save the Union without freeing any slave, I would do it; and if I could save it by freeing all the slaves, I would do it; and if I could save it by freeing some and leaving others alone, I would also do that." Whatever he did or forebore to do, he did or forebore to do for the Union, and he would try to correct errors whenever they could be shown to be errors. And in all this there was no

[1] Greeley's letter is printed in full in the New York Semi-Weekly Tribune of August 21–22, 1862, and about one-third of it in Greeley's American Conflict, ii, 249. Lincoln's letter of August 22 is in the Semi-Weekly Tribune of August 26, 1862, and in the American Conflict, ii, 250, but with different paragraphing and some italics that are not given in the copy in Lincoln's Complete Works, viii, 15. As a bit of written English, it ranks next to the Gettysburg Address.

modification of his "oft-expressed personal wish that all men everywhere could be free."

On September 13, a committee from the "Religious Denominations of Chicago" waited upon Lincoln and asked him to issue a proclamation of emancipation. Lincoln replied that the subject was one upon which he had thought much; but that he was "approached with the most opposite opinions and advice" by persons who were equally certain that they represented the Divine Will. If he could only learn what that was, he would do it. Lincoln asked what good a proclamation would do when he could not enforce the Constitution in the rebel States? He did not believe that it would influence a single judge in those States or induce the negroes to come into the Union lines and do what they could to help the cause of freedom. Slavery was at the root of the rebellion; an emancipation proclamation would help the Union cause in Europe and would weaken the rebels by drawing off their laborers. There were fifty thousand soldiers in the Union armies from the Border States. "It would be a serious matter if, in consequence of a proclamation such as you desire, they should go over to the rebels," — but that danger was decreasing every day. He had not decided against a proclamation of liberty to the slaves. This subject was on his mind day and night. "Whatever shall appear to be God's will, I will do." Four days later, the reversal of the Confederate course of victory at the South Mountain and the Antietam seemed to be the opportunity for which he had been waiting since July, when he had laid the matter before his Cabinet.

The story of the second Cabinet meeting on the question of the Emancipation Proclamation has been told over and over again. There was some general conversation, then the President read a chapter from Artemus Ward's latest book.

Then he took a graver tone and announced that he had made a promise to himself and to his God that if the Southerners should be driven out of Maryland, he would issue a Proclamation of Emancipation. That time had now come. On September 22, 1862, the Preliminary Emancipation Proclamation was issued. The first paragraph declared that the war for the restoration of the old Union would be prosecuted; the second again recommended voluntary emancipation with compensation for the loyal States and the prosecution of the colonization scheme. He then announced as "President of the United States of America and commander-in-chief of the army and navy thereof" that on the first day of January, 1863, all persons held as slaves within any State or part of a State that "shall then be in rebellion" shall be then, thenceforward, and forever free; and the Executive Government of the United States, including the military and naval authority thereof, will recognize and maintain the freedom of such persons." The Proclamation then recites acts of Congress prohibiting officers of the army and navy returning fugitive slaves and declaring free those who escape from persons in rebellion, and all slaves captured "within any place occupied by rebel forces and afterwards occupied by the forces of the United States." Three things are especially noticeable. One is that the President three times refers to his authority as commander-in-chief; the second is the prominence given to the Confiscation Act of July 17, 1862; and the third is that the Proclamation in effect did not free a single slave. It was simply a notice that the President of the United States would carry out the policy enunciated in the Confiscation Act, thus adding his own authority as commander-in-chief to that of an act of Congress in case the Supreme Court, that was still presided over by Chief Justice Taney, or any other person within the limits of the

United States, should oppose or contest the constitutional power of Congress so to act.[1]

The Emancipation Proclamation, in its historical outcome, made Abraham Lincoln one of the half-dozen out-standing figures of history. At the moment, it added greatly to his political difficulties. Looking backward from the vantage point of the close of the first quarter of the twentieth century, we realize the stupendous qualities of Abraham Lincoln's mind and heart. To the Radical Republicans of the autumn months of 1862 and to the War Democrats who cared for the restoration of the Union, Lincoln's abilities and his desire for right and justice seemed very indefinable. In August, 1861, Edwin M. Stanton, in a letter to James Buchanan, contemned "the imbecility" of the administration, — but the word "imbecile" was then often used to describe any person whom one did not happen to like at the moment. Later, Stanton declared that if McClellan had "the ability of Cæsar, Alexander, or Napoleon," [2] he could accomplish nothing and that the result of Lincoln's "running the machine" for five months had been the "ruin of all peaceful pursuits and national bankruptcy." Two months later, Lincoln appointed Stanton, Secretary of War, and some six or seven months after that, by writing at the bottom of a request, which the masterful Secretary had refused, the words "I guess you will have to do it" convinced Stanton, once for all, who was "running the machine." At the other end of the line from the War Democrats were the Radical Republicans, as the political abolitionists were designated at the time. The most prominent of these were Senator Wade of Ohio and Senator Chandler of Michigan.

[1] See the present work, vol. v, p. 168, and William Whiting's *War Powers of the President*, 79. For an intelligible discussion of the Emancipation Proclamation, see W. A. Dunning's *Essays on the Civil War and Reconstruction*, 50.

[2] J. B. Moore's *Works of James Buchanan*, xi, 213, 214.

They had no belief in Lincoln's good faith as to abolition. They thought he wished to win back the seceders by kindness and that his attitude toward emancipation was merely a cloak under which he could accomplish other designs. They pursued ruthlessly any one whom the abolition politicians of the North accused of lukewarmness in the cause of the negro.[1] Then there were the abolitionists, pure and simple; these wished for freedom for the negro now and forever, whether the Union lived or died. To some of them the Emancipation Proclamation appeared as a nullity and it actually freed slaves only within districts controlled by the military power of the United States. Absolutely opposed to these were those persons who saw in the Proclamation, a shifting of the basis of the war from a war for the restoration of the Union to a war for the freedom of the slaves. In the elections that were held in October and November, 1862, the Lincoln majority in the Federal House of Representatives almost faded away and State legislatures, as that of Indiana, became hostile to the prolongation of the war.[2]

When Congress came together in December, 1862, Lincoln renewed his plea for compensated abolition. The answer came in the form of a resolution introduced by a Kentucky Representative to the effect that the Proclamation of September was unwarranted by the Constitution. This was voted down and a resolution was adopted declaring the Preliminary Proclamation constitutional and the policy enunciated in it a legitimate war measure. On January 1, 1863, Lincoln issued the definitive Proclamation, declaring all persons held as slaves in certain areas free. He ordered

[1] See General Townsend's *Anecdotes*, 70, 71, and the *Speech of Hon. J. A. McDougall . . . April 15, 16, & 22, 1862.*

[2] D. C. Shilling's "Relation of Southern Ohio to the South during the Decade preceding the Civil War" in the Historical and Philosophical Society of Ohio's *Quarterly*, vol. viii. The maps at the end show clearly the influence of the Emancipation Proclamation on Ohio politics.

the military authorities to maintain the freedom of "said persons." He also enjoined the freedmen to abstain from violence, to "labor faithfully for reasonable wages," and to enter into the armed service of the United States. He invoked the "considerate judgment of mankind, and the gracious favor of Almighty God." As to the former, there was for some time considerable doubt, for the statesmen of Europe did not understand the peculiar provisions of the Constitution of the United States. The legal effect of the Proclamation was and is extremely doubtful. To clear up the doubt, the Thirteenth Amendment to the Constitution, providing that slavery and servitude shall never exist within the United States, was proposed by Congress. After its adoption by the requisite number of the State legislatures, human slavery definitely ceased in every part of the United States.

In the beginning, the slaves seem to have placed little confidence in the Northern soldiers. As the months went by, those slaves nearer to the Union lines visited them and remained within them. With January, 1863, there came a psychological change in the blacks. They, or many of them, became imbued with desire to leave the plantation home and follow the troops of "Massa Linkum." Wherever a Union army appeared, the negroes flocked to it and when it marched away followed in its wake. They had always been fed, clothed, and housed on their plantations and it doubtless never occurred to them that this would not continue in a state of freedom; but it placed a great tax on the army transportation in the midst of the enemy's country. General Sherman on his march from Atlanta was followed by an ever increasing army of colored people. He did not know what to do with them, and his outspoken statements on the subject brought about friction with Stanton that led to very unpleasant consequences. Curiously, side by side with this suddenly aroused desire to leave their plantation homes and see the world or, better, to share in the excitements of the town, there were countless instances most carefully related by Southern writers, of faithful negroes who remained at home, concealed the portable treasures of their masters and mistresses and did what they could to protect them from the insults of a ruffian soldiery and stragglers of both armies. Probably both pictures are correct, and this contrariety of action continued long after the war was over. The saddest part of the whole affair, perhaps, was the attempt of some Northern States to secure colored men as items in the State quotas of enlistments under the calls for troops issued by the Washington government.[1] Probably, in these instances as in others, there was gross exaggeration by searchers for the sensational, but enough undoubted facts remain to form the basis of a very unpleasant story.

[1] See F. P. Stearns's *Life and Public Services of George Luther Stearns*, 312, 324, 330. In one of these extracts, Edward Bartlett of Concord, Massachusetts, wrote that when colored men for enlistment in Northern regiments became scarce in the city of Nashville, Tennessee, "we made trips into the country, often going beyond the Union picket line, and generally reaping a harvest of slaves." Stearns wrote that at Nashville "colored men, free and slave were hunted daily through the streets, and impressed for labor"; and ultimately, those who survived "were forcibly enlisted in the Twelfth United States colored troops." From Hilton Head, S. C., John C. Gray wrote "this traffic of New England towns in the bodies of wretched negroes . . . forms too good a justification of all that is said against the Yankees." And on October 1, 1864, Albert G. Brown wrote to Governor Andrew that "the whole system of getting slave recruits is damnable. I can conceive nothing worse on the Coast of Africa. These men have been hunted like wild beasts and ruthlessly dragged from their families." This extract was made for me by Samuel Abrams from the John A. Andrew Mss. in the cabinet of the Massachusetts Historical Society. In 1868, Brown published a *Sketch of the Official Life of John A. Andrew*. It was on one of the pages noted above that General Stearns stated that he recruited thirteen hundred negroes in Pennsylvania and the West for the 54th and 55th Massachusetts Infantry regiments.

NOTE

The Emancipation Proclamation in the South. — The reaction of the Southerners to the Proclamation was as rapid and as outspoken as was that of the old anti-slavery factions in English society. The Southerners' ideas were freely expressed by Governor John Letcher of Virginia in language that reminds one of Kansas-Nebraska debates and shows that war had not tamed nor the years removed the ardor of the Southern diatriber. He informed the Senate and House of Delegates of Virginia, on January 19, 1863, that Abraham Lincoln " in violation of all the principles of humanity, and of the nobler and more generous impulses of our natures, in disregard of all the social, moral and political obligations . . . in wanton heedlessness . . . has issued a proclamation " from which Letcher took this paragraph: " That on the first day of January in the year of our Lord one thousand eight hundred and sixty-three, all persons held as slaves within any state or designated part of a state, the people whereof shall then be in rebellion against the United States, shall be then, thenceforward and forever free. . . . No public man in our country " declared the Virginia governor, " has exhibited such depravity . . . has displayed so atrocious a spirit as is manifested in this proposition." *Documents, Extra Sessions*, 1862–63, No. 10, of the Virginia legislature.

The effect of the Proclamation on English opinion is seen in Cobden's letter of February 13, 1863 (*American Historical Review*, ii, 308).

CHAPTER XVIII

FROM VICKSBURG "TO THE SEA"

THE winter of 1862–1863 in the western area was spent in preparation for the campaigns of the coming year. General Rosecrans remained in command in Tennessee and General Grant had charge of operations in the Mississippi Valley from Cairo southward.[1] Memphis having fallen, the one remaining task on the river itself was to capture Vicksburg and the fortified positions between it and Natchez. The job was one that might well have appalled any soldier, for the river bottoms afforded abundant concealment for the troops and vessels of the Confederates. By this time, David D. Porter had taken command of the Union fleet on the upper river and Farragut had retired from that portion of the Mississippi basin. The great river flows in an alluvial plain, approaching first one edge of the high ground and then another; and it is only at these high places that the interior

---

[1] Three descriptions of Grant by three Massachusetts men about a year later are as follows. Theodore Lyman, a volunteer aide on Meade's staff, writing to Mrs. Lyman, in April, 1864, described him as "a man of a good deal of rough dignity." He was rather under middle height, of strong build, with "light-brown hair, and short, light-brown beard. His eyes of a clear blue; forehead high; nose aquiline; jaw squarely set." "He wore an expression," so Lyman wrote, on April 12, 1864, "as if he had determined to drive his head through a brick wall, and was about to do it" (Theodore Lyman's *Meade's Headquarters*, 80, 81, 83). John C. Ropes saw Grant at about the same time and wrote, April 16, 1864, that Grant had "a rather strong quick eye, compact and decided-looking, like a man of decision and self-reliance and of experience." C. F. Adams commanded Meade's Headquarters Guard at the time. On May 29, 1864, he wrote to his father that no intelligent person could watch Grant, "even from such a distance as mine, without concluding that he is a remarkable man. He handles those around him so quietly and well, he so evidently has the faculty of disposing of work and managing men, he is cool and quiet, . . . and in a crisis he is one against whom all around, whether few in number or a great army as here, would instinctively lean" (*Cycle of Adams Letters*, ii, 133).

can be gained from the river itself. Vicksburg stands on a
bluff at a point where the Mississippi, in those days, flowed
almost due east and then, with one of its theatrical turns,
flowed almost west. Vicksburg had no importance then,
except as a convenient point of transshipment, now that
Memphis and Baton Rouge were in Union hands. After
the capture of New Orleans in the spring of 1862, Farragut
ran up the river passing Vicksburg. It was then slightly
fortified and could easily have been seized, but there were
not troops with which to hold it. After Farragut retired
southward, the place was strongly fortified and subsidiary
defences were established at Grand Gulf and Port Hudson
farther down. The obvious method of approach to Vicksburg from Corinth, which was then occupied by Grant, was
to advance southward to Jackson, Mississippi, and then
turn westward to Vicksburg some twenty-five or thirty
miles away. The great objection to this plan was that the
amphibious Yazoo Valley lay between the firm ground where
the army would operate and the Mississippi, where the naval
and transport services would be. In other words, a long
line of communication between Memphis and the army must
be kept open or the soldiers must live off the country. As
no Union army up to that time had done this, large supply
depots were established as the army moved southward.
This gave the Confederates their opportunity; they seized
some of these stations and compelled Grant to retrace his
steps. At this moment, Major General McClernand intervened. He visited Lincoln at Washington and laid before
him a plan to capture Vicksburg by an advance down the
Mississippi River. Lincoln fell in with the idea on condition
that McClernand should raise the necessary troops in the
Northwest. When Grant was obliged to fall back, he sent
Sherman with a large force to attack the fortifications just

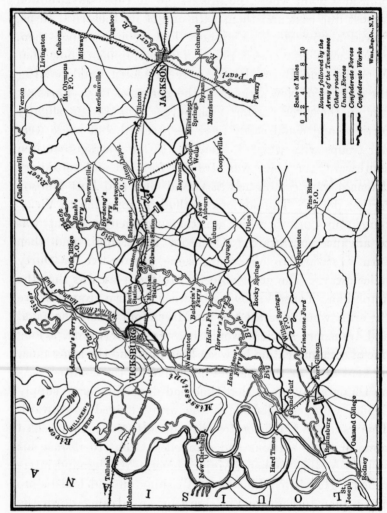

THE VICKSBURG CAMPAIGN.

Scale of Miles
0 1 2 4 6 8 10

Routes followed by the
Army of the Tennessee
Other roads
Union Forces
Confederate Forces
Confederate Works

Wम.Eng.Co., N.Y.

above Vicksburg at Hayne's Bluff on the Yazoo River; but the task proved to be impossible. It was at this juncture that McClernand appeared with troops that he had raised and took the command from Sherman as his commission as Major General of Volunteers antedated Sherman's. It occurred to one or to both of them that it would be possible to capture Arkansas Post, a fortified position on the Arkansas River, which was convenient for the Confederate supply service. Porter with a strong naval force went with the expedition. He battered the forts so effectually that the Confederates surrendered before the soldiers actually assaulted the position. It was then that Grant determined to take the control of the operations on the river into his own hands.[1] Vicksburg was clearly unassailable in front and so was Hayne's Bluff. At first, a combined naval and military force tried to get into the Yazoo River by some cut-off connecting it with the Mississippi. After the lighter draft gun-boats and transports had made a most astonishing progress, they came to a strong position occupied by the enemy and only the appearance of some of Sherman's soldiers rescued the naval vessels. They retired to the Mississippi and tried again, but again without success.[2]

[1] Besides the *Official Records* and Grant's own recollections as set forth in his *Memoirs*, there are some interesting books. Charles A. Dana lived at headquarters, during this, the Chattanooga, and parts of the Virginia campaigns, as a species of private observer for Secretary Stanton and embodied his observations in the life of Grant that he wrote with James H. Wilson and in his own *Recollections of the Civil War.* Wilson himself set forth his own recollections in his *Under the Old Flag* and in his biography of John A. Rawlins. Wilson's "Staff-Officer's Journal of the Vicksburg Campaign" is in the *Journal of the Military Service Institution* for 1908. An estimate of

"General Grant's Military Abilities By a Confederate Officer" is in the *Magazine of American History* for October, 1885, p. 341. In the Southern Historical Society's *Papers*, xii, 352–360, is a defence of General Pemberton which was "written not long after the fall of the city" by Major R. W. Memminger, his Chief of Staff. General Stephen D. Lee of the Confederate army has two articles on the campaign of Vicksburg in the *Publications* of the Mississippi Historical Society, iii, 21, 55, and on the previous campaigns of December, 1862, and January, 1863, in *ibid.*, iv, 15.

[2] On April 2, 1863, Gustavus Vasa Fox wrote to Farragut that "Grant who I judge by his proceedings has not the

Upon the failure of the Yazoo enterprise, Grant decided to march his army by Vicksburg on the western bank of the Mississippi and gain the firm ground on the eastern side below the city. At an earlier time an attempt had been made to isolate Vicksburg by digging a canal across the neck of land between the easterly and westerly bends of the river; but when the channel was dug, the Mississippi refused to flow into it, but ran swirling by. All this time the river had been high, but now it fell and it became possible to march the army by the western bank past Vicksburg. Grant and Porter now agreed that the warships with transports should run the Vicksburg batteries on the first favorable night. It was one of the most exhilarating episodes of the war. As soon as the vessels were seen from the Vicksburg shore, houses were set on fire, so that the scene was light as day — although it was midnight — until the smoke of combat settled down on the river. When one of the warships entered one of the eddying whirlpools, she became unmanageable, turned completely around, and came directly under the fire of the batteries. Nevertheless, owing to the confusion and excitement, every one of the naval vessels went through the ordeal with damages that were made good in half a day and only one or two of the transports were lost. Grant had hoped that Porter with his guns might silence the batteries at Grand Gulf, but when that was found to be impossible, the fleet ran by that point and the army gained the high land on the east side of the river at Bruinsberg, between Grand Gulf and Port Hudson. To mask his intentions, Grant had despatched Sherman with his army corps and the naval

brains for great work, has kept our Navy tailing through swamps to protect his soldiers" (*Publications* of the Naval History Society, vol. ix, 331). Probably this remark merely echoes some unprinted letter from Porter anticipating the complaints of a later letter as to the lack of appreciation of the navy by Grant.

vessels that remained above Vicksburg to make a demonstration against Hayne's Bluff. Sherman did this with such good will that the Confederate General Pemberton marched his army to that point and left the way open to Grant below Grand Gulf. Sherman then regained the western bank of the Mississippi and marched southward with such speed that he reached the crossing point before the transports were ready for him.

McClernand's corps led the way across the river and with it went Grant. At first there was no opposition of any kind, but the adventures of generals and soldiers in getting something to eat and a place to sleep were most interesting. No enemy was encountered — to speak of — and the garrison at Grand Gulf, when it realized what was going on, abandoned the post. There were attempts made to impede the march at crossings of rivers and at wooded places, but these were easily overborne. The head of the army then pushed for Jackson, where General Johnston had a considerable body of troops. Grant attacked them and drove them away and then turned westward to encounter Pemberton with the Vicksburg army. There were some thirty-five thousand Confederates, ably led, but nothing could withstand the unexpectedness and ardor of the Union attack. Instead of making every effort to march around the Union army and join Johnston, Pemberton retired toward Vicksburg. Grant pursued him vigorously until stopped at the high ground on which the town stands. It has been said that Pemberton disobeyed his orders from Johnston and also that he never received them. It has also been said that if Grant had pushed his men, he could have entered the fortification with the retreating Confederates, — but this is one of the might-have-beens that are common in war. As it was, Grant established the siege of Vicksburg on the land side and directed Sherman northward to take Hayne's Bluff and the fortifications of the Yazoo in the rear. This was done and, once again, after one of the most brilliant operations in the annals of war, the Union army and fleet regained touch with one another above Vicksburg. This plan of operation was Grant's own. It had been undertaken against the written remonstrance of General Sherman, whose letter Grant carefully retained until after the surrender, when he returned it to its author. Lincoln and the authorities at Washington had been greatly perturbed by Grant's repeated failures. But when he was again in communication with the government, Lincoln thanked him in remarkable phrase. The siege of Vicksburg now went on for a month, — the army bombarding it from the east and the navy cannonading it from the west. One assault was made, for Grant felt that his men would not be content without an attempt to overwhelm the Confederates by direct attack. It failed with severe loss, but the siege continued. On July 4, 1863, Pemberton surrendered Vicksburg to Grant,[1] with thirty thousand soldiers, four days' provisions, and plenty of ammunition. Port Hudson surrendered as soon as its commander

---

[1] On July 6, 1863, Grant wrote to his father announcing the surrender of Vicksburg and stated that he had continuously underestimated the force of the enemy and that when it surrendered, they had about four days' rations of flour and meat on hand, and a large quantity of sugar; *American Historical Review*, xii p. 109.

Several, interesting bits of original material are listed in Freeman's *Confederate Calendar* (index under "Vicksburg"). Among these on p. 395 is a letter that is printed in full from General Kirby Smith to General J. E. Johnston, saying that he had found it impossible to throw supplies into Vicksburg from the other side of the Mississippi and that Pemberton's only chance was to cut his way out. Pemberton's own account of the surrender was written in 1875 and was printed in *Progress* for July 30, 1881. In this he describes himself as saying to Grant that he had enough provisions to last "for an indefinite period." This would seem to justify the statement in the Richmond *Examiner* for July 9, 1863, that the news of the Vicksburg surrender was "astoundingly contradictory" to every recent report and the editor concluded with the statement that the soldiers at Vicksburg could have lived on half rations for months. A graphic Confederate account is A. S. Abrams's *A Full and Detailed History of the Siege of Vicksburg* that was printed at Atlanta in November, 1863.

learned of the fall of Vicksburg. Without an hour's delay after Pemberton's surrender, Grant despatched Sherman with a strong force to overwhelm Johnston, but the Confederates were too swift for him and he was obliged to content himself with the reoccupation of Jackson.

After the battle of Murfreesboro', on the last day of the year 1862, the armies in Tennessee stood still for some months. Campaigning in southern Tennessee and in northern Alabama and Georgia was very difficult, — there is no doubt about that. Supplies and transportation were very hard to get and both armies were badly shaken by the Murfreesboro' conflict. Quite in despair at the ever recurring failure to succor the Unionists of East Tennessee, the Washington government sent General Burnside over the mountains to Knoxville in September, 1863, where he and his men were warmly welcomed by the Unionists. Somewhat earlier, in the summer of 1863, Rosecrans moved forward until he gained the opening of the valley of East Tennessee at Chattanooga. The battle of Gettysburg had now been fought and the quietness that prevailed in northern Virginia induced the Confederate authorities to send Longstreet with his men, or a part of them, from Lee's army to act in conjunction with Bragg. When Longstreet reached the front, the Union army was not consolidated, its units being within ordinary supporting distance, roughly speaking, along the line of Chickamauga Creek in the vicinity of Chattanooga. By a vigorous attack the Confederates got in between two portions of the Union army. The country was densely wooded for the most part, with few roads, and it was difficult to know what was going on over any considerable space of the battlefield. Rosecrans happened to be with a portion of the army that was badly shattered. Believing retreat inevitable, he rode into Chattanooga to prepare for the reception of his soldiers and of the oncoming enemy. It happened that, at the other end of the line, Thomas, "the rock of Chickamauga," stood firm and only after repeated orders the next day retired from the field. Soon Bragg had established a strict siege of the Union army.[1] The only line of communication with the North was over very difficult country. The soldiers soon lacked food and the animals forage. The army could not retreat and a prolonged stay where it was meant surrender.

It was on October 17, 1863, that Grant received an order to meet a representative of the War Department at Louisville. Although lame from a recent accident, he at once obeyed. When he reached Indianapolis, he found Edwin M. Stanton, the Secretary of War, and together they journeyed to Louisville. Since Vicksburg and the failure of Meade to pursue Lee after Gettysburg, the Washington authorities had thought of bringing Grant to the East and placing him in command of the Army of the Potomac. In all of Grant's voluminous correspondence, there is no more characteristic letter than one he wrote on August 5, 1863, to Charles A. Dana, expressing his gratitude to Dana for having saved him from being offered the command of the Army of the Potomac. He knew the West, so he wrote, but he would have to learn the geography of the East; he knew the western army and there were many officers in the eastern army

[1] Braxton Bragg is, possibly, the most enigmatical of all the Confederate general officers, — and that is saying a good deal when one thinks of Floyd and Pillow, Albert Sydney Johnston, Beauregard, and Pemberton, and winds up with Hood and Gustavus W. Smith. After the collapse of Bragg's invasion of Kentucky, his division commanders — or whatever they were — apparently were unanimous in believing that a change in the command of the army was necessary. When this came to President Davis's attention, he directed J. E. Johnston to betake himself to Bragg's army and institute an inquiry, and, indeed, to take personal command of it. Johnston refused to do more than inquire and report and Bragg was still in command at the time of Chickamauga. This whole subject has been recently examined by Don C. Seitz in his *Braxton Bragg;* but he has not cleared up the most difficult points.

who had grown up with it. He was grateful to Dana for his "timely intercession." Grant and Stanton had never seen each other before. After they had conversed for a time, the Secretary took out of his pocket an order placing Grant in command of all the armies between the Alleghanies and the Mississippi. Stanton asked Grant whom he would like to have in command of the Army of the Cumberland, whether Rosecrans or Thomas. Grant at once replied, "Thomas." As soon as he could gather up the loose ends of his old and new commands, Grant, himself, repaired to Chattanooga.

On his arrival at Chattanooga, Grant found that plans had already been made to reopen communication between that place and the North and that Hooker with sixteen thousand men from the Army of the Potomac had arrived within reach. After days spent in reconnoitering, Grant ordered Sherman to come to him and directed Hooker to cross the Tennessee below Chattanooga and thus free the navigation of the stream from Confederate attack. Everything was pushed with vigor. Within a week food and forage were abundant, and the Confederates had been forced back from the immediate vicinity of the Union camp. After the battle of Chickamauga, Jefferson Davis had visited Bragg and, in a short time, Longstreet was detached and marched away northward toward Knoxville. Many reasons have been advanced for this movement, but they are all unsatisfactory. Grant's plan was that Hooker should attack the Confederate left by way of Lookout Valley and Mountain ; that Sherman should arrive unseen, cross the river above Chattanooga, and attack the Confederate right, and when these operations were advancing, the Army of the Cumberland should assail its old enemy in the center. Hooker and Sherman made good beginnings, but the former found the way to the Confederate left and rear longer and more difficult than had been expected, and the latter was brought to a standstill by unforeseen obstacles. In front, the nearest Confederate positions had been seized and one can picture Grant standing on Orchard Knob, looking eagerly in either direction, for Chattanooga lies in the midst of an open valley. No Union troops could be seen advancing. Grant then ordered Thomas to attack. The soldiers of the Army of the Cumberland gained the Confederate entrenchments at the foot of Missionary Ridge connecting Lookout Mountain and the hills to the northward where Sherman was stopped. With Sheridan leading, the Union men charged up the slope with the retreating Confederates and went over the entrenchments at the top with them. With his tremendous impetuosity, Sheridan pushed on into the darkness until stopped by direct orders from Grant. Chattanooga,[1] November 26, 1863, was one of the completest victories of the war.

Now, again, as at Vicksburg, without waiting for food, clothing, shoes, or supplies of any kind, Grant ordered a portion of his army to proceed at once to Knoxville, drive off Longstreet, and rescue Burnside and his men. Whatever may have been Burnside's limitations at Fredericksburg, at Knoxville he made very good use of the resources at his command. Formidable fortifications had been constructed and in front of the foremost of these, telegraph wire had been stretched from tree to tree, — apparently the first time that it was so employed in war. Longstreet's men attacked with courage and skill, but were held off, until the approach of the

---

[1] Besides the reports and usual biographies — as those of Grant, Sherman, Sheridan, and Thomas — it is interesting to read the telegrams sent by C. A. Dana to Secretary Stanton in the *Official Records*, ser. i, vol. xxxi, pt. ii, pp. 52–73, especially p. 69. The original blanks upon which these messages were written are now in the Library of Congress. An examination of them is an inspiration to historical research. Another contemporaneous description is contained in a letter from Alfred Pirtle, dated "Camp Tenth Ohio Infantry, November 27, 1863" and printed in Ohio Commandery's *Sketches of War History*, vi, 38–46.

Union forces from Chattanooga compelled their rapid retirement toward Virginia. A month or two later, an act of Congress revived the rank of lieutenant general, which had been held only by Washington and Scott. Grant was appointed to that office and an order was issued placing him in command of all the armies of the United States. In three years and less, the shopman [1] of Galena, Illinois, had become the commander of one-half a million men. The poet in his study has, oftentimes, estimated a man better than the orator or the historian; so James Russell Lowell at Elmwood in Cambridge, Massachusetts, appraised Grant: —

> "Strong, simple, silent . . . such was he
> Who helped us in our need; the eternal law
> That who can saddle Opportunity
> Is God's elect . . .
> Was verified in him."

After much consideration, Grant determined to take charge of the operations in the eastern field [2] and place Sherman in control of the campaign from Chattanooga southward. Following Sherman's advice, he also decided to take the field in person. At first Lincoln seemed inclined to make suggestions as to the strategy of the coming Virginia campaign. But after Grant had made clear to him the futility of his suggestions, Lincoln left the control of operations to the commanding officer of the armies. In the course of the year 1864, one million men were on the muster rolls of the United States armies. So many were employed "behind the lines" and in unfruitful minor operations that

[1] H. J. Eckenrode's summation of Grant's qualities as a military commander, on pages 333, 334 of his *Jefferson Davis, President of the South*, is possibly the best analysis in prose of that great commander's military career : — "Action was his sphere, not words; and in mighty action he has been surpassed by no one in our history."

[2] Two interesting articles by Captain Willey Howell entitled "Lieutenant-General Grant's Campaign of 1864–65" are in *The Military Historian and Economist*, i, 113 and 274.

Grant never had more than one hundred and fifty thousand in the field in Virginia at any one time and Sherman had to content himself with one hundred thousand, including railroad guards and the garrisons connecting his front with his base. Yet Sherman's task was to penetrate to the very vitals of the Confederacy. As for Halleck, it is noteworthy that his letter-heads no longer bore the words "General in Chief," but the words "Chief of Staff." War is no respecter of persons, but it must be said that Halleck did what in him lay to carry out the orders of his former subordinate.

Sherman's campaign had the two-fold objective of the capture or destruction of Johnston's army — once Bragg's — and the capture or the destruction of Atlanta and other centers of Southern warlike industry. Johnston's army comprised about thirty-seven thousand "effectives," according to himself, or seventy thousand, according to his successor, General Hood. Whatever the size of his army, it was strongly posted where the railroad proceeds southward from Chattanooga to Atlanta, in the vicinity of Ringgold. The campaign, from May to July, 1864, offers one of the most fascinating studies in military art. Whatever Joseph E. Johnston's abilities or limitations may have been in other respects, he certainly was a master of the art of defence, and the war probably produced no greater strategist and tactician than William Tecumseh Sherman.[1] In personal charac-

---

[1] Sherman's character and accomplishments shine through the *Official Records*, and the *Home Letters of General Sherman*, edited by M. A. DeW. Howe, contain — pp. 196–354 — private letters of the greatest value to the historical student. Sherman's *Memoirs* were published in 1875. They represent exceedingly vivid recollections; but oftentimes the dates and sequences of events are confused. This has given much pleasure to the adherents of General Thomas, see H. V. Boynton's *Sherman's Historical Raid. The Memoirs in the Light of the Record,* — it is to be noted that chs. xx–xxxi of Don Piatt's *General George H. Thomas* were written by Boynton. Grant's summaries of Sherman's career to July 22, 1863, and also of McPherson's are set forth in a letter that is printed in the *Official Records,* ser. i, vol. xxiv, pt. iii, p. 540. Edward Robins's *William T. Sherman* in the *American Crisis* biographies is a good readable brief account of a great career.

teristics, he was the antithesis of Grant. The one was silent, self-contained; the other was loquacious, but it was noticeable that Sherman's communications never gave notice of his military intentions. The alternations of mountains and rivers from Ringgold southward offered defensive positions that were exceedingly difficult to attack; but the rugged, wooded country offered admirable opportunity for concealed flanking operations. Time and again, Sherman passed his men around the flanks of the enemy, rough field fortifications[1] being thrown up every time a regiment or division halted. Whenever the pressure became too great, Johnston retired from his fortified position to another that was awaiting him in the rear. At times there was almost continuous fighting and then the roar of battle would die down for days. There was only one costly assault, that on Kenesaw Mountain. Arrived within sight of Atlanta, the problem seemed to be as insoluble as ever. Johnston's army was still in good form and spirit. It was then south of the town and Sherman and his men were south of Johnston. President Davis now intervened. He displaced Johnston[2] and appointed General Hood to the command after Hardee had declined it. Hood was expected to fight and he did so. He attacked with great vigor and promptitude. In places the Union soldiers were compelled to jump over their trenches and fight the other way about. In the end, the Confederates were driven back with direful loss, but not until a chance shot had killed General McPherson, Sherman's most trusted subordinate.

[1] The "hasty trench" was the most important contribution of the war to military science. It seems to have been used for the first time at Gaines's Mill in 1862. See "Note" in Ropes's *Story of the Civil War*, pt. ii, p. 380. This reprints in part the statement of Major A. L. Wagner in the *Journal of the Military Service Institute*, March, 1898, p. 230.

[2] President Davis's opinion of Johnston's Atlanta campaign is set forth in a paper drawn by him on February 18, 1865, and printed in Rowland's *Davis*, vi, 499 and on. Johnston's own opinion of the campaign is contained in a letter dated "Aug. 13, 1864," and printed in the *Bulletin* of the New York Public Library, vol. vi, 170.

After other attacks and further losses, Hood retired from Atlanta, and it was occupied by the Union forces on September 2, 1864.

The position of Sherman and his army in northern Georgia with Hood unfettered was one of extreme difficulty. His line of communications extended from Atlanta to Chattanooga and thence to Nashville in Tennessee. Nearly every mile of this long line was accessible to Confederate attack and needed a whole army for its protection, now that Hood had freed himself from all thought of defending posts. With his knowledge of the country and with the friendliness of the inhabitants, Hood could outmarch the swiftest Union army and it was useless to pursue him. The Confederates fell upon one post after another, capturing some and being beaten off at others. To meet the new crisis, Grant sent one of his most trusted men, James H. Wilson, to organize a force of ten thousand cavalry that could take the field against any of the mobile Confederate bands and fight any one in the western area, except the main army. The organization of this force would be the work of time, and Sherman could not stay still and permit Hood and the western horsemen to work their will. He laid before Grant a new or a revamped plan of campaign to march with sixty thousand men from Atlanta to the sea.[1] General Thomas, with the rest of the army and all the detachments within reach and an army corps from the Red River, new recruits, and Wilson's new cavalry force, could fortify himself at Nashville and await Hood. The problem was a very grave one. The solution proposed was full of risks for both Sherman and Thomas, but Grant assented to it.

[1] Vice-President Stephens, on March 16, 1864, at Atlanta, stated that to that time the Union forces had "never yet . . . reached" the heart of the Confederacy; they had been "able only to break the outer shell." This was eight months before Sherman's march through Georgia and may possibly have been a minor incitement to it.

After destroying everything in Atlanta that could be of military service to the enemy, Sherman — on November 15, 1864 — set out on his march with sixty thousand men. They proceeded in three columns, covering a front of some thirty miles. As they went on, they destroyed the railroads, wrapping the heated rails around the nearest trees. Ordinarily in war such a proceeding would be hardly worth the time, but in the Confederacy there were no reserve stores of rails and every one rendered useless brought the day of surrender nearer. Sherman's men "lived off the country" and lived well. Numberless stories have been told of Sherman's "bummers." Undoubtedly, there was a great deal of useless pillage, rough treatment of inhabitants, and removal of valuable articles, that had no place in military operations.[1] Sherman's orders were strict as to the regulation of foraging parties, but there were in the army and following it, men who were careless of right and wrong; and, oftentimes, the provocation given by the inhabitants of Southern planters' houses was great. The idea that Northerners were thieves and rascals, mudsills, and bandits, was part of a vigorous propaganda that had begun before the war. Moreover the insulting demeanor of some Southern

---

[1] Colonel O. L. Jackson in *The Colonel's Diary* (p. 168) recorded that some of the straggling soldiery behaved outrageously. He came across a soldier threatening to shoot an old man who would not tell him where his gold and silver were hidden. Jackson turned the soldier over to the Provost Marshal, who put him in irons. This man belonged to the 1st Alabama Cavalry. This regiment was composed of professed Union men, but Jackson says that they behaved like robbers. Other instances are given in *ibid.*, 164 and 166. Sherman told Gray that his soldiers had turkey for breakfast and would not eat hog and reached Savannah with seven of the eight days' bread with which they had started from Atlanta. A graphic account of the two marches from Atlanta to Savannah and thence to Raleigh, including the Columbia episode (pp. 306–320), is in Capt. G. W. Pepper's *Personal Recollections of Sherman's Campaigns in Georgia and the Carolinas* (Zanesville, Ohio, 1866). An early Union account of Sherman's three marches is G. W. Nichols's *Story of the Great March. From the Diary of a Staff Officer* (New York, 1865). The narrative is preceded by a very good map showing the marches of the different portions of Sherman's army.

women was enough to excite the rage of many a forager.
Apart from pillaging and some torturing of the men, there
seems to have been little violence; but in Southern memoirs,
a smile on the lips of a Northern officer was recorded as an
insult. The most laughable instance of the campaign and
one that occasioned great distress to Governor Brown of
Georgia was the careful removal of all his cabbages to a place
of safety before the coming of the vanguard of Sherman's
army. On the tenth day of December, 1864, Sherman
reached the seacoast and soon opened communication with
the Federal fleet.[1] Ten days later, the Confederates evacuated Savannah, leaving behind them great quantities of
cotton and other valuable products of the Southern country.
Writers on the war have often decried the value of Sherman's
"March to the Sea." Possibly the military objects gained
by it might have been more easily achieved in other ways.
Apart from these considerations, the disappearance of sixty
thousand men into the very heart of the Confederacy and
then the sudden reappearance of this great army on the seacoast impressed the foreign imagination and put absolutely
out of mind—and forever—all thoughts of recognition of the
Confederate States or of armed intervention in their behalf.

Meantime, Thomas had been having a very serious four
weeks. There were Federal garrisons in sundry places of

---

[1] At the time Sherman reached the
sea, John C. Gray was Advocate General of the Southern Department, or
whatever was the name of it at the
moment, with headquarters at Hilton
Head, S. C. He accompanied General
Foster on the steamer *Nemala* and on
December 14, 1864, met Sherman.
Writing to John C. Ropes on that day,
Gray described General Sherman as the
"most American looking man" he ever
saw. He was tall, not very erect, with
hair like thatch, "a rusty beard . . .
a wrinkled face . . . small, bright eyes,
coarse red hands; . . . dirty dickey
with the points wilted down . . . brown
field officers coat with high collar and no
shoulder straps, muddy trowsers and
one spur. He carries his hands in his
pockets, is very awkward in his gait and
motions." Gray wrote that Sherman
declared that he had Savannah surely in
his grip and "stretches out his arm and
claws his bony fingers in the air to
illustrate how he has his grip on it. . . .
He told with evident delight how on his
march he could look forty miles in each
direction and see the smoke rolling up."

strategic importance, in Georgia and Alabama, but these were too feeble to resist serious attack. Had Hood's movements been wisely directed, they might have occasioned a series of disasters to the Union arms and have led to the reoccupation of Tennessee and even of Kentucky by the Confederates. As it was, the over-confidence of Hood, coupled with the lack of faith in him by some of his subordinates, inopportune rains, and a shortage of supplies, greatly retarded his advance. On the Union side, there was good management coupled with a considerable amount of good luck. It resulted that General Schofield with a division or a corps from Atlanta, together with some reënforcements that had been gathered in Georgia and Alabama, found himself at the crossing of the Harpeth River at Franklin,[1] about twenty or twenty-five miles from Nashville, where Thomas then was with the bulk of his army. The trains got across the river and the Union forces threw up some fortifications before the Confederates appeared. Hood at once directed an attack. For a moment the assault succeeded, when General Stanley, whose men had not been engaged, changed front and overwhelmed the Confederates who were huddled in confusion within the Union lines. Another determined assault was made, but again without result. The next morning the Union force made good its retirement to Nashville where Thomas had been anxiously awaiting reënforce-

---

[1] The battle of Franklin was so important and so brilliant an exploit that many books and articles have been written about it. General J. D. Cox wrote a three-hundred-page book on the subject. General J. M. Schofield gives it a whole chapter in his *Forty-Six Years in the Army*. Colonel Henry Stone has a long article on it in vol. vii of the *Papers* of the Military Historical Society of Massachusetts. There is a thrilling account of the campaign by the Confederate General S. G. French in his *Two Wars*, 291 and fol., but its authenticity may well be doubted. Another Confederate, Captain R. W. Banks, published a small volume entitled *The Battle of Franklin . . . The Bloodiest Engagement of the War*, and there is an interesting bit of experience in the *Papers* of the Southern Historical Society, xxiv, 189. A discussion as to the command at Franklin between Generals Stanley and Cox and Colonel Stone is in the *Century* for February, 1889, pp. 628–631.

ments, especially Smith's corps from the Red River. There were entrenchments at Nashville, others were constructed, and every man capable of bearing arms was put into a uniform and placed where he could fight. At length Smith arrived. Then there was great delay, owing to Wilson's inability to mount the last thousands of his cavalrymen. Finally, when all was ready to march to the attack of Hood's entrenched position in front of the town, a storm of sleet converted the hillside into sloping fields of ice. Meantime, Grant had been very anxious. He had written Thomas to advance, but nothing seemed to stir that commander. Thomas wrote that he was willing to resign, but would not take the field until he was prepared to do so. Grant despatched Logan to Nashville with an order in his pocket to relieve Thomas in case he had remained stationary, and even he, himself, started for Tennessee. Before Logan had gone far, however, news came that entirely changed the situation.

As soon as the icy hillsides thawed, Thomas left his entrenchments. Wilson with a large detachment of Union cavalry, dismounted for action, attacked the extreme left of Hood's line, and portions of the Union infantry advancing gained positions favorable for an assault on Hood's entrenchments. The next day, December 16, 1864, Wilson gained a position in the rear of the Confederate lines and awaited the advance of the Union infantry. As it did not come, he rode six miles to headquarters and implored Thomas to give the order.[1] It was given. When the Union infantry

[1] On p. 587 of Don Piatt's *General George H. Thomas*, General H. V. Boynton states that on the second day of the Battle of Nashville, General Wilson was so impatient at the delay of the advance of the Federal infantry that he galloped from behind the rebel lines where he was with his cavalry to the position occupied by Thomas to explain to him the necessity for immediate advance of the whole line. It happened that at that moment the dismounted cavalrymen could be seen swarming into the rebel entrenchments and, writes General Boynton, "At this inspiring sight, Thomas . . . said, 'Let the whole line advance.'" A somewhat similar statement was made by General Wilson himself in his *Under the Old Flag*, ii, 116.

reached the trenches, the Confederates, attacked in front and rear, broke and fled. Their panic communicated itself to the other troops and the whole Confederate army that was not captured on the spot retreated. The dismounted Union cavalrymen regained their horses as fast as they could and rode in pursuit well into the night, but accidents and the rising of the Harpeth River prevented the capture of any large portion of the Confederate army. As it was, it dispersed in small units and not more than fifteen thousand ever reappeared in the armies of the Confederacy.

While Sherman and Thomas had been playing their parts in Georgia and Tennessee, Grant had taken control of operations in Virginia. Recognizing that Lee's army "carried the Confederacy on its bayonets," his plan of campaign was to lead the Army of the Potomac around the right of the Army of Northern Virginia, fight it wherever it might be, and follow it wherever it should go. Grant reënforced the Army of the Potomac with the Nineteenth Corps, a rather heterogeneous collection of old and new troops and negro regiments, all under General Burnside. This arrangement of command was made, so it was said, to save the feelings of Burnside from serving under Meade and to save Meade's feelings by making Grant's presence necessary, as the commander-in-chief of two military units. The Army of the James, some thirty thousand strong, was to advance from Fortress Monroe and, in conjunction with the Union fleet, capture Richmond or, at all events, threaten it. The commander of this army was General B. F. Butler, who was totally without experience in the field, but had considerable political influence. It was one of Grant's characteristics to make use of the instruments that were placed in his hands and, possibly, he had no alternative. The best he could do was to place General W. F. Smith in command of one of Butler's divisions

in the hope perhaps that Smith's remarkable knowledge as
a military engineer would be helpful,[1] but for one reason or
another the arrangement did not turn out well. Butler's
movements were not as rapid as they might have been and
his intentions were not as thoroughly concealed as they might
have been. In the end the Army of the James found itself
safely entrenched on a neck of land about midway between
Petersburg and Richmond. As someone said and Grant
repeated, Butler had bottled himself up and Beauregard, now
again in command in front of Richmond, had driven in the
stopper. The failure of Butler to engage any considerable
body of the enemy, either in the field or by making a determined attack on Richmond, was a great blow to Grant's
plans and left Lee free to thwart him as well as he might.
In the end Grant removed Smith and his corps from Butler's
army and added it to his own.

On May 5, 1864, Grant crossed the Rapidan and entered
the Wilderness on the march to Richmond. He was now on
the battlefield of Chancellorsville and Lee seems to have
thought of dealing with him as he had dealt with Hooker a
year before. But circumstances had changed, for Grant
was not Hooker and Stonewall Jackson was no longer there
to lead the "forlorn hope" in an attack on the Union flank.
As it was, the Confederates attacked with vigor and with
skill and the Union Army replied with equal vigor and equal
skill. But the conditions of battling in the Wilderness were
such that the preponderance of strength of the Federal forces
could not be used effectively, or, at all events, was not used
effectively. This was Grant's first battle with the Army of
the Potomac. It must have been distressing to him, but he

---

[1] There is an interesting article on
Butler and his campaign of 1864 by
G. M. Wolfson in the *South Atlantic
Quarterly*, x, 377. He refers with ap-
proval to C. F. Adams's statements in
the *Proceedings* of the Massachusetts
Historical Society for October, 1905,
pp. 348–355.

gave no sign of irritation of any kind. At first, there was
jealousy and opposition to Grant, — but this soon disappeared. It may be, that on May 5th and 6th, his orders
were slowly executed and, when one looks over the story of
those days, there is apparent the same disinclination to use
the full power of divisions and corps that had marked the
earlier history of the Army of the Potomac. As nothing
could be done in the Wilderness,[1] Grant decided to get out of
it. Instead of retracing his steps to the Rapidan, he directed
the head of the army southward, toward Richmond.

On this occasion, as before in its history, it was difficult
to get the Army of the Potomac to move. The roads were
very bad, this time knee-deep in dust. The trains were vast
in extent and there was far too much artillery for a densely
wooded country. Nevertheless, a cavalry division was sent
forward to seize the crossroads at Spottsylvania Court
House and the corps on the extreme right of the Union army
took up the march behind the front in the same direction
and was followed by the other corps in succession from right
to left. The movement should have been made in the night,

[1] C. F. Atkinson in *Grant's Campaigns of 1864 and 1865*, pp. 205–208,
has admirably summed up this first
contact between Grant and Lee. He
quotes Grant's statement on the
morning of May 7, 1865, that "Joe
Johnston would have retreated after
two days of such punishment!"
Grant's eyes had been opened to the
truth that with Lee and the Army of
Northern Virginia, he had to deal with
a different problem from that which had
confronted him in his Western campaigns. Atkinson further gives us to
understand that Lee likewise had met
with a different opponent and his "first
attempt to break the 'war spirit' of the
Union army ended with little more than
the loss of 18 per cent. of his small army
and the confirmation of his opponent's
resolution to renew the battle."

Two other studies of this campaign
by Englishmen are J. H. Anderson's
*Grant's Campaign in Virginia, May 1–
June 30, 1864* and Capt. Vaughan-
Sawyer's *Grant's Campaign in Virginia,
1864*. This campaign at that time,
1908, was prescribed for the British
Army Staff College Examination. *The
Virginia Campaign of '64 and '65* by
General A. A. Humphreys is a master-
piece of its kind and represents the sober
second thought of Meade's chief of staff.
One of Grant's personal aides, General
Horace Porter, in 1897, published a very
attractive volume entitled *Campaigning
with Grant*. The "Preface" states that
"these reminiscences are simply a
transcript of memoranda jotted down
at the time," but they have been
thoroughly edited.

but it had hardly begun before daylight dawned and columns of dust rising above the tree-tops apprised the Confederates of what was going on. And one may wonder at Lee's thoughts as he saw those columns of dust rise farther and farther to the southward! The days of McClellan, Pope, and Hooker were no more. A division of the Confederate army was at once directed to Spottsylvania. The Union cavalry reached the Court House first, but could not maintain itself against the onslaughts of the infantry. The best that could be done was to retire as slowly as possible until the Federal infantry appeared. Then followed battle for two days and more. The conflict was waged with a ferocity and a bloodiness that seldom has been equalled. Attack after attack was made on either side with no result at all comparable to the loss.[1] In desperation, Lee tried to place himself at the head of his charging battalions, but they refused to move until he went to the rear. Again, Grant saw that nothing could be accomplished with the conditions as they were. He skilfully removed his army from in front of Lee and set it on its southward march, — "I propose to fight it out on this line if it takes all summer," so he wrote. He summoned W. F. Smith and his corps from the Army of the James; he reorganized the cavalry and placed it under command of Sheridan, and he sent back a part of his artillery.

Up to this time Sheridan had been an infantry commander and had always acted under the orders of another. He had scarcely occupied his new position when he developed a new

---

[1] C. A. Dana's telegram to Stanton of May 9, 1864, in the Library of Congress, states that "Warren, however, proceeded with exceeding caution, and when he finally did attack, sent a single division at a time and was constantly repulsed. The general attack which Generals Grant and Meade directed was never made for reasons which I have not yet been able to learn, but successive assaults were made upon this and that point in the rebel positions, with no decisive results."

line of action for the cavalry.   Hitherto, it had been regarded
as existing for outpost duty and for the protection of transportation.   The Confederate cavalry, extremely efficient
in itself, had been superbly commanded by General J. E. B.
Stuart and had ridden at will around the Union armies and
through its lines of communication.   Sheridan thought that
the cavalry of the Army of the Potomac should be brought
together as one force and should be employed to combat the
Confederate cavalry and break up the Confederate lines of
communication.   He laid his ideas before Grant, who told
him to take them to Meade.   He did so.   It cannot be said
that Meade had much faith in the new way of looking at
cavalry, or, perhaps, in the new commander.   But his position was a peculiarly difficult one and he assented to the
plan of Grant's chosen cavalry chief.   Thereupon, Sheridan
with ten or twelve thousand cavalrymen cut loose from the
armies in the Wilderness, rode rapidly southward, destroying
whatever he could without too much waste of time, placed
himself south of Stuart, and compelled that commander to go
after him without more ado.   The two came together at
Yellow Tavern within the outer defences of Richmond.   In
the encounter, Sheridan was successful, the Confederate
cavalry was defeated and its leader killed.   It is possible
that Sheridan might have entered Richmond;   and, had
there been a soldier in command of the Army of the James,
which was not many miles away, the two might have maintained themselves there for a time, at least, and powerfully
affected the future movements of Lee.   But it was not so
to be.   Sheridan extricated himself with difficulty, took his
command to Butler's camp, refreshed it, and then rode back
to the Army of the Potomac, which now was well on its way
from Spottsylvania to the North Anna River.   In this short
expedition, he had greatly increased the confidence of the

Union cavalrymen in themselves, had shown himself to be
an independent commander of high ability, and had inflicted
a severe stroke on Southern morale, which up to that time
had not been accustomed to seeing ten or a dozen thousand
Northern soldiers riding hither and yon, over the sacred soil
of northern Virginia.

Once out of the Wilderness, the Army of the Potomac and
the Nineteenth Corps, now reënforced with the Sixteenth
Corps from the James, found conditions of marching and of
camping much improved; but it cannot be said that the
military problem had greatly altered for the better. Taught
a lesson, perhaps, by his terrible losses of the Wilderness and
Spottsylvania, Lee no longer attempted attacks. He now
placed his men behind entrenchments and awaited the on-
slaught of Grant's soldiers. At Cold Harbor, May 31–
June 12, the two armies came to the ground of McClellan's
Peninsular Campaign. Indeed, the Confederates occupied
in part of their line some of the old Union entrenchments,
fighting the other way about. The contest here was of the
most stern and bloody character. Time after time, fortune
seemed about to smile on the Northern troops and tempted
Grant to further attack, when the tide turned and nothing
but unavailing bloodshed occurred. Again, Grant took his
men away from Lee's front and this time carried them with
most skilfully directed movements to the banks of the James
and across that river to the southern side. A part of his
plan had been the capture of Petersburg; but misadventure
again occurred. By some lack of orders or absence of comprehension, Hancock and Smith, who were first across the
James, did not realize that they were expected to seize Petersburg at the very first moment of their approach. They
stopped for food and munitions, while it was unoccupied,
and when they advanced, found the trenches and forts in the

hands of Lee's soldiers. In these battles, from May 4th
to June 16th, 1864 — from the Rapidan to the James — Lee's
losses totaled 31,800 or "46 per cent. of the original force
of priceless veterans he had commanded in April." [1] The
Union army had lost "about 50,000" men or some forty per
cent of the army that had crossed the Rapidan on the 4th of
May.[2] In other words, the loss of the Confederates had been
proportionately greater than that of the Union army.
Nevertheless, Grant's casualties were used by Northern
newspaper men and politicians and by Confederate propagandists in ways that were greatly to the detriment of
Grant's military reputation and to the heroism and fighting
spirit of the Army of the Potomac, — and most unjustly in
both cases.

For eight months, the two armies confronted each other
in the lines at Petersburg and across the James to Bermuda
Hundred. Each army fortified itself strongly and the operation took on the form of a siege with recurring field campaigns
to the south of Petersburg. The object of these was to seize
the railroads and the country roads leading from Petersburg
and Richmond to the southward, for it was over these lines
of communication that Lee's army received the greater part
of its supplies. Here, again, owing to the broken and
wooded country, it was very difficult to utilize the superior
strength of the Union army. As month after month went

[1] C. F. Atkinson's *Grant's Campaigns*,
462.

[2] These estimates are from Colonel
Livermore's paper on "Grant's Campaign against Lee" in the *Papers* of the
Military Historical Society of Massachusetts, vol. iv, 448–451. General A.
A. Humphreys' *Virginia Campaign of
'64 and '65*, pp. 424, 425, points out that
the Surgeon General's "Tabular Statement" from which the figures of the
losses in the Wilderness have been
generally compiled contains "two alternative statements of losses, derived from
different sources" and that these had
been added together instead of being
averaged by the Confederate General
Wilcox in his article in the Southern
Historical Society's *Papers*, vi, 75, —
one of the most terrible and unjust
blunders in modern military history.
In C. A. Dana's *Recollections of the Civil
War*, 210, 211, is a table showing the
losses of the Union armies in Virginia,
Maryland, and Pennsylvania from May
24, 1861, to April 9, 1865.

by, Grant received accessions of new soldiers and old soldiers
from other parts of the field of war until by winter his force
very greatly outnumbered that of Lee.   The fall of Atlanta
in July at about the time of the transfer of the army from
Cold Harbor to Petersburg also exercised a very great
influence on the morale of the Southern people.   This time
the psychological loss of nerve extended to the Army of
Northern Virginia.   It was greatly increased by the ever
growing difficulty of supplying that army with food, owing to
the breaking of the lines of transportation to the south of
Petersburg and to the west of Richmond.   As the months
went by, desertions increased in volume and, on the other
hand, accessions came in very slowly to Lee's army.   The
growing lack of confidence among the Confederate soldiers
was made more noticeable by the deserters bringing their
arms with them when they came into the Union lines.   Lee
determined to repeat, in a measure, his manœuvre of 1862
and by threatening Washington to lessen the pressure on
Petersburg and to restore the spirits of the Southern soldiers
and people.   Probably he did not expect that Grant would
be ordered away from the James as McClellan had been two
years earlier, but one could not tell what panic might impel
the Washington government to do.   Lee selected Jubal A.
Early as the commander of this new expedition.   Like
Jackson, Early had been originally a Union man, and like
Jackson he had thrown in his lot with his State when it
seceded.   He was not a phenomenal commander, but he
possessed many of the attributes of military greatness.
Leading his men to the Valley of the Shenandoah, he proceeded rapidly downward to the Potomac, crossed that river
at Harper's Ferry, turned his line of march to Washington,
and came within sight of the fortifications.   Whatever
soldiers there were in the capital were placed in the forts

and as formidable an appearance of resistance was set up as possible. It happened that the Sixth Corps was on transports on the James River. Grant at once diverted it to Washington, where it arrived in good time. With the appearance of these soldiers at Washington, Early retired and was leisurely followed to Harper's Ferry. At this juncture, Grant himself came to the capital and determined to appoint Sheridan to the command of the army acting against Early. There was much opposition to this appointment, on the part of Stanton and some others at Washington, mainly on account of Sheridan's youthful appearance and lack of experience in high command. But Grant insisted and the appointment was made. Then followed a campaign in the Valley such as it had never witnessed, for now, instead of Frémont, Banks, or Hunter, the Union army was directed by one of the foremost fighters of the century, in America or in Europe.

Sheridan was of Irish parentage, his father and mother being immigrants from the Emerald Isle. He was born at Albany in the State of New York, but his parents removed to Ohio when he was a babe, and thus he became the third of the great Ohio generals to win fame in the war, — Grant, Sherman, and Sheridan. The problem that confronted Sheridan was complicated by the detachment of a considerable portion of the old Longstreet division from Petersburg to the Valley, when the pressure upon Early had become too great for him to withstand. At first Sheridan acted with caution, as was natural to a man in his new position. Possibly Grant was somewhat annoyed at this, for he wrote out a series of instructions for Sheridan and summoned him to a conference at Charlestown, ten miles above Harper's Ferry. When the two came together, Sheridan was full of abounding confidence and only asked for permission to go in and destroy his opponent.   Grant kept his instructions in his pocket and told Sheridan to go in.   The two armies marched up and down the Valley and then back again, somewhat after the old manner, except that this time the Union soldiers were the aggressors.   Sheridan adopted the expedient of sending his cavalry, in which he was strong, around the enemy's flanks and then, when the moment came, attacking with infantry.   After several battles of this kind, in which Early suffered reverse after reverse, Sheridan moved down the Valley to try to find a position that could be fortified and thus release a portion of his command for return to the main army at Petersburg.   In furtherance of this design and to explain the situation of affairs he went to Washington, leaving his men encamped at Cedar Creek.   On his return, accompanied by some engineer officers, he passed the night at Winchester, a dozen miles or so from his camp.   When the morning came, sounds of cannon were heard in the distance. After a time, they became louder and seemed to be coming nearer.   Sheridan at once mounted his horse and with his staff rode forward.   Before long, he came across fleeing Union soldiers and then the road became filled with them. Calling to them to turn back and sending his aids to either side of the road to induce others to return, he rode forward with whatever speed he could make.   When he reached the front, he found that Early had surprised his camp, had driven out the men, and that some of them had become panic stricken.   Others had held steadfast in defensible positions.   Reforming his line and adding to it many of the stragglers who had followed him to the field, Sheridan rode along the front and by his presence alone restored confidence. At the word the line swept forward and before nightfall the Confederates were in utter rout.   Sheridan now spared neither man nor horse, but followed Early wherever he went

until the Valley was cleared of the enemy. Acting under
orders from Grant, he then destroyed everything eatable by
man or beast, set fire to barns and hayricks, and left the
Valley in such condition that a crow flying over it would have
to carry his food with him. Naturally there was great
suffering in the immediate future on the part of the inhabitants of the Valley of the Shenandoah; but that the destruction was justifiable is seen in a letter from General Lee to the
effect that forage was so scarce that he could not sustain his
cavalry force.[1] Having accomplished this and leaving a
few soldiers to maintain some posts of importance, Sheridan
with his main body passed through the Blue Ridge and boldly
marched eastwardly across northern Virginia to the White
House on the Pamunky River. There he refreshed man
and beast from the stores collected and then, taking whatever he could with him, by orders from Grant, abandoned it
as a depot and marched to the James River and the Petersburg front, arriving there early in March, 1865.

Meantime, Fort Fisher had fallen before the combined
efforts of the navy and the army, and Wilmington, the last
refuge of the blockade runners, had been captured. Mobile
Bay had been occupied in August, 1864, by Admiral Farragut
after another spectacular running by forts and a most
extraordinary combat between the wooden men-of-war and
the Federal monitors, on the one side, and the Confederate
ironclad *Tennessee* on the other. Farragut had then been
offered the command of the Atlantic fleet, but borne down
with fatigue, he had declined and Admiral Porter had been
brought from the West and placed in charge of all the opera-

[1] Writing to Breckinridge on March
17, 1865, Lee stated that "Had we been
able to use the supplies which Sheridan
has destroyed in his late expedition in
maintaining our troops in the Valley in
a body, if his march could not have been
arrested it would at least have been
rendered comparatively harmless. . . .
Now, I do not see how we can sustain
even our small force of cavalry around
Richmond." A. L. Long's *Memoirs of
Robert E. Lee*, 689.

tions on the remaining Atlantic seaboard of the Confederacy. Porter believed that with the aid of an army division or two, Fort Fisher at the entrance to the Cape Fear River might be captured. If that were done, the subsidiary fortifications in the neighborhood would be abandoned, the Union fleet could lie in the river itself and put a stop to any further blockade running and Wilmington would sooner or later fall into Federal control. Grant approved the plan and despatched soldiers from the Army of the James. At that moment someone suggested that a vessel filled with powder and exploded as near Fort Fisher as it could get would so shake the walls that assault would be practicable. Although this meant extra delay, Grant acceded to it. Apparently it had never occurred to him that General Butler, the commander of the Army of the James, would proceed with a detachment from that force; but this he insisted on doing and it was difficult to displace him. After many delays the powder boat was exploded without damage to the walls of the fort and without attracting the attention of the garrison who supposed that the boiler of one of the blockading vessels had exploded. Porter then bombarded the walls, but when the time came for the troops who had been landed out of range of the fort to advance to the assault, Butler refused to permit it. They were reëmbarked and returned to Fortress Monroe, whereupon Grant, with the concurrence of the government, ordered General Butler to report for duty at his home town in Massachusetts. A larger force was sent to coöperate with Porter, the fort was again bombarded and, after a fierce contest, it was captured.[1]

[1] Besides the official accounts, there are interesting letters on the two sides of the Southern defence by General Bragg and by Colonel William Lamb, the Confederate commander at the fort at the time of the surrender, in Southern Historical Society's *Papers*, x, 346 and 350, and in the *Memoirs of the War of Secession* by Johnson Hagood, commander of the South Carolina troops at Fort Fisher, pp. 320–348.

In the month of January, 1865, Sherman and Grant anxiously planned as to what the former should do with the great army that he had brought with him to Savannah. Grant was inclined to bring Sherman's army by water from Savannah to the James and add it to his own force. Sherman thought it would be better for the Army of the Potomac itself to end the contest with the Army of Northern Virginia and for the soldiers from the West to march from Savannah northward and take care of whatever Confederates might be in their way and keep them from joining Lee at Petersburg. Grant acceded to this idea and Sherman proceeded to put the plan into execution. Leaving Savannah in February, 1865, long before the Confederates expected him, his soldiers struggled painfully through drowned river bottoms, but at last gained solid land in the rear of Charleston and on the road to Columbia, the capital of South Carolina. Charleston was plainly untenable, and General Hardee, the Confederate commander there, removed the garrison, and in no long time the city was occupied by the forces that had been blockading the harbor entrance. With its rapid stride and merciless power, Sherman's army marched forward, having outstripped a force that was being gathered to oppose it. While marching through Georgia, the soldiers had been comparatively good natured, but they, as well as the politicians, looked upon South Carolina as the author of the trouble that had torn them from their families and firesides. It was with a revengeful spirit that the western army pursued its northward march, — little mercy was shown to whomsoever resisted in the slightest degree.

In the course of Sherman's northward progress, Columbia was occupied and a great deal of property, that had been taken there from Charleston for safe-keeping, was appropriated to public or private uses. Columbia was partly

destroyed by fire,[1] and the arsenals and factories at Fayetteville suffered a similar fate. The burning of Columbia
appears to have been partly accidental and partly to have
been the result of the drunkenness and feelings of resentment
of Sherman's soldiers. He has told us that he did not order
the burning of Columbia because there was no military
necessity for so doing; had there been, he would not have
hesitated an instant to have ordered its destruction.[2] When
the army advanced beyond Fayetteville, the resistance to its
forward march stiffened. In January, 1865, the Confederate
Congress had found the courage of its convictions and made
Lee commander-in-chief of all the armies of the Confederacy.[3] One of his first acts in this new office was to draw
Joseph E. Johnston from retirement and place him in charge
of the troops, including the remains of Hood's army, once
Johnston's own, that were gathering in Sherman's way.[4]
At Bentonville, North Carolina, on March 19, 1865, there
was an encounter between the two forces. A few days later,
General Schofield and his corps, which had left Sherman's
army at Atlanta, had fought at Franklin and at Nashville,

[1] Sherman had been stationed at
Charleston before the war. On June
30, 1864, from his camp near Marietta,
Georgia, he addressed a letter to Mrs.
Annie Gilman Bowen who was then living in Baltimore, Maryland. He refers
to those old days on Sullivan's Island
and then speaks very plainly as to the
reason for the war and as to the outcome
and declares that if the fortunes of war
should ever bring "your mother or your
sisters" under the shelter of his authority, they would have no cause to regret
it (American Antiquarian Society's Proceedings for April, 1891, p. 222).

[2] On December 14, 1864, Major John
C. Gray recorded the statement of Sherman that he would rather march to
Richmond by land, and if he did, his
progress through South Carolina would
be "one of the most horrible things in
the history of the world, that the devil

himself could not restrain his men in
that state," — the cradle of secession.
Again on January 14, 1865, Gray wrote
that when Sherman started, it would be
for the interior of South Carolina and
added: "It will be a pitiless march."
Replying to these various statements,
Ropes said that "making the South feel
the horrors of war" is admirable; Sherman "has carried out the right idea,
that War is War."

[3] Pages 323–325 of *Lee's Dispatches
to Jefferson Davis* contain a long note as
to Lee's assuming chief command on
February 9, 1865.

[4] On February 18, 1865, Davis refused
to give J. E. Johnston a command. A
few days later he acceded to the
request of General Robert E. Lee and
appointed Johnston to the command of
what was left of the Army of Tennessee.
Rowland's *Davis*, vi, 503 and 491.

and thence had proceeded by rail and steamer, and again by rail to the heart of North Carolina, joined their former comrades who had marched the whole way from Atlanta to Savannah, thence to the meeting point. Together, they could successfully oppose any force that the Confederates could bring against them. But Sherman realized that their part in the closing scene was to hold Johnston and his troops where they were and leave the rest to Grant and the Army of the Potomac.

NOTE

The Burning of Columbia. — Colonel Jackson (*The Colonel's Diary*, 182, 191) under date of February 17, 1865, describes this episode.[1] He went into it with the advance corps of the army and wrote that the women looked sour or turned their heads away; "the rebels had piled the cotton in the streets for burning and had burned a little," but when he rode through the city no fires were in progress. The soldiers found quantities of spirituous liquors in the town and were joined by many escaped Union prisoners who had been penned in the neighborhood and were very bitter against the inhabitants of Columbia. Jackson crossed the river to his own regiment at night and in the evening observed "considerable fire in the city." The next morning he returned to the city and found it mostly in ruins. And there seemed to be a general acquiescence in the disaster as a fit example. He wrote that perhaps the brigade on duty "made some efforts to put out the fires, but I do not think you could have got enough men in the army disposed to stop it to have affected anything." Later he records that there was a recklessness shown by the soldiers in South Carolina that they had never exhibited before and "a sort of general 'don't care' on the part of the officers."

[1] The report of General C. R. Woods, who was in command of the division of the Fifteenth Corps that occupied Columbia, made on February 17, the day of the occupation and the conflagration, is the best possible historical evidence. This and other official reports are printed in the *Official Records*, ser. i, vol. xlvii, pt. ii, p. 457. Other accounts are in the same volume and also in pt. i, where they may easily be found by using the index under "Columbia." The question as to the responsibility for the burning of cotton at Columbia became an important item in litigation, and Sherman's testimony was taken in Egypt and again in New York and may be found in many places. Ex-parte evidence, on one side or the other, can be found in recollections of Sherman and of Howard, and in numerous Southern tracts as D. H. Trezevant's *Burning of Columbia* (Columbia, S. C., 1866); Col. J. C. Gibbes's *Who Burnt Columbia* (Newberry, S. C., 1902); and the "Sack and Destruction of the City of Columbia, S. C." This was originally published in the *Columbia Daily Phœnix*. It was written by William Gilmore Simms and was printed in pamphlet form at Columbia, in 1865. The matter was summarized by Rhodes in his *Historical Essays*, 301–313.

CHAPTER XIX

THE ELECTION OF 1864

In the summer of 1864 the war seemed to be halting; — Grant's Virginia campaign was gravely imperilled by the incapacity of many of his subordinate commanders and Sherman was still outside of Atlanta. With the oncoming of the political campaign for the control of the government for the next four years, it was necessary that there should be an assessment of men, means, and measures, of failures and achievements. Looking backward, we can see that the people of the North in 1861 undertook to reconnect the seceded States with the Union and to use the legislative power that the absence of the Secessionists from Congress placed in their hands to build up the manufacturing industries of the North and to extend its agricultural operations. This policy was the natural result of the wishes of the constituents of Congressmen in all parts of the country; and it may well be that the prolongation of the war for a year or more was distinctly a lesser evil than the retardation of Northern prosperity.

In ages past, in the times of Alexander and of Cæsar, of Wallenstein and of Napoleon, the ability to march long distances and day after day, to carry weights, and to ride on horseback were of the first necessity for the soldier. It was a man trained to outdoor life, to delving in the soil, to following the plow, or to ranging the woods, who was useful in war. It followed that an agricultural country was the strongest country for military purposes, that cattlemen, herdsmen, and shepherds were the best soldiers. By 1860, the art of war was beginning to take on the industrial phase in which machines and not marchers were to be supreme. In the future, soldiers were to be transported by rail or boat, instead of marching hundreds of miles to the fields of battle. And when in front of the enemy, artillery, and not infantry or cavalry, was oftentimes to be the deciding factor. It is a long way from the horse-frightening cannon of Cressy and Poictiers to the seventy-five-mile carrying gun of the year 1918. The War for Southern Independence came in the mid-interval. It came at the moment when machines, from the steam-locomotive to the breech-loader and the torpedo, were beginning to play their parts. The war was to be waged industrially as no war had ever been waged before. In this regard the South was hopelessly handicapped and the outcome was in the hands of the Northern people, provided they stood fast. The year 1864 was to decide whether they would stand fast or not.

The sudden boom in production in the North — due to the establishment of war industries and to the demand for the wheat of the Northwest by the dwellers on the other side of the Atlantic — has already been noted. For years, the Northern people had wished for a much more liberal attitude on the part of the Federal government toward the bestowal of vacant lands on actual occupiers. The Southerners had no wish to thus strengthen the area of Northern free-soil sentiment and had opposed every attempt to pass legislation that would bring this about. On May 20, 1862, President Lincoln affixed his signature to a bill which came to be known as the Homestead Act. By this law any person who should go and live for a specified time on an allotment of one hundred and sixty acres should become the owner of the farm, upon paying a very small sum. Two and one-half million acres of lands — more or less — were taken up by "Homesteaders" in the years from 1862 to 1865. In 1862 and in 1863, the Northern States alone produced more wheat than the whole country had grown before secession.[1]

The Know-Nothing movement and the panic of 1857, in combination, had greatly retarded the flow of foreign immigration to the United States. With the quickening of the demand for labor that the war made in the factory and on the farm, immigration began again and was greatly stimulated by the offer of free lands to the new-comer. It fell out, therefore, that in 1863 and thereafter, there was a constant increase in the number of immigrants that landed on the shores of the United States;[2] and there was a constant movement of population from the eastern part of the country and from the Old Northwest across the prairies to the silver and gold producing mountains and valleys from Colorado to the Coast. How many went in the years of the war or in any one year will never be known.[3] We read of the wagons of the migrants whitening the plains, of thousands of people dying of an epidemic on the way, and of this mining camp or that one having one inhabitant today and a thousand a month later, — or a thousand today and none a month later.[4] One man who rode in a stage from Kansas City to Denver

[1] Fite's *Social and Industrial Conditions*, p. 2.

[2] The numbers were 91,985 in 1862, 176,282 in 1863, 193,418 in 1864, and 248,120 in 1865. See *Reports of the Immigration Commission*, vol. iii, "Statistical Review of Immigration, 1820–1910," pp. 27–29. Professor Fite in the *Quarterly Journal of Economics*, xx, 271, states that Illinois in the years 1860–1865 gained 430,000 inhabitants, Wisconsin 90,000, Minnesota 78,000, Iowa 180,000, Kansas 35,000, Nebraska 30,000, or 843,000 for these six States during the war.

[3] In 1864, the Secretary of the Treasury reported that in 1860 the population of California, Nevada, Utah, Colorado, and Kansas was 554,046 and four years later 820,000; and that the population of Idaho, Montana, and Dakota was practically nothing in 1860 and 42,000 in 1863; *Senate Executive Document*, No. 55, 38th Cong., 1st Sess., pp. 212–217. In March, 1865, S. M. Worcester reported to the Massachusetts Senate that in 1860 the population of Oregon was 52,160 and over 100,000 in 1865.

[4] In March, 1863, the "great push" from California and Oregon to the Idaho mines began; see J. Hailey's *History of Idaho*, 33, 62.

states that every time he looked out of the window he saw wagons pursuing their slow westward way. But all this means little except that there was a large and constant migration westward from the Missouri River in every year of the war.[1] It was estimated that the population of Oregon almost doubled in the five years from 1860 to 1865 and that eight thousand votes were cast in the first election that was held in Idaho Territory in 1863. In the four years of the war, no less than one hundred and sixty-eight million dollars worth of gold and twenty-seven of silver were taken from the soil of the United States. Of this great gold production, forty-three millions were recorded in 1861 and fifty-three millions in 1865.[2] Plainly there must have been many workers on the Coast and in the mountains. The motives for this western migration during the war have been generally set down as the desire to gain free lands or easily acquired wealth in the shape of gold and silver taken from the newly discovered lodes and diggings. It has also been suggested that many men sought the Far Western settlements to escape the draft. Of course one cannot probe into the motives of those who sought this region in the years when the Union government was fighting for its life. Undoubtedly some of them had served their time in the Union army, had been

[1] On p. 56 of his *Great West: Emigrants', Settlers', & Travelers' Guide* (New York, 1864) E. H. Hall prints a letter dated Virginia City, July 26, 1864. The writer states that the streets were filled with pilgrims and wanderers; not less than twenty thousand having already arrived and the roads from Salt Lake and Denver were lined with emigrants. The population of Virginia City had doubled within a year. J. S. Collins in *Across the Plains in '64*, p. 11, states that at one time in the spring of 1864 there were over two hundred teams encamped opposite Fort Kearney. R. D. Ross, in the *Collections* of the State Historical Society of North Dakota (ii, 219–231), gives the impression of a very active migration in June and July, 1863. A bibliography of three hundred and forty-nine original narratives is in H. R. Wagner's *The Plains and The Rockies* (San Francisco, 1921). See also Fite's *Social and Industrial Conditions*, 34–41.

[2] *Statistical Abstract of the United States* (1916), p. 226; W. A. Goulder's *Reminiscences*, 246; *The Silver Mines of Nevada* (New York, 1865), p. 13; W. J. McConnell's *Early History of Idaho*, and Fite's *Social and Industrial Conditions*, 32–34.

disabled from further service in the field, or had had enough
of war and, therefore, sought new homes in the Western
country.[1] It is certain that among a large part of the
Northern people there was lukewarmness in 1864 as to the
further prosecution of the war. Many persons were and
always had been opposed to the coercion of their fellow
Americans in the seceded States. It is undoubtedly true
that the publication of the Emancipation Proclamation
chilled the enthusiasm of many persons for the war and
increased the number of the active opponents of it. In
older days in England, it was said that one could predict the
path that grown-up men would take as to any one matter
by the preferences, more or less vigorously expressed, by the
students at Oxford and at Cambridge. If any such prog-
nostication could be based on the doings of students of
Northern colleges in these years,[2] it would certainly seem
that there was no ardent wish for war in the North, although
some institutions — as Antioch — were depleted of students.

As the year 1864 dragged its weary length along, the
apathy of the Northern people and of the Southern toward
the war became more and more noticeable. In the South,
the demand of family, of wife, and of children for the father's

---

[1] An interesting group of settlers was
a party of marooned Confederates who
had found themselves on the western
side of the Union line and had migrated
in a body to Virginia City, Montana,
which for a time was called Varina in
honor of Mrs. Jefferson Davis. There
were also certain companies of Southern
prisoners who had been taken into the
Union army and sent to garrisons on the
plains where these "galvanized Confederates" or "whitewashed Rebs"
were safe from the vengeance of their
former comrades. See A. K. McClure's
Recollections, 383; T. J. Dimsdale's
Vigilantes of Montana, 55; and Montana Historical Society's *Contributions*,
i, 113.

[2] The catalogues of Harvard, Yale,
Columbia, and Michigan give the
combined undergraduate attendance
in 1860–61 as 1,359; in the next four
years the lowest number was 1,178 in
1864–65. The total registration of the
senior classes in the four institutions in
the five years of the war time was
268, 283, 320, 272, and 242, — at
Michigan, alone, was there any striking
falling off. Robert T. Lincoln, the
President's oldest son, remained at
Harvard from 1860 to 1864, when he
received a staff appointment that
enabled him to see something of war
in the Appomattox campaign (Nicolay
and Hay's *Abraham Lincoln*, x, 213).

or brother's labor on the farm, or his superintendence of the plantation became acute. In the North, hardly a household but had suffered loss of son or brother, or some relative who had given his life for the Union. Moreover, by this time the war had become a struggle to free the slave, and probably not one man in ten in the North cared whether the negro was a slave or a free man, and the constantly rising wages and demand for men's labor blocked the path of patriotism. Besides, the war seemed to be interminable. Now, of course, it is clear that by the summer of 1864 Grant and Sherman held the Southern armies where they could deal with them, when the time came. The only possible hope for the Confederates was to break the faith of the Northern people in success not too far away. And it was very possible that they could do it, for there seemed to be a joint movement on the part of politicians and newspaper men to destroy the confidence of the people in Lincoln and in his two great commanders. In May, 1864, two New York papers, both consistent opponents of the Lincoln government, published a proclamation dated "Executive Mansion, May 17, 1864." The names of the President and the Secretary of State were appended to it.[1] The proclamation set apart the twenty-sixth day of May following as a day of fasting, humiliation, and prayer. "With a heavy heart, but an undiminished confidence in our cause, I approach the performance of a duty rendered imperative by my sense of weakness before Almighty God and of justice to the people." In the present condition of public affairs, so the

[1] Appleton's *Annual Cyclopaedia*, iv, 389 and Nicolay and Hay's *Abraham Lincoln*, ix, 48. In June, 1863, General Burnside had ordered the Chicago *Times* to cease publication. Senator Trumbull, Isaac N. Arnold, and others at once protested and telegraphed so vigorously to Washington that Lincoln directed Burnside to revoke his order. When it was too late, some of the Chicagoans changed their minds. See *General Burnside's Order No. 84, Suppressing the Chicago Times, and Its History*.

proclamation stated, it was necessary to call out four hundred thousand more men, and in case any State did not furnish its quota, to secure the necessary soldiers by a draft. At once, on learning of the publication of this false and malicious document, the Washington government ordered the suppression of the papers and the arrest of the proprietors and publishers thereof.

In the late spring and summer of 1864, persons who were technically members of Lincoln's own party were as filled with fault-finding and as venomous in their expression of it as any Democratic governor in the land. Foremost of these opponents were three senators from the Old Northwest — Wade, Chandler, and Trumbull. They wished to have all the slaves freed at once, to hang Jeff. Davis and as many other rebels as could be caught, to seize all the property of traitors and keep it forever, and to bring the war to a short and successful conclusion by entrusting the chief command to either Butler or Frémont. The real animus at the basis of the action of these men was the question whether the President acting under his "War Powers" was the ruler of the country, or as much of it as he could control, or whether Congress was the ruler of the country or as much of it as the generals and admirals could bring under its control. These men acting through the Committee on the Conduct of the War, pursued to the death soldiers and sailors whom they did not like, either because of some lukewarmness toward the negro, or of some feeling of responsibility toward the commander-in-chief of the army as opposed to the majority in one or both Houses of Congress. The first Confiscation Act was not drastic enough to suit them, and in July, 1862, they passed a second one, providing that the forfeiture of the estates of Southern seceders should be permanent. Of course, this was contrary to the clause of the Constitution that provided that no forfeiture should work "Corruption of Blood," — in other words should extend after the life of a traitor to his children. It being discovered that Lincoln was preparing to veto this bill, they passed an explanatory resolution to meet Lincoln's objection. When the bill came before him, Lincoln signed both the bill and the amendment, and at the beginning of the next session, returned them to Congress with his proposed veto message. The fact that Lincoln was right and the Radicals were wrong had not the slightest effect upon them. The contest between the Wade-Chandler-Trumbull group in Congress and the President came to a head in the spring and summer of 1864, when Lincoln persisted in clinging to his own mode of "reconstructing" the members of the Confederacy as soon as they were conquered by the Union armies.[1] He offered to recognize any one of the old States whenever ten per cent of the voters therein should take the oath of allegiance to the United States and exercise their constitutional rights at the ballot box. He did not demand that the ten per cent of repentant seceders, or inhabitants of a State that had seceded should abolish slavery; he left that to the future, — the slaves already freed by the Emancipation Proclamation remaining free. The Radicals on their part passed through both Houses of Congress and presented to Lincoln within one hour of the time set for adjournment a bill for the reconstruction of seceded States that required a larger percentage of voters, and prescribed freedom for the slaves. Lincoln was indignant at this trying to force his hand. He refused to approve the bill, and four days later — July 8, 1864 — issued a proclamation stating his reasons. He declared that he sincerely hoped that a constitutional amendment might be adopted to abolish slavery throughout the nation, but he did not

[1] Nicolay and Hay's *Complete Works of Abraham Lincoln*, ix, 218 ; x, 58.

believe that the Constitution gave Congress the power to abolish slavery within the States. He favored the restoration of State authority, and did not much care how it was brought about so long as it was brought about. In his last address to the people of the United States, nine months later, on the eleventh of April, 1865, he said that to his mind the seceded States were "out of their proper practical relation with the Union," and the whole object of the moment is to get them again into that practical relation. And this might be done without deciding whether they had or had not been out of the Union. He would welcome within the fold any large body of men who wished to regain allegiance to the Union; he would like to see the elective franchise conferred on the very intelligent negroes, and on those "who serve our cause as soldiers." But he was opposed to any inflexible plan of reconstruction. Lincoln's pocket veto of their reconstruction bill filled the Radical leaders with indignation and dismay. It led to the publication on the fifth day of August of the "Wade-Davis Manifesto." This was addressed to the "Supporters of the Government." It informed them that they were responsible to the country for the conduct of the administration. Only the lowest personal motives could have dictated the President's action in vetoing the reconstruction bill, so they said. By so doing he held the "electoral votes of the rebel States at the dictation of his personal ambition"; it was a blow "at the friends of his Administration, at the rights of humanity, and at the principles of republican government." It was for the supporters of the government to consider the remedy for Lincoln's usurpation, and "having found it, fearlessly execute it."

Benjamin Franklin Wade, from northern Ohio, was a native of Massachusetts; Salmon Portland Chase, from southern Ohio, was born in New Hampshire. As Secretary of the Treasury, Chase had done work for the Union in value and in importance not exceeded by that of any other man in the official family of President Lincoln. His knowledge of finance and his knowledge of law were both at the instant service of the government, and were both of incalculable value in that great crisis of the Union. But Chase, like many other strong men, was not a colleague with whom it was easy to work, or a subordinate who always recognized his subordination. When things went wrong or he did not like what the President did or the way he did it, Chase offered his resignation. He was jealous of Seward and, every now and then, had small confidence in Lincoln's ability or in his good faith. Chase wanted to be President and criticized freely the doings of others. Lincoln, with the generosity that was so prominent in his make-up, shut his eyes to Chase's ambition and imperfections. He even appointed men to office who were working hard to make Chase President of the United States. Early in the spring of 1864, the matter culminated with the appearance of a "confidential circular" issued by Senator Pomeroy of Kansas, who had been selected by Chase to manage his presidential campaign. A copy of this "Pomeroy" circular came to Lincoln. He refused to look at it, but other persons told him what was in it. The circular took it for granted that the reëlection of Lincoln was undesirable and impossible, because if he were reëlected, he would be even more lenient toward his opponents than he had been and the war would "languish" until the public debt became too large to be borne. In Salmon P. Chase, the circular declared, more of the qualities needed in the next four years were to be found. It was inevitable that the circular should find its way into the newspapers.[1] When it did, Chase wrote to the President that he did not

[1] Nicolay and Hay's *Abraham Lincoln*, viii, 318.

wish to remain in the Treasury Department one day without his entire confidence and that differences of opinion had not changed the sentiments of affection that he held for the President. Chase further declared that in case of Lincoln's reëlection he should retire into private life with the sentiments he then cherished whole and unimpaired. Lincoln answered that he had not read the Pomeroy Circular. He knew of the existence of the committee and of the work that was being done, but he did not perceive "occasion for a change" in the Treasury Department. Chase remained in office, but did not entirely abandon his presidential hopes, and he continued to criticize the President. The separation finally came over an appointment to a Federal office in New York, — which has been the graveyard of many political ambitions. Lincoln refused absolutely to appoint the one person whom Chase desired and whom the President looked upon as unfit for the place. Chase at once had recourse to his usual expedient and sent his letter of resignation, which the President accepted, much to Chase's surprise and dismay. Curiously enough, Lincoln had no difficulty in finding another able Secretary of the Treasury, for he at once forced the office on William Pitt Fessenden of Maine, who, as chairman of the Senate Finance Committee, had acquired nearly as much knowledge of the business interests of the country as Chase himself.

The election of 1860 had borne weightily on the Democratic party. The Southern end of it had disappeared with secession and it was that end that had ruled the whole. What Democrats there were in the North were divided between the Douglasites and the Breckinridgers. The Douglasites, or most of them, acted with the Republicans in the measures that were taken for the prosecution of the war, with the result that the Democratic party, as a party,

was disappearing from American politics. It was rescued
from extinction by a few able men. At the head of these
was Clement L. Vallandigham of Ohio. He had many
Southern relatives and connections and desired reconciliation between the two sections of the Union at the smallest
possible cost to either of them, and this could only be done
by putting a stop to the further "effusion of blood," at once
and on almost any terms. A great many people agreed with
Vallandigham in the beginning, and in 1864, thought that
the sooner the war came to an end, the better. The movement spread in the States of the Old Northwest. Soon
there appeared a secret organization which went under
various names and which as the Knights of the Golden
Circle,[1] the Order of American Knights, and finally, the Sons
of Liberty, had very considerable influence in that part of
the country. It was supposed to have half a million members and was strong in Indiana, in Ohio, and in Illinois. The
Knights had grips and pass words; probably the secrecy of
the organization appealed to many people fully as much
as the opinions which it was supposed to represent. Those
who were opposed to the continuance of the war were called
Copperheads. Their enemies attributed the name to the
copperhead snake and they, themselves, referred it to the

[1] *Report of the Judge Advocate General
on the "Order of American Knights,"*
. . . *or "Sons of Liberty"* (Washington, 1864). Among the numerous
partisan pamphlets published at one
time or another on this matter, see *An
Authentic Exposition of the "K. G. C."*
. . . *By a Member of the Order* (Indianapolis, 1861); *Copperhead Conspiracy
in the North-West* (Printed by the Union
Congressional Committee, New York,
1864); *The Copperhead Catechism* (New
York, 1864). Modern accounts are
Fayette Hall's *The Copperhead or the
Secret Political History of Our Civil War
Unveiled* (New Haven, 1902); F. G.

Stidger's *Treason History* (Chicago,
1903); Nicolay and Hay's *Abraham
Lincoln*, viii, ch. i, and Rhodes's *United
States*, index at end of vol. vii under
"Sons of Liberty."

A great deal of interesting information of one sort or another came out in
the trials that were held before a military commission in September and
October, 1864, and is recorded in Benn
Pitman's *Trials for Treason at Indianapolis* (Cincinnati, 1865). The "Official Report" of the Judge Advocate
General is printed at the end of this
volume.

practice that grew up among them of wearing something like a medal that originally was a copper cent-piece with a hole in it and which then bore the figure of the Goddess of Liberty. Whatever its origin, the name "Copperhead" soon came to imply something hardly short of treason.[1]

On May 1, 1863, Vallandigham made an address at Mount Vernon in Ohio.[2] Army officers had been sent by the commander of the department to take down what he said. According to them, Vallandigham declared that the contest was "a wicked, cruel and unnecessary war" and that it was not waged for the preservation of the Union, but for crushing out liberty, erecting a despotism, and bringing about "the freedom of the blacks and the enslavement of the whites." Everything had gone wrong or was going wrong; and the sooner the people informed the "minions of usurped power," who were attempting "to build up a monarchy upon the ruins of our free government," that they would not submit, the better. Vallandigham was arrested, notwithstanding the disapproval of the Judge Advocate,[3] and a military commission voted him guilty and sentenced him to close confinement in some fortress during the continuance of the war. He applied to the Federal judge at Cincinnati for a writ of habeas corpus.[4] It was refused. Lincoln declined

---

[1] See "Origin of Butternut and Copperhead" by Albert Matthews in the *Publications* of the Colonial Society of Massachusetts, xx, 205–237.

There were many Union organizations of a more or less secret character as "The Union League of America"; see the *Minutes . . . of the Grand Council, U. L. A. for the State of Kansas* (Lawrence, 1864), pp. 5–15. There were Union Clubs and Union League Clubs in the Eastern cities that were convenient meeting places for Union men and that did good service in the publication of Union propaganda. See J. A. Stevens's *The Union Defence Committee of the City of New York;* H. W. Bellows's

Historical Sketch of the Union League Club of New York; and the Union League Club of New York's volume for 1887.

[2] J. L. Vallandigham's *Life of Clement L. Vallandigham,* 263, and Appleton's *American Annual Cyclopædia,* iii, 474. There is an interesting account of Vallandigham and the Peace Democrats by E. J. Benton in the *Collections* of the Western Reserve Historical Society for December, 1918.

[3] *In the Matter of . . . Captain and Bvt. Lieut. Col. J. Madison Cutts,* p. 4.

[4] See *Decision of Judge Leavitt, of Ohio, in the Vallandigham Habeas Corpus Case* (Philadelphia, 1863).

to set aside the decision of the military commission. He modified it by ordering that Vallandigham should be put "beyond our military lines" and committed to close custody in case of his return.[1] Apparently, Braxton Bragg did not like Vallandigham's society and the deportée made his way to Richmond and eventually to Canada, where he settled within sight of the United States and bided his time.

During the years 1863 and 1864, Southern propaganda from without and Southern sabotage from within were most active to turn Northern sentiment toward the Southern cause and to spread terror in one way or another through the transport and military services behind the Northern lines. President Davis, himself, set the example by sending emissaries to try to open communications with the government at Washington. There is not the remotest reason to suppose he had the slightest intention of making peace on any other basis than the independence of the Confederate States. Nor is there any reason to suppose that he had the least expectation that the Lincoln government would receive his agents, for to do so would have recognized the Confederacy as a political entity. Nevertheless, Davis employed his abilities and presumably brought in those of Benjamin to fire the Southern heart by a recital in language that takes one back to the debates in Congress on Kansas and allied topics. On August 18, 1862, Davis sent a message to the Confederate Senate and House, declaring that the enemy had small regard for the "usages of civilized war." It destroyed private property, — so he asserted, — made war on non-combatants, murdered captives, and threatened to avenge "the death of an invading soldiery by the slaughter of unarmed citizens." A year later on August 1, 1863, he

[1] Nicolay and Hay's *Abraham Lincoln*, vii, 338; see also his letter to Erastus Corning of June 12, 1863, in the *Complete Works of Abraham Lincoln*, viii, 298–314.

returned to the charge in a proclamation addressed to "The Soldiers of the Confederate States." In this he declared that the enemy continued a struggle in which the final triumph of the South was inevitable. But, at that moment, the Northerners were gathering heavy masses for a general invasion. "Their malignant rage aims at nothing less than the extermination of yourselves, your wives, and children." They purposed, so Davis asserted, that your "homes shall be partitioned among the wretches whose atrocious cruelties have stamped infamy on their Government." Realizing that they cannot prevail by legitimate means, "not daring to make peace lest they should be hurled from their seats of power," the Lincoln government has refused even to confer on the question of exchange of prisoners and similar matters. Again, in December, 1863, Davis recurred to the terrible barbarities with which the enemy conducts the war and declared that the Union authorities wherever they had gained access to "the unfortunate negroes" had forced into the ranks of the Union army every able-bodied man, leaving the aged negroes, the colored women, and the children to perish by starvation or neglect. His information on this subject, Davis declared, came not only from his own observation, but from the reports of the negroes "who succeed in escaping from the enemy."

In his beliefs as to the rightfulness of slavery and its beneficial effects on the negroes themselves, President Davis was stating in clear language what was the prevailing opinion among the white people of the South, or of most of them at any rate. Slavery was the condition of society described in the Bible. To deny it was irreligious. On August 1, 1863, the clergy of the Confederate States issued an "Address to Christians throughout the World." The separation of the Southern States from the old Union was final, — so they

said. This being so, the Proclamation of the President of
the United States seeking the emancipation of the slaves was
"a suitable occasion for solemn protest on the part of the
people of God throughout the world." This address was
signed by eighty-seven clergymen of eleven denominations.
Among the signers were the Methodist bishops of Virginia,
Alabama, and Georgia, five Protestant Episcopalian clergy-
men including James A. Latané and Robert L. Dabney,
Professor of Systematic Theology in the Union Seminary of
Virginia. The conviction that slavery was justified by the
Scriptures was not confined to the clergymen of the South.
In December, 1860, the Episcopalian Bishop, John Henry
Hopkins of Vermont, drew up a pamphlet which was printed
in January, 1861, and reprinted at New York in 1864.[1]
The reprint had been called for, according to M. A. De Wolfe
Howe,[2] because it was thought that its publication might
strengthen "the political power which notoriously favors the
perpetuation of slavery," and that if public opinion, expressed through the ballot-box, could be brought to bear
upon the administration, it might be willing to adjust "our
differences with the South."

While this ecclesiastico-philanthropic propaganda was
progressing, other Confederates were trying to break down
the Northern war spirit by acts of violence. On March
14, 1864, a person named J. W. Tucker wrote to President
Davis from the Spotswood Hotel in Richmond informing
him that in the "Lodge" at St. Louis of a secret society to
which he belonged, there were seventy-two engineers serving

---

[1] It formed pp. 5–41 of J. H. Hop-
kins's *Scriptural, Ecclesiastical, and
Historical View of Slavery, from the
Days of the Patriarch Abraham, to the
Nineteenth Century* and, as No. 8 of the
*Papers from the Society for the Diffusion
of Political Knowledge,* formed part of

the campaign literature of 1864.
[2] *Reply to the Letter of Bishop Hopkins, Addressed to Dr. Howe,* pp. 7, 8;
and *The Voice of the Clergy . . . in the
following Protest* to Bishop Hopkins's
"Letter" (Philadelphia, 1863).

on western river steamers by whom ten Federal transports
had been destroyed within ten weeks. They had burned
half a million dollars worth of hay at Memphis and designed
to strike blows at many points at one moment of time and
thus "paralyze the foe."   He needed one hundred thousand
dollars in greenbacks to carry on the work and this need not
be given to him, but might be placed in General Polk's
hands for disbursement.[1] It is possible that there was
exaggeration in these statements, but there is a good deal of
collateral evidence to bear out the truth of some of them.
In this year, 1864, there were several Confederate agents in
Canada, who seem to have been there in a more or less quasi-
diplomatic character. Acting with them, or alongside of
them, were other agents who had nothing diplomatic whatever in the character of their missions. The object seems
to have been to strike terrorism in the North and, therefore,
to aid the organization that has just been noted. At one
time, their plans contemplated the release of the Confederate
prisoners at Chicago. At another time, the scheme was to
seize the United States armed vessel *Michigan* and with
her aid to capture Johnson's Island in Lake Erie where were
lodged hundreds of Confederate officers. A third plan
was to bombard some of the unprotected Lake shore cities,
as Cleveland. The most interesting of these plots was the
St. Albans raid into Vermont and the attempt to burn New
York City. The amount of terrorism achieved was nothing
like that contemplated. In point of fact, the outraged
feelings of the Federal General Dix, culminating in an
attempt to invade Canada in pursuit of the raiders, seems to
have been the crowning achievement of this campaign of
murder and arson.[2] Nevertheless, it is with some degree

[1] Rowland's *Jefferson Davis*, vi, 204.   *tions in Canada and New York* (New
[2] J. W. Headley's *Confederate Opera-*   York, 1906) contains a mass of astonish-

of astonishment that one reflects that the cities of the Great Lakes were absolutely open to raids from the water until toward the close of 1864.

It must not be supposed that the desire for peace without emancipation and even without reunion was peculiar to the people of the Northwest. Throughout the country there were many groups of persons who wished to stop the shedding of blood and who thought that the Washington government was altogether too strait-laced in refusing to recognize Jefferson Davis as President of the Confederate States and to negotiate with him as such. In point of fact, from the very beginning of the war there had been attempt after attempt made to open negotiations between the two governments. The first of these in point of time was undertaken by Rudolf Mathias Schleiden.[1] He was a German who had found his way to the United States as diplomatic representative of the Hanseatic Republic of Bremen. In Washington, he became rather friendly with Secretary Seward. On April 24, 1861, he laid before him a plan to go to Richmond and begin confidential discussions with the Vice-President of the Confederate States, who was then in that city. Seward told him that he, himself, could not authorize such an undertaking, and Lincoln, upon being consulted, regretted Schleiden had not gone to Richmond without consulting anyone, and refused to make any definite statements what-

ing matter which can be supplemented by the *Memoir of John Yeats Beall, his Life; his Trial,* that was printed at Montreal, in 1865; the *Speech of B. Devlin, Esquire* — also printed at Montreal, in 1865; *The St. Albans Raid* that was complied by L. N. Benjamin, B.C.L., and published at Boston in 1865, the *Reminiscences of General Basil W. Duke, C.S.A.* (New York, 1911) and J. B. Castleman's *Active Service* (Louisville, 1917). J. M. Cal-

lahan brought together, within a few pages, interesting material on the matter from original papers of the time in his "Northern Lake Frontier during the Civil War" in the *Report* of the American Historical Association, for 1896, i, 337–357.

[1] R. H. Lutz's "Rudolf Schleiden and the Visit to Richmond, April 25, 1861" in American Historical Association's *Report* for 1915, p. 209.

ever. The next day, Schleiden had an interview with Stephens. It lasted for three hours. Stephens declared that all attempts to settle the differences between the two sections without war were futile. He thought that a "de facto truce through tactful avoidance of an attack on both sides" would be the best way to proceed. Schleiden wrote Stephens, after the conference had closed, asking for the terms which the South would require for the maintenance of peace. Stephens replied that the government of the Confederacy had resorted to every honorable means to avoid war and that as things were "no power on earth can arrest or prevent a most bloody conflict."

In June, 1863, Alexander H. Stephens, himself, brought forward a plan for initiating negotiations for peace. Militarily, affairs were not going well for the North at that moment. In the preceding year, the Democrats had made great gains in Ohio and Indiana and other Northern States; Fernando Wood and Vallandigham with Benjamin R. Curtis had attacked the Lincoln administration violently and everything pointed, in Stephens's eyes, to the time being ripe for the government at Washington to enter into negotiations for a general adjustment that would "stop the further effusion of blood in the contest so irrational, unchristian, and so inconsistent with all recognized American principles." Davis thought that the venture was worth taking, for, although Vicksburg was likely to surrender, he had hopes of the success of Lee's invasion of Pennsylvania. Stephens reached Hampton Roads on July 4, the day after Pickett's charge at Gettysburg, and opened communications with Admiral Lee, the cousin of the Confederate general, who was then in command of the Federal naval forces at Hampton Roads. Using the words agreed upon with Davis, Stephens stated that he had a communication from Jefferson Davis,

Commander-in-chief of the land and naval forces of the Confederate States, to Abraham Lincoln, Commander-in-chief of the land and naval forces of the United States. As soon as President Lincoln received this communication, he directed Admiral Lee to refuse to permit Mr. Stephens to proceed to Washington by water on his own vessel, or to pass the blockade in any way, and nothing must be received from him when offered in terms assuming the independence of the so-called Confederate States. Before this communication actually started on its way, Lincoln directed the Secretary of the Navy to inform Admiral Lee that the "request of A. H. Stephens is inadmissible. The customary agents and channels are adequate for all needful communication and conference between the United States forces and the insurgents." Apparently, Stephens had nothing tangible to offer, but merely hoped to give the opposition party in the North aid and comfort.[1]

The next act in this extraordinary drama centered around the person of one of the most peculiar and, in some ways, most estimable, characters in our history, Horace Greeley. By the summer of 1864, Greeley had made up his mind that the war was hopeless and that practically any sacrifice might well be made to stop the killing and maiming of the young men of the North. Greeley's private business letters about the conduct of his paper are so sane and so full of common sense that one almost shudders to contemplate the difference between them and the letters that he wrote for publication and the editorials that he placed in the "Tribune." He seemed, indeed, to have been a sort of newspaper Dr. Jekyll and Mr. Hyde. Furthermore, Greeley's hatred for Seward had in no wise diminished with time, and he gave heed to practically any story and anything that

---

[1] Nicolay and Hay's *Abraham Lincoln*, vii, 369 and fol.

could bring his old enemy into any sort of disrepute. Of course, much of this is conjecture and apart from the business of the historian; but there is no other way to account for Greeley except to think of him as a dual person, one of those personalities being full of hate for and distrust of the administration at Washington, partly because it was or was supposed to be dominated by the Secretary of State. Greeley had fallen in with an eccentric person named Jewett. According to Moran, the diarist, Jewett was "a vain weak minded man, who would be a traitor if he had brains enough." As it was he proclaimed himself to be "the self-constituted Ambassador from the people to induce European Governments to step in and settle our difficulties." In Washington, Jewett visited both Lyons and Mercier and represented himself as "a sort of Apostle of Mediation." [1] Mercier did not look upon Jewett as quite sane, but thought that the "Tribune" was changing. At all events, something about the man appealed to Greeley and he sent one of Jewett's epistles to President Lincoln on July 7, 1864, with one of the most extraordinary letters that he ever wrote! In this communication, Greeley ventured to remind the President that "our bleeding, bankrupt, almost dying country" longs for peace and shudders at the prospect of new rivers of human blood. He feared that the President did not realize how intently the people desired peace and how joyously they would bless its authors. There were, at the moment, at Niagara on the Canadian side, persons whom Jewett described as "two ambassadors of Davis & Co." [2]

[1] Among Jewett's printed pamphlets and leaflets are *Mediation in America;* it is dated London, July 25, 1863 and addressed to Napoleon III and Alexander II. Another is entitled *Mediation Position of France in Connection with A Congress of Nations.* Mr. *Jewett's Telegram to His Majesty Napoleon III . . . also Letters to Governor Horatio Seymour and President Lincoln.*

[2] This whole matter is gone into at length in W. R. Thayer's *Life and Letters of John Hay,* i, 173–183.

Greeley urged the President to invite them to "exhibit their credentials and submit their ultimatum." Lincoln had slight hope of any good coming out of the "Tribune" office, but he saw that it was desirable on every account to neutralize Greeley. He therefore sent him a letter, two days later, in which he stated : "If you can find any person, anywhere, professing to have any proposition of Jefferson Davis in writing, for peace, embracing the restoration of the Union and abandonment of slavery, whatever else it embraces," bring him or them to me and he or they shall have safe conduct back to the point where you shall have met him. This proposition troubled Greeley, and after four days, and possibly more communication with Jewett, he again wrote that there were two persons at Niagara Falls who were empowered to negotiate for peace, and it seemed to him "high time an effort should be made to terminate the wholesale slaughter," — which, by the way, had in great measure resulted from the information and exaggerations printed in the "New York Tribune." Two days later, Lincoln telegraphed to Greeley that he was disappointed, for he had not expected to receive another letter from him, but had expected that he would appear with the man or the men ; and the same day he sent one of his secretaries with a confirmatory letter to Greeley. For some inscrutable reason, Greeley thought that this letter superseded Lincoln's letter of July 9. But when he reached Niagara Falls, he found that there were no persons there who were empowered to conduct any such negotiations as the President had authorized him to open. The men in Canada asserted that they had no credentials, but if they were sent to Richmond with the "circumstances disclosed in this correspondence," namely, Greeley's letter, they were sure they could obtain credentials. Greeley returned to New York

and spent his time trying to prove that he had done right
and that the President had done wrong.

In point of fact, while Greeley was muddling matters at
Niagara, two other extraordinary characters were in Richmond with the consent of Lincoln trying to extract some
kind of possible terms from the Confederate government.
These were James F. Jaquess, a Methodist clergyman from
Illinois, who had led a regiment of volunteers into the field
as its colonel. He had an idea that as the Methodists were
strong, both North and South, although split into two
organizations on the subject of slavery, he might get into
communication with some of the Southern Methodists, and
in that way bring about peace. His early efforts were not
particularly cheering, but he fell in with a story writer, J.
R. Gilmore, who is better known by his pen name of "Edmund Kirke." Probably Lincoln had about as much faith
in the success of the efforts of Jaquess and Gilmore, as he
had in those of Jewett and Greeley, but he gave them a pass
taking them through the Union lines, although he warned
them that they might lose their liberty or their lives in the
adventure. As it was, on July 17, the very day that Greeley
was dickering with the commissioners at Niagara Falls,
Jaquess and Gilmore, from the Spotswood Hotel in Richmond, addressed a note to Judah P. Benjamin, asking for
an interview with President Davis. They were at Richmond, "only as private citizens" so they wrote, but they
were acquainted with the views of the United States government and with the sentiments of the Northern people and
they earnestly hoped that "a free interchange of views between President Davis and themselves" might bring peace
to "the two sections of our distracted country." At nine
o'clock in the evening, in the office of the Confederate Secretary of State and in his presence, President Davis and these

two Northerners held a conversation of about two hours in length. They then were escorted out of the Confederate lines and made their way safely to Washington. Davis said that the real matter in issue was "Independence or Subjugation." They tried to argue with him on various lines such as an armistice during which a plebiscite of all the voters North and South might be taken on the question of Southern independence and reunion with emancipation. Davis replied that each State of the Confederacy was sovereign and that they had gone out of the Union to escape majority rule. As to amnesty, that applied to criminals, and the Southerners, so he said, "have committed no crime." In conclusion, according to the statement that Jaquess and Gilmore printed,[1] Davis declared, "you may 'emancipate' every negro in the Confederacy, but *we will be free!* We will govern ourselves. We *will* do it, if we have to see every Southern plantation sacked, and every Southern city in flames." After another half-hour of talk as the Northerners were leaving, President Davis closed the interview: "Say to Mr. Lincoln from me, that I shall at any time be pleased to receive proposals for peace on the basis of our Independence. It will be useless to approach me with any other." And the conclusion reached by Jaquess and Gilmore, as stated by the latter, was that "We must conquer or be conquered. . . . We can have peace and union only by putting forth all our strength, crushing the Southern armies, and overthrowing the Southern government."

About a month later, Jeremiah S. Black,[2] a colleague of

---

[1] *Atlantic Monthly*, September, 1864, pp. 372–383. Years later J. R. Gilmore included this account with a statement as to "The Preliminaries" in his *Recollections*, chs. xvi, xvii.

[2] J. S. Black to E. M. Stanton from "York Pa. August 24th, 1864" and Stanton's reply of "Aug. 31, 1864" are in the Library of Congress. My attention was called to them by Mr. J. S. Fitzpatrick, Assistant Chief of the Manuscripts Division, to whom I am indebted for many valuable suggestions.

Stanton's in the later months of Buchanan's administration, visited Toronto and had a conference with Jacob Thompson of Mississippi, who had also been in Buchanan's Cabinet. In 1864, Thompson was in Canada as one of the commissioners or representatives of the Confederate government. According to his own account, Black told Thompson that he was not "in any sense, an agent of the federal government"; but if he should learn from him "any fact which it was important for the public authorities to know" he would communicate it to "some member" of Lincoln's Cabinet. Black thought that he was acting in accordance with "the wish expressed by you [Stanton] in our last conversation," — but Stanton denied that he had expressed any wish of the kind. Thompson's statement as to Southern feelings and desires was substantially a replica of those made by Davis to Jaquess and Gilmore.

From the vantage point of the twentieth century, it seems reasonably clear that at no time in the year 1864 was the reëlection of Abraham Lincoln within the realm of doubt. The plain people of the North were behind him and they greatly outnumbered the Radical Republicans, the Peace Democrats, and the extreme abolitionists put together. His opponents, however, were mighty in speech and pen and produced an appearance of power that was disproportionate to their actual vote-casting strength. For almost the first time, Lincoln's political instincts failed him. Possibly a recurrence of one of those depressive eras that marked his earlier life for a time clouded the clearness of his vision. In the summer, military affairs were gloomy from the point of view of the Federal side: Grant seemed to be marking time in front of Petersburg, Sherman had not captured Atlanta, Early had marched to within reach of the guns at Washington, gold was selling on Wall Street for nearly one to three in paper, and another draft was imminent. On the 23rd of August, Lincoln wrote a "Memorandum" to the effect that it seemed exceedingly probable that he would not be reëlected. In that case, it would be his duty to coöperate with the President-elect to save the Union between election day and March 4, 1865, because after his inauguration the new President could not possibly save the Union on any ground that would have secured him the election. Lincoln folded up this paper, pasted the edges together, took it to the Cabinet meeting, and asked each member to write his name on the back of it. He then placed it in a drawer and gave no intimation as to its contents until after election day.

One of the things that stood in the way of clear sightedness on the part of Lincoln and the Republican leaders in July and August, 1864, was the fact that there was no opponent for them to attack. It is true that John C. Frémont had been nominated by certain discontented persons at Cleveland in June. Among the sponsors of this meeting were B. Gratz Brown, Elizabeth Cady Stanton, Wendell Phillips, and sundry Germans of St. Louis. It was expected to be a gathering in mass, something like the anti-slavery conventions of the 1850's, but on May 31st only four hundred persons assembled, which reminded Mr. Lincoln of the Cave of Adullam mentioned in First Samuel, to which came "every one that was in distress, and every one that was in debt, and every one that was discontented . . . and there were with him about four hundred men." They nominated two New Yorkers, General John C. Frémont and General John Cochrane, forgetful of the prescription in the Constitution that each elector should vote for two persons, one of whom was not from his own State. A week later, on the 7th day of June, the National Union Convention met at Balti-

more.[1] The platform ratified the unconditional surrender
policy of the administration toward the Confederates, unanimously nominated Abraham Lincoln for the presidency and,
on the first ballot, nominated Andrew Johnson of Tennessee,
a Southern Union man, for the vice-presidency. The action
of the Convention was so unanimous and so speedy that Mr.
Lincoln did not reach the telegraph in the War Department until after the nomination of Johnson was announced
and hearing no mention of himself for a time wondered as
to what had happened in his own case.

On the 29th of August, 1864, the Democrats assembled
at Chicago.[2] The meeting was called to order by August
Belmont, chairman of the National Democratic Committee
and nephew of the Confederate Commissioner at Paris.
Most of the members of the Convention were violently in
favor of peace. Vallandigham crossed over from Canada,
was not molested by the Federal officers, and was made a
member of the Committee on the Platform. He induced
that body, and later the Convention itself, to adopt a resolution to the effect that the war had failed to restore the
Union, public liberty and private right had been trodden
down, and "the material prosperity of the country essentially impaired." It followed that "justice, humanity, liberty, and the public welfare" demanded that immediate
efforts be made to bring about a cessation of hostilities to
the end that "at the earliest practicable moment peace may

[1] *Proceedings of the National Union
Convention held in Baltimore, Md.,
June 7th and 8th, 1864. Reported by
D. F. Murphy* (New York, 1864).
[2] *Official Proceedings of the Democratic National Convention held in 1864
at Chicago.* The Congressional Union
Committee issued campaign documents,
several of which deserve study as *The
Chicago Copperhead Convention*, re-
printed in William Abbatt's *Magazine*
of History "Extra Number 58"; the
Copperhead Conspiracy in the North-
West. An Exposé of the Treasonable
Order of the "Sons of Liberty." Vallandigham, Supreme Commander; the
Treasonable Designs of the Democracy,
and The Chicago Copperhead Convention. Noah Brooks attended the
Convention as a reporter; see his
Washington in Lincoln's Time, 180–
190.

be restored on the basis of the Federal Union of the States."
It was on this platform that George B. McClellan was
nominated for the presidency. While he was writing his letter of acceptance, the news of Farragut's success in Mobile
Bay and Sherman's occupation of Atlanta thrilled the
country.[1] In his letter of acceptance, General McClellan
wrote that he "could not look in the face" his gallant comrades who had survived so many bloody battles and tell
them that we have abandoned the Union, — and "no peace
can be permanent without Union." It was on these terms
that he accepted the Democratic nomination.

As the weeks went by, it became more and more increas-
ingly evident that there would be but one outcome to the
political campaign as there would be but one outcome to the
military campaign. This being so, it was quite evident
that those who longed for a political future would better
cease their opposition and rejoin their comrades in the Republican organization. Until September, Chase had nursed
his wrath in resignation. Suddenly, his whole attitude
toward the President and toward the political situation
underwent a radical change. He voted the Republican
ticket in the Ohio October election and reopened communication with President Lincoln by telegraphing to him that
the result was all right in Ohio and in Indiana. Soon
afterwards, Chief Justice Taney died and the question came
up as to his successor. Chase was undoubtedly the foremost

---

[1] The historian's tendency to agree
with the actuality of the past — if he
can find out what it was — oftentimes
conceals from him the realities of the
situation. At all events, it was on
October 24, 1864, that an exceedingly
intelligent, generally well-informed, and
very successful Northern business man
wrote to a relative that he and others,
who were going to vote for McClellan,
were informed that they were traitors.

He hoped, however, that "this insanity
would stop with the re-election of
Lincoln," because he did not consider
it possible to annihilate an united nation
of six million people and there would be
a disgraceful peace. After the election,
early in the next year, he wrote that the
weakness shown by the South had
convinced him that Lincoln was right in
considering "that severity was the best
and only way of ending the war."

of the candidates, but there was fear in some quarters that he would never get over his desire for the presidency and there was some feeling that it was undesirable for a Chief Justice of the Supreme Court of the United States to regard himself as in line for the first place in the executive branch of the government.   In the end Chase was appointed and signalized the last years of his life by repudiating, as Chief Justice of the Supreme Court of the United States, three of his own most important acts as Secretary of the Treasury. Later, others of the discontented of the springtime came back into the fold at the price of the resignation of Montgomery Blair.   The cause of the Union owes a great deal to the Blair family, father and two sons; but like all positive, strong men, they were not easy to work with.   Montgomery Blair made exceedingly unpleasant remarks about men around him, and F. P. Blair, Jr., was at the same time a member of the national House of Representatives and a brigadier general in the army and he used the former position to make criticisms of his superiors that were difficult for them to bear.   It fell out that both Benjamin F. Wade and H. Winter Davis were willing to retire from their position of animosity toward the administration and that John C. Frémont was also willing to retire from his position as presidential candidate, provided that at least one of the Blairs was sacrificed and Lincoln requested Montgomery Blair, the Postmaster General, to leave the Cabinet.   Thereupon, Davis and Frémont retired into seclusion, but Wade took the stump and made stirring speeches for the administration. In October local elections were held in half a dozen States including Ohio, Indiana, and Illinois, and the result was a complete overturn in comparison with that of 1862.   The Republicans gained a majority in the State legislatures and elected their candidates for governor.   No longer was there a shadow of a doubt as to what the outcome of the national election in November would be, but probably no one had any conception of the majority that would be given to Abraham Lincoln. He received 2,213,665 votes to 1,802,237 for McClellan. The majority was not large, but, owing to the workings of the electoral system, 212 electors gave their votes to Lincoln and only 21 to McClellan.[1] It is noteworthy that in the three States with the largest electoral vote — New York, Pennsylvania, and Ohio — Lincoln received 930,269 votes to 843,862 for McClellan, a difference of only 86,407 votes, but giving to the Union candidate 80 votes in the Electoral College. Had these three States gone the other way and been joined by a couple more, the election would have been fairly close ; McClellan might have been elected ; and the history of the next few months might have been very unlike what it was ; — there would have been no march to Appomattox.

[1] The popular vote is taken from McPherson's *Hand Book of Politics for 1868*, p. 372. The electoral vote is given in the *Journal of the House of Representatives*, 38th Cong., 2nd Sess., pp. 209–211. A slightly different tabulation of the popular vote is in the *World Almanac* for 1916, p. 722.

NOTE

Constitutional Questions. — The standard work on the constitutional history of this period is William Whiting's *War Powers under the Constitution of the United States*. It was first printed in Boston in 1864 in the form of a small book of 256 pages with supplementary matter on "Military Government of Hostile Territory in Time of War." The book proved to be so useful that by 1871, it had reached the 43rd edition and was nearly double its original size, the added matter consisting of cases and opinions, with an extended index.

There is much material on this general subject in James B. Thayer's *Cases on Constitutional Law* and in Eugene Wambaugh's *Selection of Cases on Constitutional Law*, using the indexes on "Civil War," "Habeas Corpus," "Rebellion," "War," etc.[1]

[1] The pros and cons of the constitutional questions that came up in the years 1861–1865 are admirably and briefly stated in Professor W. A. Dunning's *Essays on Civil War and Reconstruction*, pp. 1–62, and in his article entitled "Disloyalty in Two Wars" in *American Historical Review*, xxiv, 625–630. The matter is treated at greater length and with abundant citations in G. C. Sellery's "Lincoln's Suspension of Habeas Corpus as Viewed by Congress" in *Bulletin*, No. 149 of the University of Wisconsin.

CHAPTER XX

IN the spring of 1865, the Confederacy collapsed with a speed and a thoroughness that was entirely unexpected, except by a few of the leading men on both sides of the line. Nor is the catastrophe easy to understand or to describe. In April, 1865, the Confederacy was not beaten from a military point of view. Lee had thirty thousand men, more or less, Joseph E. Johnston had as many and, scattered through Georgia, Alabama, and Mississippi were other thousands and, west of the Mississippi River, there were twenty or twenty-five thousand more. All in all, in the first days of April, when Lee broke away from Petersburg, there must have been from one hundred and fifty to two hundred thousand men answerable to the orders of the Adjutant General at Richmond. Of these, Lee, on his last return, February 28, 1865, reported "present for duty," that is with the colors, with arms in their hands, and ready to step into the fighting line, fifty-nine thousand out of an "aggregate" of one hundred and sixty thousand "present and absent," and Ewell, on March 20 following, reported forty-five hundred for duty and nearly ten thousand "present and absent" in the Department of Richmond.[1] Of course, an army melts away in times of stress and disaster, but the disappearance of the Confederate soldiers from the rolls between December, 1864,

---

[1] On December 11, 1864, General Gorgas gives the Confederate force in Virginia as 61,700, including artillery and cavalry. Of these 44,500 infantry were in front of Richmond. He added, "The infantry count is taken from the return of arms in the hands of troops, and is, therefore, reliable."

and April, 1865, is one of the puzzles of the history of the Confederacy.

The Southern people, had they so wished, could have held out for a long time.[1] The Texans, alone, might have fought on until the Northern people would have become so wearied that they would have preferred to let them go in peace rather than send their sons and brothers to continue useless warfare. With this opinion, Jefferson Davis was in entire agreement. At Greensboro, in April, 1865, while on his way southward from Richmond, he summoned to a conference General Breckinridge, then Secretary of War, and Joseph E. Johnston, the commander of the only considerable Confederate army east of the Mississippi River. He tried to induce them to agree to an opinion that it was possible to continue the war. Johnston absolutely disagreed with him[2] and told him that the people were beaten and knew it. Later, at Abbeville, in South Carolina, on one of the first days of May, Jefferson Davis held his last council of war, — this time, with the commanders of the brigades that still clung to him and with Generals Breckinridge and Bragg. At the beginning of the conference, he was affable, dignified, and the personification of high and undaunted courage. Upon being asked for their opinions, the brigade commanders in turn said that "They and their followers despaired of successfully conducting the war, and doubted the propriety of prolonging it." They would risk battle to secure the safety of Mr. Davis "but would not ask their men to struggle against a fate, which was inevitable, and forfeit all hope of a restoration to their homes and friends." Davis answered that he wished to hear no plan for his safety — "that twenty-five hundred men brave men were enough to prolong the

---

[1] C. F. Adams's *Studies Military and Diplomatic*, 241.
[2] J. E. Johnston's *Narrative*, 395–400.

war, until the panic had passed away, and they would then be a nucleus for thousands more." There was no reply. He then said, bitterly, that "he saw all hope was gone — that all the friends of the South were prepared to consent to her degradation." When he left the room he faltered and leaned upon General Breckinridge for support.[1] Judging from the history of other wars and other revolutions, the end had not come and was not even in sight had the Southern people, or the mass of the people of the seceded States, wished to continue the fight for Southern independence.

From the very beginning, or at all events from the year 1862, the number of soldiers actually in the Confederate field army had borne a rapidly changing proportion to the number on the rolls. There were men detailed to work in factories or on railroads, there were men detached for the conscription service, and there were men who obtained furloughs at Richmond without the knowledge of the field commanders. Besides these, who were officially absent, there were large numbers who took themselves off when fighting was done and quarters were hard and turned up, oftentimes, in one of the partisan bands. Many soldiers, apparently, visited their homes in an entirely irregular manner. By the summer of 1864, the question of absence from the army had become very serious. In January of that year, Lee had complained to Davis[2] that men from his army on passing through Richmond, joined General Morgan's command and that some twenty-five or thirty convalescents

---

[1] B. W. Duke's *History of Morgan's Cavalry* (Cincinnati, 1867), p. 575; or p. 438 of the edition of 1909.

[2] Lee's *Dispatches . . . to Jefferson Davis*, 131–133. Interesting details can be gleaned from Davis's Message of February 3, 1864 (*Journal* of the Confederate Congress, vi, 744), of February 8, 1864, in the Virginia State Library, and an earlier one of February

11, 1863, in the Confederate Museum at Richmond. In the Library at Richmond is an interesting minority report that was presented to the Confederate House of Representatives on February 15, 1865, proposing to bring into the army "the many thousands of able bodied young men, . . . whose places at home may be supplied by those exempt from physical causes or from age."

had actually gone to Morgan instead of to the Army of Northern Virginia. In another letter, Lee suggested that all details should be revoked and regranted only with the consent of an officer who had actually served in the field or was then serving with the army. In 1864, affairs were so serious in Georgia from the advance of Sherman's army toward Atlanta, and in North Carolina from the presence of thousands of deserters and fugitives from conscription in the mountains and among the foothills, that both Governor Brown and Governor Vance[1] threatened to withdraw their men from the field. The subject is a very delicate one, but the evidence would seem to point to the fact that the conscription acts had performed their part and were now, in the mode in which they were enforced, doing more harm than good. But, of course, this is a subject upon which two opinions are certain to arise. On October 6, 1864, General Gorgas wrote in his "Journal" that the harrowed and overworked soldiers were getting worn out. "They see nothing before them but certain death, and have, I fear, fallen into a sort of hopelessness and are dispirited," the only cure that occurred to Gorgas was to limit the term of service to five years and to employ slaves in every possible capacity, even as guards and soldiers. Meetings were held in North Carolina and Alabama in 1864 and, possibly, in other States at which methods of bringing about peace at once and by

---

[1] See a remarkable letter from Vance to Davis, dated May 13, 1863, in Rowland's *Davis*, v, 485. In *ibid.*, vi, p. 30, is a letter in which Vance threatens to withdraw the North Carolina troops from the field, unless the Confederate authorities protect the State of North Carolina from depredations by soldiers from other States.

In 1874, the Honorable B. H. Hill of Georgia declared that "malcontents at home and in high places . . . created dissensions among our people, and we failed to win independence because our sacrifices ceased, our purpose faltered, and our strength was divided." Southern Historical Society's *Papers*, xiv, 500. A somewhat different view is set forth by the Confederate Colonel Robert Tansill in his *Free and Impartial Exposition of the Causes which led to the Failure of the Confederate States to establish their Independence* (Washington, 1865).

State action were discussed; but these movements, whatever they amounted to, came to speedy and untimely ends.[1] It would seem that there was an available military population within the one-time limits of the Confederacy that was amply sufficient to keep up resistance to Northern armies, had there been the enthusiasm for the cause that there was in 1861. It has been usual to attribute the sudden ending of the war to scarcity of arms and munitions and to a lack of food.

Until the end of the year 1863 there is reason to suppose that the Confederate armies relied upon foreign munitions,[2] for use in the field, and it is well known that arms that came through the blockade into Charleston were used by the Confederates in the battle of Chickamauga, although what would have happened had the blockade runner containing this material been captured is of course a mere matter of guesswork. On October 29, 1863, General Josiah Gorgas, the head of the Confederate ordnance service, confided to his journal that "We are now in a condition to carry on the war for an indefinite period . . . we have war material sufficient — men, guns, powder — the real pinch is in the Treasury." Josiah Gorgas was a native of Pennsylvania. He had married Amelia Gayle, the daughter of Governor Gayle of Alabama. In 1860 Gorgas was a member of the Ordnance Board in the War Department. He resigned, "went South," and was

[1] For the North Carolina movements, see *Memoirs of W. W. Holden* (Durham, N. C., 1911), especially p. 76; Clement Dowd's *Life of Zebulon B. Vance*, 91; *The Papers of Thomas Ruffin*, edited by J. G. de Roulhac Hamilton, iii, 327 and index under "Peace Movement"; J. R. Gilmore's *Recollections*, ch. xv, and A. Sellew Roberts in *Mississippi Valley Historical Review*, xi, 190. For Alabama, see Professor W. L. Fleming's articles on "The Peace Movement in Alabama" in *South Atlantic Quarterly*, ii, 114–124, 246–260.

[2] See article by D. H. Hill, "Confederate Ordnance Department" in North Carolina Historical Commission's *Bulletin*, No. 28, pp. 80–91. Colonel William Allan described how deficiencies in ordnance equipment were overcome in Southern Historical Society's *Papers*, xiv, 137–146; and there is some interesting information in the *Report of Evidence* on the Confederate Navy Department, p. 239 and fol. See also Caleb Huse's *The Supplies for the Confederate Army* (Boston, 1904).

appointed head of the Ordnance Service of the Confederacy. In his first report dated in September, 1861, he enumerated eight or ten armories and arsenals, as forming the whole equipment of the Confederacy for the production of war materials.[1] On April 8, 1864, General Gorgas wrote in his journal that three years ago today he took charge of the Ordnance Department, and had succeeded beyond his utmost expectations. Large arsenals had been organized; a "superb powder mill" had been built at Augusta, lead smelting works established at Petersburg, and turned over to the Nitre and Mining Bureau, when it was separated from his department at his request. A cannon foundry had been established at Macon, bronze foundries there and at Augusta, besides a manufactory of carbines, and a rifle factory, and two pistol factories "where three years ago we were not making a gun, a pistol, nor a sabre, no shot nor shell (except at the Tredegar Works), a pound of powder — we now make all these in quantities to meet the demands of our large armies"; and General Gorgas felt that his time had not been passed "in vain." He had been greatly assisted by Lieutenant Colonel St. John, and by Colonel Rains. As Gorgas says, they were already in 1864 producing powder, but the "quantity production" of powder was on the point of beginning when the end came so suddenly.

One is astounded at the ingenuity and mechanical ability

---

[1] In the *Papers* of the Southern Historical Society (xii, 67–94) are "Notes on the Ordnance Department of the Confederate Government." This paper with some differences and three additional paragraphs is printed in Rowland's *Davis*, viii, 308–336. A note to the latter page states that it was written by General Gorgas for Davis's use in the preparation of his *Rise and Fall of the Confederate Government*. Other reports of Gorgas made in 1864 and 1865 are in the *Papers* of the Southern Historical Society, i, 57; ii, 58–63. A "Sketch of the Life of General Josiah Gorgas" is in *ibid.*, xiii, 216. See also *Official Records*, ser. iv, vol. i, p. 622, ii, p. 958, and Southern Historical Association's *Papers*, ii, p. 61. An interesting paragraph is in J. H. Wilson's *Under the Old Flag*, ii, p. 233 — it describes the destruction of the military factories at Selma, Alabama.

displayed by the Southerners in this emergency of their lives. In the production of munitions and of material they faced the same difficulties that they did in manufacturing textiles and in every industry, and also in transportation. There was not an adequate labor supply in the South, although the greater part of the male white population had been conscribed. Many English mechanics were imported, but they do not seem to have liked working in factories in the South. It may have been on account of the climate, or it may have been the association with work that went side by side with the slave system. Also it would seem that the Confederate government itself was not at all skilful in differentiating the classes of white working men, and utilizing the several classes to the utmost, in the factories and on the railroads. Some State governors also tried to force the imported workingmen into the military service![1]   But without much success. If any one has doubts as to the capacity of the South to continue warfare in April, 1865, so far as war materials are concerned, he has only to read Gorgas's accounts to satisfy himself that it was not any dearth of material that brought about the ending in the spring of 1865.

One of the favorite modes of accounting for the collapse of the Confederacy has been to depict the starving condition of the Confederate soldier in April, 1865. This idea is possibly most graphically expressed in the sentence: "Those twin monsters, hunger and starvation, forced our gates." Those who hold to this view, point to the prices paid for food at Richmond in the winter of 1864–1865. It is true that in February, 1865, potatoes sold for one hundred dollars a bushel at Richmond,[2] and flour for eighty-eight dollars a

---

[1] "Circular Letter" of Sept. 19, 1864, of President Davis to six governors protesting against their action in this regard. Rowland's *Davis*, vi, 338.

[2] "Ellis and Allan Cash Book," under date. On February 10, 1865, President Davis informed Congress that the uniform for a naval officer would cost

barrel. But eighty-eight dollars in Confederate money at
that time was the equivalent of eight dollars and eighty
cents in gold, and indeed the gold price of flour at Richmond
in that winter was less than it was at New York. Also it
is interesting to note that as late as the spring of 1864 it was
possible to buy brown sugar in Richmond, although the
price was six dollars a pound, and also coffee at eight dollars
a pound ; but this price was only somewhere between a quarter and a half a dollar in specie. The Southern food crops
of 1862 had been deficient and there was, no doubt, a scarcity of food in the spring and summer of 1863 and Lee's
invasion of Pennsylvania was partly in answer to that need.
The crops of 1863 and 1864 were good, and during those
years, until the latter part of 1864, quantities of bacon were
imported through the blockade to make up for the loss of
that which in the old days had been brought into the Southern
country from the Ohio Valley. There is no question but
that the operations of Sherman from Atlanta to Raleigh had
seriously interfered with the transportation service of the
Confederacy [1] so that although Commissary Northrup
reported in February, 1865, that two and a half million

$1,175.00 in Confederate currency ; but
this would have been $20 or $25 in gold.
In the "Burton Harrison Papers" in
the Library of Congress is a table of the
comparative purchasing power of gold
and United States paper money in
Richmond, from January, 1862 to
May, 1865 ; the latter would purchase
about one-half as much as gold throughout this time. In estimating gold values,
I have been greatly assisted by the use
of tables compiled by Charles W. Edwards of Enterprise, Alabama.

[1] The president of the Virginia Central Railroad wrote to Governor
Letcher, in September, 1863, that he
could not keep more than eleven
engines at work and that unless the
government would provide him with
labor, he could not promise more than

fifty per cent of the transportation
furnished in the winter of 1862–63. At
a later time, he stated that there was
gross misconception on the part of
members of Congress and of the legislature. Wages had increased eight hundred per cent, the cost of oil one hundred
per cent, the loss by depreciation was
nearly a million a year, and the in-
creases in rates had not been at all
commensurate to these rising costs. In
his opinion, if something were not done
to stop hostile legislation, the government would have to take over the railroads and operate them. There is
interesting matter in the Southern
Historical Society's *Papers*, ii, 121 and
in the report of the Assistant Quartermaster General, in President Davis's
"Message" of January 19, 1864.

rations of meat and seven hundred thousand rations of bread were on the way to Richmond, it is extremely probable that not much of it had reached that place in the first part of February,[1] for President Davis found it necessary to replace his old friend Northrup, at the head of the Commissary Bureau, by General I. M. St. John. That officer at once displayed the same energy and capacity that he had shown at the head of the Nitre and Mining Bureau. On April 1, 1865, his assistant, Lieutenant Colonel Williams, reported[2] that there were at Richmond three hundred thousand rations of bread and meat; at Danville, five hundred thousand rations of bread, and one and a half million rations of meat; and one million six hundred and eighty thousand more rations of bread and meat at Lynchburg and at Greensboro. Also it is worth noting that in October, 1864, the navy had on hand four months rations, including one hundred thousand pounds of coffee and thirty thousand pounds of sugar and one thousand pounds of tea. Confirming these statements as to food in North Carolina and Virginia, it may be noted that General Joseph E. Johnston stated that in February, 1865,[3] there were in depots between Danville and Weldon rations for sixty thousand men for more than four months; and at Charlotte "what we then regarded as large stores of sugar, coffee, tea, and brandy." "The Georgia Girl," Eliza F. Andrews, in her "War-time Journal," recounts that on February, 1865, she went to a rehearsal near Albany, Georgia, and had "a splendid supper, with ice cream and sherbet and cake made of real white sugar." Soon after, she returned to the parental home in Washington,

---

[1] Southern Historical Society's *Papers*, ii, 93.

[2] Southern Historical Society's *Papers*, iii, 99; and *Report of the Secretary of the [Confederate] Navy*, dated November 5, 1864, p. 51. See also W. L. Royall's *Some Reminiscences*, 43.

[3] Johnston's *Narrative*, 375.

also in Georgia, and fed hundreds of paroled soldiers streaming westward from Appomattox and later from Raleigh, —
and it is marvellous to read of the amount of food that
was stored away in her father's house.   Finally, Jabez L.
M. Curry, one of the most prominent of after-the-war Confederates, states in his book that "at the surrender there
was on the line of the railways and rivers, between Jackson,
Mississippi, and Montgomery, Alabama, enough corn to
supply the demand for breadstuffs for a full twelve-month
or more."   When Richmond was evacuated by the Confederates, they set fire to storehouses filled with foodstuffs and
also with munitions of war; at Farmville, and again at
Appomattox Station trainloads of food, which were waiting
for the Confederates, were captured by the Union soldiers.
There was starvation and suffering in Lee's army from
Petersburg to Appomattox Court House, but that was due
in no way to a scarcity of food within the Confederacy.[1]

It is abundantly evident to the under-surface seeker that
by the summer of 1864, and even more so by December of
that year, the will to fight had gone from large sections of
the Southern people.[2]   The literary women of the South
possessed an undying desire to fight to the bottom of the
last ditch, but was it the same with the women living in the
small towns, or on the lonely farms, — or with the wives
and sisters of the soldiers?   We have abundant diaries and
memoirs from the first, but we have little evidence as to the
feelings of the second group.   In January, 1865, a soldier
of Perote, Alabama, returned home for a month's furlough,
and a party was given in his honor.[3]   At this gathering,

[1] See beyond p. 632.
[2] Three remarkable letters written
by Howell Cobb and Senator B. H.
Hill to James A. Seddon and President
Davis in January and March, 1865
(*American Historical Review*, i, 97),
throw a flood of light on the inner
history of this time, although written
by two Georgia men.

[3] E. Y. McMorries' *History of the
First Regiment, Alabama Volunteer
Infantry, C. S. A.*, p. 113.

he "plainly saw that the ladies were becoming despondent of our ultimate success in the war. They tried to conceal it but the fact was too patent." He was deeply affected to find the women "who from start to finish had been the spirit of the war, seemed to be yielding to doubts and despondency" and he told them that if other Southern women shared their fears, that alone would ruin the cause. Earlier, in the preceding August, the wife of a Confederate officer, then living in Richmond, had written that there is "a strong feeling among the people I meet that the hour has come when we should consider the lives of the few men left to us. . . . *I* am for a tidal wave of peace — and I am not alone." [1] On January 18, 1865, and again, on March 9, the Confederate Adjutant-General issued a list of twelve hundred officers whose resignations had been accepted by President Davis. The cause for this utter demoralization, as it was, could be stated by any man according to his own preconceived ideas; but a few things may be set down with a reasonable degree of confidence. By the winter of 1864–1865, the "utter hopelessness of the struggle" was borne in upon the people by the terrible losses of life in the fearful battles in the Wilderness in which attack after attack had been made upon the Union lines.[2] Then the constant infringement on the freedom of movement and of employment seems to have been deeply felt. The Confederate soldier had never had much money to send home to his family, but the amount that his monthly wage, paid in Confederate money, would purchase for his wife and children had

[1] Printed in Mrs. Roger A. Pryor's *Reminiscences*, 293.

[2] On October 11, 1864, General Gorgas noted in his "Journal" that Colonel Chilton told him that General Lee had said: "If we can't get the men, all that is left for us is to make peace on the best terms we can." Gorgas added that he could not think that Lee was serious, but regretted "to hear such language from his mouth. . . . He must be subject to fits of despondence. Our brave President never wavers thus, in act or thought."

so diminished that the most zealous enthusiasm weakened.
And all this time "the soulless extortioner was upon his
walk seeking victims for plunder." The exaggerations with
which President Davis and other orators had appealed and
were appealing to the people now reacted to bring about a
general popular demand for surrender. "Portions of the
army," so runs the resolution adopted by Wise's Brigade
in January, 1865, are "moving upon the subject of peace."
This feeling of discontent was stated — probably over-stated
— in the Richmond "Examiner" not long after the battles
of May, 1864; — "Another series of battles, . . . another
outburst of grief throughout the Confederacy, another occasion for self congratulation to those whose duty did not call
them to share the fate of the men whose carcasses fell in
'The Wilderness,'" would mark the ending.

By the autumn and winter of 1864–1865, whatever the reason, there can be no question as to the amount of absenteeism
and desertion from the army. In September, 1864, President Davis stated that "two-thirds of our men are absent —
some sick, some wounded, but most of them absent without leave." [1] At about the same time a committee of the
Congress at Richmond reported that while the country
"notoriously swarms with skulkers from military service
and absentees and deserters from the army" they were asked
to provide new soldiers. As the autumn wore on, it became
noticeable that the deserters from the Confederate lines
from Petersburg brought their arms with them, which they
had not done before. In February and March, 1865, the
commanders constantly came across "intercepted appeals
from friends at home to the soldiers to desert." [2] On the

---

[1] In Rowland's *Davis*, vi, 327, is a
letter from Lee dated September 2,
1864, in which he argues for the substitution of negroes for whites, whenever they can be used, and putting into
the ranks all the detailed and exempted
men, whenever the reasons alleged
would not entitle a service man to his
discharge.

[2] Hagood's *Memoirs*, 317, 331, 332.

31st of December, 1864, the field return of Hagood's South
Carolina Brigade shows that 1,592 were present and 2,016
were absent; of the latter 577 were reported as "missing" and
529 as "absent without leave" and 15 of these were officers.
General Hagood noted that the number of this latter group
was "ominous of that change in popular sentiment which
now began to connive at a dereliction of duty" which earlier
had been deemed "little less shameful than desertion." He
states that Hardee left Charleston with "upward of 10,000
men" and had four thousand only when he reached the
North Carolina border, although there had been no combat
on the way, "straggling and desertion had done the work."

Parts of some States of the Confederacy were filled with
deserters and with fugitives from conscription. These joined
with Unionists and with escaped Union prisoners and held
the countryside in terror. In portions of Virginia, in parts of
the Carolinas, and in many other bits of the Confederacy, the
ordinary bonds binding together society had disappeared.
Governor P. Murrah of Texas stated that in some parts of
that State, society was demoralized, law was a dead letter,
whole communities were under a reign of terror, "and the
criminal, . . . goes unwhipped of justice." Throughout the
South there was a strange unnatural condition, "a letting
down of society" and a giving way of the "underguard" of
the State. It is noticeable that after the surrender of Johnston, the officers were obliged to stand guard over their horses
and their private belongings, for the released soldiers appeared to regard every bit of public property as fair prey, as
belonging to them as much as to its titular owner. As to the
responsibility for this condition of affairs, many Southern
men placed it squarely upon the shoulders of President Davis.

In the beginning Jefferson Davis had been the idolized
leader of the Southern people, or of those in the Slave States

who favored Southern independence and were willing to
fight for it. There were some exceptions to this rule, as
there are to all rules. In April, 1861, James H. Hammond
of South Carolina informed a correspondent that Davis was
"the most irascible man" he ever knew ; he had "no breadth
of political views or solid judgement about them." [1] By
the winter of 1864–1865, the feeling of confidence in and
love for Davis had entirely gone, except from those who were
most intimately associated with him. The Confederate
Congress had been opposed to him almost from the beginning. This was partly because some of his personal
enemies were prominent in it, but it was more especially
due to the fact that he vetoed every measure voted by it
that he did not like, and paid slight attention to the personal wishes of Congressmen. Of course, under the Confederate constitution, he had a perfect right to veto their
legislative acts ; but he certainly went beyond his bare
constitutional right and did a great many things that Congress had refused to sanction. Also, in some cases where he
had been empowered to do this thing or that by act of
Congress he went far beyond what it was supposed would
have been the limits of his prerogatives. To a Northerner,
who has grown up since the war and has studied the career
of the Confederacy as a matter of history and not of sentiment, Jefferson Davis appears to have been a man of great
natural abilities, thoroughly schooled in the arts of administration and of war, and actuated by a singleness of purpose
and a love of country — or of a section — that are rarely
found in statesmen and politicians. Granted that the
Southerners were right in desiring independence and in
fighting for it, Davis's motives and actions were above

---

[1] Elizabeth Merritt's "James Henry Hammond" (*Johns Hopkins Studies,*
xli, No. 4, p. 143).

reproach. The task that he had to perform was stupendous. The material that he had to work with was — some of it — very good, but, as a whole, was entirely inadequate to the working out of the problem in hand. Putting Davis on one side, and those within the Confederacy who opposed him on the other, one is amazed at his power and sincerity in comparison with the littleness of his opponents. These were, for the most part, Southern politicians of the pre-war type. They were much more interested in securing places and favors for themselves and their dependents than they were in upholding the hands of their chief executive. One of the charges made against Davis by many of his own people at the time and repeated over and over again by historical writers, North and South, from that day to this, is that he interfered in military matters. There is no doubt that he did so, nor is there any doubt that his selection of secretaries and generals was oftentimes unfortunate. But, looking at it coldly and calmly, as a matter of historical study, it is impossible to admit that Davis from a military point of view was always wrong and his generals right. Nevertheless the opposition to him grew until he was obliged to approve a vote of Congress taking the chief command from himself and giving it to Robert E. Lee.

The breach between President Davis and General Joseph E. Johnston, and also between the Confederate chief executive and General Beauregard, probably had an influence on Davis's position that accounts for a great deal in the history of those years. The Johnstons, husband and wife, were of the first families of Virginia; Jefferson Davis had no aristocratic roots, and Mrs. Davis was the daughter of a former governor of the State of New Jersey.[1] When the list of the

<hr/>

[1] See Josiah G. Leach's *Genealogical and Biographical Memorials of the Reading, Howell, . . . Families,* p. 139.   Mrs. Davis's cousin, John C. Howell, commanded the Union gunboat *Nereus* in the attack on Fort Fisher in Decem-

higher officers in the new Confederate military service came out, Johnston found himself ranked below Lee, whom he had ranked in the old army, and felt aggrieved because it had been understood that the officers of the old army entering the Confederate service should have the same relative rank that they had had in the Federal service. Davis wrote to Johnston, with possibly an excess of warmth, that his language was "unusual," his arguments "one-sided," and his insinuations "as unfounded as they are unbecoming."[1] Soon he became involved in friction with Beauregard. Both Johnston and Beauregard were appointed to command departments, and were given instructions which neither of them understood; but Davis held them responsible for the failures of others. On February 7, 1864, Beauregard indited a letter to Adjutant-General Cooper, asking to be relieved because he did not "possess the confidence & support of the Administration," — but on reflection he did not send the letter.[2] Moreover, Davis's peremptory style was not confined to military men. On March 31, 1864, he wrote to Governor Z. B. Vance, one of the strongest men in the Confederacy, suggesting that his "future communications be restricted to such matters as may require official action."[3] On the other hand, Davis had his "pets," and when one had gained his affections, it was impossible to displace him. He clung to men like Pemberton, and Bragg, and Northrup with the devotion of a lover. When Pemberton surrendered Vicksburg prematurely — as it seemed to many Southerners — Davis found another job for him. When Bragg was

ber, 1864 and January, 1865. Some letters from Mrs. Davis in the "Burton Harrison Papers" in the Library of Congress give a different idea of her from that gained from the perusal of Southern memoirs and diaries.

[1] Rowland's *Davis*, v, 132. See an interesting article by Leslie J. Perry on "President Davis and General Johnston" in the Southern Historical Society's *Papers*, xx, 95–108.

[2] Ms. in the Library of Congress.

[3] Rowland's *Davis*, vi, 218.

finally forced from the Army of Tennessee, Davis made him a sort of Chief of Staff, or confidential adviser. And Northrup could not be dislodged from the Commissary Department until the very end, in February, 1865. Commenting on this side of Davis's character, General Gorgas wrote in his journal, under date of August 10, 1863, that the President seemed determined to respect the opinions of no one, and had little appreciation of services rendered, "unless the party enjoys his good opinion. He seems to be an indifferent judge of men, and is guided more by prejudice than by sound discriminating judgment." As Davis's popularity waned, his enemies fell upon him with redoubled vigor and venom. They charged misfortune to him and laid it to his prejudices, his nepotism, his kingly ambition, and the nearer the hostile guns sounded, the louder was their clamor.[1] And the Vice-President of the Confederacy in February, 1864, declared that the policy foreshadowed in President Davis's latest message would lead to "a centralized, consolidated, military despotism, as absolute and execrable as that of Russia or Turkey."[2]

In January, 1865, Francis P. Blair, the elder, made his way to Richmond ostensibly to settle some question about his private property, but in reality to suggest to President Davis and others high in authority in the Confederate government that the war might somehow be brought to a close by the North and the South coöperating to drive the French and their Austrian Archduke, the Emperor Maximilian,[3] out of Mexico. The great desire for a termination of the

[1] For a very hostile view of the Davis administration, see H. S. Foote's *War of the Rebellion* (New York, 1866), p. 376 and fol.

[2] M. L. Avary's *Recollections of Alexander H. Stephens*, 168. Chapter xv, of H. J. Eckenrode's *Jefferson Davis*,

President of the South (New York, 1923) is a most discriminating argument as to why the Confederacy failed.

[3] J. F. Rippy's "Mexican Projects of the Confederates" in the *Southwestern Historical Quarterly*, xxii, 291–317, has a wider interest than its title indicates.

struggle that was then expressing itself in many ways in
many parts of the South compelled the Confederate government to temporize, and, while doing so, to use language that
would make it impossible for the Federal government to
accept any proposition and this refusal could then be used
to "fire the Southern heart" and bring back the spirit of
1861. In February, three Southerners, Vice-President
Stephens, R. M. T. Hunter, and former Judge Campbell of
the United States Supreme Court opened communications
with the Federal military authorities in front of Petersburg.
They asked to be allowed to go through the lines to Washington to confer with the United States government. Lincoln was distinctly unwilling to permit this, but he wrote
that they might be allowed to pass the lines to confer as to
bringing peace to "our one common country." They
came to City Point and were cared for by General Grant.
The four of them engaged in general conversation and Grant,
either on account of their attitude, or at the prompting of
Mrs. Grant, who was then at City Point, telegraphed to
Stanton that he thought the President should personally
confer with the Commissioners. It was in answer to this
that Lincoln went to Hampton Roads and with Seward
conferred with the three Confederates on February 3, no
one else being present. The history of those days is not
easily discernible. In every other instance, Lincoln had
refused to consider anything short of the restoration of the
Union as the price of peace. At all events, when the Southerners returned to Richmond with their negative report,[1]

---

[1] Lincoln's cold-blooded report is in
the *Official Records*, ser. i, vol. xlvi, pt.
ii, pp. 505–513. See also the *Complete
Works of Abraham Lincoln*, x, 347–356,
xi, 10–32 and *Lincoln's Account . . .
with Facsimiles from Collection of Judd
Stewart* (1910).

Benjamin's account of the drafting
of the instructions of the Confederate
Commissioners is in Rowland's *Davis*,
vii, 540; Davis's own account, also
written in 1877, is on p. 566. In 1887,
John A. Campbell published his *Reminiscences*, which included (pp. 11–19) a
"Memorandum of the Conversation at
the Conference," dated February, 1865.

President Davis summoned a meeting in the African Church. There he addressed the people before him and through them the whole Confederacy. But the response was slight to his asseveration that the Lincoln government was inexorable and that it would be content with nothing but Southern humiliation and surrender.

As the year 1865 opened, General Grant realized that the end of the Confederacy was in sight and bent every effort to hasten its demise. Roads and weather were notorious in Virginia in the early springtime, but Grant pitched upon March 29th as the day for the final movement to begin. The extreme left of the line was confided to Sheridan and his cavalry. As so often before, the plan was to attack the extreme Confederate right, seize the railroads remaining in the enemy's hands, and also the important crossings of the country roads. This plan, if successful, would force Lee to let go of Petersburg and Richmond and once again to seek the open field. With his great military sagacity, Lee apprehended fully what was about to happen and determined to forestall his opponent by attacking the Federal line in front of Petersburg.[1] This was done in the most dashing way, by Gordon and his men. They got into Fort Stedman, but soon found themselves cut off from retreat and from reënforcements by cross fires from the forts to the right and to the left. As a bit of military strategy, the attempt, though brilliant in conception and execution, had no effect on the prosecution of Grant's plans.

Other statements may be found through the index volume of the Southern Historical Society's *Papers* and in vol. xlii, 45–52. Several letters, written in 1870, are in the *Century* for July, 1896.

[1] See letter of 26th of March, 1865, in *Lee's Dispatches . . . to Jefferson Davis*, 341–346. In this letter and in others of these critical weeks, one is impressed with the constancy, devotion, and military genius of the Confederate commander-in-chief. There was not one word of complaint of others or the slightest desire to shift the burden from his own shoulders. He went into the vital operations of the next few days tranquil and unafraid.

Although the roads were deep in mud in those early spring days and the rains descended, off and on, Sheridan led the advance to the appointed task. The difficulties of the operation were very great and the unfavorable weather added to them. Nevertheless, the cavalry gained an important point, and Sheridan sent for infantry to hold what he had gained and to aid him in his further operations. In the existing lack of knowledge of the country and of the roads and the extremely unfavorable weather, great difficulty of movement was experienced and there were delays. On April 1, 1865, Sheridan gained a position at Five Forks, beyond the Confederate right, and then, with tremendous personal exertion, led or pushed one infantry division after another into the fight. When night fell, the Confederates, — those of them that were left — surrendered; and the next day, Lee was unable to retrieve the lost position. It is in his description of this day's battle that General Chamberlain drew a graphic comparison between Sheridan, with whom he then served for the first time, and his earlier commanders and his earlier experiences in the war. He tells us that Sheridan had no lines of retreat, that he gathered up his rear and his flanks and carried them forward with him, and that there was no longer any thought, when something had been accomplished, of stopping to make sure of that accomplishment, but the next step was at once and inexorably taken. On Sunday, April 2, 1865, Lee informed Davis that he could no longer maintain his lines and that Petersburg and Richmond must be abandoned.[1]

By midnight of the second day of April, the Confederate

[1] A remarkably graphic letter, describing these days in Richmond is printed in Freeman's *Calendar of Confederate Papers*, 249–253. Colonel Livermore printed interesting papers on this campaign in the *Proceedings* of the Massachusetts Historical Society for March, 1906, pp. 87–112, and in the *Papers* of the Military Historical Society of Massachusetts, vol. vi, pp. 451–506.

army had taken up its line of march toward the North
Carolina boundary where connection might be made with
Johnston's army. The march of the Confederates was
directed toward Amelia Court House where food was to be
brought for the soldiers. By one of those mishaps, not
uncommon in war, some misunderstanding had arisen
between General Lee and the supply department. Jefferson
Davis, at a later time, sought to explain the matter by
stating that Lee, instead of giving a command, oftentimes
made a suggestion. He believed that Lee "had in this
manner indicated that supplies were to be deposited at
Amelia Court-house." The testimony of General Breckinridge, then Secretary of War, of General St. John, Commissary General, and of Lewis Harvie, president of the
Richmond and Danville Railroad, conclusively prove that
no such orders were ever received by them; and it is beyond
question that there were supplies at both Richmond and
at Danville that could have been sent to the place of rendezvous, if orders had been received that they were wanted
there.[1] As it was, when Lee's retreating army reached
Amelia Court House, no food was to be found. For a day,
the movement was stopped and the soldiers dispersed to
gather whatever would sustain life for themselves and for
the animals that accompanied the army. This delay gave
Sheridan time to get up with the Confederates and the later
stoppages that were required for food and forage greatly
assisted — to say the least — the Union soldiers in getting
ahead of the Confederates and in planting themselves
squarely across the line of march to Lynchburg, — for the
pressure of the Union soldiers had been so heavy that the
route had been diverted from Danville toward the moun-

[1] See Jefferson Davis's "Robert E.
Lee" in *The North American Review* for
January, 1890, p. 64. This article is
repeated in *The Life and Reminiscences
of Jefferson Davis* (Baltimore, 1890),
p. 410.

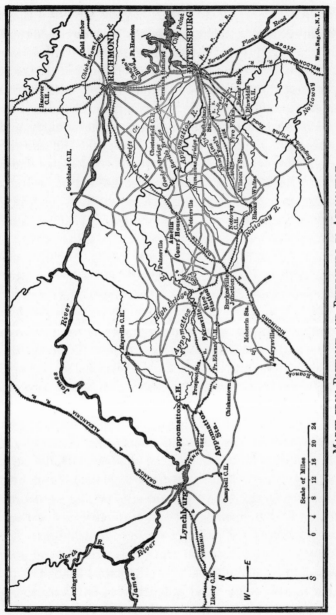

MARCH FROM RICHMOND AND PETERSBURG TO APPOMATTOX.

633

tains. A Confederate soldier graphically expressed the circumstances of that march: "Night was day, — day was night. . . . The events of morning became strangely intermingled with the events of evening. Breakfast, dinner and supper were merged into 'something to eat' whenever and wherever it could be had." [1] At one time, Sheridan sought his chief and told him that if he had some infantry under his direct command, he thought they could end the thing then and there. He was given what he asked for and for the next five days and nights pressed on and on, marching and fighting with his horsemen, the soldiers of the Army of the James, and the Fifth Corps of the Army of the Potomac.

At Sailor's Creek, where the route of march came to the Appomattox, there was, for a time, as fierce fighting as at any moment in the war. The Confederates were captured or killed or were driven back and compelled to cross the river. At Farmville, the advance of Sheridan's men found railroad trains filled with food for the enemy. The farther they went, the faster seemed to go the feet of the marching Union infantry, until at length on the morning of April 9, they caught up with the Union cavalry posted across the road leading from Appomattox Court House to Lynchburg. The Confederates, pushed rigorously onward by Meade and the main body of the army and constantly pressed by the attackers on the left, had reached the Court House on the evening of April 8th and encamped to get some rest before resuming their march in the morning. When the morning came, on April 9, dismounted Union cavalry men were seen on the high lands beyond, on the road to Lynchburg. There was hardly a brigade of the Army of Northern Virginia left in organized trim for combat; but there were enough to make up an attacking column and gallantly they advanced to over-

[1] Carlton McCarthy in Southern Historical Society's *Papers*, vi, 198.

whelm the cavalry — when it drew aside and an infantry line stood across the route. That was the end! Before four o'clock on that afternoon, terms for the surrender of the Confederate army were drawn up by Grant and assented to by Lee.

On the morning of April 12, the Army of Northern Virginia — what was left of it — marched to the appointed station to pile arms and lay down accoutrements and become men of peace. To receive them were several brigades of the Army of the Potomac, commanded for the occasion by General Joshua L. Chamberlain.[1] As the advancing gray column "with the old swinging route step and swaying battle-flags" and General Gordon riding ahead, reached the front of the first division of the "men in blue," a bugle sounded. Instantly, the whole Union line, regiment by regiment, gave the marching salute by shifting from "order arms" to "carry arms." As Gordon heard the sound of shifting arms, he looked up and, quickly realizing what it meant, dropped the point of his sword and, facing his own men, gave word for his brigades to pass with arms at "the carry," — honor answering honor. There was an awed stillness "as if it were the passing of the dead." And so it was, for it was the end of the Confederate States of America.

Well would it have been had the reconstruction of Southern society been in the hands of these men and of others who respected one another and were guided by Abraham Lincoln. On March 4, 1865, in his Second Inaugural, he had used these words: "With malice toward none; with charity for all; with firmness in the right, as God gives us to see the right, let us strive on to finish the work we are in; to bind up the nation's wounds; . . . to do all which may achieve and cherish a just and lasting peace

[1] See Chamberlain's *The Passing of the Armies*, 259.

among ourselves, and with all nations." Six weeks later, on April 14, an assassin's bullet closed the life of this greatest of Americans and delivered the Southern people into the hands of the Radical Republican politicians of the North.   As the news of Abraham Lincoln's murder travelled through the Southern land, the wisest men were depressed, but to the generality of the Southern people it seemed to be a fitting accompaniment to the tragedy that was in their own hearts.

NOTE [1]

Grant's Virginia Campaigns. — These campaigns, from the Rapidan to the Appomattox, are treated in their various aspects, including Butler's doings — or lack of them — in the *Official Records*, ser. i, vol. xxxvi, pts. i–iii, and ser. i, vol. xlvi, pts. i–iii. Of the voluminous studies of these campaigns, none better repays perusal than that of Colonel Thomas L. Livermore in the fourth volume of the *Papers* of the Military Historical Society of Massachusetts. Three comments that John C. Ropes made in letters to Major Gray in May, June, and November, 1864, deserve notice. On May 28, he asks why does not Grant abandon his base and advancing his right instead of his left, force a battle with his army facing to the east. In June, he wrote that he could not understand the use to Lee of these battles in the Wilderness and Spottsylvania; and in November, he notes one of the things that must have caused Grant great anxiety: "Somehow the enemy always finds a gap between two corps and that must be Meade's fault." With these papers, one might read "The Military Life of General Grant" by Colonel Charles C. Chesney of the British army in his *Essays* in military biography (London and New York, 1874).

[1] In closing this volume, the author wishes to thank friends and students, past and present, living in many places, whose suggestions and researches have aided him in countless different ways. The names of some of them are included in the foot-notes. Especially, he wishes to record his obligations to his colleague, Arthur M. Schlesinger, to his friend, George Parker Winship, for his valuable literary suggestions, and to his secretary, Miss Eva G. Moore, for her continuing care and her expert advice in many ways.

INDEX

Adams, C. F., 139; in 1860–61, 295; minister to Great Britain, 350, 369.

Adams, J. H., Gov. of S. C., advocates reopening of African slave trade, 214.

Alabama, Confed. cruiser, 358, 359, 491–493.

Amazon River, exploration of, 62.

Anderson, Robert, Major, at Fort Sumter, 283–285; surrenders, 314 and *n*.

Antietam, 473.

Appeal of the Independent Democrats, 158.

Appomattox campaign, 630–635.

Arms, supplying the South with, 284, 287, 401 and *n*, 402 and *n*.

Army, Northern, the, 403; numbers in, 430–434; care of sick, 436–438; casualties, 438–442.

Army, Southern, the, 402 and *n*.; numbers in, 430–434; care of sick, 436–438; casualties, 438–442; desertions from, 623.

Atlanta campaign, the, 558–560.

Baltimore, riot, 316.

Baltimore conventions, National Union, 1860, 244, 245; Democratic, 1860, 242; Bell and Everett, 1860, 244; National Union, 1864, 606.

Barton, Clara, 437; on emancipation, 524 *n*.

Battles or campaigns, Bull Run, 327–329 and *n*.; Donelson, 454–456; Shiloh, 461; Corinth, 463; Murfreesboro', 463; Seven Days, 470–472; second Bull Run, 473; Antietam, 473; Chancellorsville, 477; Gettysburg, 479–484; Vicksburg, 547–553; Chickamauga, 553; Chattanooga, 555; Knoxville, 556; Atlanta, 559; Franklin, 563; Nashville, 564; Wilderness, 565–567; Petersburg, 630; Appomattox, 631.

Beaufort, S. C., captured, 464.

Beauregard, P. G. T., Confed. Gen., 284; and Sumter, 313; at Bull Run, 327; at Shiloh, 461; at Corinth, 463.

Bell, John, on Kansas, 160; presidential candidate, 1860, 245.

Benjamin, J. P., Confed. Sec'y of State, etc., 280, 402, 603.

Bibliographies, of the period, 37; of Southern life, 38, 39; William H. Russell, 11 *n.*, 38, 307 *n.*; of California, 40 *n.*, 43 *n.*, 47 *n.*, 50 *n.*, 64; of Central America, 64; of Japan, 65; of danger of secession, 86; Anthony Burns, 111 *n.*; "Underground Railroad," 116; *Uncle Tom's Cabin*, 116–118; Know-Nothing, 147; Kansas, 179; Dred Scott, 202; Harper's Ferry, 226; Lincoln, 255; Jefferson Davis, 277 *n.*; Confed. States, 297; Fort Sumter, 310 *n.*; Bull Run, 331; cotton, 336 *n.*; general, of the war, 395–397; prisoners of war, 443; casualties, 443, 444 *n.*; of secondary works on the war, 485; general naval, 522; Grant's Virginia campaign, 637.

Black, J. S., Sec'y of State, 281; in 1864, 604.

"Black Warrior" affair, 57.

Blair, Frank P., at Chicago, 1860, 232; at Richmond, 1865, 268.

Blair, Frank P., Jr., and Missouri, 390.

Blair, Montgomery, at Chicago, 233; Postmaster Gen., 301; resigns, 609.

Blockade, the, 488–490, 511 and fol.

"Border Ruffians," the, in Kansas, 168 and fol.

Bounties, in the South, 414; in the North, 421.

Bragg, Braxton, Confed. Gen., 284; in Kentucky and Tennessee, 463; at Chickamauga, 553; military adviser to Davis, 627.

Breckinridge, John C., presidential candidate, 1860, 244–251; Confed. Sec'y of War, 613.